WUTHERING HEIGHTS

NEW RIVERSIDE EDITIONS

Series Editor for the British Volumes
Alan Richardson

Fictions of Empire: Heart of Darkness, Joseph Conrad; *The Man Who Would Be King,* Rudyard Kipling; and *The Beach of Falesá,* Robert Louis Stevenson
edited by John Kucich

Lyrical Ballads and Related Writings, William Wordsworth and Samuel Taylor Coleridge
edited by William Richey and Daniel Robinson

Making Humans: Frankenstein, Mary Shelley, and *The Island of Doctor Moreau,* H. G. Wells
edited by Judith Wilt

Sense and Sensibility, Jane Austen
edited by Beth Lau

Three Oriental Tales: History of Nourjahad, Frances Sheridan; *Vathek,* William Beckford; and *The Giaour,* Lord Byron
edited by Alan Richardson

Three Vampire Tales: Dracula, Bram Stoker; *Carmilla,* Sheridan LeFanu; and *The Vampyre,* John Polidori
edited by Anne Williams

Two Irish National Tales: Castle Rackrent, Maria Edgeworth, and *The Wild Irish Girl,* Sydney Owenson (Lady Morgan)
edited by James M. Smith

Wuthering Heights, Emily Brontë
edited by Diane Long Hoeveler

For a complete listing of our American and British New Riverside Editions, visit our web site at **http://college.hmco.com.**

NEW RIVERSIDE EDITIONS
Series Editor for the British Volumes
Alan Richardson, Boston College

EMILY BRONTË

Wuthering Heights

Complete Text with Introduction
Contexts • Critical Essays

Edited by
Diane Long Hoeveler
MARQUETTE UNIVERSITY

Houghton Mifflin Company
BOSTON • NEW YORK

MANY THANKS TO BOB DAVIS, BRUCE CANTLEY,
ALAN RICHARDSON, AND MARGARET MCPEAKE
FOR THEIR PATIENCE AND ASSISTANCE

Sponsoring Editor: Michael Gillespie
Editorial Associate: Bruce Cantley
Senior Project Editor: Tracy Patruno
Senior Cover Design Coordinator: Deborah Azerrad Savona
Manufacturing Manager: Florence Cadran
Marketing Manager: Cindy Graff Cohen

Cover image: © Neil Robinson/STONE

Credits appear on page 456, which is a continuation of the copyright page.

Printed in the U.S.A.

Library of Congress Control Number: 2001090566
ISBN: 0-618-08486-x

1 2 3 4 5 6 7 8 9-FFG-05 04 03 02 01

As part of Houghton Mifflin's ongoing
commitment to the environment, this text
has been printed on recycled paper.

CONTENTS

ABOUT THIS SERIES
Alan Richardson

The Riverside imprint, stamped on a book's spine or printed on its title page, carries a special aura for anyone who loves and values books. As well it might: by the middle of the nineteenth century, Houghton Mifflin had already established the "Riverside" edition as an important presence in American publishing. The Riverside series of British poets brought trustworthy editions of Milton and Wordsworth, Spenser and Pope, and (then) lesser-known writers like Herbert, Vaughan, and Keats to a growing nation of readers. There was both a Riverside Shakespeare and a Riverside Chaucer by the century's end, titles that would be revived and recreated as the authoritative editions of the late twentieth century. Riverside Editions of writers like Emerson, Hawthorne, Longfellow, and Thoreau helped establish the first canon of American literature. Early in the twentieth century, the Cambridge editions published by Houghton Mifflin at the Riverside Press made the complete works of dozens of British and American poets widely available in single-volume editions that can still be found in libraries and homes throughout the United States and beyond.

The Riverside Editions of the 1950s and 1960s brought attractive, affordable, and carefully edited versions of a range of British and American titles into the thriving new market for serious paperback literature. Prepared by leading scholars and critics of the time, the Riversides rapidly became known for their lively introductions, reliable texts, and lucid annotation. Though aimed primarily at the college market, the series was also created (as one editor put it) with the "general reader's private library" in mind. These were paperbacks to hold on to and read again, and many a "private" library was seeded with the colorful spines of Riverside editions kept long after graduation.

Houghton Mifflin's New Riverside Editions now bring the combination of high editorial values and wide popular appeal long associated with the Riverside imprint into line with the changing needs and desires of twenty-first century students and general readers. Inaugurated in 2000 with the first set of American titles under the general editorship of Paul Lauter, the New Riversides reflect both the changing canons of literature in English and the greater emphases on historical and cultural context that have helped a new generation of critics to extend and reenliven literary studies. The Series is not only concerned with keeping the classic works of British and American literature alive, but grows as well out of the excitement that a broader range of literary texts and cultural reference points has brought to the classroom. Works by formerly marginalized authors, including women writers and writers of color, will find a place in the Series along with titles from the traditional canons that a succession of Riverside imprints helped establish beginning a century and a half ago. New Riverside titles will reflect the recent surge of interest in the connections between literary activity, historical change, and social and political issues, including slavery, abolition, and the construction of "race"; gender relations and the history of sexuality; the rise of the British Empire and of nationalisms on both sides of the Atlantic; and changing conceptions of nature and of the human.

The New Riverside Editions respond to recent changes in literary studies not only in the range of titles but also in the design of individual volumes. Issues and debates crucial to a book's author and original audience find voice in selections from contemporary writings of many kinds as well as in early reactions and reviews. Some volumes will place contemporary writers into dialogue, as with the pairing of Irish national tales by Maria Edgeworth and Sydney Owenson or of vampire stories by Bram Stoker and Sheridan Le Fanu. Other volumes provide alternative ways of constructing literary tradition, juxtaposing Mary Shelley's *Frankenstein* with H. G. Wells' *Island of Dr. Moreau*, or Lord Byron's *The Giaour*, an "Eastern Tale" in verse, with Frances Sheridan's *Nourjahad* and William Beckford's *Vathek*, its most important predecessors in Orientalist prose fiction. Chronologies, selections from major criticism, notes on textual history, and bibliographies will allow readers to go beyond the text and explore a given writer or issue in greater depth. Seasoned critics will find fresh new contexts and juxtapositions, and general readers will find intriguing new material to read alongside of familiar titles in an attractive format.

Houghton Mifflin's New Riverside Editions maintain the values of reliability and readability that have marked the Riverside name for well over a century. Each volume also provides something new — often unexpected — and each in a distinctive way. Freed from the predictable monotony and rigidity of a set template, editors can build their volumes around the special opportunities presented by a given title or set of related works. We hope that the resulting blend of innovative scholarship, creative format, and high production values will help the Riverside imprint continue to thrive well into the new century.

INTRODUCTION
Diane Long Hoeveler

Emily Brontë's only novel, *Wuthering Heights,* has enthralled, puzzled, and annoyed readers and critics since its publication in 1847. Is it a gothic ghost story, a melodramatic romance, a metaphysical treatise on *Naturphilosophie,* or a sentimental novel twice told? The work has been assigned to all of these genres, and none of them alone captures its complexity. Critics have been equally puzzled by the character of Heathcliff, some seeing him as a devil, others as a force of natural energy, and still others as a victim of racial and class prejudices in an age that rigidly enforced such boundaries. And what should we make of the inheritance and disinheritance plot, as well as the elaborate legal maneuvering that Heathcliff manages in order to displace the privileged men who had earlier tormented him? Like the revenge plot that characterizes so much of the action in a Restoration drama or a gothic novel, *Wuthering Heights* is a peculiarly literary work, written by a woman whose reading was no doubt deeper and more extensive than her personal interactions with the world of society.

Both at the time of its publication and since, readers of *Wuthering Heights* have either loved or intensely disliked the experience. The book seems more than other works to be such an alternately abstract and concrete work that understanding it is quite different from responding to it. Put another way, a person reading this book at different points over a lifetime can see radically different meanings in it. To an adolescent, it is a love story about doomed and unfulfilled passion. To a somewhat older (and wiser) adult, it is a story of the necessary compromises that women make in order to conform to middle-class expectations about marriage and social acceptance. To the person past middle age it may seem like an anthropological account about an alien species, beings hopelessly buffeted about by emotions and irrationalities they are unable to control, which will by necessity doom them to extinction unless they can bring these feelings under some kind of control. For any reader, what is amazing is that the book was written by a motherless young woman who had been raised in near isolation in a sparsely populated area of northern England.

How did Emily Brontë come to write *Wuthering Heights,* and what does it mean? Those two questions have dominated critical discussion of the novel since its publication. After her sister's death, Charlotte Brontë attempted to answer the first question by saying, in effect, please do not judge Emily because she created Heathcliff. Later critics have been equally at a loss to explain the composition of the novel. Charlotte Brontë, who lived with her sister and knew her as well as anyone, could not account for the passion, sadism, and sheer violence that spill out of pages of the book. One of the few stories that we know about Emily Brontë concerns her reaction to being bitten by a dog. When she thought she might have contracted rabies, she calmly heated up an iron and cauterized the bite herself. It is fair to remark that many young women would not have had the courage or determination to commit such an act, and one is reminded here that M. Constantin Heger, her French teacher in Brussels, observed after instructing Emily that she should have been born a man; she would have made a great navigator.

The chronology of Brontë's life provides little more than the simple facts and dates. Only a very few autobiographical statements, such as the birthday letter that she wrote to Anne and wanted opened in five years' time, survive. Other letters and personal reflections may have been written, but they have never surfaced. There is also Charlotte Brontë's tantalizing statement that Emily was working on another novel, but that manuscript also has been lost. Given her protective nature, Charlotte has long been suspected of tidying up her sister's reputation. But we simply do not know what happened to several key pieces of written evidence—the original manuscript of *Wuthering Heights* or the prose pieces of the Gondal saga— that would allow us to form a more complete portrait of Emily Brontë as a woman and a writer.

Few lovers of British literature do not know the Brontë myth: Three talented sisters—Charlotte, Emily, and Anne—living with Branwell, their pampered and drug-addicted brother, in the Yorkshire moors of Haworth, all of them dominated by an Irish-born, eccentric, near-blind curate father who had been a widower most of their lives. While they are still children, their father leaves on a trip and returns with toy soldiers for his son, who shares them with his sisters. Instead of dashing them to pieces in a few weeks as most children would, the Brontë siblings invent increasingly elaborate narratives about each of the soldiers, giving them wives, lovers, children, and rival kingdoms to rule. More surprisingly, however, they choose to write and rewrite these narratives into miniature booklets that they maintain until well into adulthood. Reading what was available either at home or borrowed from the local Keighley Mechanics' Institute, Emily Brontë grew up using that reading as source material for her own feverish narratives of the lives and loves of the lords and ladies who inhabited the strange island of Gondal.

In addition to her early writing experiences, Emily Brontë's career as a published poet and novelist is owed in large measure to the efforts of her elder sister, Charlotte, author of the wildly successful novel *Jane Eyre* (1847). There can be no doubt that *Wuthering Heights* survived initially because of the attempts of her more famous and successful sister to explain the novel to a bewildered reading public. Charlotte Brontë was fiercely protective of Emily's reputation, and the early charges of "coarseness" made against the novel's characters and language deeply offended Charlotte's knowledge of Emily's nature. Her Biographical Notice of Ellis and Acton Bell and Editor's Preface to the 1850 edition of the novel (reprinted on pages 13–23), written after Emily's death, went a long way toward softening the perception of fierceness and nihilism that critics thought they detected in the voice of the author of the novel. We know that Emily Brontë saw a few negative reviews of the book as she was dying, but we also know that her death at thirty-one was not brought on by anything other than pulmonary tuberculosis, produced by the poor sanitation conditions around the Haworth parsonage.

By the time Charlotte Brontë died in 1855, the story of the three isolated sisters writing in the wilds of northern England, nurtured only by native genius and paternal eccentricity, had become the stuff of legend. Elizabeth Gaskell fueled the myth of the Brontë family with her biography of Charlotte (1855). Although Gaskell had met Emily Brontë, she had very little to say about her, perhaps because Emily Brontë seems always to have been aloof, solitary, deeply immersed in her own private creation of a world in which the masculine and feminine principles waged cosmic power struggles to the death. In her early years she shared and jointly created this private kingdom, Gondal, in close to one hundred poems and numerous prose pieces (all now lost) with only her younger sister, Anne, as they worked out together its elaborate scenarios of sexual power. That Emily Brontë chose to live in this self-created fantasy world until well into her twenties has puzzled and intrigued critics with a psychoanalytic bent. In order to put the Gondal saga into its fullest context as a source for the mature novel, this edition reprints Mary Visick's essay, "The Genesis of *Wuthering Heights*," on the role of this early writing as a source for the mature novel.

Emily Brontë's creativity was forced into the public spotlight only when Charlotte found her poems (in 1845) and pressed her sister to join in a collaborative publication venture, culminating in the famous first production of the pseudonymous Bell family, *Poems by Currer, Ellis, and Acton Bell* (May 1846). As "Ellis Bell," Emily Brontë revised twenty-one of her Gondal poems, removing arcane or obscure references to Gondal personages. After Emily Brontë's death, Charlotte Brontë chose seventeen of Emily's poems to reprint with the 1850 edition of *Wuthering Heights*. Some of those poems illustrate "a point in her character" at the age of sixteen, while others are among the last pieces of writing she ever composed. In addition to her abilities as a poet, Emily Brontë was also a talented artist, creating many watercolors that were not simply schoolgirl attempts at still life but accomplished paintings such as "The North Wind" and "Guwald Tower" that convey the mood and tone of the novel. The poems are included in Part Two, "The Personal Context," followed by Sylvia Plath's poetic meditation on *Wuthering Heights* as a modern reaction to the novel. Students are advised to consult Christine Alexander and Jane Sellars, *The Art of the Brontës*, for a discussion and portfolio of Emily Brontë's paintings.

The composition of *Wuthering Heights* appears to have been amazingly quick and effortless. According to Charlotte Brontë, Emily wrote the novel within the space of a year (from sometime in 1845 to July 1846), once again at the urging of her assertive elder sister. Dating the composition of the novel, however, has always been more than a bit of a mystery. How could a novel so elaborately and chronologically complex, as well as meticulously plotted over three generations, have been composed entirely within a nine-month period? The only plausible explanation is that Emily Brontë had so totally internalized the characters, action, and stylistic devices of the Gondal saga that she was able to naturalize that early collaborative narrative into a work that approached in shape and tone a conventional novel. That the novel is not realistic by Victorian standards can be appreciated if we recognize its emergence out of a deeply private and long-extended meditation on the world of Gondal. In Part Three of this edition, Edward Chitham discusses his theories about the evolution of the novel, concluding that one overlooked source must have been the family folk legend about a distant and disinherited Irish relative, a story that Reverend Brontë told his children many times. This displaced Irish ancestor bears some resemblance to the hero of Bartholomew Simmons's gothic short story set in Ireland, "The Bridegroom of Barna," which is reprinted in Part Four. Although we cannot know for certain, the two narratives, one real and the other fictional, could have entwined in Emily Brontë's mind to create the dispossessed character of Heathcliff.

Early reviews of *Wuthering Heights* are readily available in *The Brontës: The Critical Heritage*, edited by Miriam Allott (1974). Those reviews, summarized here, show that contemporary critics of Brontë did not know what to make of *Wuthering Heights*. One of the first reviews, published in the January 1848 issue of *Atlas,* called it "a strange, inartistic story [...] cast[ing] a gloom over the mind not easily to be dispelled." In the same month, Douglas Jerrold's *Weekly Newspaper* also labeled the novel "strange" and its author obsessed with "brutal cruelty, and semi-savage love." Assuming the author to be a man who should turn his skills to the stage, the reviewer notes that the "reader is shocked, disgusted, almost sickened by details of cruelty, inhumanity, and the most diabolical hate and vengeance." By the third published review, in the *Examiner* (also January 1848), the tone was set. "This is a strange book," the reviewer begins, and proceeds to condemn the novel as "wild, confused, disjointed, and improbable."

By 1850, when the second edition of the novel appeared, the critic Sydney Dobell thought he had solved the mystery of the Bell phenomenon. The novels, to his mind, were all written by one woman, "Currer Bell," who had used the other names for earlier productions. In his view, *Wuthering Heights* was "ruder in execution," "a youthful story, written for oneself in solitude, and thrown aside till other successes recall the eyes to it in hope." By this date, however, Emily Brontë was dead and there would be no further books to clarify, explain, or expand on the sudden genius of her only novel. After Charlotte Brontë's own identity was revealed and the preface and biographical account she had published in the 1850 edition of *Wuthering Heights* had circulated throughout literary London, a softened tone toward Emily Brontë began to emerge in the reviewing community. Yet even in these later reviews, "Ellis" was patronized as an isolated and eccentric spinster who should be pardoned for her peculiarities.

The critical tone throughout the early to mid-twentieth century did not stray far from this pattern of puzzlement and patronizing sympathy. F. R. Leavis omits the entire Brontë corpus from his attempt to establish the canon of important British novels in *The Great Tradition* and dismisses *Wuthering Heights* as "a kind of sport" (38). Other critics have seized on the landscapes that Emily Brontë lived in and traveled through for the physical and material sources of her work (see Christopher Heywood's "Yorkshire Landscapes in *Wuthering Heights*" in Part Three). In addition, critics such as Terry Eagleton in *Myths of Power: A Marxist Study of the Brontës* have set the novel in its various political and social milieux, arguing that Heathcliff represents the slave, the proletariat, or the displaced worker. Also representative of this school of criticism is Maja-Lisa Von Sneidern's essay "*Wuthering Heights* and the Liverpool Slave Trade," reprinted in Part Three. Many anthologies of critical essays on the novel are in print, and an extensive bibliography of secondary sources for the novel is provided in the For Further Reading section at the end of this volume.

Whether drawn on directly or indirectly echoed, literary sources for *Wuthering Heights* have been variously identified over the years. Shakespeare, Milton, E. T. A. Hoffman, Walter Scott, William Wordsworth, Samuel Taylor Coleridge, Lord Byron, and Percy Bysshe Shelley are the most frequently mentioned as influences on the composition of the work. My own focus is on the heavy use of gothic elements in the novel as well as its place in the larger phenomenon that we now label the "female gothic." In contrast to earlier critics who were inclined to view this book as a great solitary crag standing apart from literary influences, I believe that *Wuthering Heights* is part of a continuous tradition of women's gothic writings. Accordingly, I have reprinted my article "*Wuthering Heights* and Gothic Feminism" in Part Four. In addition, a likely seminal source for the novel, Bartholomew Simmons's short story, "The Bridegroom of Barna," is reprinted for the first time in conjunction with the novel in Part Four. This tale was published in 1840 in *Blackwood's Edinburgh Magazine,* a leading journal that provided favorite reading material for the Brontë family, including numerous likely sources for the exotic settings of the Gondal poems. Set in Ireland, the story concerns disinheritance, revenge, and an unconsummated marriage between a woman of good family and a man from a lower class. As in *Wuthering Heights,* much of the action is set in the proximity of windows. The most startling similarity, however, is the scene in which the frustrated bridegroom digs up his beloved's coffin in order to embrace her corpse. Leicester Bradner was the first to propose the story as a source, and John Hewish, the only critic to discuss the story at any length, says: "One feels that had Simmons read *Wuthering Heights* he might have charged Emily Brontë with plagiarism" (122). In reading "The Bridegroom of Barna" after studying the novel, students should be able to see how an earlier, obviously inferior work by one author can be transformed, expanded, and crafted into a much more significant literary production by another.

Wuthering Heights, like Charlotte Brontë's more accessible *Jane Eyre,* has continued to live in the public consciousness not simply because academic critics continue to canonize these novels. Both works have assumed living cultural currency as their stories have been translated into a variety of successful films and plays. Patsy Stoneman has recently charted their cultural permutations, from avant-garde musicals staged in local theaters to Hollywood blockbusters from the 1920s through the 1990s. The Merle Oberon–Lawrence Olivier version of *Wuthering Heights* (1939) was an extremely popular result of the attempt by U.S. filmmakers to film British literary classics just as Britain itself was approaching a war with Germany. Movie versions have not been confined to Hollywood. Luis Buñuel's Mexican version of *Wuthering Heights,* entitled *Abismos de Pasión* (1954), presents the story as a *Liebestod* (literally, a "song of death" suggesting suicide induced by mystical love) with clear incestuous overtones. Most recently, an adaptation of the novel has been produced with Ralph Fiennes playing Heathcliff and Juliette Binoche assuming the roles of both Catherines, mother and daughter (1992). A filmography is provided at the end of this volume for students and instructors interested in viewing and comparing the different film versions of the novel.

This New Riverside Edition aims, then, to present the most thoroughly examined version of the original text of *Wuthering Heights,* taking into account as much as possible the corrections that Emily Brontë made in her own hand (see the Note on Text). In the tradition of the Riverside editions, this text includes some of the best and most original new critical work as well as earlier articles that aid the student in placing the novel in its historical and cultural contexts. Besides presenting work that is not readily available elsewhere, this edition takes a strong historicist approach, attempting to show that literary works are not produced in vacuums but are reflections of the author's life, culture, and ideological beliefs. Emily Brontë is an interesting case study because she appears on the surface to be an isolated genius, exactly the sort of artist who might have created in the solitary realm of art and inspiration. But the facts even for her do not bear out this approach. As the readings in Parts Three and Four illustrate, Emily Brontë knew about the Liverpool slave trade and the Irish and Catholic emancipation issues and she read popular gothic short stories and novels. She used this reading and her limited life experiences and travels to create a work that reflects and criticizes mid-nineteenth-century ideologies about men and women, marriage and courtship, class struggle and oppression, and finally renewal and the triumph of the human spirit.

The experience of reading *Wuthering Heights* can be both intense and engaging if we are willing to suspend disbelief long enough to immerse ourselves in the Yorkshire countryside at the end of the eighteenth century, as Emily Brontë's imagination recreated it. Although men as fierce or passionate or vengeful as Heathcliff and marriages as strange as those in this book may not exist in real life, *Wuthering Heights* may nevertheless be intended as an accurate vision of life, "red in tooth and claw," with all the civilities stripped away. As horrible as such a possibility is, it may very well reflect what we all know to be true in our inner selves. There is no hypocrisy in Emily Brontë; as Charlotte Brontë emphatically stated, she had nothing but contempt for weakness or sham or false fronts. And that may be why we still circle this novel warily, uncomfortable with the possibility that it reveals, clearly and pitilessly, the beast within all of us.

Diane Long Hoeveler

Whenever the original manuscript of an author's book does not survive, controversy can arise about the exact intentions and shape of the work. Such is the case with *Wuthering Heights.* Emily Brontë's original fair copy of *Wuthering Heights* was lost or destroyed at about the time of her death, and the manuscript that she submitted to her original publisher, Thomas C. Newby, was virtually mutilated in his clumsy hands. Newby was not a publisher in the same sense as Charlotte Brontë's publisher, Smith, Elder, and Co. Instead, Newby was a printer with no experience correcting grammatical errors, or mistakes in spelling or punctuation—none of which appears to have been Emily Brontë's strong suit. In fact, he seems to have introduced additional errors throughout the text. The 1847 edition was riddled with eccentric spelling, haphazard hyphenation, and punctuation that few scholars have been willing to attribute to the original text.

The story becomes more complicated at this point, because Emily Brontë then marked a copy of the 1847 edition with her own corrections. She died in 1848, however, before she could oversee a new, corrected edition. In the 1850 edition of the novel, Charlotte Brontë diligently tried to correct all of the technical errors and to simplify the Yorkshire dialect of Joseph. She also reparagraphed the book to minimize the choppiness of the originally printed version. Purists, however, were interested not in Charlotte Brontë's editorial revisions of the book, well-intentioned and admirable as they were, but in what Emily Brontë had originally intended in her editorial notes to the 1847 printed version.

The indefatigable Clement Shorter and his cohort in purchasing Brontë manuscripts, Thomas J. Wise, emerge at this point. Shorter bought (for a pittance) all the Brontë materials available from Charlotte Brontë's widower, the Reverend Arthur Bell Nichols, who had retired to Ireland in possession of all the extant childhood writings, poetry, and miscellaneous papers produced by the entire Brontë family. In 1911 when he published the two-volume *Works of Emily Brontë,* Shorter stated that he was printing for the first time the version of the novel as "set up in type from Emily Brontë's own copy of *Wuthering Heights,* which was carried by Mr. Arthur Bell Nichols from Haworth to his later home in Banagher in Ireland, where it rested on his shelves for more than forty years (xi)." Wise republished the novel in 1931, collating the 1847 text with the corrections by both sisters in what was for many years the standard edition of all of the Brontë works, the Shakespeare Head Edition. This is where another piece of controversy arises. Shorter made a number of silent corrections in the text he published in 1911, but he never explained his authority for doing so, apart from the claim that he was in possession of Emily Brontë's corrections in her own hand. Later Wise stated that fifteen corrections had been made in Brontë's hand in the original book, but he listed only nine.

Shorter died in 1926 and his estate sold Emily Brontë's copy of *Wuthering Heights* at auction (again for a pittance) in 1928. Taking a circuitous route, the book ended up at a Sotheby's auction again in 1964, when it was purchased by an anonymous private collector for the equivalent in today's dollars of around $5,000. That purchaser has never been identified, and consequently scholars are unable to check either the claims or the editorial changes made by Shorter and Wise. Interestingly, the catalogue description of the book states that there are "twenty-three corrections written in pencil, in [Emily Brontë's] hand." Brontë scholars have diligently tried to track down this missing document, as well as several missing poems by Charlotte Brontë that are known to be in private hands. It is probable, however, that the penciled corrections by Emily Brontë, like those listed by Shorter, make no significant difference in the meaning of the text (e.g., "these" for "those" and "here" for "there"). This New Riverside Edition follows the 1956 Riverside Edition, which was based on the Shakespeare Head version, with a few changes in punctuation and capitalization. Additional changes, mostly in the removal of hyphens from compound words, have been made to accommodate the American reader.

Part One

—◆—

WUTHERING HEIGHTS

Branwell Brontë's portrait of Emily Brontë, aged about 18 (c. 1833–34).

of Ellis and Acton Bell

Charlotte Brontë

Emily Brontë died a little more than a year after her only novel was published. She had been ill for about four months before her death, and the negative reviews that had been published about her novel were found in her possession, so Charlotte Brontë knew that her sister had read them. Charlotte Brontë was a passionate woman who had served as a sort of mother-substitute to her two younger sisters since the deaths of their older sisters, Maria and Elizabeth, of typhus. It was Charlotte, as well, who had coaxed Emily to expose her writing to public view, first with the publication of *Poems* (1846) and then with the publication of the novel. No doubt there was some guilt on Charlotte Brontë's part when her sister's novel received scornful reviews and her own production, *Jane Eyre*, became an overnight literary sensation. Charlotte Brontë persuaded her publisher, Smith, Elder, to reprint *Wuthering Heights* in an edition that she herself would carefully edit and correct (see the Note on the Text). In addition to tidying up the text of the novel, Charlotte Brontë wrote a short biographical sketch of her two sisters, Emily and Anne, in order to present to the public a more sympathetic portrait of the two. Anne's reputation needed little revisionary work (although she had created an abusive alcoholic husband in *The Tenant of Wildfell Hall* that Charlotte felt compelled to explain). Emily, however, was suspect because of the perceived violence in the novel, as well as the brutal and savage character of Heathcliff.

Charlotte Brontë also wrote the Editor's Preface to the New Edition of *Wuthering Heights* and published it in the 1850 edition. This short article focuses on Emily Brontë as a singular artist in possession of "the creative gift" (22). The possessor of this gift, according to Charlotte, "owns something of which he is not always master — something that at times strangely wills and works for itself" (22). This gift had compelled Emily Brontë to create the character of Heathcliff, even though, as Charlotte points out, "it is [not] right or advisable to create beings like Heathcliff" (22). Critics have found Charlotte Brontë's defense of *Wuthering Heights* patronizing and somewhat insulting to her sister's artistry. There is no doubt, however, that Charlotte Brontë thought she was redeeming her sister's reputation by presenting her as a laborer in a "wild workshop, with simple tools, [using] homely materials" (22). [ED.]

It has been thought that all the works published under the names of Currer, Ellis, and Acton Bell, were, in reality, the production of one person. This mistake I endeavoured to rectify by a few words of disclaimer prefixed to the third edition of *Jane Eyre*. These, too, it appears, failed to gain general credence, and now, on the occasion of a reprint of *Wuthering Heights* and *Agnes Grey*, I am advised distinctly to state how the case really stands.

Indeed, I feel myself that it is time the obscurity attending those two names—Ellis and Acton—was done away. The little mystery, which formerly yielded some harmless pleasure, has lost its interest; circumstances are changed. It becomes, then, my duty to explain briefly the origin and authorship of the books written by Currer, Ellis, and Acton Bell.

About five years ago, my two sisters and myself, after a somewhat prolonged period of separation, found ourselves reunited, and at home. Resident in a remote district where education had made little progress, and where, consequently, there was no inducement to seek social intercourse beyond our own domestic circle, we were wholly dependent on ourselves and each other, on books and study, for the enjoyments and occupations of life. The highest stimulus, as well as the liveliest pleasure we had known from childhood upwards, lay in attempts at literary composition; formerly we used to show each other what we wrote, but of late years this habit of communication and consultation had been discontinued; hence it ensued, that we were mutually ignorant of the progress we might respectively have made.

One day, in the autumn of 1845, I accidentally lighted on a MS. volume of verse in my sister Emily's handwriting. Of course, I was not surprised, knowing that she could and did write verse: I looked it over, and something more than surprise seized me—a deep conviction that these were not common effusions, nor at all like the poetry women generally write. I thought them condensed and terse, vigorous and genuine. To my ear, they had also a peculiar music—wild, melancholy, and elevating.

My sister Emily was not a person of demonstrative character, nor one, on the recesses of whose mind and feelings, even those nearest and dearest to her could, with impunity, intrude unlicensed; it took hours to reconcile her to the discovery I had made, and days to persuade her that such poems merited publication. I knew, however, that a mind like hers could not be

---

From *Wuthering Heights*. 2nd ed. London: Smith, Elder, 1850.

without some latent spark of honourable ambition, and refused to be dis-couraged in my attempts to fan that spark to flame.

Meantime, my younger sister quietly produced some of her own com-positions, intimating that since Emily's had given me pleasure, I might like to look at hers. I could not but be a partial judge, yet I thought that these verses too had a sweet and sincere pathos of their own.

We had very early cherished the dream of one day becoming authors. This dream, never relinquished even when distance divided and absorbing tasks occupied us, now suddenly acquired strength and consistency: it took the character of a resolve. We agreed to arrange a small selection of our poems, and, if possible, get them printed. Averse to personal publicity, we veiled our own names under those of Currer, Ellis, and Acton Bell; the ambiguous choice being dictated by a sort of conscientious scruple at assuming Christian names positively masculine, while we did not like to declare ourselves women, because—without at that time suspecting that our mode of writing and thinking was not what is called "feminine"—we had a vague impression that authoresses are liable to be looked on with prejudice; we had noticed how critics sometimes use for their chastise-ment the weapon of personality, and for their reward, a flattery, which is not true praise.

The bringing out of our little book was hard work. As was to be ex-pected, neither we nor our poems were at all wanted; but for this we had been prepared at the outset; though inexperienced ourselves, we had read the experience of others. The great puzzle lay in the difficulty of getting an-swers of any kind from the publishers to whom we applied. Being greatly harassed by this obstacle, I ventured to apply to the Messrs. Chambers, of Edinburgh, for a word of advice; *they* may have forgotten the circumstance, but *I* have not, for from them I received a brief and business-like but civil and sensible reply, on which we acted, and at last made a way.

The book was printed: it is scarcely known, and all of it that merits to be known are the poems of Ellis Bell. The fixed conviction I held, and hold, of the worth of these poems has not indeed received the confirmation of much favourable criticism; but I must retain it notwithstanding.

Ill-success failed to crush us: the mere effort to succeed had given a wonderful zest to existence; it must be pursued. We each set to work on a prose tale: Ellis Bell produced *Wuthering Heights,* Acton Bell *Agnes Grey,* and Currer Bell also wrote a narrative in one volume. These MSS. were per-severingly obtruded upon various publishers for the space of a year and a half; usually, their fate was an ignominious and abrupt dismissal.

At last *Wuthering Heights* and *Agnes Grey* were accepted on terms some-what impoverishing to the two authors; Currer Bell's book found accep-tance nowhere, nor any acknowledgment of merit, so that something like the chill of despair began to invade his heart. As a forlorn hope, he tried one publishing house more — Messrs. Smith and Elder. Ere long, in a much shorter space than that on which experience had taught him to calculate — there came a letter, which he opened in the dreary expectation of finding two hard hopeless lines, intimating that Messrs. Smith and Elder "were not disposed to publish the MS.," and, instead, he took out of the envelope a letter of two pages. He read it trembling. It declined, indeed, to publish that tale, for business reasons, but it discussed its merits and demerits so courteously, so considerately, in a spirit so rational, with a discrimination so enlightened, that this very refusal cheered the author better than a vulgarly expressed acceptance would have done. It was added, that a work in three volumes would meet with careful attention.

I was then just completing *Jane Eyre,* at which I had been working while the one volume tale was plodding its weary round in London: in three weeks I sent it off; friendly and skilful hands took it in. This was in the commencement of September 1847; it came out before the close of October following, while *Wuthering Heights* and *Agnes Grey,* my sisters' works, which had already been in the press for months, still lingered under a different management.

They appeared at last. Critics failed to do them justice. The immature but very real powers revealed in *Wuthering Heights* were scarcely recognised; its import and nature were misunderstood; the identity of its author was misrepresented; it was said that this was an earlier and ruder attempt of the same pen which had produced *Jane Eyre.* Unjust and grievous error! We laughed at it at first, but I deeply lament it now. Hence, I fear, arose a prejudice against the book. That writer who could attempt to palm off an inferior and immature production under cover of one successful effort, must indeed be unduly eager after the secondary and sordid result of authorship, and pitiably indifferent to its true and honourable meed. If reviewers and the public truly believed this, no wonder that they looked darkly on the cheat.

Yet I must not be understood to make these things subject for reproach or complaint; I dare not do so; respect for my sister's memory forbids me. By her any such querulous manifestation would have been regarded as an unworthy, and offensive weakness.

It is my duty, as well as my pleasure, to acknowledge one exception to the general rule of criticism. One writer,[1] endowed with the keen vision and fine sympathies of genius, has discerned the real nature of *Wuthering Heights,* and has, with equal accuracy, noted its beauties and touched on

---

[1] "See the *Palladium* for September 1850." [Charlotte Brontë's note.]

its faults. Too often do reviewers remind us of the mob of Astrologers, Chaldeans, and Soothsayers gathered before the "writing on the wall," and unable to read the characters or make known the interpretation. We have a right to rejoice when a true seer comes at last, some man in whom is an excellent spirit, to whom have been given light, wisdom, and understanding; who can accurately read the "Mene, Mene, Tekel, Upharsin"[1] of an original mind (however unripe, however inefficiently cultured and partially expanded that mind may be); and who can say with confidence, "This is the interpretation thereof."

Yet even the writer to whom I allude shares the mistake about the authorship, and does me the injustice to suppose that there was equivoque in my former rejection of this honour (as an honour, I regard it). May I assure him that I would scorn in this and in every other case to deal in equivoque; I believe language to have been given us to make our meaning clear, and not to wrap it in dishonest doubt.

The Tenant of Wildfell Hall by Acton Bell, had likewise an unfavourable reception. At this I cannot wonder. The choice of subject was an entire mistake. Nothing less congruous with the writer's nature could be conceived. The motives which dictated this choice were pure, but, I think, slightly morbid. She had, in the course of her life, been called on to contemplate, near at hand and for a long tune, the terrible effects of talents misused and faculties abused; hers was naturally a sensitive, reserved, and dejected nature; what she saw sank deeply into her mind; it did her harm. She brooded over it till she believed it to be a duty to reproduce every detail (of course with fictitious characters, incidents, and situations) as a warning to others. She hated her work, but would pursue it. When reasoned with on the subject, she regarded such reasonings as a temptation to self-indulgence. She must be honest; she must not varnish, soften, or conceal. This well-meant resolution brought on her misconstruction and some abuse, which she bore, as it was her custom to bear whatever was unpleasant, with mild, steady patience. She was a very sincere and practical Christian, but the tinge of religious melancholy communicated a sad shade to her brief, blameless life.

Neither Ellis nor Acton allowed herself for one moment to sink under want of encouragement; energy nerved the one, and endurance upheld the other. They were both prepared to try again; I would fain think that hope

---

[1] The reference is to a prophecy made in Daniel 5.25–28 (*Mene:* "God hath numbered thy kingdom and finished it"; *Tekel:* "Thou art weighed in the balances, and art found wanting"; *Upharsin:* "Thy kingdom is divided, and given to the Medes and Persians"). Charlotte Brontë's use of the biblical passage suggests how rare it was for a contemporary critic to understand and appreciate her sister's novel.

and the sense of power was yet strong within them. But a great change approached: affliction came in that shape which to anticipate is dread; to look back on, grief. In the very heat and burden of the day, the labourers failed over their work.

My sister Emily first declined. The details of her illness are deep-branded in my memory, but to dwell on them, either in thought or narrative, is not in my power. Never in all her life had she lingered over any task that lay before her, and she did not linger now. She sank rapidly. She made haste to leave us. Yet, while physically she perished, mentally, she grew stronger than we had yet known her. Day by day, when I saw with what a front she met suffering, I looked on her with an anguish of wonder and love. I have seen nothing like it; but, indeed, I have never seen her parallel in anything. Stronger than a man, simpler than a child, her nature stood alone. The awful point was, that, while full of ruth for others, on herself she had no pity; the spirit was inexorable to the flesh; from the trembling hand, the unnerved limbs, the faded eyes, the same service was exacted as they had rendered in health. To stand by and witness this, and not dare to remonstrate, was a pain no words can render.

Two cruel months of hope and fear passed painfully by, and the day came at last when the terrors and pains of death were to be undergone by this treasure, which had grown dearer and dearer to our hearts as it wasted before our eyes. Towards the decline of that day, we had nothing of Emily but her mortal remains as consumption left them. She died December 19, 1848.

We thought this enough; but we were utterly and presumptuously wrong. She was not buried ere Anne fell ill. She had not been committed to the grave a fortnight, before we received distinct intimation that it was necessary to prepare our minds to see the younger sister go after the elder. Accordingly, she followed in the same path with slower step, and with a patience that equalled the other's fortitude. I have said that she was religious, and it was by leaning on those Christian doctrines in which she firmly believed, that she found support through her most painful journey. I witnessed their efficacy in her latest hour and greatest trial, and must bear my testimony to the calm triumph with which they brought her through. She died May 28, 1849.

What more shall I say about them? I cannot and need not say much more. In externals, they were two unobtrusive women; a perfectly secluded life gave them retiring manners and habits. In Emily's nature the extremes of vigour and simplicity seemed to meet. Under an unsophisticated culture, inartificial tastes, and an unpretending outside, lay a secret power and fire that might have informed the brain and kindled the veins of a hero; but she had no worldly wisdom; her powers were unadapted to the practical business of life; she would fail to defend her most manifest rights, to consult her most legitimate advantage. An interpreter ought always to have stood between her and the world. Her will was not very flexible, and it generally opposed her interest. Her temper was magnanimous, but warm and sudden; her spirit altogether unbending.

Anne's character was milder and more subdued; she wanted the power, the fire, the originality of her sister, but was well-endowed with quiet virtues of her own. Long-suffering, self-denying, reflective, and intelligent, a constitutional reserve and taciturnity placed and kept her in the shade, and covered her mind, and especially her feelings, with a sort of nun-like veil, which was rarely lifted. Neither Emily nor Anne was learned; they had no thought of filling their pitchers at the well-spring of other minds; they always wrote from the impulse of nature, the dictates of intuition, and from such stores of observation as their limited experience had enabled them to amass. I may sum up all by saying, that for strangers they were nothing, for superficial observers less than nothing; but for those who had known them all their lives in the intimacy of close relationship, they were genuinely good and truly great.

This notice has been written, because I felt it a sacred duty to wipe the dust off their gravestones, and leave their dear names free from soil.

Currer Bell

September 19, 1850

EDITOR'S PREFACE
To The New Edition of
Wuthering Heights *(1850)*

Charlotte Brontë

I have just read over *Wuthering Heights* and, for the first time, have obtained a clear glimpse of what are termed (and, perhaps, really are) its faults; have gained a definite notion of how it appears to other people — to strangers who knew nothing of the author; who are unacquainted with the locality where the scenes of the story are laid; to whom the inhabitants, the customs, the natural characteristics of the outlying hills and hamlets in the West-Riding of Yorkshire are things alien and unfamiliar.

To all such *Wuthering Heights* must appear a rude and strange production. The wild moors of the north of England can for them have no inter-

From *Wuthering Heights.* 2nd ed. London: Smith, Elder, 1850.

est; the language, the manners, the very dwellings and household customs of the scattered inhabitants of those districts, must be to such readers in a great measure unintelligible, and — where intelligible — repulsive. Men and women who, perhaps, naturally very calm, and with feelings moderate in degree, and little marked in kind, have been trained from their cradle to observe the utmost evenness of manner and guardedness of language, will hardly know what to make of the rough, strong utterance, the harshly manifested passions, the unbridled aversions, and headlong partialities of unlettered moorland hinds and rugged moorland squires, who have grown up untaught and unchecked, except by mentors as harsh as themselves. A large class of readers, likewise, will suffer greatly from the introduction into the pages of this work of words printed with all their letters, which it has become the custom to represent by the initial and final letter only — a blank line filling the interval. I may as well say at once that, for this circumstance, it is out of my power to apologize; deeming it, myself, a rational plan to write words at full length. The practice of hinting by single letters those expletives with which profane and violent persons are wont to garnish their discourse, strikes me as a proceeding which, however well meant, is weak and futile. I cannot tell what good it does — what feeling it spares — what horror it conceals.

With regard to the rusticity of *Wuthering Heights* I admit the charge, for I feel the quality. It is rustic all through. It is moorish, and wild, and knotty as a root of heath. Nor was it natural that it should be otherwise; the author being herself a native and nursling of the moors. Doubtless, had her lot been cast in a town, her writings, if she had written at all, would have possessed another character. Even had chance or taste led her to choose a similar subject, she would have treated it otherwise. Had Ellis Bell been a lady or a gentleman accustomed to what is called "the world," her view of a remote and unreclaimed region, as well as of the dwellers therein, would have differed greatly from that actually taken by the homebred country girl. Doubtless it would have been wider — more comprehensive: whether it would have been more original or more truthful is not so certain. As far as the scenery and locality are concerned, it could scarcely have been so sympathetic: Ellis Bell did not describe as one whose eye and taste alone found pleasure in the prospect; her native hills were far more to her than a spectacle; they were what she lived in, and by, as much as the wild birds, their tenants, or as the heather, their produce. Her descriptions, then, of natural scenery, are what they should be, and all they should be.

Where delineation of human character is concerned, the case is different. I am bound to avow that she had scarcely more practical knowledge of the peasantry amongst whom she lived, than a nun has of the country people who sometimes pass her convent gates. My sister's disposition was

not naturally gregarious; circumstances favoured and fostered her tendency to seclusion; except to go to church or take a walk on the hills, she
rarely crossed the threshold of home. Though her feeling for the people
round was benevolent, intercourse with them she never sought; nor, with
very few exceptions, ever experienced. And yet she knew them: knew
their ways, their language, their family histories; she could hear of them
with interest, and talk of them with detail, minute, graphic, and accurate;
but *with* them, she rarely exchanged a word. Hence it ensued that what
her mind had gathered of the real concerning them, was too exclusively
confined to those tragic and terrible traits of which, in listening to the secret annals of every rude vicinage, the memory is sometimes compelled to
receive the impress. Her imagination, which was a spirit more sombre than
sunny, more powerful than sportive, found in such traits material whence
it wrought creations like Heathcliff, like Earnshaw, like Catherine. Having
formed these beings, she did not know what she had done. If the auditor of
her work when read in manuscript, shuddered under the grinding influence of natures so relentless and implacable, of spirits so lost and fallen; if
it was complained that the mere hearing of certain vivid and fearful scenes
banished sleep by night, and disturbed mental peace by day, Ellis Bell
would wonder what was meant, and suspect the complainant of affectation. Had she but lived, her mind would of itself have grown like a strong
tree, loftier, straighter, wider-spreading, and its matured fruits would have
attained a mellower ripeness and sunnier bloom; but on that mind time
and experience alone could work: to the influence of other intellects, it was
not amenable.

Having avowed that over much of *Wuthering Heights* there broods "a
horror of great darkness"; that, in its storm-heated and electrical atmosphere, we seem at times to breathe lightning, let me point to those spots
where clouded daylight and the eclipsed sun still attest their existence. For
a specimen of true benevolence and homely fidelity, look at the character
of Nelly Dean; for an example of constancy and tenderness, remark that
of Edgar Linton. (Some people will think these qualities do not shine so
well incarnate in a man as they would do in a woman, but Ellis Bell could
never be brought to comprehend this notion: nothing moved her more
than any insinuation that the faithfulness and clemency, the long-suffering
and loving-kindness which are esteemed virtues in the daughters of Eve,
become foibles in the sons of Adam. She held that mercy and forgiveness
are the divinest attributes of the Great Being who made both man and
woman, and that what clothes the Godhead in glory, can disgrace no form
of feeble humanity.) There is a dry saturnine humour in the delineation of
old Joseph, and some glimpses of grace and gaiety animate the younger
Catherine. Nor is even the first heroine of the name destitute of a certain

strange beauty in her fierceness, or of honesty in the midst of perverted passion and passionate perversity.

Heathcliff, indeed, stands unredeemed; never once swerving in his arrow-straight course to perdition, from the time when "the little black-haired, swarthy thing, as dark as if it came from the Devil," was first un-rolled out of the bundle and set on its feet in the farmhouse kitchen, to the hour when Nelly Dean found the grim, stalwart corpse laid on its back in the panel-enclosed bed, with wide-gazing eyes that seemed "to sneer at her attempt to close them, and parted lips and sharp white teeth that sneered too."

Heathcliff betrays one solitary human feeling, and that is *not* his love for Catherine; which is a sentiment fierce and inhuman: a passion such as might boil and glow in the bad essence of some evil genius; a fire that might form the tormented centre — the ever-suffering soul of a magnate of the in-fernal world: and by its quenchless and ceaseless ravage effect the execution of the decree which dooms him to carry Hell with him wherever he wan-ders. No; the single link that connects Heathcliff with humanity is his rudely confessed regard for Hareton Earnshaw — the young man whom he has ruined; and then his half-implied esteem for Nelly Dean. These solitary traits omitted, we should say he was child neither of Lascar nor gipsy, but a man's shape animated by demon life — a Ghoul — an Afreet.

Whether it is right or advisable to create beings like Heathcliff, I do not know: I scarcely think it is. But this I know; the writer who possesses the creative gift owns something of which he is not always master — something that at times strangely wills and works for itself. He may lay down rules and devise principles, and to rules and principles it will perhaps for years lie in subjection; and then, haply without any warning of revolt, there comes a time when it will no longer consent to "harrow the vallies, or be bound with a band in the furrow" — when it "laughs at the multitude of the city, and regards not the crying of the driver" — when, refusing absolutely to make ropes out of sea-sand any longer, it sets to work on statue-hewing, and you have a Pluto or a Jove, a Tisiphone or a Psyche, a Mermaid or a Madonna, as Fate or Inspiration direct. Be the work grim or glorious, dread or divine, you have little choice left but quiescent adoption. As for you — the nominal artist — your share in it has been to work passively under dic-tates you neither delivered nor could question — that would not be uttered at your prayer, nor suppressed nor changed at your caprice. If the result be

---

Lascar: disease-ridden, swarthy seaman or soldier (*OED*).
Afreet: evil demon or monster (*OED*).
Tisiphone: mythological being who used a lash to scourge trembling sinners (*OED*).

attractive, the World will praise you, who little deserve praise; if it be repulsive, the same World will blame you, who almost as little deserve blame.

Wuthering Heights was hewn in a wild workshop, with simple tools, out of homely materials. The statuary found a granite block on a solitary moor: gazing thereon, he saw how from the crag might be elicited a head, savage, swart, sinister; a form moulded with at least one element of grandeur — power. He wrought with a rude chisel, and from no model but the vision of his meditations. With time and labour, the crag took human shape; and there it stands colossal, dark, and frowning, half statue, half rock: in the former sense, terrible and goblin-like; in the latter, almost beautiful, for its colouring is of mellow grey, and moorland moss clothes it; and heath, with its blooming bells and balmy fragrance, grows faithfully close to the giant's foot.

Currer Bell

Wuthering Heights

Emily Brontë

CHAPTER I

1801. I have just returned from a visit to my landlord—the solitary neighbour that I shall be troubled with. This is certainly, a beautiful country! In all England, I do not believe that I could have fixed on a situation so completely removed from the stir of society. A perfect misanthropist's Heaven—and Mr. Heathcliff and I are such a suitable pair to divide the desolation between us. A capital fellow! He little imagined how my heart warmed towards him when I beheld his black eyes withdraw so suspiciously under their brows, as I rode up, and when his fingers sheltered themselves, with a jealous resolution still further in his waistcoat, as I announced my name.

"Mr. Heathcliff?" I said.

A nod was the answer.

"Mr. Lockwood your new tenant, sir. I do myself the honour of calling as soon as possible, after my arrival, to express the hope that I have not inconvenienced you by my perseverance in soliciting the occupation of Thrushcross Grange: I heard, yesterday, you had some thoughts—"

"Thrushcross Grange is my own, sir," he interrupted wincing, "I should not allow anyone to inconvenience me, if I could hinder it—walk in!"

The "walk in," was uttered with closed teeth and expressed the sentiment, "Go to the Deuce!" even the gate over which he leant manifested no sympathizing movement to the words; and I think that circumstance determined me to accept the invitation: I felt interested in a man who seemed more exaggeratedly reserved than myself.

When he saw my horse's breast fairly pushing the barrier, he did pull out his hand to unchain it, and then sullenly preceded me up the causeway, calling, as we entered the court:

"Joseph, take Mr. Lockwood's horse; and bring up some wine."

"Here we have the whole establishment of domestics, I suppose," was the reflection, suggested by this compound order, "No wonder the grass grows up between the flags, and cattle are the only hedge-cutters."

Joseph was an elderly, nay, an old man, very old, perhaps, though hale and sinewy.

"The Lord help us!" he soliloquised in an undertone of peevish displeasure, while relieving me of my horse: looking, meantime, in my face so sourly that I charitably conjectured he must have need of divine aid to

---

Riverside edition, Boston: Houghton Mifflin, 1956, with minor revisions.

the Deuce: the Devil.

digest his dinner, and his pious ejaculation had no reference to my unexpected advent.

Wuthering Heights is the name of Mr. Heathcliff's dwelling. "Wuthering" being a significant provincial adjective, descriptive of the atmospheric tumult to which its station is exposed, in stormy weather. Pure, bracing ventilation they must have up there, at all times, indeed: one may guess the power of the north wind, blowing over the edge, by the excessive slant of a few, stunted firs at the end of the house; and by a range of gaunt thorns all stretching their limbs one way, as if craving alms of the sun. Happily, the architect had foresight to build it strong: the narrow windows are deeply set in the wall; and the corners defended with large jutting stones.

Before passing the threshold, I paused to admire a quantity of grotesque carving lavished over the front, and especially about the principal door, above which, among a wilderness of crumbling griffins, and shameless little boys, I detected the date "1500," and the name "Hareton Earnshaw." I would have made a few comments, and requested a short history of the place, from the surly owner, but his attitude at the door appeared to demand my speedy entrance, or complete departure, and I had no desire to aggravate his impatience, previous to inspecting the penetralium.

One step brought us into the family sitting-room, without any introductory lobby, or passage: they call it here "the house" preeminently. It includes kitchen, and parlour, generally, but I believe at Wuthering Heights, the kitchen is forced to retreat altogether, into another quarter, at least I distinguished a chatter of tongues, and a clatter of culinary utensils, deep within; and I observed no signs of roasting, boiling, or baking, about the huge fireplace; nor any glitter of copper saucepans and tin cullenders on the walls. One end, indeed, reflected splendidly both light and heat, from ranks of immense pewter dishes; interspersed with silver jugs, and tankards, towering row after row, in a vast oak dresser, to the very roof. The latter had never been underdrawn, its entire anatomy lay bare to an inquiring eye, except where a frame of wood laden with oatcakes, and clusters of legs of beef, mutton, and ham, concealed it. Above the chimney were sundry villainous old guns, and a couple of horse pistols, and, by way of ornament, three gaudily painted canisters disposed along its ledge. The floor was of smooth, white stone: the chairs, high-backed, primitive structures, painted green: one or two heavy black ones lurking in the shade. In an arch, under the dresser, reposed a huge, liver-coloured bitch pointer surrounded by a swarm of squealing puppies; and other dogs, haunted other recesses.

The apartment, and furniture would have been nothing extraordinary as belonging to a homely, northern farmer with a stubborn countenance and stalwart limbs, set out to advantage in knee-breeches, and gaiters. Such an individual, seated in his arm-chair, his mug of ale frothing on the round table before him, is to be seen in any circuit of five or six miles among these hills, if you go at the right time, after dinner. But, Mr. Heathcliff forms a singular contrast to his abode and style of living. He is a dark skinned gipsy, in aspect; in dress, and manners, a gentleman, that is, as much a gentleman as many a country squire: rather slovenly, perhaps, yet not looking amiss, with his negligence, because he has an erect and handsome figure—and rather morose—possibly, some people might suspect him of a degree of under-bred pride—I have a sympathetic chord within that tells me it is nothing of the sort; I know, by instinct, his reserve springs from an aversion to showy displays of feeling—to manifestations of mutual kindliness. He'll love and hate, equally under cover, and esteem it a species of impertinence, to be loved or hated again—No, I'm running on too fast—I bestow my own attributes over liberally on him. Mr. Heathcliff may have entirely dissimilar reasons for keeping his hand out of the way, when he meets a would be acquaintance, to those which actuate me. Let me hope my constitution is almost peculiar: my dear mother used to say I should never have a comfortable home, and only last summer, I proved myself perfectly unworthy of one.

While enjoying a month of fine weather at the sea-coast, I was thrown into the company of a most fascinating creature, a real goddess, in my eyes, as long as she took no notice of me. I "never told my love" vocally; still, if looks have language, the merest idiot might have guessed I was over head and ears; she understood me, at last, and looked a return—the sweetest of all imaginable looks—and what did I do? I confess it with shame—shrunk icily into myself, like a snail, at every glance retired colder and farther; till, finally, the poor innocent was led to doubt her own senses, and, overwhelmed with confusion at her supposed mistake, persuaded her mamma to decamp.

By this curious turn of disposition I have gained the reputation of deliberate heartlessness, how undeserved, I alone can appreciate.

I took a seat at the end of the hearthstone opposite that towards which my landlord advanced, and filled up an interval of silence by attempting to caress the canine mother, who had left her nursery, and was sneaking wolfishly to the back of my legs, her lip curled up, and her white teeth watering for a snatch.

My caress provoked a long, guttural gnarl.

"You'd better let the dog alone," growled Mr. Heathcliff, in unison, checking fiercer demonstrations with a punch of his foot. "She's not accustomed to be spoiled—not kept for a pet."

Then, striding to a side-door, he shouted again.

"Joseph!"

Joseph mumbled indistinctly in the depths of the cellar; but, gave no intimation of ascending; so, his master dived down to him, leaving me *vis-à-vis* the ruffianly bitch, and a pair of grim, shaggy sheep-dogs, who shared with her a jealous guardianship over all my movements.

Not anxious to come in contact with their fangs, I sat still—but, imagining they would scarcely understand tacit insults, I unfortunately indulged in winking and making faces at the trio, and some turn of my physiognomy so irritated madam, that she suddenly broke into a fury, and leapt on my knees. I flung her back, and hastened to interpose the table between us. This proceeding roused the whole hive. Half-a-dozen four-footed fiends, of various sizes and ages, issued from hidden dens to the common centre. I felt my heels, and coat-laps peculiar subjects of assault; and, parrying off the larger combatants, as effectually as I could, with the poker, I was constrained to demand, aloud, assistance from some of the household, in re-establishing peace.

Mr. Heathcliff and his man climbed the cellar steps with vexatious phlegm. I don't think they moved one second faster than usual, though the hearth was an absolute tempest of worrying and yelping.

Happily, an inhabitant of the kitchen made more dispatch; a lusty dame, with tucked up gown, bare arms, and fire-flushed cheeks, rushed into the midst of us flourishing a fryingpan; and used that weapon, and her tongue to such purpose, that the storm subsided magically, and she only remained, heaving like a sea after a high wind, when her master entered on the scene.

"What the devil is the matter?" he asked, eyeing me in a manner that I could ill endure after this inhospitable treatment.

"What the devil, indeed!" I muttered. "The herd of possessed swine could have had no worse spirits in them than those animals of yours, sir. You might as well leave a stranger with a brood of tigers!"

"They won't meddle with persons who touch nothing," he remarked, putting the bottle before me, and restoring the displaced table. "The dogs do right to be vigilant. Take a glass of wine?"

"No, thank you."

"Not bitten, are you?"

"If I had been, I would have set my signet on the biter."

Heathcliff's countenance relaxed into a grin.

"Come, come," he said, "you are flurried, Mr. Lockwood. Here, take a little wine. Guests are so exceedingly rare in this house that I and my dogs, I am willing to own, hardly know how to receive them. Your health, sir."

---

set my signet on the biter: struck the dog with my fist.

I bowed and returned the pledge; beginning to perceive that it would be foolish to sit sulking for the misbehaviour of a pack of curs: besides, I felt loth to yield the fellow further amusement, at my expense; since his humour took that turn.

He—probably swayed by prudential considerations of the folly of offending a good tenant—relaxed, a little, in the laconic style of chipping off his pronouns, and auxiliary verbs; and introduced, what he supposed would be a subject of interest to me, a discourse on the advantages and disadvantages of my present place of retirement.

I found him very intelligent on the topics we touched; and, before I went home, I was encouraged so far as to volunteer another visit, tomorrow.

He evidently wished no repetition of my intrusion. I shall go, notwithstanding. It is astonishing how sociable I feel myself compared with him.

CHAPTER II

Yesterday afternoon set in misty and cold. I had half a mind to spend it by my study fire, instead of wading through heath and mud to Wuthering Heights.

On coming up from dinner, however (N.B. I dine between twelve and one o'clock; the housekeeper, a matronly lady taken as a fixture along with the house, could not, or would not comprehend my request that I might be served at five.)—On mounting the stairs with this lazy intention, and stepping into the room, I saw a servant-girl on her knees, surrounded by brushes, and coal-scuttles; and raising an infernal dust as she extinguished the flames with heaps of cinders. This spectacle drove me back immediately; I took my hat, and, after a four miles' walk, arrived at Heathcliff's garden gate just in time to escape the first feathery flakes of a snow shower.

On that bleak hill top the earth was hard with a black frost, and the air made me shiver through every limb. Being unable to remove the chain, I jumped over, and, running up the flagged causeway bordered with straggling gooseberry bushes, knocked vainly for admittance, till my knuckles tingled, and the dogs howled.

"Wretched inmates!" I ejaculated, mentally, "you deserve perpetual isolation from your species for your churlish inhospitality. At least, I would not keep my doors barred in the day time—I don't care—I will get in!"

So resolved, I grasped the latch, and shook it vehemently. Vinegar-faced Joseph projected his head from a round window of the barn.

"Whet are ye for?" he shouted. "T' maister's dahn i' t' fowld. Goa rahnd by th' end ut' laith, if yah went tuh spake tull him."

"Is there nobody inside to open the door?" I hallooed, responsively.

"They's nobbut t' missis; and shoo'll nut oppen't an ye mak yer flaysome dins till nneeght."

"Why? cannot you tell her who I am, eh, Joseph?"

"Nor-ne me! Aw'll hae noa hend wi't," muttered the head vanishing.

The snow began to drive thickly. I seized the handle to essay another trial; when a young man, without coat, and shouldering a pitchfork, appeared in the yard behind. He hailed me to follow him, and, after marching through a washhouse, and a paved area containing a coal-shed, pump, and pigeon cote, we at length arrived in the large, warm, cheerful apartment, where I was formerly received.

It glowed delightfully in the radiance of an immense fire, compounded of coal, peat, and wood: and near the table, laid for a plentiful evening meal, I was pleased to observe the "missis," an individual whose existence I had never previously suspected.

I bowed and waited, thinking she would bid me take a seat. She looked at me, leaning back in her chair, and remained motionless and mute.

"Rough weather!" I remarked. "I'm afraid, Mrs. Heathcliff, the door must bear the consequence of your servants' leisure attendance: I had hard work to make them hear me!"

She never opened her mouth. I stared—she stared also. At any rate, she kept her eyes on me, in a cool, regardless manner, exceedingly embarrassing and disagreeable.

"Sit down," said the young man, gruffly. "He'll be in soon."

I obeyed; and hemmed, and called the villain Juno, who deigned, at this second interview, to move the extreme tip of her tail, in token of owning my acquaintance.

"A beautiful animal!" I commenced again. "Do you intend parting with the little ones, madam?"

"They are not mine," said the amiable hostess more repellingly than Heathcliff himself could have replied.

"Ah, your favourites are among these!" I continued, turning to an obscure cushion full of something like cats.

---

fowld: fold (fenced enclosure for domestic animals).
laith: barn.
nobbut: no one but; only.
flaysome: frightening; terrible.
Nor-ne me: Not I!

"A strange choice of favourites," she observed scornfully.

Unluckily, it was a heap of dead rabbits—I hemmed once more, and drew closer to the hearth, repeating my comment on the wildness of the evening.

"You should not have come out," she said, rising and reaching from the chimney piece two of the painted canisters.

Her position before was sheltered from the light: now, I had a distinct view of her whole figure and countenance. She was slender, and apparently scarcely past girlhood: an admirable form, and the most exquisite little face that I have ever had the pleasure of beholding: small features, very fair; flaxen ringlets, or rather golden, hanging loose on her delicate neck; and eyes—had they been agreeable in expression, they would have been irresistible—fortunately for my susceptible heart, the only sentiment they evinced hovered between scorn and a kind of desperation, singularly unnatural to be detected there.

The canisters were almost out of her reach; I made a motion to aid her; she turned upon me as a miser might turn, if anyone attempted to assist him in counting his gold.

"I don't want your help," she snapped, "I can get them for myself."

"I beg your pardon," I hastened to reply.

"Were you asked to tea?" she demanded, tying an apron over her neat black frock, and standing with a spoonful of the leaf poised over the pot.

"I shall be glad to have a cup," I answered.

"Were you asked?" she repeated.

"No," I said, half smiling. "You are the proper person to ask me."

She flung the tea back, spoon and all; and resumed her chair in a pet, her forehead corrugated, and her red under-lip pushed out, like a child's, ready to cry.

Meanwhile, the young man had slung onto his person a decidedly shabby upper garment, and, erecting himself before the blaze, looked down on me, from the corner of his eyes, for all the world as if there were some mortal feud unavenged between us. I began to doubt whether he were a servant or not; his dress and speech were both rude, entirely devoid of the superiority observable in Mr. and Mrs. Heathcliff; his thick, brown curls were rough and uncultivated, his whiskers encroached bearishly over his cheeks, and his hands were embrowned like those of a common labourer: still his bearing was free, almost haughty; and he showed none of a domestic's assiduity in attending on the lady of the house.

---

pet: sulky mood.

In the absence of clear proofs of his condition, I deemed it best to abstain from noticing his curious conduct, and, five minutes afterwards, the entrance of Heathcliff relieved me, in some measure, from my uncomfortable state.

"You see, sir, I am come, according to promise!" I exclaimed, assuming the cheerful; "and I fear I shall be weather-bound for half an hour, if you can afford me shelter during that space."

"Half an hour?" he said, shaking the white flakes from his clothes; "I wonder you should select the thick of a snow-storm to ramble about in. Do you know that you run a risk of being lost in the marshes? People familiar with these moors often miss their road on such evenings, and, I can tell you, there is no chance of a change at present."

"Perhaps I can get a guide among your lads, and he might stay at the Grange till morning—could you spare me one?"

"No, I could not."

"Oh, indeed! Well then, I must trust to my own sagacity."

"Umph!"

"Are you going to mak th' tea?" demanded he of the shabby coat, shifting his ferocious gaze from me to the young lady.

"Is *he* to have any?" she asked, appealing to Heathcliff.

"Get it ready, will you?" was the answer, uttered so savagely that I started. The tone in which the words were said revealed a genuine bad nature. I no longer felt inclined to call Heathcliff a capital fellow.

When the preparations were finished, he invited me with—

"Now, sir, bring forward your chair." And we all, including the rustic youth, drew round the table, an austere silence prevailing while we discussed our meal.

I thought, if I had caused the cloud, it was my duty to make an effort to dispel it. They could not every day sit so grim and taciturn, and it was impossible, however ill-tempered they might be, that the universal scowl they wore was their every day countenance.

"It is strange," I began in the interval of swallowing one cup of tea, and receiving another, "it is strange how custom can mould our tastes and ideas; many could not imagine the existence of happiness in a life of such complete exile from the world as you spend, Mr. Heathcliff; yet, I'll venture to say, that, surrounded by your family, and with your amiable lady as the presiding genius over your home and heart—"

"My amiable lady!" he interrupted, with an almost diabolical sneer on his face. "Where is she—my amiable lady?"

"Mrs. Heathcliff, your wife, I mean."

"Well, yes—Oh! you would intimate that her spirit has taken the post of ministering angel, and guards the fortunes of Wuthering Heights, even when her body is gone. Is that it?"

Perceiving myself in a blunder, I attempted to correct it. I might have seen there was too great a disparity between the ages of the parties to make it likely that they were man and wife. One was about forty; a period of mental vigour at which men seldom cherish the delusion of being married for love, by girls: that dream is reserved for the solace of our declining years. The other did not look seventeen.

Then it flashed upon me; "the clown at my elbow, who is drinking his tea out of a basin, and eating his bread with unwashed hands, may be her husband. Heathcliff, junior, of course. Here is the consequence of being buried alive: she has thrown herself away upon that boor, from sheer ignorance that better individuals existed! A sad pity—I must beware how I cause her to regret her choice."

The last reflection may seem conceited; it was not. My neighbour struck me as bordering on repulsive. I knew, through experience, that I was tolerably attractive.

"Mrs. Heathcliff is my daughter-in-law," said Heathcliff, corroborating my surmise. He turned, as he spoke, a peculiar look in her direction, a look of hatred unless he has a most perverse set of facial muscles that will not, like those of other people, interpret the language of his soul.

"Ah, certainly—I see now; you are the favoured possessor of the beneficent fairy," I remarked, turning to my neighbour.

This was worse than before: the youth grew crimson, and clenched his fist, with every appearance of a meditated assault. But he seemed to recollect himself, presently; and smothered the storm in a brutal curse, muttered on my behalf, which, however, I took care not to notice.

"Unhappy in your conjectures, sir!" observed my host; "we neither of us have the privilege of owning your good fairy; her mate is dead. I said she was my daughter-in-law, therefore, she must have married my son."

"And this young man is—"

"Not my son, assuredly!"

Heathcliff smiled again, as if it were rather too bold a jest to attribute the paternity of that bear to him.

"My name is Hareton Earnshaw," growled the other; "and I'd counsel you to respect it!"

"I've shown no disrespect," was my reply, laughing internally at the dignity with which he announced himself.

He fixed his eye on me longer than I cared to return the stare, for fear I might be tempted either to box his ears, or render my hilarity audible. I began to feel unmistakably out of place in that pleasant family circle. The dismal spiritual atmosphere overcame, and more than neutralized the glowing physical comforts round me; and I resolved to be cautious how I ventured under those rafters a third time.

The business of eating being concluded, and no one uttering a word of sociable conversation, I approached a window to examine the weather.

A sorrowful sight I saw; dark night coming down prematurely, and sky and hills mingled in one bitter whirl of wind and suffocating snow.

"I don't think it possible for me to get home now, without a guide," I could not help exclaiming. "The roads will be buried already; and, if they were bare, I could scarcely distinguish a foot in advance."

"Hareton, drive those dozen sheep into the barn porch. They'll be covered if left in the fold all night; and put a plank before them," said Heathcliff.

"How must I do?" I continued, with rising irritation.

There was no reply to my question; and, on looking round, I saw only Joseph bringing in a pail of porridge for the dogs; and Mrs. Heathcliff, leaning over the fire, diverting herself with burning a bundle of matches which had fallen from the chimney-piece as she restored the tea-canister to its place.

The former, when he had deposited his burden, took a critical survey of the room; and, in cracked tones, grated out:

"Aw woonder hagh yah can faishion tuh 'stand thear i' idleness un war, when all on 'em's goan aght! Bud yah're a nowt, and it's noa use talking — yah'll niver mend uh yer ill ways; bud, goa raight tuh t' divil, like yer mother afore ye!"

I imagined, for a moment, that this piece of eloquence was addressed to me; and, sufficiently enraged, stepped towards the aged rascal with an intention of kicking him out of the door.

Mrs. Heathcliff, however, checked me by her answer.

"You scandalous old hypocrite!" she replied. "Are you not afraid of being carried away bodily, whenever you mention the devil's name? I warn you to refrain from provoking me, or I'll ask your abduction as a special favour. Stop, look here, Joseph," she continued, taking a long, dark book from a shelf. "I'll show you how far I've progressed in the Black Art — I shall soon be competent to make a clear house of it. The red cow didn't die by chance; and your rheumatism can hardly be reckoned among providential visitations!"

---

faishion tuh: dare to.
un war: and worse.
a nowt: a nothing.

"Oh, wicked, wicked!" gasped the elder, "may the Lord deliver us from evil!"

"No, reprobate! you are a castaway—be off, or I'll hurt you seriously! I'll have you all modelled in wax and clay; and the first who passes the limits I fix shall—I'll not say what he shall be done to—but, you'll see! Go, I'm looking at you!"

The little witch put a mock malignity into her beautiful eyes, and Joseph, trembling with sincere horror, hurried out praying and ejaculating "wicked" as he went.

I thought her conduct must be prompted by a species of dreary fun; and, now that we were alone, I endeavoured to interest her in my distress.

"Mrs. Heathcliff," I said earnestly, "you must excuse me for troubling you—I presume, because, with that face, I'm sure you cannot help being good-hearted. Do point out some landmarks by which I may know my way home—I have no more idea how to get there than you would have how to get to London!"

"Take the road you came," she answered, ensconcing herself in a chair, with a candle, and the long book open before her. "It is brief advice; but, as sound as I can give."

"Then, if you hear of me being discovered dead in a bog, or a pit full of snow, your conscience won't whisper that it is partly your fault?"

"How so? I cannot escort you. They wouldn't let me go to the end of the garden-wall."

"*You!* I should be sorry to ask you to cross the threshold, for my convenience, on such a night," I cried. "I want you to *tell* me the way, not to *show* it; or else to persuade Mr. Heathcliff to give me a guide."

"Who? There is himself, Earnshaw, Zillah, Joseph, and I. Which would you have?"

"Are there no boys at the farm?"

"No, those are all."

"Then, it follows that I am compelled to stay."

"That you may settle with your host. I have nothing to do with it."

"I hope it will be a lesson to you, to make no more rash journeys on these hills," cried Heathcliff's stern voice from the kitchen entrance. "As to staying here, I don't keep accommodations for visiters; you must share a bed with Hareton, or Joseph, if you do."

"I can sleep on a chair in this room," I replied.

"No, no! A stranger is a stranger, be he rich or poor—it will not suit me to permit anyone the range of the place while I am off guard!" said the unmannerly wretch.

With this insult my patience was at an end. I uttered an expression of disgust, and pushed past him into the yard, running against Earnshaw in my haste. It was so dark that I could not see the means of exit, and, as I wandered round, I heard another specimen of their civil behaviour amongst each other.

At first, the young man appeared about to befriend me.

"I'll go with him as far as the park," he said.

"You'll go with him to hell!" exclaimed his master, or whatever relation he bore. "And who is to look after the horses, eh?"

"A man's life is of more consequence than one evening's neglect of the horses; somebody must go," murmured Mrs. Heathcliff, more kindly than I expected.

"Not at your command!" retorted Hareton. "If you set store on him, you'd better be quiet."

"Then I hope his ghost will haunt you; and I hope Mr. Heathcliff will never get another tenant, till the Grange is a ruin!" she answered sharply.

"Hearken, hearken, shoo's cursing on em!" muttered Joseph, towards whom I had been steering.

He sat within earshot, milking the cows, by the light of a lantern which I seized unceremoniously, and calling out that I would send it back on the morrow, rushed to the nearest postern.

"Maister, maister, he's staling t' lantern!" shouted the ancient, pursuing my retreat. "Hey, Gnasher! Hey, dog! Hey, Wolf! holld him, holld him!"

On opening the little door, two hairy monsters flew at my throat, bearing me down, and extinguishing the light, while a mingled guffaw, from Heathcliff and Hareton, put the copestone on my rage and humiliation.

Fortunately, the beasts seemed more bent on stretching their paws and yawning, and flourishing their tails, than devouring me alive; but, they would suffer no resurrection, and I was forced to lie till their malignant masters pleased to deliver me: then hatless, and trembling with wrath, I ordered the miscreants to let me out — on their peril to keep me one minute longer — with several incoherent threats of retaliation, that in their indefinite depth of virulency smacked of King Lear.

The vehemence of my agitation brought on a copious bleeding at the nose, and still Heathcliff laughed, and still I scolded. I don't know what would have concluded the scene had there not been one person at hand rather more rational than myself, and more benevolent than my entertainer. This was Zillah, the stout housewife; who at length issued forth to inquire into the nature of the uproar. She thought that some of them had been laying violent hands on me; and, not daring to attack her master, she turned her vocal artillery against the younger scoundrel.

---

copestone: topping.

"Well, Mr. Earnshaw," she cried, "I wonder what you'll have agait next! Are we going to murder folk on our very door-stones? I see this house will never do for me—look at t' poor lad, he's fair choking! Wisht, wisht! you mun'n't go on so—come in, and I'll cure that. There now, hold ye still."

With these words she suddenly splashed a pint of icy water down my neck, and pulled me into the kitchen. Mr. Heathcliff followed, his accidental merriment expiring quickly in his habitual moroseness.

I was sick exceedingly, and dizzy and faint; and thus compelled, perforce, to accept lodgings under his roof. He told Zillah to give me a glass of brandy, and then passed on to the inner room, while she condoled with me on my sorry predicament, and having obeyed his orders, whereby I was somewhat revived, ushered me to bed.

CHAPTER III

While leading the way upstairs, she recommended that I should hide the candle, and not make a noise, for her master had an odd notion about the chamber she would put me in; and never let anybody lodge there willingly.

I asked the reason.

She did not know, she answered; she had only lived there a year or two; and they had so many queer goings on, she could not begin to be curious.

Too stupified to be curious myself, I fastened my door and glanced round for the bed. The whole furniture consisted of a chair, a clothes-press, and a large oak case, with squares cut out near the top, resembling coach windows.

Having approached this structure, I looked inside, and perceived it to be a singular sort of old-fashioned couch, very conveniently designed to obviate the necessity for every member of the family having a room to himself. In fact, it formed a little closet, and the ledge of a window, which it enclosed, served as a table.

I slid back the panelled sides, got in with my light, pulled them together again, and felt secure against the vigilance of Heathcliff, and everyone else.

The ledge, where I placed my candle, had a few mildewed books piled up in one corner; and it was covered with writing scratched on the paint. This writing, however, was nothing but a name repeated in all kinds of characters, large and small—*Catherine Earnshaw;* here and there varied to *Catherine Heathcliff,* and then again to *Catherine Linton.*

---

wisht: be quiet.

In vapid listlessness I leant my head against the window, and continued spelling over Catherine Earnshaw — Heathcliff — Linton, till my eyes closed; but they had not rested five minutes when a glare of white letters started from the dark, as vivid as spectres — the air swarmed with Catherines; and rousing myself to dispel the obtrusive name, I discovered my candle wick reclining on one of the antique volumes, and perfuming the place with an odour of roasted calf-skin.

I snuffed it off, and, very ill at ease, under the influence of cold and lingering nausea, sat up, and spread open the injured tome on my knee. It was a Testament, in lean type, and smelling dreadfully musty: a fly-leaf bore the inscription — "Catherine Earnshaw, her book," and a date some quarter of a century back.

I shut it, and took up another, and another, till I had examined all. Catherine's library was select; and its state of dilapidation proved it to have been well used, though not altogether for a legitimate purpose; scarcely one chapter had escaped a pen and ink commentary, at least, the appearance of one, covering every morsel of blank that the printer had left.

Some were detached sentences; other parts took the form of a regular diary, scrawled in an unformed, childish hand. At the top of an extra page, quite a treasure probably when first lighted on, I was greatly amused to behold an excellent caricature of my friend Joseph, rudely yet powerfully sketched.

An immediate interest kindled within me for the unknown Catherine, and I began, forthwith, to decypher her faded hieroglyphics.

"An awful Sunday!" commenced the paragraph beneath. "I wish my father were back again. Hindley is a detestable substitute — his conduct to Heathcliff is atrocious — H. and I are going to rebel — we took our initiatory step this evening.

"All day had been flooding with rain; we could not go to church, so Joseph must needs get up a congregation in the garret; and, while Hindley and his wife basked downstairs before a comfortable fire, doing anything but reading their bibles, I'll answer for it; Heathcliff, myself, and the unhappy plough-boy were commanded to take our prayer books, and mount — we were ranged in a row, on a sack of corn, groaning and shivering, and hoping that Joseph would shiver too, so that he might give us a short homily for his own sake. A vain idea! The service lasted precisely three hours; and yet my brother had the face to exclaim, when he saw us descending,

" 'What, done already?'

"On Sunday evenings we used to be permitted to play, if we did not make much noise; now a mere titter is sufficient to send us into corners!

"'You forget you have a master here,' says the tyrant. 'I'll demolish the first who puts me out of temper! I insist on perfect sobriety and silence. Oh, boy! was that you? Frances, darling, pull his hair as you go by; I heard him snap his fingers.'

"Frances pulled his hair heartily; and then went and seated herself on her husband's knee, and there they were, like two babies, kissing and talking nonsense by the hour—foolish palaver that we should be ashamed of.

"We made ourselves as snug as our means allowed in the arch of the dresser. I had just fastened our pinafores together, and hung them up for a curtain; when in comes Joseph, on an errand from the stables. He tears down my handywork, boxes my ears, and croaks:

"'T' maister nobbut just buried, and Sabbath nut oe'red, und t'sahnd uh't gospel still i' yer lugs, and yah darr be laiking! shame on ye! sit ye dahn, ill childer! they's good books eneugh if ye'll read 'em; sit ye dahn and think uh yer sowls!'

"Saying this, he compelled us so to square our positions that we might receive, from the far-off fire, a dull ray to show us the text of the lumber he thrust upon us.

"I could not bear the employment. I took my dingy volume by the scroop, and hurled it into the dog kennel, vowing I hated a good book.

"Heathcliff kicked his to the same place.

"Then there was a hubbub!

"'Maister Hindley!' shouted our chaplain. 'Maister, coom hither! Miss Cathy's riven th' back off "Th' Helmet uh Salvation," un' Heathcliff's pawsed his fit intuh t' first part uh "T' Brooad Way to Destruction!" It's fair flaysome ut yah let 'em goa on this gait. Ech! th' owd man ud uh laced 'em properly—bud he's goan!'

"Hindley hurried up from his paradise on the hearth, and seizing one of us by the collar, and the other by the arm, hurled both into the back-kitchen; where, Joseph asseverated, 'owd Nick' would fetch us as sure as we were living; and, so comforted, we each sought a separate nook to await his advent.

"I reached this book, and a pot of ink from a shelf, and pushed the house-door ajar to give me light, and I have got the time on with writing for twenty minutes; but my companion is impatient, and proposes that we should appropriate the dairy woman's cloak, and have a scamper on the moors, under its shelter. A pleasant suggestion—and then, if the surly old man come in, he may believe his prophesy verified—we cannot be damper, or colder, in the rain than we are here."

Sabbath nut oe'red: The Sabbath day (Sunday) is not over yet.
scroop: a harsh, strident noise.

I suppose Catherine fulfilled her project, for the next sentence took up another subject; she waxed lachrymose.

"How little did I dream that Hindley would ever make me cry so!" she wrote. "My head aches, till I cannot keep it on the pillow; and still I can't give over. Poor Heathcliff! Hindley calls him a vagabond, and won't let him sit with us, nor eat with us any more; and, he says, he and I must not play together, and threatens to turn him out of the house if we break his orders.

"He has been blaming our father (how dared he?) for treating H. too liberally; and swears he will reduce him to his right place —"

I began to nod drowsily over the dim page; my eye wandered from manuscript to print. I saw a red ornamented title . . . "Seventy Times Seven,[1] and the First of the Seventy-First. A Pious Discourse delivered by the Reverend Jabes Branderham, in the Chapel of Gimmerton Sough." And while I was, half consciously, worrying my brain to guess what Jabes Branderham would make of his subject, I sank back in bed, and fell asleep.

Alas, for the effects of bad tea and bad temper! what else could it be that made me pass such a terrible night? I don't remember another that I can at all compare with it since I was capable of suffering.

I began to dream, almost before I ceased to be sensible of my locality. I thought it was morning; and I had set out on my way home, with Joseph for a guide. The snow lay yards deep in our road; and, as we floundered on, my companion wearied me with constant reproaches that I had not brought a pilgrim's staff: telling me that I could never get into the house without one, and boastfully flourishing a heavy-headed cudgel, which I understood to be so denominated.

For a moment I considered it absurd that I should need such a weapon to gain admittance into my own residence. Then, a new idea flashed across me. I was not going there; we were journeying to hear the famous Jabes

---

lachrymose: tearful.
First of the Seventy-First: Unforgivable sin.

[1] A reference to Matthew 18.21–35. In this passage, Peter asks Jesus how many times he should forgive his brother. Jesus answers, "Until seventy times seven." Jesus then relates a parable about a feud between two servants, the moral being, "Have compassion on thy fellow servant even as I had pity on thee." [ED.]

Branderham preach from the text—"Seventy Times Seven"; and either Joseph, the preacher, or I had committed the "First of the Seventy-First," and were to be publicly exposed and excommunicated.

We came to the chapel—I have passed it really in my walks, twice or thrice: it lies in a hollow, between two hills—an elevated hollow—near a swamp, whose peaty moisture is said to answer all the purposes of embalming on the few corpses deposited there. The roof has been kept whole hitherto, but, as the clergyman's stipend is only twenty pounds per annum, and a house with two rooms, threatening speedily to determine into one, no clergyman will undertake the duties of pastor, especially, as it is currently reported that his flock would rather let him starve than increase the living by one penny from their own pockets. However, in my dream, Jabes had a full and attentive congregation: and he preached—good God—what a sermon! Divided into *four hundred and ninety* parts—each fully equal to an ordinary address from the pulpit—and each discussing a separate sin! Where he searched for them, I cannot tell; he had his private manner of interpreting the phrase, and it seemed necessary the brother should sin different sins on every occasion.

They were of the most curious character—odd transgressions that I never imagined previously.

Oh, how weary I grew. How I writhed, and yawned, and nodded, and revived! How I pinched and pricked myself, and rubbed my eyes, and stood up, and sat down again, and nudged Joseph to inform me if he would *ever* have done!

I was condemned to hear all out—finally, he reached the *"First of the Seventy-First."* At that crisis, a sudden inspiration descended on me; I was moved to rise and denounce Jabes Branderham as the sinner of the sin that no Christian need pardon.

"Sir," I exclaimed, "sitting here, within these four walls, at one stretch, I have endured and forgiven the four hundred and ninety heads of your discourse. Seventy times seven times have I plucked up my hat, and been about to depart—seventy times seven times have you preposterously forced me to resume my seat. The four hundred and ninety-first is too much. Fellow martyrs, have at him! Drag him down, and crush him to atoms, that the place which knows him may know him no more!"

"*Thou art the Man!*" cried Jabes, after a solemn pause, leaning over his cushion. "Seventy times seven times didst thou gapingly contort thy visage—seventy times seven did I take counsel with my soul—Lo, this is human weakness; this also may be absolved! The First of the Seventy-First is come. Brethren, execute upon him the judgment written! such honour have all His saints!"

With that concluding word, the whole assembly, exalting their pilgrim's staves, rushed round me in a body, and I, having no weapon to raise in self-defence, commenced grappling with Joseph, my nearest and most ferocious assailant, for his. In the confluence of the multitude, several clubs crossed; blows, aimed at me, fell on other sconces. Presently the whole chapel resounded with rappings and counter-rappings. Every man's hand was against his neighbour; and Branderham, unwilling to remain idle, poured forth his zeal in a shower of loud taps on the boards of the pulpit which responded so smartly, that, at last, to my unspeakable relief, they woke me.

And what was it that had suggested the tremendous tumult, what had played Jabes' part in the row? Merely, the branch of a fir tree that touched my lattice, as the blast wailed by, and rattled its dry cones against the panes!

I listened doubtingly an instant; detected the disturber, then turned and dozed, and dreamt again; if possible, still more disagreeably than before.

This time, I remembered I was lying in the oak closet, and I heard distinctly the gusty wind, and the driving of the snow; I heard also, the fir bough repeat its teasing sound, and ascribed it to the right cause; but, it annoyed me so much, that I resolved to silence it, if possible; and, I thought, I rose and endeavoured to unhasp the casement. The hook was soldered into the staple, a circumstance observed by me, when awake, but forgotten.

"I must stop it, nevertheless!" I muttered, knocking my knuckles through the glass, and stretching an arm out to seize the importunate branch: instead of which, my fingers closed on the fingers of a little, ice-cold hand!

The intense horror of nightmare came over me; I tried to draw back my arm, but, the hand clung to it, and a most melancholy voice sobbed,

"Let me in—let me in!"

"Who are you?" I asked struggling, meanwhile, to disengage myself.

"Catherine Linton," it replied, shiveringly, (why did I think of *Linton*? I had read *Earnshaw*, twenty times for Linton) "I'm come home, I'd lost my way on the moor!"

As it spoke, I discerned, obscurely, a child's face looking through the window—Terror made me cruel; and, finding it useless to attempt shaking the creature off, I pulled its wrist on to the broken pane, and rubbed it to and fro till the blood ran down and soaked the bed-clothes: still it wailed, "Let me in!" and maintained its tenacious gripe, almost maddening me with fear.

"How can I?" I said at length. "Let *me* go, if you want me to let you in!"

The fingers relaxed, I snatched mine through the hole, hurriedly piled the books up in a pyramid against it, and stopped my ears to exclude the lamentable prayer.

I seemed to keep them closed above a quarter of an hour, yet, the instant I listened, again, there was the doleful cry moaning on!

"Begone!" I shouted, "I'll never let you in, not if you beg for twenty years!"

"It's twenty years," mourned the voice, "twenty years, I've been a waif for twenty years!"

Thereat began a feeble scratching outside, and the pile of books moved as if thrust forward.

I tried to jump up; but, could not stir a limb; and so, yelled aloud, in a frenzy of fright.

To my confusion, I discovered the yell was not ideal. Hasty footsteps approached my chamber door: somebody pushed it open, with a vigorous hand, and a light glimmered through the squares at the top of the bed. I sat shuddering, yet, and wiping the perspiration from my forehead: the intruder appeared to hesitate and muttered to himself.

At last, he said in a half-whisper, plainly not expecting an answer, "Is anyone here?"

I considered it best to confess my presence, for I knew Heathcliff's accents, and feared he might search further, if I kept quiet.

With this intention, I turned and opened the panels—I shall not soon forget the effect my action produced.

Heathcliff stood near the entrance, in his shirt and trousers; with a candle dripping over his fingers, and his face as white as the wall behind him. The first creak of the oak startled him like an electric shock: the light leaped from his hold to a distance of some feet, and his agitation was so extreme that he could hardly pick it up.

"It is only your guest, sir," I called out, desirous to spare him the humiliation of exposing his cowardice further. "I had the misfortune to scream in my sleep, owing to a frightful nightmare. I'm sorry I disturbed you."

"Oh, God confound you, Mr. Lockwood! I wish you were at the—" commenced my host setting the candle on a chair, because he found it impossible to hold it steady.

"And who showed you up to this room?" he continued, crushing his nails into his palms, and grinding his teeth to subdue the maxillary convulsions. "Who was it? I've a good mind to turn them out of the house, this moment!"

"It was your servant, Zillah," I replied flinging myself, on to the floor, and rapidly resuming my garments. "I should not care if you did, Mr. Heathcliff; she richly deserves it. I suppose that she wanted to get another proof that the place was haunted, at my expense—Well, it is—swarming with ghosts and goblins! You have reason in shutting it up, I assure you. No one will thank you for a doze in such a den!"

"What do you mean?" asked Heathcliff, "and what are you doing? Lie down and finish out the night, since you *are* here; but, for Heaven's sake! don't repeat that horrid noise—Nothing could excuse it, unless you were having your throat cut!"

"If the little fiend had got in at the window, she probably would have strangled me!" I returned. "I'm not going to endure the persecutions of your hospitable ancestors, again—Was not the Reverend Jabes Branderham akin to you on the mother's side? And that minx, Catherine Linton, or Earnshaw, or however she was called—she must have been a changeling—wicked little soul! She told me she had been walking the earth these twenty years: a just punishment for her mortal transgressions, I've no doubt!"

Scarcely were these words uttered, when I recollected the association of Heathcliff's with Catherine's name in the book, which had completely slipped from my memory till thus awakened. I blushed at my inconsideration; but without showing further consciousness of the offence, I hastened to add,

"The truth is, sir, I passed the first part of the night in—" Here, I stopped afresh—I was about to say "perusing those old volumes," then it would have revealed my knowledge of their written, as well as their printed contents; so correcting myself, I went on,

"In spelling over the name scratched on that window-ledge. A monotonous occupation, calculated to set me asleep, like counting, or—"

"What *can* you mean, by talking in this way to *me?*" thundered Heathcliff with savage vehemence. "How—how *dare* you, under my roof—God! he's mad to speak so!" And he struck his forehead with rage.

I did not know whether to resent this language, or pursue my explanation; but he seemed so powerfully affected that I took pity and proceeded with my dreams; affirming I had never heard the appellation of "Catherine Linton," before, but, reading it often over produced an impression which personified itself when I had no longer my imagination under control.

Heathcliff gradually fell back into the shelter of the bed, as I spoke, finally, sitting down almost concealed behind it. I guessed, however, by his irregular and intercepted breathing, that he struggled to vanquish an access of violent emotion.

Not liking to show him that I heard the conflict, I continued my toilette rather noisily, looked at my watch, and soliloquised on the length of the night:

"Not three o'clock, yet! I could have taken oath it had been six—time stagnates here—we must surely have retired to rest at eight!"

"Always at nine in winter, and always rise at four," said my host, suppressing a groan; and, as I fancied, by the motion of his shadow's arm, dashing a tear from his eyes.

"Mr. Lockwood," he added, "you may go into my room; you'll only be in the way, coming downstairs so early: and your childish outcry has sent sleep to the devil for me."

"And for me too," I replied. "I'll walk in the yard till daylight, and then I'll be off; and you need not dread a repetition of my intrusion. I am now quite cured of seeking pleasure in society, be it country or town. A sensible man ought to find sufficient company in himself."

"Delightful company!" muttered Heathcliff. "Take the candle, and go where you please. I shall join you directly. Keep out of the yard, though, the dogs are unchained; and the house—Juno mounts sentinel there—and—nay, you can only ramble about the steps and passages—but, away with you! I'll come in two minutes."

I obeyed, so far as to quit the chamber; when, ignorant where the narrow lobbies led, I stood still, and was witness, involuntarily, to a piece of superstition on the part of my landlord, which belied, oddly, his apparent sense.

He got on to the bed, and wrenched open the lattice, bursting, as he pulled at it, into an uncontrollable passion of tears.

"Come in! come in!" he sobbed. "Cathy, do come. Oh do—*once* more! Oh! my heart's darling, hear me *this* time—Catherine, at last!"

The spectre showed a spectre's ordinary caprice; it gave no sign of being; but the snow and wind whirled wildly through, even reaching my station, and blowing out the light.

There was such an anguish in the gush of grief that accompanied this raving that my compassion made me overlook its folly, and I drew off, half angry to have listened at all, and vexed at having related my ridiculous nightmare, since it produced that agony; though *why*, was beyond my comprehension.

I descended cautiously to the lower regions and landed in the back-kitchen, where a gleam of fire, raked compactly together, enabled me to rekindle my candle.

Nothing was stirring except a brindled, grey cat, which crept from the ashes, and saluted me with a querulous mew.

Two benches, shaped in sections of a circle, nearly enclosed the hearth; on one of these I stretched myself, and Grimalkin mounted the other. We were both of us nodding, ere anyone invaded our retreat; and then it was

---

Grimalkin: the cat.

Joseph shuffling down a wooden ladder that vanished in the roof, through a trap, the ascent to his garret, I suppose.

He cast a sinister look at the little flame which I had enticed to play between the ribs, swept the cat from its elevation, and bestowing himself in the vacancy, commenced the operation of stuffing a three-inch pipe with tobacco; my presence in his sanctum was evidently esteemed a piece of impudence too shameful for remark. He silently applied the tube to his lips, folded his arms, and puffed away.

I let him enjoy the luxury, unannoyed; and after sucking out the last wreath, and heaving a profound sigh, he got up, and departed as solemnly as he came.

A more elastic footstep entered next, and now I opened my mouth for a "good morning," but closed it again, the salutation unachieved; for Hareton Earnshaw was performing his orisons, *sotto voce,* in a series of curses directed against every object he touched, while he rummaged a corner, for a spade or shovel to dig through the drifts. He glanced over the back of the bench dilating his nostrils, and thought as little of exchanging civilities with me, as with my companion, the cat.

I guessed by his preparations that egress was allowed, and leaving my hard couch, made a movement to follow him. He noticed this, and thrust at an inner door with the end of his spade, intimating by an inarticulate sound, that there was the place where I must go, if I changed my locality.

It opened into the house, where the females were already astir, Zillah urging flakes of flame up the chimney with a colossal bellows; and Mrs. Heathcliff, kneeling on the hearth, reading a book by the aid of the blaze.

She held her hand interposed between the furnace-heat and her eyes; and seemed absorbed in her occupation: desisting from it only to chide the servant for covering her with sparks, or to push away a dog, now and then, that snoozled its nose over forwardly into her face.

I was surprised to see Heathcliff there also. He stood by the fire, his back towards me, just finishing a stormy scene to poor Zillah, who ever and anon interrupted her labour to pluck up the corner of her apron, and heave an indignant groan.

"And you, you worthless—" he broke out as I entered, turning to his daughter-in-law, and employing an epithet as harmless as duck, or sheep, but generally represented by a dash. "There you are at your idle tricks again! The rest of them do earn their bread—you live on my charity! Put

---

sotto voce: in a soft voice.

your trash away, and find something to do. You shall pay me for the plague of having you eternally in my sight—do you hear, damnable jade?"

"I'll put my trash away, because you can make me, if I refuse," answered the young lady, closing her book, and throwing it on a chair. "But I'll not do anything, though you should swear your tongue out, except what I please!"

Heathcliff lifted his hand, and the speaker sprang to a safer distance, obviously acquainted with its weight.

Having no desire to be entertained by a cat and dog combat, I stepped forward briskly, as if eager to partake the warmth of the hearth, and innocent of any knowledge of the interrupted dispute. Each had enough decorum to suspend further hostilities; Heathcliff placed his fists, out of temptation, in his pockets: Mrs. Heathcliff curled her lip, and walked to a seat far off; where she kept her word by playing the part of a statue during the remainder of my stay.

That was not long. I declined joining their breakfast, and, at the first gleam of dawn, took an opportunity of escaping into the free air, now clear, and still, and cold as impalpable ice.

My landlord hallooed for me to stop ere I reached the bottom of the garden, and offered to accompany me across the moor. It was well he did, for the whole hill-back was one billowy, white ocean; the swells and falls not indicating corresponding rises and depressions in the ground—many pits, at least, were filled to a level; and entire ranges of mounds, the refuse of the quarries, blotted from the chart which my yesterday's walk left pictured in my mind.

I had remarked on one side of the road, at intervals of six or seven yards, a line of upright stones, continued through the whole length of the barren: these were erected, and daubed with lime, on purpose to serve as guides in the dark, and also, when a fall, like the present, confounded the deep swamps on either hand with the firmer path: but, excepting a dirty dot pointing up, here and there, all traces of their existence had vanished; and my companion found it necessary to warn me frequently to steer to the right, or left, when I imagined I was following, correctly, the windings of the road.

We exchanged little conversation, and he halted at the entrance of Thrushcross park, saying I could make no error there. Our adieux were limited to a hasty bow, and then I pushed forward, trusting to my own resources, for the porter's lodge is untenanted as yet.

This distance from the gate to the Grange is two miles: I believe I managed to make it four; what with losing myself among the trees, and sinking up to the neck in snow, a predicament which only those who have experienced it can appreciate. At any rate, whatever were my wanderings, the clock chimed twelve as I entered the house; and that gave exactly an hour for every mile of the usual way from Wuthering Heights.

My human fixture and her satellites rushed to welcome me; exclaiming, tumultuously, they had completely given me up; everybody conjectured that I perished last night; and they were wondering how they must set about the search for my remains.

I bid them be quiet, now that they saw me returned, and, benumbed to my very heart, I dragged upstairs, whence, after putting on dry clothes, and pacing to and fro, thirty or forty minutes, to restore the animal heat, I am adjourned to my study, feeble as a kitten, almost too much so to enjoy the cheerful fire and smoking coffee which the servant has prepared for my refreshment.

CHAPTER IV

What vain weathercocks we are! I, who had determined to hold myself independent of all social intercourse, and thanked my stars that, at length, I had lighted on a spot where it was next to impracticable: I, weak wretch, after maintaining till dusk a struggle with low spirits, and solitude, was finally compelled to strike my colours; and, under pretence of gaining information concerning the necessities of my establishment, I desired Mrs. Dean, when she brought in supper, to sit down while I ate it, hoping sincerely she would prove a regular gossip, and either rouse me to animation, or lull me to sleep by her talk.

"You have lived here a considerable time," I commenced; "did you not say sixteen years?"

"Eighteen, sir; I came, when the mistress was married, to wait on her; after she died, the master retained me for his house-keeper."

"Indeed."

There ensued a pause. She was not a gossip, I feared, unless about her own affairs, and those could hardly interest me.

However, having studied for an interval, with a fist on either knee, and a cloud of meditation over her ruddy countenance, she ejaculated—

"Ah, times are greatly changed since then!"

"Yes," I remarked, "you've seen a good many alterations, I suppose?"

"I have: and troubles, too," she said.

"Oh, I'll turn the talk on my landlord's family!" I thought to myself. "A good subject to start—and that pretty girl-widow, I should like to know her history; whether she be a native of the country, or, as is more probable, an exotic that the surly indigenae will not recognise for kin."

With this intention I asked Mrs. Dean why Heathcliff let Thrushcross Grange, and preferred living in a situation and residence so much inferior.

"Is he not rich enough to keep the estate in good order?" I enquired.

"Rich, sir!" she returned. "He has nobody knows what money, and every year it increases. Yes, yes, he's rich enough to live in a finer house than this; but he's very near—close-handed; and, if he had meant to flit to Thrushcross Grange, as soon as he heard of a good tenant, he could not have borne to miss the chance of getting a few hundreds more. It is strange people should be so greedy, when they are alone in the world!"

"He had a son, it seems?"

"Yes, he had one—he is dead."

"And that young lady, Mrs. Heathcliff, is his widow?"

"Yes."

"Where did she come from originally?"

"Why, sir, she is my late master's daughter; Catherine Linton was her maiden name. I nursed her, poor thing! I did wish Mr. Heathcliff would remove here, and then we might have been together again."

"What, Catherine Linton!" I exclaimed, astonished. But a minute's reflection convinced me it was not my ghostly Catherine. "Then," I continued, "my predecessor's name was Linton?"

"It was."

"And who is that Earnshaw, Hareton Earnshaw, who lives with Mr. Heathcliff? are they relations?"

"No; he is the late Mrs. Linton's nephew."

"The young lady's cousin, then?"

"Yes; and her husband was her cousin also—one, on the mother's—the other, on the father's side—Heathcliff married Mr. Linton's sister."

"I see the house at Wuthering Heights has 'Earnshaw' carved over the front door. Are they an old family?"

"Very old, sir; and Hareton is the last of them, as our Miss Cathy is of us—I mean, of the Lintons. Have you been to Wuthering Heights? I beg pardon for asking; but I should like to hear how she is!"

"Mrs. Heathcliff? she looked very well, and very handsome; yet, I think, not very happy."

"Oh dear, I don't wonder! And how did you like the master?"

"A rough fellow, rather, Mrs. Dean. Is not that his character?"

---

indigenae: natives of the region.

"Rough as a saw-edge, and hard as whinstone. The less you meddle with him the better."

"He must have had some ups and downs in life to make him such a churl. Do you know anything of his history?"

"It's a cuckoo's, sir—I know all about it; except where he was born, and who were his parents, and how he got his money, at first—And Hareton has been cast out like an unfledged dunnock—The unfortunate lad is the only one, in all this parish, that does not guess how he has been cheated!"

"Well, Mrs. Dean, it will be a charitable deed to tell me something of my neighbours—I feel I shall not rest, if I go to bed; so, be good enough to sit, and chat an hour."

"Oh, certainly, sir! I'll just fetch a little sewing, and then I'll sit as long as you please. But you've caught cold, I saw you shivering, and you must have some gruel to drive it out."

The worthy woman bustled off; and I crouched nearer the fire: my head felt hot, and the rest of me chill: moreover I was excited, almost to a pitch of foolishness through my nerves and brain. This caused me to feel, not uncomfortable, but rather fearful, as I am still, of serious effects from the incidents of today and yesterday.

She returned presently, bringing a smoking basin, and a basket of work; and, having placed the former on the hob, drew in her seat, evidently pleased to find me so companionable.

Before I came to live here, she commenced, waiting no further invitation to her story, I was almost always at Wuthering Heights; because, my mother had nursed Mr. Hindley Earnshaw, that was Hareton's father, and I got used to playing with the children—I ran errands too, and helped to make hay, and hung about the farm ready for anything that anybody would set me to.

One fine summer morning—it was the beginning of harvest, I remember—Mr. Earnshaw, the old master, came downstairs, dressed for a journey; and, after he had told Joseph what was to be done during the day, he turned to Hindley, and Cathy, and me—for I sat eating my porridge, with them, and he said, speaking to his son,

"Now my bonny man, I'm going to Liverpool, today. . . . What shall I bring you? You may choose what you like; only let it be little, for I shall walk there and back; sixty miles each way, that is a long spell!"

whinstone: hard rock, usually basalt and chert.
dunnock: sparrow; small bird.

Hindley named a fiddle, and then he asked Miss Cathy; she was hardly six years old, but she could ride any horse in the stable, and she chose a whip.

He did not forget me; for he had a kind heart, though he was rather severe, sometimes. He promised to bring me a pocketful of apples, and pears, and then he kissed his children good-bye, and set off.

It seemed a long while to us all—the three days of his absence—and often did little Cathy ask when he would be home: Mrs. Earnshaw expected him by supper-time, on the third evening; and she put the meal off hour after hour; there were no signs of his coming, however, and at last the children got tired of running down to the gate to look—Then it grew dark, she would have had them to bed, but they begged sadly to be allowed to stay up; and, just about eleven o'clock, the door-latch was raised quietly and in stept the master. He threw himself into a chair, laughing and groaning, and bid them all stand off, for he was nearly killed—he would not have such another walk for the three kingdoms.

"And at the end of it, to be flighted to death!" he said opening his great coat, which he held bundled up in his arms. "See here, wife; I was never so beaten with anything in my life; but you must e'en take it as a gift of God; though it's as dark almost as if it came from the devil."

We crowded round, and, over Miss Cathy's head, I had a peep at a dirty, ragged, black-haired child; big enough both to walk and talk—indeed, its face looked older than Catherine's—yet, when it was set on its feet, it only stared round, and repeated over and over again, some gibberish that nobody could understand. I was frightened, and Mrs. Earnshaw was ready to fling it out of doors: she did fly up—asking how he could fashion to bring that gipsy brat into the house, when they had their own bairns to feed, and fend for? What he meant to do with it, and whether he were mad?

The master tried to explain the matter; but, he was really half dead with fatigue, and all that I could make out, amongst her scolding, was a tale of his seeing it starving, and houseless, and as good as dumb in the streets of Liverpool where he picked it up and inquired for its owner—Not a soul knew to whom it belonged, he said, and his money and time, being both limited, he thought it better, to take it home with him, at once, than run into vain expenses there; because he was determined he would not leave it as he found it.

Well, the conclusion was that my mistress grumbled herself calm; and Mr. Earnshaw told me to wash it, and give it clean things, and let it sleep with the children.

---

the three kingdoms: England, Ireland, and Scotland.

Hindley and Cathy contented themselves with looking and listening till peace was restored then both began searching their father's pockets for the presents he had promised them. The former was a boy of fourteen, but when he drew out what had been a fiddle crushed to morsels in the great coat, he blubbered aloud, and Cathy, when she learnt the master had lost her whip in attending on the stranger, showed her humour by grinning and spitting at the stupid little thing, earning for her pains a sound blow from her father to teach her cleaner manners.

They entirely refused to have it in bed with them, or even in their room, and I had no more sense, so I put it on the landing of the stairs, hoping it might be gone on the morrow. By chance, or else attracted by hearing his voice, it crept to Mr. Earnshaw's door and there he found it on quitting his chamber. Inquiries were made as to how it got there; I was obliged to confess, and in recompense for my cowardice and inhumanity was sent out of the house.

This was Heathcliff's first introduction to the family: on coming back a few days afterwards, for I did not consider my banishment perpetual, I found they had christened him "Heathcliff," it was the name of a son who died in childhood, and it has served him ever since, both for christian and surname.

Miss Cathy and he were now very thick; but Hindley hated him, and to say the truth I did the same; and we plagued and went on with him shamefully, for I wasn't reasonable enough to feel my injustice, and the mistress never put in a word on his behalf, when she saw him wronged.

He seemed a sullen, patient child; hardened, perhaps, to ill-treatment: he would stand Hindley's blows without a wink or shedding a tear, and my pinches moved him only to draw in a breath, and open his eyes as if he had hurt himself by accident, and nobody was to blame.

This endurance made old Earnshaw furious when he discovered his son persecuting the poor, fatherless child, as he called him. He took to Heathcliff strangely, believing all he said (for that matter, he said precious little, and generally the truth), and petting him up far above Cathy, who was too mischievous and wayward for a favourite.

So, from the very beginning, he bred bad feeling in the house; and at Mrs. Earnshaw's death, which happened in less than two years after, the young master had learnt to regard his father as an oppressor rather than a friend, and Heathcliff as a usurper of his parent's affections, and his privileges, and he grew bitter with brooding over these injuries.

I sympathised awhile, but, when the children fell ill of the measles and I had to tend them, and take on me the cares of a woman, at once, I changed my ideas. Heathcliff was dangerously sick, and while he lay at the worst he would have me constantly by his pillow; I suppose he felt I did a good deal for him, and he hadn't wit to guess that I was compelled to do it. However, I will say this, he was the quietest child that ever nurse watched over. The difference between him and the others forced me to be less partial: Cathy and her brother harassed me terribly: *he* was as uncomplaining as a lamb; though hardness, not gentleness, made him give little trouble.

He got through, and the doctor affirmed it was in a great measure owing to me, and praised me for my care. I was vain of his commendations, and softened towards the being by whose means I earned them, and thus Hindley lost his last ally; still I couldn't dote on Heathcliff, and I wondered often what my master saw to admire so much in the sullen boy who never, to my recollection, repaid his indulgence by any sign of gratitude. He was not insolent to his benefactor; he was simply insensible, though knowing perfectly the hold he had on his heart, and conscious he had only to speak and all the house would be obliged to bend to his wishes.

As an instance, I remember Mr. Earnshaw once bought a couple of colts at the parish fair, and gave the lads each one. Heathcliff took the handsomest, but it soon fell lame, and when he discovered it, he said to Hindley,

"You must exchange horses with me; I don't like mine, and, if you won't I shall tell your father of the three thrashings you've given me this week, and show him my arm which is black to the shoulder."

Hindley put out his tongue, and cuffed him over the ears.

"You'd better do it, at once," he persisted escaping to the porch, (they were in the stable) "you will have to, and, if I speak of these blows, you'll get them again with interest."

"Off dog!" cried Hindley, threatening him with an iron weight, used for weighing potatoes and hay.

"Throw it," he replied, standing still, "and then I'll tell how you boasted that you would turn me out of doors as soon as he died, and see whether he will not turn you out directly."

Hindley threw it, hitting him on the breast, and down he fell, but staggered up, immediately, breathless and white, and had not I prevented it he would have gone just so to the master, and got full revenge by letting his condition plead for him, intimating who had caused it.

"Take my colt, gipsy, then!" said young Earnshaw, "And I pray that he may break your neck, take him, and be damned, you beggarly interloper! and wheedle my father out of all he has, only, afterwards, show him what you are, imp of Satan — And take that, I hope he'll kick out your brains!"

Heathcliff had gone to loose the beast, and shift it to his own stall. He was passing behind it, when Hindley finished his speech by knocking him under its feet, and without stopping to examine whether his hopes were fulfilled, ran away as fast he could.

I was surprised to witness how coolly the child gathered himself up, and went on with his intention, exchanging saddles and all; and then sitting down on a bundle of hay to overcome the qualm which the violent blow occasioned, before he entered the house.

I persuaded him easily to let me lay the blame of his bruises on the horse; he minded little what tale was told since he had what he wanted. He complained so seldom, indeed, of such stirs as these, that I really thought him not vindictive—I was deceived, completely, as you will hear.

CHAPTER V

In the course of time, Mr. Earnshaw began to fail. He had been active and healthy, yet his strength left him suddenly; and when he was confined to the chimney-corner he grew grievously irritable. A nothing vexed him, and suspected slights of his authority nearly threw him into fits.

This was especially to be remarked if anyone attempted to impose upon, or domineer over his favourite: he was painfully jealous lest a word should be spoken amiss to him, seeming to have got into his head the notion that, because he liked Heathcliff, all hated, and longed to do him an ill-turn.

It was a disadvantage to the lad, for the kinder among us did not wish to fret the master, so we humoured his partiality; and that humouring was rich nourishment to the child's pride and black tempers. Still it became in a manner necessary; twice, or thrice, Hindley's manifestation of scorn, while his father was near, roused the old man to a fury. He seized his stick to strike him, and shook with rage that he could not do it.

At last, our curate (we had a curate then who made the living answer by teaching the little Lintons and Earnshaws, and farming his bit of land himself), he advised that the young man should be sent to college, and Mr. Earnshaw agreed, though with a heavy spirit, for he said—

"Hindley was nought, and would never thrive as where he wandered."

I hoped heartily we should have peace now. It hurt me to think the master should be made uncomfortable by his own good deed. I fancied the discontent of age and disease arose from his family disagreements, as he would have it that it did—really, you know, sir, it was in his sinking frame.

We might have got on tolerably, notwithstanding; but for two people, Miss Cathy, and Joseph, the servant; you saw him, I dare say, up yonder. He was, and is yet, most likely, the wearisomest self-righteous pharisee that ever ransacked a bible to rake the promises to himself, and fling the curses on his neighbours. By his knack of sermonizing and pious discoursing, he contrived to make a great impression on Mr. Earnshaw, and, the more feeble the master became, the more influence he gained.

He was relentless in worrying him about his soul's concerns, and about ruling his children rigidly. He encouraged him to regard Hindley as a reprobate; and, night after night, he regularly grumbled out a long string of tales against Heathcliff and Catherine; always minding to flatter Earnshaw's weakness by heaping the heaviest blame on the last.

Certainly, she had ways with her such as I never saw a child take up before; and she put all of us past our patience fifty times and oftener in a day: from the hour she came downstairs, till the hour she went to bed, we had not a minute's security that she wouldn't be in mischief. Her spirits were always at high-water mark, her tongue always going — singing, laughing, and plaguing everybody who would not do the same. A wild, wick slip she was — but she had the bonniest eye, and sweetest smile, and lightest foot in the parish; and, after all, I believe she meant no harm; for when once she made you cry in good earnest, it seldom happened that she would not keep you company; and oblige you to be quiet that you might comfort her.

She was much too fond of Heathcliff. The greatest punishment we could invent for her was to keep her separate from him: yet she got chided more than any of us on his account.

In play, she liked, exceedingly, to act the little mistress; using her hands freely, and commanding her companions: she did so to me, but I would not bear slapping, and ordering; and so I let her know.

Now, Mr. Earnshaw did not understand jokes from his children: he had always been strict and grave with them; and Catherine, on her part, had no idea why her father should be crosser and less patient in his ailing condition, than he was in his prime.

His peevish reproofs wakened in her a naughty delight to provoke him; she was never so happy as when we were all scolding her at once, and she defying us with her bold, saucy look, and her ready words; turning Joseph's religious curses into ridicule, baiting me, and doing just what her father hated most, showing how her pretended insolence, which he thought real, had more power over Heathcliff than his kindness. How the boy would do *her* bidding in anything, and *his* only when it suited his own inclination.

After behaving as badly as possible all day, she sometimes came fondling to make it up at night.

"Nay, Cathy," the old man would say, "I cannot love thee; thou'rt worse than thy brother. Go, say thy prayers, child, and ask God's pardon. I doubt thy mother and I must rue that we ever reared thee!"

---

wick: lively, mischevious.

That made her cry, at first; and then, being repulsed continually hardened her, and she laughed if I told her to say she was sorry for her faults, and beg to be forgiven.

But the hour came, at last, that ended Mr. Earnshaw's troubles on earth. He died quietly in his chair one October evening, seated by the fireside.

A high wind blustered round the house, and roared in the chimney: it sounded wild and stormy, yet it was not cold, and we were all together—I, a little removed from the hearth, busy at my knitting, and Joseph reading his Bible near the table (for the servants generally sat in the house then, after their work was done). Miss Cathy had been sick, and that made her still; she leant against her father's knee, and Heathcliff was lying on the floor with his head in her lap.

I remember the master, before he fell into a doze, stroking her bonny hair—it pleased him rarely to see her gentle—and saying—"Why canst thou not always be a good lass, Cathy?"

And she turned her face up to his, and laughed, and answered—"Why cannot you always be a good man, father?"

But as soon as she saw him vexed again, she kissed his hand, and said she would sing him to sleep. She began singing very low, till his fingers dropped from hers, and his head sank on his breast. Then I told her to hush, and not stir, for fear she should wake him. We all kept as mute as mice a full half-hour, and should have done longer, only Joseph, having finished his chapter, got up and said that he must rouse the master for prayers and bed. He stepped forward, and called him by name, and touched his shoulder, but he would not move—so he took the candle and looked at him.

I thought there was something wrong as he set down the light; and seizing the children each by an arm, whispered them to "frame upstairs, and make little din—they might pray alone that evening—he had summut to do."

"I shall bid father good night first," said Catherine, putting her arms round his neck, before we could hinder her.

The poor thing discovered her loss directly—she screamed out—"Oh, he's dead, Heathcliff! he's dead!"

And they both set up a heart-breaking cry.

I joined my wail to theirs, loud and bitter; but Joseph asked what we could be thinking of to roar in that way over a saint in Heaven.

He told me to put on my cloak and run to Gimmerton for the doctor and the parson. I could not guess the use that either would be of, then. However, I went, through wind and rain, and brought one, the doctor, back with me; the other said he would come in the morning.

Leaving Joseph to explain matters, I ran to the children's room; their door was ajar, I saw they had never laid down, though it was past midnight; but they were calmer, and did not need me to console them. The little souls were comforting each other with better thoughts than I could have hit on; no parson in the world ever pictured Heaven so beautifully as they did, in their innocent talk; and, while I sobbed, and listened, I could not help wishing we were all there safe together.

CHAPTER VI

Mr. Hindley came home to the funeral; and—a thing that amazed us, and set the neighbours gossiping right and left—he brought a wife with him.

What she was, and where she was born he never informed us; probably, she had neither money nor name to recommend her, or he would scarcely have kept the union from his father.

She was not one that would have disturbed the house much on her own account. Every object she saw, the moment she crossed the threshold, appeared to delight her; and every circumstance that took place about her, except the preparing for the burial, and the presence of the mourners.

I thought she was half silly from her behaviour while that went on; she ran into her chamber, and made me come with her, though I should have been dressing the children; and there she sat shivering and clasping her hands, and asking repeatedly—

"Are they gone yet?"

Then she began describing with hysterical emotion the effect it produced on her to see black; and started, and trembled, and, at last, fell a weeping—and when I asked what was the matter? answered, she didn't know; but she felt so afraid of dying!

I imagined her as little likely to die as myself. She was rather thin, but young, and fresh complexioned, and her eyes sparkled as bright as diamonds. I did remark, to be sure, that mounting the stairs made her breathe very quick, that the least sudden noise set her all in a quiver, and that she coughed troublesomely sometimes: but, I knew nothing of what these symptoms portended, and had no impulse to sympathize with her. We don't in general take to foreigners here, Mr. Lockwood, unless they take to us first.

Young Earnshaw was altered considerably in the three years of his absence. He had grown sparer, and lost his colour, and spoke and dressed quite differently: and, on the very day of his return, he told Joseph and me we must thenceforth quarter ourselves in the back-kitchen, and leave the house for him. Indeed he would have carpeted and papered a small spare room for a parlour; but his wife expressed such pleasure at the white floor, and huge glowing fireplace, at the pewter dishes and delf-case, and dog-kennel, and the wide space there was to move about in, where they usually sat, that he thought it unnecessary to her comfort, and so dropped the intention.

She expressed pleasure, too, at finding a sister among her new acquaintance, and she prattled to Catherine, and kissed her, and ran about with her, and gave her quantities of presents, at the beginning. Her affection tired very soon, however, and when she grew peevish, Hindley became tyrannical. A few words from her, evincing a dislike to Heathcliff, were enough to rouse in him all his old hatred of the boy. He drove him from their company to the servants, deprived him of the instructions of the curate, and insisted that he should labour out of doors instead, compelling him to do so, as hard as any other lad on the farm.

Heathcliff bore his degradation pretty well at first, because Cathy taught him what she learnt, and worked or played with him in the fields. They both promised fair to grow up as rude as savages, the young master being entirely negligent how they behaved, and what they did, so they kept clear of him. He would not even have seen after their going to church on Sundays, only Joseph and the curate reprimanded his carelessness when they absented themselves, and that reminded him to order Heathcliff a flogging, and Catherine a fast from dinner or supper.

But it was one of their chief amusements to run away to the moors in the morning and remain there all day, and the after punishment grew a mere thing to laugh at. The curate might set as many chapters as he pleased for Catherine to get by heart, and Joseph might thrash Heathcliff till his arm ached; they forgot everything the minute they were together again, at least the minute they had contrived some naughty plan of revenge, and many a time I've cried to myself to watch them growing more reckless daily, and I not daring to speak a syllable for fear of losing the small power I still retained over the unfriended creatures.

One Sunday evening, it chanced that they were banished from the sitting-room, for making a noise, or a light offence of the kind, and when I went to call them to supper, I could discover them nowhere.

We searched the house, above and below, and the yard, and stables; they were invisible; and, at last, Hindley in a passion told us to bolt the doors, and swore nobody should let them in that night.

The household went to bed; and I, too anxious to lie down, opened my lattice and put my head out to hearken, though it rained, determined to admit them in spite of the prohibition, should they return.

In a while, I distinguished steps coming up the road, and the light of a lantern glimmered through the gate.

I threw a shawl over my head and ran to prevent them from waking Mr. Earnshaw by knocking. There was Heathcliff, by himself; it gave me a start to see him alone.

"Where is Miss Catherine?" I cried hurriedly. "No accident, I hope?"

"At Thrushcross Grange," he answered, "and I would have been there too, but they had not the manners to ask me to stay."

"Well, you will catch it!" I said, "you'll never be content till you're sent about your business. What in the world led you wandering to Thrushcross Grange?"

"Let me get off my wet clothes, and I'll tell you all about it, Nelly," he replied.

I bid him beware of rousing the master, and while he undressed, and I waited to put out the candle, he continued—

"Cathy and I escaped from the wash-house to have a ramble at liberty, and getting a glimpse of the Grange lights, we thought we would just go and see whether the Lintons passed their Sunday evenings standing shivering in corners, while their father and mother sat eating and drinking, and singing and laughing, and burning their eyes out before the fire. Do you think they do? Or reading sermons, and being catechised by their manservant, and set to learn a column of Scripture names, if they don't answer properly?"

"Probably not," I responded. "They are good children, no doubt, and don't deserve the treatment you receive, for your bad conduct."

"Don't you cant, Nelly," he said: "nonsense! We ran from the top of the Heights to the park, without stopping—Catherine completely beaten in the race, because she was barefoot. You'll have to seek for her shoes in the bog tomorrow. We crept through a broken hedge, groped our way up the path, and planted ourselves on a flower-pot under the drawing-room window. The light came from thence; they had not put up the shutters, and the curtains were only half closed. Both of us were able to look in by standing on the basement, and clinging to the ledge, and we saw—ah! it was beautiful—a splendid place carpeted with crimson, and crimson-covered chairs and tables, and a pure white ceiling bordered by gold, a shower of glass-drops hanging in silver chains from the centre, and shimmering with little soft tapers. Old Mr. and Mrs. Linton were not there. Edgar and his sister had it entirely to themselves; shouldn't they have been happy? We should have thought ourselves in heaven! And now, guess what your good children were doing? Isabella, I believe she is eleven, a year younger than Cathy, lay screaming at the farther end of the room, shrieking as if witches were

---

cant: to recount or narrate (*OED*); in this context, to preach.

running red hot needles into her. Edgar stood on the hearth weeping silently, and in the middle of the table sat a little dog shaking its paw and yelping, which, from their mutual accusations, we understood they had nearly pulled in two between them. The idiots! That was their pleasure! to quarrel who should hold a heap of warm hair, and each begin to cry because both, after struggling to get it, refused to take it. We laughed outright at the petted things, we did despise them! When would you catch me wishing to have what Catherine wanted? or find us by ourselves, seeing entertainment in yelling, and sobbing, and rolling on the ground, divided by the whole room? I'd not exchange, for a thousand lives, my condition here, for Edgar Linton's at Thrushcross Grange—not if I might have the privilege of flinging Joseph off the highest gable, and painting the house-front with Hindley's blood!"

"Hush, hush!" I interrupted. "Still you have not told me, Heathcliff, how Catherine is left behind?"

"I told you we laughed," he answered. "The Lintons heard us, and with one accord, they shot like arrows to the door; there was silence, and then a cry, 'Oh, mamma, mamma! Oh, papa! Oh, mamma, come here. Oh, papa, oh!' They really did howl out, something in that way. We made frightful noises to terrify them still more, and then we dropped off the ledge, because somebody was drawing the bars, and we felt we had better flee. I had Cathy by the hand, and was urging her on, when all at once she fell down.

"'Run, Heathcliff, run!' she whispered. 'They have let the bulldog loose, and he holds me!'

"The devil had seized her ankle, Nelly; I heard his abominable snorting. She did not yell out—no! She would have scorned to do it, if she had been spitted on the horns of a mad cow. I did, though, I vociferated curses enough to annihilate any fiend in Christendom, and I got a stone and thrust it between his jaws, and tried with all my might to cram it down his throat. A beast of a servant came up with a lantern, at last, shouting—

"'Keep fast, Skulker, keep fast!' He changed his note, however, when he saw Skulker's game. The dog was throttled off, his huge, purple tongue hanging half a foot out of his mouth, and his pendant lips streaming with bloody slaver.

"The man took Cathy up; she was sick; not from fear, I'm certain, but from pain. He carried her in; I followed grumbling execrations and vengeance.

"'What prey, Robert?' hallooed Linton from the entrance.

"'Skulker has caught a little girl, sir,' he replied; 'and there's a lad here,' he added, making a clutch at me, 'who looks an out-and-outer! Very like, the robbers were for putting them through the window, to open the doors to the gang after all were asleep, that they might murder us at their ease.

Hold your tongue, you foul-mouthed thief, you! you shall go to the gallows for this. Mr. Linton, sir, don't lay by your gun!'

"'No, no, Robert,' said the old fool. 'The rascals knew that yesterday was my rent day; they thought to have me cleverly. Come in; I'll furnish them a reception. There, John, fasten the chain. Give Skulker some water, Jenny. To beard a magistrate in his stronghold, and on the Sabbath, too! where will their insolence stop? Oh, my dear Mary, look here! Don't be afraid, it is but a boy—yet, the villain scowls so plainly in his face, would it not be a kindness to the country to hang him at once, before he shows his nature in acts, as well as features?'

"He pulled me under the chandelier, and Mrs. Linton placed her spectacles on her nose and raised her hands in horror. The cowardly children crept nearer also, Isabella lisping—

"'Frightful thing! Put him in the cellar, papa. He's exactly like the son of the fortune-teller, that stole my tame pheasant. Isn't he, Edgar?'

"While they examined me, Cathy came round; she heard the last speech, and laughed. Edgar Linton, after an inquisitive stare, collected sufficient wit to recognise her. They see us at church, you know, though we seldom meet them elsewhere.

"'That's Miss Earnshaw!' he whispered to his mother, 'and look how Skulker has bitten her—how her foot bleeds!'

"'Miss Earnshaw! Nonsense!' cried the dame, 'Miss Earnshaw scouring the country with a gipsy! And yet, my dear, the child is in mourning— surely it is—and she may be lamed for life!'

"'What culpable carelessness in her brother!' exclaimed Mr. Linton, turning from me to Catherine. 'I've understood from Shielders'" (that was the curate, sir) "'that he lets her grow up in absolute heathenism. But who is this? Where did she pick up this companion? Oho! I declare he is that strange acquisition my late neighbour made in his journey to Liverpool— a little Lascar, or an American or Spanish castaway.'

"'A wicked boy, at all events,' remarked the old lady, 'and quite unfit for a decent house! Did you notice his language, Linton? I'm shocked that my children should have heard it.'

"I recommenced cursing—don't be angry, Nelly—and so Robert was ordered to take me off—I refused to go without Cathy—he dragged me into the garden, pushed the lantern into my hand, assured me that Mr. Earnshaw should be informed of my behaviour, and bidding me march, directly, secured the door again.

"The curtains were still looped up at one corner; and I resumed my station as spy, because, if Catherine had wished to return, I intended shattering their great glass panes to a million fragments, unless they let her out.

"She sat on the sofa quietly. Mrs. Linton took off the grey cloak of the dairy maid which we had borrowed for our excursion; shaking her head, and expostulating with her, I suppose; she was a young lady and they made a distinction between her treatment, and mine. Then the woman servant brought a basin of warm water, and washed her feet; and Mr. Linton mixed a tumbler of negus, and Isabella emptied a plateful of cakes into her lap, and Edgar, stood gaping at a distance. Afterwards, they dried and combed her beautiful hair, and gave her a pair of enormous slippers, and wheeled her to the fire, and I left her, as merry as she could be, dividing her food, between the little dog and Skulker whose nose she pinched as he ate; and kindling a spark of spirit in the vacant blue eyes of the Lintons—a dim reflection from her own enchanting face—I saw they were full of stupid admiration; she is so immeasurably superior to them—to everybody on earth; is she not, Nelly?"

"There will more come of this business than you reckon on," I answered covering him up and extinguishing the light, "You are incurable, Heathcliff, and Mr. Hindley will have to proceed to extremities, see if he won't."

My words came truer than I desired. The luckless adventure made Earnshaw furious—And then, Mr. Linton, to mend matters, paid us a visit himself, on the morrow; and read the young master such a lecture on the road he guided his family, that he was stirred to look about him, in earnest.

Heathcliff received no flogging, but he was told that the first word he spoke to Miss Catherine should ensure a dismissal; and Mrs. Earnshaw undertook to keep her sister-in-law in due restraint, when she returned home; employing art, not force—with force she would have found it impossible.

CHAPTER VII

Cathy stayed at Thrushcross Grange five weeks, till Christmas. By that time her ankle was thoroughly cured, and her manners much improved. The mistress visited her often, in the interval, and commenced her plan of reform, by trying to raise her self-respect with fine clothes, and flattery, which she took readily: so that, instead of a wild, hatless little savage jumping into the house, and rushing to squeeze us all breathless, there lighted from a handsome black pony a very dignified person with brown ringlets falling from the cover of a feathered beaver, and a long cloth habit which she was obliged to hold up with both hands that she might sail in.

Hindley lifted her from her horse exclaiming delightedly.

"Why, Cathy, you are quite a beauty! I should scarcely have known you—you look like a lady now—Isabella Linton is not to be compared with her, is she Frances?"

"Isabella has not her natural advantages," replied his wife, "but she must mind and not grow wild again here. Ellen, help Miss Catherine off with her things—Stay, dear, you will disarrange your curls—let me untie your hat."

I removed the habit, and there shone forth, beneath a grand plaid silk frock, white trousers, and burnished shoes; and, while her eyes sparkled joyfully when the dogs came bounding up to welcome her, she dare hardly touch them lest they should fawn upon her splendid garments.

She kissed me gently, I was all flour making the Christmas cake, and it would not have done to give me a hug; and, then, she looked round for Heathcliff. Mr. and Mrs. Earnshaw watched anxiously their meeting, thinking it would enable them to judge, in some measure, what grounds they had for hoping to succeed in separating the two friends.

Heathcliff was hard to discover, at first—If he were careless, and uncared for, before Catherine's absence, he had been ten times more so, since.

Nobody, but I, even did him the kindness to call him a dirty boy, and bid him wash himself, once a week; and children of his age, seldom have a natural pleasure in soap and water. Therefore, not to mention his clothes, which had seen three months' service, in mire and dust, and his thick uncombed hair; the surface of his face and hands was dismally beclouded. He might well skulk behind the settle, on beholding such a bright, graceful damsel enter the house, instead of a rough-headed counterpart to himself, as he expected.

"Is Heathcliff not here?" she demanded pulling off her gloves, and displaying fingers wonderfully whitened with doing nothing, and staying in doors.

"Heathcliff, you may come forward," cried Mr. Hindley enjoying his discomfiture and gratified to see what a forbidding young blackguard he would be compelled to present himself. "You may come and wish Miss Catherine welcome, like the other servants."

Cathy, catching a glimpse of her friend in his concealment, flew to embrace him, she bestowed seven or eight kisses on his cheek within the second, and, then, stopped, and drawing back, burst into a laugh, exclaiming,

"Why, how very black and cross you look! and how—how funny and grim! But that's because I'm used to Edgar, and Isabella Linton. Well, Heathcliff, have you forgotten me?"

She had some reason to put the question, for shame and pride threw double gloom over his countenance, and kept him immoveable.

"Shake hands, Heathcliff," said Mr. Earnshaw, condescendingly; "once in a way that is permitted."

"I shall not!" replied the boy, finding his tongue at last, "I shall not stand to be laughed at, I shall not bear it!"

And he would have broken from the circle, but Miss Cathy seized him again.

"I did not mean to laugh at you," she said, "I could not hinder myself, Heathcliff, shake hands, at least! What are you sulky for? It was only that you looked odd—If you wash your face, and brush your hair it will be all right. But you are so dirty!"

She gazed concernedly at the dusky fingers she held in her own, and also at her dress which she feared had gained no embellishment from its contact with his.

"You needn't have touched me!" he answered, following her eye and snatching away his hand. "I shall be as dirty as I please, and I like to be dirty, and I will be dirty."

With that he dashed head foremost out of the room, amid the merriment of the master and mistress, and to the serious disturbance of Catherine who could not comprehend how her remarks should have produced such an exhibition of bad temper.

After playing lady's maid to the newcomer, and putting my cakes in the oven, and making the house and kitchen cheerful with great fires befitting Christmas eve, I prepared to sit down and amuse myself by singing carols, all alone; regardless of Joseph's affirmations that he considered the merry tunes I chose as next door to songs.

He had retired to private prayer in his chamber, and Mr. and Mrs. Earnshaw were engaging Missy's attention by sundry gay trifles bought for her to present to the little Lintons, as an acknowledgment of their kindness.

They had invited them to spend the morrow at Wuthering Heights, and the invitation had been accepted, on one condition: Mrs. Linton begged that her darlings might be kept carefully apart from that "naughty, swearing boy."

Under these circumstances I remained solitary. I smelt the rich scent of the heating spices; and admired the shining kitchen utensils, the polished clock, decked in holly, the silver mugs ranged on a tray ready to be filled with mulled ale for supper; and, above all, the speckless purity of my particular care—the scoured and well-swept floor.

I gave due inward applause to every object and, then, I remembered how old Earnshaw used to come in when all was tidied, and call me a cant lass, and slip a shilling into my hand, as a Christmas box: and, from that, I went on to think of his fondness for Heathcliff, and his dread lest he should suffer neglect after death had removed him; and that naturally led me to consider the poor lad's situation now, and from singing I changed my mind to crying. It struck me soon, however, there would be more sense in endeavouring to repair some of his wrongs than shedding tears over them—I got up and walked into the court to seek him.

He was not far, I found him smoothing the glossy coat of the new pony in the stable, and feeding the other beasts, according to custom.

"Make haste, Heathcliff!" I said, "the kitchen is so comfortable—and Joseph is upstairs; make haste, and let me dress you smart before Miss Cathy comes out—and then you can sit together, with the whole hearth to yourselves, and have a long chatter till bedtime."

He proceeded with his task and never turned his head towards me.

"Come—are you coming?" I continued, "There's a little cake for each of you, nearly enough; and you'll need half an hour's donning."

I waited five minutes, but getting no answer left him. . . . Catherine supped with her brother and sister-in-law: Joseph and I joined in an unsociable meal seasoned with reproofs on one side, and sauciness on the other. His cake and cheese remained on the table all night, for the fairies. He managed to continue work till nine o'clock, and, then, marched dumb and dour to his chamber.

Cathy sat up late; having a world of things to order for the reception of her new friends: she came into the kitchen, once, to speak to her old one, but he was gone, and she only staid to ask what was the matter with him, and then went back.

In the morning, he rose early; and, as it was a holiday, carried his ill-humour onto the moors; not re-appearing till the family were departed for church. Fasting and reflection seemed to have brought him to a better spirit. He hung about me, for a while, and having screwed up his courage, exclaimed abruptly,

"Nelly, make me decent, I'm going to be good."

"High time, Heathcliff," I said, "you *have* grieved Catherine: she's sorry she ever came home, I dare say! It looks as if you envied her, because she is more thought of than you."

The notion of *envying* Catherine was incomprehensible to him, but the notion of grieving her, he understood clearly enough.

"Did she say she was grieved?" he inquired, looking very serious.

"She cried when I told her you were off again this morning."

"Well, *I* cried last night," he returned, "and I had more reason to cry than she."

"Yes, you had the reason of going to bed, with a proud heart, and an empty stomach," said I, "Proud people breed sad sorrows for themselves— But, if you be ashamed of your touchiness, you must ask pardon, mind, when she comes in. You must go up, and offer to kiss her, and say—you know best what to say, only, do it heartily, and not as if you thought her converted into a stranger by her grand dress. And now, though I have dinner to get ready, I'll steal time to arrange you so that Edgar Linton shall look quite a doll beside you: and that he does—You are younger, and yet,

I'll be bound, you are taller and twice as broad across the shoulders — you could knock him down in a twinkling; don't you feel that you could?"

Heathcliff's face brightened a moment; then, it was overcast afresh, and he sighed.

"But, Nelly, if I knocked him down twenty times, that wouldn't make him less handsome, or me more so. I wish I had light hair and a fair skin, and was dressed, and behaved as well, and had a chance of being as rich as he will be!"

"And cried for mamma, at every turn —" I added, "and trembled if a country lad heaved his fist against you, and sat at home all day for a shower of rain. — O, Heathcliff, you are showing a poor spirit! Come to the glass, and I'll let you see what you should wish. Do you mark those two lines between your eyes, and those thick brows, that instead of rising arched, sink in the middle, and that couple of black fiends, so deeply buried, who never open their windows boldly, but lurk glinting under them, like devil's spies? Wish and learn to smooth away the surly wrinkles, to raise your lids frankly, and change the fiends to confident, innocent angels, suspecting and doubting nothing, and always seeing friends where they are not sure of foes — Don't get the expression of a vicious cur that appears to know the kicks it gets are its desert, and yet hates all the world, as well as the kicker, for what it suffers."

"In other words, I must wish for Edgar Linton's great blue eyes, and even forehead," he replied. "I do — and that won't help me to them."

"A good heart will help you to a bonny face, my lad," I continued, "if you were a regular black; and a bad one will turn the bonniest into something worse than ugly. And now that we've done washing, and combing, and sulking — tell me whether you don't think yourself rather handsome? I'll tell you, I do. You're fit for a prince in disguise. Who knows, but your father was Emperor of China, and your mother an Indian queen, each of them able to buy up, with one week's income, Wuthering Heights and Thrushcross Grange together? And you were kidnapped by wicked sailors, and brought to England. Were I in your place, I would frame high notions of my birth; and the thoughts of what I was should give me courage and dignity to support the oppressions of a little farmer!"

So I chattered on; and Heathcliff gradually lost his frown, and began to look quite pleasant; when all at once, our conversation was interrupted by a rumbling sound moving up the road and entering the court. He ran to the window, and I to the door, just in time to behold the two Lintons descend from the family carriage, smothered in cloaks and furs, and the Earnshaws dismount from their horses — they often rode to church in winter. Catherine took a hand of each of the children, and brought them into the house, and set them before the fire which quickly put colour into their white faces.

I urged my companion to hasten now, and show his amiable humour; and he willingly obeyed: but ill luck would have it; that as he opened the door leading from the kitchen on one side, Hindley opened it on the other; they met, and the master irritated at seeing him clean and cheerful, or, perhaps, eager to keep his promise to Mrs. Linton shoved him back with a sudden thrust, and angrily bade Joseph "keep the fellow out of the room — send him into the garret till dinner is over. He'll be cramming his fingers in the tarts, and stealing the fruit, if left alone with them a minute."

"Nay, sir," I could not avoid answering, "he'll touch nothing, not he — and, I suppose, he must have his share of the dainties as well as we."

"He shall have his share of my hand, if I catch him downstairs again till dark," cried Hindley. "Begone, you vagabond! What, you are attempting the coxcomb, are you? Wait till I get hold of those elegant locks — see if I won't pull them a bit longer!"

"They are long enough already," observed Master Linton, peeping from the doorway, "I wonder they don't make his head ache. It's like a colt's mane over his eyes!"

He ventured this remark without any intention to insult; but Heathcliff's violent nature was not prepared to endure the appearance of impertinence from one whom he seemed to hate, even then, as a rival. He seized a tureen of hot apple-sauce, the first thing that came under his gripe, and dashed it full against the speaker's face and neck — who instantly commenced a lament that brought Isabella and Catherine hurrying to the place.

Mr. Earnshaw snatched up the culprit directly and conveyed him to his chamber, where, doubtless, he administered a rough remedy to cool the fit of passion, for he reappeared red and breathless. I got the dish-cloth, and, rather spitefully, scrubbed Edgar's nose and mouth, affirming, it served him right for meddling. His sister began weeping to go home, and Cathy stood by confounded, blushing for all.

"You should not have spoken to him!" she expostulated with Master Linton. "He was in a bad temper, and now you've spoilt your visit, and he'll be flogged — I hate him to be flogged! I can't eat my dinner. Why did you speak to him, Edgar?"

"I didn't," sobbed the youth, escaping from my hands, and finishing the remainder of the purification with his cambric pocket-handkerchief. "I promised mamma that I wouldn't say one word to him, and I didn't."

"Well, don't cry!" replied Catherine, contemptuously. "You're not killed — don't make more mischief — my brother is coming — be quiet! Give over, Isabella! Has anybody hurt *you?*"

"There, there, children—to your seats!" cried Hindley, bustling in. "That brute of a lad has warmed me nicely. Next time, Master Edgar, take the law into your own fists—it will give you an appetite!"

The little party recovered its equanimity at sight of the fragrant feast. They were hungry, after their ride, and easily consoled, since no real harm had befallen them.

Mr. Earnshaw carved bountiful platefuls; and the mistress made them merry with lively talk. I waited behind her chair, and was pained to behold Catherine, with dry eyes and an indifferent air, commence cutting up the wing of a goose before her.

"An unfeeling child," I thought to myself, "how lightly she dismisses her old playmate's troubles. I could not have imagined her to be so selfish."

She lifted a mouthful to her lips; then, she set it down again: her cheeks flushed, and the tears gushed over them. She slipped her fork to the floor, and hastily dived under the cloth to conceal her emotion. I did not call her unfeeling long, for, I perceived she was in purgatory throughout the day, and wearying to find an opportunity of getting by herself, or paying a visit to Heathcliff, who had been locked up by the master, as I discovered, on endeavouring to introduce to him a private mess of victuals.

In the evening we had a dance. Cathy begged that he might be liberated then, as Isabella Linton had no partner; her entreaties were vain, and I was appointed to supply the deficiency.

We got rid of all gloom in the excitement of the exercise, and our pleasure was increased by the arrival of the Gimmerton band, mustering fifteen strong; a trumpet, a trombone, clarionets, bassoons, French horns, and a bass viol, besides singers. They go the rounds of all the respectable houses, and receive contributions every Christmas, and we esteemed it a first-rate treat to hear them.

After the usual carols had been sung, we set them to songs and glees. Mrs. Earnshaw loved the music, and, so, they gave us plenty.

Catherine loved it too; but she said it sounded sweetest at the top of the steps, and she went up in the dark; I followed. They shut the house door below, never noting our absence, it was so full of people. She made no stay at the stair's head, but mounted farther, to the garret where Heathcliff was confined; and called him. He stubbornly declined answering for a while— she persevered, and finally persuaded him to hold communion with her through the boards.

I let the poor things converse unmolested, till I supposed the songs were going to cease, and the singers to get some refreshment: then, I clambered up the ladder to warn her.

Instead of finding her outside, I heard her voice within. The little monkey had crept by the skylight of one garret, along the roof, into the skylight of the other, and it was with the utmost difficulty I could coax her out again.

When she did come, Heathcliff came with her; and she insisted that I should take him into the kitchen, as my fellow-servant had gone to a neighbour's to be removed from the sound of our "devil's psalmody," as it pleased him to call it.

I told them I intended, by no means, to encourage their tricks; but as the prisoner had never broken his fast since yesterday's dinner, I would wink at his cheating Mr. Hindley that once.

He went down; I set him a stool by the fire, and offered him a quantity of good things; but, he was sick and could eat little: and my attempts to entertain him were thrown away. He leant his two elbows on his knees, and his chin on his hands, and remained wrapt in dumb meditation. On my inquiring the subject of his thoughts, he answered gravely—

"I'm trying to settle how I shall pay Hindley back. I don't care how long I wait, if I can only do it, at last. I hope he will not die before I do!"

"For shame, Heathcliff!" said I. "It is for God to punish wicked people; we should learn to forgive."

"No, God won't have the satisfaction that I shall," he returned. "I only wish I knew the best way! Let me alone, and I'll plan it out: while I'm thinking of that, I don't feel pain."

But, Mr. Lockwood, I forget these tales cannot divert you. I'm annoyed how I should dream of chattering on at such a rate; and your gruel cold, and you nodding for bed! I could have told Heathcliff's history, all that you need hear, in a half-a-dozen words.

Thus interrupting herself, the housekeeper rose, and proceeded to lay aside her sewing; but I felt incapable of moving from the hearth, and I was very far from nodding.

"Sit still, Mrs. Dean," I cried, "do sit still, another half hour! You've done just right to tell the story leisurely. That is the method I like; and you must finish in the same style. I am interested in every character you have mentioned, more or less."

"The clock is on the stroke of eleven, sir."

"No matter—I'm not accustomed to go to bed in the long hours. One or two is early enough for a person who lies till ten."

"You shouldn't lie till ten. There's the very prime of the morning gone long before that time. A person who has not done one half his day's work by ten o'clock, runs a chance of leaving the other half undone."

"Nevertheless, Mrs. Dean, resume your chair; because tomorrow I intend lengthening the night till afternoon. I prognosticate for myself an obstinate cold, at least."

"I hope not, sir. Well, you must allow me to leap over some three years; during that space, Mrs. Earnshaw—"

"No, no, I'll allow nothing of the sort! Are you acquainted with the mood of mind in which, if you were seated alone, and the cat licking its kitten on the rug before you, you would watch the operation so intently that puss's neglect of one ear would put you seriously out of temper?"

"A terribly lazy mood, I should say."

"On the contrary, a tiresomely active one. It is mine, at present, and, therefore, continue minutely. I perceive that people in these regions acquire over people in towns the value that the spider in a dungeon does over a spider in a cottage, to their various occupants; and yet the deepened attraction is not entirely owing to the situation of the looker-on. They *do* live more in earnest, more in themselves, and less in surface change, and frivolous external things. I could fancy a love for life here almost possible; and I was a fixed unbeliever in any love of a year's standing—one state resembles setting a hungry man down to a single dish on which he may concentrate his entire appetite, and do it justice—the other, introducing him to a table laid out by French cooks; he can perhaps extract as much enjoyment from the whole; but each part is a mere atom in his regard and remembrance."

"Oh! here we are the same as anywhere else, when you get to know us," observed Mrs. Dean, somewhat puzzled at my speech.

"Excuse me," I responded; "you, my good friend, are a striking evidence against that assertion. Excepting a few provincialisms of slight consequence, you have no marks of the manners that I am habituated to consider as peculiar to your class. I am sure you have thought a great deal more than the generality of servants think. You have been compelled to cultivate your reflective faculties, for want of occasions for frittering your life away in silly trifles."

Mrs. Dean laughed.

"I certainly esteem myself a steady, reasonable kind of body," she said; "not exactly from living among the hills, and seeing one set of faces, and one series of actions, from year's end to year's end: but I have undergone sharp discipline which has taught me wisdom; and then, I have read more than you would fancy, Mr. Lockwood. You could not open a book in this library that I have not looked into, and got something out of also; unless it be that range of Greek and Latin, and that of French—and those I know one from another, it is as much as you can expect of a poor man's daughter.

"However, if I am to follow my story in true gossip's fashion, I had better go on; and instead of leaping three years, I will be content to pass to the next summer—the summer of 1778, that is, nearly twenty-three years ago."

CHAPTER VIII

On the morning of a fine June day, my first bonny little nursling, and the last of the ancient Earnshaw stock was born.

We were busy with the hay in a far away field, when the girl that usually brought our breakfasts came running, an hour too soon, across the meadow and up the lane, calling me as she ran.

"Oh, such a grand bairn!" she panted out. "The finest lad that ever breathed! But the doctor says missis must go; he says she's been in a consumption these many months. I heard him tell Mr. Hindley — and now she has nothing to keep her, and she'll be dead before winter. You must come home directly. You're to nurse it, Nelly — to feed it with sugar and milk, and take care of it, day and night — I wish I were you, because it will be all yours when there is no missis!"

"But is she very ill?" I asked, flinging down my rake, and tying my bonnet.

"I guess she is; yet she looks bravely," replied the girl, "and she talks as if she thought of living to see it grow a man. She's out of her head for joy, it's such a beauty! If I were her I'm certain I should not die. I should get better at the bare sight of it, in spite of Kenneth. I was fairly mad at him. Dame Archer brought the cherub down to master, in the house, and his face just began to light up, then the old croaker steps forward, and, says he: 'Earnshaw, it's a blessing your wife has been spared to leave you this son. When she came, I felt convinced we shouldn't keep her long; and now, I must tell you, the winter will probably finish her. Don't take on, and fret about it too much, it can't be helped. And besides, you should have known better than to choose such a rush of a lass!'"

"And what did the master answer?" I enquired.

"I think he swore — but, I didn't mind him, I was straining to see the bairn," and she began again to describe it rapturously. I, as zealous as herself, hurried eagerly home to admire, on my part, though I was very sad for Hindley's sake; he had room in his heart only for two idols — his wife and himself — he doted on both, and adored one, and I couldn't conceive how he would bear the loss.

When we got to Wuthering Heights, there he stood at the front door; and, as I passed in, I asked, "how was the baby?"

"Nearly ready to run about, Nell!" he replied, putting on a cheerful smile.

"And the mistress?" I ventured to inquire, "the doctor says she's —"

"Damn the doctor!" he interrupted, reddening. "Frances is quite right — she'll be perfectly well by this time next week. Are you going upstairs? will

---

bairn: baby or child.

you tell her that I'll come, if she'll promise not to talk. I left her because she would not hold her tongue; and she must—tell her Mr. Kenneth says she must be quiet."

I delivered this message to Mrs. Earnshaw; she seemed in flighty spirits, and replied merrily—

"I hardly spoke a word, Ellen, and there he has gone out twice, crying. Well, say I promise I won't speak; but that does not bind me not to laugh at him!"

Poor soul! Till within a week of her death that gay heart never failed her; and her husband persisted doggedly, nay, furiously, in affirming her health improved every day. When Kenneth warned him that his medicines were useless at that stage of the malady, and he needn't put him to further expense by attending her, he retorted—

"I know you need not—she's well—she does not want any more attendance from you! She never was in a consumption. It was a fever; and it is gone—her pulse is as slow as mine now, and her cheek as cool."

He told his wife the same story, and she seemed to believe him; but one night, while leaning on his shoulder, in the act of saying she thought she should be able to get up tomorrow, a fit of coughing took her—a very slight one—he raised her in his arms; she put her two hands about his neck, her face changed, and she was dead.

As the girl had anticipated; the child, Hareton, fell wholly into my hands. Mr. Earnshaw, provided he saw him healthy, and never heard him cry, was contented, as far as regarded him. For himself, he grew desperate; his sorrow was of that kind that will not lament, he neither wept nor prayed—he cursed and defied—execrated God and man, and gave himself up to reckless dissipation.

The servants could not bear his tyrannical and evil conduct long: Joseph and I were the only two that would stay. I had not the heart to leave my charge; and besides, you know, I had been his foster sister, and excused his behaviour more readily than a stranger would.

Joseph remained to hector over tenants and labourers; and because it was his vocation to be where he had plenty of wickedness to reprove.

The master's bad ways and bad companions formed a pretty example for Catherine and Heathcliff. His treatment of the latter was enough to make a fiend of a saint. And, truly, it appeared as if the lad *were* possessed of something diabolical at that period. He delighted to witness Hindley degrading himself past redemption; and became daily more notable for savage sullenness and ferocity.

I could not half tell what an infernal house we had. The curate dropped calling, and nobody decent came near us, at last; unless, Edgar Linton's visits to Miss Cathy might be an exception. At fifteen she was the queen of the countryside; she had no peer: and she did turn out a haughty, headstrong creature! I own I did not like her, after her infancy was past; and I vexed her frequently by trying to bring down her arrogance; she never took an aversion to me though. She had a wondrous constancy to old attachments; even Heathcliff kept his hold on her affections unalterably, and young Linton, with all his superiority, found it difficult to make an equally deep impression.

He was my late master; that is his portrait over the fireplace. It used to hang on one side, and his wife's on the other; but hers has been removed, or else you might see something of what she was. Can you make that out?

Mrs. Dean raised the candle, and I discerned a soft-featured face, exceedingly resembling the young lady at the Heights, but more pensive and amiable in expression. It formed a sweet picture. The long light hair curled slightly on the temples; the eyes were large and serious; the figure almost too graceful. I did not marvel how Catherine Earnshaw could forget her first friend for such an individual. I marvelled much how he, with a mind to correspond with his person, could fancy my idea of Catherine Earnshaw.

"A very agreeable portrait," I observed to the housekeeper. "Is it like?"

"Yes," she answered; "but he looked better when he was animated, that is his everyday countenance; he wanted spirit in general."

Catherine had kept up her acquaintance with the Lintons since her five weeks' residence among them; and as she had no temptation to show her rough side in their company, and had the sense to be ashamed of being rude where she experienced such invariable courtesy, she imposed unwittingly on the old lady and gentleman, by her ingenious cordiality; gained the admiration of Isabella, and the heart and soul of her brother—acquisitions that flattered her from the first, for she was full of ambition—and led her to adopt a double character without exactly intending to deceive anyone.

In the place where she heard Heathcliff termed a "vulgar young ruffian," and "worse than a brute," she took care not to act like him; but at home she had small inclination to practise politeness that would only be laughed at, and restrain an unruly nature when it would bring her neither credit, nor praise.

Mr. Edgar seldom mustered courage to visit Wuthering Heights openly. He had a terror of Earnshaw's reputation, and shrank from encountering him, and yet, he was always received with our best attempts at civility: the master himself, avoided offending him—knowing why he came, and if he could not be gracious, kept out of the way. I rather think his appearance there was distasteful to Catherine; she was not artful, never played the coquette, and had evidently an objection to her two friends meeting at all:

for when Heathcliff expressed contempt of Linton, in his presence, she could not half coincide, as she did in his absence; and when Linton evinced disgust and antipathy to Heathcliff, she dared not treat his sentiments with indifference, as if depreciation of her playmate were of scarcely any consequence to her.

I've had many a laugh at her perplexities, and untold troubles, which she vainly strove to hide from my mockery. That sounds ill-natured—but she was so proud, it became really impossible to pity her distresses, till she should be chastened into more humility.

She did bring herself, finally, to confess, and confide in me. There was not a soul else that she might fashion into an adviser.

Mr. Hindley had gone from home, one afternoon; and Heathcliff presumed to give himself a holiday, on the strength of it. He had reached the age of sixteen then, I think, and without having bad features or being deficient in intellect, he contrived to convey an impression of inward and outward repulsiveness that his present aspect retains no traces of.

In the first place, he had, by that time, lost the benefit of his early education: continual hard work, begun soon and concluded late, had extinguished any curiosity he once possessed in pursuit of knowledge, and any love for books, or learning. His childhood's sense of superiority, instilled into him by the favours of old Mr. Earnshaw, was faded away. He struggled long to keep up an equality with Catherine in her studies and yielded with poignant though silent regret: but, he yielded completely; and there was no prevailing on him to take a step in the way of moving upward, when he found he must, necessarily, sink beneath his former level. Then personal appearance sympathised with mental deterioration; he acquired a slouching gait, and ignoble look; his naturally reserved disposition was exaggerated into an almost idiotic excess of unsociable moroseness; and he took a grim pleasure, apparently, in exciting the aversion rather than the esteem of his few acquaintance.

Catherine and he were constant companions still, at his seasons of respite from labour; but he had ceased to express his fondness for her in words, and recoiled with angry suspicion from her girlish caresses, as if conscious there could be no gratification in lavishing such marks of affection on him. On the before-named occasion he came into the house to announce his intention of doing nothing, while I was assisting Miss Cathy to arrange her dress—she had not reckoned on his taking it into his head to be idle, and imagining she would have the whole place to herself, she managed, by some means, to inform Mr. Edgar of her brother's absence, and was then preparing to receive him.

"Cathy, are you busy, this afternoon?" asked Heathcliff. "Are you going anywhere?"

"No, it is raining," she answered.

"Why have you that silk frock on, then?" he said. "Nobody coming here, I hope?"

"Not that I know of," stammered Miss, "but you should be in the field now, Heathcliff. It is an hour past dinner time; I thought you were gone."

"Hindley does not often free us from his accursed presence," observed the boy. "I'll not work any more today, I'll stay with you."

"O, but Joseph will tell," she suggested, "you'd better go!"

"Joseph is loading lime on the farther side of Penistone Crag,[2] it will take him till dark, and he'll never know."

So saying he lounged to the fire, and sat down. Catherine reflected an instant, with knitted brows — she found it needful to smooth the way for an intrusion.

"Isabella and Edgar Linton talked of calling this afternoon," she said at the conclusion of a minute's silence. "As it rains, I hardly expect them; but they may come, and if they do, you run the risk of being scolded for no good."

"Order Ellen to say you are engaged, Cathy," he persisted, "Don't turn me out for those pitiful, silly friends of yours! I'm on the point, sometimes, of complaining that they — but I'll not — "

"That they what?" cried Catherine, gazing at him with a troubled countenance. "Oh Nelly!" she added petulantly jerking her head away from my hands, "you've combed my hair quite out of curl! That's enough, let me alone. What are you on the point of complaining about, Heathcliff?"

"Nothing — only look at the almanack, on that wall," he pointed to a framed sheet hanging near the window, and continued;

"The crosses are for the evenings you have spent with the Lintons, the dots for those spent with me — Do you see, I've marked every day?"

"Yes — very foolish; as if I took notice!" replied Catherine in a peevish tone. "And where is the sense of that?"

"To show that I *do* take notice," said Heathcliff.

"And should I always be sitting with you?" she demanded, growing more irritated. "What good do I get — What do you talk about? You might be dumb or a baby for anything you say to amuse me, or for anything you do, either!"

---

[2]Penistone Crag is a quarry near the Brontë parsonage. The Fairy Cave has been identified as either Yordas Cave, a famous tourist site in Yorkshire (see Christopher Heywood's article on Yorkshire landscapes, 349–66), or as Ponden Kirk near Stanbury (see Marsden and Jack's edition of *Wuthering Heights*, 425). Spellings of both *Penistone* and *Crag* vary in earlier editions. The spelling is standardized to *Penistone Crag* in this New Riverside Edition. [ED.]

"You never told me before that I talked too little, or that you disliked my company, Cathy!" exclaimed Heathcliff, in much agitation.

"It's no company at all, when people know nothing and say nothing," she muttered.

Her companion rose up, but he hadn't time to express his feelings further, for a horse's feet were heard on the flags, and, having knocked gently, young Linton entered, his face brilliant with delight at the unexpected summons he had received.

Doubtless Catherine marked the difference between her friends as one came in, and the other went out. The contrast resembled what you see in exchanging a bleak, hilly, coal country, for a beautiful fertile valley; and his voice, and greeting were as opposite as his aspect—He had a sweet, low manner of speaking, and pronounced his words as you do, that's less gruff than we talk here and softer.

"I'm not come too soon, am I?" he said, casting a look at me. I had begun to wipe the plate, and tidy some drawers at the far end in the dresser.

"No," answered Catherine. "What are you doing there, Nelly?"

"My work, Miss," I replied. (Mr. Hindley had given me directions to make a third party in any private visits Linton chose to pay.)

She stepped behind me and whispered crossly, "Take yourself and your dusters off! when company are in the house, servants don't commence scouring and cleaning in the room where they are!"

"It's a good opportunity, now that master is away," I answered aloud, "he hates me to be fidgeting over these things in his presence—I'm sure Mr. Edgar will excuse me."

"I hate you to be fidgeting in *my* presence," exclaimed the young lady imperiously, not allowing her guest time to speak—she had failed to recover her equanimity since the little dispute with Heathcliff.

"I'm sorry for it, Miss Catherine!" was my response; and I proceeded assiduously with my occupation.

She, supposing Edgar could not see her, snatched the cloth from my hand, and pinched me, with a prolonged wrench, very spitefully on the arm.

I've said I did not love her; and rather relished mortifying her vanity, now and then; besides, she hurt me extremely, so I started up from my knees, and screamed out.

"O, Miss, that's a nasty trick! You have no right to nip me, and I'm not going to bear it!"

"I didn't touch you, you lying creature!" cried she, her fingers tingling to repeat the act, and her ears red with rage. She never had power to conceal her passion, it always set her whole complexion in a blaze.

"What's that then?" I retorted, showing a decided purple witness to refute her.

She stamped her foot, wavered a moment, and then, irresistibly impelled by the naughty spirit within her, slapped me on the cheek a stinging blow that filled both eyes with water.

"Catherine, love! Catherine!" interposed Linton, greatly shocked at the double fault of falsehood and violence which his idol had committed.

"Leave the room, Ellen!" she repeated, trembling all over.

Little Hareton, who followed me everywhere, and was sitting near me on the floor, at seeing my tears commenced crying himself, and sobbed out complaints against "wicked aunt Cathy," which drew her fury on to his unlucky head: she seized his shoulders, and shook him till the poor child waxed livid, and Edgar thoughtlessly laid hold of her hand to deliver him. In an instant one was wrung free, and the astonished young man felt it applied over his own ear in a way that could not be mistaken for jest.

He drew back in consternation—I lifted Hareton in my arms, and walked off to the kitchen with him; leaving the door of communication open, for I was curious to watch how they would settle their disagreement.

The insulted visitor moved to the spot where he had laid his hat, pale and with a quivering lip.

"That's right!" I said to myself, "Take warning and begone! It's a kindness to let you have a glimpse of her genuine disposition."

"Where are you going?" demanded Catherine, advancing to the door.

He swerved aside and attempted to pass.

"You must not go!" she exclaimed energetically.

"I must and shall!" he replied in a subdued voice.

"No," she persisted, grasping the handle; "not yet, Edgar Linton—sit down, you shall not leave me in that temper. I should be miserable all night, and I won't be miserable for you!"

"Can I stay after you have struck me?" asked Linton.

Catherine was mute.

"You've made me afraid, and ashamed of you," he continued; "I'll not come here again!"

Her eyes began to glisten and her lids to twinkle.

"And you told a deliberate untruth!" he said.

"I didn't!" she cried, recovering her speech. "I did nothing deliberately—Well, go, if you please—get away! And now I'll cry—I'll cry myself sick!"

She dropped down on her knees by a chair and set to weeping in a serious earnest.

Edgar persevered in his resolution as far as the court; there, he lingered. I resolved to encourage him.

"Miss is dreadfully wayward, sir!" I called out. "As bad as any marred child—you'd better be riding home, or else she will be sick, only to grieve us."

The soft thing looked askance through the window—he possessed the power to depart, as much as a cat possesses the power to leave a mouse half killed, or a bird half eaten.

Ah; I thought, there will be no saving him—He's doomed, and flies to his fate!

And so it was; he turned abruptly, hastened into the house again, shut the door behind him; and, when I went in a while after to inform them that Earnshaw had come home rabid drunk, ready to pull the old place about our ears, (his ordinary frame of mind in that condition) I saw the quarrel had merely effected a closer intimacy—had broken the outworks of youthful timidity, and enabled them to forsake the disguise of friendship, and confess themselves lovers.

Intelligence of Mr. Hindley's arrival drove Linton speedily to his horse, and Catherine to her chamber. I went to hide little Hareton, and to take the shot out of the master's fowling piece which he was fond of playing with in his insane excitement, to the hazard of the lives of any who provoked, or even attracted his notice too much; and I had hit upon the plan of removing it, that he might do less mischief, if he did go the length of firing the gun.

CHAPTER IX

He entered, vociferating oaths dreadful to hear; and caught me in the act of stowing his son away in the kitchen cupboard. Hareton was impressed with a wholesome terror of encountering either his wild-beast's fondness, or his madman's rage—for in one he ran a chance of being squeezed and kissed to death, and in the other of being flung into the fire, or dashed against the wall—and the poor thing remained perfectly quiet wherever I chose to put him.

"There I've found it out at last!" cried Hindley, pulling me back by the skin of the neck, like a dog. "By Heaven and Hell, you've sworn between you to murder that child! I know how it is, now, that he is always out of my way. But, with the help of Satan, I shall make you swallow the carving knife, Nelly! you needn't laugh; for I've just crammed Kenneth, head-downmost, in the Blackhorse marsh: and two is the same as one—and I want to kill some of you, I shall have no rest till I do!"

"But I don't like the carving-knife, Mr. Hindley," I answered, "it has been cutting red herrings—I'd rather be shot if you please."

"You'd rather be damned!" he said, "and so you shall—No law in England can hinder a man from keeping his house decent, and mine's abominable! open your mouth."

He held the knife in his hand, and pushed its point between my teeth: but, for my part I was never much afraid of his vagaries. I spat out, and affirmed it tasted detestably—I would not take it on any account.

"Oh!" said he releasing me, "I see that hideous little villain is not Hareton—I beg your pardon, Nell—if it be, he deserves flaying alive for not running to welcome me, and for screaming as if I were a goblin. Unnatural cub, come hither! I'll teach thee to impose on a good-hearted, deluded father—Now, don't you think the lad would be handsomer cropped? It makes a dog fiercer, and I love something fierce—Get me a scissors—something fierce and trim! Besides, it's infernal affectation—devilish conceit, it is, to cherish our ears—we're asses enough without them. Hush, child, hush! well then, it is my darling! wisht, dry thy eyes—there's a joy; kiss me; what, it won't? kiss me, Hareton! Damn thee, kiss me! By God, as if I would rear such a monster! As sure as I'm living, I'll break the brat's neck."

Poor Hareton was squalling and kicking in his father's arms with all his might, and redoubled his yells when he carried him upstairs and lifted him over the bannister. I cried out that he would frighten the child into fits, and ran to rescue him.

As I reached them, Hindley leant forward on the rails to listen to a noise below; almost forgetting what he had in his hands.

"Who is that?" he asked, hearing someone approaching the stair's foot.

I leant forward, also, for the purpose of signing to Heathcliff, whose step I recognized, not to come further; and, at the instant when my eye quitted Hareton, he gave a sudden spring, delivered himself from the careless grasp that held him, and fell.

There was scarcely time to experience a thrill of horror before he saw that the little wretch was safe. Heathcliff arrived underneath just at the critical moment; by a natural impulse, he arrested his descent, and setting him on his feet, looked up to discover the author of the accident.

A miser who has parted with a lucky lottery ticket for five shillings and finds next day he has lost in the bargain five thousand pounds, could not show a blanker countenance than he did on beholding the figure of Mr. Earnshaw above—It expressed, plainer than words could do, the intensest anguish at having made himself the instrument of thwarting his own revenge. Had it been dark, I dare say, he would have tried to remedy the mistake by smashing Hareton's skull on the steps; but, we witnessed his salvation; and I was presently below with my precious charge pressed to my heart.

Hindley descended more leisurely, sobered and abashed.

"It is your fault, Ellen," he said, "you should have kept him out of sight; you should have taken him from me! Is he injured anywhere?"

"Injured!" I cried, angrily, "If he's not killed, he'll be an idiot! Oh! I wonder his mother does not rise from her grave to see how you use him. You're worse than a heathen—treating your own flesh and blood in that manner!"

He attempted to touch the child, who on finding himself with me sobbed off his terror directly. At the first finger his father laid on him, however, he shrieked again louder than before, and struggled as if he would go into convulsions.

"You shall not meddle with him!" I continued, "He hates you—they all hate you—that's the truth! A happy family you have; and a pretty state you've come to!"

"I shall come to a prettier yet, Nelly," laughed the misguided man, recovering his hardness. "At present, convey yourself and him away—And, hark you, Heathcliff! clear you too, quite from my reach and hearing . . . I wouldn't murder you tonight, unless, perhaps, I set the house on fire; but that's as my fancy goes—"

While saying this he took a pint bottle of brandy from the dresser, and poured some into a tumbler.

"Nay don't!" I entreated, "Mr. Hindley, do take warning. Have mercy on this unfortunate boy, if you care nothing for yourself!"

"Anyone will do better for him than I shall," he answered.

"Have mercy on your own soul!" I said, endeavouring to snatch the glass from his hand.

"Not I! On the contrary, I shall have great pleasure in sending it to perdition, to punish its maker," exclaimed the blasphemer, "Here's to its hearty damnation!"

He drank the spirits, and impatiently bade us go; terminating his command with a sequel of horrid imprecations, too bad to repeat, or remember.

"It's a pity he cannot kill himself with drink," observed Heathcliff, muttering an echo of curses back when the door was shut. "He's doing his very utmost; but his constitution defies him—Mr. Kenneth says he would wager his mare, that he'll outlive any man on this side Gimmerton, and go to the grave a hoary sinner; unless, some happy chance out of the common course befall him."

I went into the kitchen and sat down to lull my little lamb to sleep. Heathcliff, as I thought, walked through to the barn. It turned out, afterwards, that he only got as far as the other side the settle, when he flung himself on a bench by the wall, removed from the fire, and remained silent.

I was rocking Hareton on my knee, and humming a song that began,

It was far in the night, and the bairnies grat,
The mither beneath the mools heard that.

when Miss Cathy, who had listened to the hubbub from her room, put her head in, and whispered, "Are you alone, Nelly?"

"Yes, Miss," I replied.

She entered and approached the hearth. I, supposing she was going to say something, looked up. The expression of her face seemed disturbed and anxious. Her lips were half asunder as if she meant to speak; and she drew a breath, but it escaped in a sigh, instead of a sentence.

I resumed my song: not having forgotten her recent behaviour.

"Where's Heathcliff?" she said, interrupting me.

"About his work in the stable," was my answer.

He did not contradict me; perhaps, he had fallen into a doze. There followed another long pause, during which I perceived a drop or two trickle from Catherine's cheek to the flags.

"Is she sorry for her shameful conduct?" I asked myself. "That will be a novelty, but she may come to the point as she will—I shan't help her!"

No, she felt small trouble regarding any subject, save her own concerns.

"Oh, dear!" she cried at last. "I'm very unhappy!"

"A pity," observed I, "you're hard to please—so many friends and so few cares, and can't make yourself content!"

"Nelly, will you keep a secret for me?" she pursued, kneeling down by me, and lifting her winsome eyes to my face with that sort of look which turns off bad temper, even when one has all the right in the world to indulge it.

"Is it worth keeping?" I inquired, less sulkily.

"Yes, and it worries me, and I must let it out! I want to know what I should do—Today, Edgar Linton has asked me to marry him, and I've given him an answer. Now, before I tell you whether it was a consent or denial—you tell me which it ought to have been."

"Really, Miss Catherine, how can I know?" I replied. "To be sure, considering the exhibition you performed in his presence, this afternoon, I might say it would be wise to refuse him—since he asked you after that, he must either be hopelessly stupid, or a venturesome fool."

"If you talk so, I won't tell you any more," she returned, peevishly, rising to her feet. "I accepted him, Nelly; be quick, and say whether I was wrong!"

"You accepted him? then, what good is it discussing the matter? You have pledged your word, and cannot retract."

---

grat: wept.
mools: earth.

"But say whether I should have done so—do!" she exclaimed in an irritated tone; chafing her hands together and frowning.

"There are many things to be considered, before that question can be answered properly," I said sententiously, "first and foremost, do you love Mr. Edgar?"

"Who can help it? Of course I do," she answered.

Then I put her through the following catechism—for a girl of twenty-two it was not injudicious.

"Why do you love him, Miss Cathy?"

"Nonsense, I do—that's sufficient."

"By no means; you must say why?"

"Well, because he is handsome, and pleasant to be with."

"Bad," was my commentary.

"And because he is young and cheerful."

"Bad, still."

"And, because he loves me."

"Indifferent, coming there."

"And he will be rich, and I shall like to be the greatest woman of the neighbourhood, and I shall be proud of having such a husband."

"Worst of all! And, now, say how you love him?"

"As anybody loves—You're silly, Nelly."

"Not at all—Answer."

"I love the ground under his feet, and the air over his head, and everything he touches, and every word he says—I love all his looks, and all his actions, and him entirely, and altogether. There now!"

"And why?"

"Nay—you are making a jest of it; it is exceedingly ill-natured! It's no jest to me!" said the young lady scowling, and turning her face to the fire.

"I'm very far from jesting, Miss Catherine," I replied, "you love Mr. Edgar, because he is handsome, and young, and cheerful, and rich, and loves you. The last, however, goes for nothing—You would love him without that, probably, and with it, you wouldn't unless he possessed the four former attractions."

"No, to be sure not—I should only pity him—hate him, perhaps, if he were ugly, and a clown."

"But, there are several other handsome, rich young men in the world; handsomer, possibly, and richer than he is—What should hinder you from loving them?"

"If there be any, they are out of my way—I've seen none like Edgar."

"You may see some; and he won't always be handsome, and young, and may not always be rich."

"He is now; and I have only to do with the present—I wish you would speak rationally."

"Well, that settles it—if you have only to do with the present, marry Mr. Linton."

"I don't want your permission for that—I *shall* marry him; and yet, you have not told me whether I'm right."

"Perfectly right; if people be right to marry only for the present. And now, let us hear what you are unhappy about. Your brother will be pleased . . . The old lady and gentleman will not object, I think—you will escape from a disorderly, comfortless home into a wealthy respectable one; and you love Edgar, and Edgar loves you. All seems smooth and easy—where is the obstacle?"

"*Here!* and *here!*" replied Catherine, striking one hand on her forehead, and the other on her breast. "In whichever place the soul lives—in my soul, and in my heart, I'm convinced I'm wrong!"

"That is very strange! I cannot make it out."

"It's my secret; but if you will not mock at me, I'll explain it; I can't do it distinctly—but I'll give you a feeling of how I feel."

She seated herself by me again: her countenance grew sadder and graver, and her clasped hands trembled.

"Nelly, do you never dream queer dreams?" she said, suddenly, after some minutes' reflection.

"Yes, now and then," I answered.

"And so do I. I've dreamt in my life dreams that have stayed with me ever after, and changed my ideas; they've gone through and through me, like wine through water, and altered the colour of my mind. And this is one—I'm going to tell it—but take care not to smile at any part of it."

"Oh! don't, Miss Catherine!" I cried. "We're dismal enough without conjuring up ghosts, and visions to perplex us. Come, come, be merry, and like yourself! Look at little Hareton—*he's* dreaming nothing dreary. How sweetly he smiles in his sleep!"

"Yes; and how sweetly his father curses in his solitude! You remember him, I dare say, when he was just such another as that chubby thing—nearly as young and innocent. However, Nelly, I shall oblige you to listen—it's not long; and I've no power to be merry tonight."

"I won't hear it, I won't hear it!" I repeated, hastily.

I was superstitious about dreams then, and am still; and Catherine had an unusual gloom in her aspect, that made me dread something from which I might shape a prophecy, and foresee a fearful catastrophe.

She was vexed, but she did not proceed. Apparently taking up another subject, she re-commenced in a short time.

"If I were in heaven, Nelly, I should be extremely miserable."

"Because you are not fit to go there," I answered. "All sinners would be miserable in heaven."

"But it is not for that. I dreamt, once, that I was there."

"I tell you I won't hearken to your dreams, Miss Catherine! I'll go to bed," I interrupted again.

She laughed, and held me down, for I made a motion to leave my chair.

"This is nothing," cried she; "I was only going to say that heaven did not seem to be my home; and I broke my heart with weeping to come back to earth; and the angels were so angry that they flung me out, into the middle of the heath on the top of Wuthering Heights; where I woke sobbing for joy. That will do to explain my secret, as well as the other. I've no more business to marry Edgar Linton than I have to be in heaven; and if the wicked man in there had not brought Heathcliff so low I shouldn't have thought of it. It would degrade me to marry Heathcliff, now; so he shall never know how I love him; and that, not because he's handsome, Nelly, but because he's more myself than I am. Whatever our souls are made of, his and mine are the same, and Linton's is as different as a moonbeam from lightning, or frost from fire."

Ere this speech ended, I became sensible of Heathcliff's presence. Having noticed a slight movement, I turned my head, and saw him rise from the bench, and steal out, noiselessly. He had listened till he heard Catherine say it would degrade her to marry him, and then he stayed to hear no farther.

My companion, sitting on the ground, was prevented by the back of the settle from remarking his presence or departure; but I started, and bade her hush.

"Why?" she asked, gazing nervously round.

"Joseph is here," I answered, catching, opportunely, the roll of his cartwheels up the road; "and Heathcliff will come in with him. I'm not sure whether he were not at the door this moment."

"Oh, he couldn't overhear me at the door!" said she. "Give me Hareton, while you get the supper, and when it is ready ask me to sup with you. I want to cheat my uncomfortable conscience, and be convinced that Heathcliff has no notion of these things—he has not, has he? He does not know what being in love is?"

"I see no reason that he should not know, as well as you," I returned; "and if *you* are his choice, he'll be the most unfortunate creature that ever was born! As soon as you become Mrs. Linton, he loses friend, and love, and all! Have you considered how you'll bear the separation, and how he'll bear to be quite deserted in the world? Because, Miss Catherine—"

"He quite deserted! we separated!" she exclaimed, with an accent of indignation. "Who is to separate us, pray? They'll meet the fate of Milo![3] Not as long as I live, Ellen—for no mortal creature. Every Linton on the face of the earth might melt into nothing, before I could consent to forsake Heathcliff. Oh, that's not what I intend—that's not what I mean! I shouldn't be Mrs. Linton were such a price demanded! He'll be as much to me as he has been all his lifetime. Edgar must shake off his antipathy, and tolerate him, at least. He will when he learns my true feelings towards him. Nelly, I see now, you think me a selfish wretch, but, did it never strike you that, if Heathcliff and I married, we should be beggars? whereas, if I marry Linton, I can aid Heathcliff to rise, and place him out of my brother's power."

"With your husband's money, Miss Catherine?" I asked. "You'll find him not so pliable as you calculate upon: and, though I'm hardly a judge, I think that's the worst motive you've given yet for being the wife of young Linton."

"It is not," retorted she, "it is the best! The others were the satisfaction of my whims; and for Edgar's sake, too, to satisfy him. This is for the sake of one who comprehends in his person my feelings to Edgar and myself. I cannot express it; but surely you and everybody have a notion that there is, or should be an existence of yours beyond you. What were the use of creation if I were entirely contained here? My great miseries in this world have been Heathcliff's miseries, and I watched and felt each from the beginning; my great thought in living is himself. If all else perished, and *he* remained, I should still continue to be; and if all else remained, and he were annihilated, the Universe would turn to a mighty stranger. I should not seem a part of it. My love for Linton is like the foliage in the woods. Time will change it, I'm well aware, as winter changes the trees—my love for Heathcliff resembles the eternal rocks beneath—a source of little visible delight, but necessary. Nelly, I *am* Heathcliff—he's always, always in my mind—not as a pleasure, any more than I am always a pleasure to myself—but, as my own being—so, don't talk of our separation again—it is impracticable; and—"

She paused, and hid her face in the folds of my gown; but I jerked it forcibly away. I was out of patience with her folly!

"If I can make any sense out of your nonsense, Miss," I said, "it only goes to convince me that you are ignorant of the duties you undertake in marrying; or else, that you are a wicked, unprincipled girl. But trouble me with no more secrets. I'll not promise to keep them."

---

[3] Milo was eaten by wild beasts after he attempted to graft two trees together. The two-trees image suggests that the two houses of Heathcliff and Catherine are antithetical and can never be merged, no matter what either party desires. [ED.]

"You'll keep that?" she asked, eagerly.

"No, I'll not promise," I repeated.

She was about to insist, when the entrance of Joseph finished our conversation; and Catherine removed her seat to a corner, and nursed Hareton, while I made the supper.

After it was cooked, my fellow servant and I began to quarrel who should carry some to Mr. Hindley; and we didn't settle it till all was nearly cold. Then we came to the agreement that we would let him ask, if he wanted any, for we feared particularly to go into his presence when he had been for some time alone.

"Und hah isn't that nowt comed in frough th' field, be this time? What is he abaht? girt eedle seeght!" demanded the old man, looking round for Heathcliff.

"I'll call him," I replied. "He's in the barn, I've no doubt."

I went and called, but got no answer. On returning, I whispered to Catherine that he had heard a good part of what she said, I was sure; and told her how I saw him quit the kitchen just as she complained of her brother's conduct regarding him.

She jumped up in a fine fright—flung Hareton onto the settle, and ran to seek for her friend herself, not taking leisure to consider why she was so flurried, or how her talk would have affected him.

She was absent such a while that Joseph proposed that we should wait no longer. He cunningly conjectured that they were staying away in order to avoid hearing his protracted blessing. They were "ill eneugh for ony fahl manners," he affirmed. And, on their behalf, he added that night a special prayer to the usual quarter of an hour's supplication before meat, and would have tacked another to the end of the grace, had not his young mistress broken in upon him with a hurried command, that he must run down the road, and, wherever Heathcliff had rambled, find and make him re-enter directly!

"I want to speak to him, and I *must*, before I go upstairs," she said. "And the gate is open, he is somewhere out of hearing; for he would not reply, though I shouted at the top of the fold as loud as I could."

Joseph objected at first; she was too much in earnest, however, to suffer contradiction; and, at last, he placed his hat on his head, and walked grumbling forth.

Meantime Catherine paced up and down the floor, exclaiming—

"I wonder where he is—I wonder where he *can* be! What did I say,

---

girt eedle seeght: great idle sight.
fahl: foul.

Nelly? I've forgotten. Was he vexed at my bad humour this afternoon? Dear! tell me what I've said to grieve him? I do wish he'd come. I do wish he would!"

"What a noise for nothing!" I cried, though rather uneasy myself. "What a trifle scares you! It's surely no great cause of alarm that Heathcliff should take a moonlight saunter on the moors, or, even lie too sulky to speak to us, in the hay-loft. I'll engage he's lurking there. See, if I don't ferret him out!"

I departed to renew my search; its result was disappointment, and Joseph's quest ended in the same.

"Yon lad gets war un war!" observed he on re-entering. "He's left th' yate ut t' full swing, and miss's pony has trodden dahn two rigs uh corn, un plottered through, raight o'er intuh t' meadow! Hahsomdiver, t' maister 'ull play t' devil to-morn, and he'll do weel. He's patience itsseln wi' sich careless, offald craters — patience itsseln he is! Bud he'll not be soa allus — yah's see, all on ye! Yah mumn't drive him aht uf his heead fur nowt!"

"Have you found Heathcliff, you ass?" interrupted Catherine. "Have you been looking for him, as I ordered?"

"Aw sud more likker look for th' horse," he replied. "It 'ud be tuh more sense. Bud, Aw can look for norther horse, nur man uf a neeght loike this — as black as t' chimbley! und Hathecliff's noan t' chap tuh coom at *maw* whistle — happen he'll be less hard uh hearing wi' *ye!*"

It *was* a very dark evening for summer: the clouds appeared inclined to thunder, and I said we had better all sit down; the approaching rain would be certain to bring him home without further trouble.

However, Catherine would not be persuaded into tranquillity. She kept wandering to and fro, from the gate to the door, in a state of agitation, which permitted no repose: and, at length, took up a permanent situation on one side of the wall, near the road; where, heedless of my expostulations, and the growling thunder, and the great drops that began to plash around her, she remained calling, at intervals, and then listening, and then crying outright. She beat Hareton, or any child, at a good, passionate fit of crying.

About midnight, while we still sat up, the storm came rattling over the Heights in full fury. There was a violent wind, as well as thunder, and either one or the other split a tree off at the corner of the building; a huge bough fell across the roof, and knocked down a portion of the east chimney-stack, sending a clatter of stones and soot into the kitchen fire.

---

war un war: worse and worse.
rigs: ridges.
offald craters: awful creatures.
mumn't: mustn't.

We thought a bolt had fallen in the middle of us, and Joseph swung onto his knees, beseeching the Lord to remember the patriarchs Noah and Lot; and, as in former times, spare the righteous, though he smote the ungodly. I felt some sentiment that it must be a judgment on us also. The Jonah, in my mind, was Mr. Earnshaw, and I shook the handle of his den that I might ascertain if he were yet living. He replied audibly enough, in a fashion which made my companion vociferate more clamorously than before that a wide distinction might be drawn between saints like himself, and sinners like his master. But the uproar passed away in twenty minutes, leaving us all unharmed, excepting Cathy, who got thoroughly drenched for her obstinacy in refusing to take shelter, and standing bonnetless and shawlless to catch as much water as she could with her hair and clothes.

She came in, and lay down on the settle, all soaked as she was, turning her face to the back, and putting her hands before it.

"Well, Miss!" I exclaimed, touching her shoulder. "You are not bent on getting your death, are you? Do you know what o'clock it is? Half-past twelve. Come! come to bed; there's no use waiting longer on that foolish boy—he'll be gone to Gimmerton, and he'll stay there now. He guesses we shouldn't wake for him till this late hour; at least, he guesses that only Mr. Hindley would be up; and he'd rather avoid having the door opened by the master."

"Nay, nay, he's noan at Gimmerton!" said Joseph. "Aw's niver wonder, bud he's at t'bothom uf a bog-hoile. This visitation worn't for nowt, und Aw wod hev ye tuh look aht, Miss—yah muh be t' next. Thank Hivin for all! All warks togither for gooid tuh them as is chozzen, and piked aht froo' th' rubbidge! Yah knaw whet t' Scripture ses—"

And he began quoting several texts; referring us to the chapters and verses, where we might find them.

I having vainly begged the wilful girl to rise and remove her wet things, left him preaching, and her shivering, and betook myself to bed with little Hareton; who slept as fast as if everyone had been sleeping round him.

I heard Joseph read on a while afterwards; then, I distinguished his slow step on the ladder, and then I dropt asleep.

Coming down somewhat later than usual, I saw, by the sunbeams piercing the chinks of the shutters, Miss Catherine still seated near the fireplace. The house-door was ajar, too; light entered from its unclosed windows, Hindley had come out, and stood on the kitchen hearth, haggard, and drowsy.

"What ails you, Cathy?" he was saying when I entered; "You look as dismal as a drowned whelp—Why are you so damp and pale, child?"

"I've been wet," she answered reluctantly, "and I'm cold, that's all."

"Oh, she is naughty!" I cried, perceiving the master to be tolerably sober; "she got steeped in the shower of yesterday evening, and there she has sat, the night through, and I couldn't prevail on her to stir."

Mr. Earnshaw stared at us in surprise. "The night through," he repeated. "What kept her up, not fear of the thunder, surely? That was over, hours since."

Neither of us wished to mention Heathcliff's absence, as long as we could conceal it; so, I replied, I didn't know how she took it into her head to sit up; and she said nothing.

The morning was fresh and cool; I threw back the lattice, and presently the room filled with sweet scents from the garden: but Catherine called peevishly to me.

"Ellen, shut the window. I'm starving!" And her teeth chattered as she shrunk closer to the almost extinguished embers.

"She's ill—" said Hindley, taking her wrist; "I suppose that's the reason she would not go to bed—Damn it! I don't want to be troubled with more sickness, here—What took you into the rain!"

"Running after t' lads, as usuald!" croaked Joseph, catching an opportunity, from our hesitation, to thrust in his evil tongue.

"If Aw wur yah, maister, Aw'd just slam t' boards i' their faces all on 'em, gentle and simple! Never a day ut yah're off, but yon cat uh Linton comes sneaking hither—and Miss Nelly, shoo's a fine lass! shoo sits watching for ye i' t' kitchen; and as yah're in at one door, he's aht at t'other—Und, then, wer grand lady goes a coorting uf hor side! It's bonny behaviour, lurking amang t' fields, after twelve ut' night, wi' that fahl, flaysome divil of a gipsy, Heathcliff! They think *Aw'm* blind; but Aw'm noan, now't ut t' soart! Aw seed young Linton, boath coming and going, and Aw seed *yah* (directing his discourse to me). Yah gooid fur nowt, slattenly witch! nip up und bolt intuh th' hahs, t' minute yah heard t' maister's horse fit clatter up t' road."

"Silence, eavesdropper!" cried Catherine, "None of your insolence, before me! Edgar Linton came yesterday, by chance, Hindley: and it was *I* who told him to be off: because, I knew you would not like to have met him as you were."

"You lie, Cathy, no doubt," answered her brother, "and you are a confounded simpleton! But, never mind Linton, at present—Tell me, were you not with Heathcliff, last night? Speak the truth now. You need not be afraid of harming him—Though I hate him as much as ever, he did me a good

---

hahs: house.

turn, a short time since, that will make my conscience tender of breaking his neck. To prevent it, I shall send him about his business, this very morning; and after he's gone, I'd advise you all to look sharp, I shall only have the more humour for you!"

"I never saw Heathcliff last night," answered Catherine, beginning to sob bitterly: "and if you do turn him out of doors, I'll go with him. But, perhaps, you'll never have an opportunity—perhaps, he's gone." Here she burst into uncontrollable grief, and the remainder of her words were inarticulate.

Hindley lavished on her a torrent of scornful abuse, and bade her get to her room immediately, or she shouldn't cry for nothing! I obliged her to obey; and I shall never forget what a scene she acted, when we reached her chamber. It terrified me—I thought she was going mad, and I begged Joseph to run for the doctor.

It proved the commencement of delirium; Mr. Kenneth, as soon as he saw her, pronounced her dangerously ill; she had a fever.

He bled her, and he told me to let her live on whey and water gruel; and take care she did not throw herself downstairs, or out of the window; and then he left; for, he had enough to do in the parish where two or three miles was the ordinary distance between cottage and cottage.

Though I cannot say I made a gentle nurse, and Joseph and the master were no better; and though our patient was as wearisome and headstrong as a patient could be, she weathered it through.

Old Mrs. Linton paid us several visits, to be sure; and set things to rights, and scolded, and ordered us all; and when Catherine was convalescent, she insisted on conveying her to Thrushcross Grange; for which deliverance we were very grateful. But the poor dame had reason to repent of her kindness; she, and her husband, both took the fever, and died within a few days of each other.

Our young lady returned to us saucier, and more passionate, and haughtier than ever. Heathcliff had never been heard of since the evening of the thunder-storm, and, one day, I had the misfortune, when she had provoked me exceedingly, to lay the blame of his disappearance on her (where indeed it belonged, as she well knew). From that period for several months, she ceased to hold any communication with me save in the relation of a mere servant. Joseph fell under a ban also; he *would* speak his mind, and lecture her all the same as if she were a little girl; and she esteemed herself a woman, and our mistress; and thought that her recent illness gave her a claim to be treated with consideration. Then the doctor had said that she would not bear crossing much, she ought to have her own way; and it was nothing less than murder, in her eyes, for anyone to presume to stand up and contradict her.

From Mr. Earnshaw and his companions she kept aloof, and tutored by Kenneth, and serious threats of a fit that often attended her rages, her brother allowed her whatever she pleased to demand, and generally avoided aggravating her fiery temper. He was rather *too* indulgent in humouring her caprices; not from affection, but from pride; he wished earnestly to see her bring honour to the family by an alliance with the Lintons, and, as long as she let him alone, she might trample us like slaves, for aught he cared!

Edgar Linton, as multitudes have been before, and will be after him, was infatuated; and believed himself the happiest man alive on the day he led her to Gimmerton Chapel, three years subsequent to his father's death.

Much against my inclination, I was persuaded to leave Wuthering Heights and accompany her here. Little Hareton was nearly five years old, and I had just begun to teach him his letters. We made a sad parting, but Catherine's tears were more powerful than ours—When I refused to go, and when she found her entreaties did not move me, she went lamenting to her husband, and brother. The former offered me munificent wages; the latter ordered me to pack up—he wanted no women in the house, he said, now that there was no mistress; and as to Hareton, the curate should take him in hand, by and bye. And so, I had but one choice left, to do as I was ordered—I told the master he got rid of all decent people only to run to ruin a little faster; I kissed Hareton good-bye; and, since then, he has been a stranger, and it's very queer to think it, but I've no doubt, he has completely forgotten all about Ellen Dean and that he was ever more than all the world to her, and she to him!

At this point of the housekeeper's story, she chanced to glance towards the time-piece over the chimney; and was in amazement, on seeing the minute-hand measure half past one. She would not hear of staying a second longer—In truth, I felt rather disposed to defer the sequel of her narrative, myself: and now, that she is vanished to her rest, and I have meditated for another hour or two, I shall summon courage to go, also, in spite of aching laziness of head and limbs.

CHAPTER X

A charming introduction to a hermit's life! Four week's torture, tossing and sickness! Oh, these bleak winds, and bitter, northern skies, and impassable roads and dilatory country surgeons! And, oh, this dearth of the human physiognomy, and, worse than all, the terrible intimation of Kenneth that I need not expect to be out of doors till spring!

Mr. Heathcliff has just honoured me with a call. About seven days ago he sent me a brace of grouse—the last of the season. Scoundrel! He is not altogether guiltless in this illness of mine; and that I had a great mind to tell him. But, alas! how could I offend a man who was charitable enough to sit at my bedside a good hour, and talk on some other subject than pills, and draughts, blisters, and leeches?

This is quite an easy interval. I am too weak to read, yet I feel as if I could enjoy something interesting. Why not have up Mrs. Dean to finish her tale? I can recollect its chief incidents, as far as she had gone. Yes, I remember her hero had run off, and never been heard of for three years: and the heroine was married. I'll ring; she'll be delighted to find me capable of talking cheerfully.

Mrs. Dean came.

"It wants twenty minutes, sir, to taking the medicine," she commenced.

"Away, away with it!" I replied; "I desire to have—"

"The doctor says you must drop the powders."

"With all my heart! Don't interrupt me. Come and take your seat here. Keep your fingers from that bitter phalanx of vials. Draw your knitting out of your pocket—that will do—now continue the history of Mr. Heathcliff, from where you left off, to the present day. Did he finish his education on the Continent, and come back a gentleman? or did he get a sizer's place at college? or escape to America, and earn honours by drawing blood from his foster country? or make a fortune more promptly, on the English highways?"

"He may have done a little in all these vocations, Mr. Lockwood; but I couldn't give my word for any. I stated before that I didn't know how he gained his money; neither am I aware of the means he took to raise his mind from the savage ignorance into which it was sunk; but, with your leave, I'll proceed in my own fashion, if you think it will amuse, and not weary you. Are you feeling better this morning?"

"Much."

"That's good news."

I got Miss Catherine and myself to Thrushcross Grange: and, to my agreeable disappointment, she behaved infinitely better than I dared to expect. She seemed almost over fond of Mr. Linton; and even to his sister, she showed plenty of affection. They were both very attentive to her comfort, certainly. It was not the thorn bending to the honeysuckles, but the honeysuckles embracing the thorn. There were no mutual concessions; one stood erect, and the other yielded; and who can be ill-natured, and bad-tempered, when they encounter neither opposition, nor indifference?

I observed that Mr. Edgar had a deep-rooted fear of ruffling her humour. He concealed it from her; but if ever he heard me answer sharply, or saw any other servant grow cloudy at some imperious order of hers, he would show his trouble by a frown of displeasure that never darkened on his own account. He, many a time, spoke sternly to me about my pertness; and averred that the stab of a knife could not inflict a worse pang than he suffered at seeing his lady vexed.

Not to grieve a kind master I learned to be less touchy; and, for the space of half a year, the gunpowder lay as harmless as sand, because no fire came near to explode it. Catherine had seasons of gloom and silence, now and then: they were respected with sympathizing silence by her husband, who ascribed them to an alteration in her constitution, produced by her perilous illness, as she was never subject to depression of spirits before. The return of sunshine was welcomed by answering sunshine from him. I believe I may assert that they were really in possession of deep and growing happiness.

It ended. Well, we *must* be for ourselves in the long run; the mild and generous are only more justly selfish than the domineering—and it ended when circumstances caused each to feel that the one's interest was not the chief consideration in the other's thoughts.

On a mellow evening in September, I was coming from the garden with a heavy basket of apples which I had been gathering. It had got dusk, and the moon looked over the high wall of the court, causing undefined shadows to lurk in the corners of the numerous projecting portions of the building. I set my burden on the house steps by the kitchen door, and lingered to rest, and draw in a few more breaths of the soft, sweet air; my eyes were on the moon, and my back to the entrance, when I heard a voice behind me say—

"Nelly, is that you?"

It was a deep voice, and foreign in tone; yet, there was something in the manner of pronouncing my name which made it sound familiar. I turned about to discover who spoke, fearfully, for the doors were shut, and I had seen nobody on approaching the steps.

Something stirred in the porch; and moving nearer, I distinguished a tall man dressed in dark clothes, with dark face and hair. He leant against the side, and held his fingers on the latch, as if intending to open for himself.

"Who can it be?" I thought. "Mr. Earnshaw? Oh, no! The voice has no resemblance to his."

"I have waited here an hour," he resumed, while I continued staring; "and the whole of that time all round has been as still as death. I dared not enter. You do not know me? Look, I'm not a stranger!"

A ray fell on his features; the cheeks were sallow, and half covered with black whiskers; the brows lowering, the eyes deep set and singular. I remembered the eyes.

"What!" I cried, uncertain whether to regard him as a worldly visitor, and I raised my hands in amazement. "What! you come back? Is it really you? Is it?"

"Yes, Heathcliff," he replied, glancing from me up to the windows which reflected a score of glittering moons, but showed no lights from within. "Are they at home—where is she? Nelly, you are not glad—you needn't be so disturbed. Is she here? Speak! I want to have one word with her—your mistress. Go, and say some person from Gimmerton desires to see her."

"How will she take it?" I exclaimed, "what will she do? The surprise bewilders me—it will put her out of her head! And you *are* Heathcliff? But altered! Nay, there's no comprehending it. Have you been for a soldier?"

"Go, and carry my message," he interrupted impatiently. "I'm in hell till you do!"

He lifted the latch, and I entered; but when I got to the parlour where Mr. and Mrs. Linton were, I could not persuade myself to proceed.

At length, I resolved on making an excuse to ask if they would have the candles lighted, and I opened the door.

They sat together in a window whose lattice lay back against the wall, and displayed beyond the garden trees, and the wild green park, the valley of Gimmerton, with a long line of mist winding nearly to its top (for very soon after you pass the chapel, as you may have noticed, the sough that runs from the marshes joins a beck which follows the bend of the glen). Wuthering Heights rose above this silvery vapour; but our old house was invisible—it rather dips down on the other side.

Both the room, and its occupants, and the scene they gazed on, looked wondrously peaceful. I shrank reluctantly from performing my errand: and was actually going away, leaving it unsaid, after having put my question about the candles, when a sense of my folly compelled me to return, and mutter:

"A person from Gimmerton wishes to see you, ma'am."

"What does he want?" asked Mrs. Linton.

"I did not question him," I answered.

"Well, close the curtains, Nelly," she said; "and bring up tea. I'll be back again directly."

She quitted the apartment; Mr. Edgar inquired, carelessly, who it was?

"Someone mistress does not expect," I replied. "That Heathcliff, you recollect him, sir, who used to live at Mr. Earnshaw's."

"What, the gipsy—the ploughboy?" he cried. "Why did you not say so to Catherine?"

"Hush! you must not call him by those names, master," I said. "She'd be sadly grieved to hear you. She was nearly heartbroken when he ran off; I guess his return will make a jubilee to her."

Mr. Linton walked to a window on the other side of the room that overlooked the court. He unfastened it and leant out. I suppose they were below, for he exclaimed, quickly:

"Don't stand there, love! Bring the person in, if it be anyone particular."

Ere long, I heard the click of the latch, and Catherine flew upstairs, breathless and wild, too excited to show gladness; indeed, by her face, you would rather have surmised an awful calamity.

"Oh, Edgar, Edgar!" she panted, flinging her arms round his neck. "Oh, Edgar, darling! Heathcliff's come back—he is!" And she tightened her embrace to a squeeze.

"Well, well," cried her husband, crossly, "don't strangle me for that! He never struck me as such a marvellous treasure. There is no need to be frantic!"

"I know you didn't like him," she answered, repressing a little the intensity of her delight. "Yet for my sake, you must be friends now. Shall I tell him to come up?"

"Here?" he said, "into the parlour?"

"Where else?" she asked.

He looked vexed, and suggested the kitchen as a more suitable place for him.

Mrs. Linton eyed him with a droll expression—half angry, half laughing at his fastidiousness.

"No," she added after a while; "I cannot sit in the kitchen. Set two tables here, Ellen; one for your master and Miss Isabella, being gentry; the other for Heathcliff and myself, being of the lower orders. Will that please you, dear? Or must I have a fire lighted elsewhere? If so, give directions. I'll run down and secure my guest. I'm afraid the joy is too great to be real!"

She was about to dart off again; but Edgar arrested her.

"*You* bid him step up," he said, addressing me; "and, Catherine, try to be glad, without being absurd! The whole household need not witness the sight of your welcoming a runaway servant as a brother."

I descended and found Heathcliff waiting under the porch, evidently anticipating an invitation to enter. He followed my guidance without waste of words, and I ushered him into the presence of the master and mistress, whose flushed cheeks betrayed signs of warm talking. But the lady's glowed with another feeling when her friend appeared at the door; she sprang forward, took both his hands, and led him to Linton; and then she seized Linton's reluctant fingers and crushed them into his.

Now fully revealed by the fire and candle-light, I was amazed, more than ever, to behold the transformation of Heathcliff. He had grown a tall, athletic, well-formed man; beside whom, my master seemed quite slender and youth-like. His upright carriage suggested the idea of his having been in the army. His countenance was much older in expression, and decision of feature than Mr. Linton's; it looked intelligent, and retained no marks of former degradation. A half-civilized ferocity lurked yet in the depressed brows, and eyes full of black fire, but it was subdued; and his manner was even dignified, quite divested of roughness though too stern for grace.

My master's surprise equalled or exceeded mine: he remained for a minute at a loss how to address the ploughboy, as he had called him. Heathcliff dropped his slight hand, and stood looking at him coolly till he chose to speak.

"Sit down, sir," he said, at length. "Mrs. Linton, recalling old times, would have me give you a cordial reception, and, of course, I am gratified when anything occurs to please her."

"And I also," answered Heathcliff, "especially if it be anything in which I have a part. I shall stay an hour or two willingly."

He took a seat opposite Catherine, who kept her gaze fixed on him as if she feared he would vanish were she to remove it. He did not raise his to her, often; a quick glance now and then sufficed; but it flashed back, each time, more confidently, the undisguised delight he drank from hers.

They were too much absorbed in their mutual joy to suffer embarrassment; not so Mr. Edgar, he grew pale with pure annoyance, a feeling that reached its climax when his lady rose — and stepping across the rug, seized Heathcliff's hands again, and laughed like one beside herself.

"I shall think it a dream tomorrow!" she cried. "I shall not be able to believe that I have seen, and touched, and spoken to you once more — and yet, cruel Heathcliff! you don't deserve this welcome. To be absent and silent for three years, and never to think of me!"

"A little more than you have thought of me!" he murmured. "I heard of your marriage, Cathy, not long since; and, while waiting in the yard below, I meditated this plan — just to have one glimpse of your face — a stare of surprise, perhaps, and pretended pleasure; afterwards settle my score with Hindley; and then prevent the law by doing execution on myself. Your welcome has put these ideas out of my mind; but beware of meeting me with another aspect next time! Nay, you'll not drive me off again — you were really sorry for me, were you? Well, there was cause. I've fought through a bitter life since I last heard your voice, and you must forgive me, for I struggled only for you!"

"Catherine, unless we are to have cold tea, please to come to the table," interrupted Linton, striving to preserve his ordinary tone, and a due measure of politeness. "Mr. Heathcliff will have a long walk, wherever he may lodge tonight; and I'm thirsty."

She took her post before the urn; and Miss Isabella came, summoned by the bell; then, having handed their chairs forward, I left the room.

The meal hardly endured ten minutes—Catherine's cup was never filled, she could neither eat nor drink. Edgar had made a slop in his saucer, and scarcely swallowed a mouthful.

Their guest did not protract his stay, that evening, above an hour longer. I asked, as he departed, if he went to Gimmerton?

"No, to Wuthering Heights," he answered: "Mr. Earnshaw invited me, when I called this morning."

Mr. Earnshaw invited *him!* and *he* called on Mr. Earnshaw! I pondered this sentence painfully, after he was gone. Is he turning out a bit of a hypocrite, and coming into the country to work mischief under a cloak? I mused—I had a presentiment, in the bottom of my heart, that he had better have remained away.

About the middle of the night, I was wakened from my first nap by Mrs. Linton gliding into my chamber, taking a seat on my bedside, and pulling me by the hair to rouse me.

"I cannot rest, Ellen," she said, by way of apology. "And I want some living creature to keep me company in my happiness! Edgar is sulky, because I am glad of a thing that does not interest him—He refuses to open his mouth, except to utter pettish, silly speeches; and he affirmed I was cruel and selfish for wishing to talk when he was so sick and sleepy. He always contrives to be sick at the least cross! I gave a few sentences of commendation to Heathcliff, and he, either for a headache or a pang of envy, began to cry: so I got up and left him."

"What use is it praising Heathcliff to him?" I answered. "As lads they had an aversion to each other, and Heathcliff would hate just as much to hear him praised—it's human nature. Let Mr. Linton alone about him, unless you would like an open quarrel between them."

"But does it not show great weakness?" pursued she. "I'm not envious—I never feel hurt at the brightness of Isabella's yellow hair, and the whiteness of her skin; at her dainty elegance, and the fondness all the family exhibit for her. Even you, Nelly, if we have a dispute sometimes, you back Isabella, at once; and I yield like a foolish mother—I call her a darling, and flatter her into a good temper. It pleases her brother to see us cordial, and that pleases me. But, they are very much alike: they are spoiled children, and fancy the world was made for their accommodation; and, though I humour both, I think a smart chastisement might improve them, all the same."

"You're mistaken, Mrs. Linton," said I, "They humour you—I know what there would be to do if they did not! You can well afford to indulge their passing whims, as long as their business is to anticipate all your desires—You may, however, fall out, at last, over something of equal consequence to both sides; and, then those you term weak are very capable of being as obstinate as you."

"And then we shall fight to the death, shan't we, Nelly?" she returned, laughing, "No! I tell you, I have such faith in Linton's love that I believe I might kill him, and he wouldn't wish to retaliate."

I advised her to value him the more for his affection.

"I do," she answered; "but, he needn't resort to whining for trifles. It is childish; and, instead of melting into tears, because I said that Heathcliff was now worthy of anyone's regard, and it would honour the first gentleman in the country to be his friend; he ought to have said it for me, and been delighted from sympathy—He must get accustomed to him, and he may as well like him—considering how Heathcliff has reason to object to him, I'm sure he behaved excellently!"

"What do you think of his going to Wuthering Heights?" I inquired. "He is reformed in every respect, apparently—quite a Christian—offering the right hand of fellowship to his enemies all round!"

"He explained it," she replied. "I wondered as much as you—He said he called to gather information concerning me, from you, supposing you resided there still; and Joseph told Hindley, who came out, and fell to questioning him of what he had been doing, and how he had been living: and finally, desired him to walk in—There were some persons sitting at cards—Heathcliff joined them; my brother lost some money to him; and, finding him plentifully supplied, he requested that he would come again in the evening, to which he consented. Hindley is too reckless to select his acquaintance prudently; he doesn't trouble himself to reflect on the causes he might have for mistrusting one whom he has basely injured—But Heathcliff affirms his principal reason for resuming a connection with his ancient persecutor is a wish to install himself in quarters at walking distance from the Grange, and an attachment to the house where we lived together, and, likewise a hope that I shall have more opportunities of seeing him there than I could have if he settled in Gimmerton. He means to offer liberal payment for permission to lodge at the Heights; and doubtless my brother's covetousness will prompt him to accept the terms; he was always greedy, though what he grasps with one hand, he flings away with the other."

"It's a nice place for a young man to fix his dwelling in!" said I. "Have you no fear of the consequences, Mrs. Linton?"

"None for my friend," she replied, "his strong head will keep him from danger—a little for Hindley; but, he can't be made morally worse than he is; and I stand between him and bodily harm—The event of this evening has reconciled me to God, and humanity! I had risen in angry rebellion against providence—Oh, I've endured very, very bitter misery. Nelly! If that creature knew how bitter, he'd be ashamed to cloud its removal with idle petulance—It was kindness for him which induced me to bear it alone: had I expressed the agony I frequently felt, he would have been taught to long for its alleviation as ardently as I—However, it's over, and I'll take no revenge on his folly—I can afford to suffer anything, hereafter! should the meanest thing alive slap me on the cheek, I'd not only turn the other, but, I'd ask pardon for provoking it—and, as a proof, I'll go make my peace with Edgar instantly—Good night—I'm an angel!"

In this self-complacent conviction she departed; and the success of her fulfilled resolution was obvious on the morrow—Mr. Linton had not only abjured his peevishness (though his spirits seemed still subdued by Catherine's exuberance of vivacity) but he ventured no objection to her taking Isabella with her to Wuthering Heights, in the afternoon; and she rewarded him with such a summer of sweetness and affection, in return, as made the house a paradise for several days; both master and servants profiting from the perpetual sunshine.

Heathcliff—Mr. Heathcliff I should say in future—used the liberty of visiting Thrushcross Grange cautiously, at first: he seemed estimating how far its owner would bear his intrusion. Catherine also, deemed it judicious to moderate her expressions of pleasure in receiving him; and he gradually established his right to be expected.

He retained a great deal of the reserve for which his boyhood was remarkable, and that served to repress all startling demonstrations of feeling. My master's uneasiness experienced a lull, and further circumstances diverted it into another channel for a space.

His new source of trouble sprang from the not anticipated misfortune of Isabella Linton evincing a sudden and irresistible attraction towards the tolerated guest—She was at that time a charming young lady of eighteen; infantile in manners, though possessed of keen wit, keen feelings, and a keen temper, too, if irritated. Her brother, who loved her tenderly, was appalled at this fantastic preference. Leaving aside the degradation of an alliance with a nameless man, and the possible fact that his property, in default of heirs male, might pass into such a one's power, he had sense to comprehend Heathcliff's disposition—to know that, though his exterior was altered, his mind was unchangeable, and unchanged. And he dreaded that mind; it revolted him; he shrank forebodingly from the idea of committing Isabella to its keeping.

He would have recoiled still more had he been aware that her attachment rose unsolicited, and was bestowed where it awakened no reciprocation of sentiment; for the minute he discovered its existence, he laid the blame on Heathcliff's deliberate designing.

We had all remarked, during some time, that Miss Linton fretted and pined over something. She grew cross and wearisome, snapping at and teasing Catherine, continually, at the imminent risk of exhausting her limited patience. We excused her to a certain extent, on the plea of ill health — she was dwindling and fading before our eyes — But, one day when she had been peculiarly wayward, rejecting her breakfast, complaining that the servants did not do what she told them; that the mistress would allow her to be nothing in the house, and Edgar neglected her; that she had caught a cold with the doors being left open, and we let the parlour fire go out on purpose to vex her; with a hundred yet more frivolous accusations; Mrs. Linton peremptorily insisted that she should get to bed; and, having scolded her heartily, threatened to send for the doctor.

Mention of Kenneth caused her to exclaim, instantly, that her health was perfect, and it was only Catherine's harshness which made her unhappy.

"How can you say I am harsh, you naughty fondling?" cried the mistress, amazed at the unreasonable assertion. "You are surely losing your reason. When have I been harsh, tell me?"

"Yesterday!" sobbed Isabella, "and now!"

"Yesterday!" said her sister-in-law. "On what occasion?"

"In our walk along the moor; you told me to ramble where I pleased, while you sauntered on with Mr. Heathcliff!"

"And that's your notion of harshness?" said Catherine, laughing. "It was no hint that your company was superfluous; we didn't care whether you kept with us or not; I merely thought Heathcliff's talk would have nothing entertaining for your ears."

"Oh, no," wept the young lady, "you wished me away, because you knew I liked to be there!"

"Is she sane?" asked Mrs. Linton, appealing to me. "I'll repeat our conversation, word for word, Isabella; and you point out any charm it could have had for you."

"I don't mind the conversation," she answered: "I wanted to be with —"

"Well!" said Catherine, perceiving her hesitate to complete the sentence.

"With him; and I won't always be sent off!" she continued, kindling up. "You are a dog in the manger, Cathy, and desire no one to be loved but yourself!"

"You are an impertinent little monkey!" exclaimed Mrs. Linton, in surprise. "But I'll not believe this idiocy! It is impossible that you can covet the admiration of Heathcliff — that you consider him an agreeable person! I hope I have misunderstood you, Isabella?"

"No, you have not," said the infatuated girl. "I love him more than ever you loved Edgar; and he might love me, if you would let him!"

"I wouldn't be you for a kingdom, then!" Catherine declared emphatically—and she seemed to speak sincerely. "Nelly, help me to convince her of her madness. Tell her what Heathcliff is—an unreclaimed creature, without refinement—without cultivation; an arid wilderness of furze and whinstone. I'd as soon put that little canary into the park on a winter's day as recommend you to bestow your heart on him! It is deplorable ignorance of his character, child, and nothing else, which makes that dream enter your head. Pray don't imagine that he conceals depths of benevolence and affection beneath a stern exterior! He's not a rough diamond—a pearl-containing oyster of a rustic; he's a fierce, pitiless, wolfish man. I never say to him let this or that enemy alone, because it would be ungenerous or cruel to harm them—I say let them alone, because *I* should hate them to be wronged: and he'd crush you, like a sparrow's egg, Isabella, if he found you a troublesome charge. I know he couldn't love a Linton; and yet he'd be quite capable of marrying your fortune, and expectations. Avarice is growing with him a besetting sin. There's my picture; and I'm his friend—so much so, that had he thought seriously to catch you, I should, perhaps, have held my tongue, and let you fall into his trap."

Miss Linton regarded her sister-in-law with indignation.

"For shame! for shame!" she repeated, angrily, "You are worse than twenty foes, you poisonous friend!"

"Ah! you won't believe me, then?" said Catherine. "You think I speak from wicked selfishness?"

"I'm certain you do," retorted Isabella; "and I shudder at you!"

"Good!" cried the other. "Try for yourself, if that be your spirit; I have done, and yield the argument to your saucy insolence."

"And I must suffer for her egotism!" she sobbed, as Mrs. Linton left the room. "All, all is against me; she has blighted my single consolation. But she uttered falsehoods, didn't she? Mr. Heathcliff is not a fiend; he has an honourable soul, and a true one, or how could he remember her?"

"Banish him from your thoughts, miss," I said. "He's a bird of bad omen; no mate for you. Mrs. Linton spoke strongly, and yet I can't contradict her. She is better acquainted with his heart than I, or anyone besides; and she never would represent him as worse than he is. Honest people don't hide their deeds. How has he been living? how has he got rich? why is he staying at Wuthering Heights, the house of a man whom he abhors? They say Mr. Earnshaw is worse and worse since he came. They sit up all night together continually: and Hindley has been borrowing money on his land; and does nothing but play and drink, I heard only a week ago; it was Joseph who told me—I met him at Gimmerton.

"'Nelly!' he said, 'we's hae a Crahnr's 'quest enah, at ahr folks. One on 'ems a'most getten his finger cut off wi' haudin t' other froo' sticking hisseln loike a cawlf. That's maister, yah knaw, 'ut's soa up uh going tuh t'grand 'sizes. He's noan feard uh t' Bench uh judges, norther Paul, nur Peter, nur John, nor Mathew, nor noan on 'em, nut he! He fair like's he langs tuh set his brazened face agean 'em! And yon bonny lad Hathecliff, yah mind, he's a rare 'un! He can girn a laugh, as weel's onybody at a raight divil's jest. Does he niver say nowt of his fine living amang us, when he goas tuh t' Grange? This is t' way on't—up at sun-dahn; dice, brandy, cloised shutters, und can'le lught till next day, at nooin—then, t' fooil gangs banning un raving to his cham'er, makking dacent fowks dig thur fingers i' thur lugs fur varry shaume; un' th' knave, wah he carn cahnt his brass, un' ate, un' sleep, un' off tuh his neighbour's tuh gossip wi' t' wife. I' course, he tells Dame Catherine hah hor fathur's goold runs intuh his pocket, and her fathur's son gallops dahn t' Broad road, while he flees afore tuh oppen t' pikes?' Now, Miss Linton, Joseph is an old rascal, but no liar; and, if his account of Heathcliff's conduct be true, you would never think of desiring such a husband, would you?"

"You are leagued with the rest, Ellen!" she replied. "I'll not listen to your slanders. What malevolence you must have to wish to convince me that there is no happiness in the world!"

Whether she would have got over this fancy if left to herself, or persevered in nursing it perpetually, I cannot say; she had little time to reflect. The day after, there was a justice meeting at the next town; my master was obliged to attend; and Mr. Heathcliff, aware of his absence, called rather earlier than usual. Catherine and Isabella were sitting in the library, on hostile terms, but silent. The latter alarmed at her recent indiscretion, and the disclosure she had made of her secret feelings in a transient fit of passion; the former, on mature consideration, really offended with her companion; and, if she laughed again at her pertness, inclined to make it no laughing matter to her.

She did laugh as she saw Heathcliff pass the window. I was sweeping the hearth, and I noticed a mischievous smile on her lips. Isabella, absorbed in her meditations, or a book, remained till the door opened, and it was too late to attempt an escape, which she would gladly have done had it been practicable.

---

we's hae a Crahnr's 'quest enah, at ahr folks: we will have a coroner's inquest soon enough at our house.
'ut's soa up uh going: who is set on going.
gangs banning: goes cursing.
t' pikes: the gates.

"Come in, that's right!" exclaimed the mistress, gaily, pulling a chair to the fire. "Here are two people sadly in need of a third to thaw the ice between them; and you are the very one we should both of us choose. Heathcliff, I'm proud to show you, at last, somebody that dotes on you more than myself. I expect you to feel flattered—nay, it's not Nelly; don't look at her! My poor little sister-in-law is breaking her heart by mere contemplation of your physical and moral beauty. It lies in your own power to be Edgar's brother! No, no, Isabella, you shan't run off," she continued, arresting, with feigned playfulness, the confounded girl who had risen indignantly. "We were quarrelling like cats about you, Heathcliff; and I was fairly beaten in protestations of devotion and admiration; and, moreover, I was informed that if I would but have the manners to stand aside, my rival, as she will have herself to be, would shoot a shaft into your soul that would fix you forever, and send my image into eternal oblivion!"

"Catherine!" said Isabella, calling up her dignity, and disdaining to struggle from the tight grasp that held her. "I'd thank you to adhere to the truth and not slander me, even in joke! Mr. Heathcliff, be kind enough to bid this friend of yours release me—she forgets that you and I are not intimate acquaintances, and what amuses her is painful to me beyond expression."

As the guest answered nothing, but took his seat, and looked thoroughly indifferent what sentiments she cherished concerning him, she turned, and whispered an earnest appeal for liberty to her tormentor.

"By no means!" cried Mrs. Linton in answer. "I won't be named a dog in the manger again. You *shall* stay, now then! Heathcliff, why don't you evince satisfaction at my pleasant news? Isabella swears that the love Edgar has for me is nothing to that she entertains for you. I'm sure she made some speech of the kind, did she not, Ellen? And she has fasted ever since the day before yesterday's walk, from sorrow and rage that I despatched her out of your society, under the idea of its being unacceptable."

"I think you belie her," said Heathcliff, twisting his chair to face them. "She wishes to be out of my society now, at any rate!"

And he stared hard at the object of discourse, as one might do at a strange repulsive animal, a centipede from the Indies, for instance, which curiosity leads one to examine in spite of the aversion it raises.

The poor thing couldn't bear that; she grew white and red in rapid succession, and, while tears beaded her lashes, bent the strength of her small fingers to loosen the firm clutch of Catherine, and perceiving that, as fast as she raised one finger off her arm, another closed down, and she could not remove the whole together, she began to make use of her nails, and their sharpness presently ornamented the detainer's with crescents of red.

"There's a tigress!" exclaimed Mrs. Linton, setting her free, and shaking her hand with pain. "Begone, for God's sake, and hide your vixen face! How foolish to reveal those talons to him! Can't you fancy the conclusions he'll draw? Look, Heathcliff! they are instruments that will do execution — you must beware of your eyes."

"I'd wrench them off her fingers, if they ever menaced me," he answered, brutally, when the door had closed after her. "But, what did you mean by teasing the creature in that manner, Cathy? You were not speaking the truth, were you?"

"I assure you I was," she returned. "She has been pining for your sake several weeks; and raving about you this morning, and pouring forth a deluge of abuse, because I represented your failings in a plain light for the purpose of mitigating her adoration. But don't notice it further. I wished to punish her sauciness, that's all — I like her too well, my dear Heathcliff, to let you absolutely seize and devour her up."

"And I like her too ill to attempt it," said he, "except in a very ghoulish fashion. You'd hear of odd things, if I lived alone with that mawkish, waxen face; the most ordinary would be painting on its white the colours of the rainbow, and turning the blue eyes, black, every day or two; they detestably resemble Linton's."

"Delectably," observed Catherine. "They are dove's eyes — angel's!"

"She's her brother's heir, is she not?" he asked, after a brief silence.

"I should be sorry to think so," returned his companion. "Half-a-dozen nephews shall erase her title, please Heaven! Abstract your mind from the subject, at present — you are too prone to covet your neighbour's goods: remember *this* neighbour's goods are mine."

"If they were *mine,* they would be none the less that," said Heathcliff, "but though Isabella Linton may be silly, she is scarcely mad; and — in short, we'll dismiss the matter as you advise."

From their tongues, they did dismiss it; and Catherine, probably, from her thoughts. The other, I felt certain, recalled it often in the course of the evening; I saw him smile to himself — grin rather — and lapse into ominous musing whenever Mrs. Linton had occasion to be absent from the apartment.

I determined to watch his movements. My heart invariably cleaved to the master's, in preference to Catherine's side; with reason, I imagined, for he was kind, and trustful, and honourable: and she — she could not be called the *opposite,* yet she seemed to allow herself such wide latitude, that I had little faith in her principles, and still less sympathy for her feelings. I wanted something to happen which might have the effect of freeing both Wuthering Heights and the Grange of Mr. Heathcliff, quietly, leaving us as we had been prior to his advent. His visits were a continual nightmare to me; and, I suspected, to my master also. His abode at the Heights was an oppression past explaining. I felt that God had forsaken the stray sheep there to its own wicked wanderings, and an evil beast prowled between it and the fold, waiting his time to spring and destroy.

CHAPTER XI

Sometimes, while meditating on these things in solitude, I've got up in a sudden terror, and put on my bonnet to go see how all was at the farm; I've persuaded my conscience that it was a duty to warn him how people talked regarding his ways; and then I've recollected his confirmed bad habits, and, hopeless of benefiting him, have flinched from re-entering the dismal house, doubting if I could bear to be taken at my word.

One time, I passed the old gate, going out of my way, on a journey to Gimmerton. It was about the period that my narrative has reached—a bright, frosty afternoon; the ground bare, and the road hard and dry.

I came to a stone where the highway branches off on to the moor at your left hand; a rough sand-pillar, with the letters W. H. cut on its north side, on the east, G., and on the southwest, T. G. It serves as a guide-post to the Grange, Heights, and village. The sun shone yellow on its grey head, reminding me of summer; and I cannot say why, but all at once, a gush of child's sensations flowed into my heart. Hindley and I held it a favourite spot twenty years before.

I gazed long at the weather-worn block; and, stooping down, perceived a hole near the bottom still full of snail-shells and pebbles which we were fond of storing there with more perishable things—and, as fresh as reality, it appeared that I beheld my early playmate seated on the withered turf; his dark, square head bent forward, and his little hand scooping out the earth with a piece of slate.

"Poor Hindley!" I exclaimed, involuntarily.

I started—my bodily eye was cheated into a momentary belief that the child lifted its face and stared straight into mine! It vanished in a twinkling; but, immediately, I felt an irresistible yearning to be at the Heights. Superstition urged me to comply with this impulse—"supposing he should be dead!" I thought—"or should die soon!—supposing it were a sign of death!"

The nearer I got to the house the more agitated I grew: and on catching sight of it, I trembled every limb. The apparition had outstripped me; it stood looking through the gate. That was my first idea on observing an elf-locked, brown-eyed boy setting his ruddy countenance against the bars.

Further reflection suggested this must be Hareton, *my* Hareton, not altered greatly since I left him, ten months since.

"God bless thee, darling!" I cried, forgetting instantaneously my foolish fears. "Hareton, it's Nelly—Nelly, thy nurse."

He retreated out of arm's length, and picked up a large flint.

"I am come to see thy father, Hareton," I added, guessing from the action that Nelly, if she lived in his memory at all, was not recognized as one with me.

He raised his missile to hurl it; I commenced a soothing speech, but could not stay his hand. The stone struck my bonnet, and then ensued, from the stammering lips of the little fellow, a string of curses which, whether he comprehended them or not, were delivered with practised emphasis, and distorted his baby features into a shocking expression of malignity.

You may be certain this grieved more than angered me. Fit to cry, I took an orange from my pocket, and offered it to propitiate him.

He hesitated, and then snatched it from my hold, as if he fancied I only intended to tempt, and disappoint him.

I showed another keeping it out of his reach.

"Who has taught you those fine words, my bairn?" I inquired. "The curate?"

"Damn the curate, and thee! Gie me that," he replied.

"Tell us where you got your lessons, and you shall have it," said I. "Who's your master?"

"Devil daddy," was his answer.

"And what do you learn from Daddy?" I continued.

He jumped at the fruit; I raised it higher. "What does he teach you?" I asked.

"Naught," said he, "but to keep out of his gait—Daddy cannot bide me, because I swear at him."

"Ah! and the devil teaches you to swear at Daddy?" I observed.

"Aye—nay," he drawled.

"Who then?"

"Heathcliff."

I asked if he liked Mr. Heathcliff.

"Aye!" he answered again.

Desiring to have his reasons for liking him, I could only gather the sentences. "I known't—he pays Dad back what he gives to me—he curses Daddy for cursing me—He says I mun do as I will."

"And the curate does not teach you to read and write, then?" I pursued.

"No, I was told the curate should have his —— teeth dashed down his

——throat, if he stepped over the threshold—Heathcliff, had promised that!"

I put the orange in his hand; and bade him tell his father that a woman called Nelly Dean, was waiting to speak with him, by the garden gate.

He went up the walk, and entered the house; but instead of Hindley, Heathcliff appeared on the door stones, and I turned directly and ran down the road as hard as ever I could race, making no halt till I gained the guide post, and feeling as scared as if I had raised a goblin.

This is not much connected with Miss Isabella's affair; except that it urged me to resolve further, on mounting vigilant guard, and doing my utmost to check the spread of such bad influence at the Grange, even though I should wake a domestic storm, by thwarting Mrs. Linton's pleasure.

The next time Heathcliff came, my young lady chanced to be feeding some pigeons in the court. She had never spoken a word to her sister-in-law, for three days; but she had likewise dropped her fretful complaining, and we found it a great comfort.

Heathcliff had not the habit of bestowing a single unnecessary civility on Miss Linton, I knew. Now, as soon as he beheld her, his first precaution was to take a sweeping survey of the housefront. I was standing by the kitchen window, but I drew out of sight. He then stepped across the pavement to her, and said something: she seemed embarrassed, and desirous of getting away; to prevent it, he laid his hand on her arm: she averted her face; he apparently put some question which she had no mind to answer. There was another rapid glance at the house, and supposing himself unseen, the scoundrel had the impudence to embrace her.

"Judas! Traitor!" I ejaculated, "you are a hypocrite, too, are you? a deliberate deceiver."

"Who is, Nelly?" said Catherine's voice at my elbow—I had been over-intent on watching the pair outside to mark her entrance.

"Your worthless friend!" I answered, warmly, "the sneaking rascal yonder—Ah, he has caught a glimpse of us—he is coming in! I wonder will he have the art to find a plausible excuse, for making love to Miss, when he told you he hated her?"

Mrs. Linton saw Isabella tear herself free, and run into the garden; and a minute after, Heathcliff opened the door.

I couldn't withhold giving some loose to my indignation; but Catherine angrily insisted on silence, and threatened to order me out of the kitchen, if I dared be so presumptuous as to put in my insolent tongue.

"To hear you, people might think *you* were the mistress!" she cried. "You want setting down in your right place! Heathcliff, what are you about, raising this stir? I said you must let Isabella alone!—I beg you will, unless you are tired of being received here, and wish Linton to draw the bolts against you!"

"God forbid that he should try!" answered the black villain—I detested him just then. "God keep him meek and patient! Every day I grow madder after sending him to heaven!"

"Hush!" said Catherine, shutting the inner door. "Don't vex me. Why have you disregarded my request? Did she come across you on purpose?"

"What is it to you?" he growled, "I have a right to kiss her, if she chooses, and you have no right to object—I'm not *your* husband, *you* needn't be jealous of me!"

"I'm not jealous of you;" replied the mistress, "I'm jealous for you. Clear your face, you shan't scowl at me! If you like Isabella, you shall marry her. But do you like her, tell the truth, Heathcliff? There, you won't answer. I'm certain you don't!"

"And would Mr. Linton approve of his sister marrying that man?" I inquired.

"Mr. Linton should approve," returned my lady decisively.

"He might spare himself the trouble," said Heathcliff, "I could do as well without his approbation—And, as to you, Catherine, I have a mind to speak a few words, now, while we are at it—I want you to be aware that I *know* you have treated me infernally—infernally! Do you hear? And, if you flatter yourself that I don't perceive it you are a fool—and if you think I can be consoled by sweet words you are an idiot—and if you fancy I'll suffer unrevenged, I'll convince you of the contrary, in a very little while! Meantime, thank you for telling me your sister-in-law's secret—I swear I'll make the most of it, and stand you aside!"

"What new phase of his character is this?" exclaimed Mrs. Linton, in amazement. "I've treated you infernally—and you'll take your revenge! How will you take it, ungrateful brute? How have I treated you infernally?"

"I seek no revenge on you," replied Heathcliff, less vehemently. "That's not the plan—The tyrant grinds down his slaves and they don't turn against him, they crush those beneath them—You are welcome to torture me to death for your amusement, only allow me to amuse myself a little in the same style—And refrain from insult, as much as you are able. Having levelled my palace, don't erect a hovel and complacently admire your own charity in giving me that for a home. If I imagined you really wished me to marry Isabella, I'd cut my throat!"

"Oh, the evil is that I am *not* jealous, is it?" cried Catherine. "Well, I won't repeat my offer of a wife—It is as bad as offering Satan a lost soul—Your bliss lies, like his, in inflicting misery—You prove it—Edgar is restored from the ill-temper he gave way to at your coming; I begin to be secure and tranquil; and you, restless to know us at peace, appear resolved on exciting a quarrel—quarrel with Edgar if you please, Heathcliff, and deceive his sister; you'll hit on exactly the most efficient method of revenging yourself on me."

The conversation ceased—Mrs. Linton sat down by the fire, flushed and gloomy. The spirit which served her was growing intractable: she could neither lay nor control it. He stood on the hearth, with folded arms brooding on his evil thoughts; and in this position I left them, to seek the master who was wondering what kept Catherine below so long.

"Ellen," said he, when I entered, "have you seen your mistress?"

"Yes; she is in the kitchen, sir," I answered. "She's sadly put out by Mr. Heathcliff's behaviour: and, indeed, I do think it's time to arrange his visits on another footing. There's harm in being too soft, and now it's come to this—." And I related the scene in the court, and, as near as I dared, the whole subsequent dispute. I fancied it could not be very prejudicial to Mrs. Linton, unless she made it so, afterwards, by assuming the defensive for her guest.

Edgar Linton had difficulty in hearing me to the close—His first words revealed that he did not clear his wife of blame.

"This is insufferable!" he exclaimed. "It is disgraceful that she should own him for a friend, and force his company on me! Call me two men out of the hall, Ellen—Catherine shall linger no longer to argue with the low ruffian—I have humoured her enough."

He descended, and bidding the servants wait in the passage, went, followed by me, to the kitchen. Its occupants had recommenced their angry discussion; Mrs. Linton, at least, was scolding with renewed vigour; Heathcliff had moved to the window, and hung his head somewhat cowed by her violent rating apparently.

He saw the master first, and made a hasty motion that she should be silent; which she obeyed, abruptly, on discovering the reason of his intimation.

"How is this?" said Linton, addressing her; "what notion of propriety must you have to remain here, after the language which has been held to you by that blackguard? I suppose, because it is his ordinary talk, you think nothing of it—you are habituated to his baseness, and, perhaps, imagine I can get used to it too!"

"Have you been listening at the door, Edgar?" asked the mistress, in a tone particularly calculated to provoke her husband, implying both carelessness and contempt of his irritation.

Heathcliff, who had raised his eyes at the former speech, gave a sneering laugh at the latter, on purpose, it seemed, to draw Mr. Linton's attention to him.

He succeeded; but Edgar did not mean to entertain him with any high flights of passion.

"I have been so far forbearing with you, sir," he said, quietly; "not that I was ignorant of your miserable, degraded character, but, I felt you were only partly responsible for that; and Catherine wishing to keep up your acquaintance, I acquiesced—foolishly. Your presence is a moral poison that would contaminate the most virtuous—for that cause, and to prevent worse consequences, I shall deny you, hereafter, admission into this house and give notice, now, that I require your instant departure. Three minutes' delay will render it involuntary and ignominious."

Heathcliff measured the height and breadth of the speaker with an eye full of derision.

"Cathy, this lamb of yours threatens like a bull!" he said. "It is in danger of splitting its skull against my knuckles. By God, Mr. Linton, I'm mortally sorry that you are not worth knocking down!"

My master glanced towards the passage, and signed me to fetch the men—he had no intention of hazarding a personal encounter. I obeyed the hint; but Mrs. Linton suspecting something, followed, and when I attempted to call them, she pulled me back, slammed the door to, and locked it.

"Fair means!" she said, in answer to her husband's look of angry surprise. "If you have not courage to attack him, make an apology, or allow yourself to be beaten. It will correct you of feigning more valour than you possess. No, I'll swallow the key before you shall get it! I'm delightfully rewarded for my kindness to each! After constant indulgence of one's weak nature, and the other's bad one, I earn, for thanks, two samples of blind ingratitude, stupid to absurdity! Edgar, I was defending you, and yours; and I wish Heathcliff may flog you sick, for daring to think an evil thought of me!"

It did not need the medium of a flogging to produce that effect on the master. He tried to wrest the key from Catherine's grasp; and for safety she flung it into the hottest part of the fire; whereupon Mr. Edgar was taken with a nervous trembling, and his countenance grew deadly pale. For his life he could not avert that access of emotion—mingled anguish and humiliation overcame him completely. He leant on the back of a chair, and covered his face.

"Oh! heavens! In old days this would win you knighthood!" exclaimed Mrs. Linton. "We are vanquished! we are vanquished! Heathcliff would as soon lift a finger at you as a king would march his army against a colony of mice. Cheer up, you shan't be hurt! Your type is not a lamb, it's a sucking leveret."

"I wish you joy of the milk-blooded coward, Cathy!" said her friend. "I compliment you on your taste: and that is the slavering, shivering thing you preferred to me! I would not strike him with my fist, but I'd kick him with my foot, and experience considerable satisfaction. Is he weeping, or is he going to faint for fear?"

The fellow approached and gave the chair on which Linton rested a push. He'd better have kept his distance: my master quickly sprang erect, and struck him full on the throat a blow that would have levelled a slighter man.

It took his breath for a moment; and, while he choked, Mr. Linton walked out by the back door into the yard, and from thence, to the front entrance.

"There! you've done with coming here," cried Catherine. "Get away, now—he'll return with a brace of pistols, and half-a-dozen assistants. If he did overhear us, of course, he'd never forgive you. You've played me an ill turn, Heathcliff! But, go—make haste! I'd rather see Edgar at bay than you."

"Do you suppose I'm going with that blow burning in my gullet?" he thundered. "By Hell, no! I'll crush his ribs in like a rotten hazel-nut, before I cross the threshold! If I don't floor him now, I shall murder him some time, so, as you value his existence, let me get at him!"

"He's not coming," I interposed, framing a bit of a lie. "There's the coachman, and the two gardeners; you'll surely not wait to be thrust into the road by them! Each has a bludgeon, and master will, very likely, be watching from the parlour windows to see that they fulfill his orders."

The gardeners and coachman *were* there; but Linton was with them. They had already entered the court—Heathcliff, on second thoughts, resolved to avoid a struggle against the three underlings; he seized the poker, smashed the lock from the inner door, and made his escape as they tramped in.

Mrs. Linton, who was very much excited, bid me accompany her upstairs. She did not know my share in contributing to the disturbance, and I was anxious to keep her in ignorance.

"I'm nearly distracted, Nelly!" she exclaimed, throwing herself on the sofa. "A thousand smiths' hammers are beating in my head! Tell Isabella to shun me—this uproar is owing to her; and should she or anyone else aggravate my anger at present, I shall get wild. And, Nelly, say to Edgar, if you see him again tonight, that I'm in danger of being seriously ill—I wish it may prove true. He has startled and distressed me shockingly! I want to frighten him. Besides, he might come and begin a string of abuse, or complainings; I'm certain I should recriminate, and God knows where we should end! Will you do so, my good Nelly? You are aware that I am no way blameable in this matter. What possessed him to turn listener? Heathcliff's talk was outrageous, after you left us; but I could soon have diverted him from Isabella, and the rest meant nothing. Now, all is dashed wrong by the fool's craving to hear evil of self that haunts some people like a demon! Had Edgar never gathered our conversation, he would never have been the worse for it. Really, when he opened on me in that unreasonable tone of displeasure, after I had scolded Heathcliff till I was hoarse for *him;* I did not care, hardly, what they did to each other, especially as I felt that, however the scene closed, we should all be driven asunder for nobody knows how long! Well, if I cannot keep Heathcliff for my friend—if Edgar will be mean and jealous, I'll try to break their hearts by breaking my own. That will be a prompt way of finishing all, when I am pushed to extremity! But it's a deed to be reserved for a forlorn hope—I'd not take Linton by surprise with it. To this point he has been discreet in dreading to provoke me; you must represent the peril of quitting that policy; and remind him of my passionate temper, verging, when kindled, on frenzy—I wish you could dismiss that apathy out of your countenance, and look rather more anxious about me!"

The stolidity with which I received these instructions was, no doubt, rather exasperating; for they were delivered in perfect sincerity, but I believed a person who could plan the turning of her fits of passion to account, beforehand, might, by exerting her will, manage to control herself tolerably even while under their influence; and I did not wish to "frighten" her husband, as she said, and multiply his annoyances for the purpose of serving her selfishness. Therefore I said nothing when I met the master coming towards the parlour; but I took the liberty of turning back to listen whether they would resume their quarrel together.

He began to speak first.

"Remain where you are, Catherine," he said, without any anger in his voice, but with much sorrowful despondency. "I shall not stay. I am neither come to wrangle, nor be reconciled; but I wish just to learn whether, after this evening's events, you intend to continue your intimacy with—"

"Oh, for mercy's sake," interrupted the mistress, stamping her foot, "for mercy's sake, let us hear no more of it now! Your cold blood cannot be worked into a fever—your veins are full of ice-water—but mine are boiling, and the sight of such chillness makes them dance."

"To get rid of me—answer my question," persevered Mr. Linton. "You *must* answer it; and that violence does not alarm me. I have found that you can be as stoical as anyone, when you please. Will you give up Heathcliff hereafter, or will you give up me? It is impossible for you to be *my* friend, and *his* at the same time; and I absolutely *require* to know which you choose."

"I require to be let alone!" exclaimed Catherine, furiously. "I demand it! Don't you see I can scarcely stand? Edgar, you—you leave me!"

She rang the bell till it broke with a twang: I entered leisurely. It was enough to try the temper of a saint, such senseless, wicked rages! There she lay dashing her head against the arm of the sofa, and grinding her teeth, so that you might fancy she would crash them to splinters!

Mr. Linton stood looking at her in sudden compunction and fear. He told me to fetch some water. She had no breath for speaking.

I brought a glass full; and as she would not drink, I sprinkled it on her face. In a few seconds she stretched herself out stiff, and turned up her eyes, while her cheeks, at once blanched and livid, assumed the aspect of death.

Linton looked terrified.

"There is nothing in the world the matter," I whispered. I did not want him to yield, though I could not help being afraid in my heart.

"She has blood on her lips!" he said, shuddering.

"Never mind!" I answered, tartly. And I told him how she had resolved, previous to his coming, on exhibiting a fit of frenzy.

I incautiously gave the account aloud, and she heard me, for she started up — her hair flying over her shoulders, her eyes flashing, the muscles of her neck and arms standing out preternaturally. I made up my mind for broken bones, at least; but she only glared about for an instant, and then rushed from the room. The master directed me to follow; I did, to her chamber door; she hindered me from going farther by securing it against me.

As she never offered to descend to breakfast next morning, I went to ask whether she would have some carried up.

"No!" she replied, peremptorily.

The same question was repeated at dinner, and tea; and again on the morrow after, and received the same answer.

Mr. Linton, on his part, spent his time in the library, and did not inquire concerning his wife's occupations. Isabella and he had had an hour's interview, during which he tried to elicit from her some sentiment of proper horror for Heathcliff's advances; but he could make nothing of her evasive replies, and was obliged to close the examination, unsatisfactorily; adding, however, a solemn warning, that if she were so insane as to encourage that worthless suitor, it would dissolve all bonds of relationship between herself and him.

CHAPTER XII

While Miss Linton moped about the park and garden, always silent, and almost always in tears; and her brother shut himself up among books that he never opened; wearying, I guessed, with a continual vague expectation that

Catherine, repenting her conduct, would come of her own accord to ask pardon, and seek a reconciliation; and *she* fasted pertinaciously, under the idea, probably, that at every meal, Edgar was ready to choke for her absence, and pride alone held him from running to cast himself at her feet; I went about my household duties, convinced that the Grange had but one sensible soul in its walls, and that lodged in my body.

I wasted no condolences on Miss, nor any expostulations on my mistress, nor did I pay attention to the sighs of my master, who yearned to hear his lady's name, since he might not hear her voice.

I determined they should come about as they pleased for me; and although it was a tiresomely slow process, I began to rejoice at length in a faint dawn of its progress, as I thought at first.

Mrs. Linton, on the third day, unbarred her door; and having finished the water in her pitcher and decanter, desired a renewed supply, and a basin of gruel, for she believed she was dying. That I set down as a speech meant for Edgar's ears; I believed no such thing, so I kept it to myself, and brought her some tea and dry toast.

She eat and drank eagerly; and sank back on her pillow again clenching her hands and groaning.

"Oh, I will die," she exclaimed, "since no one cares anything about me. I wish I had not taken that."

Then a good while after I heard her murmur,

"No, I'll not die—he'd be glad—he does not love me at all—he would never miss me!"

"Did you want anything, ma'am?" I enquired, still preserving my external composure, in spite of her ghastly countenance, and strange exaggerated manner.

"What is that apathetic being doing?" she demanded, pushing her thick entangled locks from her wasted face. "Has he fallen into a lethargy, or is he dead?"

"Neither," replied I; "if you mean Mr. Linton. He's tolerably well, I think, though his studies occupy him rather more than they ought; he is continually among his books, since he has no other society."

I should not have spoken so, if I had known her true condition, but I could not get rid of the notion that she acted a part of her disorder.

"Among his books!" she cried, confounded. "And I dying! I on the brink of the grave! My God! does he know how I'm altered?" continued she, staring at her reflection in a mirror, hanging against the opposite wall. "Is that Catherine Linton? He imagines me in a pet—in play, perhaps. Cannot you inform him that it is frightful earnest? Nelly, if it be not too late, as soon as I learn how he feels, I'll choose between these two—either to starve, at once, that would be no punishment unless he had a heart—or to recover and leave the country. Are you speaking the truth about him now? Take care. Is he actually so utterly indifferent for my life?"

"Why, ma'am," I answered, "the master has no idea of your being deranged; and, of course, he does not fear that you will let yourself die of hunger."

"You think not? Cannot you tell him I will?" she returned; "persuade him—speak of your own mind—say you are certain I will!"

"No, you forget, Mrs. Linton," I suggested, "that you have eaten some food with a relish this evening, and tomorrow you will perceive its good effects."

"If I were only sure it would kill him," she interrupted, "I'd kill myself directly! These three awful nights, I've never closed my lids—and oh, I've been tormented! I've been haunted, Nelly! But I begin to fancy you don't like me. How strange! I thought, though everybody hated and despised each other, they could not avoid loving me—and they have all turned to enemies in a few hours. *They* have, I'm positive; the people *here*. How dreary to meet death, surrounded by their cold faces. Isabella, terrified and repelled, afraid to enter the room, it would be so dreadful to watch Catherine go. And Edgar standing solemnly by to see it over; then offering prayers of thanks to God for restoring peace to his house, and going back to his *books!* What in the name of all that feels, has he to do with *books,* when I am dying?"

She could not bear the notion which I had put into her head of Mr. Linton's philosophical resignation. Tossing about, she increased her feverish bewilderment to madness, and tore the pillow with her teeth, then raising herself up all burning, desired that I would open the window. We were in the middle of winter, the wind blew strong from the northeast, and I objected.

Both the expressions flitting over her face, and the changes of her moods, began to alarm me terribly; and brought to my recollection her former illness, and the doctor's injunction that she not be crossed.

A minute previously she was violent; now, supported on one arm, and not noticing my refusal to obey her, she seemed to find childish diversion in pulling the feathers from the rents she had just made, and ranging them on the sheet according to their different species: her mind had strayed to other associations.

"That's a turkey's," she murmured to herself; "and this is a wild duck's; and this is a pigeon's. Ah, they put pigeons' feathers in the pillows—no wonder I couldn't die! Let me take care to throw it on the floor when I lie down. And here is a moor-cock's; and this—I should know it among a thousand—it's a lapwing's. Bonny bird; wheeling over our heads in the middle of the moor. It wanted to get to its nest, for the clouds touched the swells, and it felt rain coming. This feather was picked up from the heath, the bird was not shot—we saw its nest in the winter, full of little skeletons. Heathcliff set a trap over it, and the old ones dare not come. I made him promise he'd never shoot a lapwing, after that, and he didn't. Yes, here are more! Did he shoot my lapwings, Nelly? Are they red, any of them? Let me look."

"Give over with that baby-work!" I interrupted, dragging the pillow away, and turning the holes towards the mattress, for she was removing its contents by handfuls. "Lie down and shut your eyes, you're wandering. There's a mess! The down is flying about like snow!"

I went here and there collecting it.

"I see in you, Nelly," she continued, dreamily, "an aged woman—you have grey hair, and bent shoulders. This bed is the Fairy Cave under Penistone Crag, and you are gathering elf-bolts to hurt our heifers; pretending, while I am near, that they are only locks of wool. That's what you'll come to fifty years hence; I know you are not so now. I'm not wandering, you are mistaken, or else I should believe you really *were* that withered hag, and I should think I *was* under Penistone Crag, and I'm conscious it's night, and there are two candles on the table making the black press shine like jet."

"The black press? where is that?" I asked. "You are talking in your sleep!"

"It's against the wall, as it always is," she replied. "It *does* appear odd—I see a face in it!"

"There's no press in the room, and never was," said I, resuming my seat, and looping up the curtain that I might watch her.

"Don't *you* see that face?" she enquired, gazing earnestly at the mirror.

And say what I could, I was incapable of making her comprehend it to be her own; so I rose and covered it with a shawl.

"It's behind there still!" she pursued, anxiously. "And it stirred. Who is it? I hope it will not come out when you are gone! Oh! Nelly, the room is haunted! I'm afraid of being alone!"

I took her hand in mine, and bid her be composed, for a succession of shudders convulsed her frame, and she *would* keep straining her gaze towards the glass.

"There's nobody here!" I insisted. "It was *yourself,* Mrs. Linton; you knew it a while since."

---

elf-bolts: relates to a superstition that elves inhabiting the cave can send out arrows.
press: oak cupboard used to store clothing.

"Myself!" she gasped, "and the clock is striking twelve! It's true, then, that's dreadful!"

Her fingers clutched the clothes, and gathered them over her eyes. I attempted to steal to the door with an intention of calling her husband; but I was summoned back by a piercing shriek. The shawl had dropped from the frame.

"Why what *is* the matter?" cried I. "Who is coward now? Wake up! That is the glass—the mirror, Mrs. Linton; and you see yourself in it, and there am I too by your side."

Trembling and bewildered, she held me fast, but the horror gradually passed from her countenance; its paleness gave place to a glow of shame.

"Oh, dear! I thought I was at home," she sighed. "I thought I was lying in my chamber at Wuthering Heights. Because I'm weak, my brain got confused, and I screamed unconsciously. Don't say anything; but stay with me. I dread sleeping, my dreams appal me."

"A sound sleep would do you good, ma'am," I answered; "and I hope this suffering will prevent your trying starving again."

"Oh, if I were but in my own bed in the old house!" she went on bitterly, wringing her hands, "And that wind sounding in the firs by the lattice. Do let me feel it—it comes straight down the moor—do let me have one breath!"

To pacify her, I held the casement ajar, a few seconds. A cold blast rushed through, I closed it, and returned to my post.

She lay still now: her face bathed in tears—Exhaustion of body had entirely subdued her spirit; our fiery Catherine was no better than a wailing child.

"How long is it since I shut myself in here?" she asked suddenly reviving.

"It was Monday evening," I replied, "and this is Thursday night, or rather Friday morning, at present."

"What! of the same week?" she exclaimed. "Only that brief time?"

"Long enough to live on nothing but cold water, and ill temper," observed I.

"Well, it seems a weary number of hours," she muttered doubtfully, "it must be more—I remember being in the parlour, after they had quarrelled; and Edgar being cruelly provoking, and me running into this room desperate—As soon as ever I had barred the door, utter blackness overwhelmed me, and I fell on the floor—I couldn't explain to Edgar how certain I felt of having a fit, or going raging mad, if he persisted in teasing me! I had no command of tongue, or brain, and he did not guess my agony, perhaps; it barely left me sense to try to escape from him and his voice—

Before I recovered sufficiently to see, and hear, it began to be dawn; and, Nelly, I'll tell you what I thought, and what has kept recurring and recurring till I feared for my reason — I thought as I lay there, with my head against that table leg, and my eyes dimly discerning the grey square of the window, that I was enclosed in the oak-panelled bed at home; and my heart ached with some great grief which, just waking, I could not recollect — I pondered, and worried myself to discover what it could be; and most strangely, the whole last seven years of my life grew a blank! I did not recall that they had been at all. I was a child; my father was just buried, and my misery arose from the separation that Hindley had ordered between me and Heathcliff — I was laid alone, for the first time, and, rousing from a dismal doze after a night of weeping — I lifted my hand to push the panels aside, it struck the table-top! I swept it along the carpet, and then, memory burst in — my late anguish was swallowed in a paroxysm of despair — I cannot say why I felt so wildly wretched — it must have been temporary derangement for there is scarcely cause — But, supposing at twelve years old, I had been wrenched from the Heights, and every early association, and my all in all, as Heathcliff was at that time, and been converted, at a stroke into Mrs. Linton, the lady of Thrushcross Grange, and the wife of a stranger; an exile, and outcast, thenceforth, from what had been my world — You may fancy a glimpse of the abyss where I grovelled! Shake your head, as you will, Nelly, *you* have helped to unsettle me! You should have spoken to Edgar, indeed you should, and compelled him to leave me quiet! Oh, I'm burning! I wish I were out of doors — I wish I were a girl again, half savage and hardy, and free . . . and laughing at injuries, not maddening under them! Why am I so changed? why does my blood rush into a hell of tumult at a few words? I'm sure I should be myself were I once among the heather on those hills. . . . Open the window again wide, fasten it open! Quick, why don't you move?"

"Because I won't give you your death of cold," I answered.

"You won't give me a chance of life, you mean," she added sullenly. "However, I'm not helpless yet, I'll open it myself."

And sliding from the bed before I could hinder her, she crossed the room, walking very uncertainly, threw it back, and bent out, careless of the frosty air that cut about her shoulders as keen as a knife.

I entreated, and finally attempted to force her to retire. But I soon found her delirious strength much surpassed mine; (she *was* delirious, I became convinced by her subsequent actions, and ravings).

There was no moon, and everything beneath lay in misty darkness; not a light gleamed from any house, far or near; all had been extinguished long ago; and those at Wuthering Heights were never visible . . . still she asserted she caught their shining.

"Look!" she cried eagerly, "that's my room, with the candle in it, and the trees swaying before it . . . and the other candle is in Joseph's garret . . . Joseph sits up late, doesn't he? He's waiting till I come home that he may lock the gate. Well, he'll wait a while yet. It's a rough journey, and a sad heart to travel it; and we must pass by Gimmerton Kirk, to go that journey! We've braved its ghosts often together, and dared each other to stand among the graves and ask them to come . . . But Heathcliff, if I dare you now, will you venture? If you do, I'll keep you. I'll not lie there by myself: they may bury me twelve feet deep, and throw the church down over me; but I won't rest till you are with me . . . I never will!"

She paused, and resumed with a strange smile. "He's considering . . . he'd rather I'd come to him! Find a way, then! not through that kirkyard . . . You are slow! Be content, you always followed me!"

Perceiving it vain to argue against her insanity, I was planning how I could reach something to wrap about her, without quitting my hold of herself, for I could not trust her alone by the gaping lattice, when, to my consternation, I heard the rattle of the door handle, and Mr. Linton entered. He had only then come from the library; and, in passing through the lobby, had noticed our talking and been attracted by curiosity, or fear, to examine what it signified, at that late hour.

"Oh, sir!" I cried, checking the exclamation risen to his lips at the sight which met him, and the bleak atmosphere of the chamber.

"My poor Mistress is ill, and she quite masters me; I cannot manage her at all, pray, come and persuade her to go to bed. Forget your anger, for she's hard to guide any way but her own."

"Catherine ill?" he said, hastening to us. "Shut the window, Ellen! Catherine! Why . . ."

He was silent; the haggardness of Mrs. Linton's appearance smote him speechless, and he could only glance from her to me in horrified astonishment.

"She's been fretting here," I continued, "and eating scarcely anything, and never complaining, she would admit none of us till this evening, and so we couldn't inform you of her state, as we were not aware of it ourselves, but it is nothing."

I felt I uttered my explanations awkwardly; the master frowned. "It is nothing, is it, Ellen Dean?" he said sternly. "You shall account more clearly for keeping me ignorant of this!" And he took his wife in his arms, and looked at her with anguish.

At first she gave him no glance of recognition . . . he was invisible to her abstracted gaze. The delirium was not fixed, however; having weaned her eyes from contemplating the outer darkness; by degrees, she centred her attention on him, and discovered who it was that held her.

"Ah! you are come, are you, Edgar Linton?" she said, with angry animation . . . "You are one of those things that are ever found when least wanted, and when you are wanted, never! I suppose we shall have plenty of lamentations, now . . . I see we shall . . . but they can't keep me from my narrow home out yonder—My resting place where I'm bound before Spring is over! There it is, not among the Lintons, mind, under the chapel-roof; but in the open air with a head-stone, and you may please yourself, whether you go to them, or come to me!"

"Catherine, what have you done?" commenced the master. "Am I nothing to you, any more? Do you love that wretch, Heath—"

"Hush!" cried Mrs. Linton. "Hush, this moment! You mention that name and I end the matter, instantly, by a spring from the window! What you touch at present, you may have; but my soul will be on that hilltop before you lay hands on me again. I don't want you, Edgar; I'm past wanting you . . . Return to your books . . . I'm glad you possess a consolation, for all you had in me is gone."

"Her mind wanders, sir," I interposed. "She has been talking nonsense the whole evening; but let her have quiet and proper attendance, and she'll rally . . . Hereafter, we must be cautious how we vex her."

"I desire no further advice from you," answered Mr. Linton. "You knew your mistress's nature, and you encouraged me to harass her. And not to give me one hint of how she has been these three days! It was heartless! months of sickness could not cause such a change!"

I began to defend myself, thinking it too bad to be blamed for another's wicked waywardness!

"I knew Mrs. Linton's nature to be headstrong and domineering," cried I; "but I didn't know that you wished to foster her fierce temper! I didn't know that, to humour her, I should wink at Mr. Heathcliff. I performed the duty of a faithful servant in telling you, and I have got a faithful servant's wages! Well, it will teach me to be careful next time. Next time you may gather intelligence for yourself!"

"The next time you bring a tale to me, you shall quit my service, Ellen Dean," he replied.

"You'd rather hear nothing about it, I suppose, then, Mr. Linton?" said I. "Heathcliff has your permission to come a courting to Miss, and to drop in at every opportunity your absence offers, on purpose to poison the mistress against you?"

Confused as Catherine was, her wits were alert at applying our conversation.

"Ah! Nelly has played traitor," she exclaimed, passionately. "Nelly is my hidden enemy—you witch! So you do seek elf-bolts to hurt us! Let me go, and I'll make her rue! I'll make her howl a recantation!"

A maniac's fury kindled under her brows; she struggled desperately to disengage herself from Linton's arms. I felt no inclination to tarry the event; and resolving to seek medical aid on my own responsibility, I quitted the chamber.

In passing the garden to reach the road, at a place where a bridle hook is driven into the wall, I saw something white moved irregularly, evidently by another agent than the wind. Notwithstanding my hurry, I stayed to ex-amine it, lest ever after I should have the conviction impressed on my imagination that it was a creature of the other world.

My surprise and perplexity were great to discover, by touch more than vision, Miss Isabella's springer Fanny, suspended to a handkerchief, and nearly at its last gasp.

I quickly released the animal, and lifted it into the garden. I had seen it follow its mistress upstairs, when she went to bed, and wondered much how it could have got out there, and what mischievous person had treated it so.

While untying the knot round the hook, it seemed to me that I repeat-edly caught the beat of horses' feet galloping at some distance; but there was such a number of things to occupy my reflections that I hardly gave the circumstance a thought, though it was a strange sound, in that place, at two o'clock in the morning.

Mr. Kenneth was fortunately just issuing from his house to see a patient in the village as I came up the street; and my account of Catherine Linton's malady induced him to accompany me back immediately.

He was a plain rough man; and he made no scruple to speak his doubts of her surviving this second attack; unless she were more submissive to his directions than she had shown herself before.

"Nelly Dean," said he, "I can't help fancying there's an extra cause for this. What has there been to do at the Grange? We've odd reports up here. A stout, hearty lass like Catherine does not fall ill for a trifle; and that sort of people should not either. It's hard work bringing them through fevers, and such things. How did it begin?"

"The master will inform you," I answered; "but you are acquainted with the Earnshaws' violent dispositions, and Mrs. Linton caps them all. I may say this; it commenced in a quarrel. She was struck during a tempest of pas-sion with a kind of fit. That's her account, at least; for she flew off in the height of it, and locked herself up. Afterwards, she refused to eat, and now she alternately raves, and remains in a half dream, knowing those about her, but having her mind filled with all sorts of strange ideas and illusions."

"Mr. Linton will be sorry?" observed Kenneth, interrogatively.

"Sorry? he'll break his heart should anything happen!" I replied. "Don't alarm him more than necessary."

"Well, I told him to beware," said my companion, "and he must bide the consequences of neglecting my warning! Hasn't he been thick with Mr. Heathcliff lately?"

"Heathcliff frequently visits at the Grange," answered I, "though more on the strength of the mistress having known him when a boy, than because the master likes his company. At present, he's discharged from the trouble of calling; owing to some presumptuous aspirations after Miss Linton which he manifested. I hardly think he'll be taken in again."

"And does Miss Linton turn a cold shoulder on him?" was the doctor's next question.

"I'm not in her confidence," returned I, reluctant to continue the subject.

"No, she's a sly one," he remarked, shaking his head. "She keeps her own counsel! But she's a real little fool. I have it from good authority, that, last night, and a pretty night it was! she and Heathcliff were walking in the plantation at the back of your house, above two hours; and he pressed her not to go in again, but just mount his horse and away with him! My informant said she could only put him off by pledging her word of honour to be prepared on their first meeting after that, when it was to be, he didn't hear, but you urge Mr. Linton to look sharp!"

This news filled me with fresh fears: I outstripped Kenneth, and ran most of the way back. The little dog was yelping in the garden yet. I spared a minute to open the gate for it, but instead of going to the house door, it coursed up and down snuffing the grass, and would have escaped to the road, had I not seized and conveyed it in with me.

On ascending to Isabella's room, my suspicions were confirmed; it was empty. Had I been a few hours sooner, Mrs. Linton's illness might have arrested her rash step. But what could be done now? There was a bare possibility of overtaking them if pursued instantly. *I* could not pursue them, however; and I dare not rouse the family, and fill the place with confusion; still less unfold the business to my master, absorbed as he was in his present calamity, and having no heart to spare for a second grief!

I saw nothing for it, but to hold my tongue, and suffer matters to take their course: and Kenneth being arrived, I went with a badly composed countenance to announce him.

Catherine lay in a troubled sleep; her husband had succeeded in soothing the access of frenzy; he now hung over her pillow, watching every shade, and every change of her painfully expressive features.

The doctor, on examining the case for himself, spoke hopefully to him of its having a favourable termination, if we could only preserve around her perfect and constant tranquillity. To me, he signified the threatening danger was, not so much death, as permanent alienation of intellect.

I did not close my eyes that night, nor did Mr. Linton; indeed, we never went to bed: and the servants were all up long before the usual hour, moving through the house with stealthy tread, and exchanging whispers as they encountered each other in their vocations. Everyone was active, but Miss Isabella; and they began to remark how sound she slept—her brother too asked if she had risen, and seemed impatient for her presence, and hurt that she showed so little anxiety for her sister-in-law.

I trembled lest he should send me to call her; but I was spared the pain of being the first proclaimant of her flight. One of the maids, a thoughtless girl, who had been on an early errand to Gimmerton, came panting upstairs, open-mouthed, and dashed into the chamber, crying,

"Oh, dear, dear! What mun we have next? Master, master, our young lady—"

"Hold your noise!" cried I hastily, enraged at her clamorous manner.

"Speak lower, Mary—What is the matter?" said Mr. Linton. "What ails your young lady?"

"She's gone, she's gone! Yon' Heathcliff's run off wi' her!" gasped the girl.

"That is not true!" exclaimed Linton, rising in agitation. "It cannot be—how has the idea entered your head? Ellen Dean, go and seek her—it is incredible—it cannot be."

As he spoke he took the servant to the door, and, then, repeated his demand to know her reasons for such an assertion.

"Why, I met on the road a lad that fetches milk here," she stammered, "and he asked whether we weren't in trouble at the Grange—I thought he meant for Missis's sickness, so I answered, yes. Then says he, 'They's some body gone after 'em, I guess?' I stared. He saw I knew naught about it, and he told how a gentleman and lady had stopped to have a horse's shoe fastened at a blacksmith's shop, two miles out of Gimmerton, not very long after midnight! and how the blacksmith's lass had got up to spy who they were: she knew them both directly—And she noticed the man, Heathcliff it was, she felt certain, nob'dy could mistake him, besides—put a sovereign in her father's hand for payment. The lady had a cloak about her face; but having desired a sup of water, while she drank, it fell back, and she saw her very plain—Heathcliff held both bridles as they rode on, and they set their faces from the village, and went as fast as the rough roads would let them. The lass said nothing to her father, but she told it all over Gimmerton this morning."

I ran and peeped, for form's sake into Isabella's room: confirming, when I returned, the servant's statement—Mr. Linton had resumed his seat by the bed; on my re-entrance, he raised his eyes, read the meaning of my blank aspect, and dropped them without giving an order, or uttering a word.

"Are we to try any measures for overtaking and bringing her back?" I inquired. "How should we do?"

"She went of her own accord," answered the master; "she had a right to go if she pleased—Trouble me no more about her—Hereafter she is only my sister in name; not because I disown her, but because she has disowned me."

And that was all he said on the subject; he did not make a single inquiry further, or mention her in any way, except directing me to send what property she had in the house to her fresh home, wherever it was, when I knew it.

CHAPTER XIII

For two months the fugitives remained absent; in those two months, Mrs. Linton encountered and conquered the worst shock of what was denominated a brain fever. No mother could have nursed an only child more devotedly than Edgar tended her. Day and night, he was watching, and patiently enduring all the annoyances that irritable nerves and a shaken reason could inflict: and, though Kenneth remarked that what he saved from the grave would only recompense his care by forming the source of constant future anxiety, in fact, that his health and strength were being sacrificed to preserve a mere ruin of humanity, he knew no limits in gratitude and joy, when Catherine's life was declared out of danger; and hour after hour, he would sit beside her, tracing the gradual return to bodily health, and flattering his too sanguine hopes with the illusion that her mind would settle back to its right balance also, and she would soon be entirely her former self.

The first time she left her chamber was at the commencement of the following March. Mr. Linton had put on her pillow, in the morning, a handful of golden crocuses; her eye, long stranger to any gleam of pleasure, caught them in waking, and shone delighted as she gathered them eagerly together.

"These are the earliest flowers at the Heights!" she exclaimed. "They remind me of soft thaw winds, and warm sunshine, and nearly melted snow—Edgar, is there not a south wind, and is not the snow almost gone?"

"The snow is quite gone down here, darling!" replied her husband; "and I only see two white spots on the whole range of moors—The sky is blue, and the larks are singing, and the becks and brooks are all brim full. Catherine; last spring at this time, I was longing to have you under this roof—now, I wish you were a mile or two up those hills, the air blows so sweetly, I feel that it would cure you."

"I shall never be there, but once more!" said the invalid; "and then you'll leave me, and I shall remain, forever. Next spring you'll long again to have me under this roof, and you'll look back and think you were happy today."

Linton lavished on her the kindest caresses, and tried to cheer her by the fondest words; but, vaguely regarding the flowers, she let the tears collect on her lashes, and stream down her cheeks unheeding.

We knew she was really better, and therefore decided that long confinement to a single place produced much of this despondency, and it might be partially removed by a change of scene.

The master told me to light a fire in the many-weeks-deserted parlour, and to set an easy-chair in the sunshine by the window; and then he brought her down, and she sat a long while enjoying the genial heat, and, as we expected, revived by the objects round her, which, though familiar, were free from the dreary associations investing her hated sick-chamber. By evening, she seemed greatly exhausted; yet no arguments could persuade her to return to that apartment, and I had to arrange the parlour sofa for her bed, till another room could be prepared.

To obviate the fatigue of mounting and descending the stairs, we fitted up this, where you lie at present; on the same floor with the parlour: and she was soon strong enough to move from one to the other, leaning on Edgar's arm.

Ah, I thought myself, she might recover, so waited on as she was. And there was double cause to desire it, for on her existence depended that of another; we cherished the hope that in a little while, Mr. Linton's heart would be gladdened, and his lands secured from a stranger's gripe, by the birth of an heir.

I should mention that Isabella sent to her brother, some six weeks from her departure a short note, announcing her marriage with Heathcliff. It appeared dry and cold; but at the bottom, was dotted in with pencil, an obscure apology, and an entreaty for kind remembrance, and reconciliation, if her proceeding had offended him; asserting that she could not help it then, and being done, she had now no power to repeal it.

Linton did not reply to this, I believe; and in a fortnight more, I got a long letter which I considered odd coming from the pen of a bride just out of the honeymoon. I'll read it, for I keep it yet. Any relic of the dead is precious, if they were valued living.

DEAR ELLEN, it begins.

I came last night to Wuthering Heights, and heard, for the first time, that Catherine has been, and is yet, very ill. I must not write to her I suppose, and my brother is either too angry, or too distressed to answer what I send him. Still, I must write to somebody, and the only choice left me is you.

Inform Edgar that I'd give the world to see his face again—that my heart returned to Thrushcross Grange in twenty-four hours after I left it, and is there at this moment, full of warm feelings for him and Catherine! *I can't follow it though*—(those words are underlined)—they need not expect me, and they may draw what conclusions they please; taking care however, to lay nothing at the door of my weak will, or deficient affection.

The remainder of the letter is for yourself alone. I want to ask you two questions: the first is,

How did you contrive to preserve the common sympathies of human nature when you resided here? I cannot recognize any sentiment which those around share with me.

The second question, I have great interest in; it is this—

Is Mr. Heathcliff a man? If so, is he mad? And if not, is he a devil? I shan't tell my reasons for making this inquiry; but, I beseech you to explain, if you can, what I have married—that is, when you call to see me; and you must call, Ellen, very soon. Don't write, but come, and bring me something from Edgar.

Now, you shall hear how I have been received in my new home, as I am led to imagine the Heights will be. It is to amuse myself that I dwell on such subjects as the lack of external comforts; they never occupy my thoughts, except at the moment when I miss them—I should laugh and dance for joy, if I found their absence was the total of my miseries, and the rest was an unnatural dream!

The sun set behind the Grange, as we turned on to the moors; by that, I judged it to be six o'clock; and my companion halted half an hour, to inspect the park, and the gardens, and, probably, the place itself, as well as he could; so it was dark when we dismounted in the paved yard of the farmhouse, and your old fellow-servant, Joseph, issued out to receive us by the light of a dip candle. He did it with a courtesy that redounded to his credit. His first act was to elevate his torch to a level with my face, squint malignantly, project his upper lip, and turn away.

Then he took the two horses, and led them into the stables; reappearing for the purpose of locking the outer gate, as if we lived in an ancient castle.

Heathcliff stayed to speak to him, and I entered the kitchen—a dingy, untidy hole; I dare say you would not know it, it is so changed since it was in your charge.

By the fire stood a ruffianly child, strong in limb, and dirty in garb, with a look of Catherine in his eyes, and about his mouth.

"This is Edgar's legal nephew," I reflected—"mine in a manner; I must shake hands, and—yes—I must kiss him. It is right to establish a good understanding at the beginning."

I approached, and, attempting to take his chubby fist, said—

"How do you do, my dear?"

He replied in a jargon I did not comprehend.

"Shall you and I be friends, Hareton?" was my next essay at conversation.

An oath, and a threat to set Throttler on me if I did not "frame off" rewarded my perseverance.

"Hey, Throttler, lad!" whispered the little wretch, rousing a half-bred bulldog from its lair in a corner. "Now, wilt tuh be ganging?" he asked authoritatively.

Love for my life urged a compliance; I stepped over the threshold to wait till the others should enter. Mr. Heathcliff was nowhere visible; and Joseph, whom I followed to the stables, and requested to accompany me in, after staring and muttering to himself, screwed up his nose, and replied—

"Mim! mim! mim! Did iver Christian body hear owt like it? Minching un' munching! Hah can Aw tell whet ye say?"

"I say, I wish you to come with me into the house!" I cried, thinking him deaf, yet highly disgusted at his rudeness.

"Nor nuh me! Aw getten summut else to do," he answered, and continued his work, moving his lantern jaws meanwhile, and surveying my dress and countenance (the former a great deal too fine, but the latter, I'm sure, as sad as he could desire) with sovereign contempt.

I walked round the yard, and through a wicket, to another door, at which I took the liberty of knocking, in hopes some more civil servant might show himself.

After a short suspense it was opened by a tall, gaunt man, without neckerchief, and otherwise extremely slovenly, his features were lost in masses of shaggy hair that hung on his shoulders; and *his* eyes, too, were like a ghostly Catherine's, with all their beauty annihilated.

"What's your business here?" he demanded, grimly. "Who are you?"

"My name *was* Isabella Linton," I replied. "You've seen me before, sir. I'm lately married to Mr. Heathcliff; and he has brought me here—I suppose by your permission."

"Is he come back, then?" asked the hermit, glaring like a hungry wolf.

"Yes—we came just now," I said; "but he left me by the kitchen door; and when I would have gone in, your little boy played sentinel over the place, and frightened me off by the help of a bulldog."

"It's well the hellish villain has kept his word!" growled my future host, searching the darkness beyond me in expectation of discovering Heathcliff,

---

mim: prim; genteel.
Minching un' munching: mincing and phony speech.

and then he indulged in a soliloquy of execrations, and threats of what he would have done had the "fiend" deceived him.

I repented having tried this second entrance; and was almost inclined to slip away before he finished cursing, but ere I could execute that intention, he ordered me in, and shut and re-fastened the door.

There was a great fire, and that was all the light in the huge apartment, whose floor had grown a uniform grey; and the once brilliant pewter dishes which used to attract my gaze when I was a girl partook of a similar obscurity, created by tarnish and dust.

I inquired whether I might call the maid, and be conducted to my bedroom? Mr. Earnshaw vouchsafed no answer. He walked up and down, with his hands in his pockets, apparently quite forgetting my presence; and his abstraction was evidently so deep, and his whole aspect so misanthropical, that I shrank from disturbing him again.

You'll not be surprised, Ellen, at my feeling particularly cheerless, seated in worse than solitude, on that inhospitable hearth, and remembering that four miles distant lay my delightful home, containing the only people I loved on earth: and there might as well be the Atlantic to part us, instead of those four miles, I could not overpass them!

I questioned with myself—where must I turn for comfort? and—mind you don't tell Edgar, or Catherine—above every sorrow beside, this rose pre-eminent—despair at finding nobody who could or would be my ally against Heathcliff!

I had sought shelter at Wuthering Heights, almost gladly, because I was secured by that arrangement from living alone with him; but he knew the people we were coming amongst, and he did not fear their intermeddling.

I sat and thought a doleful time; the clock struck eight, and nine, and still my companion paced to and fro, his head bent on his breast, and perfectly silent, unless a groan, or a bitter ejaculation forced itself out at intervals.

I listened to detect a woman's voice in the house, and filled the interim with wild regrets, and dismal anticipations, which, at last, spoke audibly in irrepressible sighing, and weeping.

I was not aware how openly I grieved, till Earnshaw halted opposite, in his measured walk, and gave me a stare of newly awakened surprise. Taking advantage of his recovered attention, I exclaimed—

"I'm tired with my journey, and I want to go to bed! Where is the maid-servant? Direct me to her, as she won't come to me!"

"We have none," he answered; "you must wait on yourself!"

"Where must I sleep, then?" I sobbed—I was beyond regarding self-respect, weighed down by fatigue and wretchedness.

"Joseph will show you Heathcliff's chamber," said he; "open that door—he's in there."

I was going to obey, but he suddenly arrested me, and added in the strangest tone —

"Be so good as to turn your lock, and draw your bolt — don't omit it!"

"Well!" I said. "But why, Mr. Earnshaw?" I did not relish the notion of deliberately fastening myself in with Heathcliff.

"Look here!" he replied, pulling from his waistcoat a curiously constructed pistol, having a double-edged spring knife attached to the barrel. "That's a great tempter to a desperate man, is it not? I cannot resist going up with this every night, and trying his door. If once I find it open he's done for! I do it invariably, even though the minute before I have been recalling a hundred reasons that should make me refrain — it is some devil that urges me to thwart my own schemes by killing him — you fight against that devil, for love, as long as you may; when the time comes, not all the angels in heaven shall save him!"

I surveyed the weapon inquisitively; a hideous notion struck me. How powerful I should be possessing such an instrument! I took it from his hand, and touched the blade. He looked astonished at the expression my face assumed during a brief second. It was not horror, it was covetousness. He snatched the pistol back, jealously; shut the knife, and returned it to its concealment.

"I don't care if you tell him," said he. "Put him on his guard, and watch for him. You know the terms we are on, I see; his danger does not shock you."

"What has Heathcliff done to you?" I asked. "In what has he wronged you, to warrant this appalling hatred? Wouldn't it be wiser to bid him quit the house?"

"No!" thundered Earnshaw, "should he offer to leave me, he's a dead man, persuade him to attempt it, and you are a murderess! Am I to lose *all*, without a chance of retrieval? Is Hareton to be a beggar? Oh, damnation! I *will* have it back; and I'll have *his* gold too; and then his blood; and hell shall have his soul! It will be ten times blacker with that guest than ever it was before!"

You've acquainted me, Ellen, with your old master's habits. He is clearly on the verge of madness — he was so, last night, at least. I shuddered to be near him, and thought on the servant's ill-bred moroseness as comparatively agreeable.

He now recommenced his moody walk, and I raised the latch, and escaped into the kitchen.

Joseph was bending over the fire, peering into a large pan that swung above it; and a wooden bowl of oatmeal stood on the settle close by. The contents of the pan began to boil, and he turned to plunge his hand into the bowl; I conjectured that this preparation was probably for our supper, and, being hungry, I resolved it should be eatable—so, crying out, sharply—"*I'll* make the porridge!" I removed the vessel out of his reach, and proceeded to take off my hat and riding habit. "Mr. Earnshaw," I continued, "directs me to wait on myself—I will—I'm not going to act the lady among you, for fear I should starve."

"Gooid Lord!" he muttered, sitting down, and stroking his ribbed stockings from the knee to the ankle. "If they's tuh be fresh ortherings— just when Aw getten used tuh two maisters, if Aw mun hev a *mistress* set o'er my heead, it's loike time tuh be flitting. Aw niver *did* think tuh say t' day ut Aw mud lave th' owld place—but Aw daht it's nigh at hend!"

This lamentation drew no notice from me; I went briskly to work; sighing to remember a period when it would have been all merry fun; but compelled speedily to drive off the remembrance. It racked me to recall past happiness, and the greater peril there was of conjuring up its apparition, the quicker the thible ran round, and the faster the handfuls of meal fell into the water.

Joseph beheld my style of cookery with growing indignation.

"Thear!" he ejaculated, "Hareton, thah willn't sup thy porridge tuh neeght; they'll be nowt bud lumps as big as maw nave. Thear, agean! Aw'd fling in bowl un all, if Aw wer yah! Thear, pale t' guilp off, un' then yah'll hae done wi't. Bang, bang. It's a marcy t' bothom isn't deaved aht!"

It *was* rather a rough mess, I own, when poured into the basins; four had been provided, and a gallon pitcher of new milk was brought from the dairy, which Hareton seized and commenced drinking and spilling from the expansive lip.

I expostulated, and desired that he should have his in a mug; affirming that I could not taste the liquid treated so dirtily. The old cynic chose to be vastly offended at this nicety; assuring me, repeatedly, that "the bairn was every bit as gooid" as I, "and every bit as wollsome," and wondering how I could fashion to be so conceited; meanwhile, the infant ruffian continued sucking; and glowered up at me defyingly, as he slavered into the jug.

"I shall have my supper in another room," I said. "Have you no place you call a parlour?"

If they's tuh be fresh ortherings: If there's going to be new ways.
Aw daht: I'm afraid.
thible: spoon.
maw nave: my fist.
pale t' guilp off: skim the top off.
deaved aht: knocked out.
wollsome: wholesome.

"*Parlour!*" he echoed, sneeringly, "*parlour!* Nay, we've noa *parlours.* If yah dunnut loike wer company, they's maister's; un' if yah dunnut loike maister, they's us."

"Then I shall go upstairs," I answered; "show me a chamber."

I put my basin on a tray, and went myself to fetch some more milk.

With great grumblings, the fellow rose, and preceded me in my ascent: we mounted to the garrets; he opening a door, now and then, to look into the apartments we passed.

"Here's a rahm," he said, at last, flinging back a cranky board on hinges. "It's weel eneugh tuh ate a few porridge in. They's a pack uh corn i' t' corner, thear, meeterly clane; if yah're feared uh muckying yer grand silk cloes, spread her hankerchir ut t' top on't."

The "rahm" was a kind of lumber-hole smelling strong of malt and grain; various sacks of which articles were piled around, leaving a wide, bare space in the middle.

"Why, man!" I exclaimed, facing him angrily, "this is not a place to sleep in. I wish to see my bedroom."

"*Bed-rume!*" he repeated, in a tone of mockery. "Yah's see all t' *bed-rumes* thear is—yon's mine."

He pointed into the second garret, only differing from the first in being more naked about the walls, and having a large, low, curtainless bed, with an indigo-coloured quilt, at one end.

"What do I want with yours?" I retorted. "I suppose Mr. Heathcliff does not lodge at the top of the house, does he?"

"Oh! it's Maister *Hathecliff's* yah're wenting!" cried he, as if making a new discovery. "Couldn't ye uh said soa, at onst? un' then, Aw mud ha' telled ye, baht all this wark, ut that's just one yah cannut sea—he allas keeps it locked, un' nob'dy iver mells on't but hisseln."

"You've a nice house, Joseph," I could not refrain from observing, "and pleasant inmates; and I think the concentrated essence of all the madness in the world took up its abode in my brain the day I linked my fate with theirs! However, that is not to the present purpose—there are other rooms. For Heaven's sake, be quick, and let me settle somewhere!"

He made no reply to this adjuration; only plodding doggedly down the wooden steps, and halting before an apartment which, from that halt, and the superior quality of its furniture, I conjectured to be the best one.

---

meeterly clane: tolerably clean.
at onst: at once.
nob'dy iver mells on't but hisseln: nobody ever meddles with it except him.

There was a carpet, a good one; but the pattern was obliterated by dust; a fireplace hung with cut paper dropping to pieces; a handsome oak bedstead with ample crimson curtains of rather expensive material, and modern make. But they had evidently experienced rough usage, the valances hung in festoons, wrenched from their rings; and the iron rod supporting them was bent in an arc, on one side, causing the drapery to trail upon the floor. The chairs were also damaged, many of them severely; and deep indentations deformed the panels of the walls.

I was endeavouring to gather resolution for entering, and taking possession, when my fool of a guide announced—

"This here is t' maister's."

My supper by this time was cold, my appetite gone, and my patience exhausted. I insisted on being provided instantly with a place of refuge, and means of repose.

"Whear the divil," began the religious elder. "The Lord bless us! The Lord forgive us! Whear the *hell* wold ye gang? ye marred, wearisome nowt! Yah seen all bud Hareton's bit uf a cham'er. There's nut another hoile tuh lig dahn in i' th' hahse!"

I was so vexed, I flung my tray and its contents on the ground; and then seated myself at the stairs-head, hid my face in my hands, and cried.

"Ech! ech!" exclaimed Joseph. "Weel done, Miss Cathy! weel done, Miss Cathy! Hahsiver, t' maister sall just tum'le o'er them brocken pots; un' then we's hear summut; we's hear hah it's tuh be. Gooid-for-nowt madling! yah desarve pining froo this tuh Churstmas, flinging t' precious gifts uh God under fooit i' yer flaysome rages! Bud, Aw'm mista'en if yah shew yer sperrit long. Will Hathecliff bide sich bonny ways, think ye? Aw nobbut wish he muh cotch ye i' that plisky. Aw nobbut wish he may."

And so he went scolding to his den beneath, taking the candle with him, and I remained in the dark.

The period of reflection succeeding this silly action, compelled me to admit the necessity of smothering my pride, and choking my wrath, and bestirring myself to remove its effects.

An unexpected aid presently appeared in the shape of Throttler, whom I now recognized as a son of our old Skulker; it had spent its whelphood at the Grange, and was given by my father to Mr. Hindley. I fancy it knew me—it pushed its nose against mine by way of salute, and then hastened to devour the porridge, while I groped from step to step, collecting the shat-

---

valances: curtain decorations.
madling: fool.
pining: staring.
plisky: rage.

tered earthenware, and drying the splatters of milk from the bannisters with my pocket-handkerchief.

Our labours were scarcely over when I heard Earnshaw's tread in the passage; my assistant tucked in his tail, and pressed to the wall; I stole into the nearest doorway. The dog's endeavour to avoid him was unsuccessful; as I guessed by a scutter downstairs, and a prolonged, piteous yelping. I had better luck. He passed on, entered his chamber, and shut the door.

Directly after Joseph came up with Hareton, to put him to bed. I had found shelter in Hareton's room, and the old man on seeing me, said—

"They's rahm fur boath yah, un' yer pride, nah, Aw sud think i' the' hahse. It's empty; yah muh hev it all tuh yerseln, un Him as allas makes a third, i' sich ill company!"

Gladly did I take advantage of this intimation; and the minute I flung myself into a chair, by the fire, I nodded, and slept.

My slumber was deep, and sweet; though over far too soon. Mr. Heathcliff awoke me; he had just come in, and demanded, in his loving manner, what I was doing there.

I told him the cause of my staying up so late—that he had the key of our room in his pocket.

The adjective *our* gave mortal offence. He swore it was not, nor ever should be mine; and he'd—but I'll not repeat his language, nor describe his habitual conduct; he is ingenious and unresting in seeking to gain my abhorrence! I sometimes wonder at him with an intensity that deadens my fear: yet, I assure you, a tiger, or a venomous serpent could not rouse terror in me equal to that which he wakens. He told me of Catherine's illness, and accused my brother of causing it; promising that I should be Edgar's proxy in suffering, till he could get a hold of him.

I do hate him—I am wretched—I have been a fool! Beware of uttering one breath of this to anyone at the Grange. I shall expect you every day—don't disappoint me!

Isabella

CHAPTER XIV

As soon as I had perused this epistle, I went to the master, and informed him that his sister had arrived at the Heights, and sent me a letter expressing her sorrow for Mrs. Linton's situation, and her ardent desire to see him;

Him as allas makes a third: reference to the Devil.

with a wish that he would transmit to her, as early as possible, some token of forgiveness by me.

"Forgiveness?" said Linton, "I have nothing to forgive her, Ellen—you may call at Wuthering Heights this afternoon, if you like, and say that I am not *angry*, but I'm *sorry* to have lost her: especially as I can never think she'll be happy. It is out of the question my going to see her, however; we are eternally divided; and should she really wish to oblige me, let her persuade the villain she has married to leave the country."

"And you won't write her a little note, sir?" I asked, imploringly.

"No," he answered. "It is needless. My communication with Heathcliff's family shall be as sparing as his with mine. It shall not exist!"

Mr. Edgar's coldness depressed me exceedingly; and all the way from the Grange, I puzzled my brains how to put more heart into what he said, when I repeated it; and how to soften his refusal of even a few lines to console Isabella.

I daresay she had been on the watch for me since morning: I saw her looking through the lattice, as I came up the garden causeway, and I nodded to her; but she drew back, as if afraid of being observed.

I entered without knocking. There never was such a dreary, dismal scene as the formerly cheerful house presented! I must confess that, if I had been in the young lady's place, I would, at least, have swept the hearth, and wiped the tables with a duster. But she already partook of the pervading spirit of neglect which encompassed her. Her pretty face was wan and listless; her hair uncurled; some locks hanging lankly down, and some carelessly twisted round her head. Probably she had not touched her dress since yester evening.

Hindley was not there. Mr. Heathcliff sat at a table, turning over some papers in his pocket-book; but he rose when I appeared, asked me how I did, quite friendly, and offered me a chair.

He was the only thing there that seemed decent, and I thought he never looked better. So much had circumstances altered their positions, that he would certainly have struck a stranger as a born and bred gentleman, and his wife as a thorough little slattern!

She came forward eagerly to greet me; and held out one hand to take the expected letter.

I shook my head. She wouldn't understand the hint, but followed me to a sideboard, where I went to lay my bonnet, and importuned me in a whisper to give her directly what I had brought.

Heathcliff guessed the meaning of her manoeuvres, and said—

"If you have got anything for Isabella, as no doubt you have, Nelly, give it to her. You needn't make a secret of it; we have no secrets between us."

"Oh, I have nothing," I replied, thinking it best to speak the truth at once. "My master bid me tell his sister that she must not expect either a letter or a visit from him at present. He sends his love, ma'am, and his wishes for your happiness, and his pardon for the grief you have occasioned; but he thinks that after this time, his household, and the household here, should drop inter-communication; as nothing could come of keeping it up."

Mrs. Heathcliff's lip quivered slightly, and she returned to her seat in the window. Her husband took his stand on the hearthstone, near me, and began to put questions concerning Catherine.

I told him as much as I thought proper of her illness, and he extorted from me, by cross-examination, most of the facts connected with its origin.

I blamed her, as she deserved, for bringing it all on herself; and ended by hoping that he would follow Mr. Linton's example, and avoid future interference with his family, for good or evil.

"Mrs. Linton is now just recovering," I said, "she'll never be like she was, but her life is spared, and if you really have a regard for her, you'll shun crossing her way again. Nay, you'll move out of this country entirely; and that you may not regret it, I'll inform you Catherine Linton is as different now, from your old friend Catherine Earnshaw, as that young lady is different from me! Her appearance is changed greatly, her character much more so; and the person, who is compelled, of necessity, to be her companion, will only sustain his affection hereafter, by the remembrance of what she once was, by common humanity, and a sense of duty!"

"That is quite possible," remarked Heathcliff, forcing himself to seem calm, "quite possible that your master should have nothing but common humanity, and a sense of duty to fall back upon. But do you imagine that I shall leave Catherine to his *duty* and *humanity?* and can you compare my feelings respecting Catherine, to his? Before you leave this house, I must exact a promise from you, that you'll get me an interview with her — consent, or refuse, I *will* see her! What do you say?"

"I say, Mr. Heathcliff," I replied, "you must not — you never shall through my means. Another encounter between you and the master, would kill her altogether!"

"With your aid, that may be avoided," he continued, "and should there be danger of such an event — should he be the cause of adding a single trouble more to her existence — Why, I think, I shall be justified in going to extremes! I wish you had sincerity enough to tell me whether Catherine would suffer greatly from his loss. The fear that she would restrains me: and there you see the distinction between our feelings — Had he been in my place, and I in his, though I hated him with a hatred that turned my life to gall, I never would have raised a hand against him. You may look incredulous, if you please! I never would have banished him from her society, as long as she desired his. The moment her regard ceased, I would have torn his heart out, and drunk his blood! But, till then, if you don't believe me, you don't know me—till then, I would have died by inches before I touched a single hair of his head!"

"And yet," I interrupted, "you have no scruples in completely ruining all hopes of her perfect restoration, by thrusting yourself in to her remembrance, now, when she has nearly forgotten you, and involving her in a new tumult of discord, and distress."

"You suppose she has nearly forgotten me?" he said. "Oh! Nelly, you know she has not! You know as well as I do, that for every thought she spends on Linton, she spends a thousand on me! At a most miserable period of my life, I had a notion of the kind, it haunted me on my return to the neighborhood, last summer, but only her own assurance, could make me admit the horrible idea again. And then, Linton would be nothing, nor Hindley, nor all the dreams that ever I dreamt. Two words would comprehend my future—*death* and *hell*—existence, after losing her, would be hell.

"Yet I was a fool to fancy for a moment that she valued Edgar Linton's attachment more than mine—If he loved with all the powers of his puny being, he couldn't love as much in eighty years, as I could in a day. And Catherine has a heart as deep as I have; the sea could be as readily contained in that horse-trough, as her whole affection be monopolized by him— Tush! He is scarcely a degree dearer to her than her dog, or her horse—It is not in him to be loved like me, how can she love in him what he has not?"

"Catherine and Edgar are as fond of each other, as any two people can be!" cried Isabella with sudden vivacity. "No one has a right to talk in that manner, and I won't hear my brother depreciated in silence!"

"Your brother is wondrous fond of you too, isn't he?" observed Heathcliff scornfully. "He turns you adrift on the world with surprising alacrity."

"He is not aware of what I suffer," she replied. "I didn't tell him that."

"You have been telling him something, then—you have written, have you?"

"To say that I was married, I did write—you saw the note."

"And nothing since?"

"No."

"My young lady is looking sadly the worse for her change of condition," I remarked. "Somebody's love comes short in her case, obviously—whose I may guess; but, perhaps, I shouldn't say."

"I should guess it was her own," said Heathcliff. "She degenerates into a mere slut! She is tired of trying to please me, uncommonly early—You'd hardly credit it, but the very morrow of our wedding, she was weeping to go home. However, she'll suit this house so much the better for not being over nice, and I'll take care she does not disgrace me by rambling abroad."

"Well, sir," returned I, "I hope you'll consider that Mrs. Heathcliff is accustomed to be looked after, and waited on; and that she has been brought up like an only daughter whom everyone was ready to serve — You must let her have a maid to keep things tidy about her, and you must treat her kindly — Whatever be your notion of Mr. Edgar, you cannot doubt that she has a capacity for strong attachments or she wouldn't have abandoned the elegancies, and comforts, and friends of her former home, to fix contentedly, in such a wilderness as this, with you."

"She abandoned them under a delusion," he answered; "picturing in me a hero of romance, and expecting unlimited indulgences from my chivalrous devotion. I can hardly regard her in the light of a rational creature, so obstinately has she persisted in forming a fabulous notion of my character, and acting on the false impressions she cherished. But at last, I think she begins to know me — I don't perceive the silly smiles and grimaces that provoked me, at first; and the senseless incapability of discerning that I was in earnest when I gave her my opinion of her infatuation, and herself — It was a marvellous effort of perspicacity to discover that I did not love her. I believed at one time, no lessons could teach her that! and yet it is poorly learnt; for this morning she announced, as a piece of appalling intelligence, that I had actually succeeded in making her hate me! A positive labour of Hercules, I assure you! If it be achieved, I have cause to return thanks — Can I trust your assertion, Isabella? are you sure you hate me? If I let you alone for half-a-day, won't you come sighing and wheedling to me again? I dare say she would rather I had seemed all tenderness before you; it wounds her vanity to have the truth exposed. But I don't care who knows that the passion was wholly on one side, and I never told her a lie about it. She cannot accuse me of showing a bit of deceitful softness. The first thing she saw me do, on coming out of the Grange, was to hang up her little dog, and when she pleaded for it, the first words I uttered, were a wish that I had the hanging of every being belonging to her, except one: possibly, she took that exception for herself — But no brutality disgusted her — I suppose, she has an innate admiration of it, if only her precious person were secure from injury! Now, was it not the depth of absurdity — of genuine idiocy, for that pitiful, slavish, mean-minded brach to dream that I could love her? Tell your master, Nelly, that I never, in all my life, met with such an abject thing as she is. She even disgraces the name of Linton; and I've sometimes relented, from pure lack of invention, in my experiments on what she could

---

brach: dog, bitch mongrel.

endure, and still creep shamefully cringing back! But tell him also, to set his fraternal and magisterial heart at ease, that I keep strictly within the limits of the law—I have avoided, up to this period, giving her the slightest right to claim a separation; and what's more, she'd thank nobody for dividing us—if she desired to go she might—the nuisance of her presence outweighs the gratification to be derived from tormenting her!"

"Mr. Heathcliff," said I, "this is the talk of a madman, and your wife most likely is convinced you are mad; and, for that reason, she has borne with you hitherto: but now that you say she may go, she'll doubtless avail herself of the permission—You are not so bewitched, ma'am, are you, as to remain with him of your own accord?"

"Take care, Ellen!" answered Isabella, her eyes sparkling irefully—there was no misdoubting by their expression the full success of her partner's endeavours to make himself detested. "Don't put faith in a single word he speaks. He's a lying fiend, a monster, and not a human being! I've been told I might leave him before; and I've made the attempt, but I dare not repeat it! Only Ellen, promise you'll not mention a syllable of his infamous conversation to my brother or Catherine—whatever he may pretend, he wishes to provoke Edgar to desperation—he says he has married me on purpose to obtain power over him; and he shan't obtain it—I'll die first! I just hope, I pray that he may forget his diabolical prudence, and kill me! The single pleasure I can imagine is to die, or to see him dead!"

"There—that will do for the present!" said Heathcliff. "If you are called upon in a court of law, you'll remember her language, Nelly! And take a good look at that countenance—she's near the point which would suit me. No, you're not fit to be your own guardian, Isabella, now; and I, being your legal protector, must retain you in my custody, however distasteful the obligation may be—Go upstairs; I have something to say to Ellen Dean, in private. That's not the way—upstairs, I tell you! Why this is the road upstairs, child!"

He seized, and thrust her from the room; and returned muttering,

"I have no pity! I have no pity! The more the worms writhe, the more I yearn to crush out their entrails! It is a moral teething, and I grind with greater energy, in proportion to the increase of pain."

"Do you understand what the word pity means?" I said hastening to resume my bonnet. "Did you ever feel a touch of it in your life?"

"Put that down!" he interrupted, perceiving my intention to depart. "You are not going yet—Come here now, Nelly—I must either persuade, or compel you to aid me in fulfilling my determination to see Catherine, and that without delay—I swear that I meditate no harm; I don't desire to cause any disturbance, or to exasperate, or insult Mr. Linton; I only wish to hear from herself how she is, and why she has been ill; and to ask, if anything that I could do would be of use to her. Last night, I was in the Grange garden six hours, and I'll return there tonight; and every night I'll haunt the place, and every day, till I find an opportunity of entering. If Edgar Linton meets me, I shall not hesitate to knock him down, and give him enough to insure his quiescence while I stay—If his servants oppose me, I shall threaten them off with these pistols—But wouldn't it be better to prevent my coming in contact with them, or their master? And you could do it so easily! I'd warn you when I came, and then you might let me in unobserved, as soon as she was alone, and watch till I departed—your conscience quite calm, you would be hindering mischief."

I protested against playing that treacherous part in my employer's house; and besides, I urged the cruelty and selfishness of his destroying Mrs. Linton's tranquillity, for his satisfaction.

"The commonest occurrence startles her painfully," I said. "She's all nerves, and she couldn't bear the surprise, I'm positive—Don't persist, sir! or else, I shall be obliged to inform my master of your designs, and he'll take measures to secure his house and its inmates from any such unwarrantable intrusions!"

"In that case, I'll take measures to secure you, woman!" exclaimed Heathcliff, "you shall not leave Wuthering Heights till tomorrow morning. It is a foolish story to assert that Catherine could not bear to see me; and as to surprising her, I don't desire it, you must prepare her—ask her if I may come. You say she never mentions my name, and that I am never mentioned to her. To whom should she mention me if I am a forbidden topic in the house? She thinks you are all spies for her husband—Oh, I've no doubt she's in hell among you! I guess, by her silence as much as anything, what she feels. You say she is often restless, and anxious-looking—is that a proof of tranquillity? You talk of her mind being unsettled—How the devil could it be otherwise, in her frightful isolation? And that insipid, paltry creature attending her from *duty* and *humanity!* From *pity* and *charity.* He might as well plant an oak in a flower-pot, and expect it to thrive, as imagine he can restore her to vigour in the soil of his shallow cares! Let us settle it at once; will you stay here, and am I to fight my way to Catherine over Linton, and his footmen? Or will you be my friend, as you have been hitherto, and do what I request? Decide! because there is no reason for my lingering another minute, if you persist in your stubborn ill-nature!"

Well, Mr. Lockwood, I argued, and complained, and flatly refused him fifty times; but in the long run he forced me to an agreement—I engaged to carry a letter from him to my mistress; and, should she consent, I promised to let him have intelligence of Linton's next absence from home, when he might come, and get in as he was able—I wouldn't be there, and my fellow servants should be equally out of the way.

Was it right, or wrong? I fear it was wrong, though expedient. I thought I prevented another explosion by my compliance; and I thought too, it might create a favourable crisis in Catherine's mental illness: and then I remembered Mr. Edgar's stern rebuke of my carrying tales; and I tried to smooth away all disquietude on the subject, by affirming, with frequent iteration, that, that betrayal of trust, if it merited so harsh an appellation, should be the last.

Notwithstanding, my journey homeward was sadder than my journey thither; and many misgivings I had, ere I could prevail on myself to put the missive in Mrs. Linton's hand.

But here is Kenneth—I'll go down, and tell him how much better you are. My history is *dree,* as we say, and will serve to wile away another morning.

Dree, and dreary! I reflected as the good woman descended to receive the doctor; and not exactly of the kind which I should have chosen to amuse me; but never mind! I'll extract wholesome medicines from Mrs. Dean's bitter herbs; and firstly, let me beware of the fascination that lurks in Catherine Heathcliff's brilliant eyes. I should be in a curious taking if I surrendered my heart to that young person, and the daughter turned out a second edition of the mother![4]

CHAPTER XV

Another week over—and I am so many days nearer health, and spring! I have now heard all my neighbour's history, at different sittings, as the housekeeper could spare time from more important occupations. I'll continue it in her own words, only a little condensed. She is, on the whole, a very fair narrator and I don't think I could improve her style.

In the evening, she said, the evening of my visit to the Heights, I knew as well as if I saw him, that Mr. Heathcliff was about the place; and I shunned going out, because I still carried his letter in my pocket, and didn't want to be threatened, or teased any more.

I had made up my mind not to give it till my master went somewhere; as I could not guess how its receipt would affect Catherine. The conse-

---

dree: sad, pitiable.
taking: situation.

[4] End of Volume I of the 1847 edition. [ED.]

quence was that it did not reach her before the lapse of three days. The fourth was Sunday, and I brought it into her room, after the family were gone to church.

There was a man servant left to keep the house with me, and we generally made a practice of locking the doors during the hours of service; but on that occasion, the weather was so warm and pleasant that I set them wide open; and to fulfil my engagement, as I knew who would be coming, I told my companion that the mistress wished very much for some oranges, and he must run over to the village, and get a few, to be paid for on the morrow. He departed, and I went upstairs.

Mrs. Linton sat in a loose, white dress, with a light shawl over her shoulders, in the recess of the open window, as usual. Her thick, long hair had been partly removed at the beginning of her illness; and now, she wore it simply combed in its natural tresses over her temples and neck. Her appearance was altered, as I had told Heathcliff, but when she was calm, there seemed unearthly beauty in the change.

The flash of her eyes had been succeeded by a dreamy and melancholy softness: they no longer gave the impression of looking at the objects around her; they appeared always to gaze beyond, and far beyond—you would have said out of this world—Then, the paleness of her face, its haggard aspect having vanished as she recovered flesh, and the peculiar expression arising from her mental state, though painfully suggestive of their causes, added to the touching interest, which she awakened, and invariably to me, I know, and to any person who saw her, I should think, refuted more tangible proofs of convalescence and stamped her as one doomed to decay.

A book lay spread on the sill before her, and the scarcely perceptible wind fluttered its leaves at intervals. I believe Linton had laid it there, for she never endeavoured to divert herself with reading, or occupation of any kind; and he would spend many an hour in trying to entice her attention to some subject which had formerly been her amusement.

She was conscious of his aim, and in her better moods, endured his efforts placidly; only showing their uselessness by now and then suppressing a wearied sigh, and restraining him at last with the saddest of smiles and kisses. At other times, she would turn petulantly away, and hide her face in her hands, or even push him off angrily; and then he took care to let her alone, for he was certain of doing no good.

Gimmerton chapel bells were still ringing; and the full, mellow flow of the beck in the valley came soothingly on the ear. It was a sweet substitute for the yet absent murmur of the summer foliage which drowned that music about the Grange when the trees were in leaf. At Wuthering Heights it always sounded on quiet days, following a great thaw, or a season of steady rain—and of Wuthering Heights Catherine was thinking as she listened;

that is, if she thought, or listened, at all; but she had the vague, distant look I mentioned before, which expressed no recognition of material things either by ear or eye.

"There's a letter for you, Mrs. Linton," I said, gently inserting it in one hand that rested on her knee. "You must read it immediately, because it wants an answer. Shall I break the seal?"

"Yes," she answered, without altering the direction of her eyes.

I opened it—it was very short.

"Now," I continued, "read it."

She drew away her hand, and let it fall. I replaced it in her lap, and stood waiting till it should please her to glance down; but that movement was so long delayed that at last I resumed—

"Must I read it, ma'am? It is from Mr. Heathcliff."

There was a start, and a troubled gleam of recollection, and a struggle to arrange her ideas. She lifted the letter, and seemed to peruse it; and when she came to the signature she sighed; yet still I found she had not gathered its import; for upon my desiring to hear her reply she merely pointed to the name, and gazed at me with mournful and questioning eagerness.

"Well, he wishes to see you," said I, guessing her need of an interpreter. "He's in the garden by this time, and impatient to know what answer I shall bring."

As I spoke, I observed a large dog lying on the sunny grass beneath raise its ears, as if about to bark; and then smoothing them back, announce by a wag of the tail that someone approached whom it did not consider a stranger.

Mrs. Linton bent forward, and listened breathlessly. The minute after a step traversed the hall; the open house was too tempting for Heathcliff to resist walking in: most likely he supposed that I was inclined to shirk my promise, and so resolved to trust to his own audacity.

With straining eagerness Catherine gazed towards the entrance of her chamber. He did not hit the right room directly; she motioned me to admit him; but he found it out, ere I could reach the door, and in a stride or two was at her side, and had her grasped in his arms.

He neither spoke, nor loosed his hold, for some five minutes, during which period he bestowed more kisses than ever he gave in his life before, I dare say; but then my mistress had kissed him first, and I plainly saw that he could hardly bear, for downright agony, to look into her face! The same conviction had stricken him as me, from the instant he beheld her, that there was no prospect of ultimate recovery there—she was fated, sure to die.

"Oh, Cathy! Oh my life! how can I bear it?" was the first sentence he uttered, in a tone that did not seek to disguise his despair.

And now he stared at her so earnestly that I thought the very intensity of his gaze would bring tears into his eyes; but they burned with anguish, they did not melt.

"What now?" said Catherine, leaning back, and returning his look with a suddenly clouded brow—her humour was a mere vane for constantly varying caprices. "You and Edgar have broken my heart, Heathcliff! And you both come to bewail the deed to me, as if you were the people to be pitied! I shall not pity you, not I. You have killed me—and thriven on it, I think. How strong you are! How many years do you mean to live after I am gone?"

Heathcliff had knelt on one knee to embrace her; he attempted to rise, but she seized his hair, and kept him down.

"I wish I could hold you," she continued bitterly, "till we were both dead! I shouldn't care what you suffered. I care nothing for your sufferings. Why shouldn't you suffer? I do! Will you forget me—will you be happy when I am in the earth? Will you say twenty years hence, 'That's the grave of Catherine Earnshaw. I loved her long ago, and was wretched to lose her; but it is past. I've loved many others since—my children are dearer to me than she was, and, at death, I shall not rejoice that I am going to her. I shall be sorry that I must lose them!' Will you say so Heathcliff?"

"Don't torture me till I am as mad as yourself," cried he, wrenching his head free, and grinding his teeth.

The two, to a cool spectator, made a strange and fearful picture. Well might Catherine deem that heaven would be a land of exile to her, unless, with her mortal body, she cast away her mortal character also. Her present countenance had a wild vindictiveness in its white cheek, and a bloodless lip, and scintillating eye; and she retained, in her closed fingers, a portion of the locks she had been grasping. As to her companion, while raising himself with one hand, he had taken her arm with the other; and so inadequate was his stock of gentleness to the requirements of her condition, that on his letting go, I saw four distinct impressions left blue in the colourless skin.

"Are you possessed with a devil," he pursued, savagely, "to talk in that manner to me, when you are dying? Do you reflect that all those words will be branded in my memory, and eating deeper eternally, after you have left me? You know you lie to say I have killed you; and, Catherine, you know that I could as soon forget you as my existence! Is it not sufficient for your infernal selfishness, that while you are at peace I shall writhe in the torments of hell?"

"I shall not be at peace," moaned Catherine, recalled to a sense of physical weakness by the violent, unequal throbbing of her heart, which beat visibly, and audibly under this excess of agitation.

She said nothing further till the paroxysm was over; then she continued, more kindly—

"I'm not wishing you greater torment than I have, Heathcliff! I only wish us never to be parted—and should a word of mine distress you hereafter, think I feel the same distress underground, and for my own sake, forgive me! Come here and kneel down again! You never harmed me in your life. Nay, if you nurse anger, that will be worse to remember than my harsh words! Won't you come here again? Do!"

Heathcliff went to the back of her chair, and leant over, but not so far as to let her see his face, which was livid with emotion. She bent round to look at him; he would not permit it; turning abruptly, he walked to the fireplace, where he stood, silent, with his back towards us.

Mrs. Linton's glance followed him suspiciously: every movement woke a new sentiment in her. After a pause, and a prolonged gaze, she resumed, addressing me in accents of indignant disappointment.

"Oh, you see, Nelly! he would not relent a moment, to keep me out of the grave! *That* is how I'm loved! Well, never mind! That is not *my* Heathcliff. I shall love mine yet; and take him with me—he's in my soul. And," added she, musingly, "the thing that irks me most is this shattered prison, after all. I'm tired, tired of being enclosed here. I'm wearying to escape into that glorious world, and to be always there; not seeing it dimly through tears, and yearning for it through the walls of an aching heart; but really with it, and in it. Nelly, you think you are better and more fortunate than I; in full health and strength—you are sorry for me—very soon that will be altered. I shall be sorry for *you.* I shall be incomparably beyond and above you all. I *wonder* he won't be near me!" She went on to herself. "I thought he wished it. Heathcliff dear! you should not be sullen now. Do come to me, Heathcliff."

In her eagerness she rose, and supported herself on the arm of the chair. At that earnest appeal, he turned to her, looking absolutely desperate. His eyes wide, and wet, at last, flashed fiercely on her; his breast heaved convulsively. An instant they held asunder; and then how they met I hardly saw, but Catherine made a spring, and he caught her, and they were locked in an embrace from which I thought my mistress would never be released alive. In fact, to my eyes, she seemed directly insensible. He flung himself into the nearest seat, and on my approaching hurriedly to ascertain if she had fainted, he gnashed at me, and foamed like a mad dog, and gathered her to him with greedy jealousy. I did not feel as if I were in the company of a creature of my own species; it appeared that he would not understand, though I spoke to him; so, I stood off, and held my tongue, in great perplexity.

A movement of Catherine's relieved me a little presently: she put up her hand to clasp his neck, and bring her cheek to his, as he held her: while he, in return, covering her with frantic caresses, said wildly—

"You teach me now how cruel you've been—cruel and false. *Why* did you despise me? *Why* did you betray your own heart, Cathy? I have not one word of comfort—you deserve this. You have killed yourself. Yes, you may kiss me, and cry; and wring out my kisses and tears. They'll blight you— they'll damn you. You loved me—then what *right* had you to leave me? What right—answer me—for the poor fancy you felt for Linton? Because misery, and degradation, and death, and nothing that God or Satan could inflict would have parted us, *you,* of you own will, did it. I have not broken your heart—*you* have broken it—and in breaking it, you have broken mine. So much the worse for me, that I am strong. Do I want to live? What kind of living will it be when you—oh God! would *you* like to live with your soul in the grave?"

"Let me alone. Let me alone," sobbed Catherine. "If I have done wrong, I'm dying for it. It is enough! You left me too; but I won't upbraid you! I forgive you. Forgive me!"

"It is hard to forgive, and to look at those eyes, and feel those wasted hands," he answered. "Kiss me again; and don't let me see your eyes! I forgive what you have done to me. I love *my* murderer—but *yours!* How can I?"

They were silent—their faces hid against each other, and washed by each other's tears. At least, I suppose the weeping was on both sides; as it seemed Heathcliff *could* weep on a great occasion like this.

I grew very uncomfortable, meanwhile; for the afternoon wore fast away, the man whom I had sent off returned from his errand, and I could distinguish, by the shine of the westering sun up the valley, a concourse thickening outside Gimmerton chapel porch.

"Service is over," I announced. "My master will be here in half an hour."

Heathcliff groaned a curse, and strained Catherine closer—she never moved.

Ere long I perceived a group of the servants passing up the road towards the kitchen wing. Mr. Linton was not far behind; he opened the gate himself, and sauntered slowly up, probably enjoying the lovely afternoon that breathed as soft as summer.

"Now he is here," I exclaimed. "For Heaven's sake, hurry down! You'll not meet anyone on the front stairs. Do be quick; and stay among the trees till he is fairly in."

"I must go, Cathy," said Heathcliff, seeking to extricate himself from his companion's arms. "But, if I live, I'll see you again before you are asleep. I won't stray five yards from your window."

"You must not go!" she answered, holding him as firmly as her strength allowed. "You shall not, I tell you."

"For one hour," he pleaded earnestly.

"Not for one minute," she replied.

"I *must*—Linton will be up immediately," persisted the alarmed intruder.

He would have risen, and unfixed her fingers by the act—she clung fast gasping; there was mad resolution in her face.

"No!" she shrieked. "Oh, don't, don't go. It is the last time! Edgar will not hurt us. Heathcliff, I shall die! I shall die!"

"Damn the fool! There he is," cried Heathcliff, sinking back into his seat. "Hush, my darling! Hush, hush, Catherine! I'll stay. If he shot me so, I'd expire with a blessing on my lips."

And there they were fast again. I heard my master mounting the stairs— the cold sweat ran from my forehead; I was horrified.

"Are you going to listen to her ravings?" I said, passionately. "She does not know what she says. Will you ruin her, because she has not wit to help herself? Get up! You could be free instantly. That is the most diabolical deed that ever you did. We are all done for—master, mistress, and servant."

I wrung my hands, and cried out; and Mr. Linton hastened his step at the noise. In the midst of my agitation, I was sincerely glad to observe that Catherine's arms had fallen relaxed, and her head hung down.

"She's fainted or dead," I thought, "so much the better. Far better that she should be dead, than lingering a burden, and a misery-maker to all about her."

Edgar sprang to his unbidden guest, blanched with astonishment and rage. What he meant to do, I cannot tell; however, the other stopped all demonstrations, at once, by placing the lifeless-looking form in his arms.

"Look there!" he said, "unless you be a fiend, help her first—then you shall speak to me!"

He walked into the parlour, and sat down, Mr. Linton summoned me, and with great difficulty, and after resorting to many means, we managed to restore her to sensation; but she was all bewildered; she sighed, and moaned, and knew nobody. Edgar, in his anxiety for her, forgot her hated friend. I did not. I went, at the earliest opportunity, and besought him to depart, affirming that Catherine was better, and he should hear from me in the morning, how she passed the night.

"I shall not refuse to go out of doors," he answered; "but I shall stay in the garden; and, Nelly, mind you keep your word tomorrow. I shall be under those larch trees, mind! or I pay another visit, whether Linton be in or not."

He sent a rapid glance through the half-open door of the chamber, and ascertaining that what I stated was apparently true, delivered the house of his luckless presence.

CHAPTER XVI

About twelve o'clock that night, was born the Catherine you saw at Wuthering Heights, a puny, seven months' child; and two hours after the mother died, having never recovered sufficient consciousness to miss Heathcliff or know Edgar.

The latter's distraction at his bereavement is a subject too painful to be dwelt on; its after effects showed how deep the sorrow sunk.

A great addition, in my eyes, was his being left without an heir. I bemoaned that, as I gazed on the feeble orphan; and I mentally abused old Linton for what was only natural partiality, the securing his estate to his own daughter, instead of his son's.

An unwelcomed infant it was, poor thing! It might have wailed out of life, and nobody cared a morsel, during those first hours of existence. We redeemed the neglect afterwards; but its beginning was as friendless as its end is likely to be.

Next morning—bright and cheerful out of doors—stole softened in through the blinds of the silent room, and suffused the couch and its occupant with a mellow, tender glow.

Edgar Linton had his head laid on the pillow, and his eyes shut. His young and fair features were almost as deathlike as those of the form beside him, and almost as fixed; but *his* was the hush of exhausted anguish, and *hers* of perfect peace. Her brow smooth, her lids closed, her lips wearing the expression of a smile. No angel in heaven could be more beautiful than she appeared; and I partook of the infinite calm in which she lay. My mind was never in a holier frame, than while I gazed on that untroubled image of Divine rest. I instinctively echoed the words she had uttered, a few hours before. "Incomparably beyond, and above us all! Whether still on earth or now in heaven her spirit is at home with God!"

I don't know if it be a peculiarity in me, but I am seldom otherwise than happy while watching in the chamber of death, should no frenzied or despairing mourner share the duty with me. I see a repose that neither earth nor hell can break; and I feel an assurance of the endless and shadowless hereafter—the Eternity they have entered—where life is boundless in its duration, and love in its sympathy, and joy in its fulness. I noticed on that occasion how much selfishness there is even in a love like Mr. Linton's, when he so regretted Catherine's blessed release!

To be sure one might have doubted, after the wayward and impatient existence she had led, whether she merited a haven of peace at last. One might doubt in seasons of cold reflection, but not then, in the presence of her corpse. It asserted its own tranquillity, which seemed a pledge of equal quiet to its former inhabitant.

"Do you believe such people *are* happy in the other world, sir? I'd give a great deal to know."

I declined answering Mrs. Dean's question, which struck me as something heterodox. She proceeded:

"Retracing the course of Catherine Linton, I fear we have no right to think she is: but we'll leave her with her Maker."

The master looked asleep, and I ventured soon after sunrise to quit the room and steal out to the pure, refreshing air. The servants thought me gone to shake off the drowsiness of my protracted watch; in reality my chief motive was seeing Mr. Heathcliff. If he had remained among the larches all night he would have heard nothing of the stir at the Grange, unless, perhaps, he might catch the gallop of the messenger going to Gimmerton. If he had come nearer, he would probably be aware, from the lights flitting to and fro, and the opening and shutting of the outer doors, that all was not right within.

I wished yet feared to find him. I felt the terrible news must be told, and I longed to get it over, but *how* to do it I did not know.

He was there—at least a few yards further in the park; leant against an old ash tree, his hat off, and his hair soaked with the dew that had gathered on the budded branches, and fell pattering round him. He had been standing a long time in that position, for I saw a pair of ousels passing and repassing, scarcely three feet from him, busy in building their nest, and regarding his proximity no more than that of a piece of timber. They flew off at my approach, and he raised his eyes and spoke:

"She's dead!" he said; "I've not waited for you to learn that. Put your handkerchief away—don't snivel before me. Damn you all! she wants none of *your* tears!"

I was weeping as much for him as her: we do sometimes pity creatures that have none of the feeling either for themselves or others; and

---

ousels: diving birds.

when I first looked into his face I perceived that he had got intelligence of the catastrophe; and a foolish notion struck me that his heart was quelled, and he prayed, because his lips moved, and his gaze was bent on the ground.

"Yes, she's dead!" I answered, checking my sobs, and drying my cheeks. "Gone to heaven, I hope, where we may, everyone, join her, if we take due warning, and leave our evil ways to follow good!"

"Did *she* take due warning, then?" asked Heathcliff, attempting a sneer. "Did she die like a saint? Come, give me a true history of the event. How did—"

He endeavored to pronounce the name, but could not manage it; and compressing his mouth, he held a silent combat with his inward agony, defying, meanwhile, my sympathy with an unflinching, ferocious stare.

"How did she die?" he resumed, at last—fain, notwithstanding his hardihood, to have a support behind him, for, after the struggle, he trembled, in spite of himself, to his very finger ends.

"Poor wretch!" I thought; "you have a heart and nerves the same as your brother men! Why should you be anxious to conceal them? your pride cannot blind God! You tempt him to wring them, till he forces a cry of humiliation!"

"Quietly as a lamb!" I answered, aloud. "She drew a sigh, and stretched herself, like a child reviving, and sinking again to sleep; and five minutes after I felt one little pulse at her heart, and nothing more!"

"And—did she ever mention me?" he asked, hesitating, as if he dreaded the answer to his question would introduce details that he could not bear to hear.

"Her senses never returned—she recognized nobody from the time you left her," I said. "She lies with a sweet smile on her face; and her latest ideas wandered back to pleasant early days. Her life closed in a gentle dream— may she wake as kindly in the other world!"

"May she wake in torment!" he cried, with frightful vehemence, stamping his foot, and groaning in a sudden paroxysm of ungovernable passion. "Why, she's a liar to the end! Where is she? Not *there*—not in heaven—not perished—where? Oh! you said you cared nothing for my sufferings! And I pray one prayer—I repeat it till my tongue stiffens—Catherine Earnshaw, may you not rest, as long as I am living! You said I killed you—haunt me then! The murdered *do* haunt their murderers. I believe—I know that ghosts *have* wandered on earth. Be with me always—take any form—drive me mad! only *do* not leave me in this abyss, where I cannot find you! Oh, God! it is unutterable! I *cannot* live without my life! I *cannot* live without my soul!"

He dashed his head against the knotted trunk; and, lifting up his eyes, howled, not like a man, but like a savage beast being goaded to death with knives and spears.

I observed several splashes of blood about the bark of the tree, and his hand and forehead were both stained; probably the scene I witnessed was a repetition of others acted during the night. It hardly moved my compassion—it appalled me; still I felt reluctant to quit him so. But the moment he recollected himself enough to notice me watching, he thundered a command for me to go, and I obeyed. He was beyond my skill to quiet or console!

Mrs. Linton's funeral was appointed to take place on the Friday following her decease; and till then her coffin remained uncovered, and strewn with flowers and scented leaves, in the great drawing-room. Linton spent his days and nights there, a sleepless guardian; and—a circumstance concealed from all but me—Heathcliff spent his nights, at least, outside, equally a stranger to repose.

I held no communication with him; still I was conscious of his design to enter, if he could; and on the Tuesday, a little after dark, when my master from sheer fatigue, had been compelled to retire a couple of hours, I went and opened one of the windows, moved by his perseverance to give him a chance of bestowing on the fading image of his idol one final adieu.

He did not omit to avail himself of the opportunity, cautiously and briefly; too cautiously to betray his presence by the slightest noise; indeed, I shouldn't have discovered that he had been there, except for the disarrangement of the drapery about the corpse's face, and for observing on the floor a curl of light hair, fastened with a silver thread, which, on examination, I ascertained to have been taken from a locket hung round Catherine's neck. Heathcliff had opened the trinket, and cast out its contents, replacing them by a black lock of his own. I twisted the two, and enclosed them together.

Mr. Earnshaw was, of course, invited to attend the remains of his sister to the grave; and he sent no excuse, but he never came; so that besides her husband, the mourners were wholly composed of tenants and servants. Isabella was not asked.

The place of Catherine's interment, to the surprise of the villagers, was neither in the chapel, under the carved monument of the Lintons, nor yet by the tombs of her own relations, outside. It was dug on a green slope, in a corner of the kirkyard, where the wall is so low that heath and bilberry plants have climbed over it from the moor; and peat mould almost buries it. Her husband lies in the same spot, now; and they have each a simple headstone, above, and a plain grey block at their feet, to mark the graves.

CHAPTER XVII

That Friday made the last of our fine days, for a month. In the evening, the weather broke; the wind shifted from south to northeast, and brought rain, first, and then sleet, and snow.

On the morrow one could hardly imagine that there had been three weeks of summer: the primroses and crocuses were hidden under wintry drifts: the larks were silent, the young leaves of the early trees smitten and blackened—And dreary, and chill, and dismal that morrow did creep over! My master kept his room—I took possession of the lonely parlour, converting it into a nursery; and there I was sitting, with the moaning doll of a child laid on my knee; rocking it to and fro, and watching, meanwhile, the still driving flakes build up the uncurtained window, when the door opened, and some person entered out of breath, and laughing!

My anger was greater than my astonishment for a minute; I supposed it one of the maids, and I cried, "Have done! How dare you show your giddiness, here? What would Mr. Linton say if he heard you?"

"Excuse me!" answered a familiar voice, "but I know Edgar is in bed, and I cannot stop myself."

With that, the speaker came forward to the fire, panting and holding her hand, to her side.

"I have run the whole way from Wuthering Heights!" she continued, after a pause. "Except where I've flown—I couldn't count the number of falls I've had—Oh, I'm aching all over! Don't be alarmed—There shall be an explanation as soon as I can give it—only just have the goodness to step out, and order the carriage to take me on to Gimmerton, and tell a servant to seek up a few clothes in my wardrobe."

The intruder was Mrs. Heathcliff—she certainly seemed in no laughing predicament: her hair streamed on her shoulders dripping with snow and water; she was dressed in the girlish dress she commonly wore, befitting her age more than her position; a low frock, with short sleeves, and nothing on either head, or neck. The frock was of light silk, and clung to her with wet; and her feet were protected merely by thin slippers; add to this a deep cut under one ear, which only the cold prevented from bleeding profusely, a white face scratched and bruised, and a frame hardly able to support itself through fatigue, and you may fancy my first fright was not much allayed when I had leisure to examine her.

"My dear young lady," I exclaimed, "I'll stir nowhere, and hear nothing, till you have removed every article of your clothes, and put on dry things; and certainly you shall not go to Gimmerton tonight, so it is needless to order the carriage."

"Certainly, I shall," she said; "walking or riding—yet I've no objection to dress myself decently; and—ah, see how it flows down my neck now! The fire does make it smart."

She insisted on my fulfilling her directions, before she would let me touch her; and not till after the coachman had been instructed to get ready, and a maid set to pack up some necessary attire, did I obtain her consent for binding the wound, and helping to change her garments.

"Now, Ellen," she said when my task was finished, and she was seated in an easy chair on the hearth, with a cup of tea before her, "You sit down opposite me, and put poor Catherine's baby away—I don't like to see it! You mustn't think I care little for Catherine, because I behaved so foolishly on entering—I've cried too, bitterly—yes, more than anyone else has reason to cry—we parted unreconciled, you remember, and I shan't forgive myself. But for all that, I was not going to sympathise with him—the brute beast! O give me the poker! This is the last thing of his I have about me," she slipped the gold ring from her third finger, and threw it on the floor. "I'll smash it!" she continued striking it with childish spite. "And then I'll burn it!" and she took and dropped the misused article among the coals. "There! he shall buy another, if he gets me back again. He'd be capable of coming to seek me, to tease Edgar—I dare not stay, lest that notion should possess his wicked head! And besides, Edgar has not been kind, has he? And I won't come suing for his assistance; nor will I bring him into more trouble—Necessity compelled me to seek shelter here; though if I had not learnt he was out of the way, I'd have halted at the kitchen, washed my face, warmed myself, got you to bring what I wanted, and departed again to anywhere out of reach of my accursed—of that incarnate goblin! Ah, he was in such a fury—if he had caught me! It's a pity, Earnshaw is not his match in strength—I wouldn't have run, till I'd seen him all but demolished, had Hindley been able to do it!"

"Well, don't talk so fast, Miss!" I interrupted, "you'll disorder the handkerchief I have tied round your face, and make the cut bleed again—Drink your tea, and take breath and give over laughing—Laughter is sadly out of place under this roof, and in your condition!"

"An undeniable truth," she replied, "Listen to that child! It maintains a constant wail—send it out of my hearing, for an hour; I shan't stay any longer."

I rang the bell, and committed it to a servant's care; and then I inquired what had urged her to escape from Wuthering Heights in such an unlikely plight—and where she meant to go, as she refused remaining with us?

---

tease: torment.

"I ought, and I wish to remain," answered she; "to cheer Edgar, and take care of the baby, for two things, and because the Grange is my right home — but I tell you, he wouldn't let me! Do you think he could bear to see me grow fat, and merry; and could bear to think that we were tranquil, and not resolve on poisoning our comfort? Now, I have the satisfaction of being sure that he detests me to the point of its annoying him seriously to have me within earshot, or eyesight — I notice, when I enter his presence, the muscles of his countenance are involuntarily distorted into an expression of hatred; partly arising from his knowledge of the good causes I have to feel that sentiment for him, and partly from original aversion — It is strong enough to make me feel pretty certain that he would not chase me over England, supposing I contrived a clear escape; and therefore I must get quite away. I've recovered from my first desire to be killed by him. I'd rather he'd kill himself! He has extinguished my love effectually, and so I'm at my ease. I can recollect yet how I loved him; and can dimly imagine that I could still be loving him, if — No, no! Even if he had doted on me, the devilish nature would have revealed its existence, somehow. Catherine had an awfully perverted taste to esteem him so dearly, knowing him so well — Monster! would that he could be blotted out of creation, and out of my memory!"

"Hush, hush! He's a human being," I said. "Be more charitable; there are worse men than he is yet!"

"He's not a human being," she retorted; "and he has no claim on my charity — I gave him my heart, and he took and pinched it to death; and flung it back to me — people feel with their hearts, Ellen, and since he has destroyed mine, I have not power to feel for him, and I would not, though he groaned from this, to his dying day; and wept tears of blood for Catherine! No, indeed, indeed, I wouldn't!" And here Isabella began to cry; but, immediately dashing the water from her lashes, she recommenced.

"You asked, what has driven me to flight at last? I was compelled to attempt it, because I had succeeded in rousing his rage a pitch above his malignity. Pulling out the nerves with red hot pincers requires more coolness than knocking on the head. He was worked up to forget the fiendish prudence he boasted of, and proceeding to murderous violence: I experienced pleasure in being able to exasperate him: the sense of pleasure woke my instinct of self-preservation; so, I fairly broke free, and if ever I come into his hands again he is welcome to a signal revenge.

"Yesterday, you know, Mr. Earnshaw should have been at the funeral. He kept himself sober, for the purpose — tolerably sober; not going to bed mad at six o'clock and getting up drunk at twelve. Consequently, he rose, in suicidal low spirits; as fit for the church, as for a dance; and instead, he sat down by the fire, and swallowed gin or brandy by tumblerfuls.

"Heathcliff—I shudder to name him! has been a stranger in the house from last Sunday till today—Whether the angels have fed him, or his kin beneath, I cannot tell; but, he has not eaten a meal with us for nearly a week—He has just come home at dawn, and gone upstairs to his chamber; locking himself in—as if anybody dreamt of coveting his company! There he has continued, praying like a Methodist; only the deity he implored is senseless dust and ashes; and God, when addressed, was curiously confounded with his own black father! After concluding these precious orisons—and they lasted generally till he grew hoarse, and his voice was strangled in his throat, he would be off again; always straight down to the Grange! I wonder Edgar did not send for a constable, and give him into custody! For me, grieved as I was about Catherine, it was impossible to avoid regarding this season of deliverance from degrading oppression as a holiday.

"I recovered spirits sufficient to hear Joseph's eternal lectures without weeping; and to move up and down the house, less with the foot of a frightened thief, than formerly. You wouldn't think that I should cry at anything Joseph could say, but he and Hareton are detestable companions. I'd rather sit with Hindley, and hear his awful talk, than with 't' little maister,' and his staunch supporter, that odious old man!

"When Heathcliff is in, I'm often obliged to seek the kitchen, and their society, or starve among the damp, uninhabited chambers; when he is not, as was the case this week, I establish a table, and chair, at one corner of the house fire, and never mind how Mr. Earnshaw may occupy himself; and he does not interfere with my arrangements: he is quieter, now, than he used to be, if no one provokes him; more sullen and depressed, and less furious. Joseph affirms he's sure he's an altered man; that the Lord has touched his heart, and he is saved 'so as by fire.' [5] I'm puzzled to detect signs of the favorable change, but it is not my business.

"Yester-evening, I sat in my nook reading some old books, till late on towards twelve. It seemed so dismal to go upstairs, with the wild snow blowing outside, and my thoughts continually reverting to the kirkyard, and the new made grave! I dared hardly lift my eyes from the page before me, that melancholy scene so instantly usurped its place.

---

orisons: hymns.

[5] "So as by fire" refers to I Corinthians 3.15: "If any man's work shall be burned, he shall suffer loss; but he himself shall be saved, yet as by fire." The reference suggests that the loss of Earnshaw's estate to Heathcliff has actually made Earnshaw a more spiritual man, at least in Joseph's eyes. [ED.]

"Hindley sat opposite; his head leant on his hand, perhaps meditating on the same subject. He had ceased drinking at a point below irrationality, and had neither stirred, nor spoken during two or three hours. There was no sound through the house, but the moaning wind which shook the windows every now and then: the faint crackling of the coals; and the click of my snuffers as I removed at intervals the long wick of the candle. Hareton and Joseph were probably fast asleep in bed. It was very, very sad, and while I read, I sighed, for it seemed as if all joy had vanished from the world, never to be restored.

"The doleful silence was broken, at length, by the sound of the kitchen latch—Heathcliff had returned from his watch earlier than usual, owing, I suppose, to the sudden storm.

"That entrance was fastened; and we heard him coming round to get in by the other. I rose with an irrepressible expression of what I felt on my lips, which induced my companion, who had been staring towards the door, to turn and look at me.

"'I'll keep him out five minutes,' he exclaimed. 'You won't object?'

"'No, you may keep him out the whole night, for me,' I answered. 'Do! put the key in the lock, and draw the bolts.'

"Earnshaw accomplished this, ere his guest reached the front; he then came, and brought his chair to the other side of my table; leaning over it, and searching in my eyes a sympathy with the burning hate that gleamed from his: as he both looked, and felt like an assassin, he couldn't exactly find that; but he discovered enough to encourage him to speak.

"'You, and I,' he said, 'have each a great debt to settle with the man out yonder! If we were neither of us cowards, we might combine to discharge it. Are you as soft as your brother? Are you willing to endure to the last, and not once attempt a repayment?'

"'I'm weary of enduring now,' I replied, 'and I'd be glad of a retaliation that wouldn't recoil on myself; but treachery and violence are spears pointed at both ends—they wound those who resort to them, worse than their enemies.'

"'Treachery and violence are a just return for treachery and violence!' cried Hindley. 'Mrs. Heathcliff, I'll ask you to do nothing, but sit still, and be dumb—Tell me now, can you? I'm sure you would have as much pleasure as I, in witnessing the conclusion of the fiend's existence, he'll be *your* death unless you overreach him—and he'll be *my* ruin—Damn the hellish villain! He knocks at the door, as if he were master here, already! Promise to hold your tongue, and before that clock strikes—it wants three minutes of one—you're a free woman!'

"He took the implements which I described to you in my letter from his breast, and would have turned down the candle—I snatched it away, however, and seized his arm.

"'I'll not hold my tongue!' I said, 'You mustn't touch him . . . Let the door remain shut and be quiet!'

"'No! I've formed my resolution, and by God, I'll execute it!' cried the desperate being, 'I'll do you a kindness, in spite of yourself, and Hareton justice! And you needn't trouble your head to screen me, Catherine is gone—Nobody alive would regret me, or be ashamed though I cut my throat, this minute—and it's time to make an end!'

"I might as well have struggled with a bear; or reasoned with a lunatic. The only resource left me was to run to a lattice, and warn his intended victim of the fate which awaited him.

"'You'd better seek shelter somewhere else tonight!' I exclaimed in a rather triumphant tone. 'Mr. Earnshaw has a mind to shoot you, if you persist in endeavouring to enter.'

"'You'd better open the door, you—' he answered, addressing me by some elegant term that I don't care to repeat.

"'I shall not meddle in the matter,' I retorted again. 'Come in, and get shot, if you please! I've done my duty.'

"With that I shut the window, and returned to my place by the fire; having too small a stock of hypocrisy at my command to pretend any anxiety for the danger that menaced him.

"Earnshaw swore passionately at me; affirming that I loved the villain yet: and calling me all sorts of names for the base spirit I evinced. And I, in my secret heart, (and conscience never reproached me) thought what a blessing it would be for *him*, should Heathcliff put him out of misery: and what a blessing for *me*, should he send Heathcliff to his right abode! As I sat nursing these reflections, the casement behind me was banged on to the floor by a blow from the latter individual; and his black countenance looked blightingly through. The stanchions stood too close to suffer his shoulders to follow; and I smiled, exulting in my fancied security. His hair and clothes were whitened with snow, and his sharp cannibal teeth, revealed by cold and wrath, gleamed through the dark.

"'Isabella, let me in, or I'll make you repent!' he 'girned,' as Joseph calls it.

"'I cannot commit murder,' I replied. 'Mr. Hindley stands sentinel with a knife, and loaded pistol.'

"'Let me in by the kitchen door!' he said.

'girned': snarled.

"'Hindley will be there before me,' I answered. 'And that's a poor love of yours, that cannot bear a shower of snow! We were left at peace in our beds, as long as the summer moon shone, but the moment a blast of winter returns, you must run for shelter! Heathcliff, if I were you, I'd go stretch myself over her grave, and die like a faithful dog . . . The world is surely not worth living in now, is it? You had distinctly impressed on me the idea that Catherine was the whole joy of your life—I can't imagine how you think of surviving her loss.'

"'He's there . . . is he?' exclaimed my companion, rushing to the gap. 'If I can get my arm out I can hit him!'

"I'm afraid, Ellen, you'll set me down, as really wicked—but you don't know all, so don't judge! I wouldn't have aided or abetted an attempt on even *his* life, for anything—Wish that he were dead, I must; and therefore, I was fearfully disappointed, and unnerved by terror for the consequences of my taunting speech when he flung himself on Earnshaw's weapon and wrenched it from his grasp.

"The charge exploded, and the knife, in springing back, closed into its owner's wrist. Heathcliff pulled it away by main force, slitting up the flesh as it passed on, and thrust it dripping into his pocket. He then took a stone, struck down the division between two windows and sprung in. His adversary had fallen senseless with excessive pain, and the flow of blood that gushed from an artery, or a large vein.

"The ruffian kicked and trampled on him, and dashed his head repeatedly against the flags; holding me with one hand, meantime, to prevent me summoning Joseph.

"He exerted preter-human self-denial in abstaining from finishing him, completely; but getting out of breath, he finally desisted, and dragged the apparently inanimate body onto the settle.

"There he tore off the sleeve of Earnshaw's coat, and bound up the wound with brutal roughness, spitting and cursing, during the operation, as energetically as he had kicked before.

"Being at liberty, I lost no time in seeking the old servant; who, having gathered by degrees the purport of my hasty tale, hurried below, gasping, as he descended the steps two at once.

"'Whet is thur tuh do, nah? whet is thur tuh do, nah?'

"'There's this to do,' thundered Heathcliff, 'that your master's mad; and should he last another month, I'll have him to an asylum. And how the devil did you come to fasten me out, you toothless hound? Don't stand

---

preter: super.

muttering and mumbling there. Come, I'm not going to nurse him. Wash that stuff away; and mind the sparks of your candle—it is more than half brandy!'

"'And soa, yah been murthering on him?' exclaimed Joseph, lifting his hands and eyes in horror. 'If iver Aw seed a seeght loike this! May the Lord—'

"Heathcliff gave him a push onto his knees, in the middle of the blood; and flung a towel to him; but instead of proceeding to dry it up, he joined his hands, and began a prayer which excited my laughter from its odd phraseology. I was in the condition of mind to be shocked at nothing; in fact, I was as reckless as some malefactors show themselves at the foot of the gallows.

"'Oh, I forgot you,' said the tyrant, 'you shall do that. Down with you. And you conspire with him against me, do you, viper? There, that is work fit for you!'

"He shook me till my teeth rattled, and pitched me beside Joseph, who steadily concluded his supplications, and then rose, vowing he would set off for the Grange directly. Mr. Linton was a magistrate, and though he had fifty wives dead, he should inquire into this.

"He was so obstinate in his resolution that Heathcliff deemed it expedient to compel, from my lips, a recapitulation of what had taken place; standing over me, heaving with malevolence, as I reluctantly delivered the account in answer to his questions.

"It required a great deal of labour to satisfy the old man that he was not the aggressor; especially with my hardly wrung replies. However, Mr. Earnshaw soon convinced him that he was alive still; he hastened to administer a dose of spirits, and by their succour his master presently regained motion and consciousness.

"Heathcliff, aware that he was ignorant of the treatment received while insensible, called him deliriously intoxicated; and said he should not notice his atrocious conduct further; but advised him to get to bed. To my joy, he left us after giving this judicious counsel, and Hindley stretched himself on the hearthstone. I departed to my own room, marvelling that I had escaped so easily.

"This morning, when I came down, about half an hour before noon, Mr. Earnshaw was sitting by the fire, deadly sick; his evil genius, almost as gaunt and ghastly, leant against the chimney. Neither appeared inclined to dine; and having waited till all was cold on the table, I commenced alone.

"Nothing hindered me from eating heartily; and I experienced a certain sense of satisfaction and superiority, as, at intervals, I cast a look towards my silent companions, and felt the comfort of a quiet conscience within me.

"After I had done, I ventured on the unusual liberty of drawing near the fire; going round Earnshaw's seat, and kneeling in the corner beside him.

"Heathcliff did not glance my way, and I gazed up, and contemplated his features, almost as confidently as if they had been turned to stone. His forehead, that I once thought so manly, and that I now think so diabolical, was shaded with a heavy cloud; his basilisk eyes were nearly quenched by sleeplessness—and weeping, perhaps, for the lashes were wet then: his lips devoid of their ferocious sneer, and sealed in an expression of unspeakable sadness. Had it been another, I would have covered my face, in the presence of such grief. In *his* case, I was gratified: and ignoble as it seems to insult a fallen enemy, I couldn't miss this chance of sticking in a dart; his weakness was the only time when I could taste the delight of paying wrong for wrong."

"Fie, fie, Miss!" I interrupted. "One might suppose you had never opened a Bible in your life. If God afflict your enemies, surely that ought to suffice you. It is both mean and presumptuous to add your torture to his!"

"In general, I'll allow that it would be, Ellen," she continued. "But what misery laid on Heathcliff could content me, unless I have a hand in it? I'd rather he suffered *less*, if I might cause his sufferings, and he might *know* that I was the cause. Oh, I owe him so much. On only one condition can I hope to forgive him. It is, if I may take an eye for an eye, a tooth for a tooth, for every wrench of agony, return a wrench, reduce him to my level. As he was the first to injure, make him the first to implore pardon; and then— why then, Ellen, I might show you some generosity. But it is utterly impossible I can ever be revenged, and therefore I cannot forgive him. Hindley wanted some water, and I handed him a glass, and asked him how he was.

"'Not as ill as I wish,' he replied. 'But leaving out my arm, every inch of me is as sore as if I had been fighting with a legion of imps!'

"'Yes, no wonder,' was my next remark. 'Catherine used to boast that she stood between you and bodily harm—she meant that certain persons would not hurt you, for fear of offending her. It's well people don't *really* rise from their grave, or, last night, she might have witnessed a repulsive scene! Are not you bruised, and cut over your chest and shoulders?'

"'I can't say,' he answered; 'but what do you mean? Did he dare to strike me when *I* was down?'

"'He trampled on, and kicked you, and dashed you on the ground,' I whispered. 'And his mouth watered to tear you with his teeth; because, he's only half a man—not so much.'

"Mr. Earnshaw looked up, like me, to the countenance of our mutual foe; who, absorbed in his anguish, seemed insensible to anything around him; the longer he stood, the plainer his reflections revealed their blackness through his features.

"'Oh, if God would but give me strength to strangle him in my last agony, I'd go to hell with joy,' groaned the impatient man writhing to rise, and sinking back in despair, convinced of his inadequacy for the struggle.

"'Nay, it's enough that he has murdered one of you,' I observed aloud. 'At the Grange, everyone knows your sister would have been living now, had it not been for Mr. Heathcliff. After all, it is preferable to be hated than loved by him. When I recollect how happy we were—how happy Catherine was before he came—I'm fit to curse the day.'

"Most likely, Heathcliff noticed more the truth of what was said, than the spirit of the person who said it. His attention was roused, I saw, for his eyes rained down tears among the ashes, and he drew his breath in suffocating sighs.

"I stared full at him, and laughed scornfully. The clouded windows of hell flashed, a moment towards me; the fiend which usually looked out, however, was so dimmed and drowned that I did not fear to hazard another sound of derision.

"'Get up, and begone out of my sight,' said the mourner.

"I guessed he uttered those words, at least, though his voice was hardly intelligible.

"'I beg your pardon,' I replied. 'But I loved Catherine too; and her brother requires attendance which, for her sake, I shall supply. Now that she's dead, I see her in Hindley; Hindley has exactly her eyes, if you had not tried to gouge them out, and made them black and red, and her—'

"'Get up, wretched idiot, before I stamp you to death!' he cried, making a movement that caused me to make one also.

"'But then,' I continued, holding myself ready to flee; 'if poor Catherine had trusted you, and assumed the ridiculous, contemptible, degrading title of Mrs. Heathcliff, she would soon have presented a similar picture! *She* wouldn't have borne your abominable behaviour quietly; her detestation and disgust must have found voice.'

"The back of the settle, and Earnshaw's person interposed between me and him; so instead of endeavouring to reach me, he snatched a dinner knife from the table, and flung it at my head. It struck beneath my ear, and stopped the sentence I was uttering; but pulling it out, I sprang to the door, and delivered another which I hope went a little deeper than his missile.

"The last glimpse I caught of him was a furious rush, on his part, checked by the embrace of his host; and both fell locked together on the hearth.

"In my flight through the kitchen I bid Joseph speed to his master; I knocked over Hareton, who was hanging a litter of puppies from a chair-back in the doorway; and, blest as a soul escaped from purgatory, I bounded, leaped, and flew down the steep road: then, quitting its windings, shot direct across the moor, rolling over banks, and wading through marshes; precipitating myself, in fact, towards the beacon light of the Grange. And far rather would I be condemned to a perpetual dwelling in the infernal regions, than even for one night abide beneath the roof of Wuthering Heights again."

Isabella ceased speaking, and took a drink of tea; then she rose, and bidding me put on her bonnet, and a great shawl I had brought, and turning a deaf ear to my entreaties for her to remain another hour, she stepped onto a chair, kissed Edgar's and Catherine's portraits, bestowed a similar salute on me, and descended to the carriage accompanied by Fanny, who yelped wild with joy at recovering her mistress. She was driven away, never to revisit this neighbourhood; but a regular correspondence was established between her and my master when things were more settled.

I believe her new abode was in the south, near London; there she had a son born, a few months subsequent to her escape. He was christened Linton, and, from the first, she reported him to be an ailing, peevish creature.

Mr. Heathcliff, meeting me one day in the village, inquired where she lived. I refused to tell. He remarked that it was not of any moment, only she must beware of coming to her brother: she should not be with him, if he had to keep her himself.

Though I would give no information, he discovered, through some of the other servants, both her place of residence, and the existence of the child. Still he didn't molest her; for which forbearance she might thank his aversion, I suppose.

He often asked about the infant, when he saw me; and on hearing its name, smiled grimly, and observed:

"They wish me to hate it too, do they?"

"I don't think they wish you to know anything about it," I answered.

"But I'll have it," he said, "when I want it. They may reckon on that!"

Fortunately, its mother died before the time arrived, some thirteen years after the decease of Catherine, when Linton was twelve, or a little more.

On the day succeeding Isabella's unexpected visit, I had no opportunity of speaking to my master: he shunned conversation, and was fit for discussing nothing. When I could get him to listen, I saw it pleased him that his sister had left her husband, whom he abhorred with an intensity which the mildness of his nature would scarcely seem to allow. So deep and sensitive was his aversion, that he refrained from going anywhere where he was likely to see or hear of Heathcliff. Grief, and that together, transformed him into a complete hermit: he threw up his office of magistrate, ceased even to attend church, avoided the village on all occasions, and spent a life of entire seclusion within the limits of his park and grounds: only varied by solitary rambles on the moors, and visits to the grave of his wife, mostly at evening, or early morning, before other wanderers were abroad.

But he was too good to be thoroughly unhappy long. *He* didn't pray for Catherine's soul to haunt him: Time brought resignation, and a melancholy sweeter than common joy. He recalled her memory with ardent, tender love, and hopeful aspiring to the better world, where he doubted not she was gone.

And he had earthly consolation and affections, also. For a few days, I said, he seemed regardless of the puny successor to the departed: the coldness melted as fast as snow in April, and ere the tiny thing could stammer a word or totter a step, it wielded a despot's sceptre in his heart.

It was named Catherine, but he never called it the name in full as he had never called the first Catherine short, probably because Heathcliff had a habit of doing so. The little one was always Cathy, it formed to him a distinction from the mother, and yet, a connection with her; and his attachment sprang from its relation to her, far more than from its being his own.

I used to draw a comparison between him, and Hindley Earnshaw and perplex myself to explain satisfactorily, why their conduct was so opposite in similar circumstances. They had both been fond husbands, and were both attached to their children; and I could not see how they shouldn't both have taken the same road, for good or evil. But, I thought in my mind, Hindley with apparently the stronger head, has shown himself sadly the worse and the weaker man. When his ship struck, the captain abandoned his post; and the crew, instead of trying to save her, rushed into riot, and confusion, leaving no hope for their luckless vessel. Linton, on the contrary, displayed the true courage of a loyal and faithful soul: he trusted God; and God comforted him. One hoped, and the other despaired; they chose their own lots, and were righteously doomed to endure them.

But you'll not want to hear my moralizing, Mr. Lockwood: you'll judge as well as I can, all these things; at least, you'll think you will and that's the same.

The end of Earnshaw was what might have been expected: it followed fast on his sister's, there was scarcely six months between them. We at the Grange never got a very succinct account of his state preceding it; all that I did learn, was on occasion of going to aid in the preparations for the funeral. Mr. Kenneth came to announce the event to my master.

"Well, Nelly," said he, riding into the yard, one morning, too early not to alarm me with an instant presentiment of bad news. "It's yours, and my turn to go into mourning at present. Who's given us the slip, now do you think?"

"Who?" I asked in a flurry.

"Why, guess!" he returned, dismounting, and slinging his bridle on a hook by the door. "And nip up the corner of your apron; I'm certain you'll need it."

"Not Mr. Heathcliff, surely?" I exclaimed.

"What! would you have tears for him?" said the doctor. "No, Heathcliff's a tough young fellow; he looks blooming today — I've just seen him. He's rapidly regaining flesh since he lost his better half."

"Who is it, then, Mr. Kenneth?" I repeated impatiently.

"Hindley Earnshaw! Your old friend Hindley —" he replied. "And my wicked gossip; though he's been too wild for me this long while. There! I said we should draw water — But cheer up! He died true to his character drunk as a lord — Poor lad; I'm sorry too. One can't help missing an old companion; though he had the worst tricks with him that ever man imagined; and has done me many a rascally turn — He's barely twenty-seven, it seems; that's your own age; who would have thought you were born in one year?"

I confess this blow was greater to me than the shock of Mrs. Linton's death: ancient associations lingered round my heart; I sat down in the porch, and wept as for a blood relation, desiring Kenneth to get another servant to introduce him to the master.

I could not hinder myself from pondering on the question — "Had he had fair play?" Whatever I did that idea would bother me: it was so tiresomely pertinacious that I resolved on requesting leave to go to Wuthering Heights, and assist in the last duties to the dead. Mr. Linton was extremely reluctant to consent, but I pleaded eloquently for the friendless condition in which he lay; and I said my old master, and foster brother had a claim on my services as strong as his own. Besides, I reminded him that the child, Hareton, was his wife's nephew; and, in the absence of nearer kin, he ought to act as its guardian; and he ought to and must inquire how the property was left, and look over the concerns of his brother-in-law.

He was unfit for attending to such matters then, but he bid me speak to his lawyer; and at length, permitted me to go. His lawyer had been Earnshaw's also: I called at the village, and asked him to accompany me. He shook his head, and advised that Heathcliff should be let alone; affirming, if the truth were known, Hareton would be found little else than a beggar.

"His father died in debt," he said; "the whole property is mortgaged, and the sole chance for the natural heir is to allow him an opportunity of creating some interest in the creditor's heart, that he may be inclined to deal leniently towards him."

When I reached the Heights, I explained that I had come to see everything carried on decently, and Joseph, who appeared in sufficient distress, expressed satisfaction at my presence. Mr. Heathcliff said he did not perceive that I was wanted, but I might stay and order the arrangements for the funeral, if I chose.

"Correctly," he remarked, "that fool's body should be buried at the crossroads, without ceremony of any kind—I happened to leave him ten minutes, yesterday afternoon; and, in that interval, he fastened the two doors of the house against me, and he has spent the night in drinking himself to death deliberately! We broke in this morning, for we heard him snorting like a horse; and there he was, laid over the settle—flaying and scalping would not have wakened him—I sent for Kenneth, and he came; but not till the beast had changed into carrion—he was both dead and cold, and stark; and so you'll allow, it was useless making more stir about him!"

The old servant confirmed this statement, but muttered, "Aw'd rayther he'd goan hisseln fur t' doctor! Aw sud uh taen tent uh t' maister better nur him—un he warn't deead when Aw left, nowt uh t' soart!"

I insisted on the funeral being respectable—Mr. Heathcliff said I might have my own way there too; only, he desired me to remember, that the money for the whole affair came out of his pocket.

He maintained a hard, careless deportment, indicative of neither joy nor sorrow; if anything, it expressed a flinty gratification at a piece of difficult work, successfully executed. I observed once, indeed, something like exultation in his aspect. It was just when the people were bearing the coffin from the house; he had the hypocrisy to represent a mourner; and previous to following with Hareton he lifted the unfortunate child on to the table, and muttered with peculiar gusto,

"Now, my bonny lad, you are *mine!* And we'll see if one tree won't grow as crooked as another, with the same wind to twist it!"

The unsuspecting thing was pleased at this speech; he played with Heathcliff's whiskers, and stroked his cheek, but I divined its meaning and observed tartly,

"That boy must go back with me to Thrushcross Grange, Sir—There is nothing in the world less yours than he is!"

"Does Linton say so?" he demanded.

"Of course—he has ordered me to take him," I replied.

"Well," said the scoundrel, "we'll not argue the subject now; but I have a fancy to try my hand at rearing a young one, so intimate to your master, that I must supply the place of this with my own, if he attempt to remove it; I don't engage to let Hareton go, undisputed; but, I'll be pretty sure to make the other come! remember to tell him."

---

taen tent: taken care.

This hint was enough to bind our hands. I repeated its substance on my return, and Edgar Linton, little interested at the commencement, spoke no more of interfering. I'm not aware that he could have done it to any purpose, had he been ever so willing.

The guest was now the master of Wuthering Heights: he held firm possession, and proved to the attorney, who, in his turn, proved it to Mr. Linton, that Earnshaw had mortgaged every yard of land he owned for cash to supply his mania for gaming: and he, Heathcliff, was the mortgagee.

In that manner, Hareton, who should now be the first gentleman in the neighbourhood, was reduced to a state of complete dependence on his father's inveterate enemy; and lives in his own house as a servant deprived of the advantage of wages, and quite unable to right himself, because of his friendlessness, and his ignorance that he has been wronged.

CHAPTER XVIII

The twelve years, continued Mrs. Dean, following that dismal period, were the happiest of my life: my greatest troubles, in their passage, rose from our little lady's trifling illnesses which she had to experience in common with all children, rich and poor.

For the rest, after the first six months, she grew like a larch; and could walk and talk too, in her own way, before the heath blossomed a second time over Mrs. Linton's dust.

She was the most winning thing that ever brought sunshine into a desolate house—a real beauty in face—with the Earnshaws' handsome dark eyes, but the Lintons' fair skin, and small features, and yellow curling hair. Her spirit was high, though not rough, and qualified by a heart, sensitive and lively to excess in its affections. That capacity for intense attachments reminded me of her mother; still she did not resemble her; for she could be soft and mild as a dove, and she had a gentle voice, and pensive expression: her anger was never furious; her love never fierce; it was deep and tender.

However, it must be acknowledged, she had faults to foil her gifts. A propensity to be saucy was one; and a perverse will that indulged children invariably acquire, whether they be good tempered or cross. If a servant chanced to vex her, it was always: "I shall tell papa!" And if he reproved her, even by a look, you would have thought it a heart-breaking business: I don't believe he ever did speak a harsh word to her.

---

larch: tree of heavy, durable wood.

He took her education entirely on himself, and made it an amusement: fortunately, curiosity and a quick intellect urged her into an apt scholar; she learnt rapidly and eagerly, and did honour to his teaching.

Till she reached the age of thirteen, she had not once been beyond the range of the park by herself. Mr. Linton would take her with him, a mile or so outside, on rare occasions; but he trusted her to no one else. Gimmerton was an unsubstantial name in her ears; the chapel, the only building she had approached, or entered, except her own home; Wuthering Heights and Mr. Heathcliff did not exist for her; she was a perfect recluse; and, apparently, perfectly contented. Sometimes, indeed, while surveying the country from her nursery window, she would observe—

"Ellen, how long will it be before I can walk to the top of those hills? I wonder what lies on the other side—is it the sea?"

"No, Miss Cathy," I would answer, "it is hills again, just like these."

"And what are those golden rocks like, when you stand under them?" she once asked.

The abrupt descent of Penistone Crag[6] particularly attracted her notice, especially when the setting sun shone on it, and the topmost Heights; and the whole extent of landscape besides lay in shadow.

I explained that they were bare masses of stone, with hardly enough earth in their clefts to nourish a stunted tree.

"And why are they bright so long after it is evening here?" she pursued.

"Because they are a great deal higher up than we are," replied I; "you could not climb them, they are too high and steep. In winter the frost is always there before it comes to us; and, deep into summer, I have found snow under that black hollow on the northeast side!"

"Oh, you have been on them!" she cried, gleefully. "Then I can go, too, when I am a woman. Has papa been, Ellen?"

"Papa would tell you, Miss," I answered hastily, "that they are not worth the trouble of visiting. The moors, where you ramble with him, are much nicer; and Thrushcross park is the finest place in the world."

"But I know the park, and I don't know those," she murmured to herself. "And I should delight to look round me, from the brow of that tallest point—my little pony, Minny, shall take me sometime."

One of the maids mentioning the Fairy Cave, quite turned her head with a desire to fulfil this project; she teased Mr. Linton about it; and he promised she should have the journey when she got older: but Miss Catherine measured her age by months, and—

---

[6] For Penistone Crag, see note 2, page 73.

"Now, am I old enough to go to Penistone Crag?" was the constant question in her mouth.

The road thither wound close by Wuthering Heights. Edgar had not the heart to pass it; so she received as constantly the answer,

"Not yet, love, not yet."

I said Mrs. Heathcliff lived above a dozen years after quitting her husband. Her family were of a delicate constitution: she and Edgar both lacked the ruddy health that you will generally meet in these parts. What her last illness was, I am not certain; I conjecture, they died of the same thing, a kind of fever, slow at its commencement, but incurable, and rapidly consuming life towards the close.

She wrote to inform her brother of the probable conclusion of a four months' indisposition, under which she had suffered; and entreated him to come to her, if possible, for she had much to settle, and she wished to bid him adieu, and deliver Linton safely into his hands. Her hope was, that Linton might be left with him, as he had been with her; his father, she would fain convince herself, had no desire to assume the burden of his maintenance or education.

My master hesitated not a moment in complying with her request; reluctant as he was to leave home at ordinary calls, he flew to answer this; commending Catherine to my peculiar vigilance, in his absence; with reiterated orders that she must not wander out of the park, even under my escort; he did not calculate on her going unaccompanied.

He was away three weeks: the first day or two, my charge sat in a corner of the library, too sad for either reading or playing: in that quiet state she caused me little trouble; but it was succeeded by an interval of impatient, fretful weariness; and being too busy, and too old then, to run up and down amusing her, I hit on a method by which she might entertain herself.

I used to send her on her travels round the grounds—now on foot, and now on a pony; indulging her with a patient audience of all her real and imaginary adventures, when she returned.

The summer shone in full prime; and she took such a taste for this solitary rambling that she often contrived to remain out from breakfast till tea; and then the evenings were spent in recounting her fanciful tales. I did not fear her breaking bounds, because the gates were generally locked, and I thought she would scarcely venture forth alone, if they had stood wide open.

Unluckily, my confidence proved misplaced. Catherine came to me, one morning, at eight o'clock, and said she was that day an Arabian merchant, going to cross the desert with his caravan; and I must give her plenty of provision for herself, and beasts, a horse, and three camels, personated by a large hound, and a couple of pointers.

I got together a good store of dainties, and slung them in a basket on one side of the saddle; and she sprang up as gay as a fairy, sheltered by her wide-brimmed hat and gauze veil from the July sun, and trotted off with a merry laugh, mocking my cautious counsel to avoid galloping, and come back early.

The naughty thing never made her appearance at tea. One traveller, the hound, being an old dog, and fond of its ease, returned; but neither Cathy, nor the pony, nor the two pointers were visible in any direction; and I despatched emissaries down this path, and that path, and, at last, went wandering in search of her myself.

There was a labourer working at a fence round a plantation, on the borders of the grounds I enquired of him if he had seen our young lady.

"I saw her at morn," he replied, "she would have me to cut her a hazel switch; and then she leapt her galloway over the hedge yonder, where it is lowest, and galloped out of sight."

You may guess how I felt at hearing this news. It struck me directly she must have started for Penistone Crag.

"What will become of her?" I ejaculated, pushing through a gap which the man was repairing, and making straight to the high road.

I walked as if for a wager, mile after mile, till a turn brought me in view of the Heights, but no Catherine could I detect, far or near.

The Crag lies about a mile and a half beyond Mr. Heathcliff's place, and that is four from the Grange, so I began to fear night would fall ere I could reach them.

"And what if she should have slipped in clambering among them," I reflected, "and been killed, or broken some of her bones?"

My suspense was truly painful; and, at first, it gave me delightful relief to observe, in hurrying by the farmhouse, Charlie, the fiercest of the pointers, lying under a window, with swelled head, and bleeding ear.

I opened the wicket, and ran to the door, knocking vehemently for admittance. A woman whom I knew, and who formerly lived at Gimmerton, answered—she had been servant there since the death of Mr. Earnshaw.

"Ah," said she, "you are come a seeking your little mistress! don't be frightened. She's here safe—but I'm glad it isn't the master."

"He is not at home then, is he?" I panted, quite breathless with quick walking and alarm.

---

galloway: horse bred in the southwest of Scotland.

"No, no," she replied: "both he and Joseph are off, and I think they won't return this hour or more. Step in and rest you a bit."

I entered, and beheld my stray lamb, seated on the hearth, rocking herself in a little chair that had been her mother's, when a child. Her hat was hung against the wall, and she seemed perfectly at home, laughing and chattering, in the best spirits imaginable, to Hareton, now a great, strong lad of eighteen, who stared at her with considerable curiosity and astonishment; comprehending precious little of the fluent succession of remarks and questions which her tongue never ceased pouring forth.

"Very well, Miss," I exclaimed, concealing my joy under an angry countenance. "This is your last ride, till papa comes back. I'll not trust you over the threshold again, you naughty, naughty girl."

"Aha, Ellen!" she cried gaily, jumping up, and running to my side. "I shall have a pretty story to tell tonight—and so you've found me out. Have you ever been here in your life before?"

"Put that hat on, and home at once," said I. "I'm dreadfully grieved at you, Miss Cathy, you've done extremely wrong! It's no use pouting and crying; that won't repay the trouble I've had, scouring the country after you. To think how Mr. Linton charged me to keep you in; and you stealing off so; it shows you are a cunning little fox, and nobody will put faith in you any more."

"What have I done?" sobbed she, instantly checked. "Papa charged me nothing—he'll not scold me, Ellen—he's never cross, like you!"

"Come, come!" I repeated. "I'll tie the riband. Now, let us have no petulance. Oh, for shame. You thirteen years old, and such a baby!"

This exclamation was caused by her pushing the hat from her head, and retreating to the chimney out of my reach.

"Nay," said the servant, "don't be hard on the bonny lass, Mrs. Dean. We made her stop—she'd fain have ridden forwards, afeard you should be uneasy. But Hareton offered to go with her, and I thought he should. It's a wild road over the hills."

Hareton, during the discussion, stood with his hands in his pockets, too awkward to speak, though he looked as if he did not relish my intrusion.

"How long am I to wait?" I continued, disregarding the woman's interference. "It will be dark in ten minutes. Where is the pony, Miss Cathy? And where is Phenix? I shall leave you, unless you be quick, so please yourself."

---

riband: ribbon.

"The pony is in the yard," she replied, "and Phenix is shut in there. He's bitten—and so is Charlie. I was going to tell you all about it; but you are in a bad temper, and don't deserve to hear."

I picked up her hat, and approached to reinstate it; but perceiving that the people of the house took her part, she commenced capering round the room; and, on my giving chase, ran like a mouse, over and under, and behind the furniture, rendering it ridiculous for me to pursue.

Hareton and the woman laughed; and she joined them, and waxed more impertinent still; till I cried, in great irritation,

"Well, Miss Cathy, if you were aware whose house this is, you'd be glad enough to get out."

"It's *your* father's, isn't it?" said she, turning to Hareton.

"Nay," he replied, looking down, and blushing bashfully.

He could not stand a steady gaze from her eyes, though they were just his own.

"Whose then—your master's?" she asked.

He coloured deeper, with a different feeling, muttered an oath, and turned away.

"Who is his master?" continued the tiresome girl, appealing to me. "He talked about 'our house,' and 'our folk.' I thought he had been the owner's son. And he never said, Miss; he should have done, shouldn't he, if he's a servant?"

Hareton grew black as a thunder-cloud, at this childish speech. I silently shook my questioner, and, at last, succeeded in equipping her for departure.

"Now, get my horse," she said, addressing her unknown kinsman as she would one of the stable-boys at the Grange. "And you may come with me. I want to see where the goblin hunter rises in the marsh, and to hear about the *fairishes,* as you call them—but, make haste! What's the matter? Get my horse, I say."

"I'll see thee damned, before I be *thy* servant!" growled the lad.

"You'll see me *what?*" asked Catherine in surprise.

"Damned—thou saucy witch!" he replied.

"There, Miss Cathy! you see you have got into pretty company," I interposed. "Nice words to be used to a young lady! Pray don't begin to dispute with him—Come, let us seek for Minny ourselves, and begone."

"But, Ellen," cried she, staring, fixed in astonishment. "How dare he speak so to me? Mustn't he be made to do as I ask him? You wicked creature, I shall tell papa what you said—Now then!"

---

fairishes: fairies.

Hareton did not appear to feel this threat; so the tears sprang into her eyes with indignation. "You bring the pony," she exclaimed, turning to the woman, "and let my dog free this moment!"

"Softly, Miss," answered the addressed. "You'll lose nothing, by being civil. Though Mr. Hareton, there, be not the master's son, he's your cousin; and I was never hired to serve you."

"*He* my cousin!" cried Cathy with a scornful laugh.

"Yes, indeed," responded her reprover.

"Oh, Ellen! don't let them say such things," she pursued in great trouble. "Papa is gone to fetch my cousin from London—my cousin is a gentleman's son—That my—" she stopped, and wept outright; upset at the bare notion of relationship with such a clown.

"Hush, hush!" I whispered, "people can have many cousins and of all sorts, Miss Cathy, without being any the worse for it; only they needn't keep their company, if they be disagreeable, and bad."

"He's not, he's not my cousin, Ellen!" she went on, gathering fresh grief from reflection, and flinging herself into my arms for refuge from the idea.

I was much vexed at her and the servant for their mutual revelations; having no doubt of Linton's approaching arrival, communicated by the former, being reported to Mr. Heathcliff; and feeling as confident that Catherine's first thought on her father's return, would be to seek an explanation of the latter's assertion, concerning her rude-bred kindred.

Hareton, recovering from his disgust at being taken for a servant, seemed moved by her distress; and, having fetched the pony round to the door, he took, to propitiate her, a fine crooked-legged terrier-whelp from the kennel; and putting it into her hand, bid her wisht! for he meant naught.

Pausing in her lamentations, she surveyed him with a glance of awe, and horror, then burst forth anew.

I could scarcely refrain from smiling at this antipathy to the poor fellow; who was a well-made, athletic youth, good looking in features, and stout and healthy, but attired in garments befitting his daily occupations of working on the farm, and lounging among the moors after rabbits and game. Still, I thought I could detect in his physiognomy a mind owning better qualities than his father ever possessed. Good things lost amid a wilderness of weeds, to be sure, whose rankness far over-topped their neglected growth; yet notwithstanding, evidence of a wealthy soil that might yield luxuriant crops, under other and favourable circumstances. Mr. Heathcliff, I believe, had not treated him physically ill; thanks to his fearless nature which offered no temptation to that course of oppression;

---

bid her wisht: told her to be quiet.

it had none of the timid susceptibility that would have given zest to ill-treatment, in Heathcliff's judgment. He appeared to have bent his malevolence on making him a brute: he was never taught to read or write; never rebuked for any bad habit which did not annoy his keeper; never led a single step towards virtue, or guarded by a single precept against vice. And from what I heard, Joseph contributed much to his deterioration, by a narrow-minded partiality which prompted him to flatter, and pet him, as a boy, because he was the head of the old family. And as he had been in the habit of accusing Catherine Earnshaw, and Heathcliff, when children, of putting the master past his patience, and compelling him to seek solace in drink, by what he termed, their "offald ways," so at present, he laid the whole burden of Hareton's faults on the shoulders of the usurper of his property.

If the lad swore he wouldn't correct him; nor however culpably he behaved. It gave Joseph satisfaction, apparently, to watch him go the worst lengths. He allowed that he was ruined; that his soul was abandoned to perdition; but then, he reflected that Heathcliff must answer for it. Hareton's blood would be required at his hands; and there lay immense consolation in that thought.

Joseph had instilled into him a pride of name, and of his lineage; he would had he dared, have fostered hate between him and the present owner of the Heights, but his dread of that owner amounted to superstition; and he confined his feelings, regarding him, to muttered inuendoes and private comminations.

I don't pretend to be intimately acquainted with the mode of living customary in those days, at Wuthering Heights. I only speak from hearsay; for I saw little. The villagers affirmed Mr. Heathcliff was *near,* and a cruel hard landlord to his tenants; but the house, inside, had regained its ancient aspect of comfort under female management; and the scenes of riot common in Hindley's time, were not now enacted within its walls. The master was too gloomy to seek companionship with any people, good or bad, and he is yet —

This, however, is not making progress with my story. Miss Cathy rejected the peace offering of the terrier, and demanded her own dogs, Charlie and Phenix. They came limping, and hanging their heads; and we set out for home, sadly out of sorts, everyone of us.

I could not wring from my little lady how she had spent the day; except that, as I supposed, the goal of her pilgrimage was Penistone Crag; and she arrived without adventure to the gate of the farmhouse, when Hareton

---

near: stingy.

happened to issue forth, attended by some canine followers who attacked her train.

They had a smart battle, before their owners could separate them: that formed an introduction. Catherine told Hareton who she was, and where she was going; and asked him to show her the way; finally, beguiling him to accompany her.

He opened the mysteries of the Fairy Cave,[7] and twenty other queer places; but, being in disgrace, I was not favoured with the description of the interesting objects she saw.

I could gather however, that her guide had been a favourite till she hurt his feelings by addressing him as a servant, and Heathcliff's housekeeper hurt hers, by calling him her cousin.

Then the language he had held to her rankled in her heart; she who was always "love," and "darling," and "queen," and "angel," with everybody at the Grange; to be insulted so shockingly by a stranger! She did not comprehend it; and hard work I had, to obtain a promise that she would not lay the grievance before her father.

I explained how he objected to the whole household at the Heights, and how sorry he would be to find she had been there; but, I insisted most on the fact, that if she revealed my negligence of his orders, he would perhaps, be so angry that I should have to leave; and Cathy couldn't bear that prospect: she pledged her word, and kept it, for my sake—after all, she was a sweet little girl.

CHAPTER XIX

A letter, edged with black, announced the day of my master's return. Isabella was dead; and he wrote to bid me get mourning for his daughter, and arrange a room, and other accommodations, for his youthful nephew.

Catherine ran wild with joy at the idea of welcoming her father back: and indulged most sanguine anticipations of the innumerable excellencies of her "real" cousin.

The evening of their expected arrival came. Since early morning, she had been busy, ordering her own small affairs; and now, attired in her new black frock—poor thing! her aunt's death impressed her with no definite sorrow—she obliged me, by constant worrying, to walk with her, down through the grounds, to meet them.

---

[7] For the Fairy Cave, see note 2, page 75, and the illustration on page 348.

"Linton is just six months younger than I am," she chattered as we strolled leisurely over the swells and hollows of mossy turf. under shadow of the trees. "How delightful it will be to have him for a playfellow! Aunt Isabella sent papa a beautiful lock of his hair; it was lighter than mine—more flaxen, and quite as fine. I have it carefully preserved in a little glass box; and I've often thought what pleasure it would be to see its owner—Oh! I am happy—and papa, dear, dear papa! come, Ellen, let us run! come run."

She ran, and returned and ran again, many times before my sober footsteps reached the gate, and then she seated herself on the grassy bank beside the path, and tried to wait patiently; but that was impossible; she couldn't be still a minute.

"How long they are!" she exclaimed. "Ah, I see some dust on the road—they are coming! No! When will they be here? May we not go a little way—half a mile, Ellen, only just half a mile? Do say yes, to that clump of birches at the turn!"

I refused staunchily: and, at length, her suspense was ended: the travelling carriage rolled in sight.

Miss Cathy shrieked, and stretched out her arms, as soon as she caught her father's face, looking from the window. He descended, nearly as eager as herself; and a considerable interval elapsed, ere they had a thought to spare for any but themselves.

While they exchanged caresses, I took a peep in to see after Linton. He was asleep, in a corner, wrapped in a warm, fur-lined cloak, as if it had been winter. A pale, delicate, effeminate boy, who might have been taken for my master's younger brother, so strong was the resemblance, but there was a sickly peevishness in his aspect, that Edgar Linton never had.

The latter saw me looking; and having shaken hands, advised me to close the door, and leave him undisturbed; for the journey had fatigued him.

Cathy would fain have taken one glance; but her father told her to come on, and they walked together up the park, while I hastened before, to prepare the servants.

"Now, darling," said Mr. Linton, addressing his daughter, as they halted at the bottom of the front steps. "Your cousin is not strong, or merry as you are, and he has lost his mother, remember, a very short time since, therefore, don't expect him to play, and run about with you directly. And don't harass him much by talking—let him be quiet this evening, at least, will you?"

"Yes, yes, papa," answered Catherine; "but I do want to see him; and he hasn't once looked out."

The carriage stopped; and the sleeper, being roused, was lifted to the ground by his uncle.

"This is your cousin Cathy, Linton," he said, putting their little hands together. "She's fond of you already; and mind you don't grieve her by crying tonight. Try to be cheerful now; the travelling is at an end, and you have nothing to do but rest and amuse yourself as you please."

"Let me go to bed, then," answered the boy, shrinking from Catherine's salute; and he put his fingers to his eyes to remove incipient tears.

"Come, come, there's a good child," I whispered, leading him in. "You'll make her weep too—see how sorry she is for you!"

I do not know whether it were sorrow for him, but his cousin put on as sad a countenance as himself, and returned to her father. All three entered, and mounted to the library where tea was laid ready.

I proceeded to remove Linton's cap and mantle, and placed him on a chair by the table; but he was no sooner seated than he began to cry afresh. My master inquired what was the matter.

"I can't sit on a chair," sobbed the boy.

"Go to the sofa then; and Ellen shall bring you some tea," answered his uncle, patiently.

He had been greatly tried during the journey, I felt convinced, by his fretful, ailing charge.

Linton slowly trailed himself off, and lay down. Cathy carried a footstool and her cup to his side.

At first she sat silent; but that could not last; she had resolved to make a pet of her little cousin, as she would have him to be; and she commenced stroking his curls, and kissing his cheek, and offering him tea in her saucer, like a baby. This pleased him, for he was not much better; he dried his eyes, and lightened into a faint smile.

"Oh, he'll do very well," said the master to me, after watching them a minute. "Very well, if we can keep him, Ellen. The company of a child of his own age will instil new spirit into him soon: and by wishing for strength he'll gain it."

"Aye, if we can keep him!" I mused to myself; and sore misgivings came over me that there was slight hope of that. And then, I thought, however will that weakling live at Wuthering Heights, between his father and Hareton? What playmates and instructors they'll be.

Our doubts were presently decided; even earlier than I expected. I had just taken the children upstairs, after tea was finished; and seen Linton asleep—he would not suffer me to leave him, till that was the case—I had come down, and was standing by the table in the hall, lighting a bedroom candle for Mr. Edgar, when a maid stepped out of the kitchen, and informed me that Mr. Heathcliff's servant, Joseph, was at the door, and wished to speak with the master.

"I shall ask him what he wants first," I said, in considerable trepidation. "A very unlikely hour to be troubling people, and the instant they have returned from a long journey. I don't think the master can see him."

Joseph had advanced through the kitchen, as I uttered these words, and now presented himself in the hall. He was donned in his Sunday garments, with his most sanctimonious and sourest face; and holding his hat in one hand, and his stick in the other, he proceeded to clean his shoes on the mat.

"Good evening, Joseph," I said, coldly. "What business brings you here tonight?"

"It's Maister Linton Aw mun spake tull," he answered, waving me disdainfully aside.

"Mr. Linton is going to bed; unless you have something particular to say, I'm sure he won't hear it now," I continued. "You had better sit down in there, and entrust your message to me."

"Which is his rahm?" pursued the fellow, surveying the range of closed doors.

I perceived he was bent on refusing my mediation; so very reluctantly, I went up to the library, and announced the unseasonable visiter; advising that he should be dismissed till next day.

Mr. Linton had no time to empower me to do so, for Joseph mounted close at my heels, and pushing into the apartment, planted himself at the far side of the table, with his two fists clapped on the head of his stick, and began in an elevated tone, as if anticipating opposition.

"Hathecliff has sent me for his lad, and Aw 'munn't goa back 'baht him."

Edgar Linton was silent a minute; an expression of exceeding sorrow overcast his features; he would have pitied the child on his own account; but, recalling Isabella's hopes and fears, and anxious wishes for her son, and her commendations of him to his care, he grieved bitterly at the prospect of yielding him up, and searched in his heart how it might be avoided. No plan offered itself: the very exhibition of any desire to keep him would have rendered the claimant more peremptory: there was nothing left but to resign him. However, he was not going to rouse him from his sleep.

"Tell Mr. Heathcliff," he answered, calmly, "that his son shall come to Wuthering Heights tomorrow. He is in bed, and too tired to go the distance now. You may also tell him that the mother of Linton desired him to remain under my guardianship; and, at present, his health is very precarious."

"Noa!" said Joseph, giving a thud with his prop on the floor, and assuming an authoritative air. "Noa! that manes nowt—Hathecliff maks noa 'cahnt uh t' mother, nur yah norther—bud he'll hev his lad; und Aw mun tak him—soa now yah knaw!"

"You shall not tonight!" answered Linton, decisively. "Walk downstairs at once, and repeat to your master what I have said. Ellen, show him down. Go—"

And, aiding the indignant elder with a lift by the arm, he rid the room of him, and closed the door.

"Varrah weel!" shouted Joseph, as he slowly drew off. "Tuh morn, he's come hisseln, and thrust *him* aht, if yah darr!"

CHAPTER XX

To obviate the danger of this threat being fulfilled, Mr. Linton commissioned me to take the boy home early, on Catherine's pony, and, said he—

"As we shall now have no influence over his destiny, good or bad, you must say nothing of where he is gone to my daughter; she cannot associate with him hereafter; and it is better for her to remain in ignorance of his proximity, lest she should be restless, and anxious to visit the Heights—merely tell her, his father sent for him suddenly, and he has been obliged to leave us."

Linton was very reluctant to be roused from his bed, at five o'clock, and astonished to be informed that he must prepare for further travelling: but I softened off the matter by stating that he was going to spend some time with his father, Mr. Heathcliff, who wished to see him so much, he did not like to defer the pleasure till he should recover from his late journey.

"My father?" he cried, in strange perplexity. "Mamma never told me I had a father. Where does he live? I'd rather stay with uncle."

"He lives a little distance from the Grange," I replied, just beyond those hills—not so far, but you may walk over here, when you get hearty. And you should be glad to go home, and to see him. You must try to love him, as you did your mother, and then he will love you."

"But why have I not heard of him before?" asked Linton; "why didn't mamma and he live together as other people do?"

"He had business to keep him in the north," I answered; "and your mother's health required her to reside in the south."

---

maks noa 'cahnt uh t' mother: does not care about the mother nor you.
nur yah norther: nor you, neither.

"And why didn't mamma speak to me about him?" persevered the child. "She often talked of uncle, and I learnt to love him long ago. How am I to love papa? I don't know him."

"Oh, all children love their parents," I said. "Your mother, perhaps, thought you would want to be with him, if she mentioned him often to you. Let us make haste. An early ride on such a beautiful morning is much preferable to an hour's more sleep."

"Is *she* to go with us," he demanded. "The little girl I saw yesterday?"

"Not now," replied I.

"Is uncle?" he continued.

"No, I shall be your companion there," I said.

Linton sank back on his pillow, and fell into a brown study.

"I won't go without uncle," he cried at length; "I can't tell where you mean to take me."

I attempted to persuade him of the naughtiness of showing reluctance to meet his father: still he obstinately resisted any progress towards dressing; and I had to call for my master's assistance, in coaxing him out of bed.

The poor thing was finally got off with several delusive assurances that his absence should be short; that Mr. Edgar and Cathy would visit him; and other promises, equally ill-founded, which I invented and reiterated, at intervals, throughout the way.

The pure heather-scented air, and the bright sunshine, and the gentle canter of Minny relieved his despondency, after a while. He began to put questions concerning his new home, and its inhabitants, with greater interest, and liveliness.

"Is Wuthering Heights as pleasant a place as Thrushcross Grange?" he inquired, turning to take a last glance into the valley, whence a light mist mounted, and formed fleecy cloud, on the skirts of the blue.

"It is not so buried in trees," I replied, "and it is not quite so large, but you can see the country beautifully, all round; and the air is healthier for you—fresher, and dryer. You will, perhaps, think the building old and dark, at first—though it is a respectable house, the next best in the neighbourhood. And you will have such nice rambles on the moors! Hareton Earnshaw—that is Miss Cathy's other cousin; and so yours in a manner—will show you all the sweetest spots; and you can bring a book in fine weather, and make a green hollow your study; and, now and then, your uncle may join you in a walk; he does, frequently, walk out on the hills."

"And what is my father like?" he asked. "Is he as young and handsome as uncle?"

"He's as young," said I, "but he has black hair, and eyes; and looks sterner, and he is taller and bigger altogether. He'll not seem to you so gentle and kind at first, perhaps, because, it is not his way—still, mind you be frank and cordial with him; and naturally, he'll be fonder of you than any uncle, for you are his own."

"Black hair and eyes!" mused Linton. "I can't fancy him. Then I am not like him, am I?"

"Not much," I answered . . . Not a morsel, I thought: surveying with regret the white complexion, and slim frame of my companion, and his large languid eyes . . . his mother's eyes save that, unless a morbid touchiness kindled them, a moment, they had not a vestige of her sparkling spirit.

"How strange that he should never come to see mama and me," he murmured. "Has he ever seen me? If he have, I must have been a baby—I remember not a single thing about him!"

"Why, Master Linton," said I, "three hundred miles is a great distance: and ten years seem very different in length, to a grown up person, compared with what they do to you. It is probable Mr. Heathcliff proposed going, from summer to summer, but never found a convenient opportunity: and now it is too late—Don't trouble him with questions on the subject: it will disturb him for no good."

The boy was fully occupied with his own cogitations for the remainder of the ride, till we halted before the farmhouse garden gate. I watched to catch his impressions in his countenance. He surveyed the carved front, and low-browed lattices; the straggling gooseberry bushes, and crooked firs, with solemn intentness, and then shook his head: his private feelings entirely disapproved of the exterior of his new abode; but he had sense to postpone complaining—there might be compensation within.

Before he dismounted, I went and opened the door. It was half-past six; the family had just finished breakfast; the servant was clearing and wiping down the table: Joseph stood by his master's chair telling some tale concerning a lame horse; and Hareton was preparing for the hay-field.

"Hallo, Nelly!" cried Mr. Heathcliff, when he saw me. "I feared I should have to come down and fetch my property, myself—You've brought it have you? Let us see what we can make of it."

He got up and strode to the door: Hareton and Joseph followed in gaping curiosity. Poor Linton ran a frightened eye over the faces of the three.

"Surely," said Joseph, after a grave inspection, "he's swopped wi' ye, maister, an' yon's his lass!"

Heathcliff having stared his son into an ague of confusion, uttered a scornful laugh.

"God! what a beauty! what a lovely, charming thing!" he exclaimed. "Haven't they reared it on snails, and sour milk, Nelly? Oh, damn my

---

ague: attack of fever.

soul! but that's worse than I expected—and the devil knows I was not sanguine!"

I bid the trembling and bewildered child get down, and enter. He did not thoroughly comprehend the meaning of his father's speech, or whether it were intended for him: indeed, he was not yet certain that the grim, sneering stranger was his father; but he clung to me with growing trepidation; and on Mr. Heathcliff's taking a seat, and bidding him "come hither," he hid his face on my shoulder, and wept.

"Tut, tut!" said Heathcliff, stretching out a hand and dragging him roughly between his knees, and then holding up his head by the chin. "None of that nonsense! We're not going to hurt thee, Linton—isn't that thy name? Thou art thy mother's child, entirely! Where is *my* share in thee, puling chicken?"

He took off the boy's cap and pushed back his thick flaxen curls, felt his slender arms, and his small fingers; during which examination, Linton ceased crying, and lifted his great blue eyes to inspect the inspector.

"Do you know me?" asked Heathcliff, having satisfied himself that the limbs were all equally frail and feeble.

"No," said Linton, with a gaze of vacant fear.

"You've heard of me, I daresay?"

"No," he replied again.

"No! What a shame of your mother, never to waken your filial regard for me! You are my son, then, I'll tell you; and your mother was a wicked slut to leave you in ignorance of the sort of father you possessed—Now, don't wince, and colour up! Though it *is* something to see you have not white blood—Be a good lad; and I'll do for you—Nelly, if you be tired you may sit down, if not get home again—I guess you'll report what you hear, and see, to the cipher at the Grange; and this thing won't be settled while you linger about it."

"Well," replied I, "I hope you'll be kind to the boy, Mr. Heathcliff, or you'll not keep him long, and he's all you have akin, in the wide world that you will ever know—remember."

"I'll be *very* kind to him, you needn't fear," he said laughing. "Only nobody else must be kind to him—I'm jealous of monopolizing his affection—And, to begin my kindness, Joseph! bring the lad some breakfast—Hareton, you infernal calf, begone to your work. Yes, Nell," he added when they were departed, "my son is prospective owner of your place, and I should not wish him to die till I was certain of being his successor. Besides, he's *mine,* and I want the triumph of seeing *my* descendent fairly lord of their estates; my child hiring their children, to till their fathers' land for wages—That is the sole consideration which can make me endure the whelp—I despise him for himself, and hate him for the memories he revives! But that consideration is sufficient; he's as safe with me, and shall be tended as carefully, as your master tends his own—I have a room upstairs, furnished for him, in handsome style—I've engaged a tutor, also, to come three times a week, from twenty miles distance, to teach him what he pleases to learn. I've ordered Hareton to obey him: and in fact, I've arranged everything with a view to preserve the superior, and the gentleman in him, above his associates—I do regret however, that he so little deserves the trouble—if I wished any blessing in the world, it was to find him a worthy object of pride, and I'm bitterly disappointed with the whey-faced whining wretch!"

While he was speaking, Joseph returned, bearing a basin of milk-porridge, and placed it before Linton. He stirred round the homely mess with a look of aversion, and affirmed that he could not eat it.

I saw the old man servant shared largely in his master's scorn of the child, though he was compelled to retain the sentiment in his heart, because Heathcliff plainly meant his underlings to hold him in honour.

"Cannot ate it?" repeated he, peering in Linton's face, and subduing his voice to a whisper, for fear of being overheard. "But Maister Hareton nivir ate nowt else, when he wer a little un: und what wer gooid eneugh fur him's gooid eneugh fur yah, Aw's rayther think!"

"I *shan't* eat it!" answered Linton, snappishly. "Take it away."

Joseph snatched up the food indignantly, and brought it to us.

"Is there owt ails th' victuals?" he asked, thrusting the tray under Heathcliff's nose.

"What should ail them?" he said.

"Wah!" answered Joseph, "yon dainty chap says he cannut ate 'em. Bud Aw guess it's raight! His mother wer just soa—we wer a'most too mucky tuh sow t' corn for makking her breead."

"Don't mention his mother to me," said the master, angrily. "Get him something that he can eat, that's all. What is his usual food, Nelly?"

I suggested boiled milk or tea; and the housekeeper received instructions to prepare some.

Come, I reflected, his father's selfishness may contribute to his comfort. He perceives his delicate constitution, and the necessity of treating him tolerably. I'll console Mr. Edgar by acquainting him with the turn Heathcliff's humour has taken.

Having no excuse for lingering longer, I slipped out, while Linton was engaged in timidly rebuffing the advances of a friendly sheepdog. But he was too much on the alert to be cheated—as I closed the door, I heard a cry, and a frantic repetition of the words—

"Don't leave me! I'll not stay here! I'll not stay here!"

Then the latch was raised and fell—they did not suffer him to come forth. I mounted Minny, and urged her to a trot; and so my brief guardianship ended.

CHAPTER XXI

We had sad work with little Cathy that day: she rose in high glee, eager to join her cousin; and such passionate tears and lamentations followed the news of his departure, that Edgar himself was obliged to soothe her, by affirming he should come back soon; he added, however, "if I can get him;" and there were no hopes of that.

This promise poorly pacified her; but time was more potent; and though still, at intervals, she inquired of her father, when Linton would return; before she did see him again, his features had waxed so dim in her memory that she did not recognise him.

When I chanced to encounter the housekeeper of Wuthering Heights, in paying business visits to Gimmerton, I used to ask how the young master got on; for he lived almost as secluded as Catherine herself, and was never to be seen. I could gather from her that he continued in weak health, and was a tiresome inmate. She said Mr. Heathcliff seemed to dislike him ever longer and worse, though he took some trouble to conceal it. He had an antipathy to the sound of his voice, and could not do at all with his sitting in the same room with him many minutes together.

There seldom passed much talk between them; Linton learnt his lessons, and spent his evenings in a small apartment they called the parlour; or else lay in bed all day; for he was constantly getting coughs, and colds, and aches, and pains of some sort.

"And I never knew such a faint-hearted creature," added the woman; "nor one so careful of hisseln. He *will* go on, if I leave the window open, a bit late in the evening. Oh! it's killing, a breath of night air! And he must have a fire in the middle of summer; and Joseph's bacca pipe is poison; and he must always have sweets and dainties, and always milk, milk forever—heeding naught how the rest of us are pinched in winter—and there he'll sit, wrapped in his furred cloak in his chair by the fire, and some toast and water, or other slop on the hob to sip at; and if Hareton, for pity, comes to amuse him—Hareton is not bad-natured, though he's rough—they're sure

---

hob: shelf at the back of a fireplace for keeping food or utensils warm.

to part, one swearing, and the other crying. I believe the master would relish Earnshaw's thrashing him to a mummy, if he were not his son: and I'm certain, he would be fit to turn him out of doors, if he knew half the nursing he gives hisseln. But then, he won't go into danger of temptation; he never enters the parlour, and should Linton show those ways in the house where he is, he sends him upstairs directly."

I divined, from this account, that utter lack of sympathy had rendered young Heathcliff selfish and disagreeable, if he were not so originally; and my interest in him, consequently, decayed; though still I was moved by a sense of grief at his lot, and a wish that he had been left with us.

Mr. Edgar encouraged me to gain information; he thought a great deal about him, I fancy, and would have run some risk to see him; and he told me once to ask the housekeeper whether he ever came into the village?

She said he had only been twice, on horseback, accompanying his father: and both times he pretended to be quite knocked up for three or four days afterwards.

The housekeeper left, if I recollect rightly, two years after he came; and another, whom I did not know, was her successor: she lives there still.

Time wore on at the Grange in its former pleasant way, till Miss Cathy reached sixteen. On the anniversary of her birth we never manifested any signs of rejoicing, because it was, also, the anniversary of my late mistress's death. Her father invariably spent that day alone in the library; and walked, at dusk, as far as Gimmerton kirkyard, where he would frequently prolong his stay beyond midnight. Therefore Catherine was thrown on her own resources for amusement.

This twentieth of March was a beautiful spring day, and when her father had retired, my young lady came down dressed for going out, and said she had asked to have a ramble on the edge of the moors with me; and Mr. Linton had given her leave, if we went only a short distance, and were back within the hour.

"So make haste, Ellen!" she cried. "I know where I wish to go; where a colony of moor game are settled; I want to see whether they have made their nests yet."

"That must be a good distance up," I answered; "they don't breed on the edge of the moor."

"No, it's not," she said. "I've gone very near with papa."

I put on my bonnet, and sallied out; thinking nothing more of the matter. She bounded before me, and returned to my side, and was off again like a young greyhound; and, at first, I found plenty of entertainment in listening to the larks singing far and near; and enjoying the sweet, warm sunshine; and watching her, my pet, and my delight, with her golden ringlets flying loose behind, and her bright cheek, as soft and pure in its bloom, as a wild rose, and her eyes radiant with cloudless pleasure. She was a happy creature, and an angel, in those days. It's a pity she could not be content.

"Well," said I, "where are your moor-game, Miss Cathy? We should be at them—the Grange park fence is a great way off now."

"Oh, a little further—only a little further, Ellen," was her answer, continually. "Climb to that hillock, pass that bank, and by the time you reach the other side, I shall have raised the birds."

But there were so many hillocks and banks to climb and pass that, at length, I began to be weary, and told her we must halt, and retrace our steps.

I shouted to her, as she had outstripped me, a long way; she either did not hear, or did not regard, for she still sprang on, and I was compelled to follow. Finally, she dived into a hollow; and before I came in sight of her again, she was two miles nearer Wuthering Heights than her own home; and I beheld a couple of persons arrest her, one of whom I felt convinced was Mr. Heathcliff himself.

Cathy had been caught in the act of plundering, or, at least, hunting out the nests of the grouse.

The Heights were Heathcliff's land, and he was reproving the poacher.

"I've neither taken any nor found any," she said, as I toiled to them, expanding her hands in corroboration of the statement. "I didn't mean to take them; but papa told me there were quantities up here, and I wished to see the eggs."

Heathcliff glanced at me with an ill-meaning smile, expressing his acquaintance with the party, and, consequently, his malevolence towards it, and demanded who "papa" was.

"Mr. Linton of Thrushcross Grange," she replied. "I thought you did not know me, or you wouldn't have spoken in that way."

"You suppose papa is highly esteemed and respected then?" he said, sarcastically.

"And what are you?" inquired Catherine, gazing curiously on the speaker. "That man I've seen before. Is he your son?"

She pointed to Hareton, the other individual; who had gained nothing but increased bulk and strength by the addition of two years to his age: he seemed as awkward and rough as ever.

"Miss Cathy," I interrupted, "it will be three hours instead of one, that we are out, presently. We really must go back."

"No, that man is not my son," answered Heathcliff, pushing me aside. "But I have one, and you have seen him before too; and, though your nurse is in a hurry, I think both you and she would be the better for a little rest. Will you just turn this nab of heath, and walk into my house? You'll get home earlier for the ease; and you shall receive a kind welcome."

I whispered to Catherine that she mustn't, on any account, accede to the proposal; it was entirely out of the question.

"Why?" she asked, aloud. "I'm tired of running, and the ground is dewy—I can't sit here. Let us go, Ellen! Besides, he says I have seen his son. He's mistaken, I think; but I guess where he lives, at the farmhouse I visited in coming from Penistone Crag. Don't you?"

"I do. Come, Nelly, hold your tongue—it will be a treat for her to look in on us. Hareton, get forwards with the lass. You shall walk with me, Nelly."

"No, she's not going to any such place," I cried, struggling to release my arm which he had seized; but she was almost at the door-stones already, scampering round the brow at full speed. Her appointed companion did not pretend to escort her; he shyed off by the road side, and vanished.

"Mr. Heathcliff, it's very wrong," I continued, "you know you mean no good; and there she'll see Linton, and all will be told, as soon as ever we return; and I shall have the blame."

"I want her to see Linton," he answered: "he's looking better these few days; it's not often he's fit to be seen. And we'll soon persuade her to keep the visit secret—where is the harm of it?"

"The harm of it is, that her father would hate me, if he found I suffered her to enter your house; and I am convinced you have a bad design in encouraging her to do so," I replied.

"My design is as honest as possible. I'll inform you of its whole scope," he said. "That the two cousins may fall in love, and get married. I'm acting generously to your master; his young chit has no expectations, and should she second my wishes, she'll be provided for, at once, as joint successor with Linton."

"If Linton died," I answered, "and his life is quite uncertain, Catherine would be the heir."

"No, she would not," he said. "There is no clause in the will to secure it so; his property would go to me; but, to prevent disputes, I desire their union, and am resolved to bring it about."

"And I'm resolved she shall never approach your house with me again," I returned, as we reached the gate, where Miss Cathy waited our coming.

Heathcliff bid me be quiet; and, preceding us up the path, hastened to open the door. My young lady gave him several looks, as if she could not exactly make up her mind what to think of him; but now he smiled when he met her eye, and softened his voice in addressing her, and I was foolish enough to imagine the memory of her mother might disarm him from desiring her injury.

Linton stood on the hearth. He had been out, walking in the fields; for his cap was on, and he was calling to Joseph to bring him dry shoes.

He had grown tall of his age, still wanting some months of sixteen. His features were pretty yet, and his eye and complexion brighter than I remembered them, though with merely temporary lustre borrowed from the salubrious air and genial sun.

"Now, who is that?" asked Mr. Heathcliff, turning to Cathy. "Can you tell?"

"Your son?" she said, having doubtfully surveyed, first one, and then the other.

"Yes, yes," answered he: "but is this the only time you have beheld him? Think! Ah! you have a short memory. Linton, don't you recall your cousin, that you used to tease us so, with wishing to see?"

"What, Linton!" cried Cathy, kindling into joyful surprise at the name. "Is that little Linton? He's taller than I am! Are you Linton?"

The youth stepped forward, and acknowledged himself: she kissed him fervently, and they gazed with wonder at the change time had wrought in the appearance of each.

Catherine had reached her full height; her figure was both plump and slender, elastic as steel, and her whole aspect sparkling with health and spirits. Linton's looks and movements were very languid, and his form extremely slight; but there was a grace in his manner that mitigated these defects, and rendered him not unpleasing.

After exchanging numerous marks of fondness with him, his cousin went to Mr. Heathcliff, who lingered by the door, dividing his attention between the objects inside, and those that lay without, pretending, that is, to observe the latter, and really noting the former alone.

"And you are my uncle, then!" she cried, reaching up to salute him. "I thought I liked you, though you were cross, at first. Why don't you visit at the Grange with Linton? To live all these years such close neighbours, and never see us, is odd; what have you done so for?"

"I visited it once or twice too often before you were born," he answered. "There—damn it! If you have any kisses to spare, give them to Linton—they are thrown away on me."

"Naughty Ellen!" exclaimed Catherine, flying to attack me next with her lavish caresses. "Wicked Ellen! to try to hinder me from entering. But I'll take this walk every morning in future—may I, uncle—and sometimes bring papa? Won't you be glad to see us?"

"Of course!" replied the uncle, with a hardly suppressed grimace, resulting from his deep aversion to both the proposed visiters. "But stay," he continued, turning towards the young lady. "Now I think of it, I'd better tell you. Mr. Linton has a prejudice against me; we quarrelled at one time of our lives, with unchristian ferocity; and, if you mention coming here to him, he'll put a veto on your visits altogether. Therefore, you must not mention it, unless you be careless of seeing your cousin hereafter — you may come, if you will, but you must not mention it."

"Why did you quarrel?" asked Catherine, considerably crestfallen.

"He thought me too poor to wed his sister," answered Heathcliff, "and was grieved that I got her — his pride was hurt, and he'll never forgive it."

"That's wrong!" said the young lady: "some time, I'll tell him so; but Linton and I have no share in your quarrel. I'll not come here, then, he shall come to the Grange."

"It will be too far for me," murmured her cousin, "to walk four miles would kill me. No, come here, Miss Catherine, now and then, not every morning, but once or twice a week."

The father launched towards his son a glance of bitter contempt.

"I am afraid, Nelly, I shall lose my labour," he muttered to me. "Miss Catherine, as the ninny calls her, will discover his value, and send him to the devil. Now, if it had been Hareton — do you know that, twenty times a day, I covet Hareton, with all his degradation? I'd have loved the lad had he been someone else. But I think he's safe from *her* love. I'll pit him against that paltry creature, unless it bestir itself briskly. We calculate it will scarcely last till it is eighteen. Oh, confound the vapid thing. He's absorbed in drying his feet, and never looks at her — Linton!"

"Yes, father," answered the boy.

"Have you nothing to show your cousin, anywhere about; not even a rabbit, or a weasel's nest? Take her into the garden, before you change your shoes; and into the stable to see your horse."

"Wouldn't you rather sit here?" asked Linton, addressing Cathy in a tone which expressed reluctance to move again.

"I don't know," she replied, casting a longing look to the door, and evidently eager to be active.

He kept his seat, and shrank closer to the fire.

Heathcliff rose, and went into the kitchen, and from thence to the yard, calling out for Hareton.

Hareton responded, and presently the two re-entered. The young man had been washing himself, as was visible by the glow on his cheeks, and his wetted hair.

"Oh, I'll ask *you*, uncle," cried Miss Cathy, recollecting the housekeeper's assertion. "That's not my cousin, is he?"

"Yes," he replied, "your mother's nephew. Don't you like him?"

Catherine looked queer.

"Is he not a handsome lad?" he continued.

The uncivil little thing stood on tiptoe, and whispered a sentence in Heathcliff's ear.

He laughed; Hareton darkened; I perceived he was very sensitive to suspected slights, and had obviously a dim notion of his inferiority. But his master or guardian chased the frown by exclaiming—

"You'll be the favourite among us, Hareton! She says you are a—What was it? Well, something very flattering—Here! you go with her round the farm. And behave like a gentleman, mind! Don't use any bad words; and don't stare, when the young lady is not looking at you, and be ready to hide your face when she is; and, when you speak, say your words slowly, and keep your hands out of your pockets. Be off, and entertain her as nicely as you can."

He watched the couple walking past the window. Earnshaw had his countenance completely averted from his companion. He seemed studying the familiar landscape with a stranger's, and an artist's interest.

Catherine took a sly look at him, expressing small admiration. She then turned her attention to seeking out objects of amusement for herself, and tripped merrily on, lilting a tune to supply the lack of conversation.

"I have tied his tongue," observed Heathcliff. "He'll not venture a single syllable, all the time! Nelly, you recollect me at his age—nay, some years younger—Did I ever look so stupid, so 'gaumless,' as Joseph calls it?"

"Worse," I replied, "because more sullen with it."

"I've a pleasure in him!" he continued reflecting aloud. "He has satisfied my expectations—If he were a born fool I should not enjoy it half so much—But he's no fool; and I can sympathize with all his feelings, having felt them myself—I know what he suffers now, for instance, exactly—it is merely a beginning of what he shall suffer, though. And he'll never be able to emerge from his bathos of coarseness and ignorance. I've got him faster than his scoundrel of a father secured me, and lower; for he takes a pride in his brutishness. I've taught him to scorn everything extra-animal, as silly and weak—Don't you think Hindley would be proud of his son, if he could see him? almost as proud as I am of mine—But there's this difference, one is gold put to the use of paving stones; and the other is tin polished to ape a service of silver—*Mine* has nothing valuable about it; yet I shall have the merit of making it go as far as such poor stuff can go. *His* had first-rate qualities, and they are lost—rendered worse than unavailing—I have nothing to regret; he would have more than any, but I, are aware of—And the best of it is, Hareton is damnably fond of me! You'll own that I've outmatched Hindley there—If the dead villain could rise from his grave to abuse me for his offspring's wrongs, I should have the fun of seeing the said offspring fight him back again, indignant that he should dare to rail at the one friend he has in the world!"

Heathcliff chuckled a fiendish laugh at the idea; I made no reply, because I saw that he expected none.

Meantime, our young companion, who sat too removed from us to hear what was said, began to evince symptoms of uneasiness: probably repenting that he denied himself the treat of Catherine's society, for fear of a little fatigue.

His father remarked the restless glances wandering to the window, and the hand irresolutely extended towards his cap.

"Get up, you idle boy!" he exclaimed with assumed heartiness. "Away after them . . . they are just at the corner, by the stand of hives."

Linton gathered his energies, and left the hearth. The lattice was open and, as he stepped out, I heard Cathy inquiring of her unsociable attendant, what was that inscription over the door?

Hareton stared up, and scratched his head like a true clown.

"It's some damnable writing," he answered. "I cannot read it."

"Can't read it?" cried Catherine, "I can read it . . . It's English . . . but I want to know, why it is there."

Linton giggled—the first appearance of mirth he had exhibited.

"He does not know his letters," he said to his cousin. "Could you believe in the existence of such a colossal dunce?"

"Is he all as he should be?" asked Miss Cathy seriously, "or is he simple . . . not right? I've questioned him twice now, and each time he looked so stupid, I think he does not understand me; I can hardly understand *him* I'm sure!"

Linton repeated his laugh, and glanced at Hareton tauntingly, who certainly did not seem quite clear of comprehension at that moment.

"There's nothing the matter, but laziness, is there, Earnshaw?" he said. "My cousin fancies you are an idiot . . . There you experience the consequence of scorning 'book-larning,' as you would say . . . Have you noticed, Catherine, his frightful Yorkshire pronunciation?"

"Why, where the devil is the use on't?" growled Hareton, more ready in answering his daily companion. He was about to enlarge further, but the two youngsters broke into a noisy fit of merriment; my giddy Miss being delighted to discover that she might turn his strange talk to matter of amusement.

"Where is the use of the devil in that sentence?" tittered Linton. "Papa told you not to say any bad words, and you can't open your mouth without one . . . Do try to behave like a gentleman, now do!"

"If thou weren't more a lass than a lad, I'd fell thee this minute, I would; pitiful lath of a crater!" retorted the angry boor retreating, while his face

---

lath: weakling, stupid creature.

burnt with mingled rage and mortification; for he was conscious of being insulted, and embarrassed how to resent it.

Mr. Heathcliff having overheard the conversation, as well as I, smiled when he saw him go, but immediately afterwards, cast a look of singular aversion on the flippant pair, who remained chattering in the doorway. The boy finding animation enough while discussing Hareton's faults, and deficiencies, and relating anecdotes of his goings on; and the girl relishing his pert and spiteful sayings, without considering the ill-nature they evinced: but I began to dislike, more than to compassionate, Linton, and to excuse his father, in some measure, for holding him cheap.

We staid till afternoon: I could not tear Miss Cathy away, before: but happily my master had not quitted his apartment, and remained ignorant of our prolonged absence.

As we walked home, I would fain have enlightened my charge on the characters of the people we had quitted; but she got it into her head that I was prejudiced against them.

"Aha!" she cried, "you take papa's side, Ellen—you are partial . . . I know, or else you wouldn't have cheated me so many years, into the notion that Linton lived a long way from here. I'm really extremely angry, only I'm so pleased I can't show it! But you must hold your tongue about my uncle . . . he's *my* uncle remember, and I'll scold papa for quarrelling with him."

And so she ran on, till I dropped endeavouring to convince her of her mistake.

She did not mention the visit that night, because she did not see Mr. Linton. Next day it all came out, sadly to my chagrin; and still I was not altogether sorry: I thought the burden of directing and warning would be more efficiently borne by him than me, but he was too timid in giving satisfactory reasons for his wish that she would shun connection with the household of the Heights, and Catherine liked good reasons for every restraint that harassed her petted will.

"Papa!" she exclaimed after the morning's salutations, "guess whom I saw yesterday, in my walk on the moors . . . Ah, papa, you started! you've not done right, have you, now? I saw—But listen, and you shall hear how I found you out, and Ellen, who is in league with you, and yet pretended to pity me so, when I kept hoping, and was always disappointed about Linton's coming back!"

She gave a faithful account of her excursion and its consequences; and my master, though he cast more than one reproachful look at me, said nothing, till she had concluded. Then he drew her to him, and asked if she knew why he had concealed Linton's near neighbourhood from her? Could she think it was to deny her a pleasure that she might harmlessly enjoy?

"It was because you disliked Mr. Heathcliff," she answered.

"Then you believe I care more for my own feelings than yours, Cathy?" he said. "No, it was not because I disliked Mr. Heathcliff; but because Mr. Heathcliff dislikes me; and is a most diabolical man, delighting to wrong and ruin those he hates, if they give him the slightest opportunity. I knew that you could not keep up an acquaintance with your cousin, without being brought into contact with him; and I knew he would detest you, on my account; so, for your own good, and nothing else, I took precautions that you should not see Linton again—I meant to explain this sometime as you grew older, and I'm sorry I delayed it!"

"But Mr. Heathcliff was quite cordial, papa," observed Catherine, not at all convinced; "and *he* didn't object to our seeing each other: he said I might come to his house, when I pleased, only I must not tell you, because you had quarrelled with him, and would not forgive him for marrying Aunt Isabella. And you won't—*you* are the one to be blamed—he is willing to let *us* be friends, at least; Linton and I—and you are not."

My master, perceiving that she would not take his word for her uncle-in-law's evil disposition, gave a hasty sketch of his conduct to Isabella, and the manner in which Wuthering Heights became his property. He could not bear to discourse long upon the topic, for though he spoke little of it, he still felt the same horror, and detestation of his ancient enemy that had occupied his heart ever since Mrs. Linton's death. "She might have been living yet, if it had not been for him!" was his constant bitter reflection; and, in his eyes, Heathcliff seemed a murderer.

Miss Cathy, conversant with no bad deeds except her own slight acts of disobedience, injustice, and passion, rising from hot temper, and thoughtlessness, and repented of on the day they were committed, was amazed at the blackness of spirit that could brood on, and cover revenge for years; and deliberately prosecute its plans, without a visitation of remorse. She appeared so deeply impressed and shocked at this new view of human nature—excluded from all her studies and all her ideas till now—that Mr. Edgar deemed it unnecessary to pursue the subject. He merely added,

"You will know hereafter, darling, why I wish you to avoid his house and family—now, return to your old employments and amusements, and think no more about them!"

Catherine kissed her father, and sat down quietly to her lessons for a couple of hours, according to custom: then she accompanied him into the grounds, and the whole day passed as usual: but in the evening, when she had retired to her room, and I went to help her to undress, I found her crying, on her knees by the bedside.

"Oh, fie, silly child!" I exclaimed. "If you had any real griefs, you'd be ashamed to waste a tear on this little contrariety. You never had one shadow of substantial sorrow, Miss Catherine. Suppose, for a minute, that master and I were dead, and you were by yourself in the world—how would you feel, then? Compare the present occasion with such an affliction as that, and be thankful for the friends you have, instead of coveting more."

"I'm not crying for myself, Ellen," she answered, "it's for him—He expected to see me again, tomorrow, and there, he'll be so disappointed— and he'll wait for me, and I shan't come!"

"Nonsense," said I: "do you imagine he has thought as much of you, as you have of him? Hasn't he Hareton for a companion? Not one in a hundred would weep at losing a relation they had just seen twice, for two afternoons—Linton will conjecture how it is, and trouble himself no further about you."

"But may I not write a note to tell him why I cannot come?" she asked rising to her feet. "And just send those books, I promised to lend him—his books are not as nice as mine, and he wanted to have them extremely, when I told him how interesting they were—May I not, Ellen?"

"No, indeed, no, indeed!" replied I with decision. "Then he would write to you, and there'd never be an end of it—No, Miss Catherine, the acquaintance must be dropped entirely—so papa expects, and I shall see that it is done."

"But how can one little note—" she recommenced, putting on an imploring countenance.

"Silence!" I interrupted. "We will not begin with your little notes—Get into bed."

She threw at me a very naughty look, so naughty that I would not kiss her good night at first: I covered her up, and shut her door, in great displeasure—but, repenting halfway, I returned softly, and lo! there was Miss, standing at the table with a bit of blank paper before her, and a pencil in her hand, which she guiltily slipped out of sight, on my re-entrance.

"You'll get nobody to take that, Catherine," I said, "if you write it; and at present I shall put out your candle."

I set the extinguisher on the flame, receiving as I did so, a slap on my hand, and a petulant "cross thing!" I then quitted her again, and she drew the bolt in one of her worst, most peevish humours.

The letter was finished and forwarded to its destination by a milk-fetcher who came from the village, but that I didn't learn till some time afterwards. Weeks passed on, and Cathy recovered her temper, though she grew wondrous fond of stealing off to corners by herself, and often, if I came near her suddenly while reading she would start, and bend over the book, evidently desirous to hide it; and I detected edges of loose paper sticking out beyond the leaves.

She also got a trick of coming down early in the morning, and lingering about the kitchen, as if she were expecting the arrival of something; and she had a small drawer in a cabinet in the library which she would trifle over for hours, and whose key she took special care to remove when she left it.

One day, as she inspected this drawer, I observed that the playthings, and trinkets which recently formed its contents, were transmuted into bits of folded paper.

My curiosity and suspicions were roused; I determined to take a peep at her mysterious treasures; so, at night, as soon as she and my master were safe upstairs, I searched and readily found among my house keys, one that would fit the lock. Having opened, I emptied the whole contents into my apron, and took them with me to examine at leisure in my own chamber.

Though I could not but suspect, I was still surprised to discover that they were a mass of correspondence, daily almost, it must have been, from Linton Heathcliff, answers to documents forwarded by her. The earlier dated were embarrassed and short; gradually however they expanded into copious love letters, foolish as the age of the writer rendered natural, yet with touches, here and there, which I thought, were borrowed from a more experienced source.

Some of them struck me as singularly odd compounds of ardour, and flatness; commencing in strong feeling, and concluding in the affected, wordy way that a school-boy might use to a fancied, incorporeal sweetheart.

Whether they satisfied Cathy, I don't know, but they appeared very worthless trash to me.

After turning over as many as I thought proper, I tied them in a handkerchief, and set them aside, re-locking the vacant drawer.

Following her habit, my young lady descended early, and visited the kitchen: I watched her go to the door, on the arrival of a certain little boy; and, while the dairy maid filled his can, she tucked something into his jacket pocket, and plucked something out.

I went round by the garden, and laid wait for the messenger; who fought valorously to defend his trust, and we spilt the milk between us; but I succeeded in abstracting the epistle; and threatening serious consequences if he did not look sharp home, I remained under the wall, and perused Miss Cathy's affectionate composition. It was more simple and more eloquent than her cousin's, very pretty and very silly. I shook my head, and went meditating into the house.

The day being wet, she could not divert herself with rambling about the park; so, at the conclusion of her morning studies, she resorted to the solace of the drawer. Her father sat reading at the table; and I, on purpose, had sought a bit of work in some unripped fringes of the window curtain, keeping my eye steadily fixed on her proceedings.

Never did any bird flying back to a plundered nest which it had left brimful of chirping young ones, express more complete despair in its anguished cries, and flutterings, than she by her single "Oh!" and the change that transfigured her late happy countenance. Mr. Linton looked up.

"What is the matter, love? Have you hurt yourself?" he said.

His tone and look assured her *he* had not been the discoverer of the hoard.

"No, papa—" she gasped. "Ellen! Ellen! come upstairs—I'm sick!"

I obeyed her summons, and accompanied her out.

"Oh, Ellen! you have got them," she commenced immediately, dropping on her knees, when we were enclosed alone. "O, give them to me, and I'll never never do so again! Don't tell papa—You have not told papa, Ellen, say you have not! I've been exceedingly naughty, but I won't do it any more!"

With a grave severity in my manner, I bid her stand up.

"So," I exclaimed, "Miss Catherine, you are tolerably far on, it seems— you may well be ashamed of them! A fine bundle of trash you study in your leisure hours, to be sure—Why, it's good enough to be printed! And what do you suppose the master will think, when I display it before him? I haven't shown it yet, but you needn't imagine I shall keep your ridiculous secrets—For shame! And you must have led the way in writing such absurdities, he would not have thought of beginning, I'm certain."

"I didn't! I didn't!" sobbed Cathy, fit to break her heart. "I didn't once think of loving him till—"

"*Loving!*" cried I, as scornfully as I could utter the word. "*Loving!* Did anybody ever hear the like! I might just as well talk of loving the miller who comes once a year to buy our corn. Pretty loving, indeed, and both times together you have seen Linton hardly four hours, in your life! Now here is the babyish trash. I'm going with it to the library; and we'll see what your father says to such *loving.*"

She sprang at her precious epistles, but I held them above my head; and then she poured out further frantic entreaties that I would burn them—do anything rather than show them. And being really fully as inclined to laugh as scold, for I esteemed it all girlish vanity, I at length relented in a measure, and asked.

"If I consent to burn them, will you promise faithfully neither to send, nor receive a letter again, nor a book, for I perceive you have sent him books, nor locks of hair, nor rings, nor playthings?"

"We don't send playthings!" cried Catherine, her pride overcoming her shame.

"Nor anything at all, then, my lady!" I said. "Unless you will, here I go."

"I promise, Ellen!" she cried catching my dress. "Oh, put them in the fire, do, do!"

But when I proceeded to open a place with the poker, the sacrifice was too painful to be borne—She earnestly supplicated that I would spare her one or two.

"One or two, Ellen, to keep for Linton's sake!"

I unknotted the handkerchief, and commenced dropping them in from an angle, and the flame curled up the chimney.

"I will have one, you cruel wretch!" she screamed, darting her hand into the fire, and drawing forth some half consumed fragments, at the expense of her fingers.

"Very well—and I will have some to exhibit to papa!" I answered shaking back the rest into the bundle, and turning anew to the door.

She emptied her blackened pieces into the flames, and motioned me to finish the immolation. It was done; I stirred up the ashes, and interred them under a shovel full of coals; and she mutely, and with a sense of intense injury, retired to her private apartment. I descended to tell my master that the young lady's qualm of sickness was almost gone, but I judged it best for her to lie down a while.

She wouldn't dine; but she re-appeared at tea, pale and red about the eyes, and marvellously subdued in outward aspect.

Next morning I answered the letter by a slip of paper inscribed, "Master Heathcliff is requested to send no more notes to Miss Linton as she will not receive them." And thenceforth the little boy came with vacant pockets.

CHAPTER XXII

Summer drew to an end, and early Autumn—it was past Michaelmas, but the harvest was late that year, and a few of our fields were still uncleared.

Mr. Linton and his daughter would frequently walk out among the reapers: at the carrying of the last sheaves, they stayed till dusk, and the evening happening to be chill and damp, my master caught a bad cold, that settling obstinately on his lungs, confined him indoors throughout the whole of the winter, nearly without intermission.

Poor Cathy, frightened from her little romance, had been considerably sadder and duller since its abandonment: and her father insisted on her reading less, and taking more exercise. She had his companionship no longer; I esteemed it a duty to supply its lack, as much as possible, with mine; an inefficient substitute, for I could only spare two or three hours, from my numerous diurnal occupations, to follow her footsteps, and then, my society was obviously less desirable than his.

On an afternoon in October, or the beginning of November, a fresh watery afternoon, when the turf and paths were rustling with moist, withered leaves, and the cold, blue sky was half hidden by clouds, dark grey streamers, rapidly mounting from the west, and boding abundant rain, I requested my young lady to forego her ramble because I was certain of showers. She refused; and I unwillingly donned a cloak, and took my umbrella to accompany her on a stroll to the bottom of the park; a formal walk which she generally affected if low-spirited; and that she invariably was when Mr. Edgar had been worse than ordinary; a thing never known from his confession, but guessed both by her and me from his increased silence, and the melancholy of his countenance.

She went sadly on; there was no running or bounding now; though the chill wind might well have tempted her to a race. And often, from the side of my eye, I could detect her raising a hand, and brushing something off her cheek.

I gazed round for a means of diverting her thoughts. On one side of the road rose a high, rough bank, where hazels and stunted oaks, with their roots half exposed, held uncertain tenour: the soil was too loose for the latter; and strong winds had blown some nearly horizontal. In summer, Miss Catherine delighted to climb along these trunks, and sit in the branches, swinging twenty feet above the ground; and I pleased with her agility, and her light, childish heart, still considered it proper to scold every time I caught her at such an elevation; but so that she knew there was no necessity for descending. From dinner to tea she would lie in her breeze-rocked cradle, doing nothing except singing old songs—my nursery lore—to herself, or watching the birds, joint tenants, feed and entice their young ones to fly, or nestling with closed lids, half thinking, half dreaming, happier than words can express.

"Look, Miss!" I exclaimed, pointing to a nook under the roots of one twisted tree. "Winter is not here yet. There's a little flower up yonder, the last bud from the multitude of blue-bells that clouded those turf steps in July with a lilac mist. Will you clamber up, and pluck it to show to papa?"

Cathy stared a long time at the lonely blossom trembling in its earthy shelter, and replied, at length—

"No, I'll not touch it—but it looks melancholy, does it not, Ellen?"

"Yes," I observed, "about as starved and sackless as you—your cheeks

---

tenour: hold.

are bloodless; let us take hold of hands and run. You're so low, I dare say I shall keep up with you."

"No," she repeated, and continued sauntering on, pausing, at intervals, to muse over a bit of moss, or a tuft of blanched grass, or a fungus spreading its bright orange among the heaps of brown foliage; and, ever and anon, her hand was lifted to her averted face.

"Catherine, why are you crying, love?" I asked, approaching and putting my arm over her shoulder. "You mustn't cry because papa has a cold; be thankful it is nothing worse."

She now put no further restraint on her tears; her breath was stifled by sobs.

"Oh, it *will* be something worse," she said. "And what shall I do when papa and you leave me, and I am by myself? I can't forget your words, Ellen, they are always in my ear. How life will be changed, how dreary the world will be, when papa and you are dead."

"None can tell, whether you won't die before us," I replied. "It's wrong to anticipate evil—we'll hope there are years and years to come before any of us go—master is young, and I am strong, and hardly forty-five. My mother lived till eighty, a canty dame to the last. And suppose Mr. Linton were spared till he saw sixty, that would be more years than you have counted, Miss. And would it not be foolish to mourn a calamity above twenty years beforehand?"

"But Aunt Isabella was younger than papa," she remarked, gazing up with timid hope to seek further consolation.

"Aunt Isabella had not you and me to nurse her," I replied. "She wasn't as happy as master; she hadn't as much to live for. All you need do, is to wait well on your father, and cheer him by letting him see you cheerful; and avoid giving him anxiety on any subject—mind that, Cathy! I'll not disguise, but you might kill him, if you were wild and reckless, and cherished a foolish, fanciful affection for the son of a person who would be glad to have him in his grave—and allowed him to discover that you fretted over the separation, he has judged it expedient to make."

"I fret about nothing on earth except papa's illness," answered my companion. "I care for nothing in comparison with papa. And I'll never—never—oh, never, while I have my senses, do an act or say a word to vex him. I love him better than myself, Ellen; and I know it by this—I pray every night that I may live after him; because I would rather be miserable than that he should be—that proves I love him better than myself."

"Good words," I replied. "But deeds must prove it also; and after he is well, remember you don't forget resolutions formed in the hour of fear."

As we talked, we neared a door that opened on the road: and my young lady, lightening into sunshine again, climbed up, and seated herself on the top of the wall, reaching over to gather some hips that bloomed scarlet on the summit branches of the wild rose trees, shadowing the highway side, the lower fruit had disappeared, but only birds could touch the upper, except from Cathy's present station.

In stretching to pull them, her hat fell off; and as the door was locked, she proposed scrambling down to recover it. I bid her be cautious lest she got a fall, and she nimbly disappeared.

But the return was no such easy matter; the stones were smooth and neatly cemented, and the rosebushes, and blackberry stragglers could yield no assistance in re-ascending. I, like a fool, didn't recollect that till I heard her laughing, and exclaiming—

"Ellen, you'll have to fetch the key, or else I must run round to the porter's lodge. I can't scale the ramparts on this side!"

"Stay where you are," I answered, "I have my bundle of keys in my pocket; perhaps I may manage to open it, if not, I'll go."

Catherine amused herself with dancing to and fro before the door, while I tried all the large keys in succession. I had applied the last, and found that none would do; so, repeating my desire that she would remain there, I was about to hurry home as fast as I could, when an approaching sound arrested me. It was the trot of a horse; Cathy's dance stopped; and in a minute the horse stopped also.

"Who is that?" I whispered.

"Ellen, I wish you could open the door," whispered back my companion, anxiously.

"Ho, Miss Linton!" cried a deep voice (the rider's). "I'm glad to meet you. Don't be in haste to enter, for I have an explanation to ask and obtain."

"I shan't speak to you, Mr. Heathcliff!" answered Catherine. "Papa says you are a wicked man, and you hate both him and me; and Ellen says the same."

"That is nothing to the purpose," said Heathcliff. (He it was.) "I don't hate my son, I suppose, and it is concerning him that I demand your attention. Yes! you have cause to blush. Two or three months since, were you not in the habit of writing to Linton? making love in play, eh? You deserved, both of you, flogging for that! You especially, the elder, and less sensitive, as it turns out. I've got your letters, and if you give me any pertness, I'll send them to your father. I presume you grew weary of the amusement, and dropped it, didn't you? Well, you dropped Linton with it, into a Slough of Despond.[8] He was in earnest—in love—really. As true as I live, he's dying

---

[8] A reference to John Bunyan's *The Pilgrim's Progress,* suggesting that on the journey through life one frequently sinks into depression and fears. [ED.]

for you—breaking his heart at your fickleness, not figuratively, but actually. Though Hareton has made him a standing jest for six weeks, and I have used more serious measures, and attempted to frighten him out of his idiocy, he gets worse daily, and he'll be under the sod before summer, unless you restore him!"

"How can you lie so glaringly to the poor child!" I called from the inside. "Pray ride on! How can you deliberately get up such paltry falsehoods? Miss Cathy, I'll knock the lock off with a stone: you won't believe that vile nonsense. You can feel in yourself, it is impossible that a person should die for love of a stranger."

"I was not aware there were eavesdroppers," muttered the detected villain. "Worthy Mrs. Dean, I like you, but I don't like your double dealing," he added, aloud. "How could *you* lie so glaringly, as to affirm I hated the 'poor child'? And invent bugbear stories to terrify her from my doorstones? Catherine Linton, (the very name warms me), my bonnie lass, I shall be from home all this week, go and see if I have not spoken truth; do, there's a darling! Just imagine your father in my place, and Linton in yours; then think how you would value your careless lover, if he refused to stir a step to comfort you, when your father, himself, entreated him; and don't, from pure stupidity, fall into the same error. I swear, on my salvation, he's going to his grave, and none but you can save him!"

The lock gave way, and I issued out.

"I swear Linton is dying," repeated Heathcliff, looking hard at me. "And grief and disappointment are hastening his death. Nelly, if you won't let her go, you can walk over yourself. But I shall not return till this time next week; and I think your master himself would scarcely object to her visiting her cousin!"

"Come in," said I, taking Cathy by the arm and half forcing her to re-enter, for she lingered, viewing, with troubled eyes, the features of the speaker, too stern to express his inward deceit.

He pushed his horse close, and, bending down, observed—

"Miss Catherine, I'll own to you that I have little patience with Linton—and Hareton and Joseph have less. I'll own he's with a harsh set. He pines for kindness, as well as love; and a kind word from you would be his best medicine. Don't mind Mrs. Dean's cruel cautions, but be generous, and contrive to see him. He dreams of you day and night, and cannot be persuaded that you don't hate him, since you neither write nor call."

I closed the door, and rolled a stone to assist the loosened lock in holding it; and spreading my umbrella, I drew my charge underneath, for the rain began to drive through the moaning branches of the trees, and warned us to avoid delay.

Our hurry prevented any comment on the encounter with Heathcliff, as we stretched towards home; but I divined instinctively that Catherine's heart was clouded now in double darkness. Her features were so sad, they did not seem hers: she evidently regarded what she had heard as every syllable true.

The master had retired to rest before we came in. Cathy stole to his room to inquire how he was; he had fallen asleep. She returned, and asked me to sit with her in the library. We took our tea together; and afterwards she lay down on the rug, and told me not to talk for she was weary.

I got a book, and pretended to read. As soon as she supposed me absorbed in my occupation, she recommenced her silent weeping: it appeared, at present, her favourite diversion. I suffered her to enjoy it a while; then, I expostulated; deriding and ridiculing all Mr. Heathcliff's assertions about his son; as if I were certain she would coincide. Alas! I hadn't skill to counteract the effect his account had produced; it was just what he intended.

"You may be right, Ellen," she answered; "but I shall never feel at ease till I know—and I must tell Linton it is not my fault that I don't write; and convince him that I shall not change."

What use were anger and protestations against her silly credulity? We parted that night hostile—but next day beheld me on the road to Wuthering Heights, by the side of my wilful young mistress's pony. I couldn't bear to witness her sorrow, to see her pale, dejected countenance, and heavy eyes; and I yielded in the faint hope that Linton himself might prove by his reception of us, how little of the tale was founded on fact.

CHAPTER XXIII

The rainy night had ushered in a misty morning—half frost, half drizzle—and temporary brooks crossed our path, gurgling from the uplands. My feet were thoroughly wetted; I was cross and low, exactly the humour suited for making the most of these disagreeable things.

We entered the farm-house by the kitchen way to ascertain whether Mr. Heathcliff were really absent; because I put slight faith in his own affirmation.

Joseph seemed sitting in a sort of elysium alone, beside a roaring fire; a quart of ale on the table near him, bristling with large pieces of toasted oat cake; and his black, short pipe in his mouth.

Catherine ran to the hearth to warm herself. I asked if the master were in?

My question remained so long unanswered, that I thought the old man had grown deaf, and repeated it louder.

"Na—ay!" he snarled, or rather screamed through his nose. "Na-ay! yah mun goa back whear yah coom frough."

"Joseph," cried a peevish voice, simultaneously with me, from the inner room. "How often am I to call you? There are only a few red ashes now. Joseph! come this moment."

Vigorous puffs, and a resolute stare into the grate declared he had no ear for this appeal. The housekeeper and Hareton were invisible; one gone on an errand, and the other at his work, probably. We knew Linton's tones and entered.

"Oh, I hope you'll die in a garret! starved to death," said the boy, mistaking our approach for that of his negligent attendant.

He stopped, on observing his error; his cousin flew to him.

"Is that you, Miss Linton?" he said, raising his head from the arm of the great chair, in which he reclined. "No—don't kiss me. It takes my breath—dear me! Papa said you would call," continued he, after recovering a little from Catherine's embrace; while she stood by looking very contrite. "Will you shut the door, if you please? you left it open—and those—those *detestable* creatures won't bring coals to the fire. It's so cold!"

I stirred up the cinders, and fetched a scuttle full myself. The invalid complained of being covered with ashes; but he had a tiresome cough, and looked feverish and ill, so I did not rebuke his temper.

"Well, Linton," murmured Catherine, when his corrugated brow relaxed. "Are you glad to see me? Can I do you any good?"

"Why didn't you come before?" he asked. "You should have come, instead of writing. It tired me dreadfully, writing those long letters. I'd far rather have talked to you. Now, I can neither bear to talk nor anything else. I wonder where Zillah is! will you (looking at me) step into the kitchen and see?"

I had received no thanks for my other service; and being unwilling to run to and fro at his behest, I replied—

"Nobody is out there but Joseph."

"I want to drink," he exclaimed, fretfully, turning away. "Zillah is constantly gadding off to Gimmerton since papa went. It's miserable! And I'm obliged to come down here—they resolved never to hear me upstairs."

"Is your father attentive to you, Master Heathcliff?" I asked, perceiving Catherine to be checked in her friendly advances.

"Attentive? He makes *them* a little more attentive, at least," he cried. "The wretches! Do you know, Miss Linton, that brute Hareton laughs at me—I hate him—indeed, I hate them all—they are odious beings."

Cathy began searching for some water; she lighted on a pitcher in the dresser; filled a tumbler, and brought it. He bid her add a spoonful of wine from a bottle on the table; and having swallowed a small portion, appeared more tranquil, and said she was very kind.

"And are you glad to see me?" asked she, reiterating her former question, and pleased to detect the faint dawn of a smile.

"Yes, I am—It's something new to hear a voice like yours!" he replied, "But I *have* been vexed, because you wouldn't come—And papa swore it was owing to me; he called me a pitiful, shuffling, worthless thing; and said you despised me; and if he had been in my place, he would be more the master of the Grange than your father, by this time. But you don't despise me, do you Miss—"

"I wish you would say Catherine, or Cathy," interrupted my young lady. "Despise you? No! Next to papa, and Ellen, I love you better than anybody living. I don't love Mr. Heathcliff, though; and I dare not come when he returns; will he stay away many days?"

"Not many," answered Linton, "but he goes onto the moors frequently, since the shooting season commenced, and you might spend an hour or two with me, in his absence—Do! say you will! I think I should not be peevish with you; you'd not provoke me, and you'd always be ready to help me, wouldn't you?"

"Yes," said Catherine, stroking his long soft hair, "if I could only get papa's consent, I'd spend half my time with you—Pretty Linton! I wish you were my brother!"

"And then you would like me as well as your father?" observed he more cheerfully. "But papa says you would love me better than him, and all the world, if you were my wife—so I'd rather you were that!"

"No! I should never love anybody better than papa," she returned gravely. "And people hate their wives, sometimes; but not their sisters and brothers, and if you were the latter, you would live with us, and papa would be as fond of you, as he is of me."

Linton denied that people ever hated their wives; but Cathy affirmed they did, and in her wisdom, instanced his own father's aversion to her aunt.

I endeavoured to stop her thoughtless tongue—I couldn't succeed, till everything she knew was out. Master Heathcliff, much irritated, asserted her relation was false.

"Papa told me; and papa does not tell falsehoods!" she answered pertly.

"*My* papa scorns yours!" cried Linton. "He calls him a sneaking fool!"

"Yours is a wicked man," retorted Catherine, "and you are very naughty to dare to repeat what he says—He must be wicked, to have made Aunt Isabella leave him as she did!"

"She didn't leave him," said the boy, "you shan't contradict me!"

"She did!" cried my young lady.

"Well, I'll tell *you* something!" said Linton. "Your mother hated your father, now then."

"Oh!" exclaimed Catherine, too enraged to continue.

"And she loved mine!" added he.

"You little liar! I hate you now," she panted, and her face grew red with passion.

"She did! she did!" sang Linton sinking into the recess of his chair, and leaning back his head to enjoy the agitation of the other disputant who stood behind.

"Hush, Master Heathcliff!" I said, "that's your father's tale too, I suppose."

"It isn't—you hold your tongue!" he answered, "she did, she did, Catherine, she did, she did!"

Cathy, beside herself, gave the chair a violent push, and caused him to fall against one arm. He was immediately seized by a suffocating cough that soon ended his triumph.

It lasted so long that it frightened even me. As to his cousin, she wept with all her might, aghast at the mischief she had done, though she said nothing.

I held him, till the fit exhausted itself. Then he thrust me away; and leant his head down, silently—Catherine quelled her lamentations also, took a seat opposite, and looked solemnly into the fire.

"How do you feel now, Master Heathcliff," I inquired after waiting ten minutes.

"I wish *she* felt as I do," he replied, "spiteful, cruel thing! Hareton never touches me, he never struck me in his life—And I was better today—and there—" his voice died in a whimper.

"*I* didn't strike you!" muttered Cathy chewing her lip to prevent another burst of emotion.

He sighed and moaned like one under great suffering; and kept it up for a quarter of an hour, on purpose to distress his cousin, apparently, for whenever he caught a stifled sob from her, he put renewed pain and pathos into the inflexions of his voice.

"I'm sorry I hurt you, Linton!" she said at length, racked beyond endurance. "But *I* couldn't have been hurt by that little push; and I had no idea that you could, either—you're not much, are you, Linton? Don't let me go home thinking I've done you harm! answer, speak to me."

"I can't speak to you," he murmured, "you've hurt me so, that I shall lie awake all night, choking with this cough! If you had it you'd know what it was—but *you'll* be comfortably asleep, while I'm in agony—and nobody near me! I wonder how you would like to pass those fearful nights!" And he began to wail aloud for very pity of himself.

"Since you are in the habit of passing dreadful nights," I said, "it won't be Miss who spoils your ease; you'd be the same, had she never come — However, she shall not disturb you, again — and perhaps, you'll get quieter when we leave you."

"Must I go?" asked Catherine dolefully, bending over him. "Do you want me to go, Linton?"

"You can't alter what you've done," he replied pettishly, shrinking from her, "unless you alter it for the worse, by teasing me into a fever!"

"Well, then I must go?" she repeated.

"Let me alone, at least," said he. "I can't bear your talking!"

She lingered, and resisted my persuasions to departure, a tiresome while, but as he neither looked up, nor spoke, she finally made a movement to the door, and I followed.

We were recalled by a scream — Linton had slid from his seat on to the hearthstone, and lay writhing in the mere perverseness of an indulged plague of a child, determined to be as grievous and harassing as it can.

I thoroughly gauged his disposition from his behaviour, and saw at once it would be folly to attempt humouring him. Not so my companion, she ran back in terror, knelt down, and cried, and soothed, and entreated, till he grew quiet from lack of breath, by no means from compunction at distressing her.

"I shall lift him on to the settle," I said, "and he may roll about as he pleases; we can't stop to watch him — I hope you are satisfied, Miss Cathy, that *you* are not the person to benefit him, and that his condition of health is not occasioned by attachment to you. Now then, there he is! Come away, as soon as he knows there is nobody by to care for his nonsense, he'll be glad to lie still!"

She placed a cushion under his head, and offered him some water, he rejected the latter and tossed uneasily on the former as if it were a stone, or a block of wood.

She tried to put it more comfortably.

"I can't do that," he said, "it's not high enough!"

Catherine brought another to lay above it.

"That's *too* high," murmured the provoking thing.

"How must I arrange it, then?" she asked despairingly.

He twined himself up to her, as she half knelt by the settle, and converted her shoulder into a support.

"No, that won't do!" I said. "You'll be content with the cushion, Master Heathcliff! Miss has wasted too much time on you, already; we cannot remain five minutes longer."

"Yes, yes, we can!" replied Cathy. "He's good and patient, now—He's beginning to think I shall have far greater misery than he will, tonight, if I believe he is the worse for my visit; and then, I dare not come again—Tell the truth about it, Linton—for I mustn't come, if I have hurt you."

"You must come, to cure me," he answered. "You ought to come because you have hurt me—You know you have, extremely! I was not as ill, when you entered, as I am at present—was I?"

"But you've made yourself ill by crying, and being in a passion."

"I didn't do it all," said his cousin. "However, we'll be friends now. And you want me—you would wish to see me sometimes, really?"

"I told you, I did!" he replied impatiently. "Sit on the settle and let me lean on your knee—That's as mamma used to do, whole afternoons together—Sit quite still, and don't talk, but you may sing a song if you can sing, or you may say a nice, long interesting ballad—one of those you promised to teach me, or a story—I'd rather have a ballad though, begin."

Catherine repeated the longest she could remember. The employment pleased both mightily. Linton would have another, and after that another; notwithstanding my strenuous objections; and so, they went on, until the clock struck twelve, and we heard Hareton in the court, returning for his dinner.

"And tomorrow, Catherine, will you be here tomorrow?" asked young Heathcliff, holding her frock, as she rose reluctantly.

"No!" I answered, "nor next day neither." She, however, gave a different response, evidently, for his forehead cleared as she stooped, and whispered in his ear.

"You won't go tomorrow, recollect, Miss!" I commenced when we were out of the house. "You are not dreaming of it, are you?"

She smiled.

"Oh, I'll take good care!" I continued, "I'll have that lock mended, and you can escape by no way else."

"I can get over the wall," she said laughing. "The Grange is not a prison, Ellen, and you are not my jailer. And besides I'm almost seventeen. I'm a woman—and I'm certain Linton would recover quickly if he had me to look after him—I'm older than he is, you know, and wiser, less childish, am I not? And he'll soon do as I direct him with some slight coaxing—He's a pretty little darling when he's good. I'd make such a pet of him, if he were mine—We should never quarrel, should we, after we were used to each other? Don't you like him, Ellen?"

"Like him?" I exclaimed. "The worst tempered bit of a sickly slip that ever struggled into its teens! Happily, as Mr. Heathcliff conjectured, he'll not win twenty! I doubt whether he'll see spring indeed—and small loss to his family, whenever he drops off; and lucky it is for us that his father took him—The kinder he was treated, the more tedious and selfish he'd be! I'm glad you have no chance of having him for a husband, Miss Catherine!"

My companion waxed serious at hearing this speech—To speak of his death so regardlessly wounded her feelings.

"He's younger than I," she answered, after a protracted pause of meditation, "and he ought to live the longest, he will—he must live as long as I do. He's as strong now as when he first came into the North, I'm positive of that! It's only a cold that ails him, the same as papa has—You say papa will get better, and why shouldn't he?"

"Well, well," I cried, "after all, we needn't trouble ourselves; for listen, Miss, and mind, I'll keep my word—If you attempt going to Wuthering Heights again, with, or without me, I shall inform Mr. Linton, and unless he allow it, the intimacy with your cousin must not be revived."

"It has been revived!" muttered Cathy sulkily.

"Must not be continued, then!" I said.

"We'll see!" was her reply, and she set off at a gallop, leaving me to toil in the rear.

We both reached home before our dinner-time: my master supposed we had been wandering through the park, and therefore, he demanded no explanation of our absence. As soon as I entered, I hastened to change my soaked shoes and stockings; but sitting such a while at the Heights had done the mischief. On the succeeding morning, I was laid up; and during three weeks I remained incapacitated for attending to my duties—a calamity never experienced prior to that period, and never, I am thankful to say, since.

My little mistress behaved like an angel in coming to wait on me, and cheer my solitude: the confinement brought me exceedingly low—It is wearisome, to a stirring active body—but few have slighter reasons for complaint than I had. The moment Catherine left Mr. Linton's room, she appeared at my bedside. Her day was divided between us; no amusement usurped a minute: she neglected her meals, her studies, and her play; and she was the fondest nurse that ever watched: she must have had a warm heart, when she loved her father so, to give so much to me!

I said her days were divided between us; but the master retired early, and I generally needed nothing after six o'clock, thus the evening was her own.

Poor thing, I never considered what she did with herself after tea. And though frequently, when she looked in to bid me good night I remarked a fresh colour in her cheeks, and a pinkness over her slender fingers; instead of fancying the hue borrowed from a cold ride across the moors, I laid it to the charge of a hot fire in the library.

CHAPTER XXIV

At the close of three weeks, I was able to quit my chamber, and move about the house. And on the first occasion of my sitting up in the evening, I asked Catherine to read to me, because my eyes were weak. We were in the library, the master having gone to bed: she consented, rather unwillingly, I fancied; and imagining my sort of books did not suit her, I bid her please herself in the choice of what she perused.

She selected one of her own favourites, and got forward steadily about an hour; then came frequent questions.

"Ellen, are you not tired? Hadn't you better lie down now? You'll be sick, keeping up so long, Ellen."

"No, no, dear, I'm not tired," I returned, continually.

Perceiving me immovable, she essayed another method of showing her dis-relish for her occupation. It changed to yawning, and stretching, and—

"Ellen, I'm tired."

"Give over then and talk," I answered.

That was worse; she fretted and sighed, and looked at her watch till eight; and finally went to her room, completely over-done with sleep, judging by her peevish, heavy look, and the constant rubbing she inflicted on her eyes.

The following night she seemed more impatient still; and on the third from recovering my company, she complained of a headache, and left me.

I thought her conduct odd; and having remained alone a long while, I was resolved on going, and inquiring whether she were better, and asking her to come and lie on the sofa, instead of upstairs, in the dark.

No Catherine could I discover upstairs, and none below. The servants affirmed they had not seen her. I listened at Mr. Edgar's door—all was silence. I returned to her apartment, extinguished my candle, and seated myself in the window.

The moon shone bright; a sprinkling of snow covered the ground, and I reflected that she might, possibly, have taken it into her head to walk about the garden, for refreshment. I did detect a figure creeping along the inner fence of the park; but it was not my young mistress; on its emerging into the light, I recognized one of the grooms.

He stood a considerable period, viewing the carriage road through the grounds; then started off at a brisk pace, as if he had detected something, and reappeared, presently, leading Miss's pony; and there she was, just dismounted, and walking by its side.

The man took his charge stealthily across the grass towards the stable. Cathy entered by the casement-window of the drawing-room, and glided noiselessly up to where I awaited her.

She put the door gently to, slipped off her snowy shoes, untied her hat, and was proceeding, unconscious of my espionage, to lay aside her mantle, when I suddenly rose, and revealed myself. The surprise petrified her an instant: she uttered an inarticulate exclamation, and stood fixed.

"My dear Miss Catherine," I began, too vividly impressed by her recent kindness to break into a scold, "where have you been riding out at this hour? And why should you try to deceive me, by telling a tale. Where have you been? Speak!"

"To the bottom of the park," she stammered. "I didn't tell a tale."

"And nowhere else?" I demanded.

"No," was the muttered reply.

"Oh, Catherine," I cried, sorrowfully. "You know you have been doing wrong, or you wouldn't be driven to uttering an untruth to me. That does grieve me. I'd rather be three months ill, than hear you frame a deliberate lie."

She sprang forward, and bursting into tears, threw her arms round my neck.

"Well, Ellen, I'm so afraid of you being angry," she said. "Promise not to be angry, and you shall know the very truth. I hate to hide it."

We sat down in the window-seat; I assured her I would not scold, whatever her secret might be, and I guessed it, of course, so she commenced—

"I've been to Wuthering Heights, Ellen, and I've never missed going a day since you fell ill; except thrice before, and twice after you left your room. I gave Michael books and pictures to prepare Minny every evening, and to put her back in the stable; you mustn't scold *him* either, mind. I was at the Heights by half-past six, and generally stayed till half-past eight, and then galloped home. It was not to amuse myself that I went; I was often wretched all the time. Now and then, I was happy, once in a week perhaps. At first, I expected there would be sad work persuading you to let me keep my word to Linton, for I had engaged to call again next day, when we quitted him; but, as you stayed upstairs on the morrow, I escaped that trouble; and while Michael was refastening the lock of the park door in the afternoon, I got possession of the key, and told him how my cousin wished me to visit him, because he was sick, and couldn't come to the Grange: and how papa would object to my going. And then I negotiated with him about the pony. He is fond of reading, and he thinks of leaving soon to get married, so he offered, if I would lend him books out of the library, to do what I wished; but I preferred giving him my own, and that satisfied him better.

"On my second visit, Linton seemed in lively spirits; and Zillah, that is their housekeeper, made us a clean room, and a good fire, and told us that as Joseph was out at a prayer-meeting, and Hareton Earnshaw was off with his dogs, robbing our woods of pheasants, as I heard afterwards, we might do what we liked.

"She brought me some warm wine and gingerbread; and appeared exceedingly good-natured; and Linton sat in the armchair, and I in the little rocking chair, on the hearth-stone, and we laughed and talked so merrily, and found so much to say; we planned where we would go, and what we would do in summer. I needn't repeat that, because you would call it silly.

"One time, however, we were near quarrelling. He said the pleasantest manner of spending a hot July day was lying from morning till evening on a bank of heath in the middle of the moors, with the bees humming dreamily about among the bloom, and the larks singing high up over head, and the blue sky, and bright sun shining steadily and cloudlessly. That was his most perfect idea of heaven's happiness — mine was rocking in a rustling green tree, with a west wind blowing, and bright, white clouds flitting rapidly above; and not only larks, but throstles, and blackbirds, and linnets, and cuckoos pouring out music on every side, and the moors seen at a distance, broken into cool dusky dells; but close by great swells of long grass undulating in waves to the breeze; and woods and sounding water, and the whole world awake and wild with joy. He wanted all to lie in an ecstasy of peace; I wanted all to sparkle, and dance in a glorious jubilee.

"I said his heaven would be only half alive, and he said mine would be drunk; I said I should fall asleep in his, and he said he could not breathe in mine, and began to grow very snappish. At last, we agreed to try both as soon as the right weather came; and then we kissed each other and were friends. After sitting still an hour, I looked at the great room with its smooth, uncarpeted floor; and thought how nice it would be to play in, if we removed the table; and I asked Linton to call Zillah in to help us — and we'd have a game at blind-man's buff — she should try to catch us — you used to, you know, Ellen. He wouldn't, there was no pleasure in it, he said; but he consented to play ball with me. We found two, in a cupboard, among a heap of old toys; tops, and hoops, and battledoors, and shuttlecocks. One was marked C., and the other H.; I wished to have the C., because that stood for Catherine, and the H. might be for Heathcliff, his name; but the bran came out of H., and Linton didn't like it.

"I beat him constantly; and he got cross again, and coughed, and returned to his chair: that night, though, he easily recovered his good humour; he was charmed with two or three pretty songs — *your* songs, Ellen; and when I was obliged to go, he begged and entreated me to come the following evening, and I promised.

"Minny and I went flying home as light as air: and I dreamt of Wuthering Heights, and my sweet, darling cousin, till morning.

"On the morrow, I was sad; partly because you were poorly, and partly that I wished my father knew, and approved of my excursions: but it was beautiful moonlight after tea; and, as I rode on, the gloom cleared.

"I shall have another happy evening, I thought to myself; and what delights me more, my pretty Linton will.

"I trotted up their garden, and was turning round to the back, when that fellow Earnshaw met me, took my bridle, and bid me go in by the front entrance. He patted Minny's neck, and said she was a bonny beast, and appeared as if he wanted to speak to him. I only told him to leave my horse alone, or else it would kick him.

"He answered in his vulgar accent.

"'It wouldn't do mitch hurt if it did;' and surveyed its legs with a smile.

"I was half inclined to make it try; however, he moved off to open the door, and, as he raised the latch, he looked up to the inscription above, and said, with a stupid mixture of awkwardness, and elation:

"'Miss Catherine! I can read yon, nah.'

"'Wonderful,' I exclaimed. 'Pray let us hear you—you *are* grown clever!'

"He spelt, and drawled over by syllables, the name—

"'Hareton Earnshaw.'

"'And the figures?' I cried, encouragingly, perceiving that he came to a dead halt.

"'I cannot tell them yet,' he answered.

"'Oh, you dunce!' I said, laughing heartily at his failure.

"The fool stared, with a grin hovering about his lips, and a scowl gathering over his eyes, as if uncertain whether he might not join in my mirth; whether it were not pleasant familiarity, or what it really was, contempt.

"I settled his doubts by suddenly retrieving my gravity, and desiring him to walk away, for I came to see Linton not him.

"He reddened—I saw that by the moonlight—dropped his hand from the latch, and skulked off, a picture of mortified vanity. He imagined himself to be as accomplished as Linton, I suppose, because he could spell his own name; and was marvellously discomfited that I didn't think the same."

"Stop, Miss Catherine, dear!" I interrupted. "I shall not scold, but I don't like your conduct there. If you had remembered that Hareton was your cousin, as much as Master Heathcliff, you would have felt how improper it was to behave in that way. At least, it was praiseworthy ambition for him to desire to be as accomplished as Linton: and probably he did not learn merely to show off; you had made him ashamed of his ignorance before, I have no doubt; and he wished to remedy it and please you. To sneer at his imperfect attempt was very bad breeding—had *you* been brought up in his circumstances, would you be less rude? He was as quick and as intelligent a child as ever you were, and I'm hurt that he should be despised now, because that base Heathcliff has treated him so unjustly."

"Well, Ellen, you won't cry about it, will you?" she exclaimed, surprised at my earnestness. "But wait, and you shall hear if he conned his abc, to please me; and if it were worthwhile being civil to the brute. I entered, Linton was lying on the settle and half got up to welcome me.

"'I'm ill tonight, Catherine, love,' he said, 'and you must have all the talk, and let me listen. Come, and sit by me—I was sure you wouldn't break your word, and I'll make you promise again, before you go.'

"I knew now that I mustn't tease him, as he was ill; and I spoke softly and put no questions, and avoided irritating him in any way. I had brought some of my nicest books for him; he asked me to read a little of one, and I was about to comply, when Earnshaw burst the door open, having gathered venom with reflection. He advanced direct to us; seized Linton by the arm, and swung him off the seat.

"'Get to thy own room!' he said, in a voice almost inarticulate with passion, and his face looked swelled and furious. 'Take her there if she comes to see thee—thou shalln't keep me out of this. Begone, wi' ye both!'

"He swore at us, and left Linton no time to answer, nearly throwing him into the kitchen; and he clenched his fist, as I followed, seemingly longing to knock me down. I was afraid, for a moment, and I let one volume fall; he kicked it after me, and shut us out.

"I heard a malignant, crackly laugh by the fire, and turning beheld that odious Joseph, standing rubbing his bony hands, and quivering.

"'Aw wer sure he'd sarve ye eht! He's a grand lad! He's getten t' raight sperrit in him! *He* knaws—Aye, he knaws, as weel as Aw do, who sud be t' maister yonder—Ech, ech, ech! He made ye skift properly! Ech, ech, ech!'

"'Where must we go? I said to my cousin, disregarding the old wretch's mockery.

"Linton was white and trembling. He was not pretty then—Ellen. Oh! no, he looked frightful! for his thin face and large eyes were wrought into an expression of frantic, powerless fury. He grasped the handle of the door, and shook it—it was fastened inside.

"'If you don't let me in I'll kill you; if you don't let me in I'll kill you!' he rather shrieked than said. 'Devil! devil! I'll kill you, I'll kill you!'

---

conned: learned.
abc: alphabet.
sarve ye eht: get the best of you.
skift: jump.

"Joseph uttered his croaking laugh again.

"'Thear, that's t' father!' he cried. 'That's father! We've allas summat uh orther side in us—Niver heed Hareton, lad—dunnut be 'feard—he cannot get at thee!'

"I took hold of Linton's hands, and tried to pull him away; but he shrieked so shockingly that I dared not proceed. At last, his cries were choked by a dreadful fit of coughing; blood gushed from his mouth, and he fell on the ground.

"I ran into the yard, sick with terror; and called for Zillah, as loud as I could. She soon heard me; she was milking the cows in a shed behind the barn; and hurrying from her work, she inquired what there was to do?

"I hadn't breath to explain; dragging her in, I looked about for Linton. Earnshaw had come out to examine the mischief he had caused, and he was then conveying the poor thing upstairs. Zillah and I ascended after him; but he stopped me, at the top of the steps, and said I shouldn't go in, I must go home.

"I exclaimed that he had killed Linton and I *would* enter.

"Joseph locked the door, and declared I should do 'no sich stuff,' and asked me whether I were 'bahn to be as mad as him.'

"I stood crying, till the housekeeper re-appeared; she affirmed that he would be better in a bit; but he couldn't do with that shrieking, and din, and she took me, and nearly carried me into the house.

"Ellen, I was ready to tear my hair off my head! I sobbed and wept so that my eyes were almost blind: and the ruffian you have such sympathy with stood opposite; presuming every now and then to bid me 'wisht,' and denying that it was his fault; and finally, frightened by my assertions that I would tell papa, and that he should be put in prison, and hanged, he commenced blubbering himself, and hurried out to hide his cowardly agitation.

"Still, I was not rid of him: when at length they compelled me to depart, and I had gone some hundred yards off the premises, he suddenly issued from the shadow of the roadside, and checked Minny and took hold of me.

"'Miss Catherine, I'm ill grieved,' he began, 'but it's rayther too bad—'

"I gave him a cut with my whip, thinking, perhaps he would murder me—He let go, thundering one of his horrid curses, and I galloped home more than half out of my senses.

"I didn't bid you good night, that evening; and I didn't go to Wuthering Heights, the next—I wished to, exceedingly; but I was strangely excited, and dreaded to hear that Linton was dead, sometimes; and sometimes shuddered at the thought of encountering Hareton.

"On the third day I took courage; at least, I couldn't bear longer suspense and stole off, once more. I went at five o'clock, and walked, fancying I might manage to creep into the house, and up to Linton's room, unobserved. However, the dogs gave notice of my approach: Zillah received me, and saying 'the lad was mending nicely,' showed me into a small, tidy, carpeted apartment, where, to my inexpressible joy, I beheld Linton laid on a little sofa, reading one of my books. But he would neither speak to me, nor look at me, through a whole hour, Ellen — He has such an unhappy temper — and what quite confounded me, when he did open his mouth it was to utter the falsehood, that I had occasioned the uproar, and Hareton was not to blame!

"Unable to reply, except passionately, I got up, and walked from the room. He sent after me a faint 'Catherine!' he did not reckon on being answered so — but I wouldn't turn back; and the morrow was the second day on which I stayed at home, nearly determined to visit him no more.

"But it was so miserable going to bed, and getting up, and never hearing anything about him, that my resolution again melted into air, before it was properly formed. It *had* appeared wrong to take the journey once; now it seemed wrong to refrain. Michael came to ask if he must saddle Minny; I said 'Yes,' and considered myself doing a duty as she bore me over the hills.

"I was forced to pass the front windows to get to the court; it was no use trying to conceal my presence.

"'Young master is in the house,' said Zillah, as she saw me making for the parlour.

"I went in, Earnshaw was there also, but he quitted the room directly. Linton sat in the great armchair half asleep; walking up to the fire, I began in a serious tone, partly meaning it to be true.

"'As you don't like me, Linton, and as you think I come on purpose to hurt you, and pretend that I do so every time, this is our last meeting — let us say good-bye; and tell Mr. Heathcliff that you have no wish to see me, and that he mustn't invent any more falsehoods on the subject.'

"'Sit down and take your hat off, Catherine,' he answered. 'You are so much happier than I am, you ought to be better. Papa talks enough of my defects, and shows enough scorn of me, to make it natural I should doubt myself — I doubt whether I am not altogether as worthless as he calls me, frequently; and then I feel so cross and bitter, I hate everybody! I *am* worthless, and bad in temper, and bad in spirit, almost always — and if you choose, you *may* say good-bye — you'll get rid of an annoyance — Only, Catherine, do me this justice; believe that if I might be as sweet, and as kind, and as good as you are, I would be, as willingly, and more so, than as happy and as healthy. And, believe that your kindness has made me love you deeper than if I deserved your love, and though I couldn't, and cannot help showing my nature to you, I regret it, and repent it, and shall regret, and repent it, till I die!'

"I felt he spoke the truth; and I felt I must forgive him; and, though he should quarrel the next moment, I must forgive him again. We were reconciled, but we cried, both of us, the whole time I stayed. Not entirely for sorrow, yet I *was* sorry Linton had that distorted nature. He'll never let his friends be at ease, and he'll never be at ease himself!

"I have always gone to his little parlour, since that night; because his father returned the day after. About three times, I think, we have been merry, and hopeful, as we were the first evening; the rest of my visits were dreary and troubled—now with his selfishness and spite; and now with his sufferings: but I've learned to endure the former with nearly as little resentment as the latter.

Mr. Heathcliff purposely avoids me. I have hardly seen him at all. Last Sunday, indeed, coming earlier than usual, I heard him abusing poor Linton, cruelly, for his conduct of the night before. I can't tell how he knew of it, unless he listened. Linton had certainly behaved provokingly; however, it was the business of nobody but me; and I interrupted Mr. Heathcliff's lecture, by entering, and telling him so. He burst into a laugh, and went away, saying he was glad I took that view of the matter. Since then, I've told Linton he must whisper his bitter things.

"Now, Ellen, you have heard all; and I can't be prevented from going to Wuthering Heights, except by inflicting misery on two people—whereas, if you'll only not tell papa, my going need disturb the tranquillity of none. You'll not tell, will you? It will be very heartless if you do."

"I'll make up my mind on that point by tomorrow, Miss Catherine," I replied. "It requires some study; and so I'll leave you to your rest, and go think it over."

I thought it over aloud, in my master's presence; walking straight from her room to his, and relating the whole story, with the exception of her conversations with her cousin, and any mention of Hareton.

Mr. Linton was alarmed and distressed more than he would acknowledge to me. In the morning, Catherine learnt my betrayal of her confidence, and she learnt also that her secret visits were to end.

In vain she wept and writhed against the interdict; and implored her father to have pity on Linton: all she got to comfort her was a promise that he would write, and give him leave to come to the Grange when he pleased; but explaining that he must no longer expect to see Catherine at Wuthering Heights. Perhaps, had he been aware of his nephew's disposition and state of health, he would have seen fit to withhold even that slight consolation.

CHAPTER XXV

"These things happened last winter, sir," said Mrs. Dean; "hardly more than a year ago. Last winter, I did not think, at another twelve months' end, I should be amusing a stranger to the family with relating them! Yet, who knows how long you'll be a stranger? You're too young to rest always contented, living by yourself; and I some way fancy, no one could see Catherine Linton, and not love her. You smile; but why do you look so lively and interested, when I talk about her—and why have you asked me to hang her picture over your fireplace? and why—"

"Stop, my good friend!" I cried. "It may be very possible that *I* should love her; but would she love me? I doubt it too much to venture my tranquillity, by running into temptation; and then my home is not here. I'm of the busy world, and to its arms I must return. Go on. Was Catherine obedient to her father's commands?"

She was, (continued the housekeeper). Her affection for him was still the chief sentiment in her heart; and he spoke without anger; he spoke in the deep tenderness of one about to leave his treasure amid perils and foes, where his remembered words would be the only aid that he could bequeath to guide her.

He said to me, a few days afterwards,

"I wish my nephew would write, Ellen, or call. Tell me, sincerely, what you think of him—is he changed for the better, or is there a prospect of improvement, as he grows a man?"

"He's very delicate, sir," I replied; "and scarcely likely to reach manhood; but this I can say, he does not resemble his father; and if Miss Catherine had the misfortune to marry him, he would not be beyond her control, unless she were extremely and foolishly indulgent. However, master, you'll have plenty of time to get acquainted with him, and see whether he would suit her—it wants four years and more to his being of age."

Edgar sighed; and, walking to the window, looked out towards Gimmerton Kirk. It was a misty afternoon, but the February sun shone dimly, and we could just distinguish the two fir trees in the yard, and the sparely scattered gravestones.

"I've prayed often," he half soliloquized, "for the approach of what is coming; and now I begin to shrink, and fear it. I thought the memory of the hour I came down that glen a bridegroom, would be less sweet than the anticipation that I was soon, in a few months, or, possibly, weeks, to be carried up, and laid in its lonely hollow! Ellen, I've been very happy with my little Cathy. Through winter nights and summer days she was a living hope at my side—but I've been as happy musing by myself among those stones, under that old church—lying, through the long June evenings, on the green mound of her mother's grave, and wishing, yearning for the time when I might lie beneath it. What can I do for Cathy? How must I quit her? I'd not care one moment for Linton being Heathcliff's son; nor for his taking her from me, if he could console her for my loss. I'd not care that Heathcliff gained his ends, and triumphed in robbing me of my last blessing! But should Linton be unworthy—only a feeble tool to his father— I cannot abandon her to him! And, hard though it be to crush her buoyant spirit, I must persevere in making her sad while I live, and leaving her solitary when I die. Darling! I'd rather resign her to God, and lay her in the earth before me."

"Resign her to God, as it is, sir," I answered, "and if we should lose you—which may He forbid—under His providence, I'll stand her friend and counsellor to the last. Miss Catherine is a good girl; I don't fear that she will go wilfully wrong; and people who do their duty are always finally rewarded."

Spring advanced; yet my master gathered no real strength, though he resumed his walks in the grounds, with his daughter. To her inexperienced notions, this itself was a sign of convalescence; and then his cheek was often flushed, and his eyes were bright, she felt sure of his recovering. On her seventeenth birthday, he did not visit the churchyard, it was raining, and I observed—

"You'll surely not go tonight, sir?"

He answered—

"No, I'll defer it, this year, a little longer."

He wrote again to Linton, expressing his great desire to see him; and, had the invalid been presentable, I've no doubt his father would have permitted him to come. As it was, being instructed, he returned an answer, intimating that Mr. Heathcliff objected to his calling at the Grange; but his uncle's kind remembrance delighted him, and he hoped to meet him, sometimes, in his rambles, and personally to petition that his cousin and he might not remain long so utterly divided.

That part of his letter was simple, and probably his own. Heathcliff knew he could plead eloquently enough for Catherine's company, then—

"I do not ask," he said, "that she may visit here; but, am I never to see her, because my father forbids me to go to her home, and you forbid her to come to mine? Do, now and then, ride with her towards the Heights; and let us exchange a few words, in your presence! we have done nothing to deserve this separation; and you are not angry with me—you have no reason to dislike me—you allow yourself. Dear uncle! send me a kind note tomorrow; and leave to join you anywhere you please, except at Thrushcross Grange. I believe an interview would convince you that my father's character is not mine; he affirms I am more your nephew than his son; and though I have faults which render me unworthy of Catherine, she has excused them, and, for her sake, you should also. You inquire after my health—it is better; but while I remain cut off from all hope, and doomed to solitude, or the society of those who never did, and never will like me, how can I be cheerful and well?"

Edgar, though he felt for the boy, could not consent to grant his request; because he could not accompany Catherine.

He said, in summer, perhaps, they might meet: meantime, he wished him to continue writing at intervals, and engaged to give him what advice and comfort he was able by letter; being well aware of his hard position in his family.

Linton complied; and had he been unrestrained, would probably have spoiled all by filling his epistles with complaints and lamentations; but his father kept a sharp watch over him; and, of course, insisted on every line that my master sent being shown; so, instead of penning his peculiar personal sufferings, and distresses, the themes constantly uppermost in his thoughts, he harped on the cruel obligation of being held asunder from his friend and love; and gently intimated that Mr. Linton must allow an interview soon, or he should fear he was purposely deceiving him with empty promises.

Cathy was a powerful ally at home: and, between them, they, at length, persuaded my master to acquiesce in their having a ride or a walk together, about once a week, under my guardianship, and on the moors nearest the Grange; for June found him still declining; and, though he had set aside, yearly, a portion of his income for my young lady's fortune, he had a natural desire that she might retain, or, at least return, in a short time, to the house of her ancestors; and he considered her only prospect of doing that was by a union with his heir: he had no idea that the latter was failing almost as fast as himself; nor had anyone, I believe; no doctor visited the Heights, and no one saw Master Heathcliff to make report of his condition, among us.

I, for my part, began to fancy my forebodings were false, and that he must be actually rallying, when he mentioned riding and walking on the moors, and seemed so earnest in pursuing his object.

I could not picture a father treating a dying child as tyrannically and wickedly as I afterwards learnt Heathcliff had treated him, to compel this apparent eagerness; his efforts redoubling the more imminently his avaricious and unfeeling plans were threatened with defeat by death.

CHAPTER XXVI

Summer was already past its prime, when Edgar reluctantly yielded his assent to their entreaties, and Catherine and I set out on our first ride to join her cousin.

It was a close, sultry day; devoid of sunshine, but with a sky too dappled and hazy to threaten rain; and our place of meeting had been fixed at the guidestone, by the crossroads. On arriving there, however, a little herdboy, despatched as a messenger, told us that—

"Maister Linton wer just ut this side th' Heights: and he'd be mitch obleeged to us to gang on a bit further."

"Then Master Linton has forgot the first injunction of his uncle," I observed: "he bid us keep on the Grange land, and here we are, off at once."

"Well, we'll turn our horses' heads round, when we reach him," answered my companion, "our excursion shall lie towards home."

But when we reached him, and that was scarcely a quarter of a mile from his own door, we found he had no horse, and we were forced to dismount, and leave ours to graze.

He lay on the heath, awaiting our approach, and did not rise till we came within a few yards. Then, he walked so feebly, and looked so pale, that I immediately exclaimed—

"Why, Master Heathcliff, you are not fit for enjoying a ramble, this morning. How ill you do look!"

Catherine surveyed him with grief and astonishment; she changed the ejaculation of joy on her lips, to one of alarm; and the congratulation on their long postponed meeting, to an anxious inquiry, whether he were worse than usual?

"No—better—better!" he panted, trembling, and retaining her hand as if he needed its support, while his large blue eyes wandered timidly over her; the hollowness round them, transforming to haggard wildness, the languid expression they once possessed.

"But you have been worse," persisted his cousin, "worse than when I saw you last—you are thinner, and—"

"I'm tired," he interrupted, hurriedly. "It is too hot for walking, let us rest here. And, in the morning, I often feel sick—papa says I grow so fast."

Badly satisfied, Cathy sat down, and he reclined beside her.

"This is something like your paradise," said she, making an effort at cheerfulness. "You recollect the two days we agreed to spend, in the place and way each thought pleasantest? This is nearly yours, only there are clouds; but then, they are so soft and mellow, it is nicer than sunshine. Next week, if you can, we'll ride down to the Grange park, and try mine."

Linton did not appear to remember what she talked of; and he had evidently great difficulty in sustaining any kind of conversation. His lack of interest in the subjects she started, and his equal incapacity to contribute to her entertainment were so obvious, that she could not conceal her disappointment. An indefinite alteration had come over his whole person and manner. The pettishness that might be caressed into fondness, had yielded to a listless apathy; there was less of the peevish temper of a child which frets and teases on purpose to be soothed, and more of the self-absorbed moroseness of a confirmed invalid, repelling consolation, and ready to regard the good-humoured mirth of others as an insult.

Catherine perceived, as well as I did, that he held it rather a punishment, than a gratification, to endure our company; and she made no scruple of proposing, presently, to depart.

That proposal, unexpectedly, roused Linton from his lethargy, and threw him into a strange state of agitation. He glanced fearfully towards the Heights, begging she would remain another half-hour, at least.

"But I think," said Cathy, "you'd be more comfortable at home than sitting here; and I cannot amuse you today, I see, by my tales, and songs, and chatter; you have grown wiser than I, in these six months; you have little taste for my diversions now; or else, if I could amuse you, I'd willingly stay."

"Stay to rest yourself," he replied. "And, Catherine, don't think, or say that I'm *very* unwell—it is the heavy weather, and heat that make me dull; and I walked about, before you came, a great deal, for me. Tell uncle, I'm in tolerable health, will you?"

"I'll tell him that *you* say so, Linton. I couldn't affirm that you are," observed my young lady, wondering at his pertinacious assertion of what was evidently an untruth.

"And be here again next Thursday," continued he, shunning her puzzled gaze. "And give him my thanks for permitting you to come—my best thanks, Catherine. And—and, if you *did* meet my father, and he asked you about me, don't lead him to suppose that I've been extremely silent and stupid—don't look sad and downcast, as you *are* doing—he'll be angry."

"I care nothing for his anger," exclaimed Cathy, imagining she would be its object.

"But I do," said her cousin, shuddering. "*Don't* provoke him against me, Catherine, for he is very hard."

"Is he severe to you, Master Heathcliff?" I inquired. "Has he grown weary of indulgence, and passed from passive, to active hatred?"

Linton looked at me, but did not answer; and, after keeping her seat by his side, another ten minutes, during which his head fell drowsily on his breast, and he uttered nothing except suppressed moans of exhaustion, or pain, Cathy began to seek solace in looking for bilberries, and sharing the produce of her researches with me: she did not offer them to him, for she saw further notice would only weary and annoy.

"Is it half an hour now, Ellen?" she whispered in my ear, at last. "I can't tell why we should stay. He's asleep, and papa will be wanting us back."

"Well, we must not leave him asleep," I answered; "wait till he wakes and be patient. You are mighty eager to set off, but your longing to see poor Linton has soon evaporated!"

"Why did *he* wish to see me?" returned Catherine. "In his crossest humours, formerly, I liked him better than I do in his present curious mood. It's just as if it were a task he was compelled to perform—this interview— for fear his father should scold him. But, I'm hardly going to come to give Mr. Heathcliff pleasure; whatever reason he may have for ordering Linton to undergo this penance. And, though I'm glad he's better in health, I'm sorry he's so much less pleasant, and so much less affectionate to me."

"You think he *is* better in health, then?" I said.

"Yes," she answered; "because he always made such a great deal of his sufferings, you know. He is not tolerably well, as he told me to tell papa, but he's better, very likely."

"There you differ with me, Miss Cathy," I remarked; "I should conjecture him to be far worse."

Linton here started from his slumber in bewildered terror, and asked if anyone had called his name.

"No," said Catherine; "unless in dreams. I cannot conceive how you manage to doze, out of doors, in the morning."

"I thought I heard my father," he gasped, glancing up to the frowning nab above us. "You are sure nobody spoke?"

"Quite sure," replied his cousin. "Only Ellen and I were disputing concerning your health. Are you truly stronger, Linton, than when we separated in winter? If you be, I'm certain one thing is not stronger—your regard for me—speak, are you?"

The tears gushed from Linton's eyes as he answered—

"Yes, yes, I am!"

And, still under the spell of the imaginary voice, his gaze wandered up and down to detect its owner.

Cathy rose.

"For today we must part," she said. "And I won't conceal that I have been sadly disappointed with our meeting, though I'll mention it to nobody but you—not that I stand in awe of Mr. Heathcliff!"

"Hush," murmured Linton; "for God's sake, hush! He's coming." And he clung to Catherine's arm, striving to detain her; but, at that announcement, she hastily disengaged herself, and whistled to Minny, who obeyed her like a dog.

"I'll be here next Thursday," she cried, springing to the saddle. "Good-bye. Quick, Ellen!"

And so we left him, scarcely conscious of our departure, so absorbed was he in anticipating his father's approach.

Before we reached home, Catherine's displeasure softened into a perplexed sensation of pity and regret, largely blended with vague, uneasy doubts about Linton's actual circumstances, physical and social; in which I partook, though I counselled her not to say much, for a second journey would make us better judges.

My master requested an account of our ongoings: his nephew's offering of thanks was duly delivered, Miss Cathy gently touching on the rest: I also, threw little lights on his inquiries, for I hardly knew what to hide, and what to reveal.

CHAPTER XXVII

Seven days glided away, everyone marking its course by the henceforth rapid alteration of Edgar Linton's state. The havoc that months had previously wrought, was now emulated by the inroads of hours.

Catherine we would fain have deluded yet, but her own quick spirit refused to delude her. It divined, in secret, and brooded on the dreadful probability, gradually ripening into certainty.

She had not the heart to mention her ride, when Thursday came round; I mentioned it for her; and obtained permission to order her out of doors; for the library, where her father stopped a short time daily—the brief period he could bear to sit up, and his chamber had become her whole world. She grudged each moment that did not find her bending over his pillow, or seated by his side. Her countenance grew wan with watching and sorrow, and my master gladly dismissed her to what he flattered himself would be a happy change of scene and society, drawing comfort from the hope that she would not now be left entirely alone after his death.

He had a fixed idea, I guessed by several observations he let fall, that as his nephew resembled him in person, he would resemble him in mind; for Linton's letters bore few, or no indications of his defective character. And I through pardonable weakness refrained from correcting the error; asking myself what good there would be in disturbing his last moments with information that he had neither power nor opportunity to turn to account.

We deferred our excursion till the afternoon; a golden afternoon of August—every breath from the hills so full of life, that it seemed whoever respired it, though dying, might revive.

Catherine's face was just like the landscape—shadows and sunshine flitting over it, in rapid succession; but the shadows rested longer and the sunshine was more transient, and her poor little heart reproached itself for even that passing forgetfulness of its cares.

We discerned Linton watching at the same spot he had selected before. My young mistress alighted, and told me that as she was resolved to stay a very little while, I had better hold the pony and remain on horseback; but I dissented, I wouldn't risk losing sight of the charge committed to me a minute; so we climbed the slope of heath, together.

Master Heathcliff received us with greater animation on this occasion; not the animation of high spirits though, nor yet of joy; it looked more like fear.

"It is late!" he said, speaking short, and with difficulty. "Is not your father very ill? I thought you wouldn't come."

"*Why* won't you be candid?" cried Catherine, swallowing her greeting. "Why cannot you say at once, you don't want me? It is strange, Linton, that for the second time, you have brought me here on purpose, apparently, to distress us both, and for no reason besides!"

Linton shivered, and glanced at her, half supplicating, half ashamed, but his cousin's patience was not sufficient to endure this enigmatical behaviour.

"My father *is* very ill," she said, "and why am I called from his bedside—why didn't you send to absolve me from my promise, when you wished I wouldn't keep it? Come! I desire an explanation—playing and trifling are completely banished out of my mind: and I can't dance attendance on your affectations, now!"

"My affectations!" he murmured, "what are they? For Heaven's sake Catherine, don't look so angry! Despise me as much as you please; I am a worthless, cowardly wretch—I can't be scorned enough! but I'm too mean for your anger—hate my father, and spare me, for contempt!"

"Nonsense!" cried Catherine in a passion. "Foolish, silly boy! And there! he trembles, as if I were really going to touch him! You needn't bespeak contempt, Linton; anybody will have it spontaneously, at your service. Get off! I shall return home—it is folly dragging you from the hearthstone, and pretending—what do we pretend? Let go my frock—if I pitied you for crying, and looking so very frightened, you should spurn such pity! Ellen, tell him how disgraceful this conduct is. Rise, and don't degrade yourself into an abject reptile—*don't!*"

With streaming face and an expression of agony, Linton had thrown his nerveless frame along the ground; he seemed convulsed with exquisite terror.

"Oh!" he sobbed, "I cannot bear it! Catherine, Catherine, I'm a traitor too, and I dare not tell you! But leave me and I shall be killed! *Dear*

Catherine, my life is in your hands; and you have said you loved me—and if you did, it wouldn't harm you. You'll not go, then? kind, sweet, good Catherine! And perhaps you *will* consent—and he'll let me die with you!"

My young lady, on witnessing his intense anguish, stooped to raise him. The old feeling of indulgent tenderness overcame her vexation, and she grew thoroughly moved and alarmed.

"Consent to what?" she asked. "To stay? Tell me the meaning of this strange talk, and I will. You contradict your own words, and distract me! Be calm and frank, and confess at once, all that weighs on your heart. You wouldn't injure me, Linton, would you? You wouldn't let any enemy hurt me, if you could prevent it? I'll believe you are a coward, for yourself, but not a cowardly betrayer of your best friend."

"But my father threatened me," gasped the boy, clasping his attenuated fingers, "and I dread him—I dread him! I *dare* not tell!"

"Oh well!" said Catherine, with scornful compassion, "keep your secret, *I'm* no coward—save yourself, I'm not afraid!"

Her magnanimity provoked his tears; he wept wildly, kissing her supporting hands, and yet could not summon courage to speak out.

I was cogitating what the mystery might be, and determined Catherine should never suffer to benefit him or anyone else, by my good will. When hearing a rustle among the ling, I looked up, and saw Mr. Heathcliff almost close upon us, descending the Heights. He didn't cast a glance towards my companions, though they were sufficiently near for Linton's sobs to be audible; but hailing me in the almost hearty tone he assumed to none besides, and the sincerity of which, I couldn't avoid doubting, he said:

"It is something to see you so near to my house, Nelly! How are you at the Grange? Let us hear! The rumour goes," he added in a lower tone, "that Edgar Linton is on his deathbed—perhaps they exaggerate his illness?"

"No; my master is dying," I replied, "it is true enough. A sad thing it will be for us all, but a blessing for him!"

"How long will he last, do you think?" he asked.

"I don't know," I said.

"Because," he continued, looking at the two young people, who were fixed under his eye—Linton appeared as if he could not venture to stir, or raise his head, and Catherine could not move, on his account—"Because that lad yonder seems determined to beat me—and I'd thank his uncle to be quick, and go before him—Hallo! Has the whelp been playing that game long? I *did* give him some lessons about snivelling. Is he pretty lively with Miss Linton generally?"

---

ling: heather.

"Lively? no—he has shown the greatest distress," I answered. "To see him, I should say, that instead of rambling with his sweetheart on the hills, he ought to be in bed, under the hands of a doctor."

"He shall be, in a day or two," muttered Heathcliff. "But first—get up, Linton! Get up!" he shouted. "Don't grovel on the ground there—up this moment!"

Linton had sunk prostrate again in another paroxysm of helpless fear, caused by his father's glance towards him, I suppose, there was nothing else to produce such humiliation. He made several efforts to obey, but his little strength was annihilated, for the time, and he fell back again with a moan.

Mr. Heathcliff advanced, and lifted him to lean against a ridge of turf.

"Now," said he with curbed ferocity, "I'm getting angry—and if you don't command that paltry spirit of yours—*Damn* you! Get up, directly!"

"I will, father!" he panted. "Only, let me alone, or I shall faint! I've done as you wished—I'm sure. Catherine will tell you that I—that I—have been cheerful. Ah! keep by me Catherine; give me your hand."

"Take mine," said his father, "stand on your feet! There now—she'll lend you her arm . . . that's right, look at *her*. You would imagine I was the devil himself, Miss Linton, to excite such horror. Be so kind as to walk home with him, will you? He shudders, if I touch him."

"Linton, dear!" whispered Catherine, "I can't go to Wuthering Heights . . . papa has forbidden me . . . He'll not harm you, why are you so afraid?"

"I can never re-enter that house," he answered. "I am *not* to re-enter it without you!"

"Stop . . . " cried his father. "We'll respect Catherine's filial scruples. Nelly, take him in, and I'll follow your advice concerning the doctor, without delay."

"You'll do well," replied I, "but I must remain with my mistress. To mind your son is not my business."

"You are very stiff!" said Heathcliff, "I know that—but you'll force me to pinch the baby, and make it scream, before it moves your charity. Come then, my hero. Are you willing to return, escorted by me?"

He approached once more, and made as if he would seize the fragile being; but shrinking back, Linton clung to his cousin, and implored her to accompany him with a frantic importunity that admitted no denial.

However I disapproved, I couldn't hinder her; indeed how could she have refused him herself? What was filling him with dread, we had no means of discerning, but there he was, powerless under its gripe, and any addition seemed capable of shocking him into idiocy.

We reached the threshold; Catherine walked in; and I stood waiting till she had conducted the invalid to a chair, expecting her out, immediately; when Mr. Heathcliff pushing me forward, exclaimed—

"My house is not stricken with the plague, Nelly; and I have a mind to be hospitable today; sit down, and allow me to shut the door."

He shut and locked it also; I started.

"You shall have tea, before you go home," he added. "I am by myself. Hareton is gone with some cattle to the Lees — and Zillah and Joseph are off on a journey of pleasure. And, though I'm used to being alone, I'd rather have some interesting company, if I can get it. Miss Linton, take your seat by *him*. I give you what I have; the present is hardly worth accepting; but, I have nothing else to offer. It is Linton, I mean. How she does stare! It's odd what a savage feeling I have to anything that seems afraid of me! Had I been born where laws are less strict, and tastes less dainty, I should treat myself to a slow vivisection of those two, as an evening's amusement."

He drew in his breath, struck the table, and swore to himself.

"By hell! I hate them."

"I'm not afraid of you!" exclaimed Catherine, who could not hear the latter part of his speech.

She stepped close up; her black eyes flashing with passion and resolution.

"Give me that key — I will have it!" she said. "I wouldn't eat or drink here, if I were starving."

Heathcliff had the key in his hand that remained on the table. He looked up, seized with a sort of surprise at her boldness, or, possibly, reminded by her voice and glance, of the person from whom she inherited it.

She snatched at the instrument, and half succeeded in getting it out of his loosened fingers; but her action recalled him to the present; he recovered it speedily.

"Now, Catherine Linton," he said, "stand off, or I shall knock you down; and that will make Mrs. Dean mad."

Regardless of this warning, she captured his closed hand, and its contents again.

"We *will* go!" she repeated, exerting her utmost efforts to cause the iron muscles to relax; and finding that her nails made no impression, she applied her teeth pretty sharply.

Heathcliff glanced at me a glance that kept me from interfering a moment. Catherine was too intent on his fingers to notice his face. He opened them, suddenly, and resigned the object of dispute; but, ere she had well secured it, he seized her with the liberated hand, and, pulling her on his knee, administered, with the other, a shower of terrific slaps on both sides of the head, each sufficient to have fulfilled his threat, had she been able to fall.

At this diabolical violence, I rushed on him furiously.

"You villain!" I began to cry, "you villain!"

A touch on the chest silenced me; I am stout, and soon put out of breath; and, what with that and the rage, I staggered dizzily back, and felt ready to suffocate, or to burst a blood-vessel.

The scene was over in two minutes; Catherine, released, put her two hands to her temples, and looked just as if she were not sure whether her ears were off or on. She trembled like a reed, poor thing, and leant against the table perfectly bewildered.

"I know how to chastise children, you see," said the scoundrel, grimly, as he stooped to repossess himself of the key, which had dropped to the floor. "Go to Linton now, as I told you; and cry at your ease! I shall be your father tomorrow—all the father you'll have in a few days—and you shall have plenty of that—you can bear plenty—you're no weakling—you shall have a daily taste, if I catch such a devil of a temper in your eyes again!"

Cathy ran to me instead of Linton, and knelt down, and put her burning cheek on my lap, weeping aloud. Her cousin had shrunk into a corner of the settle, as quiet as a mouse, congratulating himself, I dare say, that the correction had lighted on another than him.

Mr. Heathcliff, perceiving us all confounded, rose, and expeditiously made the tea himself. The cups and saucers were laid ready. He poured it out, and handed me a cup.

"Wash away your spleen," he said. "And help your own naughty pet and mine. It is not poisoned, though I prepared it. I'm going out to seek your horses."

Our first thought, on his departure, was to force an exit somewhere. We tried the kitchen door, but that was fastened outside; we looked at the windows—they were too narrow for even Cathy's little figure.

"Master Linton," I cried, seeing we were regularly imprisoned. "You know what your diabolical father is after, and you shall tell us, or I'll box your ears, as he has done your cousin's."

"Yes, Linton; you must tell," said Catherine. "It was for your sake I came; and it will be wickedly ungrateful if you refuse."

"Give me some tea, I'm thirsty, and then I'll tell you," he answered. "Mrs. Dean, go away. I don't like you standing over me. Now, Catherine, you are letting your tears fall into my cup! I won't drink that. Give me another."

Catherine pushed another to him, and wiped her face. I felt disgusted at the little wretch's composure, since he was no longer in terror for himself. The anguish he had exhibited on the moor subsided as soon as ever he entered Wuthering Heights; so, I guessed he had been menaced with an awful visitation of wrath, if he failed in decoying us there; and, that accomplished, he had no further immediate fears.

"Papa wants us to be married," he continued, after sipping some of the liquid. "And he knows your papa wouldn't let us marry now; and he's afraid of my dying, if we wait; so we are to be married in the morning, and you are to stay here all night; and, if you do as he wishes, you shall return home next day, and take me with you."

"Take you with her, pitiful changeling?" I exclaimed. "*You* marry? Why, the man is mad, or he thinks us fools, everyone. And, do you imagine that beautiful young lady, that healthy, hearty girl, will tie herself to a little perishing monkey like you? Are you cherishing the notion that *anybody*, let alone Miss Catherine Linton, would have you for a husband? You want whipping for bringing us in here at all, with your dastardly, puling tricks; and — don't look so silly now! I've a very good mind to shake you severely, for your contemptible treachery, and your imbecile conceit."

I did give him a slight shaking, but it brought on the cough, and he took to his ordinary resource of moaning and weeping, and Catherine rebuked me.

"Stay all night? No!" she said, looking slowly round. "Ellen, I'll burn that door down, but I'll get out."

And she would have commenced the execution of her threat directly, but Linton was up in alarm, for his dear self, again. He clasped her in his two feeble arms, sobbing —

"Won't you have me, and save me — not let me come to the Grange? Oh! darling Catherine! you mustn't go, and leave me, after all. You *must* obey my father, you *must!*"

"I must obey my own," she replied, "and relieve him from this cruel suspense. The whole night! What would he think? he'll be distressed already. I'll either break or burn a way out of the house. Be quiet! You're in no danger — but, if you hinder me — Linton, I love papa better than you!"

The mortal terror he felt of Mr. Heathcliff's anger, restored to the boy his coward's eloquence. Catherine was near distraught — still, she persisted that she must go home, and tried entreaty, in her turn, persuading him to subdue his selfish agony.

While they were thus occupied, our jailer re-entered.

"Your beasts have trotted off," he said, "and — Now, Linton! snivelling again? What has she been doing to you? Come, come — have done, and get to bed. In a month or two, my lad, you'll be able to pay her back her present tyrannies, with a vigorous hand — you're pining for pure love, are you not? nothing else in the world — and she shall have you! There, to bed! Zillah won't be here tonight; you must undress yourself. Hush! hold your noise! Once in your own room, I'll not come near you, you needn't fear. By chance, you've managed tolerably. I'll look to the rest."

He spoke these words, holding the door open for his son to pass; and the latter achieved his exit exactly as a spaniel might which suspected the person who attended on it of designing a spiteful squeeze.

The lock was re-secured. Heathcliff approached the fire, where my mistress and I stood silent. Catherine looked up, and instinctively raised her hand to her cheek—his neighbourhood revived a painful sensation. Anybody else would have been incapable of regarding the childish act with sternness, but he scowled on her, and muttered—

"Oh, you are not afraid of me? Your courage is well disguised—you *seem* damnably afraid!"

"I *am* afraid now," she replied; "because if I stay, papa will be miserable; and how can I endure making him miserable—when he—when he—Mr. Heathcliff, *let* me go home! I promise to marry Linton—papa would like me to, and I love him—and why should you wish to force me to do what I'll willingly do of myself?"

"Let him dare to force you!" I cried. "There's law in the land, thank God, there is! though we *be* in an out-of-the-way place. I'd inform, if he were my own son, and it's felony without benefit of clergy!"

"Silence!" said the ruffian. "To the devil with your clamour! I don't want *you* to speak. Miss Linton, I shall enjoy myself remarkably in thinking your father will be miserable; I shall not sleep for satisfaction. You could have hit on no surer way of fixing your residence under my roof, for the next twenty-four hours, than informing me that such an event would follow. As to your promise to marry Linton; I'll take care you shall keep it, for you shall not quit the place till it is fulfilled."

"Send Ellen then, to let papa know I'm safe!" exclaimed Catherine, weeping bitterly. "Or marry me now. Poor papa! Ellen, he'll think we're lost. What shall we do?"

"Not he! He'll think you are tired of waiting on him, and run off, for a little amusement," answered Heathcliff. "You cannot deny that you entered my house of your own accord, in contempt of his injunctions to the contrary. And it is quite natural that you should desire amusement at your age; and that you should weary of nursing a sick man, and that man, *only* your father. Catherine, his happiest days were over when your days began. He cursed you, I daresay, for coming into the world, (I did, at least). And it would just do if he cursed you as *he* went out of it. I'd join him. I don't love you! How should I? Weep away. As far as I can see, it will be your chief diversion hereafter: unless Linton make amends for other losses; and your provident parent appears to fancy he may. His letters of advice and consolation entertained me vastly. In his last, he recommended my jewel to be careful of his; and kind to her when he got her. Careful and kind—that's paternal! But Linton requires his whole stock of care and kindness for himself. Linton can play the little tyrant well. He'll undertake to torture any number of cats if their teeth be drawn, and their claws pared. You'll be able to tell his uncle fine tales of his *kindness,* when you get home again, I assure you."

"You're right there!" I said, "explain your son's character. Show his resemblance to yourself; and then, I hope, Miss Cathy will think twice, before she takes the cockatrice!"

"I don't much mind speaking of his amiable qualities now," he answered, "because she must either accept him, or remain a prisoner, and you along with her, till your master dies. I can detain you both, quite concealed, here. If you doubt, encourage her to retract her word, and you'll have an opportunity of judging!"

"I'll not retract my word," said Catherine. "I'll marry him, within this hour, if I may go to Thrushcross Grange afterwards. Mr. Heathcliff, you're a cruel man, but you're not a fiend; and you won't, from *mere* malice, destroy, irrevocably, all my happiness. If papa thought I had left him, on purpose; and if he died before I returned, could I bear to live? I've given over crying; but I'm going to kneel here, at your knee; and I'll not get up, and I'll not take my eyes from your face, till you look back at me! No, don't turn away! *do* look! You'll see nothing to provoke you. I don't hate you. I'm not angry that you struck me. Have you never loved *anybody,* in all your life, uncle? *never?* Ah! you must look once—I'm so wretched—you can't help being sorry and pitying me."

"Keep your eft's fingers off; and move, or I'll kick you!" cried Heathcliff, brutally repulsing her. "I'd rather be hugged by a snake. How the devil can you dream of fawning on me? I *detest* you!"

He shrugged his shoulders—shook himself, indeed, as if his flesh crept with aversion; and thrust back his chair: while I got up, and opened my mouth, to commence a downright torrent of abuse; but I was rendered dumb in the middle of the first sentence, by a threat that I should be shown into a room by myself, the very next syllable I uttered.

It was growing dark—we heard a sound of voices at the garden gate. Our host hurried out, instantly; *he* had his wits about him; *we* had not. There was a talk of two or three minutes, and he returned alone.

"I thought it had been your cousin Hareton," I observed to Catherine. "I wish he would arrive! Who knows but he might take our part?"

"It was three servants sent to seek you from the Grange," said Heathcliff, overhearing me. "You should have opened a lattice, and called out; but I

---

eft's: lizard's.

could swear that chit is glad you didn't. She's glad to be obliged to stay, I'm certain."

At learning the chance we had missed, we both gave vent to our grief without control; and he allowed us to wail on till nine o'clock; then he bid us go upstairs, through the kitchen, to Zillah's chamber; and I whispered my companion to obey; perhaps, we might contrive to get through the window there, or into a garret, and out by its skylight.

The window, however, was narrow like those below, and the garret trap was safe from our attempts; for we were fastened in as before.

We neither of us lay down: Catherine took her station by the lattice, and watched anxiously for morning—a deep sigh being the only answer I could obtain to my frequent entreaties that she would try to rest.

I seated myself in a chair, and rocked, to and fro, passing harsh judgment on my many derelictions of duty; from which, it struck me then, all the misfortunes of all my employers sprang. It was not the case, in reality, I am aware; but it was, in my imagination, that dismal night, and I thought Heathcliff himself less guilty than I.

At seven o'clock he came, and inquired if Miss Linton had risen.

She ran to the door immediately, and answered—

"Yes."

"Here then," he said, opening it, and pulling her out.

I rose to follow, but he turned the lock again. I demanded my release.

"Be patient," he replied; "I'll send up your breakfast in a while."

I thumped on the panels, and rattled the latch angrily; and Catherine asked why I was still shut up? He answered, I must try to endure it another hour, and they went away.

I endured it two or three hours; at length, I heard a footstep, not Heathcliff's.

"I've brought you something to eat," said a voice; "oppen t' door!"

Complying eagerly, I beheld Hareton, laden with food enough to last me all day.

"Tak it!" he added, thrusting the tray into my hand.

"Stay one minute," I began.

"Nay!" cried he, and retired, regardless of any prayers I could pour forth to detain him.

And there I remained enclosed, the whole day, and the whole of the next night; and another, and another. Five nights and four days I remained, altogether, seeing nobody but Hareton, once every morning, and he was a model of a jailer—surly, and dumb, and deaf to every attempt at moving his sense of justice or compassion.

CHAPTER XXVIII

On the fifth morning, or rather afternoon, a different step approached—lighter and shorter—and, this time, the person entered the room. It was Zillah; donned in her scarlet shawl, with a black silk bonnet on her head, and a willow basket swung to her arm.

"Eh, dear! Mrs. Dean," she exclaimed. "Well! there is a talk about you at Gimmerton. I never thought, but you were sunk in the Blackhorse march, and Missy with you, till master told me you'd been found, and he'd lodged you here! What, and you must have got on an island, sure? And how long were you in the hole? Did master save you, Mrs. Dean? But you're not so thin—you've not been so poorly, have you?

"Your master is a true scoundrel!" I replied. "But he shall answer for it. He needn't have raised that tale—it shall all be laid bare!"

"What do you mean?" asked Zillah. "It's not his tale—they tell that in the village—about your being lost in the marsh; and I calls to Earnshaw, when I come in—

"'Eh, they's queer things, Mr. Hareton, happened since I went off. It's a sad pity of that likely young lass, and cant Nelly Dean.'

"He stared, I thought he had not heard aught, so I told him the rumour.

"The master listened, and he just smiled to himself, and said—

"'If they have been in the marsh, they are out now, Zillah. Nelly Dean is lodged, at this minute, in your room. You can tell her to flit, when you go up; here is the key. The bog-water got into her head, and she would have run home, quite flighty, but I fixed her, till she came round to her senses. You can bid her go to the Grange, at once, if she be able, and carry a message from me, that her young lady will follow in time to attend the squire's funeral.'"

"Mr. Edgar is not dead?" I gasped. "Oh! Zillah, Zillah!"

"No, no—sit you down, my good mistress," she replied, "you're right sickly yet. He's not dead: Dr. Kenneth thinks he may last another day—I met him on the road and asked."

Instead of sitting down, I snatched my outdoor things, and hastened below, for the way was free.

On entering the house, I looked about for someone to give information of Catherine.

The place was filled with sunshine, and the door stood wide open, but nobody seemed at hand.

---

cant: lively, gossipy.

As I hesitated whether to go off at once, or return and seek my mistress, a slight cough drew my attention to the hearth.

Linton lay on the settle, sole tenant, sucking a stick of sugarcandy, and pursuing my movements with apathetic eyes.

"Where is Miss Catherine?" I demanded, sternly, supposing I could frighten him into giving intelligence, by catching him thus alone.

He sucked on like an innocent.

"Is she gone?" I said.

"No," he replied; "she's upstairs — she's not to go; we won't let her."

"You won't let her, little idiot!" I exclaimed. "Direct me to her room immediately, or I'll make you sing out sharply."

"Papa would make you sing out, if you attempted to get there," he answered. "He says I'm not to be soft with Catherine — she's my wife, and it's shameful that she should wish to leave me! He says, she hates me, and wants me to die, that she may have my money, but she shan't have it; and she shan't go home! she never shall! she may cry, and be sick as much as she pleases!"

He resumed his former occupation, closing his lids, as if he meant to drop asleep.

"Master Heathcliff," I resumed, "have you forgotten all Catherine's kindness to you, last winter, when you affirmed you loved her, and when she brought you books, and sung you songs, and came many a time through wind and snow to see you? She wept to miss one evening, because you would be disappointed; and you felt then, that she was a hundred times too good to you; and now you believe the lies your father tells, though you know he detests you both! And you join him against her. That's fine gratitude, is it not?"

The corner of Linton's mouth fell, and he took the sugarcandy from his lips.

"Did she come to Wuthering Heights, because she hated you?" I continued. "Think for yourself! As to your money, she does not even know that you will have any. And you say she's sick; and yet, you leave her alone, up there in a strange house! You, who have felt what it is to be so neglected! You could pity your own sufferings, and she pitied them, too, but you won't pity hers! I shed tears, Master Heathcliff, you see — an elderly woman, and a servant merely — and you, after pretending such affection, and having reason to worship her, almost, store every tear you have for yourself, and lie there quite at ease. Ah! you're a heartless, selfish boy!"

"I can't stay with her," he answered crossly. "I'll not stay, by myself. She cries so I can't bear it. And she won't give over, though I say I'll call my father — I did call him once; and he threatened to strangle her, if she was not quiet, but she began again, the instant he left the room; moaning and grieving, all night long, though I screamed for vexation that I couldn't sleep."

"Is Mr. Heathcliff out," I inquired, perceiving that the wretched creature had no power to sympathise with his cousin's mental tortures.

"He's in the court," he replied, "talking to Doctor Kenneth who says uncle is dying, truly, at last—I'm glad for I shall be master of the Grange after him—and Catherine always spoke of it, as *her* house. It isn't hers! It's mine—papa says everything she has is mine. All her nice books are mine—she offered to give me them, and her pretty birds, and her pony Minny, if I would get the key of our room, and let her out: but I told her she had nothing to give, they were all, all mine. And then she cried, and took a little picture from her neck, and said I should have that—two pictures in a gold case—on one side her mother, and on the other, uncle, when they were young. That was yesterday—I said *they* were mine, too; and tried to get them from her. The spiteful thing wouldn't let me; she pushed me off, and hurt me. I shrieked out—that frightens her—she heard papa coming, and she broke the hinges, and divided the case and gave me her mother's portrait; the other she attempted to hide; but papa asked what was the matter and I explained it. He took the one I had away; and ordered her to resign hers to me; she refused, and he—he struck her down, and wrenched it off the chain, and crushed it with his foot."

"And you were pleased to see her struck?" I asked: having my designs in encouraging his talk.

"I winked," he answered. "I wink to see my father strike a dog, or a horse, he does it so hard—yet I was glad at first—she deserved punishing for pushing me: but when papa was gone, she made me come to the window and showed me her cheek cut on the inside, against her teeth, and her mouth filling with blood: and then she gathered up the bits of the picture, and went and sat down with her face to the wall, and she has never spoken to me since; and I sometimes think she can't speak for pain. I don't like to think so! but she's a naughty thing for crying continually; and she looks so pale and wild, I'm afraid of her!"

"And you can get the key if you choose?" I said.

"Yes, when I am upstairs," he answered; "but I can't walk upstairs now."

"In what apartment is it?" I asked.

"Oh!" he cried, "I shan't tell *you* where it is! It is our secret. Nobody, neither Hareton nor Zillah are to know. There! you've tired me—go away, go away!" And he turned his face onto his arm, and shut his eyes, again.

I considered it best to depart without seeing Mr. Heathcliff; and bring a rescue for my young lady, from the Grange.

On reaching it the astonishment of my fellow servants to see me, and their joy also, was intense; and when they heard that their little mistress was safe, two or three were about to hurry up, and shout the news at Mr. Edgar's door: but I bespoke the announcement of it, myself.

How changed I found him, even in those few days! He lay an image of sadness, and resignation, waiting his death. Very young he looked: though his actual age was thirty-nine; one would have called him ten years younger, at least. He thought of Catherine for he murmured her name. I touched his hand, and spoke.

"Catherine is coming, dear master!" I whispered, "she is alive, and well; and will be here I hope tonight."

I trembled at the first effects of this intelligence: he half rose up, looked eagerly round the apartment, and then sunk back in a swoon.

As soon as he recovered, I related our compulsory visit, and detention at the Heights: I said Heathcliff forced me to go in, which was not quite true; I uttered as little as possible against Linton; nor did I describe all his father's brutal conduct—my intentions being to add no bitterness, if I could help it, to his already overflowing cup.

He divined that one of his enemy's purposes was to secure the personal property as well as the estate to his son, or rather himself; yet why he did not wait till his decease was a puzzle to my master; because ignorant how nearly he and his nephew would quit the world together.

However, he felt that his will had better be altered—instead of leaving Catherine's fortune at her own disposal, he determined to put it in the hands of trustees, for her use during life; and for her children, if she had any, after her. By that means, it could not fall to Mr. Heathcliff should Linton die.

Having received his orders, I despatched a man to fetch the attorney, and four more, provided with serviceable weapons, to demand my young lady of her jailer. Both parties were delayed very late. The single servant returned first.

He said Mr. Green, the lawyer, was out when he arrived at his house, and he had to wait two hours for his re-entrance: and then Mr. Green told him he had a little business in the village, that must be done, but he would be at Thrushcross Grange before morning.

The four men came back unaccompanied, also. They brought word that Catherine was ill, too ill to quit her room, and Heathcliff would not suffer them to see her.

I scolded the stupid fellows well, for listening to that tale, which I would not carry to my master; resolving to take a whole bevy up to the Heights, at daylight, and storm it, literally, unless the prisoner were quietly surrendered to us.

Her father *shall* see her, I vowed, and vowed again, if that devil be killed on his own door stones, in trying to prevent it!

Happily, I was spared the journey, and the trouble.

I had gone downstairs at three o'clock to fetch a jug of water; and was passing through the hall, with it in my hand, when a sharp knock, at the front door, made me jump.

"Oh! it is Green—I said, recollecting myself—only Green," and I went on, intending to send someone else to open it; but the knock was repeated, not loud, and still importunately.

I put the jug on the bannister, and hastened to admit him, myself.

The harvest moon shone clear outside. It was not the attorney. My own sweet little mistress sprung on my neck sobbing,

"Ellen! Ellen! is papa alive?"

"Yes!" I cried, "yes, my angel, he is! God be thanked, you are sage with us again!"

She wanted to run, breathless as she was, upstairs to Mr. Linton's room; but I compelled her to sit down on a chair, and made her drink, and washed her pale face, chafing it into a faint colour with my apron. Then I said I must go first, and tell of her arrival; imploring her to say, she should be happy, with young Heathcliff. She stared, but soon comprehended why I counselled her to utter the falsehood, she assured me she would not complain.

I couldn't abide to be present at their meeting. I stood outside the chamber-door, a quarter of an hour, and hardly ventured near the bed, then.

All was composed, however; Catherine's despair was as silent as her father's joy. She supported him calmly, in appearance; and he fixed on her features his raised eyes that seemed dilating with ecstasy.

He died blissfully, Mr. Lockwood; he died so, kissing her cheek, he murmured,

"I am going to her, and you darling child shall come to us;" and never stirred or spoke again, but continued that rapt, radiant gaze, till his pulse imperceptibly stopped, and his soul departed. None could have noticed the exact minute of his death, it was so entirely without a struggle.

Whether Catherine had spent her tears, or whether the grief were too weighty to let them flow, she sat there dry-eyed till the sun rose—she sat till noon, and would still have remained, brooding over that deathbed, but I insisted on her coming away, and taking some repose.

It was well I succeeded in removing her, for at dinnertime appeared the lawyer, having called at Wuthering Heights to get his instructions how to behave. He had sold himself to Mr. Heathcliff, and that was the cause of his delay in obeying my master's summons. Fortunately, no thought of worldly affairs crossed the latter's mind, to disturb him, after his daughter's arrival.

Mr. Green took upon himself to order everything and everybody about the place. He gave all the servants but me, notice to quit. He would have carried his delegated authority to the point of insisting that Edgar Linton should not be buried beside his wife, but in the chapel, with his family. There was the will however, to hinder that, and my loud protestations against any infringement of its directions.

The funeral was hurried over; Catherine, Mrs. Linton Heathcliff now, was suffered to stay at the Grange, till her father's corpse had quitted it.

She told me that her anguish had at last spurred Linton to incur the risk of liberating her. She heard the men I sent, disputing at the door, and she gathered the sense of Heathcliff's answer. It drove her desperate—Linton, who had been conveyed up to the little parlour soon after I left, was terrified into fetching the key before his father re-ascended.

He had the cunning to unlock, and re-lock the door, without shutting it; and when he should have gone to bed, he begged to sleep with Hareton, and his petition was granted, for once.

Catherine stole out before break of day. She dare not try the doors, lest the dogs should raise an alarm; she visited the empty chambers, and examined their windows; and, luckily, lighting on her mother's, she got easily out of its lattice, and onto the ground, by means of the fir tree, close by. Her accomplice suffered for his share in the escape, notwithstanding his timid contrivances.

CHAPTER XXIX

The evening after the funeral, my young lady and I were seated in the library; now musing mournfully, one of us despairingly, on our loss; now venturing conjectures as to the gloomy future.

We had just agreed the best destiny which could await Catherine, would be a permission to continue resident at the Grange, at least, during Linton's life: he being allowed to join her there, and I to remain as housekeeper. That seemed rather too favourable an arrangement to be hoped for, and yet I did hope, and began to cheer up under the prospect of retaining my home, and my employment, and, above all, my beloved young mistress, when a servant—one of the discarded ones, not yet departed—rushed hastily in, and said, "that devil Heathcliff" was coming through the court, should he fasten the door in his face?

If we had been mad enough to order that proceeding, we had not time. He made no ceremony of knocking, or announcing his name; he was master, and availed himself of the master's privilege to walk straight in, without saying a word.

The sound of our informant's voice directed him to the library: he entered; and motioning him out, shut the door.

It was the same room into which he had been ushered, as a guest, eighteen years before: the same moon shone through the window; and the same autumn landscape lay outside. We had not yet lighted a candle, but all the apartment was visible, even to the portraits on the wall—the splendid head of Mrs. Linton, and the graceful one of her husband.

Heathcliff advanced to the hearth. Time had little altered his person either. There was the same man; his dark face rather sallower, and more composed, his frame a stone or two heavier, perhaps, and no other difference.

Catherine had risen with an impulse to dash out, when she saw him.

"Stop!" he said, arresting her by the arm. "No more runnings away! Where would you go? I'm come to fetch you home; and I hope you'll be a dutiful daughter, and not encourage my son to further disobedience. I was embarrassed how to punish him, when I discovered his part in the business—he's such a cobweb, a pinch would annihilate him—but, you'll see by his look that he has received his due! I brought him down one evening, the day before yesterday, and just set him in a chair, and never touched him afterwards. I sent Hareton out, and we had the room to ourselves. In two hours, I called Joseph to carry him up again; and, since then, my presence is as potent on his nerves as a ghost; and I fancy he sees me often, though I am not near. Hareton says he wakes and shrieks in the night by the hour together; and calls you to protect him from me; and, whether you like your precious mate or not, you must come—he's your concern now; I yield all my interest in him to you."

"Why not let Catherine continue here?" I pleaded, "and send Master Linton to her. As you hate them both, you'd not miss them—they *can* only be a daily plague to your unnatural heart."

"I'm seeking a tenant for the Grange," he answered; "and I want my children about me, to be sure—besides, that lass owes me her services for her bread; I'm not going to nurture her in luxury and idleness after Linton is gone. Make haste and get ready now. And don't oblige me to compel you."

"I shall," said Catherine. "Linton is all I have to love in the world, and, though you have done what you could to make him hateful to me, and me to him, you *cannot* make us hate each other! and I defy you to hurt him when I am by, and I defy you to frighten me!"

"You are a boastful champion!" replied Heathcliff; "but I don't like you well enough to hurt him—you shall get the full benefit of the torment, as long as it lasts. It is not I who will make him hateful to you—it is his own sweet spirit. He's as bitter as gall at your desertion, and its consequences—

don't expect thanks for this noble devotion. I heard him draw a pleasant picture to Zillah of what he would do, if he were as strong as I—the inclination is there, and his very weakness will sharpen his wits to find a substitute for strength."

"I know he has a bad nature," said Catherine: "he's your son. But I'm glad I've a better, to forgive it; and I know he loves me and for that reason I love him. Mr. Heathcliff, *you* have *nobody* to love you; and, however miserable you make us, we shall still have the revenge of thinking that your cruelty rises from your greater misery! You *are* miserable, are you not? Lonely, like the devil, and envious like him? *Nobody* loves you—*nobody* will cry for you, when you die! I wouldn't be you!"

Catherine spoke with a kind of dreary triumph: she seemed to have made up her mind to enter into the spirit of her future family, and draw pleasure from the griefs of her enemies.

"You shall be sorry to be yourself presently," said her father-in-law, "if you stand there another minute. Begone, witch, and get your things."

She scornfully withdrew.

In her absence, I began to beg for Zillah's place at the Heights, offering to resign her mine; but he would suffer it on no account. He bid me be silent, and then, for the first time, allowed himself a glance round the room, and a look at the pictures. Having studied Mrs. Linton, he said—

"I shall have that at home. Not because I need it, but—"

He turned abruptly to the fire, and continued, with what, for lack of a better word, I must call a smile—

"I'll tell you what I did yesterday! I got the sexton, who was digging Linton's grave, to remove the earth off her coffin lid, and I opened it. I thought, once, I would have stayed there, when I saw her face again—it is hers yet[9]—he had hard work to stir me; but he said it would change, if the air blew on it, and so I struck one side of the coffin loose—and covered it up—not Linton's side, damn him! I wish he'd been soldered in lead—and I bribed the sexton to pull it away, when I'm laid there, and slide mine out too, I'll have it made so, and then, by the time Linton gets to us, he'll not know which is which!"

"You were very wicked, Mr. Heathcliff!" I exclaimed; "were you not ashamed to disturb the dead?"

"I disturbed nobody, Nelly," he replied; "and I gave some ease to myself. I shall be a great deal more comfortable now; and you'll have a better chance of keeping me underground, when I get there. Disturbed her? No!

---

suffer: allow.

[9] See the conclusion of "The Bridegroom of Barna" (432–33 in this volume). [ED.]

she has disturbed me, night and day, through eighteen years — incessantly — remorselessly — till yesternight — and yesternight, I was tranquil. I dreamt I was sleeping the last sleep, by that sleeper, with my heart stopped, and my cheek frozen against hers."

"And if she had been dissolved into earth, or worse, what would you have dreamt of then?" I said.

"Of dissolving with her, and being more happy still!" he answered. "Do you suppose I dread any change of that sort? I expected such a transformation on raising the lid, but I'm better pleased that it should not commence till I share it. Besides, unless I had received a distinct impression of her passionless features, that strange feeling would hardly have been removed. It began oddly. You know, I was wild after she died, and eternally, from dawn to dawn, praying her to return to me — her spirit — I have a strong faith in ghosts; I have a conviction that they can, and do exist, among us!

"The day she was buried there came a fall of snow. In the evening I went to the churchyard. It blew bleak as winter — all round was solitary: I didn't fear that her fool of a husband would wander up the den so late — and no one else had business to bring them there.

"Being alone, and conscious two yards of loose earth was the sole barrier between us, I said to myself —

"'I'll have her in my arms again! If she be cold, I'll think it is this north wind that chills *me;* and if she be motionless, it is sleep.'

"I got a spade from the toolhouse, and began to delve with all my might — it scraped the coffin; I fell to work with my hands; the wood commenced cracking about the screws, I was on the point of attaining my object, when it seemed that I heard a sigh from someone above, close at the edge of the grave, and bending down. — 'If I can only get this off,' I muttered, 'I wish they may shovel in the earth over us both!' and I wrenched at it more desperately still. There was another sigh, close at my ear I appeared to feel the warm breath of it displacing the sleet-laden wind. I knew no living thing in flesh and blood was by — but as certainly as you perceive the approach to some substantial body in the dark, though it cannot be discerned, so certainly I felt that Cathy was there, not under me, but on the earth.

"A sudden sense of relief flowed from my heart through every limb. I relinquished my labour of agony, and turned consoled at once, unspeakably consoled. Her presence was with me; it remained while I re-filled the grave, and led me home. You may laugh, if you will, but I was sure I should see her there. I was sure she was with me, and I could not help talking to her.

"Having reached the Heights, I rushed eagerly to the door. It was fastened; and, I remember, that accursed Earnshaw and my wife opposed my entrance. I remember stopping to kick the breath out of him, and then hurrying upstairs, to my room, and hers—I looked round impatiently—I felt her by me—I could *almost* see her, and yet I *could not!* I ought to have sweat blood then, from the anguish of my yearning, from the fervour of my supplications to have but one glimpse! I had not one. She showed herself, as she often was in life, a devil to me! And, since then, sometimes more, and sometimes less, I've been the sport of that intolerable torture! Infernal—keeping my nerves at such a stretch, that, if they had not resembled catgut, they would, long ago, have relaxed to the feebleness of Linton's.

"When I sat in the house with Hareton, it seemed that on going out, I should meet her; when I walked on the moors I should meet her coming in. When I went from home, I hastened to return, she *must* be somewhere at the Heights, I was certain! And when I slept in her chamber—I was beaten out of that—I couldn't lie there; for the moment I closed my eyes, she was either outside the window, or sliding back the panels, or entering the room, or even resting her darling head on the same pillow as she did when a child. And I must open my lids to see. And so I opened and closed them a hundred times a night—to be always disappointed! It racked me! I've often groaned aloud, till that old rascal Joseph no doubt believed that my conscience was playing the fiend inside of me.

"Now since I've seen her, I'm pacified—a little. It was a strange way of killing, not by inches, but by fractions of hair-breadths, to beguile me with the spectre of a hope, through eighteen years!"

Mr. Heathcliff paused and wiped his forehead—his hair clung to it, wet with perspiration; his eyes were fixed on the red embers of the fire; the brows not contracted, but raised next the temples, diminishing the grim aspect of his countenance, but imparting a peculiar look of trouble, and a painful appearance of mental tension towards one absorbing subject. He only half addressed me, and I maintained silence—I didn't like to hear him talk!

After a short period, he resumed his meditation on the picture, took it down and leant it against the sofa to contemplate it at better advantage; and while so occupied Catherine entered, announcing that she was ready, when her pony should be saddled.

"Send that over tomorrow," said Heathcliff to me, then turning to her he added, "You may do without your pony—it is a fine evening, and you'll need no ponies at Wuthering Heights, for what journies you take, your own feet will serve you—Come along."

"Good-bye, Ellen!" whispered my dear little mistress. As she kissed me, her lips felt like ice. "Come and see me, Ellen, don't forget."

"Take care you do no such thing, Mrs. Dean!" said her new father. "When

I wish to speak to you I'll come here. I want none of your prying at my house!"

He signed her to precede him; and casting back a look that cut my heart, she obeyed.

I watched them, from the window, walk down the garden. Heathcliff fixed Catherine's arm under his, though she disputed the act, at first, evidently, and with rapid strides, he hurried her into the alley, whose trees concealed them.

CHAPTER XXX

I have paid a visit to the Heights, but I have not seen her since she left; Joseph held the door in his hand, when I called to ask after her, and wouldn't let me pass. He said Mrs. Linton was "thrang," and the master was not in. Zillah has told me something of the way they go on, otherwise I should hardly know who was dead, and who living.

She thinks Catherine haughty, and does not like her, I can guess by her talk. My young lady asked some aid of her, when she first came, but Mr. Heathcliff told her to follow her own business, and let his daughter-in-law look after herself, and Zillah willingly acquiesced, being a narrow-minded selfish woman. Catherine evinced a child's annoyance at this neglect; repaid it with contempt, and thus enlisted my informant among her enemies, as securely as if she had done her some great wrong.

I had a long talk with Zillah, about six weeks ago, a little before you came, one day, when we foregathered on the moor; and this is what she told me.

"The first thing Mrs. Linton did," she said, "on her arrival at the Heights, was to run upstairs without even wishing good evening to me and Joseph; she shut herself into Linton's room, and remained till morning — then, while the master and Earnshaw were at breakfast, she entered the house and asked all in a quiver if the doctor might be sent for? her cousin was very ill.

"'We know that!' answered Heathcliff, 'but his life is not worth a farthing, and I won't spend a farthing on him.'

"'But I cannot tell how to do,' she said; 'and if nobody will help me, he'll die!'

---

thrang: busy.

"'Walk out of the room!' cried the master, 'and let me never hear a word more about him! None here care what becomes of him; if you do, act the nurse; if you do not, lock him up and leave him.'

"Then she began to bother me, and I said I'd had enough plague with the tiresome thing; we each had our tasks, and hers was to wait on Linton, Mr. Heathcliff bid me leave that labour to her.

"How they managed together, I can't tell. I fancy he fretted a great deal, and moaned hisseln, night and day; and she had precious little rest, one could guess by her white face, and heavy eyes—she sometimes came into the kitchen all wildered like, and looked as if she would fain beg assistance: but I was not going to disobey the master—I never dare disobey him, Mrs. Dean, and though I thought it wrong that Kenneth should not be sent for, it was no concern of mine, either to advise or complain; and I always refused to meddle.

"Once or twice, after we had gone to bed, I've happened to open my door again, and seen her sitting crying, on the stairs' top; and then I've shut myself in, quick, for fear of being moved to interfere. I did pity her then, I'm sure; still I didn't wish to lose my place, you know!

"At last, one night she came boldly into my chamber, and frightened me out of my wits, by saying,

"'Tell Mr. Heathcliff that his son is dying—I'm sure he is, this time—Get up, instantly, and tell him!'

"Having uttered this speech, she vanished again. I lay a quarter of an hour listening and trembling—Nothing stirred—the house was quiet.

"'She's mistaken,' I said to myself. 'He's got over it. I needn't disturb them.' And I began to doze. But my sleep was marred a second time by a sharp ringing of the bell—the only bell we have, put up on purpose for Linton, and the master called to me, to see what was the matter, and inform them that he wouldn't have that noise repeated.

"I delivered Catherine's message. He cursed to himself, and in a few minutes, came out with a lighted candle, and proceeded to their room. I followed—Mrs. Heathcliff was seated by the bedside, with her hands folded on her knees. Her father-in-law went up, held the light to Linton's face, looked at him, and touched him, afterwards he turned to her.

"'Now—Catherine,' he said, 'how do you feel?'

"She was dumb.

"'How do you feel, Catherine?' he repeated.

"'He's safe, and I'm free,' she answered, 'I should feel well—but,' she continued with a bitterness she couldn't conceal, 'You have left me so long to struggle against death, alone, that I feel and see only death! I feel like death!'

"And she looked like it, too! I gave her a little wine. Hareton and Joseph, who had been wakened by the ringing, and the sound of feet, and heard our talk from outside, now entered. Joseph was fain, I believe, of the lad's removal: Hareton seemed a thought bothered, though he was more taken up with staring at Catherine than thinking of Linton. But the master bid him get off to bed again—we didn't want his help. He afterwards made Joseph remove the body to his chamber, and told me to return to mine, and Mrs. Heathcliff remained by herself.

"In the morning, he sent me to tell her she must come down to breakfast—she had undressed, and appeared going to sleep; and said she was ill; at which I hardly wondered. I informed Mr. Heathcliff, and he replied,

"'Well, let her be till after the funeral; and go up now and then to get her what is needful; and as soon as she seems better, tell me.'"

Cathy stayed upstairs a fortnight, according to Zillah, who visited her twice a day, and would have been rather more friendly, but her attempts at increasing kindness were proudly and promptly repelled.

Heathcliff went up once, to show her Linton's will. He had bequeathed the whole of his, and what had been her moveable property to his father. The poor creature was threatened, or coaxed into that act, during her week's absence, when his uncle died. The lands, being a minor he could not meddle with. However, Mr. Heathcliff has claimed, and kept them in his wife's right, and his also—I suppose legally, at any rate Catherine, destitute of cash and friends, cannot disturb his possession.

"Nobody," said Zillah, "ever approached her door, except that once, but I . . . and nobody asked anything about her. The first occasion of her coming down into the house, was on a Sunday afternoon.

"She had cried out, when I carried up her dinner that she couldn't bear any longer being in the cold; and I told her the master was going to Thrushcross Grange; and Earnshaw and I needn't hinder her from descending; so, as soon as she heard Heathcliff's horse trot off, she made her appearance, donned in black, and her yellow curls combed back behind her ears, as plain as a quaker, she couldn't comb them out.

"Joseph and I generally go to chapel on Sundays," (the Kirk, you know, has no minister, now, explained Mrs. Dean, and they call the Methodists' or Baptists' place, I can't say which it is, at Gimmerton, a chapel.) "Joseph had gone," she continued, "but I thought proper to bide at home. Young folks are always the better for an elder's overlooking, and Hareton with all his bashfulness isn't a model of nice behaviour. I let him know that his cousin would very likely sit with us, and she had been always used to see the Sabbath respected, so he had as good leave his guns, and bits of indoor work alone, while she stayed.

"He coloured up at the news; and cast his eyes over his hands and clothes. The train-oil and gunpowder were shoved out of sight in a minute. I saw he meant to give her his company; and I guessed, by this way, he wanted to be presentable; so, laughing, as I durst not laugh when the master is by, I offered to help him, if he would, and joked at his confusion. He grew sullen, and began to swear.

"Now, Mrs. Dean," she went on, seeing me not pleased by her manner, "you happen think your young lady too fine for Mr. Hareton, and happen you're right—but, I own, I should love well to bring her pride a peg lower. And what will all her learning and her daintiness do for her, now? She's as poor as you, or I—poorer—I'll be bound, you're saving—and I'm doing my little all, that road."

Hareton allowed Zillah to give him her aid; and she flattered him into a good humour; so, when Catherine came, half forgetting her former insults, he tried to make himself agreeable, by the house-keeper's account.

"Missis walked in," she said, "as chill as an icicle, and as high as a princess. I got up and offered her my seat in the armchair. No, she turned up her nose at my civility. Earnshaw rose too, and bid her come to the settle, and sit close by the fire; he was sure she was starved.

"'I've been starved a month and more,' she answered, resting on the word, as scornful as she could.

"And she got a chair for herself, and placed it at a distance from both of us.

"Having sat till she was warm, she began to look round, and discovered a number of books in the dresser; she was instantly upon her feet again, stretching to reach them, but they were too high up.

"Her cousin, after watching her endeavours a while, at last summoned courage to help her; she held her frock, and he filled it with the first that came to hand.

"That was a great advance for the lad—she didn't thank him; still, he felt gratified that she had accepted his assistance, and ventured to stand behind as she examined them, and even to stoop and point out what struck his fancy in certain old pictures which they contained—nor was he daunted by the saucy style in which she jerked the page from his finger; he contented himself with going a bit farther back, and looking at her, instead of the book.

"She continued reading, or seeking for something to read. His attention became, by degrees, quite centred in the study of her thick, silky curls—her face he couldn't see, and she couldn't see him. And, perhaps, not quite awake to what he did, but attracted like a child to a candle, at last, he proceeded from staring to touching; he put out his hand and stroked one curl, as gently as if it were a bird. He might have stuck a knife into her neck, she started round in such a taking.

"'Get away, this moment! How dare you touch me? Why are you stopping there?' she cried, in a tone of disgust. 'I can't endure you! I'll go upstairs again, if you come near me.'

"Mr. Hareton recoiled, looking as foolish as he could do; he sat down in the settle, very quiet, and she continued turning over her volumes, another half hour—finally, Earnshaw crossed over, and whispered to me.

"'Will you ask her to read to us, Zillah? I'm stalled of doing naught—and I do like—I could like to hear her! dunnot say I wanted it, but ask of yourseln.'

"'Mr. Hareton wishes you would read to us, ma'am,' I said, immediately. 'He'd take it very kind—he'd be much obliged.'

"She frowned; and, looking up, answered,

"'Mr. Hareton, and the whole set of you will be good enough to understand that I reject any pretence at kindness you have the hypocrisy to offer! I despise you, and will have nothing to say to any of you! When I would have given my life for one kind word, even to see one of your faces, you all kept off. But I won't complain to you! I'm driven down here by the cold, not either to amuse you, or enjoy your society.'

"'What could I ha' done?' began Earnshaw. 'How was I to blame?'

"'Oh! you are an exception,' answered Mrs. Heathcliff. 'I never missed such a concern as you.'

"'But, I offered more than once, and asked,' he said, kindling up at her pertness, 'I asked Mr. Heathcliff to let me wake for you—'

"'Be silent! I'll go out of doors, or anywhere, rather than have your disagreeable voice in my ear!' said my lady.

"Hareton muttered she might go to hell, for him! and unslinging his gun, restrained himself from his Sunday occupations no longer.

"He talked now, freely enough; and she presently saw fit to retreat to her solitude: but the frost had set in, and, in spite of her pride, she was forced to condescend to our company, more and more. However, I took care there should be no further scorning at my good nature—ever since, I've been as stiff as herself—and she has no lover, or liker among us—and she does not deserve one—for, let them say the least word to her, and she'll curl back without respect of anyone! She'll snap at the master himself; and, as good as dares him to thrash her; and the more hurt she gets, the more venomous she grows."

At first, on hearing this account from Zillah, I determined to leave my situation, take a cottage, and get Catherine to come and live with me; but Mr. Heathcliff would as soon permit that, as he would set up Hareton in an independent house; and I can see no remedy, at present, unless she could marry again; and that scheme, it does not come within my province to arrange.

Thus ended Mrs. Dean's story. Notwithstanding the doctor's prophecy, I am rapidly recovering strength, and, though it be only the second week in January, I propose getting out on horseback, in a day or two, and riding over to Wuthering Heights, to inform my landlord that I shall spend the next six months in London; and, if he likes, he may look out for another tenant to take the place, after October—I would not pass another winter here, for much.

CHAPTER XXXI

Yesterday was bright, calm, and frosty. I went to the Heights as I proposed; my housekeeper entreated me to bear a little note from her to her young lady, and I did not refuse, for the worthy woman was not conscious of anything odd in her request.

The front door stood open, but the jealous gate was fastened, as at my last visit; I knocked and invoked Earnshaw from among the garden beds; he unchained it, and I entered. The fellow is as handsome a rustic as need be seen. I took particular notice of him this time; but then, he does his best, apparently, to make the least of his advantages.

I asked if Mr. Heathcliff were at home? He answered, no; but he would be in at dinner-time. It was eleven o'clock, and I announced my intention of going in, and waiting for him, at which he immediately flung down his tools and accompanied me, in the office of watchdog, not as a substitute for the host.

We entered together; Catherine was there, making herself useful in preparing some vegetables for the approaching meal; she looked more sulky, and less spirited than when I had seen her first. She hardly raised her eyes to notice me, and continued her employment with the same disregard to common forms of politeness, as before; never returning my bow and good-morning by the slightest acknowledgment.

"She does not seem so amiable," I thought, "as Mrs. Dean would persuade me to believe. She's a beauty, it is true; but not an angel."

Earnshaw surlily bid her remove her things to the kitchen.

"Remove them yourself," she said; pushing them from her, as soon as she had done; and retiring to a stool by the window, where she began to carve figures of birds and beasts, out of the turnip parings in her lap.

I approached her, pretending to desire a view of the garden; and, as I fancied, adroitly dropped Mrs. Dean's note onto her knee, unnoticed by Hareton—but she asked aloud—

"What is that?" And chucked it off.

"A letter from your old acquaintance, the housekeeper at the Grange," I answered, annoyed at her exposing my kind deed, and fearful lest it should be imagined a missive of my own.

She would gladly have gathered it up, at this information, but Hareton beat her; he seized, and put it in his waistcoat, saying Mr. Heathcliff should look at it first.

Thereat, Catherine silently turned her face from us, and, very stealthily, drew out her pocket-handkerchief and applied it to her eyes; and her cousin, after struggling a while to keep down his softer feelings, pulled out the letter and flung it on the floor beside her as ungraciously as he could.

Catherine caught, and perused it eagerly; then she put a few questions to me concerning the inmates, rational and irrational, of her former home; and gazing towards the hills, murmured in soliloquy.

"I should like to be riding Minny down there! I should like to be climbing up there—Oh! I'm tired—I'm *stalled,* Hareton!"

And she leant her pretty head back against the sill, with half a yawn and half a sigh, and lapsed into an aspect of abstracted sadness, neither caring, nor knowing whether we remarked her.

"Mrs. Heathcliff," I said, after sitting some time mute, "you are not aware that I am an acquaintance of yours? so intimate, that I think it strange you won't come and speak to me. My housekeeper never wearies of talking about and praising you; and she'll be greatly disappointed if I return with no news of, or from you, except that you received her letter, and said nothing!"

She appeared to wonder at this speech and asked, "Does Ellen like you?"

"Yes, very well," I replied unhesitatingly.

"You must tell her," she continued, "that I would answer her letter, but I have no materials for writing, not even a book from which I might tear a leaf."

"No books!" I exclaimed. "How do you contrive to live here without them? If I may take the liberty to enquire—Though provided with a large library, I'm frequently very dull at the Grange—take my books away, and I should be desperate!"

"I was always reading, when I had them," said Catherine, "and Mr. Heathcliff never reads; so he took it into his head to destroy my books.

---

stalled: bored.

I have not had a glimpse of one, for weeks. Only once, I searched through Joseph's store of theology; to his great irritation: and once, Hareton, I came upon a secret stock in your room . . . some Latin and Greek, and some tales and poetry; all old friends—I brought the last here—and you gathered them, as a magpie gathers silver spoons, for the mere love of stealing! They are of no use to you—or else you concealed them in the bad spirit, that as you cannot enjoy them, nobody else shall. Perhaps *your* envy counselled Mr. Heathcliff to rob me of my treasures? But, I've most of them written on my brain and printed in my heart, and you cannot deprive me of those!"

Earnshaw blushed crimson, when his cousin made this revelation of his private literary accumulations, and stammered an indignant denial of her accusations.

"Mr. Hareton is desirous of increasing his amount of knowledge," I said, coming to the rescue. "He is not *envious* but *emulous* of your attainments—He'll be a clever scholar in a few years!"

"And he wants *me* to sink into a dunce, meantime," answered Catherine. "Yes, I hear him trying to spell and read to himself, and pretty blunders he makes! I wish you would repeat Chevy Chase,[10] as you did yesterday— It was extremely funny! I heard you . . . and I heard you turning over the dictionary, to seek out the hard words, and then cursing, because you couldn't read their explanations!"

The young man evidently thought it too bad that he should be laughed at for his ignorance, and then laughed at for trying to remove it. I had a similar notion, and, remembering Mrs. Dean's anecdote of his first attempt at enlightening the darkness in which he had been reared, I observed,

"But, Mrs. Heathcliff, we have each had a commencement, and each stumbled and tottered on the threshold, and had our teachers scorned, instead of aiding us, we should stumble and totter yet."

"Oh!" she replied, "I don't wish to limit his acquirements . . . still, he has no right to appropriate what is mine, and make it ridiculous to me with his vile mistakes and mispronunciations! Those books, both prose and verse, were consecrated to me by other associations, and I hate to have them debased and profaned in his mouth! Besides, of all, he has selected my favourite pieces that I love the most to repeat, as if out of deliberate malice!"

Hareton's chest heaved in silence a minute; he laboured under a severe sense of mortification and wrath, which it was no easy task to suppress.

---

[10] "Chevy Chase" is a fifteenth-century traditional ballad published in Thomas Percy's (1729–1811) *Reliques of Ancient English Poetry* (1765), a collection of sonnets, ballads, historical songs, and metrical romances drawn in part from ancient sources but also from sources as recent as the time of King Charles I (reigned 1625–49). [ED.]

I rose, and, from a gentlemanly idea of relieving his embarrassment, took up my station in the doorway surveying the external prospect, as I stood.

He followed my example, and left the room, but presently reappeared, bearing half-a-dozen volumes in his hands, which he threw into Catherine's lap, exclaiming,

"Take them! I never want to hear, or read, or think of them again!"

"I won't have them now!" she answered. "I shall connect them with you, and hate them."

She opened one that had obviously been often turned over, and read a portion in the drawling tone of a beginner; then laughed, and threw it from her.

"And listen," she continued provokingly, commencing a verse of an old ballad in the same fashion.

But his self-love would endure no further torment—I heard, and not altogether disapprovingly, a manual check given to her saucy tongue—The little wretch had done her utmost to hurt her cousin's sensitive though uncultivated feelings, and a physical argument was the only mode he had of balancing the account, and repaying its effects on the inflicter.

He afterwards gathered the books and hurled them on the fire. I read in his countenance what anguish it was to offer that sacrifice to spleen—I fancied that as they consumed, he recalled the pleasure they had already imparted; and the triumph, and ever-increasing pleasure he had anticipated from them—and I fancied, I guessed the incitement to his secret studies, also. He had been content with daily labour and rough animal enjoyments, till Catherine crossed his path—Shame at her scorn, and hope of her approval were his first prompters to higher pursuits; and instead of guarding him from one, and winning him the other, his endeavours to raise himself had produced just the contrary result.

"Yes, that's all the good such a brute as you can get from them!" cried Catherine, sucking her damaged lip, and watching the conflagration with indignant eyes.

"You'd *better* hold your tongue, now!" he answered fiercely.

And his agitation precluding further speech, he advanced hastily to the entrance, where I made way for him to pass. But ere he had crossed the door-stones, Mr. Heathcliff, coming up the causeway, encountered him, and laying hold of his shoulder, asked,

"What's to do now, my lad?"

"Naught, naught!" he said, and broke away, to enjoy his grief and anger in solitude.

Heathcliff gazed after him, and sighed.

"It will be odd, if I thwart myself!" he muttered, unconscious that I was behind him. "But when I look for his father in his face, I find *her* every day more! How the devil is he so like? I can hardly bear to see him."

He bent his eyes to the ground, and walked moodily in. There was a restless, anxious expression in his countenance, I had never remarked there before, and he looked sparer in person.

His daughter-in-law on perceiving him through the window, immediately escaped to the kitchen, so that I remained alone.

"I'm glad to see you out of doors again, Mr. Lockwood," he said in reply to my greeting, "from selfish motives partly, I don't think I could readily supply your loss in this desolation. I've wondered, more than once, what brought you here."

"An idle whim, I fear, sir," was my answer, "or else an idle whim is going to spirit me away—I shall set out for London, next week, and I must give you warning, that I feel no disposition to retain Thrushcross Grange, beyond the twelve-months I agreed to rent it. I believe I shall not live there anymore."

"Oh, indeed! you're tired of being banished from the world, are you?" he said. "But, if you be coming to plead off paying for a place you won't occupy, your journey is useless—I never relent in exacting my due, from anyone."

"I'm coming to plead off nothing about it!" I exclaimed, considerably irritated. "Should you wish it, I'll settle with you now," and I drew my notebook from my pocket.

"No, no," he replied coolly, "you'll leave sufficient behind, to cover your debts, if you fail to return. . . . I'm not in such a hurry—sit down and take your dinner with us—a guest that is safe from repeating his visit, can generally be made welcome—Catherine! bring the things in—where are you?"

Catherine re-appeared, bearing a tray of knives and forks.

"You may get your dinner with Joseph," muttered Heathcliff aside, "and remain in the kitchen till he is gone."

She obeyed his directions very punctually—perhaps she had no temptation to transgress. Living among clowns and misanthropists, she probably cannot appreciate a better class of people, when she meets them.

With Mr. Heathcliff, grim and saturnine, on the one hand, and Hareton absolutely dumb, on the other, I made a somewhat cheerless meal, and bid adieu early—I would have departed by the back way to get a last glimpse of Catherine, and annoy old Joseph; but Hareton received orders to lead up my horse, and my host himself escorted me to the door, so I could not fulfil my wish.

"How dreary life gets over in that house!" I reflected, while riding down the road. "What a realization of something more romantic than a fairy tale it would have been for Mrs. Linton Heathcliff, had she and I struck up an attachment, as her good nurse desired, and migrated together, into the stirring atmosphere of the town!"

CHAPTER XXXII

1802. This September, I was invited to devastate the moors of a friend, in the North; and, on my journey to his abode, I unexpectedly came within fifteen miles of Gimmerton. The hostler, at a roadside public-house, was holding a pail of water to refresh my horses, when a cart of very green oats, newly reaped, passed by, and he remarked—

"Yon's frough Gimmerton, nah! They're allas three wick' after other folk wi' ther harvest."

"Gimmerton?" I repeated, my residence in that locality had already grown dim and dreamy. "Ah! I know! How far is it from this?"

"Happen fourteen mile' o'er th' hills, and a rough road," he answered.

A sudden impulse seized me to visit Thrushcross Grange. It was scarcely noon, and I conceived that I might as well pass the night under my own roof, as in an inn. Besides, I could spare a day easily, to arrange matters with my landlord, and thus save myself the trouble of invading the neighbourhood again.

Having rested a while, I directed my servant to inquire the way to the village; and, with great fatigue to our beasts, we managed the distance in some three hours.

I left him there, and proceeded down the valley alone. The grey church looked greyer, and the lonely churchyard lonelier. I distinguished a moor sheep cropping the short turf on the graves. It was sweet, warm weather—too warm for travelling; but the heat did not hinder me from enjoying the delightful scenery above and below; had I seen it nearer August, I'm sure it would have tempted me to waste a month among its solitudes. In winter, nothing more dreary, in summer, nothing more divine, than those glens shut in by hills, and those bluff, bold swells of heath.

I reached the Grange before sunset, and knocked for admittance; but the family had retreated into the back premises, I judged by one thin, blue wreath curling from the kitchen chimney, and they did not hear.

---

wick': weeks (*OED*).
Happen: about.

I rode into the court. Under the porch, a girl of nine or ten, sat knitting, and an old woman reclined on the horse-steps, smoking a meditative pipe.

"Is Mrs. Dean within?" I demanded of the dame.

"Mistress Dean? Nay!" she answered, "shoo doesn't bide here; shoo's up at th' Heights."

"Are you the housekeeper, then?" I continued.

"Eea, Aw keep th' hause," she replied.

"Well, I'm Mr. Lockwood, the master—Are there any rooms to lodge me in, I wonder? I wish to stay here all night."

"T'maister!" she cried in astonishment, "Whet, whoiver knew yah wur coming? Yah sud ha' send word. They's now't norther dry—nor mensful abaht t' place—nowt there isn't!"

She threw down her pipe and bustled in, the girl followed, and I entered too; soon perceiving that her report was true, and, moreover, that I had almost upset her wits by my unwelcome apparition.

I bid her be composed—I would go out for a walk; and, meantime, she must try to prepare a corner of a sitting-room for me to sup in, and a bedroom to sleep in—No sweeping and dusting, only good fires and dry sheets were necessary.

She seemed willing to do her best; though she thrust the hearth-brush into the grates in mistake for the poker; and malappropriated several other articles of her craft; but I retired, confiding in her energy for a resting-place against my return.

Wuthering Heights was the goal of my proposed excursion. An afterthought brought me back, when I had quitted the court.

"All well at the Heights?" I inquired of the woman.

"Eea, f'r owt Ee knaw!" she answered, skurrying away with a pan of hot cinders.

I would have asked why Mrs. Dean had deserted the Grange; but it was impossible to delay her at such a crisis, so, I turned away and made my exit, rambling leisurely along with the glow of a sinking sun behind, and the mild glory of a rising moon in front; one fading, and the other brightening, as I quitted the park, and climbed the stony by-road branching off to Mr. Heathcliff's dwelling.

Before I arrived in sight of it, all that remained of day was a beamless, amber light along the west; but I could see every pebble on the path, and every blade of grass by that splended moon.

I had neither to climb the gate, nor to knock—it yielded to my hand.

They's now't norther dry—nor mensful abaht t'place: There is nothing either dry or presentable in the place.

Eea, f'r owt Ee knaw: Yes, for all I know.

That is an improvement! I thought. And I noticed another, by the aid of my nostrils; a fragrance of stocks and wall flowers, wafted on the air, from amongst the homely fruit trees.

Both doors and lattices were open; and, yet, as is usually the case in a coal district, a fine, red fire illumined the chimney; the comfort which the eyes derives from it, renders the extra heat endurable. But the house of Wuthering Heights is so large that the inmates have plenty of space for withdrawing out of its influence; and, accordingly, what inmates there were had stationed themselves not far from one of the windows. I could both see them and hear them talk before I entered; and looked and listened in consequence, being moved thereto by a mingled sense of curiosity, and envy that grew as I lingered.

"Con-*trary!*" said a voice, as sweet as a silver bell—"That for the third time, you dunce! I'm not going to tell you, again—Recollect, or I'll pull your hair!"

"Contrary, then," answered another, in deep, but softened tones. "And now, kiss me, for minding so well."

"No, read it over first correctly, without a single mistake."

The male speaker began to read—he was a young man, respectably dressed, and seated at a table, having a book before him. His handsome features glowed with pleasure, and his eyes kept impatiently wandering from the page to a small white hand over his shoulder, which recalled him by a smart slap on the cheek, whenever its owner detected such signs of inattention.

Its owner stood behind; her light shining ringlets blending, at intervals, with his brown locks, as she bent to superintend his studies; and her face— it was lucky he could not see her face, or he would never have been so steady—I could, and I bit my lip, in spite, at having thrown away the chance I might have had, of doing something else besides staring at its smiting beauty.

The task was done, not free from further blunders, but the pupil claimed a reward and received at least five kisses, which, however, he generously returned. Then, they came to the door, and from their conversation, I judged they were about to issue out and have a walk on the moors. I supposed I should be condemned in Hareton Earnshaw's heart, if not by his mouth, to the lowest pit in the infernal regions if I showed my unfortunate person in his neighborhood then, and feeling very mean and malignant, I skulked round to seek refuge in the kitchen.

There was unobstructed admittance on that side also; and, at the door, sat my old friend, Nelly Dean, sewing and singing a song, which was often interrupted from within, by harsh words of scorn and intolerance, uttered in far from musical accents.

"Aw'd rayther, by th' haulf, hev'em swearing i' my lugs frough morn tuh neeght, nur hearken yah, hahsiver! said the tenant of the kitchen, in answer to an unheard speech of Nelly's. "It's a blazing shaime, ut Aw cannut oppen t' Blessed Book, bud yah set up them glories tuh sattan, un' all t' flaysome wickednesses ut iver wer born intuh t' warld! Oh! yah're a raight nowt; un' shoo's another; un' that poor lad 'ull be lost atween ye. Poor lad!" he added, with a groan; "he's witched, Aw'm sartin on't! O, Lord, judge 'em, fur they's norther law nur justice amang wer rullers!"

"No! or we should be sitting in flaming fagots, I suppose," retorted the singer. "But wisht, old man, and read your Bible like a Christian, and never mind me. This is 'Fairy Annie's Wedding'[11]—a bonny tune—it goes to a dance."

Mrs. Dean was about to recommence, when I advanced, and recognizing me directly, she jumped to her feet, crying—

"Why, bless you, Mr. Lockwood! How could you think of returning in this way? All's shut up at Thrushcross Grange. You should have given us notice!"

"I've arranged to be accommodated there, for as long as I shall stay," I answered. "I depart again tomorrow. And how are you transplanted here, Mrs. Dean? tell me that."

"Zillah left, and Mr. Heathcliff wished me to come, soon after you went to London, and stay till you returned. But step in, pray! Have you walked from Gimmerton this evening?"

"From the Grange," I replied; "and, while they make me lodging room there, I want to finish my business with your master, because I don't think of having another opportunity in a hurry."

"What business, sir?" said Nelly, conducting me into the house. "He's gone out, at present, and won't return soon."

"About the rent," I answered.

"Oh! then it is with Mrs. Heathcliff you must settle," she observed, "or rather with me. She had not learnt to manage her affairs yet, and I act for her; there's nobody else."

I looked surprised.

"Ah! you have not heard of Heathcliff's death, I see!" she continued.

"Heathcliff dead?" I exclaimed, astonished. "How long ago?"

---

lugs: ears.

nur hearken yah: nor have to listen to you.

hahsiver: whatsoever.

[11] See Chitham, pages 333–35 in this volume, for a discussion of "Fairy Annie's Wedding." [ED.]

"Three months since—but sit down, and let me take your hat, and I'll tell you all about it. Stop, you have had nothing to eat, have you?"

"I want nothing. I have ordered supper at home. You sit down too. I never dreamt of his dying! Let me hear how it came to pass. You say you don't expect them back for some time—the young people?"

"No—I have to scold them every evening, for their late rambles—but they don't care for me. At least, have a drink of our old ale—it will do you good—you seem weary."

She hastened to fetch it, before I could refuse, and I heard Joseph asking, whether "it warn't a crying scandal that she should have fellies at her time of life? And then, to get them jocks but uh t' Maister's cellar! He fair shaamed to 'bide still and see it."

She did not stay to retaliate, but re-entered, in a minute, bearing a reaming, silver pint, whose contents I lauded with becoming earnestness. And afterwards she furnished me with the sequel of Heathcliff's history. He had a "queer" end, as she expressed it.

I was summoned to Wuthering Heights, within a fortnight of your leaving us, she said; and I obeyed joyfully, for Catherine's sake.

My first interview with her grieved and shocked me! she had altered so much since our separation. Mr. Heathcliff did not explain his reasons for taking a new mind about my coming here; he only told me he wanted me, and he was tired of seeing Catherine, I must make the little parlour my sitting room, and keep her with me. It was enough if he were obliged to see her once or twice a day.

She seemed pleased at this arrangement; and, by degrees, I smuggled over a great number of books, and other articles, that had formed her amusement at the Grange; and flattered myself we should get on in tolerable comfort.

The delusion did not last long. Catherine, contented at first, in a brief space grew irritable and restless. For one thing, she was forbidden to move out of the garden, and it fretted her sadly to be confined to its narrow bounds, as Spring drew on—for another, in following the house, I was forced to quit her frequently, and she complained of loneliness: she preferred quarrelling with Joseph in the kitchen, to sitting at peace in her solitude.

I did not mind their skirmishes; but Hareton was often obliged to seek the kitchen also, when the master wanted to have the house to himself; and, though, in the beginning, she either left it at his approach, or quietly joined

---

jocks: food.

in my occupations, and shunned remarking, or addressing him—and though he was always as sullen and silent, as possible—after a while, she changed her behavior, and became incapable of letting him alone. Talking at him; commenting on his stupidity and idleness; expressing her wonder how he could endure the life he lived—how he could sit a whole evening staring into the fire, and dozing.

"He's just like a dog, is he not, Ellen?" she once observed, "or a cart-horse? He does his work, eats his food, and sleeps, eternally! What a blank, dreary mind he must have! Do you ever dream, Hareton? And, if you do, what is it about? But you can't speak to me!"

Then she looked at him; but he would neither open his mouth, nor look again.

"He's perhaps, dreaming now," she continued. "He twitched his shoulder as Juno twitches hers. Ask him, Ellen."

"Mr. Hareton will ask the master to send you upstairs, if you don't behave!" I said. He had not only twitched his shoulder, but clenched his fist, as if tempted to use it.

"I know why Hareton never speaks, when I am in the kitchen," she exclaimed, on another occasion. "He is afraid I shall laugh at him. Ellen, what do you think? He began to teach himself to read once; and, because I laughed, he burned his books, and dropped it—was he not a fool?"

"Were not you naughty?" I said; "answer me that."

"Perhaps I was," she went on, "but I did not expect him to be so silly. Hareton, if I gave you a book, would you take it now? I'll try!"

She placed one she had been perusing on his hand; he flung it off, and muttered, if she did not give over, he would break her neck.

"Well, I shall put it here," she said, "in the table drawer, and I'm going to bed."

Then she whispered me to watch whether he touched it, and departed. But he would not come near it, and so I informed her in the morning, to her great disappointment. I saw she was sorry for his persevering sulkiness and indolence—her conscience reproved her for frightening him off improving himself—she had done it effectually.

But her ingenuity was at work to remedy the injury; while I ironed, or pursued other stationary employments I could not well do in the parlour— she would bring some pleasant volume, and read it aloud to me. When Hareton was there, she generally paused in an interesting part, and left the book lying about—that she did repeatedly; but he was as obstinate as a mule, and, instead of snatching at her bait, in wet weather he took to smoking with Joseph, and they sat like automatons, one on each side of the fire, the elder happily too deaf to understand her wicked nonsense, as he would have called it, the younger doing his best to seem to disregard it. On fine evenings the latter followed his shooting expeditions, and Catherine yawned and sighed, and teased me to talk to her, and ran off into the court or garden, the moment I began; and, as a last resource, cried, and said she was tired of living, her life was useless.

Mr. Heathcliff, who grew more and more disinclined to society, had almost banished Earnshaw out of his apartment. Owing to an accident, at the commencement of March, he became for some days a fixture in the kitchen. His gun burst, while out on the hills, by himself; a splinter cut his arm, and he lost a good deal of blood before he could reach home. The consequence was, that, perforce, he was condemned to the fire-side and tranquillity, till he made it up again.

It suited Catherine to have him there: at any rate, it made her hate her room upstairs, more than ever; and she would compel me to find out business below, that she might accompany me.

On Easter Monday, Joseph went to Gimmerton fair with some cattle; and, in the afternoon, I was busy getting up linen in the kitchen — Earnshaw sat, morose as usual, at the chimney corner, and my little mistress was beguiling an idle hour with drawing pictures on the window panes, varying her amusement by smothered bursts of songs, and whispered ejaculations, and quick glances of annoyance and impatience in the direction of her cousin, who steadfastly smoked, and looked into the grate.

At a notice that I could do with her no longer, intercepting my light, she removed to the hearthstone. I bestowed little attention on her proceedings, but, presently, I heard her begin —

"I've found out, Hareton, that I want — that I'm glad — that I should like you to be my cousin, now, if you had not grown so cross to me, and so rough."

Hareton returned no answer.

"Hareton, Hareton, Hareton! do you hear?" she continued.

"Get off wi' ye!" he growled, with uncompromising gruffness.

"Let me take that pipe," she said, cautiously advancing her hand, and abstracting it from his mouth.

Before he could attempt to recover it, it was broken, and behind the fire. He swore at her and seized another.

"Stop," she cried, "you must listen to me, first; and I can't speak while those clouds are floating in my face."

"Will you go to the devil!" he exclaimed, ferociously, "and let me be!"

"No," she persisted, "I won't — I can't tell what to do to make you talk to me, and you are determined not to understand. When I call you stupid, I don't mean anything — I don't mean that I despise you. Come, you shall take notice of me, Hareton — you are my cousin, and you shall own me."

"I shall have naught to do wi' you, and your mucky pride, and your damned, mocking tricks!" he answered. "I'll go to hell, body and soul, before I look sideways after you again! Side out o' t' gait, now; this minute!"

Catherine frowned, and retreated to the windowseat, chewing her lip, and endeavouring, by humming an eccentric tune, to conceal a growing tendency to sob.

"You should be friends with your cousin, Mr. Hareton," I interrupted, "since she repents of her sauciness! It would do you a great deal of good — it would make you another man, to have her for a companion."

"A companion?" he cried; "when she hates me, and does not think me fit to wipe her shoon! Nay! if it made me a king, I'd not be scorned for seeking her goodwill any more."

"It is not I who hate you, it is you who hate me!" wept Cathy, no longer disguising her trouble. "You hate me as much as Mr. Heathcliff does, and more."

"You are a damned liar," began Earnshaw; "why have I made him angry, by taking your part then, a hundred times? and that, when you sneered at, and despised me, and — Go on plaguing me, and I'll step in yonder, and say you worried me out of the kitchen!"

"I didn't know you took my part," she answered, drying her eyes; "and I was miserable and bitter at everybody; but, now I thank you, and beg you to forgive me, what can I do besides?"

She returned to the hearth, and frankly extended her hand.

He blackened, and scowled like a thunder cloud, and kept his fists resolutely clenched, and his gaze fixed on the ground.

Catherine, by instinct, must have divined it was obdurate perversity, and not dislike, that prompted this dogged conduct; for, after remaining an instant, undecided, she stooped and impressed on his cheek a gentle kiss.

The little rogue thought I had not seen her, and, drawing back, she took her former station by the window, quite demurely.

I shook my head reprovingly; and then she blushed, and whispered —

"Well, what should I have done, Ellen? He wouldn't shake hands, and he wouldn't look — I must show him some way that I like him, that I want to be friends."

Whether the kiss convinced Hareton, I cannot tell; he was very careful, for some minutes, that his face should not be seen; and when he did raise it, he was sadly puzzled where to turn his eyes.

Catherine employed herself in wrapping a handsome book neatly in white paper; and having tied it with a bit of ribband, and addressed it to

---

Side out o' t' gait: Get out of my way.

"Mr. Hareton Earnshaw," she desired me to be her ambassadress, and convey the present to its destined recipient.

"And tell him, if he'll take it, I'll come and teach him to read it right," she said, "and, if he refuse it, I'll go upstairs, and never tease him again."

I carried it, and repeated the message, anxiously watched by my employer. Hareton would not open his fingers, so I laid it on his knee. He did not strike it off either. I returned to my work: Catherine leaned her head and arms on the table, till she heard the slight rustle of the covering being removed, then she stole away, and quietly seated herself beside her cousin. He trembled, and his face glowed—all his rudeness, and all his surly harshness had deserted him—he could not summon courage, at first, to utter a syllable, in reply to her questioning look, and her murmured petition.

"Say you forgive me, Hareton, do! You can make me so happy, by speaking that little word."

He muttered something inaudible.

"And you'll be my friend?" added Catherine interrogatively.

"Nay! you'll be ashamed of me every day of your life," he answered. "And the more, the more you know me, and I cannot bide it."

"So, you won't be my friend?" she said, smiling as sweet as honey, and creeping close up.

I overheard no further distinguishable talk; but on looking round again, I perceived two such radiant countenances bent over the page of the accepted book, that I did not doubt the treaty had been ratified, on both sides, and the enemies were, thenceforth, sworn allies.

The work they studied was full of costly pictures; and those, and their position had charm enough to keep them unmoved, till Joseph came home. He, poor man, was perfectly aghast at the spectacle of Catherine seated on the same bench with Hareton Earnshaw, leaning her hand on his shoulder; and confounded at his favourite's endurance of her proximity. It affected him too deeply to allow an observation on the subject that night. His emotion was only revealed by the immense sighs he drew, as he solemnly spread his large Bible on the table, and overlaid it with dirty bank-notes from his pocket-book, the produce of the day's transactions. At length, he summoned Hareton from his seat.

"Tak' these in tuh t' maister, lad," he said, "un' bide theare; Aw's gang up tuh my awn rahm. This hoile's norther mensful, nor seemly fur us—we mun side aht, and seearch another!"

This hoile's norther mensful, nor seemly fur us: This room is not decent as it is infected with a female presence.

"Come, Catherine," I said, "we must 'side out,' too—I've done my ironing, are you ready to go?"

"It is not eight o'clock!" she answered, rising unwillingly, "Hareton, I'll leave this book on the chimney-piece, and I'll bring some more tomorrow."

"Ony books ut yah leave, Aw shall tak' intuh th' hahse," said Joseph, "un' it 'ull be mitch'n yah find 'em agean; soa, yah muh plase yerseln!"

Cathy threatened that his library should pay for hers; and, smiling as she passed Hareton, went singing upstairs, lighter of heart, I venture to say, than ever she had been under that roof before; except, perhaps, during her earliest visits to Linton.

The intimacy, thus commenced, grew rapidly; though it encountered temporary interruptions. Earnshaw was not to be civilized with a wish; and my young lady was no philosopher, and no paragon of patience; but both their minds tending to the same point—one loving and desiring to esteem; and the other loving and desiring to be esteemed—they contrived in the end to reach it.

You see, Mr. Lockwood, it was easy enough to win Mrs. Heathcliff's heart; but now, I'm glad you did not try—the crown of all my wishes will be the union of those two; I shall envy no one on their wedding-day—there won't be a happier woman than myself in England!

CHAPTER XXXIII

On the morrow of that Monday, Earnshaw being still unable to follow his ordinary employments, and, therefore, remaining about the house, I speedily found it would be impracticable to retain my charge beside me, as heretofore.

She got downstairs before me, and out into the garden; where she had seen her cousin performing some easy work; and when I went to bid them come to breakfast, I saw she had persuaded him to clear a large space of ground from currant and gooseberry bushes, and they were busy planning together an importation of plants from the Grange.

I was terrified at the devastation which had been accomplished in a brief half hour; the black currant trees were the apple of Joseph's eye, and she had just fixed her choice of a flower bed in the midst of them!

---

mitch'n: odd, very strange.

"There! That will be all shewn to the master," I exclaimed, "the minute it is discovered. And what excuse have you to offer for taking such liberties with the garden? We shall have a fine explosion on the head of it: see if we don't! Mr. Hareton, I wonder you should have no more wit, than to go and make that mess at her bidding!"

"I'd forgotten they were Joseph's," answered Earnshaw, rather puzzled, "but I'll tell him I did it."

We always ate our meals with Mr. Heathcliff. I held the mistress's post in making tea and carving; so I was indispensable at table. Catherine usually sat by me; but today, she stole nearer to Hareton, and I presently saw she would have no more discretion in her friendship, than she had in her hostility.

"Now, mind you don't talk with and notice your cousin too much," were my whispered instructions as we entered the room; "it will certainly annoy Mr. Heathcliff, and he'll be mad at you both."

"I'm not going to," she answered.

The minute after, she had sidled to him, and was sticking primroses in his plate of porridge.

He dared not speak to her, there; he dared hardly look; and yet she went on teasing, till he was twice on the point of being provoked to laugh; and I frowned, and then she glanced towards the master, whose mind was occupied on other subjects than his company, as his countenance evinced, and she grew serious for an instant, scrutinizing him with deep gravity. Afterwards she turned, and re-commenced her nonsense; at last, Hareton uttered a smothered laugh.

Mr. Heathcliff started; his eye rapidly surveyed our faces. Catherine met it with her accustomed look of nervousness, and yet defiance, which he abhorred.

"It is well you are out of my reach," he exclaimed. "What fiend possesses you to stare back at me, continually, with those infernal eyes? Down with them! and don't remind me of your existence again. I thought I had cured you of laughing!"

"It was me," muttered Hareton.

"What do you say?" demanded the master.

Hareton looked at his plate, and did not repeat the confession.

Mr. Heathcliff looked at him a bit, and then silently resumed his breakfast, and his interrupted musing.

We had nearly finished, and the two young people prudently shifted wider asunder, so I anticipated no further disturbance during that sitting; when Joseph appeared at the door, revealing by his quivering lip, and furious eyes, that the outrage committed on his precious shrubs was detected.

He must have seen Cathy and her cousin about the spot, before he ex-amined it, for while his jaws worked like those of a cow chewing its cud, and rendered his speech difficult to understand, he began:

"Aw mun hev my wage, and Aw mun goa! Aw *hed* aimed tuh dee, wheare Aw'd sarved fur sixty year; un' Aw thowt Aw'd lug my books up in-tuh t' garret, un' all my bits uh stuff, un' they sud hev t' kitchen tuh theirseln; fur t' sake uh quietness. It wur hard tuh gie up my awn hearth-stun, bud Aw thowt Aw *could* do that! Bud, nah, shoo's taan my garden frough me, un' by th' heart! Maister, Aw cannot stand it! Yah muh bend tuh th' yoak, an ye will—Aw' noan used to 't and an ow'd man doesn't sooin get used tuh new barthens—Aw'd rayther arn my bite, an' my sup, wi' a ham-mer in th' road!"

"Now, now, idiot!" interrupted Heathcliff, "cut it short! What's your grievance? I'll interfere in no quarrels between you and Nelly—She may thrust you into the coal-hole for anything I care."

"It's noan Nelly!" answered Joseph. "Aw sudn't shift fur Nelly—Nasty, ill nowt as shoo is. Thank God! *shoo* cannot stale t' sowl uh nob'dy! Shoo wer niver soa handsome, bud whet a body mud look at her 'baht winking. It's yon flaysome, graceless quean, ut's witched ahr lad, wi' her bold een, un' her forrard ways—till—Nay! it fair brusts my heart! He's forgotten all E done for him, un' made on him, un' goan un' riven up a whole row ut t' grandest currant trees i' t' garden." And here he lamented outright, un-manned by a sense of his bitter injuries, and Earnshaw's ingratitude and dangerous condition.

"Is the fool drunk?" asked Mr. Heathcliff. "Hareton, is it you he's find-ing fault with?"

"I've pulled up two or three bushes," replied the young man, "but I'm going to set 'em again."

"And why have you pulled them up?" said the master.

Catherine wisely put in her tongue.

"We wanted to plant some flowers there," she cried. "I'm the only per-son to blame, for I wished him to do it."

"And who the devil gave *you* leave to touch a stick about the place?" de-manded her father-in-law, much surprised. "And who ordered *you* to obey her?" he added turning to Hareton.

The latter was speechless; his cousin replied—

"You shouldn't grudge a few yards of earth, for me to ornament, when you have taken all my land!"

---

barthens: barns, places for cattle.
shoo **cannot stale t' sowl uh nob'dy:** she cannot steal a man's soul.

"Your land, insolent slut? You never had any!" said Heathcliff.

"And my money," she continued, returning his angry glare, and meantime, biting a piece of crust, the remnant of her breakfast.

"Silence!" he exclaimed. "Get done, and begone!"

"And Hareton's land, and his money," pursued the reckless thing. "Hareton and I are friends now; and I shall tell him all about you!"

The master seemed confounded a moment, he grew pale, and rose up, eyeing her all the while, with an expression of mortal hate.

"If you strike me, Hareton will strike you!" she said, "so you may as well sit down."

"If Hareton does not turn you out of the room, I'll strike him to Hell," thundered Heathcliff. "Damnable witch! dare you pretend to rouse him against me? Off with her! Do you hear? Fling her into the kitchen! I'll kill her, Ellen Dean, if you let her come into my sight again!"

Hareton tried under his breath to persuade her to go.

"Drag her away!" he cried savagely. "Are you staying to talk?" And he approached to execute his own command.

"He'll not obey you, wicked man, any more" said Catherine, "and he'll soon detest you, as much as I do."

"Wisht! wisht!" muttered the young man reproachfully. "I will not hear you speak so to him—Have done!"

"But you won't let him strike me?" she cried.

"Come then!" he whispered earnestly.

It was too late—Heathcliff had caught hold of her.

"Now *you* go!" he said to Earnshaw. "Accursed witch! this time she has provoked me, when I could not bear it; and I'll make her repent it forever!"

He had his hand in her hair; Hareton attempted to release the locks, entreating him not to hurt her that once. His black eyes flashed, he seemed ready to tear Catherine in pieces, and I was just worked up to risk coming to the rescue, when of a sudden, his fingers relaxed, he shifted his grasp from her head, to her arm, and gazed intently in her face—Then, he drew his hand over his eyes, stood a moment to collect himself apparently, and turning anew to Catherine, said with assumed calmness.

"You must learn to avoid putting me in a passion, or I shall really murder you sometime! go with Mrs. Dean, and keep with her, and confine your insolence to her ears. As to Hareton Earnshaw, if I see him listen to you, I'll send him seeking his bread where he can get it! your love will make him an outcast, and a beggar—Nelly, take her, and leave me, all of you! Leave me!"

I led my young lady out; she was too glad of her escape to resist; the other followed, and Mr. Heathcliff had the room to himself, till dinner.

I had counselled Catherine to get hers upstairs; but, as soon as he perceived her vacant seat, he sent me to call her. He spoke to none of us, ate very little, and went out directly afterwards, intimating that he should not return before evening.

The two new friends established themselves in the house, during his absence, where I heard Hareton sternly check his cousin, on her offering a revelation of her father-in-law's conduct to his father.

He said he wouldn't suffer a word to be uttered to him, in his disparagement; if he were the devil, it didn't signify; he would stand by him; and he'd rather she would abuse himself, as she used to, than begin on Mr. Heathcliff.

Catherine was waxing cross at this; but he found means to make her hold her tongue, by asking, how she would like *him* to speak ill of her father? and then she comprehended that Earnshaw took the master's reputation home to himself: and was attached by ties stronger than reason could break—chains, forged by habit, which it would be cruel to attempt to loosen.

She showed a good heart, thenceforth, in avoiding both complaints and expressions of antipathy concerning Heathcliff; and confessed to me her sorrow that she had endeavoured to raise a bad spirit between him and Hareton—indeed, I don't believe she has ever breathed a syllable, in the latter's hearing, against her oppressor, since.

When this slight disagreement was over, they were thick again, and as busy as possible, in their several occupations, of pupil and teacher. I came in to sit with them, after I had done my work, and I felt so soothed, and comforted to watch them, that I did not notice how time got on. You know, they both appeared in a measure, my children: I had long been proud of one, and now, I was sure, the other would be a source of equal satisfaction. His honest, warm, and intelligent nature shook off rapidly the clouds of ignorance and degradation in which it had been bred; and Catherine's sincere commendations acted as a spur to his industry. His brightening mind brightened his features, and added spirit and nobility to their aspect—I could hardly fancy it the same individual I had beheld on the day I discovered my little lady at Wuthering Heights, after her expedition to the Crag.

While I admired, and they laboured, dusk grew on, and with it returned the master. He came upon us quite unexpectedly, entering by the front way, and had a full view of the whole three, ere we could raise our heads to glance at him.

Well, I reflected, there never was a pleasanter, or more harmless sight; and it will be a burning shame to scold them. The red fire-light glowed on their two bonny heads, and revealed their faces, animated with the eager interest of children; for, though he was twenty-three, and she eighteen, each had so much of novelty to feel, and learn, that neither experienced nor evinced the sentiments of sober disenchanted maturity.

They lifted their eyes together, to encounter Mr. Heathcliff—perhaps you have never remarked that their eyes are precisely similar, and they are those of Catherine Earnshaw. The present Catherine has no other likeness to her, except a breadth of forehead, and a certain arch of the nostril that makes her appear rather haughty, whether she will, or not. With Hareton the resemblance is carried farther, it is singular, at all times—then it was particularly striking: because his senses were alert, and his mental faculties wakened to unwonted activity.

I suppose this resemblance disarmed Mr. Heathcliff: he walked to the hearth in evident agitation, but it quickly subsided, as he looked at the young man; or, I should say, altered its character, for it was there yet.

He took the book from his hand, and glanced at the open page, then returned it without any observation; merely signing Catherine away—her companion lingered very little behind her, and I was about to depart also, but he bid me sit still.

"It is a poor conclusion, is it not," he observed, having brooded a while on the scene he had just witnessed. "An absurd termination to my violent exertions? I get levers and mattocks to demolish the two houses, and train myself to be capable of working like Hercules, and when everything is ready, and in my power, I find the will to lift a slate off either roof has vanished! My old enemies have not beaten me—now would be the precise time to revenge myself on their representatives—I could do it; and none could hinder me—But where is the use? I don't care for striking, I can't take the trouble to raise my hand! That sounds as if I had been labouring the whole time, only to exhibit a fine trait of magnanimity. It is far from being the case—I have lost the faculty of enjoying their destruction, and I am too idle to destroy for nothing.

"Nelly, there is a strange change approaching—I'm in its shadow at present—I take so little interest in my daily life, that I hardly remember to eat, and drink—Those two, who have left the room are the only objects which retain a distinct material appearance to me; and, that appearance causes me pain, amounting to agony. About *her* I won't speak; and I don't desire to think; but I earnestly wish she were invisible—her presence invokes only maddening sensations. *He* moves me differently; and yet if I could do it without seeming insane, I'd never see him again! You'll perhaps think me rather inclined to become so," he added, making an effort to smile, "if I try to describe the thousand forms of past associations, and ideas he awakens, or embodies—But you'll not talk of what I tell you, and my mind is so eternally secluded in itself, it is tempting, at last, to turn it out to another.

"Five minutes ago, Hareton seemed a personification of my youth, not a human being—I felt to him in such a variety of ways, that it would have been impossible to have accosted him rationally.

"In the first place, his startling likeness to Catherine connected him fearfully with her — That however which you may suppose the most potent to arrest my imagination, is actually the least — for what is not connected with her to me? and what does not recall her? I cannot look down to this floor, but her features are shaped in the flags! In every cloud, in every tree — filling the air at night, and caught by glimpses in every object, by day I am surrounded with her image! The most ordinary faces of men, and women — my own features mock me with a resemblance. The entire world is a dreadful collection of memoranda that she did exist, and that I have lost her!

"Well, Hareton's aspect was the ghost of my immortal love, of my wild endeavours to hold my right, my degradation, my pride, my happiness, and my anguish —

"But it is frenzy to repeat these thoughts to you; only it will let you know, why, with a reluctance to be always alone, his society is no benefit, rather an aggravation of the constant torment I suffer — and it partly contributes to render me regardless how he and his cousin go on together. I can give them no attention, any more."

"But what do you mean by a *change*, Mr. Heathcliff?" I said, alarmed at his manner, though he was neither in danger of losing his senses, nor dying, according to my judgment he was quite strong and healthy; and, as to his reason, from childhood he had a delight in dwelling on dark things, and entertaining odd fancies — he might have had a monomania on the subject of his departed idol; but on every other point his wits were as sound as mine.

"I shall not know that, till it comes," he said, "I'm only half conscious of it now."

"You have no feeling of illness, have you?" I asked.

"No, Nelly, I have not," he answered.

"Then, you are not afraid of death?" I pursued.

"Afraid? No!" he replied. "I have neither a fear, nor a presentiment, nor a hope of death. Why should I? With my hard constitution, and temperate mode of living, and unperilous occupations, I ought to, and probably *shall* remain above ground, till there is scarcely a black hair on my head — And yet I cannot continue in this condition! — I have to remind myself to breathe — almost to remind my heart to beat! And it is like bending back a stiff spring . . . it is by compulsion that I do the slightest act, not prompted by one thought, and by compulsion, that I notice anything alive, or dead, which is not associated with one universal idea . . . I have a single wish, and my whole being, and faculties are yearning to attain it. They have yearned towards it so long, and so unwaveringly, that I'm convinced it *will* be reached — and *soon* — because it has devoured my existence — I am swallowed in the anticipation of its fulfillment.

"My confessions have not relieved me—but, they may account for some otherwise unaccountable phases of humour, which I show. O, God! It is a long fight, I wish it were over!"

He began to pace the room, muttering terrible things to himself; till I was inclined to believe, as he said Joseph did, that conscience had turned his heart to an earthly hell—I wondered greatly how it would end.

Though he seldom before had revealed this state of mind, even by looks, it was his habitual mood, I had no doubt: he asserted it himself—but, not a soul, from his general bearing would have conjectured the fact. You did not, when you saw him, Mr. Lockwood—and at the period of which I speak, he was just the same as then, only fonder of continued solitude, and perhaps still more laconic in company.

CHAPTER XXXIV

For some days after that evening, Mr. Heathcliff shunned meeting us at meals; yet he would not consent, formally, to exclude Hareton and Cathy. He had an aversion to yielding so completely to his feelings, choosing, rather, to absent himself—And eating once in twenty-four hours seemed sufficient sustenance for him.

One night, after the family were in bed, I heard him go downstairs, and out at the front door: I did not hear him re-enter and, in the morning, I found he was still away.

We were in April then, the weather was sweet and warm, the grass as green as showers and sun could make it, and the two dwarf apple trees, near the southern wall, in full bloom. After breakfast, Catherine insisted on my bringing a chair, and sitting, with my work, under the fir trees, at the end of the house; and she beguiled Hareton, who had perfectly recovered from his accident, to dig and arrange her little garden, which was shifted to that corner by the influence of Joseph's complaints.

I was comfortably revelling in the spring fragrance around, and the beautiful soft blue overhead, when my young lady, who had run down near the gate to procure some primrose roots for a border, returned only half laden, and informed us that Mr. Heathcliff was coming in.

"And he spoke to me," she added with a perplexed countenance.

"What did he say?" asked Hareton.

"He told me to begone as fast as I could," she answered. "But he looked so different from his usual look that I stopped a moment to stare at him."

"How?" he inquired.

"Why, almost bright and cheerful—No, almost nothing—*very much* excited, and wild and glad!" she replied.

"Night-walking amuses him, then," I remarked, affecting a careless manner: in reality, as surprised as she was; and, anxious to ascertain the truth of her statement, for to see the master looking glad would not be an everyday spectacle, I framed an excuse to go in.

Heathcliff stood at the open door; he was pale, and he trembled; yet, certainly, he had a strange joyful glitter in his eyes, that altered the aspect of his whole face.

"Will you have some breakfast?" I said. "You must be hungry rambling about all night!"

I wanted to discover where he had been; but I did not like to ask directly.

"No, I'm not hungry," he answered, averting his head, and speaking rather contemptuously, as if he guessed I was trying to divine the occasion of his good humour.

I felt perplexed—I didn't know whether it were not a proper opportunity to offer a bit of admonition.

"I don't think it right to wander out of doors," I observed, "instead of being in bed: it is not wise, at any rate, this moist season. I dare say you'll catch a bad cold, or a fever—you have something the matter with you now!"

"Nothing but what I can bear," he replied, "and with the greatest pleasure, provided you'll leave me alone—get in, and don't annoy me."

I obeyed; and, in passing, I noticed he breathed as fast as a cat.

"Yes!" I reflected to myself, "we shall have a fit of illness. I cannot conceive what he has been doing!"

That noon, he sat down to dinner with us, and received a heaped-up plate from my hands, as if he intended to make amends for previous fasting.

"I've neither cold, nor fever, Nelly," he remarked, in allusion to my morning's speech. "And I'm ready to do justice to the food you give me."

He took his knife and fork, and was going to commence eating, when the inclination appeared to become suddenly extinct. He laid them on the table, looked eagerly towards the window, then rose and went out.

We saw him walking to and fro, in the garden, while we concluded our meal; and Earnshaw said he'd go, and ask why he would not dine; he thought we had grieved him some way.

"Well, is he coming?" cried Catherine, when her cousin returned.

"Nay," he answered; "but he's not angry; he seemed rare and pleased indeed; only, I made him impatient by speaking to him twice; and then he bid me off to you; he wondered how I could want the company of anybody else."

I set his plate, to keep warm, on the fender: and after an hour or two, he re-entered, when the room was clear, in no degree calmer—the same unnatural—it was unnatural—appearance of joy under his black brows; the same bloodless hue: and his teeth visible, now and then, in a kind of smile; his frame shivering, not as one shivers with chill or weakness, but as a tight-stretched cord vibrates—a strong thrilling, rather than trembling.

I will ask what is the matter, I thought, or who should? And I exclaimed—

"Have you heard any good news, Mr. Heathcliff? You look uncommonly animated."

"Where should good news come from, to me?" he said. "I'm animated with hunger; and, seemingly, I must not eat."

"Your dinner is here," I returned; "why won't you get it?"

"I don't want it now," he muttered, hastily. "I'll wait till supper. And, Nelly, once for all, let me beg you to warn Hareton and the other away from me. I wish to be troubled by nobody—I wish to have this place to myself."

"Is there some new reason for this banishment?" I inquired. "Tell me why you are so queer, Mr. Heathcliff? Where were you last night? I'm not putting the question through idle curiosity, but—"

"You are putting the question through very idle curiosity," he interrupted, with a laugh. "Yet, I'll answer it. Last night, I was on the threshold of hell. Today, I am within sight of my heaven—I have my eyes on it—hardly three feet to sever me! And now you'd better go—You'll neither see nor hear anything to frighten you, if you refrain from prying."

Having swept the hearth, and wiped the table, I departed more perplexed than ever.

He did not quit the house again that afternoon, and no one intruded on his solitude, till, at eight o'clock, I deemed it proper, though unsummoned, to carry a candle, and his supper to him.

He was leaning against the ledge of an open lattice, but not looking out; his face was turned to the interior gloom. The fire had smouldered to ashes; the room was filled with the damp, mild air of the cloudy evening, and so still, that not only the murmur of the beck down Gimmerton was distinguishable, but its ripples and its gurgling over the pebbles, or through the large stones which it could not cover.

I uttered an ejaculation of discontent at seeing the dismal grate, and commenced shutting the casements, one after another, till I came to his.

"Must I close this?" I asked, in order to rouse him, for he would not stir.

The light flashed on his features, as I spoke. Oh, Mr. Lockwood, I cannot express what a terrible start I got, by the momentary view! Those deep black eyes! That smile, and ghastly paleness! It appeared to me, not

Mr. Heathcliff, but a goblin; and, in my terror, I let the candle bend towards the wall, and it left me in darkness.

"Yes, close it," he replied, in his familiar voice. "There, that is pure awkwardness! Why did you hold the candle horizontally? Be quick, and bring another."

I hurried out in a foolish state of dread, and said to Joseph—

"The master wishes you to take him a light, and rekindle the fire." For I dare not go in myself again just then.

Joseph rattled some fire into the shovel, and went; but he brought it back, immediately, with the supper tray in his other hand, explaining that Mr. Heathcliff was going to bed, and he wanted nothing to eat till morning.

We heard him mount the stairs directly; he did not proceed to his ordinary chamber, but turned into that with the panelled bed—its window, as I mentioned before, is wide enough for anybody to get through, and it struck me, that he plotted another midnight excursion, which he had rather we had no suspicion of.

"Is he a ghoul, or a vampire?" I mused. I had read of such hideous, incarnate demons. And then, I set myself to reflect, how I had tended him in infancy; and watched him grow to youth; and followed him almost through his whole course; and what absurd nonsense it was to yield to that sense of horror.

"But, where did he come from, the little dark thing, harboured by a good man to his bane?" muttered superstition, as I dozed into unconsciousness. And I began, half dreaming, to weary myself with imaging some fit parentage for him; and repeating my waking meditations, I tracked his existence over again, with grim variations; at last, picturing his death and funeral; of which, all I can remember is being exceedingly vexed at having the task of dictating an inscription for his monument, and consulting the sexton about it; and, as he had no surname, and we could not tell his age, we were obliged to content ourselves with the single word, "Heathcliff." That came true; we were. If you enter the kirkyard, you'll read on his headstone only that, and the date of his death.

Dawn restored me to common sense. I rose, and went into the garden, as soon as I could see, to ascertain if there were any footmarks under his window. There were none.

"He has stayed at home," I thought, "and he'll be all right, today!"

I prepared breakfast for the household, as was my usual custom, but told Hareton and Catherine to get theirs, ere the master came down, for he lay late. They preferred taking it out of doors, under the trees, and I set a little table to accommodate them.

On my re-entrance, I found Mr. Heathcliff below. He and Joseph were conversing about some farming business; he gave clear, minute directions concerning the matter discussed, but he spoke rapidly, and turned his head continually aside, and had the same excited expression, even more exaggerated.

When Joseph quitted the room, he took his seat in the place he generally chose, and I put a basin of coffee before him. He drew it nearer, and then rested his arms on the table, and looked at the opposite wall, as I supposed, surveying one particular portion, up and down, with glittering, restless eyes, and with such eager interest, that he stopped breathing, during half a minute together.

"Come now," I exclaimed, pushing some bread against his hand. "Eat and drink that, while it is hot. It has been waiting near an hour."

He didn't notice me, and yet he smiled. I'd rather have seen him gnash his teeth than smile so.

"Mr. Heathcliff! master!" I cried. "Don't, for God's sake, stare as if you saw an unearthly vision."

"Don't, for God's sake, shout so loud," he replied. "Turn round, and tell me, are we by ourselves?"

"Of course," was my answer, "of course we are!"

Still, I involuntarily obeyed him, as if I were not quite sure.

With a sweep of his hand, he cleared a vacant space in front among the breakfast things, and leant forward to gaze more at his ease.

Now I perceived he was not looking at the wall, for when I regarded him alone, it seemed, exactly, that he gazed at something within two yards distance. And whatever it was, it communicated, apparently, both pleasure and pain, in exquisite extremes, at least, the anguished, yet raptured expression of his countenance suggested that idea.

The fancied object was not fixed, either; his eyes pursued it with unwearied diligence; and, even in speaking to me, were never weaned away.

I vainly reminded him of his protracted abstinence from food; if he stirred to touch anything in compliance with my entreaties, if he stretched his hand out to get a piece of bread, his fingers clenched, before they reached it, and remained on the table, forgetful of their aim.

I sat a model of patience, trying to attract his absorbed attention from its engrossing speculation; till he grew irritable, and got up, asking, why I would not allow him to have his own time in taking his meals? and saying that, on the next occasion, I needn't wait, I might set the things down, and go.

Having uttered these words, he left the house; slowly sauntered down the garden path, and disappeared through the gate.

The hours crept anxiously by: another evening came. I did not retire to rest till late, and when I did, I could not sleep. He returned after midnight, and, instead of going to bed, shut himself into the room beneath. I listened, and tossed about; and, finally, dressed, and descended. It was too irksome to lie up there, harassing my brain with a hundred idle misgivings.

I distinguished Mr. Heathcliff's step, restlessly measuring the floor; and he frequently broke the silence, by a deep inspiration, resembling a groan. He muttered detached words, also; the only one, I could catch, was the name of Catherine, coupled with some wild term of endearment, or suffering; and spoken as one would speak to a person present—low and earnest, and wrung from the depth of his soul.

I had not courage to walk straight into the apartment; but I desired to divert him from his reverie, and, therefore, fell foul of the kitchen fire; stirred it, and began to scrape the cinders. It drew him forth sooner than I expected. He opened the door immediately, and said—

"Nelly, come here—is it morning? Come in with your light."

"It is striking four," I answered; "you want a candle to take upstairs— you might have lit one at this fire."

"No, I don't wish to go upstairs," he said. "Come in, and kindle *me* a fire, and do anything there is to do about the room."

"I must blow the coals red first, before I can carry any," I replied, getting a chair and the bellows.

He roamed to and fro, meantime, in a state approaching distraction: his heavy sighs succeeding each other so thick as to leave no space for common breathing between.

"When day breaks, I'll send for Green," he said; "I wish to make some legal inquires of him, while I can bestow a thought on those matters, and while I can act calmly. I have not written my will yet, and how to leave my property, I cannot determine! I wish I could annihilate it from the face of the earth."

"I would not talk so, Mr. Heathcliff," I interposed. "Let your will be, awhile—you'll be spared to repent of your many injustices, yet! I never expected that your nerves would be disordered—they are, at present, marvellously so, however; and, almost entirely, through your own fault. The way you've passed these three last days might knock up a Titan. Do take some food, and some repose. You need only look at yourself, in the glass, to see how you require both. Your cheeks are hollow, and your eyes bloodshot, like a person starving with hunger, and going blind with loss of sleep."

"It is not my fault, that I cannot eat or rest," he replied. "I assure you it is through no settled designs. I'll do both, as soon as I possibly can. But you might as well bid a man struggling in the water, rest within arms-length of the shore! I must reach it first, and then I'll rest. Well, never mind

Mr. Green; as to repenting of my injustices, I've done no injustice, and I repent of nothing—I'm too happy, and yet I'm not happy enough. My soul's bliss kills my body, but does not satisfy itself."

"Happy, master?" I cried. "Strange happiness! If you would hear me without being angry, I might offer some advice that would make you happier."

"What is that?" he asked. "Give it."

"You are aware, Mr. Heathcliff," I said, "that from the time you were thirteen years old, you have lived a selfish, unchristian life; and probably hardly had a Bible in your hands, during all that period. You must have forgotten the contents of the book, and you may not have space to search it now. Could it be hurtful to send for someone—some minister of any denomination, it does not matter which, to explain it, and show you how very far you have erred from its precepts, and how unfit you will be for its heaven, unless a change takes place before you die?"

"I'm rather obliged than angry, Nelly," he said, "for you remind me of the manner that I desire to be buried in—It is to be carried to the churchyard, in the evening. You, and Hareton may, if you please, accompany me—and mind, particularly, to notice that the sexton obeys my directions concerning the two coffins! No minister need come; nor need anything be said over me—I tell you, I have nearly attained *my* heaven; and that of others is altogether unvalued, and uncoveted by me!"

"And supposing you persevered in your obstinate fast, and died by that means, and they refused to bury you in the precincts of the Kirk?" I said shocked at his godless indifference. "How would you like it?"

"They won't do that," he replied, "if they did, you must have me removed secretly: and if you neglect it, you shall prove, practically, that the dead are not annihilated!"

As soon as he heard the other members of the family stirring he retired to his den, and I breathed freer—But in the afternoon, while Joseph and Hareton were at their work, he came into the kitchen again, and with a wild look, bid me come, and sit in the house—he wanted somebody with him.

I declined, telling him plainly, that his strange talk and manner frightened me, and I had neither the nerve, nor the will to be his companion, alone.

"I believe you think me a fiend!" he said, with his dismal laugh, "something too horrible to live under a decent roof."

Then turning to Catherine, who was there, and who drew behind me at his approach, he added, half sneeringly,

"Will *you* come, chuck? I'll not hurt you. No! to you, I've made myself worse than the devil. Well, there is *one* who won't shrink from my

---

chuck: term of endearment, here used ironically.

company! By God! she's relentless. Oh, damn it! It's unutterably too much for flesh and blood to bear, even mine."

He solicited the society of no one more. At dusk, he went into his chamber—through the whole night, and far into the morning, we heard him groaning, and murmuring to himself. Hareton was anxious to enter, but I bid him fetch Mr. Kenneth, and he should go in, and see him.

When he came, and I requested admittance and tried to open the door, I found it locked; and Heathcliff bid us be damned. He was better, and would be left alone; so the doctor went away.

The following evening was very wet, indeed it poured down, till day-dawn; and, as I took my morning walk round the house, I observed the master's window swinging open, and the rain driving straight in.

"He cannot be in bed," I thought, "those showers would drench him through! He must either be up, or out. But, I'll make no more ado, I'll go boldly, and look!"

Having succeeded in obtaining entrance with another key, I ran to un-close the panels, for the chamber was vacant—quickly pushing them aside, I peeped in. Mr. Heathcliff was there—laid on his back. His eyes met mine so keen, and fierce, I started; and then, he seemed to smile.

I could not think him dead—but his face and throat were washed with rain; the bed-clothes dripped, and he was perfectly still. The lattice, flapping to and fro, had grazed one hand that rested on the sill—no blood trickled from the broken skin, and when I put my fingers to it, I could doubt no more—he was dead and stark!

I hasped the window; I combed his black long hair from his forehead; I tried to close his eyes—to extinguish, if possible, that frightful, life-like gaze of exultation, before anyone else beheld it. They would not shut—they seemed to sneer at my attempts, and his parted lips, and sharp, white teeth sneered too! Taken with another fit of cowardice, I cried out for Joseph. Joseph shuffled up, and made a noise, but resolutely refused to meddle with him.

"Th' divil's harried off his soul," he cried, "and he muh hev his carcass intuh t' bargin, for ow't Aw care! Ech! what a wicked un he looks girnning at death!" and the old sinner grinned in mockery.

I thought he intended to cut a caper round the bed; but suddenly composing himself, he fell on his knees, and raised his hands, and returned thanks that the lawful master and the ancient stock were restored to their rights.

I felt stunned by the awful event; and my memory unavoidably recurred

---

girnning: grinning.

to former times with a sort of oppressive sadness. But poor Hareton, the most wronged, was the only one that really suffered much. He sat by the corpse all night, weeping in bitter earnest. He pressed its hand, and kissed the sarcastic, savage face that everyone else shrank from contemplating; and bemoaned him with that strong grief which springs naturally from a generous heart, though it be tough as tempered steel.

Kenneth was perplexed to pronounce of what disorder the master died. I concealed the fact of his having swallowed nothing for four days, fearing it might lead to trouble, and then, I am persuaded he did not abstain on purpose; it was the consequence of his strange illness, not the cause.

We buried him, to the scandal of the whole neighbourhood, as he had wished. Earnshaw, and I, the sexton and six men to carry the coffin, comprehended the whole attendance.

The six men departed when they had let it down into the grave: we stayed to see it covered. Hareton, with a streaming face, dug green sods, and laid them over the brown mould himself, at present it is as smooth and verdant as its companion mounds—and I hope its tenant sleeps as soundly. But the country folks, if you asked them, would swear on their Bible that he *walks*. There are those who speak to having met him near the church, and on the moor, and even within this house—Idle tales, you'll say, and so say I. Yet that old man by the kitchen fire affirms he has seen two on' em looking out of his chamber window, on every rainy night, since his death—and an odd thing happened to me about a month ago.

I was going to the Grange one evening—a dark evening threatening thunder—and, just at the turn of the Heights, I encountered a little boy with a sheep and two lambs before him, he was crying terribly, and I supposed the lambs were skittish, and would not be guided.

"What's the matter, my little man?" I asked.

"They's Heathcliff, and a woman, yonder, under t' Nab," he blubbered, "un' Aw darnut pass' em."

I saw nothing; but neither the sheep nor he would go on, so I bid him take the road lower down.

He probably raised the phantoms from thinking, as he traversed the moors alone, on the nonsense he had heard his parents and companions repeat—yet still, I don't like being out in the dark, now—and I don't like being left by myself in this grim house—I cannot help it, I shall be glad when they leave it, and shift to the Grange!

"They are going to the Grange then?" I said.

"Yes," answered Mrs. Dean, "as soon as they are married; and that will be on New Year's day."

"And who will live here then?"

"Why, Joseph will take care of the house, and, perhaps, a lad to keep him company. They will live in the kitchen, and the rest will be shut up."

"For the use of such ghosts as choose to inhabit it," I observed.

"No, Mr. Lockwood," said Nelly, shaking her head. "I believe the dead are at peace, but it is not right to speak of them with levity."

At that moment the garden gate swung to; the ramblers were returning.

"*They* are afraid of nothing," I grumbled, watching their approach through the window. "Together they would brave Satan and all his legions."

As they stepped onto the door-stones, and halted to take a last look at the moon, or, more correctly, at each other, by her light, I felt irresistibly impelled to escape them again; and, pressing a remembrance into the hand of Mrs. Dean, and disregarding her expostulations at my rudeness, I vanished through the kitchen, as they opened the house-door, and so, should have confirmed Joseph in his opinion of his fellow-servant's gay indiscretions, had he not, fortunately, recognized me for a respectable character by the sweet ring of a sovereign at his feet.

My walk home was lengthened by a diversion in the direction of the kirk. When beneath its walls, I perceived decay had made progress, even in seven months—many a window showed black gaps deprived of glass; and slates jutted off, here and there, beyond the right line of the roof, to be gradually worked off in coming autumn storms.

I sought, and soon discovered, the three head-stones on the slope next the moor—the middle one, gray, and half buried in heath—Edgar Linton's only harmonized by the turf and moss, creeping up its foot—Heathcliff's still bare.

I lingered round them, under that benign sky; watched the moths fluttering among the heath, and hare-bells; listened to the soft wind breathing through the grass; and wondered how anyone could ever imagine unquiet slumbers for the sleepers in that quiet earth.

---

sovereign: a gold coin.

Part Two

THE PERSONAL CONTEXT

Branwell Brontë's portrait of his three sisters, Anne, Emily, and Charlotte (c. 1834). Originally he had included himself between Emily and Charlotte, but later he blotted out his self-portrait.

After Emily Brontë's death in December 1848, Charlotte Brontë took it upon herself as a sacred duty to defend her sister's character and reputation from misunderstanding. Charlotte's publisher, Smith Elder, agreed to reprint *Wuthering Heights* in an edition over which she would have complete control. Charlotte Brontë wrote an editor's preface, seeking to answer the critics' objections to the language, characters, and action in *Wuthering Heights*. She also wrote brief biographical sketches of her sisters Emily and Anne. (See pages 14–19). In addition, Charlotte Brontë included seventeen pieces of poetry in an attempt to reveal Emily Brontë's "true" and womanly character. A close analysis of the manuscripts reveals that Charlotte Brontë revised these poems, and one editor thinks that she actually wrote one of them—"Often Rebuked"—herself. Other critics disagree, believing that Charlotte would not have gone so far as actually to fabricate a poem ostensibly written by Emily. All seventeen poems are reprinted here. A full discussion of the reprinting of these poems and the changes Charlotte Brontë made to them can be found in Roper and Chitham (24).

POEMS

The poems selected by Charlotte Brontë for inclusion in the 1850 edition of *Wuthering Heights* represent only a fraction of the poetic output of Emily Brontë, who considered herself a poet first, a novelist only secondarily. This section begins with Charlotte Brontë's Prefatory Note to "Selections from Poems by Ellis Bell," printed in the 1850 edition. The first three poems she chose ("A Little While," "The Bluebell," and "Loud Without the Wind was Roaring") were, she claimed, written by Emily Brontë while she was sixteen and a very unhappy student at Miss Wooler's school at Roe Head. But scholars date these three poems to Emily Brontë's equally unhappy stint as a teacher at Law Hill school, where she served for only about six months.

We can recall that Emily Brontë had revised her poems for inclusion in the 1846 volume, *Poems*, that she jointly published with her sisters by eliminating references to Gondal characters and events. This time, Charlotte Brontë took it upon herself to eliminate the Gondal allusions that would prove confusing to the reader who knew nothing about Emily's other major literary endeavor. So in "A Little While," a poem where Emily is debating about where to go in her imagination during her very few spare hours at Law Hill—to the moors of her childhood home or to the kingdom of Gondal—

Charlotte removed the mention of "wandering deer" (l. 40) and substituted the more homely image of "sheep." [ED.]

[Preface]

CHARLOTTE BRONTË

*It would not have been difficult to compile a volume out of the papers
left by my sisters, had I, in making the selection, dismissed from my
consideration the scruples and the wishes of those whose written
thoughts these papers held. But this was impossible: an influence,
stronger than could be exercised by any motive of expediency, necessarily regulated the selection. I have, then, culled from the mass only
a little poem here and there. The whole makes but a tiny nosegay,
and the colour and perfume of the flowers are not such as fit them for
festal uses.*

*It has been already said that my sisters wrote much in childhood
and girlhood. Usually, it seems a sort of injustice to expose in print the
crude thoughts of the unripe mind, the rude efforts of the unpractised
hand; yet I venture to give three little poems of my sister Emily's,
written in her sixteenth year, because they illustrate a point in her
character.*

*At that period she was sent to school. Her previous life, with the ex-
ception of a single half-year, had been passed in the absolute retirement of a village parsonage, amongst the hills bordering Yorkshire and
Lancashire. The scenery of these hills is not grand—it is not romantic;
it is scarcely striking. Long low moors, dark with heath, shut in little
valleys, where a stream waters, here and there, a fringe of stunted
copse. Mills and scattered cottages chase romance from these valleys;
it is only higher up, deep in amongst the ridges of the moors, that
Imagination can find rest for the sole of her foot: and even if she finds
it there, she must be a solitude-loving raven—no gentle dove. If she*

From *The Poems of Emily Brontë.* Ed. Derek Roper with Edward Chitham.
Oxford: Clarendon, 1995. (Transpositions and similar spelling errors
have been corrected in this New Riverside Edition, but regionalisms and
nineteenth-century spellings, including some inconsistencies, have been
retained to reflect Brontë's distinctive style.)

demand beauty to inspire her, she must bring it inborn: these moors
are too stern to yield any product so delicate. The eye of the gazer must
itself brim with a "purple light," intense enough to perpetuate the
brief flower-flush of August on the heather, or the rare sunset-smile of
June; out of his heart must well the freshness, that in latter spring and
early summer brightens the bracken, nurtures the moss, and cherishes
the starry flowers that spangle for a few weeks the pasture of the moor
sheep. Unless that light and freshness are innate and self-sustained,
the drear prospect of a Yorkshire moor will be found as barren of poetic
as of agricultural interest: where the love of wild nature is strong, the
locality will perhaps be clung to with the more passionate constancy,
because from the hill-lover's self comes half its charm.

My sister Emily loved the moors. Flowers brighter than the rose
bloomed in the blackest of the heath for her; out of a sullen hollow in a
livid hillside her mind could make an Eden. She found in the bleak
solitude many and dear delights; and not the least and best loved
was—liberty.

Liberty was the breath of Emily's nostrils; without it, she perished.
The change from her own home to a school, and from her own very
noiseless, very secluded, but unrestricted and inartificial mode of life,
to one of disciplined routine (though under the kindliest auspices) was
what she failed in enduring. Her nature proved here too strong for her
fortitude. Every morning when she woke, the vision of home and the
moors rushed on her, and darkened and saddened the day that lay before her. Nobody knew what ailed her but me—I knew only too well.
In this struggle her health was quickly broken: her white face, attenuated form, and failing strength threatened rapid decline. I felt in my
heart she would die, if she did not go home and with this conviction
obtained her recall. She had only been three months at school; and it
was some years before the experiment of sending her from home was
again ventured on. After the age of twenty, having meantime studied
alone with diligence and perseverance, she went with me to an establishment on the Continent: the same suffering and conflict ensued,
heightened by the strong recoil of her upright, heretic and English
spirit from the gentle Jesuitry of the foreign and Romish system. Once
more she seemed sinking, but this time she rallied through the mere
force of resolution: with inward remorse and shame she looked back on
her former failure, and resolved to conquer in this second ordeal. She
did conquer: but the victory cost her dear. She was never happy till she

carried her hard-won knowledge back to the remote English village,
the old parsonage-house, and desolate Yorkshire hills. A very few years
more, and she looked her last on those hills, and breathed her last in
that house, and under the aisle of that obscure village church found
her last lowly resting-place. Merciful was the decree that spared her
when she was a stranger in a strange land, and guarded her dying bed
with kindred love and congenial constancy.

The following pieces were composed at twilight, in the schoolroom,
when the leisure of the evening play-hour brought back in full tide the
thoughts of home.

Stanzas

December 4th 1838

A little while, a little while,
The noisy crowd are barred away;
And I can sing and I can smile —
A little while I've holyday!

5 Where wilt thou go, my harassed heart?
Full many a land invites thee now;
And places near, and far apart
Have rest for thee, my weary brow —

There is a spot mid barren hills
10 Where winter howls and driving rain
But if the dreary tempest chills
There is a light that warms again

The house is old, the trees are bare
And moonless bends the misty dome
15 But what on earth is half so dear —
So longed for as the hearth of home?

The mute bird sitting on the stone,
The dank moss dripping from the wall,
The garden-walk with weeds o'er-grown
20 I love them — how I love them all!

Shall I go there? or shall I seek
Another clime, another sky —
Where tongues familiar music speak
In accents dear to memory?

₂₅ Yes, as I mused, the naked room,
The flickering firelight died away
And from the midst of cheerless gloom
I passed to bright, unclouded day—

A little and a lone green lane
₃₀ That opened on a common wide
A distant, dreamy, dim blue chain
Of mountains circling every side—

A heaven so clear, an earth so calm,
So sweet, so soft, so hushed an air
₃₅ And, deepening still the dreamlike charm,
Wild moor sheep feeding every where—

That was the scene—I knew it well
I knew the pathways far and near
That winding o'er each billowy swell
₄₀ Marked out the tracks of the wandering deer

Could I have lingered but an hour
It well had paid a week of toil,
But truth has banished fancy's power
I hear my dungeon bars recoil—

₄₅ Even as I stood with raptured eye
Absorbed in bliss so deep and dear
My hour of rest had fleeted by
And given me back to weary care.

The Bluebell [1]

December 18th 1838

The bluebell is the sweetest flower
That waves in summer air
Its blossoms have the mightiest power
To soothe my spirit's care.

---

holyday: holiday.

[1]Charlotte Brontë eliminated sixteen lines from "The Bluebell" and altered Emily Brontë's reference to the "heather-bell" (line 21) to "sweet Bluebell" in the 1850 edition. [ED.]

5 There is a spell in purple heath
    Too wildly, sadly dear
    The violet has a fragrant breath
    But fragrance will not cheer.

    The trees are bare, the sun is cold
10 And seldom, seldom seen —
    The heavens have lost their zone of gold
    The earth its robe of green.

    And ice upon the glancing stream
    Has cast its sombre shade
15 And distant hills and valleys seem
    In frozen mist arrayed —

    The blue bell cannot charm me now
    The heath has lost its bloom
    The violets in the glen below
20 They yield no sweet perfume.

    But though I mourn the heather-bell
    'Tis better far, away
    I know how fast my tears would swell
    To see it smile to day.

25 And that wood flower that hides so shy
    Beneath the mossy stone
    Its balmy scent and dewy eye
    'Tis not for them I moan.

    It is the slight and stately stem
30 The blossom's silvery blue
    The buds hid like a sapphire gem
    In sheaths of emerald hue.

    'Tis these that breathe upon my heart
    A calm and softening spell
35 That if it makes the tear-drop start
    Has power to soothe as well.

    For these I weep, so long divided
    Through winter's dreary day
    In longing weep — but most when guided
40 On withered banks to stray.

---

zone: belt.

If chilly then the light should fall
Adown the dreary sky
And gild the dank and darkened wall
With transient brilliancy.

45 How do I yearn, how do I pine
For the time of flowers to come
And turn me from that fading shine
To mourn the fields of home.

Stanzas

November 11th 1838

Loud without the wind was roaring
   Through the waned autumnal sky,
Drenching wet, the cold rain pouring
   Spoke of stormy winters nigh.

5 All Too like that dreary eve
Sighed within repining grief—
Sighed at first—but sighed not long
Sweet—How softly sweet it came!
Wild words of an ancient song—
10 Undefined, without a name—

"It was spring, for the skylark was singing."
Those words they awakened a spell—
They unlocked a deep fountain whose springing
Nor Absence nor Distance can quell.

15 In the gloom of a cloudy November
They uttered the music of May—
They kindled the perishing ember
Into fervour that could not decay

Awaken on all my dear moorlands
20 The wind in its glory and pride!
O call me from valleys and highlands
To walk by the hill-river's side!

It is swelled with the first snowy weather;
The rocks they are icy and hoar
25 And darker waves round the long heather
And the fern-leaves are sunny no more

There are no yellow-stars on the mountain
The blue-bells have long died away
From the brink of the moss-bedded fountain,
30 From the side of the wintery brae —

But lovelier than corn-fields all waving
In emerald and scarlet and gold
Are the slopes where the north-wind is raving
And the glens where I wandered of old —

35 "It was morning, the bright sun was beaming —"
How sweetly that brought back to me
The time when nor labour nor dreaming
Broke the sleep of the happy and free

But blithely we rose as the dusk heaven
40 Was melting to amber and blue
And swift were the wings to our feet given
While we traversed the meadows of dew.

For the moors, for the moors where the short grass
Like velvet beneath us should lie!
45 For the moors, for the moors where each high pass
Rose sunny against the clear sky!

For the moors, where the linnet was trilling
Its song on the old granite stone —
Where the lark — the wild sky-lark was filling
50 Every breast with delight like its own.

What language can utter the feeling
That rose when, in exile afar,
On the brow of a lonely hill kneeling
I saw the brown heath growing there:

55 It was scattered and stunted, and told me
That soon even that would be gone
It whispered; "The grim walls enfold me
"I have bloomed in my last summer's sun —"

But not the loved music whose waking
60 Makes the soul of the swiss die away

---

brae: hillside.

Has a spell—more adored and heart-breaking
Than in its half-blighted bells lay—

The spirit that bent 'neath its power
How it longed, how it burned to be free!
65 If I could have wept in that hour
Those tears had been heaven to me—

Well, well, the sad minutes are moving
Though loaded with trouble and pain—
And sometime the loved and the loving
70 Shall meet on the mountains again.

"Shall Earth no more inspire thee" [1]

May 16th 1841

Shall Earth no more inspire thee,
Thou lonely dreamer now?
Since passion may not fire thee
Shall Nature cease to bow?

5 Thy mind is ever moving
In regions dark to thee;
Recall its useless roving—
Come back and dwell with me—

I know my mountain breezes
10 Enchant and soothe thee still—
I know my sunshine pleases
Despite thy wayward will—

When day with evening blending
Sinks from the summer sky,
15 I've seen thy spirit bending
In fond idolatry—

I've watched thee every hour—
I know my mighty sway—

---

[1] "The following little piece has no title, but in it the genius [spirit] of a solitary region seems to address his wandering and wayward votary, and to recall within his influences the proud mind which rebelled at times against what it most loved." [Charlotte Brontë's note.]

I know my magic power
20 To drive thy griefs away —

Few hearts to mortals given
On earth so wildly pine
Yet none would ask a Heaven
More like this Earth than thine —

25 Then let my winds caress thee —
Thy comrade let me be —
Since nought beside can bless thee —
Return and dwell with me.

The Night Wind [1]

September 11th 1840

In summer's mellow midnight
A cloudless moon shone through
Our open parlour window
And rosetrees wet with dew —

5 I sat in silent musing —
The soft wind waved my hair
It told me Heaven was glorious
And sleeping Earth was fair —

I needed not its breathing
10 To bring such thoughts to me
But still it whispered lowly
"How dark the woods will be! —

"The thick leaves in my murmur
Are rustling like a dream,
15 And all their myriad voices
Instinct with spirit seem."

I said, "go gentle singer,
Thy wooing voice is kind

---

[1] "The Night Wind" recalls such English Romantic poems as Samuel Taylor Coleridge's "Eolian Harp" or Percy Bysshe Shelley's "Ode to the West Wind" in which a poet addresses the wind as a creative and artistic force. Charlotte Brontë corrected the meter of the last two lines of this poem. [ED.]

But do not think its music
20 Has power to reach my mind—

"Play with the scented flower,
The young tree's supple bough—
And leave my human feelings
In their own course to flow."

25 The Wanderer would not leave me
Its kiss grew warmer still—
"O come," it sighed so sweetly
"I'll win thee 'gainst thy will—

"Have we not been from childhood friends?
30 Have I not loved thee long?
As long as thou hast loved the night
Whose silence wakes my song?

"And when thy heart is laid at rest
Beneath the churchyard stone
35 I shall have time for mourning
And thou for being alone."

"Aye, there it is!" [1]

July 6th 1841

Aye, there it is! It wakes to night
Sweet thoughts that will not die
And feeling's fires flash all as bright
As in the years gone by!—

5 And I can tell by thine altered cheek
And by thy kindled gaze
And by the words thou scarce dost speak,
How wildly fancy plays—

Yes, I could swear that glorious wind
10 Has swept the world aside

---

[1] "In these stanzas a louder gale has roused the sleeper on her pillow: the wakened soul struggles to blend with the storm by which it is swayed." [Charlotte Brontë's note.] Charlotte Brontë added five lines to this poem, since eliminated, that attempt to portray Emily Brontë as a traditional believer in eternal life. [ED.]

Has dashed its memory from thy mind
Like foam-bells from the tide —

And thou art now a spirit pouring
Thy presence into all —
15 The essence of the Tempest's roaring
And of the Tempest's fall —

A universal influence
From Thine own influence free —
A principle of life intense
20 Lost to mortality —

Thus truly when that breast is cold
Thy prisoned soul shall rise
The Dungeon mingle with the mould —
The captive with the skies.

Love and Friendship [1]

*[undated, transcribed
February 1844]*

Love is like the wild rose briar,
Friendship like the holly tree
The holly is dark when the rose briar blooms,
But which will bloom most constantly?

5 The wild rose briar is sweet in spring,
Its summer blossoms scent the air;
Yet wait till winter comes again
And who will call the wild-briar fair?

Then scorn the silly rose-wreath now
10 And deck thee with the holly's sheen
That when December blights thy brow
He still may leave thy garland green.

---

[1] Although "Love and Friendship" recalls William Blake's "The Sick Rose," a meditation on death and decay, Emily Brontë's meditation on flowers and holly as emblems of love is a conventional treatment of a familiar topic, the instability of romantic love. Charlotte Brontë made no revisions to this poem. [ED.]

The Elder's Rebuke [1]

Nov 11th 1844

From a Dungeon Wall in the Southern College —
J B Sept. 1825 [2]

"Listen! when your hair like mine
Takes a tint of silver grey,
When your eyes, with dimmer shine,
Watch life's bubbles float away,

5 "When you, young man, have borne like me
The weary weight of sixty three
Then shall penance sore be paid
For these hours so wildly squandered
And the words that now fall dead
10 On your ears be deeply pondered
pondered and approved at last
But their virtue will be past!

"Glorious is the prize of Duty
Though she be a serious power
15 Treacherous all the lures of Beauty
Thorny bud and poisonous flower!

"Mirth is but a mad beguiling
Of the golden gifted Time —
Love — a demon meteor wiling
20 Heedless feet to gulfs of crime —

"Those who follow earthly pleasure
Heavenly knowledge will not lead
Wisdom hides from them her treasure,
Virtue bids them evil speed!

[1] Charlotte Brontë added six of her own lines to "The Elder's Rebuke" that have since been eliminated. Again, her intention was to portray Emily Brontë as a conventional moralist. She also eliminated lines 29–60 in the 1850 version of the poem, presumably because of the specific references to the Gondal character Rosina Alcona. [Ed.]

[2] The epigraph reveals the Gondal origin of the poem, ostensibly written by Julius Brenzaida, emperor of Gondal and Gaaldine. [Ed.]

25 "Vainly may their hearts, repenting,
Seek for aid in future years —
Wisdom scorned knows no relenting —
Virtue is not won by tears.

"Fain would we your steps reclaim
30 Waken fear and holy shame
And to this end, our council well
And kindly doomed you to a cell
Whose darkness, may perchance, disclose
A beacon-guide from sterner woes —"

35 So spake my Judge — then seized his lamp
And left me in the dungeon damp.
A vault-like place whose stagnant air
Suggests and nourishes despair!

Rosina, this had never been
40 Except for you, my despot queen
Except for you the billowy sea
Would now be tossing under me
The winds' wild voice my bosom thrill
And my glad heart bound wilder still

45 Flying before the rapid gale
Those wondrous southern isles to hail
Which wait for my companions free
But thank your passion — not for me!

You know too well — and so do I
50 Your haughty beauty's soveriegnty
Yet have I read those falcon eyes —
Have dived into their mysteries —
Have studied long their glance and feel
It is not love those eyes reveal —

55 They Flash — they burn with lightning shine
But not with such fond fire as mine;
The tender star fades faint and wan
Before Ambition's scorching sun —
So deem I now — and Time will prove
60 If I have wronged Rosina's love.

The Wanderer from the Fold[1]

March 11th 1844

E. W. to A.G.A.

How few, of all the hearts that loved,
Are grieving for thee now!
And why should mine, to night, be moved
With such a sense of woe?

5   Too often, thus, when left alone
Where none my thoughts can see,
Comes back a word, a passing tone
From thy strange history —

Sometimes I seem to see thee rise
10   A glorious child again —
All virtues beaming from thine eyes
That ever honoured men —

Courage and Truth, a generous breast
Where Love and Gladness lay;
15   A being whose very Memory blest
And made the mourner gay —

O, fairly spread thy early sail
And fresh and pure and free
Was the first impulse of the gale
20   That urged life's wave for thee!

Why did the pilot, too confiding,
Dream o'er that Ocean's foam?
And trust in Pleasure's careless guiding
To bring his vessel home?

---

[1]"The Wanderer from the Fold" was thought by early critics to concern Emily's grief
for her brother Branwell Brontë, whose decline into drugs and alcohol eventually led to
his death. But the poem was written in March 1844, when Branwell was working successfully as a private tutor. The handwritten note on the poem, "E. W. to A.G.A.," reveals that the poem is actually part of the Gondal saga in which the faithful servant Lord
Eldred W. mourns the decline and death of his beloved queen, Augusta Geraldine
Almeda, queen of Gondal. [ED.]

25 For, well he knew what dangers frowned,
   What mists would gather dim,
   What rocks and shelves and sands lay round
   Between his port and him—

   The very brightness of the sun,
30 The splendour of the main,
   The wind that bore him wildly on
   Should not have warned in vain

   An anxious gazer from the shore,
   I marked the whitening wave
35 And wept above thy fate the more
   Because I could not save—

   It recks not now, when all is over,
   But, yet my heart will be
   A mourner still, though friend and lover
40 Have both forgotten thee!

Warning and Reply[1]

September 6th 1843

   In the earth, the earth thou shalt be laid
   A grey stone standing over thee;
   Black mould beneath thee spread
   And black mould to cover thee—

5 "Well, there is rest there
   So fast come thy prophecy—
   The time when my sunny hair
   Shall with grass roots twined be."

   But cold, cold is that resting place
10 Shut out from Joy and Liberty,
   And all who loved thy living face
   Will shrink from its gloom and thee.

   "Not so, *here* the world is chill
   And sworn friends fall from me;

---

[1]"Warning and Reply" is another Gondal poem in which an unnamed speaker reflects on death, which she does not fear but welcomes. [ED.]

15 But *there,* they'll own me still
   And prize my memory."

   Farewell, then, all that love,
   All that deep sympathy;
   Sleep on, heaven laughs above—
20 Earth never misses thee.

   Turf-sod and tombstone drear
   Part human company;
   One heart broke, only, there—
   That heart was worthy thee!

Last Words,
or Song by J. Brenzaida to G. S.[1]

October 17th 1838

I knew not 't was so dire a crime
To say the word, Adieu—
But this shall be the only time
My slighted heart shall sue.

5 The wild moorside, the winter morn,
   The gnarled and ancient tree—
   If in your breast they waken scorn
   Shall wake the same in me.

   I can forget black eyes and brows
10 And lips of rosy charm,
   If you forget the sacred vows
   Those faithless lips could form—

   If hard commands can tame your love,
   Or prison walls can hold,
15 I would not wish to grieve above
   A thing so false and cold—

---

[1] "Last Words" is another poem from the Gondal cycle, in which the Emperor of Gondal, Julius Brenzaida, asks Augusta Geraldine Almeda to leave her husband, Lord Alfred, and marry him. The depiction of a triangular love affair and a woman forced to choose between two men anticipates the plot of *Wuthering Heights.* [Ed.]

And there are bosoms bound to mine
With links both tried and strong;
And there are eyes, whose lightning shine
20 Has warmed and blessed me long:

Those eyes shall make my only day,
Shall set my spirit free,
And chase the foolish thoughts away
That mourn your memory!

The Lady to Her Guitar [1]

August 30th 1838

A.G.A.

For him who struck thy foreign string
I ween this heart hath ceased to care;
Then why dost thou such feelings bring
To my sad spirit, Old guitar?

5 It is as if the warm sunlight
In some deep glen should lingering stay,
When clouds of tempest and of night
Had wrapt the parent Orb away—

It is as if the glassy brook
10 Should image still its willows fair,
Though years ago the woodman's stroke
Laid low in dust their gleaming hair:

Even so, guitar, thy magic tone
Hath moved the tear and woke the sigh,
15 Hath bid the ancient torrent flow
Although its very source is dry!

---

[1] "The Lady to Her Guitar" also has a Gondal context. Emily Brontë wrote "A.G.A." at the top of the manuscript version of the poem, revealing that the piece is meant to be spoken by Augusta Geraldine Almeda to her former lover Fernando De Samara, a singer. In his edition of *The Poems of Emily Brontë,* Roper points out a number of similarities to Percy Shelley's poem "With a Guitar, to Jane" (233n32). [ED.]

The Two Children [1]

May 28th 1845

A. E. AND R. C.

[1]

Heavy bangs the raindrop
From the burdened spray;
Heavy broods the damp mist
On Uplands far away;

5 Heavy looms the dull sky,
Heavy rolls the sea —
And heavy beats the young heart
Beneath that lonely Tree —

Never has a blue streak
10 Cleft the clouds since morn —
Never has his grim Fate
Smiled since he was born —

Frowning on the infant,
Shadowing childhood's joy;
15 Guardian angel knows not
That melancholy boy.

Day is passing swiftly
Its sad and sombre prime;
Youth is fast invading
20 Sterner manhood's time —

All the flowers are praying
For sun before they close,
And he prays too, unknowing,
That sunless human rose!

25 Blossoms, that the westwind
Has never wooed to blow,

---

[1] "The Two Children," parts one and two, reveals a persistent theme in Emily Brontë's imagination, contrasting temperaments and fates doled out to children at birth that follow them throughout their lives. The "melancholy boy" in part one recalls Heathcliff and later Hareton, while the "Child of Delight! With sunbright hair" in part two suggests Catherine Earnshaw and her daughter, determined at least initially to act as their redeemers. The dark-light, male-female dichotomy permeates Emily Brontë's Gondal saga in which numerous characters also embody this split. [ED.]

Scentless are your petals,
Your dew as cold as snow—

Soul, where kindred kindness
30   No early promise woke,
Barren is your beauty
As weed upon the rock—

Wither, Brothers, wither,
You were vainly given—
35   Earth reserves no blessing
For the unblessed of Heaven!

[21]

Child of Delight! with sunbright hair
And seablue, sea-deep eyes;
Spirit of Bliss, what brings thee here,
Beneath these sullen skies?

5   Thou shouldest live in eternal spring,
Where endless day is never dim;
Why, seraph, has thy erring wing
Borne thee down to weep with him?

"Ah, not from heaven am I descended,
10   And I do not come to mingle tears;
But sweet is day though with shadows blended;
And, though clouded, sweet are youthful years—

"I, the image of light and gladness,
Saw and pitied that mournful boy;
15   And I swore to take his gloomy sadness,
And give to him my beamy joy—

"Heavy and dark the night is closing;
Heavy and dark may its biding be;
Better for all from grief reposing,
20   And better for all who watch like me—

"Guardian angel, he lacks no longer;
Evil fortune he need not fear;
Fate is strong—but Love is stronger,
And more unsleeping than angel's care."

The Visionary[1]

October 9th 1845

JULIAN M——AND
A. G. ROCHELLE—

Silent is the House—all are laid asleep;
One, alone, looks out o'er the snow-wreaths deep;
Watching every cloud, dreading every breeze
That whirls the wildering drift and bends the groaning trees—

5   Cheerful is the hearth, soft the matted floor;
Not one shivering gust creeps through pane or door.
The little lamp burns straight; its rays shoot strong and far;
I trim it well to be the Wanderer's guiding star—

Frown my haughty sire; chide my angry Dame;
10 Set your slaves to spy, threaten me with shame;
But neither sire nor dame, nor prying serf shall know,
What angel nightly tracks that waste of winter snow.

In the dungeon crypts idly did I stray,
Reckless of the lives wasting there away;
15 "Draw the ponderous bars, open Warder stern!"
He dare not say me nay—the hinges harshly turn—

"Our guests are darkly lodged," I whispered gazing through
The vault whose grated eye showed heaven more grey than blue;
(—This was when glad Spring laughed in awaking pride.)
20 "Aye, darkly lodged enough!" returned my sullen guide.

Then, God forgive my youth, forgive my careless tongue!
I scoffed as the chill chains on the damp flagstones rung;
"Confined in triple walls, art thou so much to fear,
That we must bind thee down and clench thy fetters here?"

25 The captive raised her face; it was as soft and mild
As sculptured marble saint, or slumbering, unweaned child;

---

[1] In the 1850 version of this poem, Charlotte Brontë eliminated lines 13–152 and wrote instead her own eight-line conclusion to the poem, changing its meaning completely. The original version is a Gondal poem about a thwarted love affair, reminiscent of John Keats's "Eve of St. Agnes," as well as Shakespeare's *Romeo and Juliet,* but set during the Royalist–Republican wars. A shorter version, published in the 1846 volume as "The Prisoner," is one of Emily Brontë's best-known poems. [ED.]

It was so soft and mild, it was so sweet and fair,
Pain could not trace a line nor grief a shadow there!

The captive raised her hand and pressed it to her brow
30 "I have been struck," she said, "and I am suffering now;
Yet these are little worth, your bolts and irons strong
And were they forged in steel they could not hold me long—"

Hoarse laughed the jailer grim, "Shall I be won to hear?
Dost think fond, dreaming wretch that *I* shall grant thy prayer?
35 Or better still, wilt melt my master's heart with groans?
Ah sooner might the sun thaw down these granite stones!—

"My master's voice is low, his aspect bland and kind,
But hard as hardest flint the soul that lurks behind:
And I am rough and rude, yet, not more rough to see
40 Than is the hidden ghost which has its home in me!"

About her lips there played a smile of almost scorn
"My friend," she gently said, "you have not heard me mourn,
When you, my parent's lives— *my* lost life can restore;
Then may I weep and sue, but, never, Friend, before!"

45 Her head sank on her hands its fair curls swept the ground
The Dungeon seemed to swim in strange confusion round—
"Is she so near to death?" I murmured half aloud
And kneeling, parted back the floating golden cloud.

Alas, how former days upon my heart were borne,
50 How Memory mirrored then the prisoners joyous morn—
Too blithe, too loving child, too warmly, wildly gay!
Was that the wintry close of thy celestial May?

She knew me and she sighed, "Lord Julian, can it be,
Of all my playmates, you, alone, remember me?
55 Nay start not at my words, unless you deem it shame
To own from conquered foe, a once familiar name—

"I can not wonder now at aught the world will do,
And insult and contempt I lightly brook from you,
Since those who vowed away their souls to win my love
60 Around this living grave like utter strangers move!

"Nor has one voice been raised to plead that I might die,
Not buried under earth but in the open sky;
By ball or speedy knife or headsman's skillful blow—
A quick and welcome pang instead of lingering woe!

65 "Yet, tell them, Julian, all, I am not doomed to wear
Year after year in gloom and desolate despair;
A messenger of Hope comes every night to me,
And offers, for short life, eternal liberty—

"He comes with western winds, with evening's wandering airs,
70 With that clear dusk of heaven that brings the thickest stars;
Winds take a pensive tone and stars a tender fire,
And visions rise and change which kill me with desire—

"Desire for nothing known in my maturer years
When joy grew mad with awe at counting future tears;
75 When, if my spirit's sky was full of flashes warm,
I knew not whence they came from sun or thunder storm;

"But first a hush of peace, a soundless calm descends;
The struggle of distress and fierce impatience ends;
Mute music soothes my breast—unuttered harmony
80 That I could never dream till earth was lost to me.

"Then dawns the Invisible, the Unseen its truth reveals;
My outward sense is gone, my inward essence feels—
Its wings are almost free, its home, its harbour found;
Measuring the gulf it stoops and dares the final bound!

85 "O, dreadful is the check—intense the agony—
When the ear begins to hear, and the eye begins to see;
When the pulse begins to throb, the brain to think again,
The soul to feel the flesh, and the flesh to feel the chain!

"Yet I would lose no sting, would wish no torture less;
90 The more that anguish racks, the earlier it will bless;
And robed in fires of Hell, or bright with heavenly shine,
If it but herald Death, the vision is divine—"

She ceased to speak and I, unanswering, watched her there;
Not daring now to touch one lock of silken hair—
95 As I had knelt in scorn, on the dank floor I knelt still,
My fingers on the links of that iron hard and chill—

I heard and yet heard not the surly keeper growl;
I saw, yet did not see, the flagstones damp and foul;
The keeper, to and fro, paced by the bolted door,
100 And shivered as he walked and as he shivered, swore—

While my cheek glowed in flame, I marked that he did rave,
Of air that froze his blood and moisture like the grave—

"We have been two hours good!" he muttered peevishly,
Then, losing off his belt the rusty dungeon key,

105 He said, "you may be pleased, Lord Julian, still to stay,
But duty will not let me linger here all day;
If I might go, I'd leave this badge of mine with you
Not doubting that you'd prove a jailor stern and true."

I took the proffered charge; the captive's drooping lid
110 Beneath its shady lash a sudden lightning hid;
Earth's hope was not so dead, heaven's home was not so dear;
I read it in that flash of longing quelled by fear.

Then like a tender child whose hand did just enfold
Safe in its eager grasp a bird it wept to hold,
115 When pierced with one wild glance from the troubled hazel eye
It gushes into tears and lets its treasure fly,

Thus ruth and selfish love together striving tore
The heart all newly taught to pity and adore;
If I should break the chain, I felt my bird would go;
120 Yet I must break the chain, or seal the prisoner's woe.

Short strife what rest could soothe — what peace could visit me —
While she lay pining there for Death to set her free?
"Rochelle, the dungeons teem with foes to gorge our hate —
Thou art too young to die by such a bitter fate!"

125 With hurried blow on blow I struck the fetters through
Regardless how that deed my after hours might rue.
Oh, I was over-blest by the warm unasked embrace —
By the smile of grateful joy that lit her angel face!

And I was overblest — aye, more than I could dream,
When, faint, she turned aside from noon's unwonted beam;
130 When though the cage was wide — the heaven around it lay —
Its pinion would not waft my wounded dove away —

Through thirteen anxious weeks of terror-blent delight,
I guarded her by day and guarded her by night,
135 While foes were prowling near and Death gazed greedily,
And only Hope remained a faithful friend to me —

Then oft with taunting smile, I heard my kindred tell
How Julian loved his hearth and sheltering rooftree well;
How the trumpet's voice might call, the battle-standard wave
140 But Julian had no heart to fill a patriot's grave.

And I, who am so quick to answer sneer with sneer;
So ready to condemn to scorn a coward's fear —
I held my peace like one whose conscience keeps him dumb,
And saw my kinsmen go — and lingered still at home —

145 Another hand than mine, my rightful banner held,
And gathered my renown on Freedom's crimson field;
Yet I had no desire the glorious prize to gain —
It needed braver nerve to face the world's disdain —

And by the patient strength that could that world defy;
150 By suffering with calm mind, contempt and calumny;
By never-doubting love, unanswering constancy,
Rochelle, I earned at last an equal love from thee!

Encouragement[1]

December 19th 1841

A. S. TO G. S.
    I do not weep, I would not weep;
    Our Mother needs no tears;
    Dry thine eyes, too, 'tis vain to keep
    This causeless grief for years.

5 What though her brow be changed and cold,
    Her sweet eyes closed for ever?
    What though the stone — the darksome mould —
    Our mortal bodies sever?

    What though her hand smoothe ne'er again
10 Those silken locks of thine —
    Nor through long hours of future pain
    Her kind face o'er thee shine?

    Remember still she is not dead
    She sees us, Gerald, now
15 Laid where her angel spirit fled
    'Mid heath and frozen snow.

---

[1]"Encouragement" initially appears to concern Emily Brontë's memory of her mother's death, which occurred when she was three years old. But the use of the name "Gerald" (line 14) places the poem once again within the context of the Gondal saga. Roper has observed that Gerald, Geraldine, and Alfred were all children of the reigning Exina family, so that this poem is presumably spoken by Alfred to encourage his brother Gerald after the death of their mother (269n123). [ED.]

And from that world of heavenly light
Will she not always bend,
To guide us in our lifetime's night
20 And guard us to the end?

Thou know'st she will, and well may'st mourn
That we are left below,
But not that she can ne'er return
To share our earthly woe.

Stanzas [1]

Often rebuked, yet always back returning
　　To those first feelings that were born with me,
And leaving busy chase of wealth and learning
　　For idle dreams of things which cannot be:

5　Today, I will seek not the shadowy region,
　　Its unsustaining vastness waxes drear;
And visions rising, legion after legion,
　　Bring the unreal world too strangely near.

I'll walk, but not in old heroic traces,
10　And not in paths of high morality,
And not among the half-distinguished faces,
　　The clouded forms of long-past history.

I'll walk where my own nature would be leading:
　　It vexes me to choose another guide:
15　Where the grey flocks in ferny glens are feeding;
　　Where the wild wind blows on the mountain side.

What have those lonely mountains worth revealing?
　　More glory and more grief than I can tell:

---

[1] "Stanzas" or "Often rebuked" has been the subject of a great deal of speculation among Brontë scholars. It is the only poem attributed to Emily Brontë for which a manuscript copy does not exist. Some scholars have thought that Anne Brontë wrote the poem, others that Charlotte Brontë wrote it after Emily's death to make her sister appear more orthodox. The sentiments expressed in the poem are remarkably similar to William Wordsworth's pantheism as expressed in his poem "Tintern Abbey." Roper points out that the iambic pentameter used in the poem is not characteristic of Emily Brontë's poems, while the heavy use of feminine rhymes (in which the final syllable is unstressed) is more characteristic of Charlotte's poems than of Emily's (277n201). Other critics argue that Charlotte Brontë felt free to revise Emily's poems but that she would not have stooped to outright fabrication in order to defend her sister. [ED.]

The earth that wakes *one* human heart to feeling
20 Can centre both the worlds of Heaven and Hell.

No Coward Soul[1]

Jan 2d 1846

No coward soul is mine,
No trembler in the world's storm troubled sphere;
I see Heaven's glories shine,
And Faith shines equal arming me from Fear.

5 O God within my breast,
Almighty ever-present Deity,
Life, that in me has rest,
As I, Undying Life, have power in thee.

Vain are the thousand creeds
10 That move men's hearts, unutterably vain;
Worthless as withered weeds
Or idlest froth amid the boundless main.

To waken doubt in one
Holding so fast by thy infinity,
15 So surely anchored on
The steadfast rock of Immortality.

With wide-embracing love
Thy Spirit animates eternal years,
Pervades and broods above,
20 Changes, sustains, dissolves, creates, and rears.

Though Earth and moon were gone,
And suns and universes ceased to be;
And Thou wert left alone,
Every Existence would exist in thee

---

[1] "No Coward Soul" was published with the following claim by Charlotte Brontë: "The following are the last lines my sister Emily ever wrote." Charlotte Brontë, however, was not being truthful when she made this statement. In fact, Emily Brontë wrote *Wuthering Heights,* revised many of her early poems, and may even have begun a second novel that has been lost or destroyed after she wrote this poem. Roper points out that the title recalls Hester Chapone's poem "No More Repine, My Coward Soul," published as a preface to Elizabeth Carter's translation of *All the Works of Epictetus* (1758). Epictetus's central tenet was that humans have to overcome the fear of death before they can successfully live (Roper 271n125). The poem condemns religious sectarianism and presents God as a personal divinity who lives "within my breast" (line 5). [ED.]

25 There is not room for Death,
    Nor atom that his might could render void,
    Since Thou art Being and Breath,
    And what thou art may never be destroyed.

WUTHERING HEIGHTS

Sylvia Plath

Emily Brontë's solitary life dedicated to artistic creativity has stood as a model for numerous women writers who have admired and emulated her achievement. American poet Sylvia Plath (1932-1963) is only one of many women writers who have felt this fascination. (Virginia Woolf wrote an essay on the Brontës, and Emily Dickinson requested that Emily Brontë's poem "No Coward Soul" be read at her funeral.) At the time she wrote this poem, Plath was living in England with her husband, British poet Ted Hughes. She had suffered a miscarriage in February 1961 but became pregnant again within the next two months. She was five months pregnant when she visited Haworth and meditated on the landscape and on Emily Brontë's life. Plath had tried to commit suicide more than once in her youth, and this poem reflects the strong pull toward death that she sensed in Emily Brontë's novel *Wuthering Heights*. [Ed.]

The horizons ring me like faggots,
Tilted and disparate, and always unstable
Touched by a match, they might warm me,
And their fine lines singe
5 The air to orange
Before the distances they pin evaporate,
Weighting the pale sky with a solider color.
But they only dissolve and dissolve
Like a series of promises, as I step forward.

Collected Poems. Ed. Ted Hughes. London: Faber, 1961.

10 There is no life higher than the grasstops
Or the hearts of sheep, and the wind
Pours by like destiny, bending
Everything in one direction.
I can feel it trying
15 To funnel my heat away.
If I pay the roots of the heather
Too close attention, they will invite me
To whiten my bones among them.

The sheep know where they are,
20 Browsing in their dirty wool-clouds,
Gray as the weather.
The black slots of their pupils take me in.
It is like being mailed into space,
A thin, silly message.
25 They stand about in grandmotherly disguise,
All wig curls and yellow teeth
And hard, marbly baas.

I come to wheel ruts, and water
Limpid as the solitudes
30 That flee through my fingers.
Hollow doorsteps go from grass to grass;
Lintel and sill have unhinged themselves.
Of people the air only
Remembers a few odd syllables.
35 It rehearses them moaningly:
Black stone, black stone.

The sky leans on me, me, the one upright
Among all horizontals.
The grass is beating its head distractedly.
40 It is too delicate
For a life in such company;
Darkness terrifies it.
Now, in valleys narrow
And black as purses, the house lights
45 Gleam like small change.

The Gondal Saga

Mary Visick

There is no agreement on the meaning of the poems that have come to be known as the Gondal saga, more than a hundred poems written exclusively by Emily Brontë and about fictional personae who bear some resemblance to the later novelistic characters in *Wuthering Heights*. We do know, however, that the prose pieces accompanying these poems, some of them written by Anne Brontë, have all been lost or destroyed. The controversy about these poems centers on one question: Are they meant to be read as a coherent, chronological poetic narrative recounting the adventures of Augusta Geraldine Almeda and Lord Alfred, or are they apprentice pieces, randomly composed, with no central organizing principle? The most forceful advocate for the consistent narrative thesis is Fannie Ratchford, who has assembled the poems and provided hypothetical links that fill in for the lost prose writings to make sense of the story.

Because Ratchford's method has been subject to a fair amount of criticism, Mary Visick has taken another approach to explain the meaning of the Gondal poems. Visick sees the poems primarily as Brontë's effort to present her belief in a god who can be understood as "a creedless, immortal energy. Presumably the parson's daughter paid her formal respects to Christianity, but the mystical experiences of this sense of infinity and immortality are not, in her poetry, couched in Christian terms or given Christian explanations. She sought to find expression for them not through orthodox religion but through the fantasy of Gondal" (35). In other words, the Gondal poems, as well as the later *Wuthering Heights,* can be read as Emily Brontë's attempt to rewrite the Bible. As Visick indicates, Brontë's imagination seems to have worked by pairing oppositions and presenting all of life as a cosmic struggle between life and death, light and dark, male and female, night and day, fire and ice. These bifurcations are familiar to the reader of Charlotte Brontë's novels, and certainly it is fair to claim that the religious rigidity of the home and

---

From *The Genesis of* Wuthering Heights. Hong Kong: Hong Kong UP, 1948. (References to Roper's edition of Brontë's poems have been substituted for Visick's references to the outdated Hatfield edition.)

church was being dismantled and transformed in the imaginations of these daughters of an Anglican curate. [ED.]

[. . .] To investigate the origins of this amazing novel [*Wuthering Heights*] is a critical task worth undertaking. These origins may be found quite specifically in the Gondal poems. Emily Brontë's earliest dated poem was written towards the end of her eighteenth year; by February 1844, when she was nearly twenty-six, she had accumulated enough poetry to begin transcribing it into two manuscript books, which presumably contain all she wished to preserve. Fortunately other manuscripts have survived which, although the verse they contain is often inferior, occasionally supply some significant variations, or provide Gondal poems which help us to piece the story together. Of the two transcript books one bears simply her initials and the date; the other is headed *Gondal Poems*. Of the 151 fully finished poems in Mr. Hatfield's edition, these two books account for seventy-six. There is a third manuscript book, now in the British Museum, and there are also three collections of loose sheets, in the hands of various collectors; but neither the third book nor the sheets contains any poem dated later than February 1844. The two transcript books, then, superseded them. The books escaped the holocaust which consumed all the Gondal prose, and were obviously prepared with great care—whether for publication or not it is impossible to say. The story they can be shown to tell is the story of *Wuthering Heights.*

Charlotte's well-known account of her accidental discovery of 'a MS volume of verse in my sister Emily's handwriting' implies that Emily Brontë did not intend to publish her poems, that in fact she shrank from the idea and had to be persuaded by Charlotte that her poems 'merited publication'.[1] On this a good deal of fine writing on Emily's morbidly fastidious shyness has been produced; it seems rather beside the point, for the poems which finally appeared in *Poems by Currer, Ellis, and Acton Bell* published in 1846 are not the least personal—they include the most personal of all her poems, *The Prisoner, Stars, The Old Stoic, Plead for me, The Philosopher;* they are, quite simply, the best poems. If she had shrunk from revealing her 'quivering sensibility' to the world these would, one imagines, have been the ones she would have torn from Charlotte's rapacious grasp. We may make the not-very-rash assumption that Charlotte was right when

---

[1] Charlotte Brontë's "Biographical Notice of Ellis and Action Bell" prefixed to the 1850 edition of *Wuthering Heights,* [pages 13–19 in this edition—ED.]

she represented the diffidence mingled with Emily's anger (and it seems she was angry: 'it took hours to reconcile her to the discovery') as doubt whether the poems would be acceptable. Furthermore, although Charlotte only mentions one book, the poems in the sisters' volume are actually drawn from two manuscripts. Either Charlotte found two, or Emily voluntarily produced the second, and selected from both those poems which she felt to be the most satisfactory. Possibly she was ready to let the poems go because her mind was turning towards her novel, of which the poems represent a kind of foreshadowing.

To return to the manuscripts themselves. It is clear by the inscription 'Gondal Poems' that Emily Brontë made a distinction in her mind between Gondal and non-Gondal verse. This manuscript (referred to by Mr. Hatfield as MS B) was begun in 1844, but contains poems of a much earlier date. These poems are not copied in the order of their composition; it seems fair to assume that there is some other order rather than that their sequence is purely haphazard, especially since Emily Brontë seems to have been a methodical worker. The verse dates back some years. A note written by Anne Brontë in July 1845 says that she and her sister began writing the (presumably prose) Gondal Chronicles 'three and a half years ago'; but some of the poems are dated much earlier. The birthday notes written by Emily and Anne in 1845, exchanged, and intended to be opened on Emily's birthday in 1848, suggest that the prose chronicles related to a later generation of Gondalians than that of the chief characters of the verse, the heroes and heroines of *Gondal's Queen* [see Ratchford] and also, I believe, recognizably the chief characters of *Wuthering Heights*: probably the people belonging to this older generation were evolved in the early stages of the Gondal game, and matured in their creator's mind. If, in 1845, the current Gondal prose might be regarded as an account of contemporary Gondal, the people of the poems were historical figures out of a stormier past. The main action of *Wuthering Heights* takes place in the past—about the year 1775 and onwards. It is in fact a historical novel.

A clue to the Gondal story, then, might be found in the order in which Emily Brontë arranged the poems in her *Gondal Poems* manuscript. Poems written before 1844 are copied in their sequence in the Gondal story. For poems written after April 1844, however, the order is roughly chronological, as if she copied them in as they were written without regard for their place in the Gondal story. Many of them amplify sections of the story already told in the earlier part of the manuscript. On this theory there are two poems in the later part which are out of sequence; but since there are other Gondal poems preserved in the 'odd' manuscripts but not transcribed she may originally have intended to reject these, and changed her mind later.

The first seventeen poems in the manuscript fall into five sections each referring to an episode in the life of the heroine, Augusta Geraldine Almeda or Rosina. Miss Ratchford thinks these are two names for the same heroine; Miss Laura Hinkley thinks they are in fact two people. This sounds like a fundamental and violent difference; but it is unimportant when we are considering the relationship between Gondal and *Wuthering Heights,* since if they were indeed two their personalities coalesced in the figure of Catherine Earnshaw.

Emily Brontë usually refers to the heroine as 'A.G.A.', which is a useful abbreviation for a somewhat cumbersome name. A.G.A.-Rosina, then, has four lovers. The first is Alexander, Lord of Elbë, to whom the first two poems refer. He is killed in battle. An early figure in the saga, he contributes nothing to the *Wuthering Heights* theme, and has no particular interest. One might, of course, catch a whiff of the Napoleonic legend in his title 'Elbë': and the foundling Heathcliff might well be a quasi-Napoleonic figure. Charlotte was a great partisan of the Duke of Wellington who appears, somewhat translated, in her imaginary kingdom of Angria; Emily who does not seem to have shared Charlotte's high Toryism may have felt some admiration for Napoleon. However, conjecture cannot build on this. The next six poems relate to Lord Alfred of Aspin Castle, another lover of A.G.A. He looks like a prototype of Edgar Linton; and the poems show that the original story of his relationship with the heroine was altered, becoming more like that of Catherine and Edgar in *Wuthering Heights.* This point will be developed later. The third group, of four poems, refers to a political assassination; it is not clear whether the 'sovereign' who has been murdered is a man or a woman, but Miss Ratchford's earlier reconstruction identified him with one Julius Brenzaida, another of A.G.A.'s lovers, who, though apparently of obscure birth, rose to be emperor of Gondal. The poem *Rosina,* which seems to belong to this group, certainly refers to the murder of Julius. The fourth group obviously preceded the third, since it concerns a relationship between Julius and a girl called Geraldine; and the fifth concerns yet another lover, Fernando de Samara, who was driven to suicide by A.G.A. and in whose reproaches we can catch a note of Heathcliff. Thus each group is defined but the groups are not in sequence in the story. It is as if already in 1844 Emily Brontë was dissecting the Gondal story, seeing it as isolated episodes. Possibly she was already considering the regrouping of the episodes into another story, which in the end led her beyond Gondal to the novel.

After these sets of poems come three which have a rather obscure relation to the main story. Then the twenty-first and twenty-third refer to the death of the heroine A.G.A. This brings us to the point at which Emily Brontë caught up with herself in transcribing; from now on most of the poems bear dates which suggest that they were copied into the transcript book as soon as, or soon after, they were written. Two concern Julius, of which one is Rosina's lament 'Cold in the earth, and the deep snow piled above thee . . .' which has struck many readers as prefiguring the eighteen years of Heathcliff's mourning for Catherine. However another poem which also occurs late in the manuscript is even closer in verbal expression to Heathcliff; and here, as in 'No coward soul . . .' the reference is not to ordinary human love but to some other order of experience. It is a long Gondal narrative of which some self-contained stanzas were published in the 1846 volume as *The Prisoner, a fragment:*

> Then dawns the Invisible, the Unseen its truth reveals;
> My outward sense is gone, my inward essence feels —
> Its wings are almost free, its home, its harbour found;
> Measuring the gulf it stoops and dares the final bound!
>
> Oh, dreadful is the check — intense the agony
> When the ear begins to hear, and the eye begins to see;
> When the pulse begins to throb, the brain to think again,
> The soul to feel the flesh, and the flesh to feel the chain.[2]

In *Wuthering Heights* Heathcliff's dead love, or rather the sense of her presence, is at the core of the invisible world he cannot reach:

> I have neither a fear, nor a presentiment, nor a hope of death. Why should I? With my hard constitution and temperate mode of living, and unperilous occupation, I ought to, and probably *shall* remain above ground, till there is scarcely a black hair on my head — And yet I cannot continue in this condition! I have to remind myself to breathe — almost to remind my heart to beat! And it is like bending back a stiff spring: it is by compulsion that I do the slightest act not prompted by one thought, and by compulsion that I notice anything alive or dead, which is not associated with one universal idea. I have a single wish, and my whole being and faculties are yearning to attain it. They have yearned towards it so long, and so unwaveringly, that I'm convinced it *will* be reached — and soon — because it has devoured my existence: I am swallowed up in the anticipation of its fulfilment. . . . O, God! It is a long fight, I wish it were over! (266)

Here is another indication that the love between Catherine and Heathcliff is Emily Brontë's way of giving expression to some all-devouring spiritual experience.

Among several other themes in *Gondal Poems,* many of which are undeveloped and may or may not have any relation to the novel, we find one

---

[2] See "The Visionary," pages 298–302 in this volume. [ED.]

emerging as a well-marked interest towards the end of the manuscript. The figures in the foreground are two children, a dark boy and a fair and happy girl, who seem to belong to a different generation. The former is to be found in several very early Gondal poems, but by 1845 he is becoming rather like Hareton Earnshaw, and the girl is beginning to look like Cathy Linton.

In two poems grouped together by Charlotte Brontë in her edition of 1850, and which she called *The Two Children*[3] it is possible that the second-generation theme of *Wuthering Heights* is beginning to appear. This statement assumes that Emily Brontë intended the two poems to be read as one, for which there is some evidence. The first has a Gondal heading, 'A. E. and R. C.' and the date, May 28, 1845. The second poem has no heading and no date. It is rare for Emily Brontë not to date a poem, and from the two sets of initials we might expect to find two characters in the poems; but there is only one in the first. It seems safe to assume, then, that A. E. is the boy and R. C. the girl. This double poem is certainly one of the loveliest of Emily Brontë's lyrics—a too-little-known Song of Innocence:

> Heavy hangs the raindrop
> From the burdened spray;
> Heavy broods the damp mist
> On uplands far away;
>
> Heavy looms the dull sky,
> Heavy rolls the sea—
> And heavy beats the young heart
> Beneath that lonely tree.
>
> Never has a blue streak
> Cleft the clouds since morn—
> Never has his grim Fate
> Smiled since he was born.
>
> Frowning on the infant,
> Shadowing childhood's joy,
> Guardian angel knows not
> That melancholy boy.
>
> Day is passing swiftly
> Its sad and sombre prime;
> Youth is fast invading
> Sterner manhood's time.
>
> All the flowers are praying
> For sun before they close,

---

[3] See "The Two Children" (296–98). [ED.]

And he prays too, unknowing,
That sunless human rose!

Blossoms, that the west wind
Has never wooed to blow,
Scentless are your petals,
Your dew as cold as snow.
Soul, where kindred kindness
No early promise woke,
Barren is your beauty
As weeds upon the rock.

Wither, brothers, wither,
You were vainly given—
Earth reserves no blessing
For the unblessed of Heaven!

———

Child of Delight! with sunbright hair,
And seablue, seadeep eyes;
Spirit of Bliss, what brings thee here,
Beneath these sullen skies?

Thou should'st live in eternal spring,
Where endless day is never dim;
Why, seraph, has thy erring wing
Borne thee down to weep with him?

'Ah, not from heaven am I descended,
And I do not come to mingle tears;
But sweet is day, though with shadows blended;
And, though clouded, sweet are youthful years.

'I, the image of light and gladness
Saw and pitied that mournful boy,
And I swore to take his gloomy sadness,
And give to him my beamy joy.

'Heavy and dark the night is closing;
Heavy and dark may its biding be:
Better for all from grief reposing,
And better for all who watch like me.

'Guardian angel he lacks no longer;
Evil fortune he needs not fear:
Fate is strong, but Love is stronger;
And more unsleeping than angel's care.'

Another poem, written much earlier—in May 1842—is placed nearly next to *The Two Children* in the manuscript and, like it, is concerned with a dark boy and a fair girl:

> In the same place, when Nature wore
> The same celestial glow,
> I'm sure I've seen those forms before
> But many springs ago;
>
> And only *he* had locks of light,
> And *she* had raven hair;
> While now, his curls are dark as night,
> And hers as morning fair . . .[4]

The place of this poem is obscure; but the older generation sound like Edgar and Catherine, and the children might well foreshadow Hareton and Cathy. It is interesting to see Emily Brontë working out that relation between inner self and personal appearance which is so important in *Wuthering Heights*.

Thus we may summarise the parts of the Gondal story which concern A.G.A.: After the death of Alexander Elbë the heroine is associated with three men, one of whom, Julius Brenzaida, Emperor of Gondal, is murdered, leaving her to lament him through 'fifteen wild Decembers'. At some period in her career she has deserted him for the gentle, fair-haired Lord Alfred (whose fate will be discussed later). She is also loved by the guitar-player Fernando de Samara, who commits suicide. After her death a dark boy is rescued from some kind of misery by a fair girl.

In the unfolding story of Lord Alfred of Aspin Castle as it is told in *Gondal Poems* I believe we can see a significant modification of both the Gondal people and the story—a change which entails a much deeper scrutiny of the motives of the characters than is usual in Gondal and which also brings the Gondal plot much closer to that of the novel. Other Gondal poems not in the transcript book help to make the stages of this revision clear.

The contention that the third to the eighth entries in *Gondal Poems* refer to Lord Alfred can only be upheld at risk of some disagreement with Miss Ratchford's reconstruction. But she has not taken into account the arrangement Emily Brontë imposed on her poems in transcribing them, and that Emily Brontë did make a deliberate arrangement of at least the

---

[4] Roper (129–30). [ED.]

earlier poems in the manuscript seems clear. We find, then, the following poems, in the order in which they are placed in *Gondal Poems* [. . .]:

A.G.A. TO A. S.[5]

May 6, 1840
July 28, 1843

Here the heroine expresses her happiness in the love of Alfred, for whom she feels something like veneration:

> At such a time, in such a spot,
> The world seems made of light;
> Our blissful hearts remember not
> How surely follows night.
>
> I cannot, Alfred, dream of aught
> That casts a shade of woe;
> That heaven is reigning in my thought,
> Which wood and wave and earth have caught
> From skies that overflow.
>
> That heaven which my sweet lover's brow
> Has won me to adore,
> Which from his blue eyes beaming now
> Reflects a still intenser glow
> Than nature's heaven can pour.
>
> I know our souls are all divine;
> I know that when we die,
> What seems the vilest, even like thine
> A part of God himself shall shine
> In perfect purity.
>
> But coldly breaks November's day;
> Its changes, charmless all;
> Unmarked, unloved, they pass away;
> We do not wish one hour to stay,
> Nor sigh at evening's fall.
>
> And glorious is the gladsome rise
> Of June's rejoicing morn;
> And who with unregretful eyes
> Can watch the lustre leave its skies
> To twilight's shade forlorn?
>
> And art thou not my golden June
> All mist and tempest free?

---

[5] See Roper (104–06). [ED.]

As shines earth's sun in summer noon,
So heaven's sun shines in thee.

Let others seek its beams divine
In cell and cloister drear;
But I have found a fairer shrine
And happier worship here.

By dismal rites they win their bliss —
By penance, fasts and fears;
I have one rite: a gentle kiss;
One penance: tender tears.

O could it thus forever be
That I might so adore;
I'd ask for all eternity
To make a paradise for me.
My love — and nothing more!

This recalls Catherine in the first days of her marriage in the summer world of Thrushcross Grange — 'almost over-fond' of Edgar. Again, the mainspring of Edgar's character is a gentle, firm Christianity, at the opposite pole from the hell-fire cant of old Joseph: ineffectual against Heathcliff and Catherine, but none the less real. He might well have developed from the Alfred of this poem. It would seem that the mood of this poem, highly uncharacteristic of A.G.A., is shattered by the appearance of another lover, who is to Lord Alfred as the sun is to the moon.

TO A.G.A.[6]
This poem is undated. In it someone taxes A.G.A. with unfaithfulness and she replies that 'morning . . . and ardent noon' have destroyed her 'moon of life':

'Thou standest in the greenwood now
The place, the hour the same —
And here the fresh leaves gleam and glow
And there, down in the lake below,
The tiny ripples flame.

'The breeze sings like a summer breeze
Should sing in summer skies
And tower-like rocks and tent-like trees
In mingled glory rise.

'But where is he to-day, to-day?'
'O question not with me.'

---

[6]See Roper (196–97). [ED.]

'I will not, Lady; only say
Where may thy lover be?

'Is he upon some distant shore
Or is he on the sea
Or is the heart thou dost adore
A faithless heart to thee?'

'The heart I love, whate'er betide,
Is faithful as the grave
And neither foreign lands divide
Nor yet the rolling wave.'

'Then why should sorrow cloud that brow
And tears those eyes bedim?
Reply this once — is it that thou
Hast faithless been to him?'

'I gazed upon the cloudless moon
And loved her all the night
Till morning came, and ardent noon,
Then I forgot her light —

'No — not forgot — eternally
Remains its memory dear;
But could the day seem dark to me
Because the night was fair?

'I well may mourn that only one
Can light my future sky
Even though by such a radiant sun
My moon of life must die.'

[. . .] A. G. A. to A. S. is a farewell, penitent but irrevocable, to the gentle
lover she is deserting. Its date is March 2, 1844:

This summer wind, with thee and me
Roams in the dawn of day;
But thou must be where it shall be,
Ere Evening — far away.

The farewell's echo from thy soul
Shall not depart before
Hills rise and distant rivers roll
Between us evermore.

I know that I have done thee wrong —
Have wronged both thee and Heaven —
And I may mourn my lifetime long
Yet may not be forgiven.

Repentant tears will vainly fall
To cancel deeds untrue;
But for no grief can I recall
The dreary word—Adieu.

Yet thou a future peace shalt win
Because thy soul is clear;
And I who had the heart to sin
Will find a heart to bear.

Till far beyond earth's frenzied strife
That makes destruction joy,
Thy perished faith shall spring to life
And my remorse shall die.

A.G.A. TO A. S.[7]

[May] 20, 1838

In this much earlier poem, A.G.A. laments not her desertion but the death of her lover. Miss Ratchford's rigid reconstruction of the plot forces her to see in this A. S. an unidentified lover: but A. S. often, though not always, stands for Lord Alfred, and the poem suggests the same gentle personality in the same summery setting as the first of the Lord Alfred poems.

... The woods—even now their small leaves hide
The blackbird and the stockdove well;
And high in heaven, so blue and wide,
A thousand strains of music swell ...

... Well, pass away with the other flowers:
Too dark for them, too dark for thee
Are the hours to come, the joyless hours
That Time is treasuring up for me.

If thou hast sinned in this world of care,
'Twas but the dust of thy drear abode—
Thy soul was pure when it entered here,
And pure it will go again to God.

A.G.A. TO THE BLUEBELL[8]

May 9, 1839

Miss Ratchford takes this to be a lament for a child; but there seems no reason why, coming where it does in the manuscript, it should not refer to Lord Alfred:

Sacred watcher, wave thy bells!
Fair hill flower and woodland child!

---

[7]See Roper (54). [ED.]
[8]See Roper (78–80). [ED.]

Dear to me in deep green dells —
Dearest on the mountains wild.

Bluebell, even as all divine
I have seen my darling shine —
Bluebell, even as wan and frail
I have seen my darling fail —
Thou hast found a voice for me,
And soothing words are breathed by thee.

Thus they murmur, 'Summer's sun
Warms me till my life is done.
Would I rather choose to die
Under winter's ruthless sky?

'Glad I bloom and calm I fade;
Weeping twilight dews my bed;
Mourner, mourner, dry thy tears —
Sorrow comes with lengthened years!'

WRITTEN IN ASPIN CASTLE[9]

There are two dates at the head of this long semi-narrative poem: 20 August 1842 and 6 February 1843.

It would seem that the ghost of Lord Alfred 'walks' unquietly: that he died far away and in despair; and that the heroine of the saga in some way destroyed him. This poem may thus be taken to refer to the desertion of A.G.A's 'moon of life'. In passing, we may notice that a portrait of Lord Alfred is described, and it sounds not unlike the portrait of Edgar which Nelly shows Lockwood in *Wuthering Heights*.

While it is not certain that all these poems refer to Lord Alfred it is clear that they all refer to some gentle, fair character, the prototype of Edgar Linton. It seems that as late as May 1839 the Gondal story included the death of this character simply; the more intricate situation in which A.G.A. forsakes him for another man is worked out by 1842; Emily Brontë was in Brussels this year, away from Anne with whom she planned new stories. Perhaps it was a time for meditating on past Gondal games and even modifying the story. The undated poem 'Thou standest in the green-wood now . . .' contains a hint of the kind of contrast which is drawn in *Wuthering Heights* between Heathcliff and Linton. In her confession to Nelly Catherine says:

I've no more business to marry Edgar Linton than I have to be in heaven . . . It would degrade me to marry Heathcliff now; so he shall never

[9] See Roper (131–33). [ED.]

know how I love him: and that, not because he's handsome, Nelly, but because he's more myself than I am. Whatever our souls are made of, his and mine are the same; and Linton's is as different as a moonbeam from lightning, or frost from fire. (84)

The mention of heaven here, and its association with Linton, seems a link with the cruder personality of the Gondal man as we see it in the poem 'At such a time, in such a spot . . .'; but the main point is the use of natural imagery to point the contrast. The stanzas about the 'cloudless moon' and the bright day, which suggest two kinds of love, appear only in the later draft of the poem, the one which was copied into *Gondal Poems*. It seems as if some new experience is being worked into the story of A.G.A. and Alfred.

The earliest draft of 'Thou standest in the greenwood now . . .' is to be found on a loose sheet.[10] The poem is undated; but the poem on the reverse side is dated July 19, 1839.[11] Thus there is some indication that the idea of a forsaken lover, probably already Lord Alfred, comes later than those poems in which the fair-haired lover is represented as dying rather than as committing suicide. The first draft ends with the line 'Hast faithless been to him,' and with two following lines which do not appear in any other draft: 'I dreamt, one dark and stormy night When winter winds were wild'. Here the draft stops abruptly.

On another sheet appear two stanzas later worked into 'Thou standest in the greenwood now . . .' which make the contrast between the sun and the moon. The final stanza of the *Gondal Poems* version ('I needs must mourn . . .') is found only in that, the final, form.

Like the earliest draft, the two stanzas may be tentatively dated by another poem occupying the same sheet. This poem also concerns forsaking, and must also be mentioned. Mr. Hatfield gives the date as July 26, 1843, though he points out that the last figure of the date is obscure, and might be a '2'; in any case the two stanzas are later than the early draft, and show no connection with it.

Thus in its final form 'Thou standest in the greenwood . . .' is made up of three strata: the first, unfinished draft probably written in 1839; the two stanzas ending 'But could the day seem dark to me Because the night was fair?'; and the final summing-up stanza. No other poem shows such evidence that the writer was preoccupied with it over an extended period. It seems as if this part of the Gondal story underwent severe revision.

---

[10] See Roper (196–97). [ED.]
[11] See Roper (88–89). [ED.]

Furthermore, the poem dated July 26, 1843 — or 1842[12] — may be assumed to be on the same theme; Emily Brontë did not copy it into *Gondal Poems* but the final stanza is nearly identical with the first stanza of the repentant poem 'This summer wind . . .' which she did use in *Gondal Poems,* and which she headed 'A.G.A. to A. S.' It is an expression of the mood which the writer is later to associate with Thrushcross Grange:

Yes, holy be thy resting-place
Wherever thou mayst lie;
The sweetest winds breathe on thy face,
The softest of the sky.

And will not guardian Angels send
Kind dreams and thoughts of love,
Though I no more may watchful bend
Thy loved repose above?

And will not heaven itself bestow
A beam of glory there
That summer's grass more green may grow,
And summer's flowers more fair?

Farewell, farewell, 'tis hard to part
Yet, loved one, it must be:
I would not rend another heart
Not even by blessing thee.

Go! we must break affection's chain,
Forget the hope of years:
Nay, grieve not — willest thou remain
To waken wilder tears?

This wild breeze with thee and me
Roved in the dawning day;
And thou shouldst be where it shall be
Ere evening, far away.

Here is a Linton-like figure — entitled to a 'holy' resting-place, religious, slightly devitalized (even Nelly, Edgar's most consistent partisan, says 'he wanted spirits in general') and also, like Edgar, not small or ridiculous. Successive revisions have brought him closer and closer to the later figure of Edgar. From his personality and fate spring the sense of irretrievable wrong, which checks even the passionate A.G.A. and which destroys Catherine. 'If I have done wrong, I'm dying for it' she moans; but in the more complex world of *Wuthering Heights* it is hard to see who has been most

[12] See Roper (203–04). [ED.]

deeply wronged. Emily Brontë makes Nelly acknowledge this when, although she dislikes Catherine, distrusts Heathcliff and admires Edgar, she twists a lock of Heathcliff's hair round one of Edgar's, and lays them together in the locket round the dead Catherine's neck.

As for the sunlike lover, Miss Ratchford argues convincingly that he is Julius Brenzaida, the low-born emperor of Gondal. Julius wins power by violence and treachery; so Heathcliff deliberately corrupts Hindley, gets possession of the Heights, possibly murders him, or at least does not encourage him to live, traps Isabella and later Cathy, ruthlessly exploits his own son, and so becomes master of the fate of all the people round him. Julius, like him, is vivid, unscrupulous and violent.

Gondal Poems also contains two songs 'by Julius Brenzaida' addressed to 'Geraldine': the first is a kind of serenade, in which he recalls to her the moors where they have once been happy:

> . . . Wild the road, and rough and dreary;
> Barren all the moorland round;
> Rude the couch that rests us weary;
> Mossy stone and heathy ground.
>
> But, when winter storms were meeting
> In the moonless, midnight dome,
> Did we heed the tempest's beating,
> Howling round our spirits' home?
>
> No; that tree with branches riven,
> Whitening in the whirl of snow,
> As it tossed against the heaven,
> Sheltered happy hearts below . . .[13]

There is no need to labour the parallel; in October 1838 the two figures who were to become Heathcliff and Catherine in their childhood at the Heights were already sketched out in Emily Brontë's mind. And the second *Song,* of the same date, shows how the story was shaping:

> I knew not 'twas so dire a crime
> To say the word, Adieu;
> But this shall be the only time
> My slighted heart shall sue.
>
> The wild moorside, the winter morn,
> The gnarled and ancient tree —
> If in your breast they waken scorn,
> Shall wake the same in me . . .[14]

---

[13] See Roper (62–63). [ED.]
[14] See Roper (63–64). [ED.].

Miss Ratchford's reconstruction, in which the heroine first loves Julius, then abandons him for various lovers the last of whom is Lord Alfred, and finally leaves Alfred and returns to him, seems justified, among other reasons, because it is a sketch of the relations between Catherine, Heathcliff and Edgar in the first part of *Wuthering Heights*. [. . .]

Part Three

THE HISTORICAL
AND SOCIAL CONTEXTS

Very few writers have been so completely confined to their homes as Emily Brontë. Certainly Charlotte Brontë fostered the image of her sister as isolated on the moors, but Emily clearly read widely and traveled abroad to study in Brussels. One of the central questions about *Wuthering Heights* is how much of it is meant to be a realistic examination of life in late eighteenth and early nineteenth-century England and how much is meant to be a symbolic analysis of opposing characters, ways of life, and values. Those two positions—not mutually exclusive in my opinion—have been the subject of endless critical debate. Recent critics, however, have tended to place the novel in its historical and economic contexts, arguing that Emily Brontë grew up in a cotton- and wool-producing area of the country where she routinely would have seen thousands of displaced or unemployed workers, often homeless and desperate. The character of Heathcliff, moreover, is clearly marked as "other" than the powerful white male bourgeois Britons in the text. In Terry Eagleton's view, he could be an Irish immigrant, or a gypsy, or a Creole (*Heathcliff* 3). Christopher Heywood argues that Heathcliff is a Jamaican and that the novel should be read as a satire on the families prospering in Yorkshire off their investments in the Jamaican sugar factories (see 349–66).

In addition to the class and race issues present in the novel, gender oppression and the legalized disinheritance of women form central concerns in this work. Emily Brontë's "feminism" has been the subject of debate as well, some critics arguing that at best she is merely an "accidental" feminist. But her novel clearly depicts the legalized system of primogeniture (inheritance by the eldest son) as a corrupt and corrupting force on social stability and familial security. The ghost of Catherine Earnshaw, desperately trying to claw her way back into her family home, stands as the first image in the novel of disinheritance and displacement, associating women with the slaves, workers, and immigrants wandering around a rapidly industrialized England that had transformed itself too quickly for its inhabitants to adapt to the changes.

From *The Brontës' Irish Background*

Edward Chitham

In this selection, scholar Edward Chitham describes some real-life antecedents to the characters in *Wuthering Heights* from the Brontë family's forebears in Ireland. His source for some of this information is William Wright (1837–99), who was born in County Down, Ireland, and grew up within a few miles of the Rev. Patrick Brontë's birthplace. Hearing stories about the Brontë (Brunty) family throughout his childhood, he returned to Ireland as an adult in order to track down the family history and publish his account in *The Brontës in Ireland* (1893). Wright's major discovery was that the father of Patrick Brontë, Hugh Brunty, was adopted at a young age by a cruel and vengeful uncle named Welsh. This story, discussed by Chitham, assumed the status of folklore within the Brontë household in Haworth, as the Rev. Patrick Brontë told the ancestral story of their grandfather Hugh's virtual kidnapping and childhood abuse to his own children. Welsh himself was a central figure in the legend. An orphan found on a boat journeying from Liverpool to Drogheda, he was adopted by Hugh's grandfather. Like Heathcliff, Welsh was eventually able to turn all the legitimate heirs off the family property. Also like Heathcliff, he fell in love with the daughter of the house but was unable to marry her. [Ed.]

[. . .] Looked at from one point of view, *Wuthering Heights* is 'about' family history. Continuity with the past is important. Second and third generations repeat the characteristics of the first, reordering the traits and recombining them. A Cathy will be like Catherine, but not exactly. Linton Heathcliff is part Heathcliff, part Linton, and so on. Hareton, who will carry on the story, is born in 1778, one year after Patrick Brontë, while the

---

New York: St. Martin's, 1986.

main events of the novel take place in 1801–2, the year of Patrick's upheaval, as he vanished from his native land and sailed for Liverpool. (The Gondal saga, too, though we know very little about it, seems to be family history, the story of feuds and civil strife.) Nelly tells much of the story with vividness, recalling the 1770s and 1780s, the days when Patrick Brontë would be a child in Imdel and Ballynaskeagh. Emily, 'Ellis Bell', tells the story with a vividness that suggests she has dwelt in it and changed it organically, as a folk-artist lives his songs and stories. Possibly, through Nelly, Ellis reaches back to Allie or Ellie, in Ireland. (It may appear far-fetched to stress the narrator's name and the author's pseudonym in this way, but oddly similar 'variations on a theme' may be discerned in Emily's Gondal names.) There was an Isabella Linton in Imdel, who married a member of the Glascar meeting, James Stewart, in the late 1790s. She must have been about the same age as Patrick. As neither 'Isabella' nor 'Linton' are Yorkshire names, it seems quite probable that Emily heard her father speak of the girl and was attracted by the name. We may also note the frequence in County Down of the name 'Edgar', regarded there as a surname.

Liverpool is one of the very few real place names in *Wuthering Heights*. It may have been a familiar one to Emily Brontë, for the family were creatures of habit. (One example of this is Patrick Brontë's long-standing preference for the Chapter coffee-house in London.) Thus Branwell sought the sea at Liverpool years before he saw Scarborough; one of his tasks on his visit of 1839 was to attend the Evangelical church of St. Jude to hear the Revd. Hugh McNeile, a virulently anti-Catholic Irishman, and bring back an account of his preaching to Patrick Brontë.[1] In the novel, the function of Liverpool seems to be to represent a place known to be real, within walking distance for a healthy man, but through which unusual elements enter the closed Yorkshire world. Such elements cannot quite be naturalised in Yorkshire, though there is an affinity between them and the wind-swept uplands.

Emily Brontë was not compelled to choose Liverpool as the place of entry for her child of storm. She could have chosen Hull, for example, if she wished to imply an overseas descent. Or if she had wished merely to imply an urban and therefore alien background, she could have allowed Heathcliff to be discovered in the streets of Leeds or Sheffield. The choice of Liverpool may well be important. Winifred Gérin points out that Branwell was again in Liverpool in August 1845 and suggests that the form of Heathcliff was influenced by his reports of children newly arrived from Ireland and starving in the city streets.[2] She might well have gone further and reminded

---

[1] Daphne du Maurier, *The Infernal World of Branwell Brontë*, pp. 44–5.
[2] Winifred Gérin, *Emily Brontë*, p. 226.

us that the starving Irish children were from Patrick's homeland. Welsh, the starving and abandoned child of Hugh's alleged story, also enters upon the scene at Liverpool.

Of course, some of the imaginative ingredients of *Wuthering Heights* come from the narratives told by the Haworth kitchen-servants, especially old Tabby, who is said to have recalled the fairies living in the valley bottoms. Tabby apparently joined the household in 1824, when Emily was six.[3] This was a crucial year for Emily, as her poems show. At about the time when Tabby arrived she was banished to Cowan Bridge for six months. But she must have been listening to stories well before this time, and it is likely that her interest in fairies and the supernatural was well kindled by the time Tabby's stories could have been available to her, on her return from the clergy school in 1825. Unless we distrust Ellen Nussey's account, it seems likely that there was a layer of fairy-lore in Emily's mind before she encountered either Yorkshire folk-tale or the supernatural of Scott and the romantic poets. If the Irish background of the home was strong enough for Charlotte to be speaking with an Irish accent in 1831, it was strong enough for Emily to absorb it before the age of six or seven.

The most basic level of *Wuthering Heights,* then, may have been laid down in Emily's infancy. I have mentioned two aspects of this basic level: family history and the 'stage door' of Liverpool. But there are other deeply fundamental elements in the book which seem traceable to the early 1820s, Emily's formative years. At this time *The Maid of Killarney,* with its pagan keening over the dead, was Patrick Brontë's latest work. The breakfast-time sessions, including the fairy tales which Emily could repeat 'by the hour together' were in full swing. Mrs. Brontë was dead. Over the water, Eilís the never-seen grandmother probably died in 1822, and Maria and Elizabeth were to die in 1825. Death was a central matter in the Brontë household, as it was in some of the 'fairy tales'. Five out of six of our source passages considered these fairy tales to be partly Irish.

In a number of ways, at its deepest level, *Wuthering Heights* bears resemblances to Classic Irish legend or to Anglo-Irish folk tradition. In his assertion that he had heard the outline of the novel before it was published, Wright may not have been thinking of these matters at all; he may have been primarily concerned with the 'story-line' as he perceived it. We shall return to his comment [later]. At the moment we shall examine: (i) the pagan, animist nature of the relations between man and nature in the novel; (ii) the intense and amoral nature of 'love' and its capacity to nullify death;

---

[3] Letter from Patrick Brontë to Mr. Marriner, 10 November 1824; qtd. Gérin, *Emily Brontë,* p. 7.

and (iii) the oral character of the story, with its Ancient Mariner–like capacity to hypnotise the reader. All these characteristics are to be found in greater or less degree in the Romantics and there is no need to deny their influence on Emily Brontë; yet she gives the impression of concurring with them rather than deriving from them, in that her level of soul-felt intensity appears greater and more constant.

Perhaps the most mysterious place in the area of the Heights is Penistone Crag. The elder Catherine, in delirium, sees Nelly as a hag there:

> "I see in you, Nelly," she continued dreamily, "an aged woman — you have grey hair, and bent shoulders. This bed is the Fairy Cave under Penistone Crag, and you are gathering elf-bolts to hurt our heifers; pretending, while I am there, that they are only locks of wool. That's what you'll come to fifty years hence: I know you are not so now. I'm not wandering, you're mistaken, or else I should believe you really *were* that withered hag, and I should think I *was* under Penistone Crag." (116)

Penistone Crag, like Liverpool, casts a shadow of place over the Heights. The younger Catherine too is drawn by it as though by the magic of a witch or fairy. Indeed, at Penistone Crag, as at New Grange, there is a fairy cave. The crag and its inhabitants cast a spell on young Catherine which is not referred to afterwards but touches her with supernatural power.

Both English and Irish fairies have harmed cattle with 'elf-shot' in tradition. In Ireland a grey-haired hag called cailleach Vera presided over such pursuits and was imitated by local witches. T. G. F. Paterson gives an example from County Armagh in *Harvest Home*.[4] Emily's folklore is genuine, though it would be impossible to say whether she obtained it from a Yorkshire or an Irish source.

The haunting of the countryside near ''t Nab' by the ghosts of Heathcliff and 'a woman' near the end of the novel shows mankind, dead or alive, as part of Nature. Country people have met Heathcliff since his death near the church, but town people, of which Lockwood is one, will dismiss such evidence. 'Lockwood's' final comment (or is it Emily Brontë's?) has been the subject of much conjecture and comment. Has the townee become any the wiser for his exposure to the story-telling genius of Nelly, who has striven to lay before him the startling facts of life lived near Nature? Is his calm depiction of the scene at the edge of the churchyard Emily's unequivocal indication that the spirits of Catherine, Edgar Linton and Heathcliff are now at rest? It may be so, but the fluttering of moths among the heath may give us pause, for the notion that butterflies are the souls of the dead is recorded in Lady Wilde's *Ancient Legends, Mystic Charms and*

---

[4] T. G. F. Paterson, *Harvest Home*, p. 208.

Superstitions of Ireland and in Joseph Ferguson's *Statistical Account of the Parish of Ballymoyer,* though the belief is not confined to Ireland. After mentioning these examples, Wood-Martin says

> In some parts of Ireland the soul is supposed after death to remain in the form of a butterfly, or of a small bird, in the neighbourhood of the body, and then to follow it to the grave.[5]

In an article in *Folklore* [. . .], Dr. Jacqueline Simpson lists examples of superstitions used in *Jane Eyre* and *Wuthering Heights.* These include the notion that it is hard to die when birds' feathers have been used for the pillow; that midnight ('the clock striking twelve') is a fatal time to see a ghost or funeral; that a child in a dream indicates bad fortune or death. The first two are referred to in Seán Ó Súilleabháin's *The Types of Irish Folktale,* though it cannot be sure that Emily might not have encountered them or the third one in Yorkshire. Of course, Patrick Brontë's attitude to these legends, if he told them, would be that of Albion in *The Maid of Killarney*: curiosity rather than belief. Emily's attitude reminds us of Hugh Brunty who 'made his listeners see and feel as well as hear'.[6]

Among the other superstitions which Emily may have obtained either from a Yorkshire or an Irish source are the idea that witches run red-hot needles into the feet of their victims; that food should be left on the table at night for fairies to eat; and that a white creature seen at night may be a ghost portending death.[7] The last-mentioned occurs in the scene where Nelly goes to fetch a doctor for Catherine and sees Isabella's spaniel, which Heathcliff has hanged. With this we may compare the activities of the Brontë uncles, using a white sheet to scare their superstitious neighbours in Ballynaskeagh. Such beliefs are widespread in the British Isles and elsewhere. Emily Brontë is quite content to naturalise them in a Yorkshire context, but of their origin we must remain uncertain.

Many European ballads, alive in oral tradition in the eighteenth and nineteenth centuries, see 'love' as an amoral force, producing such positives as cohesion and continuity, even survival after death (though such survival often brings disaster); on the other hand, it also produces jealousy and hate, sometimes in the form of the triangular relationship which leads to murder. Emily Brontë's literary exemplars, such as Coleridge and Shelley, were fully aware of this tradition of course. As well as 'The Ancient Mariner' the Brontës knew 'Christabel', 'John Gilpin', and the poems of

---

[5] William Wood-Martin, *Traces of the Elder Faiths of Ireland,* vol. II, p. 296.
[6] William Wright, *Brontës in Ireland,* p. 47.
[7] J. Simpson, 'The Function of Folklore in *Jane Eyre* and *Wuthering Heights*', *Folklore,* vol. 85 (1974) pp. 47ff.

Burns, together with many narrative poems of the late eighteenth and early nineteenth centuries which bore a ballad influence. But perhaps this literary tradition is not quite enough to account for Emily's intensely oral style.

As we have seen, Wright credits Patrick Brontë with a number of folk-songs, one of which deals with the vengeance of a betrayed maiden upon her lover. He also mentions the 'Vision of Hell' poem, which seems much nearer to Irish Classic tradition. If the attributions are correct, or if at any rate Patrick Brontë knew and performed these songs, this may be one source of Emily's ear for folk-song. She does, however, mention in *Wuthering Heights* two ballads which can be recognised. These are 'The Ghaist's Warning' and 'Fairy Annie's Wedding'. J. F. Goodrich considers that the first of these is most likely to have been found in the notes to *The Lady of the Lake*.[8] The second is a puzzle we need to discuss below. The quotation from 'The Ghaist's Warning' is in Scots form, and illustrates the Brontë enthusiasm for all things Scottish which may in part be due to a wish to emphasise the respectable Scots part of their Ulster heritage. This ballad is linked with 'Sweet William's Ghost', a story of a revenant continuing relations with a lover lost through death.

The view of the balladists and their successors seems to be that death will not separate ghost and lover, but that this is not necessarily a good thing. It may be that the lover, by his or her grief, disturbs the peace of the corpse. The corpse will return, sometimes in a form barely recognisable, to the lover's room. Many versions of such ballads and their derivatives are found in the Irish tradition, though they are often supposed to be Scandinavian in origin. In many versions the dead lover cannot stay long, and spends the time persuading the other to relax the grip of affection, so that the corpse can rest. Emily's poetry contains many lovers who retain a yearning affection for the dead person, and it is hard not to see this as a matter Emily faced within herself, as she contemplated the death and separation of her mother, Maria and Elizabeth. Lockwood's intense vision of Catherine as a child-ghost seems to the point here, since it is not quite in all ways appropriate to the plot that the dream should be presented as a ghost at this point in the story: yet this 'nightmare' seems very like a ghost.

There is no known ballad called 'Fairy Annie's Wedding'. It is possible that the title may represent a confusion in Emily's mind. Two ballads have versions in which a girl called Fair Annie appears. These are numbers 62

---

[8] J. F. Goodrich, 'A New Heaven and a New Earth', in Anne Smith (ed.), *The Art of Emily Brontë*, p. 172.

and 74 in Child's *The English and Scottish Popular Ballads*.[9] There appears to be a connection between the two, and both have themes which occur in *Wuthering Heights*. 'Fair Annie' (no. 62) tells of a girl stolen by a knight in her childhood and later bearing a number of children to him. She is replaced by a legitimate wife, whom she must welcome as a bride to the household. She plays her part well, but at night retires to mourn. The bride hears her complaints and discovers her story, then leaves the knight and Fair Annie, returning to her own home beyond the seas. Child prints a partial version from County Meath, and other Irish versions have been collected since.[10]

In 'Sweet William and Fair Annie' (no. 74), William courts the fair-haired Annie, but decides to marry the 'brown girl' for her houses and land. He bids Annie to the wedding, where there is an angry exchange between the girls. In most versions the brown girl attacks Annie and kills her, only to be viciously killed in her turn by William (or Lord Thomas, as he more often becomes). Child collected a version of this ballad in Killarney, and many versions have since been collected in Ireland as well as Scotland and England.

It will be seen that either of these two ballads might have been called 'Fair Annie's Wedding', since in both the crucial point is the wedding of a usurper to Annie's true love at a marriage which should have been hers. The second of the two introduces Emily Brontë's favourite opposition (found in the poems as well as the novel) of dark-haired to light-haired. It will be recalled that 'Welsh', in Wright's version of Hugh's alleged story, is persistently dark, while the Brontës, exemplified by the aunts and Eilís McClory, are light. Of course, in *Wuthering Heights* the triangle is stood on its head. It is Catherine who has a choice between light-haired socially respectable Edgar and dark-haired outcast Heathcliff. But it does seem possible that some version or other of this ballad lurked below the surface of Emily's consciousness and became one source of the book.

However, the title of the song as given by Nelly is '*Fairy* Annie's Wedding'. No version in Child suggests a supernatural origin for Annie, but it may possibly be that the heroine has become confused with the Irish goddess Anna or Ania, whose memory lingered on in folklore for centuries after Christianity had replaced her. Nelly's comment that the ballad 'goes to a dance' for all its sadness is typical of the known versions of the ballad, and indeed many ballads with sad words use lively tunes. Emily had apparently

---

[9] Francis James Child, *The English and Scottish Popular Ballads* (New York, 1882) vol. II, pp. 63ff, 199ff. The collection does not exclude Irish ballads, but there are comparatively few of them.

[10] Ibid., p. 77.

heard this ballad sung, whether in the Haworth kitchen or by Patrick, or by James Brontë on his visit about 1846. As *Fairy* Annie was the heroine, we may think it possible that this was one of the 'fairy' tales which Emily repeated 'by the hour' in her childhood.

Though I have cited versions of both the ballads in *Wuthering Heights* from Ireland, it is right to say that Child did not draw many of his examples from there. In fact, the ballad tradition seems to have been relatively weak in most counties of Ireland, as appears from work done by Hugh Shields, the Irish folk-song collector.[11] The Gaelic tradition favours prose for narrative and verse for lyric. However, ballads were invading Ireland from Britain at least as early as plantation times. Some were translated into Irish while many waited for acceptance until English became the dominant language. Thus it is hard to see these narratives becoming well known in County Down before Hugh Brunty's generation, though we have the ascription of the folk-songs in the following generation as indications that such words and stories would be well known by the beginning of the nineteenth century. Hugh Shields does, however, list both the ballads we have considered likely to have influenced *Wuthering Heights* among a very limited list of ballads he has traced in Ireland.

Folk-ballads are, of course, only one example of oral narrative art. In previous pages I have argued that such hints as Wright gives of the content of Hugh Brunty's stories suggest that he was a *seanchaí* [storyteller], with both some of the old hero-legends and some more modern legends in his repertoire. If Hugh could write Irish from childhood (and he may have been taken from his 'comfortable home' too early for this) he is considered largely illiterate on his arrival in the neighbourhood of Donaghmore. On the other hand, his oral technique, according to the accounts Wright heard, partook of the stock-in-trade of the Gaelic storyteller of whom Seamus Delargey wrote.[12]

Patrick's art too was often oral. He frightened his breakfast-time guests, wove webs of words in the pulpit 'with nothin'' in his hand' and even in old age entertained Mrs. Gaskell with his voluble charm and courtesy. Though Mr. Brontë had enormous reverence for the book, which he passed on to all his children, the whole family listened acutely. The conversation recorded on the 1837 diary paper is a good example of this, with words accurately written so that as we read [them] we can imagine the conversation between Emily and Anne. Listening and telling were in the family. Paper was sometimes merely a means of recording the spoken word, not a fresh medium.

[11] Hugh Shields, 'Old British Ballads in Ireland', *Folklife*, vol. 10 (1972) pp. 68ff.
[12] James [Seamus] H. Delargey, 'The Gaelic Storyteller', *Proceedings of the British Academy* (1945).

Hence Nelly, who gives little away about herself throughout the novel, still seems intensely real. The origin of this oral alertness is the Irish story-telling tradition of Hugh and perhaps Pádraig Ó Pronntaigh [Patrick Brontë].

But very little of the matters we have considered sprang to the mind of the lively but unliterary Wright on first reading *Wuthering Heights*. 'I read the Brontë novels with the feeling that I had already known what was coming', he says.[13] It was the story-line that Wright thought he knew. It might be valuable at this point to discuss the similarities between what Emily actually wrote and what Wright had heard from the old men who remembered Hugh Brunty.

Many things are dissimilar. The rivalry in love between the old farmer Burns and Hugh Brunty for the hand of Eilís bears no relation at all to the rivalry between Heathcliff and Edgar Linton. The outcome is also quite different, and the runaway marriage has no parallel except with the escapade after which Heathcliff marries Isabella. The major theme of the dead lover holding the attention of the live has no trace in *The Brontës in Ireland:* all Wright's ghosts are trivial ones. The Boyne farm is a deserted ruin, while Wuthering Heights is at least habitable. The ironic parallel of the second generation does not occur in Wright's story, while in the novel it is vital. It begins to seem far-fetched to compare the story of Hugh Brunty with *Wuthering Heights* at all.

But, of course, the element that Wright thought he recognised was the identity of Heathcliff and Welsh. The latter appears, like Heathcliff, in the vicinity of Liverpool. He is adopted for no good reason except perhaps that of charity, but he worms his way into the family like a changeling and soon becomes his adopted parents' mainstay. He schemes until he wins the property, just like Heathcliff. He then warps the character of the genuine heir in the next generation; we may compare Hareton with Hugh Brunty. Ill-treatment is his constant delight, though he is not considered to be literally a tool of the devil as is sometimes hinted of Heathcliff. But he is the perpetual alien, throwing the house out of its destiny. He has gained his influence through an almost incestuous marriage with a foster-sister (in the novel, this marriage remains a matter of the soul).

It may be worth noting that Heathcliff has only one name which does for both Christian and surname. He is said to be named after a child of the old Earnshaws but he is never called Heathcliff Earnshaw in the book and the singularity of his name increases his oddness. Welsh, too, possesses only one name, said to be a nickname descriptive of his looks and origin. In Wright's narrative he is always called Welsh, though at one point he is

[13] Wright, *Brontës in Ireland,* p. 8.

said to have assumed the name Brontë. He is depicted as wily, violent, and passionate, but like Heathcliff he is capable of gentlemanly behaviour. It is odd that Emily Brontë simply tells us of Heathcliff's three-year absence and never explains or hints where he has been. At this point it almost does seem as if she is following an exemplar and has no interest in the side-issue.

In both stories the ancestral hall collapses under the influence of the cuckoo, though the Boyne house is much worse. The motif of the house in collapse is found in Emily's poems too, and the wild orphan persists throughout her work until the last lengthy fragment of 1846. When Wright describes his feeling that he had read *Wuthering Heights* before, it may have been the orphan story he had particularly in mind. [. . .]

Wright was no literary critic. His reaction to *Wuthering Heights* was spontaneous. The orphan story is the part of the Hugh Brunty legend which corresponds most clearly with *Wuthering Heights*. As I have suggested earlier in this chapter, there is reason to believe it possible that other aspects of the novel have an Irish, or at least a ballad, origin; but it is the orphan story and the story of the orphan's vengeance which bears the closest similarity to the dark legend from eighteenth-century Ireland. It is hard to see how William Wright's identification of this element with the legend of Hugh Brunty which his first Classical teacher made him write in various versions could have no basis whatever in reality.

Wuthering Heights
The First Phase

Edward Chitham

As noted in the Introduction, there is considerable controversy over exactly when Emily Brontë composed *Wuthering Heights*. Some critics believe that the entire novel was written during a nine-month period in 1845–46. Other critics believe that a novel so complexly plotted had to have taken much longer to write, and they point to a much earlier beginning date. Again, no written documentation exists to prove either theory. Here, Edward Chitham presents his

From *The Birth of* Wuthering Heights. New York: St. Martin's, 1998. (Chitham's footnotes have been slightly modified for clarity.)

argument for the way in which *Wuthering Heights* unfolded. Students wishing to follow Chitham's argument throughout the entire text of the novel should consult the book from which this essay is excerpted. [ED.]

It will not be possible to give a page-by-page account of the whole of *Wuthering Heights*, but since my view is, not surprisingly, that the first three chapters were the first section of the book to be written, it seems best to begin by giving an account of their content, in the light of the thesis proposed, namely that there was a major revision of the whole novel in 1846–7 and that though this did affect the first three chapters, some of the core of the story had been established in them, and was not susceptible of change. I assign the date of the first writing of these chapters, for reasons that will become apparent, to the months January to March 1845.

The whole book begins with a date, 1801. Once this date has been given it sets up a timescale which has to be maintained. In itself, however, it is not crucial. Though it turns out that Emily Brontë was using an almanack to perceive the phases of the moon during the progress of her novel, and indeed the same almanack had been used for Gondal before this and was also used by Anne [Brontë] in [*The Tenant of*] *Wildfell Hall*, the actual phases of the moon in 1801 were not the same as those in the 1826 almanack which she used.[1] If '1805' or '1810' had been chosen, would this have made any difference to the story? If not, why choose 1801? There are two possible reasons for this choice. One possible reason, which may have been subconscious, was that this date brings the substance of the action in the first generation to a time when Patrick Brontë was a child. He was born on 17 March 1777 when Catherine was about 12, and Hareton would be born the next year (1778). One of the lowest layers of *Wuthering Heights* is the 'Irish outcast' story, and Emily's choice of date may have enabled her to deal with her father's own memories and her own personal feeling of involvement with them.

The other, and perhaps more likely, point of origin for the date is Ponden Hall, which has a plaque on it describing its rebuilding in 1801 by one Robert Heaton, whose initials close the inscription on the plaque: 'R. H. 1801'. Ponden Hall was one of Emily Brontë's early haunts and it is most likely that the 1801 had stamped itself on her memory as a child, along with some stories from the hall's history which are also in her mind as she writes

---

[1] For Emily Brontë's use of the same almanack as Anne, see Marsden and Jack, eds. *Wuthering Heights* (Oxford, Clarendon, 1976), Introduction, etc.

Wuthering Heights.[2] After its publication a coolness grew up between the Heaton family and Mr. Brontë, and it seems probable that they thought Emily had derived some of her material from their history, perhaps even the character of Heathcliff himself. Nevertheless, it is not at all certain that the date, 1801, was in the earliest writing of the story. I hope to show that it was added later, at the time when it became necessary for Emily to systematise her chronology. As she began to write the 'tale' (after Anne went back to Thorpe Green, perhaps) she need not have thought of any detailed time-scale.

By the end of the first page, some characters are being deployed. Lockwood, whose name could have had various Yorkshire origins, is, as Ian Jack notes in the introduction to the Oxford 'World's Classics' *Wuthering Heights,* a Waverley figure.[3] His function appears to be the stranger-observer, who will mediate the odd world of the Heights to the reader. As the chapter advances Emily becomes interested in his character, making him a fop, later enamoured of the young girl he meets, with a 'susceptible heart' and a good opinion of his own attractiveness. Lockwood's interest in the girl fades as the book proceeds and is not a live issue with the reader for very long. The girl, who turns out to be the second Catherine, does not appear in Chapter I and the possibility of a link between her and Lockwood does not seem to be integral.

Much of this first chapter is given over to a careful description of the house itself. It corresponds very closely with the old delapidated house near Halifax, High Sunderland, whose owners, the Priestley family, were no longer living there when Emily knew it in 1838. There are many ways in which Wuthering Heights reflects High Sunderland. An important one is its name, which Emily has reversed and modified, making:

It seems, then, that the name of the mysterious house which is to be the central dramatic locale of the book was chosen right at the start, and that the original intention was to explore associations formed in the Law Hill

---

[2] Stories of Ponden Hall have been explored by Winifred Gérin (*Emily Brontë,* Chapter 3). It appears in some maps and documents as Ponden House. A particularly useful account of the history of the Heaton family is Mary Butterfield's *The Heatons of Ponden Hall* (Stanbury, 1976).

[3] *Wuthering Heights,* Oxford World's Classics (1981), pp. vii–xii. ["Waverley figure" refers to the protagonist of Sir Walter Scott's 1814 novel, *Waverley.* ED.]

years. Within the next pages, written, it may well seem, in the first few weeks after Anne returned to Thorpe Green, in late January to February 1845, there are 15 or 16 characteristics of the mansion. These were briefly explored in *A Life of Emily Brontë*, but we shall now look at them again, considering whether they are possibly applicable to a whole group of West Yorkshire farmhouses, to only a few, or to High Sunderland particularly. It is clear that Emily Brontë visualises this old house with great clarity, and she makes no mistakes in portraying it, either in this introductory passage or later.[4] Either she had drawn out a plan of the imagined house, or she had a vivid recall of High Sunderland.

Here is the passage in which features of Wuthering Heights are detailed, omitting material that is not relevant to the topography of the house and its contents.

1. [Heathcliff] sullenly preceded me up the *causeway*, calling,
2. as we entered the *court*:
   "Joseph, take Mr. Lockwood's horse; and bring up some wine."
3. ... "No wonder *the grass grows up between the flags,* and cattle are the only hedge cutters."...
4. *Wuthering Heights* is the name of Mr. Heathcliff's dwelling, "Wuthering" being a significant provincial adjective, descriptive of the atmospheric tumult to which its station is exposed in stormy weather. Pure, bracing ventilation they must have up there at all times, indeed: one
5. may guess the power of *the north wind, blowing over the edge,* by
6. the excessive slant of a *few stunted firs at the end of the house;* and by
7. *a range of gaunt thorns* all stretching their limbs one way, as if craving alms of the sun. Happily, the architect had foresight to build
8. it strong: the *narrow windows are deeply set in the wall,* and the
9. *corners defended with large jutting stones.*
   Before passing the threshold, I paused to admire a quantity of
10. *grotesque carving* lavished over the front, and *especially about the*
11. *principal door,* above which, among a wilderness of crumbling
12. *griffins,* and *shameless little boys,* I detected the date "1500," and the name "Hareton Earnshaw." I would have made a few comments, and
13. requested a *short history of the place* ... but ...

---

[4] In general it has been left to residents of the Halifax area to realise how closely *Wuthering Heights* mirrors the geography of the north end of Halifax. Among the pioneers in these matters are T. W. Hanson, for long a member of the Halifax Antiquarian Society, and Hilda Marsden. Some of this material is summarised in [my] *Life of Emily Brontë* and elsewhere, since I consider the period which Emily Brontë spent at Law Hill vital.

14. *One step brought us into the family sitting-room,* without any introductory lobby, or passage: they call it here "the house" pre-eminently . . . I believe at Wuthering Heights the kitchen is forced *to retreat*

15. *altogether into another quarter* . . . I observed no signs of roasting, boiling, or baking . . .

16. . . . to the very roof. The latter had never been underdrawn, its entire anatomy laid bare to an enquiring eye . . .

It is my contention that Emily Brontë actually began writing her story with a description of the house and the Gondal-like character who is being naturalised in Yorkshire, discovered by a Waverley-like interloper. At this point she has no idea how the story will progress, but she sets her scene in intricate detail, summoning up the memory of High Sunderland. Additional details consistent with High Sunderland appear later in the novel.

Evidence on the architectural features of High Sunderland is scattered and contradictory. A visitor to the site now can still see what its situation was, can understand its geographical relationship with Halifax and Law Hill. But for detail it is necessary to rely on secondary material from Halifax record office and elsewhere. This material should be treated with caution. One well-known book prints its illustration back to front and the nineteenth-century print drawn by Briggs and engraved by Wright includes fanciful features of Gothic style which were not originally there. During its demolition in 1950 photographs were taken and are now kept at Shibden Hall, but they do not represent the hall as it was earlier, and it is hard to discover exactly when various features were added or taken away. An 1885 plan shows a barn which appears rarely in illustrations, but an unidentified press cutting at the Brontë Parsonage reproduces a watercolour said to be in the possession of Halifax Antiquarian Society. This shows the barn appearing to be of stone and with drip-moulds over the windows which may be seventeenth-century, or may be in the early nineteenth-century cottage Gothic style. In either case, the barn will have been there during Emily Brontë's stay in the neighbourhood. A large building to the East of the hall (the right in most pictures) was built as a slaughterhouse and would not be there in Emily's day.[5]

Horner (1835) shows that one way to the house was along a flagged causeway to the West of the gateway. A photograph in Raymond's *In the Steps of the Brontës* shows grass growing up through the flags on the extension of this causeway along the front of the house.[6] 'Entered the court'

---

[5] e.g. in Ernest Raymond, *In the Steps of the Brontës* (London: Rich, 1948), facing p. 209.
[6] Ibid., facing p. 96.

implies passing through a barrier such as a gateway, and the entrance from the West was through such a gateway. This disposes of points 1–3 above. The enclosure was not a court, but could well have looked like it, having a field or possibly garden on one side and the south wall of the house on the other. The relation between the name of the house in the novel and the house on which it is based has already been explained. The geographical situation and details of vegetation can be experienced on site, but the illustration in *In the Steps of the Brontës* facing p. 209 looks due North and shows the meaning of the word 'edge' in the novel. Horner's engravings and the later watercolours show a scattering of trees which do not look like thorns and are certainly not firs. They may be sycamores, which is also the case in early pictures of Top or High Withens. That has no thorns either, though many West Yorkshire farmhouses have. Old photographs of Old Ponden Hall show a gnarled oak tree. We may see the range of gaunt thorns in the light of a neglected hawthorn hedge, but it may be that Emily Brontë imported it into her decaying mansion.[7] (Ernest Raymond concludes his chapter with "We can assert with some confidence, I think, that Law Hill and High Sunderland between them gave a first birth to *Wuthering Heights*." Possibly the thorns may be from Law Hill.)

Points 8 and 9 above relate to the narrow windows and corner buttressing. The deep-set, narrow nature of the mullioned windows at High Sunderland is because of the stone casing, which is not original, but perhaps dates from the seventeenth century. There are two prominent buttresses at the hall. One is to the north of the west gateway, through which Emily seems to have passed on a visit to the house. Its function is not clear, but it is shown on Horner's drawing as well as later photographs. It is not precisely 'at the corner' and neither is the other prominent buttress, which is shown at the east end of the south front in the photograph in [Phyllis] Bentley's *The Brontës and Their World*.[8] There are no buttresses at Top Withens, and little to connect it with Wuthering Heights; the identification seems to stem from Ellen Nussey, who is most unlikely to have seen or known of High Sunderland.

The carving at High Sunderland seems a unique feature. It consists of both free-standing and relief carving in three main places: outside the west gateway, inside the west gateway and at the front door. Putting together the various illustrations, it seems to have included:

---

[7] There are some stunted thorns near Law Hill, but the layout of Emily's school is most unlike Wuthering Heights. Other suggestions for the origin of Wuthering Heights have included Emmott Hall, Colne. (Romer Wilson, *All Alone* [London: Chatto, 1928], facing p. 252.)

[8] Photo by G. Bernard Wood, Bentley, op. cit., p. 90.

1. • a naked hairy giant, free-standing, on the buttress;
   • relief or free-standing heads over the gateway;
   • a frieze over the gateway, consisting of animals, perhaps stags, and faces;
   • patterns of relief sculpture including two flying birds, a coat of arms, a head on the keystone, and possibly five other human heads, all small in comparison; stylised plants and other architectural features. These are inside the west gateway.
2. • two naked male figures of large scale, twisted and grotesque, of which one still had its head in the first part of this century, while the other head is missing;
   • a relief carving of a stylised sun;
   • a lozenge shape and other minor abstract carving. These are over the front door.

During the demolition process in 1950, some of this carving was bought by a Mr. West of Halifax, who intended to have the gateway rebuilt in his garden. This project was never fulfilled, but at least he saved some of the carving, and was subsequently able to return it to Shibden Hall, where part of the collection still is. If these identifications are accepted, we may see the Lintons in final ascendancy, incorporating some of the wildest elements of Wuthering Heights in their own lowland mansion!

These sculptured figures are prominent in the novel's description of the house, and even those who think Top Withens is a model for Wuthering Heights accept that this element is from High Sunderland. There appears to be no other West Yorkshire hall that Emily could have seen which has anything like these sculptures. Comparing the description above with Emily's words in the novel, we can surely see identity. The carving *was* grotesque, it *was* crumbling, it *was* above both principal doorways, there were birds, though they may not precisely have been griffins, the three naked male figures correspond to the shameless boys. The date 1500 and the name 'Hareton Earnshaw' are not on the front of High Sunderland, but there are some engraved Latin mottoes one of which was placed over the front door, and the sun sculpture occupied a position where a date might have been expected. '1500' is pure fiction, and not very accurate in view of the style of the house. However, most of the features in my points 10–12 are accounted for.

One interesting small point from *Wuthering Heights* links with a point above. In Chapter 21, Catherine the younger is being taken on a tour of the house by Hareton. She asks him about the inscription over the door. He cannot read it and calls it 'some damnable writing'. 'Can't read it?' cries

Catherine . . . 'I can read it . . . It's English' (189). Behind this remark could possibly lurk a dim memory of Emily's when in 1838 she had been shown High Sunderland and looked up to see writing which was not English, but Latin, a language she could probably read but her companions could not. Otherwise there seems no reason to mention the language of the inscription, which would naturally be expected to be in English.

No one would ask for a history of Top Withens, but as point 13 above shows, Wuthering Heights looked as if it merited a place in the history books, just as High Sunderland has had a place in such books as [Louis] Ambler's *The Old Halls and Manor Houses of Yorkshire* (London, 1913). The point is elaborated later in the novel, where Wuthering Heights is compared to a castle. This comparison would be out of place with any of the farmhouses nearer Haworth.

High Sunderland in the nineteenth century is quite badly documented so far, though we must hope more evidence will emerge. Photographs show a small porch, so that two or three steps would have been needed to take the visitor from the causeway to the living room (the 'house'). There is certainly no passage, but perhaps this might be considered a small lobby. High Sunderland kitchen was on the right of the living room, and this coincides with Wuthering Heights, as later descriptions show. A problem which seems hard to settle is the matter of the ceiling (point 16). Shibden Hall museum possesses photographs taken in 1950 when High Sunderland was being demolished.[9] These seem to confirm a plan of *c.* 1905 apparently showing separate chambers on the first floor. This is the only point in which the description of Wuthering Heights flatly contradicts the evidence about High Sunderland. It is possible that nineteenth-century alterations are responsible for this anomaly. We can certainly hope for more evidence to emerge.

The name of Thrushcross Grange is also found on the first page of our text, but there is almost no focus on it, or the contrast between it and Wuthering Heights for the first few chapters. I shall defer consideration of the name and the factual basis for descriptions of the house to a later stage. Though the name Hareton Earnshaw stands over the door of the mansion, it is some time before we are told that the boor-like man who helps around the house is Hareton Earnshaw. Chapters 1 and 3 are mainly concerned with establishing the ambience of Wuthering Heights, while Chapter 2 concerns a series of blunders and confusions suffered by Lockwood and felt too by the reader. It does not seem to me to be quite of a piece with the rest

---

[9] Copies at BPM [the Brontë Parsonage Museum], e.g. No. SB 4115.

of the opening section. However, Hareton's name is significant, and comes from a different strand of Emily Brontë's imagination.

'Hareton' sounds like a West Yorkshire name of the type of Hartley, Sutcliffe, etc., but in fact this is not so. Emily uses the same principle she has already adopted for the name of her mysterious house. She takes a local character and scrambles him: R. HEATON becomes in anagram HARETON. Quite probably she used more than just the name of the Brontës' neighbours at Ponden Hall, and this may be the reason for the Heaton family's antipathy towards the book. It seems likely that Robert Heaton of Ponden was particularly kind to Emily, so that the emergence of a young man with uncouth characteristics and a dubious history which coincides with elements of Heaton history seems inappropriate. Her use of the name, even in garbled form, seems less than tactful.[10]

For several reasons, the end of Chapter 2 and most of Chapter 3 seem to have been written during February and March 1845. Two major ones stand out. First, there is the snow. As has already been shown, Emily likes to portray weather that is actually present at the time of writing. It would certainly be rash to say she always does so, but the poems have shown us that this is usual. According to Shackleton, the Keighley meteorologist, February was 'very cold and dry'. Emily reflects this at the start of Chapter 2 with: 'On that bleak hill top the earth was hard with black frost, and the air made me shiver through every limb' (paragraph 3). By 3 March the wind had turned to the north-east, and a month began which Shackleton calls 'mostly severe'. On 3 March itself there was sleet and snow.

The second point is the parallel with Emily's poetry, especially the well known 'Cold in the earth', dated 3 March. This poem is ostensibly a Gondal piece, with the superscription 'R. Alcona to J. Brenzaida'. It laments the separation between the two, which took place 'fifteen wild Decembers' ago ('fifteen wild Decembers . . . have melted into spring'—again we note the precise timing).[11] Emily's mood is very sadly nostalgic, and though the 'fifteen' may have to do with Gondal chronology, now reasonably well established, there is more to this than a light fiction. The pain of separation in the poem is exactly paralleled by the pain of separation from Catherine expressed by Heathcliff in Chapter 3 of *Wuthering Heights* when Lockwood cries out after seeing her ghost. This theme was on Emily's mind in the first part of March 1845, and we may reasonably date Chapter 3 to that month.

---

[10] Robert Heaton was a churchwarden at Haworth. He also seems to have been responsible for sheltering the Brontë family on the day of the alarming 'bog burst' (2 September 1824). It is alleged that he planted a pear tree for Emily at Ponden. (Mary Butterfield, *The Heatons of Ponden Hall*, p. 19.)

[11] See Roper (166–67). [ED.]

Chapter 3 continues the material of Chapter 1 and parts of Chapter 2. The Waverley figure, Lockwood, is ensconsed in a rarely used chamber, dreams and suffers a strange experience. We first learn that Heathcliff has an 'odd notion' about the room from the housekeeper, whose name has been given as Zillah in the second part of Chapter 2. If Zillah had been in his employment long, she would have known why he had this 'odd notion', and we shall return to discuss housekeepers in the novel later. Organisation must by this time have been pressing Emily, and this section may be an interpolation. Of the earliest stratum, however, are Lockwood's two dreams.

First, he dreams about an affray at the 'Chapel of Gimmerden Sough'. This form of the name does not recur. Hilda Marsden has an ingenious suggestion about the derivation of 'Gimmerden', which if true makes Emily Brontë a philologist.[11] Whether we accept her point or not, the final element in the place-name, -DEN, does reflect Shibden and suggests that Shibden Hall was already in Emily's mind. When the name next occurs it is as Gimmerton. Lockwood's dream of a chapel riot introduces material which is never used again, and which has puzzled commentators. Why is it necessary to bring in 'Jabes Branderham'? What does Lockwood mean by his curious remark to the fevered Heathcliff a page or two later when he asks, 'Was not the Reverend Jabes Branderham akin to you on the mother's side?' What sort of first name is 'Jabes' anyway? Editions from 1850 onward have 'Jabez' suggesting an emendment by Charlotte, but these two strange and anomalous spellings are retained in 1847, and they do pose a problem.

It is Joseph who leads Lockwood to the old chapel. Joseph's part in the novel has been much disputed. His rough eloquence has been variously interpreted: he is a chorus, he balances Nelly, he is a canting sample of Christianity to pose against the paganism of the book's message.[12] What seems clear is that he is integral to the book from the start. He is as much a part of Wuthering Heights as the Earnshaws. It seems likely that he was taken over by Emily with High Sunderland and is based on actuality. Here he drives Lockwood, in this early written chapter, to dream about the harshness of a sectarian sermon.

The long sermon is not revisited; the pilgrims' staves remain in the dream. One can suppose that Emily Brontë left this episode in at revision because of its nightmare qualities, which allow it to lead up to the Cather-

---

[11] *Brontë Society Transactions*, Vol. 57 (1967).

[12] Melvin R. Watson in *Nineteenth Century Fiction* (1949), 'more ironic than comic'; David Cecil in *Early Victorian Novelists* (1935), 'drawn in the flat rather than in the round, made individual by a few strongly marked, personal idiosyncrasies' (of Nelly Dean also); 'a source of burlesque', Stevie Davies in *Emily Brontë: Heretic* (1994), p. 187, are other viewpoints.

ine episode. Without it the novel would be paler, but it is not structural, it is part of the original conception of the book. Likewise the ghostly child is also part of the very first writing of *Wuthering Heights,* and is prepared for by the books Catherine has been using as a diary. Her habit is very like that of her creator, using every scrap of space on pieces of paper. Surely this episode of a dream of a lost child derives from Emily's experience in spring 1845 of the heartache at 20 years' separation from her elder sister, Maria? The 'twenty years' of the child's answer, the fact that this is a child not an adult, and therefore not the ghost at the time of her separation from Heathcliff (when she bears a child herself as a married woman), suggests that Emily's vision *started* with the frozen child. Catherine was not 'Linton' 20 years previously, according to the chronology which Emily was so carefully to work out, but had not yet apparently done. By the time she had worked it out, she may have realised that the child episode would not fit, but it was the germ of her whole book, and to lose it would have been disaster. The crucial illness and death of Maria Brontë took place 20 *years* before this chapter in real time, and Emily was going to keep this in even though it was an anomaly in her chronological pattern. There seems no other explanation of this, and the consequences of the decision were far-reaching.

Heathcliff's arrival leads to a conversation which emphasises the primary material of this part of *Wuthering Heights:* the haunting of an old, derelict house which Emily had seen at Halifax. The haunted house at this point is, as Lockwood says, 'swarming with ghosts and goblins!' (The word has already been used at the beginning of the chapter of his vision of air 'swarming with Catherines'.) It is here that Emily first begins to suggest an origin for Heathcliff, whom she has created as an anomaly in Yorkshire. Lockwood suggests that Catherine might be a changeling. In the outcome it is Heathcliff whose life is portrayed as possibly that of a changeling, while Catherine is of 'the old stock', but we can suppose that it was at this point, probably in March 1845, that the changeling story became associated with the primitive 'desolate High Sunderland' story, which may be in focus because of a joint decision with Anne.

In the rest of the chapter Emily's imagination transfers the feelings she has over the loss and haunting of Maria and possibly Elizabeth to her created Heathcliff. The tone of this is very similar to the tone of 'Cold in the earth', as has many times been pointed out. The poetic intensity of this episode led to a period when Emily concentrated on poetry. It seems highly likely that these first three chapters, in an early form, now languished as so many poem beginnings languished, awaiting continuation. This would need to wait at least for the return of Anne from Thorpe Green in June.

Etching of the celebrated Yordas Cave, the real-life counterpart of Emily Brontë's Fairy Cave, located beneath Penistone Quarry (called Penistone Crag in the novel).

FROM WILLIAM WESTALL, *VIEWS OF THE CAVES NEAR INGLETON, GORDALE SCAR, AND MALHAM COVE* (LONDON: MURRAY, 1818).

Yorkshire Landscapes
in *Wuthering Heights*

Christopher Heywood

As the controversy over the Gondal poems presented in Part Two reveals, there has been considerable debate about the intent and context of *Wuthering Heights*. Because Emily Brontë appears to have led
such a sheltered life, she has been approached as a mystic, a recluse,
or an eccentric who knew little about the realities of the world around
her. This was not at all the case. From a very early age, Emily and her
sisters and brother followed very closely the political and intellectual
developments of their time. Their father was a diligent newspaper
reader who faithfully read to his children the latest military news or
the most recent parliamentary debate about Catholic Emancipation.
We know that Emily Brontë left her home for extended periods only
three times during her life, once to study at Roe Head School, once
to teach at Law Hill, and once to accompany her sister Charlotte to
study in Brussels. She heard stories of rival neighboring families
while at Law Hill, and she made extensive walking tours not only in
Yorkshire but also in the Law Hill area. Christopher Heywood argues
that the landscape depicted in *Wuthering Heights* is a composite of all
of the areas in which she lived, no matter how briefly. [ED.]

When Matthew Arnold visited Haworth in 1852 in his capacity as Inspector
of Schools, his busy timetable prevented him from visiting the churchyard.
As a result, his poem 'Haworth Churchyard' invokes a part of the town
which he had not seen, and is a literary borrowing from Emily Brontë's
novel. Charlotte's death prompted an elegy in which Arnold envisaged
Branwell, Anne and Emily awaiting reunion with their sister in grass-
covered, open-air graves among rural moors. In sharp contrast, Haworth
churchyard was dangerously overcrowded in the mid-Victorian decades,
and like other graveyards in towns and villages with expanding popula-
tions, it had the appearance of being paved with horizontal slabs.[1] Besides,

---

Essays in Criticism 48 (1998): 13–34. (All parenthetical references are to this
New Riverside Edition.)

[1] 'Haworth Church', frontispiece to J. Horsfall Turner, *Haworth — Past and Present,*
(1879).

the Brontës are not buried in the churchyard: Anne's grave is at Scarborough, and the rest of her family are entombed in a family vault inside Haworth church. Disconcerted by Elizabeth Gaskell's letter of congratulation and correction when his poem first appeared, Arnold wrote in reply: 'I am almost sorry you told me about the place of their burial'.[2]

Arnold's error arose from Emily's use of the two landscapes of the old West Riding, the Pennine region running from Sheffield to Sedbergh. Northwards from Skipton, the mountainous limestone highlands run past Cowan Bridge. The low-lying gritstone moorland runs southwards through Haworth to Hathersage. The two landscapes are geologically and geographically distinct, but in *Wuthering Heights,* both appear in a single setting. As though in a dream, a moorland of southern Pennine type appears in the second part of the story, carpeting a limestone mountain landscape of the northern type. The limestone landscape, identified in clues scattered across the first eighteen chapters, is haunted by betrayal, oppression, and death. With no change of setting, the moorland landscape is first glimpsed at the grave of the elder Catherine (150). In the last seventeen chapters it is the setting for the younger Catherine's restoration of order in a blighted pastoral society.

Not suspecting a composite landscape in *Wuthering Heights,* Arnold supposed that Emily had merely described her father's parish. His lapse followed from Charlotte's unfulfilled offer, in her Preface to the 1850 edition of *Wuthering Heights,* to take the reader on a tour of 'the outlying hills and hamlets in the West-Riding of Yorkshire and their inhabitants', in order to satisfy the curiosity of 'strangers [. . .] who are unacquainted with the locality where the scenes of the story are laid'.[3] Instead, her next two paragraphs dwell on the rusticity of Yorkshire, and assert the nun-like seclusion of Emily, here presented as a 'home-bred, country girl.' The digression is pervaded, however, by an ironic impersonation of a supposed metropolitan reader's patronising response to *Wuthering Heights.* It leaves the Yorkshire originals for Emily's novel unidentified. Having hinted that Emily was remote from her father's parishioners, Charlotte puzzlingly adds that 'she knew them, knew their ways, their language, and their family histories; she could hear of them with interest and talk of them with detail, minute, graphic, and accurate'. Certainly, Emily rendered the Haworth dialect with precision,[4] but no sustained match for her fictional families and their re-

---

[2] 'Haworth Churchyard', *Matthew Arnold. A Critical Edition of the Major Works,* ed. Miriam Allott and R. H. Super, (1992), pp. 216–220 (ll. 79–85); also, pp. 548–9, 530.
[3] Charlotte Brontë, Preface to the 1850 edition (19–23 in this volume).
[4] K. M. Petyt, *Wuthering Heights and the Haworth Dialect,* (1970).

gion has been found among towns set, like Haworth, amidst the eastward facing moorlands of the gritstone southern Pennines. Charlotte's phrase, 'outlying hills and hamlets', does not fit Haworth, an industrialised community since the expansion of the woollen industry in Tudor times. Until the early decades of the nineteenth century it had been the most populous chapelry in the rapidly expanding parish of Bradford. The widespread presumption of an unbridgable gulf between Emily's novel and its Yorkshire subject matter has followed from the perplexing disparity between the Haworth region and the landscape she created.[5]

An early step towards resolving this difficulty was taken by James Henry Dixon in his *Chronicles and Stories of the Craven Dales*, a posthumously published collection of essays which had appeared, according to his publisher's note, in a Skipton monthly publication between 1853 and 1857.[6] In what we may take as a gloss on Charlotte's veiled phrasing in the 1850 Preface, Dixon noted that Emily's fictional landscape was a recognisable portrayal of a limestone landscape from the Yorkshire Dales. He wrote:

> Let the reader turn to *Wuthering Heights,* and if he know anything of Craven [the Pennine limestone highlands] or its scenery, he will find in that wonderful novel some truly graphic sketching. Long before we knew anything of the author, we said 'This is Craven!' and we knew where to find the bleak and barren moorland solitudes, where the misanthropic hero had his crazy dwelling. Perhaps, we could have pointed out the misanthrope himself.[7]

The region around Ingleton, Thornton in Lonsdale and Cowan Bridge fits this veiled reference. Dixon's insight was ignored for the time being by the early Brontë scholars, who were scantily versed in Yorkshire topography and literary tradition, but it matches and illumines Charlotte's hints. Emily's oral, written and topographical sources appear in the northern limestone parishes of Hornby, Sedbergh, Thornton in Lonsdale, and Tunstall, among prominent families of the region: Harrington, Mason, Redmayne, Sill, Stanley, Sutton and Tatham. In addition, following the lead given by Robert Story, a prominent member of Branwell's literary circle, Emily drew on the history and associations of the Clifford family of Skipton. The core of her narrative came from Dent, a chapelry of Sedbergh and

---

[5] See, for example, David Daiches and N. Flower, *The Literary Topography of the British Isles,* (1986), pp. 148–9.

[6] On the basis of Dixon's contributions in April to June 1853 in a sole surviving copy of the first few months' issue, the unnamed periodical can be identified with reasonable certainty as *The Craven Herald,* (Skipton Public Library).

[7] J. H. Dixon, *Chronicles and Stories of the Craven Dales,* (Skipton, 1881), p. 18.

the source of widely publicised stories about the Masons and the Sills. These two families appear in *Jane Eyre* as the Masons and the Rochesters, and in *Wuthering Heights* as the Lintons and the Earnshaws.[8] Charlotte maintained silence about this shared material, but betrayed her insight into Emily's Yorkshire sources by noting in the Preface that her sister's novel contained stories 'gathered from the real'.

Arnold's notion that Emily was 'in art [. . .] Inferior' (ll. 82–3) reflects his adherence to Charlotte's presentation of her sister as a 'nursling of the moors', confined by 'convent gates', hewing an amorphous novel, 'rustic all through', 'moorish and wild, and knotty as the root of heath', in a 'wild workshop', using 'a rude chisel', and working 'from no model but the vision of [her] meditations'. None the less, Emily's skilfully wrought landscape pervades his poem. 'Haworth Churchyard' emerges, indeed, as a sustained homage to Emily rather than to Charlotte, who appears only in the poet's guarded handling, in his opening lines, of their meeting in the company of Harriet Martineau. Arnold's references to the music of plover, bee, and grouse in summer (ll. 134, 112–124) are borrowings from the second part of *Wuthering Heights*. In a frequently cited passage, Catherine Linton debates with her cousin whether the boisterous or the becalmed aspect of moorland life—the Shelleyan or the Keatsian—resembles heaven more closely:

> rocking in a rustling green tree, with a west wind blowing, and bright, white clouds flitting rapidly above, and not only larks, but throstles, and blackbirds, and linnets, and cuckoos pouring out music on every side, and the moors seen at a distance

or 'lying from morning till evening on a bank of heath in the middle of the moors, with the bees humming dreamily about among the bloom' (209). Lacking close knowledge of the old West Riding, however, Arnold was unable to detect that the graveyard in his poem, another borrowing from *Wuthering Heights,* derives ultimately from a scantily occupied rural churchyard which Emily had seen in the Yorkshire Dales. Lockwood observes 'the three headstones on the slope next the moor—the middle one, grey, and half buried in heath', and muses 'how anyone could ever imagine unquiet slumbers, for the sleepers in that quiet earth' (276). Unknown to himself, Arnold's rural graveyard reproduces Emily's accurate memory of

---

[8] C. Heywood, 'A Yorkshire Background for *Wuthering Heights*', *Modern Language Review*, 88, (1993), 817–830; also, C. Heywood, '"The Helks Lady" and other Legends Surrounding *Wuthering Heights*', *Lore and Language*, 11, (1992–3), 127–142; and C. Heywood, 'Yorkshire Slavery in *Wuthering Heights*', *Review of English Studies*, 38, (1987), 184–98.

the graveyard at St. Oswald's Church, Thornton in Lonsdale, the last coaching stop before Cowan Bridge.[9]

Emily's powers of observation at an early age are suggested by her teachers' memories of her at Cowan Bridge during the half-year preceding her seventh birthday: 'a darling child [...] quite the pet nursling of the school', who 'reads prettily'.[10] Her exact memory of the scenery along the coaching road appears in her handling of the view of Ingleborough from Thornton in Lonsdale. To the right in the view north-eastwards, matching Nelly's recollection of Wuthering Heights hill in the view north-east from the Grange window (Chs. 10, 11, 15), Ingleborough rises above White Scars. In that view, the neighbouring Whernside (Yorkshire's highest hill) is invisible. This local peculiarity explains the omission of Whernside from several early maps.[11] The layout of the hills in Emily's novel departs slightly from the standard maps at this point, yet she remained faithful, it appears, to her memory of the landscape she had seen. In that view, too, Gragareth forms a lofty horizon on the left, matching the fictional peak named Penistone Crag. The Pennine model for the eponymous hill in *Wuthering Heights* rises to the right: the appearance, locality and atmosphere of the hills in the novel exactly match those around Ingleborough, Yorkshire's most celebrated natural landmark, as they appear in the view from the coaching road. Emily's masterly handling of that landscape in her maturity justifies the later impression of her teacher in Brussels, Constantin Heger: 'She should have been a man—a great navigator. Her powerful reason would have deduced new spheres of discovery from the knowledge of the old; and her strong, imperious will would never have been daunted by opposition or difficulty; never have given way but with life'.[12]

Based on exceptional powers of reading and observation, Emily's mature handling of the landscape around Cowan Bridge reflects her command of the conventions of mountain landscape description associated with the Picturesque movement. The Sublime or heightened Picturesque occurred, William Gilpin had maintained, in the mind's reflection upon moments of turbulence in nature:

If the imagination be thus fired by these romantic scenes even in their *common* state, how much more may we suppose it wrought on, when

---

[9] Heywood, 'A Yorkshire Background' op. cit., loc cit.

[10] Esther Chadwick, *In the Footsteps of the Brontës,* (1914), pp. 75–6; Clergy Daughters' School Register 1824–5, Cumbria Record Office, Kendal: Casterton School, WDS/38.

[11] J. E. Rawnsley, *Antique Maps of Yorkshire and Their Makers,* (Leeds, 1970); also, Heywood, 'Yorkshire Background', op. cit., loc. cit.

[12] Cited in Winifrid Gérin, *Emily Brontë,* (1967), p. 127.

they strike us under some *extraordinary* circumstance of beauty, or terror—in the tranquillity of a calm, or the agitation of a storm?[13]

Gilpin's insights were expanded and modified by his extensive literary following. Wordsworth associated the Sublime with the creation of the earth,
and beauty with later activity: 'Sublimity is the result of Nature's first great
dealings with the superficies of the earth; but the general tendency of her
subsequent operations is towards the production of beauty'.[14] In numerous guides to the northern mountain landscapes, Gilpin's admirers praised
the highlands north of Skipton as a nursery of ancient virtue, and stigma-
tised the southern moorland as a featureless bed of industry, vice, and
overpopulation. William Hutchinson wrote of Stainmoor: 'a dreary prospect extended to the eye, the hills were cloathed in heath, and all around a
scene of barrenness and deformity'.[15] John Housman offered further dis-
approval: 'The country, after leaving Bradford, has a naked appearance.
Manufactures continue; and the population great, and increasing'. Around
Keighley, Housman observed, 'The surface of the country is rather uneven,
and the general appearance somewhat barren'.[16] T. D. Whitaker presented
Haworth in similar guise: 'On the whole, Haworth is to Bradford as Hep-
tenstall to Halifax—almost at the extremity of population, high, bleak,
dirty and difficult of access'.[17] The contrast is embodied in a pair of pictures by Gilpin, showing the same hills in two forms, as a menacing and
Non-Picturesque moorland in one, and in the other, as Picturesque, light-
drenched limestone crags.[18]

Probably taking Gilpin's double landscape as a model, Emily portrayed
a single setting under two aspects. Her Picturesque but dangerous limestone hills (Chs. 1–18) are suddenly clad in a Non-Picturesque but fertile
moorland, patterned on Haworth Moor (Chs. 16–34) and laid like a mantle
over a topography taken from the hills around Thornton in Lonsdale. Ex-

---

[13] William Gilpin, *Observations on [. . .] the Mountains and Lakes of Cumberland and
Westmoreland, Relative Chiefly to Picturesque Beauty, Made in the Year 1772*, 2 vols.,
(1808), vol. I, p. 131. See also C. Heywood, 'The Romantic Non-Picturesque: Emily
Brontë's Yorkshire Landscape', in *Romanticism and Wild Places*, ed. Paul Hullah, (Edinburgh: forthcoming).

[14] William Wordsworth, *Guide to the Lakes*, ed. E. de Sélincourt, (1906), p. 35.

[15] W. Hutchinson, *An Excursion to the Lakes in Westmoreland and Cumberland: with a
Tour through part of the Northern Counties*, (1776), p. 12.

[16] J. Housman, *A Descriptive Tour and Guide to the Lakes, Caves, Mountains, and other
Natural Curiosities, in Cumberland, Westmoreland, Lancashire, and a Part of the West
Riding of Yorkshire*, (1800), pp. 18–19.

[17] T. D. Whitaker, *Loidis and Elmete*, (1817), p. 356.

[18] W. Gilpin, 'Picturesque and Non-Picturesque Mountain Landscapes', in W. Gilpin,
Three Essays, (1792), pp. 18–19.

ploiting and boldly recasting the Picturesque writers' ideas about the York-shire landscape, Emily framed her story within Lockwood's experience of a Sublime or terrifying storm at the beginning and a complementary calm at the close of his narrative. In portraying the moorland landscape as a source of life and regeneration, Emily inverted the moral values which Gilpin had assigned to the Picturesque limestone and Lake landscapes and the Non-Picturesque southern moorland. Nelly Dean's four brief vignettes are miniature masterpieces in the language of the Picturesque movement (Chs. 10, 11, 15, 18). They construct a landscape closely matching the setting around Thornton in Lonsdale. In the manner of Picturesque guides, com-pass points on the guidestone at the crossroads (Ch. 11), together with other clues, define the positions of Wuthering Heights hill and its neigh-bouring hills, and of the farmhouse, beck, cave, glen, village, and Grange. In the Picturesque idiom the beck sounds musically over stones, and is heard through trees (Ch. 15). Pale limestone crags, the source of the white building materials and of lime production at Gimmerton (Chs. 1, 8), soar above the darkening western seaboard plain in the golden light at sunset (Ch. 18), or appear swathed in ground mist at moonrise (Ch. 10). Unlike the Picturesque guides, however, Nelly presents the landscape in scattered and occasionally cryptic phrases. Reassembled, her clues yield a sustained map of her parish.

Sources available to the Brontës give counterparts in matching positions around Thornton in Lonsdale for the fictional farmhouse, manor, cross-roads, cave, limestone, coal mines, beck, sough, glen, churchyard, and the late and scanty crops in a pastoral region. Before the opening of the present Ingleton bypass road in the summer of 1825, the coach's halt at Thornton in Lonsdale was bracketed by steep hills in both directions. This suggests that the halts made by the Brontës at the Marton Arms, then named the Church Stile Inn, at the end and beginning of their two journeys, would have included pauses for the horses. These would be long enough for a sharp-sighted child to observe the churchyard and Hallsteads, the small manor screened by trees to the south-west of the inn, and the surrounding hills. From the corresponding station, at an hour matching that of the ar-rival of the coach from Keighley, Isabella views the sunset across the Grange park in *Wuthering Heights* (Ch. 13). Matching the novel, contem-porary maps show the two-mile track northwards from the church to Braeda Garth, the isolated farmhouse in Kingsdale. A mile and half beyond Braeda Garth, at a point exactly matching that of Emily's Fairy Cave, they indicate its Yorkshire counterpart, the celebrated Yordas Cave. [See the il-lustration on page 348.]

Minor alterations conform with the Picturesque doctrine that parts of a landscape may have to be moved: 'it cannot be supposed, that every scene

[. . .] is *correctly picturesque*', Gilpin observed.[19] In *Wuthering Heights,* the northern arm of the complex crossroads at Thornton in Lonsdale occupies a position a few hundred yards to the east of its Yorkshire counterpart, and the Grange park has grown from the few hundred yards of Hallsteads to two miles. As in many Dales parishes, the parish church in the novel stands away from the village, calling as a result for the direction eastwards to 'G' on the guidestone at the crossroads by the church (Ch. 11). Emily positioned Gimmerton at a place matching that of Ingleton, but moved its parish church to a position closer to the village than that of its Yorkshire counterpart, St. Oswald's Church in the neighbouring hamlet of Thornton in Lonsdale. Another move placed the Grange two miles southwest from the crossroads among woods near the road along the beck, in the position corresponding to that of Burton in Lonsdale or Black Burton, a village with numerous early coal pits. Some of the clues are presented as enigmas. Clearly the farmhouse is two miles up the valley to the north, but that distance is nowhere stated. Emily allows us to detect that distance by subtracting the two miles across the park from four between farmhouse and Grange (Ch. 3). Similarly, Gretna Green is not named, yet the clandestine marriages (Chs. 11, 27) depend on its location to the northwest, a direction omitted on the fictional guidestone. The seemingly anomalous distance to London (Ch. 20) gives the required proximity to the Scottish border. Other peculiarities of the outlying Yorkshire topography, as in the distances from Settle and Sedbergh, are recognisable but not named. These are clues in a topographical game which Emily plays with her imagined reader in order to sharpen and clarify her meaning or intention.

Emily's sharp childhood memory was amplified, it appears, by her mature reading of Picturesque writing and the available maps. Details not to be seen in the view from the coaching road appear in the two maps titled *Map of the County of York,* by John Tuke (1780) and Thomas Jeffreys (1767). The 1816 edition of Tuke's map shows the modern drainage ditch in the waterlogged Kingsdale, a feature which cannot be seen from the road but which exactly matches Emily's 'sough [ditch] that drains the marshes' (Ch. 10). Distances between towns are shown in the numerous editions between the 1780s and the 1820s of Daniel Paterson's *Roads of Britain.* Emily's knowledge of Yorkshire topographical and travel literature reappears in her adaptations from such Picturesque guides as J. Hutton's *Tour to the Caves* (1780), which appeared among the Addenda to the second and later editions of Thomas West's *Guide to the Lakes* (1784). This work was

---

[19] W. Gilpin, *Observations,* op. cit., p. 127.

available to the Brontës among books at Ponden House. The tradition of writing on the Yorkshire Dales in the Picturesque mode culminated in T. D. Whitaker's *The History and Antiquities of the Deanery of Craven* (1805) and *An History of Richmondshire* (1821), the former listed among books at the Keighley Mechanics' Institute Library and the latter illustrated by Turner. Whitaker's phrasing reappears in a book which he inspired and which the Brontës probably read, *Gleanings in Craven* (1838), by Frederic Montagu. Adaptations of phrases and ideas from these and other writers on the Dales occur in Emily's landscape descriptions, sharpened by her terse lyricism, and masked by their appearance among Nelly's scattered asides. The presentation of the story through a southern memoirist's diary is foreshadowed in Montagu's narrative of his travels through the eyes of a southern letter-writer. Viewing Gordale Scar and Malham Cove, he observed that among 'the clefts in the rocks' sides, or wherever a lodgment of earth appears, the deep and glossy green of the yew refreshes the eye in its wandering over the pale grey of the vast rock'.[20] His phrasing echoes Whitaker's view of the same formation in the *Deanery of Craven:* 'Wherever a cleft in the rock, or a lodgment of earth appears, the yew-tree [. . .] contrasts its deep and glossy green with the pale grey of the lime-stone'.[21] The phrases reappear in Emily's more compact description of Wuthering Heights hill and its companion, Penistone Crag: 'bare masses of stone, with hardly enough earth in their clefts to nourish a stunted tree' (Ch. 18). Nelly's panoramic view of those hills at sunset exactly matches the view of Leck Fell, Gragareth and Ingleborough from Cowan Bridge.

Further landscape descriptions in *Wuthering Heights* echo and improve the repertoire of early writing on the Dales. Lockwood's wandering in the park of Thrushcross Grange (Ch. 3) is anticipated by William Seward, who notes in his *Tour to Yordes Cave* (1802) that the small size of the park at Hall-steads is forgotten by the wanderer among its trees. Hutton's *Tour,* apparently among the most closely read of Emily's literary sources, includes a description of the valley of the Twiss and the Greta, the counterpart of the 'glen' referred to by Nelly Dean (Ch. 10). Hutton notes the 'deep grotesque glen' formed by Kingsdale Beck, the isolation of Kingsdale, and the gusts which produce peculiar clouds at the summit of Ingleborough. He remarks on the horrific qualities of the caves around Ingleborough, and their association with fairies. He observes the pure manners and morals of Dales society in this region: 'Having little intercourse with the luxurious, vicious, and designing part of mankind, they were temperate, substantial, sincere,

---

[20]T. D. Whitaker, *The History and Antiquities of the Deanery of Craven,* (1805), p. 194.
[21]Frederic Montagu, *Gleanings in Craven,* (1838), p. 102.

and hospitable'.[22] In Kingsdale he discovers a refuge: 'seldom visited by man, and never by the sun for near half a year. No monk or anchoret could desire a more retired situation for his cell, or disappointed lover to moralize on the inconstancy of his nymph, and the vanity of the world'.[23] Hutton's impressions reappear in the 'atmospheric tumult' found by Lockwood at Gimmerton (26), and his 'hermit's life' (91) among people who '*do* live more in earnest, more in themselves, and less in surface, change, and frivolous external things' (70). Unlike Hutton's, however, Emily's amorist is a 'weak wretch' who views himself through female eyes: 'what did I do? I confess it with shame—shrunk icily into myself, like a snail; at every glance retired colder and farther; till finally the poor innocent was led to doubt her own senses' (27).

Emily's presentation of the most celebrated of the Picturesque Yorkshire Dales echoes the widespread knowledge that picturesque settings had been tainted by slavery. William Blake's illustrations of grotesque cruelty darken *The Narrative of a Five Years' Expedition Against the Revolted Negroes of Surinam* (1795), by John Gabriel Stedman. Comparable pictures appear in the *Voyage pittoresque dans le Brésil* (1827–39), by Johan Moritz Rugendas, and Jean-Baptiste Debret's *Voyage pittoresque et historique au Brésil* (1834–39). An informative work was William Beckford's *Remarks upon the Situation of Negroes in Jamaica* (1788), translated as *Vues pittoresques de la Jamaïque, avec une description [. . .] du traitement et des moeurs des nègres* (1793). Perhaps the Brontës had seen these in Brussels, or among books belonging to Theodore Dury, founder of the Keighley Mechanics' Institute, or among books belonging to the Taylors of Gomersal. T. D. Whitaker's history of the Clifford family of Skipton in his *Craven Deanery* (1805) includes a fragment from a sea-captain's journal of a Tudor mission to West Africa, under the patronage of George Clifford of Skipton, third Earl of Cumberland, a founder of the English slave trade. 'The following passage', Whitaker wrote, 'may be commended to the captain and crew of a modern slave ship: "Nov. 5, our men went on shor and fet rys abord, and burnt the rest of the housys in the negers towne; and our bot went doune to the outermoste pointe of the river, and burnt a toune, and brout away all the rys that was in the toune"'. Whitaker adds: 'After this humane and honest employment on the Saturday, mark the next article, "the 6th day we sarvyd God, being Sunday!!" Surely the barefaced irreligion of the present day is more tolerable than such sanctified iniquity'.[24]

---

[22] John Hutton, *A Tour to the Caves, in the Environs of Ingleborough and Settle,* (1781), in Thomas West, *Guide to the Lakes,* (1784), Article VII, pp. 235–281, (pp. 243, 247, 251, 252).
[23] Hutton, op. cit., p. 244.
[24] Whitaker, *Craven,* op cit., p. 271.

Like Wilberforce's Emancipationist spies, who dogged plantation proprietors and their patrons at public meetings with detailed information about their activities, the Brontës presented the region around Cowan Bridge as a main centre for the Parliamentary and rural patronage of the northern slave trade. Emily's sombre handling reflects her awareness of its prominence in the rise and fall of the plantation economy. A stark example of English slaveholding appeared near Cowan Bridge. In 1757, the Sill family of Dent, the neighbouring village over Leck Fell, offered a reward in *Williamson's Liverpool Advertiser* for the capture of their runaway slave: 'Run away from Dent, Thomas Anson, a negro man [. . .]'.[25] Emily probably knew that Hallsteads in Thornton in Lonsdale (her topographical model for Thrushcross Grange) had been the seat of the Foxcroft family, partners in Welch & Co., the largest slave shipping house in eighteenth-century Liverpool. The partnership was founded by the Welch family of Leck Hall, across the road from the Clergy Daughters' School. An adjustment gave Thrushcross Grange its enormous size of two miles across, and enhanced its Picturesque and geometrical features by mirroring the two miles from the crossroads to the farmhouse. More pointedly, the two miles match the park around Harewood House, near Leeds, the seat of the Lascelles family, at that time Yorkshire's principal West Indies plantation proprietors and a conventional butt of satire among Wilberforce's supporters. Emily's 'wild green park' (Ch. 15) matches Harewood's vast park, marked prominently in green in the 1816 edition of Tuke's *Map of the County of York*. At Hornby Castle, a centre for the Parliamentary patronage of slavery in the Cowan Bridge region, dinner guests included William Wilson Carus Wilson, MP, the founding Patron of the Clergy Daughters' School and father of its Principal. Until he resigned his seat in 1826 as Member of Parliament for Cockermouth, a pocket borough of the Lowther family, William Wilson Carus Wilson would have been required to lend support in Parliament to the Lowthers' extensive slave and plantation interests in the Caribbean.[26]

The Brontës portrayed that society in two Parliamentary phases related to slavery, at the approach of the Abolition of the Slave Trade Act (1807) in *Wuthering Heights*, and at the approach to the Abolition of Slavery Act (1833) in *Jane Eyre*. They were constrained, however, partly by the confidentiality expected of the clergy and their families, partly by their contrasted temperaments, and partly by the difficulty that by the time they

---

[25] Heywood, 'Yorkshire Slavery', op. cit., loc. cit., note 19 and others.
[26] Alexander Fraser, *Tatham v. Wright. A Verbatim Report of the Cause Doe Dem. Tatham v. Wright*, 2 vols, Lancaster, (1834), vol. I, pp. 151, 182; also Heywood, 'Yorkshire Background', op. cit., notes 26, 27, 32, 33, 34.

wrote their novels, the problems they explored had been resolved at the Parliamentary level. In their hands, slavery became a metaphor for disorders of mind and society. In a letter to her publisher, Charlotte remarked: 'Nor can I take up a philanthropic scheme, though I honour philanthropy; and voluntarily and sincerely veil my face before such a mighty subject as that handled in Mrs. Beecher Stowe's work, *Uncle Tom's Cabin*'.[27] Her novel and Emily's are veiled forerunners of Harriet Beecher Stowe's massive confrontation. *Jane Eyre* reflects Charlotte's experience of families who were directly or indirectly involved in the patronage of English and Caribbean slaveholding. Plantation society is exposed as a corrupting influence on manners, morals and the domestic order. Emily's impersonal portrayal of the region and its family histories emphasises the impact of slaveholding society on a slave who seeks to wield its powers. Lockwood's moment of Sublime calm on a late summer's evening in 1802, shortly before the Abolition of the Slave Trade Act, is Emily's elegy upon that age of violence.

Wuthering Heights has a double focus on past and present. It was written after the abolition of slavery, but comparable social conditions remained.[28] Despite Emily's oblique treatment of slaveholding society, its outlines are recognisable in her text.[29] In an extremity of grief Heathcliff 'dashed his head against the knotted trunk; and, lifting up his eyes, howled, not like a man, but like a savage beast getting goaded to death with knives and spears' (150); Isabella exclaims that 'the single pleasure I can imagine is to die, or to see him dead!' (138); and 'Pulling out the nerves with red hot pincers, requires more coolness than knocking on the head' (153). Edgar Linton's courtship of Catherine Earnshaw exemplifies man's predatory instinct: 'he possessed the power to depart, as much as a cat possesses the power to leave a mouse half killed, or a bird half eaten' (78). The Lunesdale locality explains Heathcliff's activities during his three years' absence from Gimmerton. Military service, Nelly's first but mistaken thought on his return (94), would have consigned him to the unprofitable ranks. More probably, this dark-skinned foundling from Europe's largest slave port would have entered a lucrative branch of the slaveholding industry. He hints at the experience which produced his new wealth: 'The tyrant grinds

---

[27] Elizabeth Gaskell, *The Life of Charlotte Brontë*, (Harmondsworth, 1985), p. 483.

[28] See: C. Heywood, '"Alas! Poor Caunt": Branwell's Emancipationist Cartoon', *Brontë Society Transactions*, 21, (1995), 177–185.

[29] Independent recognitions of this element in the Brontës' writing appear in Maja-Lisa von Sneidern, '*Wuthering Heights* and the Liverpool Slave Trade', (366–90 in this volume) and Christine Alexander, 'Imagining Africa: The Brontës' Creations of Glass Town and Angria', in *Africa Today*, edited by Peter F. Alexander, Ruth Hutchinson, and Deryck Schreuder (Canberra: Humanities Research Centre, 1996), pp. 201–219.

down his slaves—and they don't turn against him, they crush those beneath them' (108). Fraud and ruthlessness distinguish his attempted construction of a male line of succession to the estate. He pursues his goal by exacerbating the male lust for gambling and drink, and exploiting a young female's infatuation.

Overturning Picturesque doctrine, Emily construed the moorland as a source of regeneration for a society corrupted by slavery and its moral counterpart, enslavement to appetite, egotism, and passion. Moorland excursions prepare the younger Catherine for her role as restorer and liberator of the estate. At the age of twelve, in the guise of an Arabian merchant and his camels she makes a first clandestine outing on Minny (167). At the excursion on her sixteenth birthday, Nelly Dean watches 'her golden ringlets flying loose behind, and her bright cheek, as soft and pure in its bloom as a wild rose, and her eyes radiant with cloudless pleasure'. They make their way towards the farmhouse among 'hillocks and banks [. . .] hunting out the nests of the grouse'. Nelly complains: 'there were so many hillocks and banks to climb and pass, that, at length, I began to be weary' (184). Catherine Linton encounters her two cousins in that setting, and marries each in turn. The defeated paternal cousin is a sterile child of slavery. Her chosen partner, a maternal cousin, is an injured but indomitable child of nature. The moorland encounters prepare the younger Catherine for her triumph over the disruption afflicting her mother's generation. Through her story, Emily proposes love beyond desire as the way to achieve Wilberforce's dual purpose of emancipating the slaves from their English captors, and English society from its enslavement to passion. Heathcliff is swept towards a belated confession of the solace he discovered after howling at the grave of Catherine. In a vision her spirit had appeared at the graveside and led him home. At that point, he relates, he had been 'unspeakably consoled' (239). His confession is the moment of recognition or *anagnorisis* in a modern slave's tragic narrative.

Emily's mastery of the topography and family histories around Cowan Bridge was reconstructed by Isabella Banks (Mrs. G. Linnaeus Banks) in her novel *Wooers and Winners* (1880), a *roman à clef* written after the death of all the participants in the Lunesdale emancipation struggle behind *Wuthering Heights* and *Jane Eyre*. Unlike the Brontës' early literary admirers and followers, Isabella Banks was versed in Yorkshire social and literary tradition, and a skilled reader of northern history and topography. Re-setting Emily's themes and characters in Ribblesdale, the neighbouring Dale to the south of Lunesdale, she built her story around Archibald Thorpe, a thinly veiled portrayal of Adam Sedgwick (1785–1873), Woodwardian Professor of Geology at Cambridge University. A native of Dent, a friend of the Carus and Welch families of Tunstall and Cowan Bridge, and a cousin of the Sidgwicks of Skipton, Sedgwick was a commanding figure in the Brontës' Yorkshire world and in the emerging scientific world of the nineteenth century. His multifarious activities included assisting the Birkbecks of Settle in founding Mechanics' Institute Libraries and London University, advising on the reform of Cambridge University, and acting as Executor and protector to the Mason and Sill families of his native Dent. In the latter connection his protégés included Richard Sutton, one of the Dales models for the character of Heathcliff and a sidesman of St. Andrew's Church, Dent, during the incumbency there of his brother, the Revd. John Sedgwick.[30]

As the wife of George Linnaeus Banks, Secretary of the Association of Mechanics' Institutes in the north of England, Isabella Banks was strategically placed to penetrate the concealment which Charlotte had maintained in her Preface and in her contact with Elizabeth Gaskell. Through her fictional portrayal of Adam Sedgwick, she surveyed Emily's handling of his position as founder of geological studies and custodian of the West Riding family secrets appearing in *Wuthering Heights*. Mrs. Gaskell and Charlotte had written within the long lifetime of the widely admired Sedgwick; Isabella Banks appears to have felt that his death opened the way for an outline of his role in the formation of Emily's novel. Elements drawn both from Emily's fiction and from the reality she had mastered are cross-woven in *Wooers and Winners*. Archibald Thorpe is guardian of the Earnshaw children and of the hero Martin Pickersgill, a dark-complexioned orphan from Jamaica who is adopted into the Earnshaw family. Martin eventually marries the daughter of the house after the collapse of her engagement to marry the fickle Jasper Ellis, and at the resolution of his long estrangement from her brother. Martin inherits an interest in the south Yorkshire coalfield, a resource which Archibald Thorpe had helped to exploit, as Sedgwick had through his encouragement of the Revd. William Thorp, whose charting of the south Yorkshire coalfield initiated its subsequent industrial development.[31] After his death in a rock fall, the fictional Thorpe's body is faithfully guarded by his dog named Keeper. The references to Emily Brontë's pets and fictional characters, and to her penetration of

[30] C. Heywood, 'Yorkshire Slavery', *Review of English Studies,* op. cit., loc. cit; and 'A Yorkshire Background', *Modern Language Review,* op. cit., loc. cit.
[31] For the probable origins of Isabella Banks's fictional name among followers of Sedgwick's geological researches, see the section on Sedgwick in Archibald Geikie, *The Founders of Geology,* (1897), pp. 256–269; and William Thorp, *Map of the Yorkshire Coalfield,* (1840), West Yorkshire County Library, Wakefield; also, *Leeds Mercury,* 10 Oct. 1840, p. 7, (presentation of Thorp's Map to the Yorkshire Geological and Polytechnic Society, with Sedgwick as guest speaker).

Sedgwick's secrets and interpretation of the landscape and society around Ingleborough, Dent, and Settle, could hardly have been more explicit.

From the 1820s onwards, Sedgwick expounded the Pennine rock system in papers and monographs, and at public lectures in Cambridge and elsewhere. His extensive following included Lyell, Darwin, Murchison, and Archibald Geikie. His exposition of the northern mountain system appeared in his Letters to Wordsworth, published as an appendix to the 1842 edition of Wordsworth's *Guide to the Lakes* (1810). He explained the mountains and lakes as products of intermittent volcanic or plutonic (as they were termed) upheavals, interspersed with oceanic flooding and glacial movements over vast ages. Like the Lake mountains, he explained, the Pennines were formed by a volcanic upheaval falling short of eruption. The underlying limestone rose to great heights in the northern sector, exposing the more recent mantle of gritstone, the foundation of the dark moorland, to the abrasive action of torrential downpours and glaciers. To the north of Skipton, the overlying gritstone was scrubbed off all but the crests of the highest hills: Ingleborough, Whernside, and Penyghent. Except for the shallow southern ridges or *edges* of the type appearing around Hathersage and Haworth, the less energetic southern upheaval had left the gritstone mantle little altered. As a result, the more ancient northern limestone adopted its enigmatic position, soaring above the more recent but low-lying southern moorland. In his third Letter to Wordsworth, Sedgwick divided the earth's formative period into ten alternating stages of turbulence and 'comparative repose'.[32] The world was formed, he explained, in a 'deep sea [. . .] filled with a formation many thousand feet in thickness', under 'the beating of an ancient surf', with 'great oscillations between the levels of land and sea'. He replaced the miscellaneous plurality of earlier rock classifications with a new paradigm of three rock types: sedimentary, igneous and metamorphic. Chalk beds of enormous thickness, laid over the violently upturned sedimentary slates, were metamorphosed to limestone by volcanic heat, and mantled over by more recent sandstone or gritstone shelves. Besides clarifying the origins of the Yorkshire landscape, Sedgwick secured recognition for earthquakes and volcanoes as evidence of natural creative powers, exerted with scarcely imaginable force over inconceivably vast periods of time.

Sedgwick's knowledge of Yorkshire family histories and his mastery of the Pennine rock system reappear in *Wuthering Heights*. The two

---

[32] Adam Sedgwick, 'Letters to Wordsworth', in *A Complete Guide to the Lakes [. . .] with Mr. Wordsworth's Description of the Scenery of the Country*, etc., 4th edn., (1853), pp. 214–5.

landscapes of the old West Riding can be seen together in the view north-wards from Withins Height, the summit of Haworth Moor and the model for Emily's title. The moorland unrolls underfoot; the limestone hills appearing to the south of Cowan Bridge are aligned in reverse order along the skyline. Among the Brontës, only Emily had the ability to reconstruct that landscape from that vantage point, and to dramatise Sedgwick's reading of it. As in Sedgwick's reading of the rock formation underlying the view from Withins Height, the moorland in *Wuthering Heights* is laid over the underlying limestone. The three generations of Lintons and Earnshaws match his paradigm of the sedimentary, igneous and metamorphic rocks. Gimmerton's fiery encounter with the world of slaveholding disrupts the old calm, but leads to a society which has been toughened by experience. Sedgwick's four disruptive epochs in the formation of the earth reappear in the disruptions among the Earnshaws and the Lintons: dissension leading to the flight of the newly arrived Heathcliff; violence on his return, leading to the flight of Isabella and the deaths of Catherine and Hindley Earnshaw; the ensnarement of Catherine Linton in Heathcliff's attempt to gain possession of the Grange; and his confession, followed by his death after the rise and reconciliation at Easter of Hareton and Catherine. The old order of dominance and passion yields to their humour and affection.

In an apocalyptic moment, Sedgwick maintained that Wordsworth's idea of the end of the world would outlast the advances of theoretical knowledge:

> But there is another 'mighty voice', muttered in the dark recesses of the earth [:] the voice of wisdom, or inspiration, and of gladness [. . .] to have their full consummation only in the end of time, when all the bonds of matter shall be cast away, and there shall begin the reign of knowledge and universal love.[33]

Sedgwick's reading of Wordsworth is re-stated in Emily's poem 'No coward soul is mine', where the speaker discards 'the thousand creeds' in favour of an atomic view of eternity: 'There is not room for Death / Nor atom that his might could render void'.[34] Her breadth of reading appears in her exposition of the atomic ideas of Epictetus which had been advocated by Ellis Walker, a name influencing her choice of the literary name Ellis Bell.[35] In 'Haworth Churchyard', Arnold wrote of this poem that 'her too bold dying song / Stirr'd, like a clarion-blast, my soul' (ll. 99–100). It encouraged his venture into the atomic philosophy of mortality. Her vision of the end of

[33] Sedgwick, op. cit., p. 219.
[34] See pages 305–06 in this volume. [ED.]
[35] Margaret Maison, 'Emily Brontë and Epictetus', *Notes & Queries*, 223, (1978), 230–1.

things, and Lockwood's vision of peace for the dead in *Wuthering Heights,* are echoed in Arnold's epilogue in the revised text of 'Haworth Church-yard'. Adhering to Emily's phrasing, Arnold proposes a final reunion for the 'unquiet' Brontës as atoms rather than as ghosts:

> In the dark fermentation of earth,
> In the never idle workshop of nature,
> In the eternal movement,
> Ye shall find yourselves again! (ll. 134–7)

Like Adam Sedgwick, Emily Brontë viewed the Pennine region as a life's ex-perience; also, as a picture to be understood and enjoyed. She was among the first, it appears, to recognise that his geological exposition had super-seded the Picturesque interpretation of the Yorkshire landscapes, and that the modern reading of their formation and appearance had emerged.[36] He proposed that:

> We must, in imagination, sweep off the drifted matter that clogs the sur-face of the ground; we must suppose all the covering of moss and heath and wood to be torn away from the sides of the mountains, and the green mantle that lies near their feet to be lifted up; we may then see the mus-cular integuments, and sinews, and bones of our mother Earth, and so judge of the part played by each of them during those old convulsive movements whereby her limbs were contorted and drawn up into their present posture.[37]

Catherine Earnshaw's familiar explanation of her relationship to Heathcliff and Linton is made through a metaphor patterned on Sedgwick's thinking. Appetite or desire draws her to the neighbouring manor and its pic-turesque park, but the adoptive siblings are bound as though by fraternal kinship and by their fiery, plutonic natures:

> My love for Linton is like the foliage in the woods. Time will change it, I'm well aware, as winter changes the trees. My love for Heathcliff re-sembles the eternal rocks beneath — a source of little visible delight, but necessary. Nelly, I *am* Heathcliff — he's always, always in my mind — not as a pleasure, any more than I am always a pleasure to myself — but as my own being (85).

Lockwood's confusion about the enigmatic relationships at the farmhouse, the products of a social upheaval of volcanic intensity, is resolved by Nelly

---

[36] Robert Speight, *The Craven and North-West Yorkshire Highlands,* (1892); P. F. Kendall and H. E. Wroot, *Geology of Yorkshire,* 2 vols., (1924); Arthur Raistrick, *The Pennine Dales,* (1972).

[37] Sedgwick, op. cit., p. 180.

Dean's exposition, and confirmed by his observations. These match Emily Brontë's mature decipherment of the types of Yorkshire landscape and society she had observed in childhood.

Wuthering Heights and the Liverpool Slave Trade

Maja-Lisa Von Sneidern

Emily Brontë's political leanings are not easy to discern in *Wuthering Heights,* although her sympathies appear to be with the dispossessed and the exploited. Maja-Lisa Von Sneidern reads the novel against the reality of slavery, providing a rich context for understanding the character of Heathcliff as more than simply a diabolical usurper. Heathcliff's "darkness" and his mysterious genetic origins have led many critics to speculate that he was intended by Brontë to represent the displaced, dispossessed "others" (whether Jamaican, Irish, African, or Indian) who had been used and exploited by the growing British imperialist interests but who very well might in the future avenge themselves on the empire itself (through seizure of its property and women). We know that Brontë's reading was broad and that she was familiar with the Liverpool newspapers, which had been full of shocking stories about the thriving slave trade conducted through that port. Like Heywood, Von Sneidern adopts a critical-materialistic approach to the novel in contrast to the symbolic or psychoanalytical critiques that have previously dominated Brontë's criticism. [ED.]

[T]hey were simply trying to master the racial
disorder from which they had formed themselves.
— Michel Foucault

ELH 62 (1995): 171–96.

"The tyrant grinds down his slaves and they don't
turn against him, they crush those beneath them—
You are welcome to torture me to death for your
amusement, only allow me to amuse myself a little
in the same style."

—*Heathcliff*

London, 1 October 1771: James Sommersett, a black slave, "absented himself from the service" of his master "and absolutely refused to return." Abolitionist Granville Sharp hired counsel, secured a writ of Habeas Corpus and pursued the case to trial. Lord Chief Justice Mansfield of the King's Bench was asked to decide if a black slave who accompanied his master to England could be forcibly returned to the colonies for resale. The judge ruled reluctantly, encouraging both parties to reach an out of court settlement. Mansfield repeatedly asserted that the decision was narrow, but his language was unequivocal: "The state of slavery is of such a nature, . . . is so odious, that nothing can be suffered to support it but positive law." [1] Technically, the Mansfield decision abolished neither slavery in Britain nor involuntary transportation of slaves to the colonies, as newspaper accounts and correspondence by such notables as Hannah More testify. [2] But it did reverse the Yorke-Talbot opinion of 1729, define the crisis of slavery with new clarity, hearten its opponents, and alarm those with an investment in human capital. [3] Edward Long, the most famous advocate of the planter's interest, wrote in *Candid Reflections:* "How far the late judicial sentence may be consistent with the spirit of *English law,* I will not take upon me to determine; sure I am, that it cannot be made compatible with the spirit of English commerce." [4]

---

[1] James Walvin, *The Black Presence: A Documentary of the Negro in England, 1555–1860* (New York: Schocken, 1972), 98, 114.

[2] Folarin Shyllon, *Black People in Britain, 1555–1833* (London: Oxford UP, 1977), 25.

[3] See Walvin, *Black Presence* (note 1), 95: "We are of opinion, that a slave coming from the West Indies to Great Britain or Ireland, with or without his master, doth not become free, and that his master's property or right in him is not thereby determined or varied; and that baptism doth not bestow freedom on him, or make any alteration in his temporal condition in these kingdoms. We are also of opinion, that his master may legally compel him to return to the plantations." P. Yorke, Solicitor-General, and C. Talbot, Attorney-General. The opinion did not have the power of "positive law" sufficient for Mansfield to uphold it.

[4] Quoted Walvin, *Black Presence,* 74.

The English city with the most spirited commerce in slaves was Liverpool. At mid-century Liverpool ranked third behind London and Bristol, but by the inter-bellum period (1763–1776) she had eclipsed her competitors and was the premier slaving port in Britain. The New Exchange/Town Hall was ornamented with "busts of blackamoors and elephants, emblematical of the African trade."[5] By 1764 Liverpool boasted more than twice the number of vessels engaged in the triangular trade than Bristol, and by 1804 Liverpool merchants were responsible for more than eighty-four percent of the British transatlantic slave trade. At the close of the eighteenth century, Britain accounted for nearly fifty-five percent of the traffic world wide, and the percentage grew until the month of its abolition.[6] It is little wonder that in 1804 Liverpool merchants, in response to a bill seeking abolition, petitioned Parliament to observe that "under the protection of the Legislature [the petitioners] embarked a considerable part of their property in that Trade, [and] will be very materially injured if the said Bill should pass into a Law," nor is it surprising that none of the several versions and revisions of Thomas Southerne's *Oroonoko*, increasingly popularized and polemic in the eighteenth century, ever appeared on a Liverpool stage.[7]

According to C. P. Sanger's chronology of *Wuthering Heights*, Mr. Earnshaw's walk to Liverpool occurred at the "beginning of harvest" in 1771, the eve of the Sommersett case and the Mansfield decision.[8] In lieu of a whip

---

[5] Gomer Williams, *History of the Liverpool Privateers and Letters of Marque with an Account of the Liverpool Slave Trade* (1887; rpt., New York: Augustus M. Kelley, 1966), 494.

[6] Percentages have been derived from Williams (note 5), 494, 680, 678 and David Eltis, *Economic Growth and the Ending of the Transatlantic Slave Trade* (New York: Oxford Univ. Press, 1987), 248.

[7] For the petition, see Averil Mackenzie-Grieve, *The Last Years of the English Slave Trade: Liverpool, 1750–1807* (1941; reprint, London: Frank Cass, 1968), 17. For information on *Oroonoko* see the Clarendon editors of Southerne, who note: "*Oroonoko* went on to become one of the most frequently performed works in the eighteenth-century theatre. Indeed in the first third of the century it seems to have been the most commonly produced of all the post-Shakespearean tragedies." After 1759, the play's popularity in the major playhouses dwindled. However, it "became the property of relatively minor performers" and "appeal[ed] to the amateurs and the inexperienced." *The Works of Thomas Southerne*, ed. Robert Jordan and Harold Love, 2 vols. (Oxford: Clarendon, 1988), 2:91–92. The editors of the Regents Restoration Drama Series edition assert that by 1760 "revisions of the play were apparently becoming a fad" and they list Hawkesworth's 1759 adaptation and John Ferriar's version, *The Prince of Angola*, an unabashedly anti-slave play, as instances (*Oroonoko*, ed. Maximillian E. Novak and David Stuart Rodes [Lincoln: Univ. of Nebraska Press, 1976], xx). From the early eighteenth century, some critics objected to the comic sub-plot, and the versions and adaptations minimized or removed the breeches comedy considered ill-suited to the loftiness of the tragic plot.

[8] Charles Percy Sanger, "The Structure of *Wuthering Heights*," in *Wuthering Heights: An Authoritative Text with Essays in Criticism*, 2d ed. (New York: Norton, 1972), 296.

for Cathy and a fiddle for Hindley, objects emblematic of the cruelty and indolence nurtured by institutionalized slavery, Earnshaw substitutes Heathcliff, "'dark almost as if it came from the devil.'"[9] Earnshaw found "it . . . in the streets of Liverpool where he picked it up and inquired for its owner—Not a soul knew to whom it belonged" (51). Heathcliff's racial otherness cannot be a matter of dispute; Brontë makes that explicit. From the first and frequently thereafter he is termed a "gipsy" (51); Mr. Linton recognizes him as "'that strange acquisition my late neighbor made in his journey to Liverpool—a little Lascar, or an American or Spanish cast-away'" (61); Nelly encourages Heathcliff to "frame high notions of [his] birth"—his father might have been the "Emperor of China" and his mother "an Indian queen." Heathcliff may not be "a regular black" (66), and Nelly cannot "image some fit parentage" for "the dark little thing" (270), but his bloodline is unambiguously tainted by color.[10] In effect, he is an irregular black, a mongrel, a source of great anxiety for the mid-nineteenth-century Victorian.

Institutionalized slavery as manifested in the eighteenth and nineteenth centuries was fundamentally incompatible with a British ethos, in part that "spirit of English Law" that Long avoids confronting. David Eltis notes that "from the viewpoint of economic self-interest, British anti-slavery policy appears wrongheaded enough to qualify for inclusion in Barbara Tuchman's catalog of folly in government."[11] Despite Adam Smith's treatise

---

[9] All parenthetical citations of *Wuthering Heights* and Charlotte Brontë's "Editor's Preface" refer to this New Riverside Edition.

[10] Like Nelly, we strain to "image some fit parentage" for Heathcliff. His blackness, which is repeatedly evoked, seems always deflected and recast into "high notions of [his] birth." "Race" in *Wuthering Heights* is rendered both anachronistically (see note 28) and in terms of its contemporary discourses. In doing so, this novel constantly threatens the limits of the "enunciative possibilities" of a Victorian novel; to visualize Heathcliff's blackness as sub-Saharan African features irrevocably revises the impact of Brontë's story. According to Michel Foucault, the principles that regulate the emergence of statements in the "episteme," the "archive" or the "discipline" limit what can be said. See *Power/Knowledge: Selected Interviews and Other Writings, 1972–1977,* ed. Colin Gordon, trans. Colin Gordon, Leo Marshall, John Mepham, and Kate Soper (New York: Pantheon, 1980), 197; *The Archaeology of Knowledge and the Discourse on Language,* trans. A. M. Sheridan Smith and Rupert Swyer (New York: Pantheon, 1972), 128–29, 222–25. In recognizing that there are rules that regulate "the enunciative possibilities and impossibilities" of any discursive system including the novel, we should not assume that what can be enunciated in one system can be adequately translated into another. However, a familiarity with contemporary racialist discourses can offer an interpretation for some of the behaviors and characteristics of Heathcliff and his son that have been problematic for readers since the book was published. For "enunciative possibilities and impossibilities" see Foucault, *Archaeology of Knowledge,* 129.

[11] Eltis, *Economic Growth* (note 6), 7.

arguing the advantages of a laissez-faire labor economy (1776), Britain's abolition of the slave trade in 1807, then her active naval suppression of it, and finally her emancipation of slaves throughout the colonies in 1834, cost her subjects dearly. The compensation to the West Indian planters for their capital loss equalled forty percent of British revenue in 1833, "almost three times the annual outlay for the English poor." [12] One might imagine that after bitter struggles over the legitimacy of the slave trade at the turn of the century, thirty years of military suppression, and the ultimate emancipation of slaves throughout the empire, that popular interest would have flagged and sentiment dulled. On the contrary, the *Anti-Slavery Reporter* began a new series in 1846, which continued until the midst of World War I. Concerns had shifted from the evils of the "middle passage" to the evils of coolie labor, but the monthly magazine with increasing subscribership continued to focus on the diverse elements intimately and problematically bound to a slave economy: the technological advances thought to herald the obsolescence of slave labor, the production figures of cotton and sugar (the two commodities most dependent on slave labor), and the moral threat of prostitution, exacerbated by the short-sighted economics of a slavery that privileged male productivity. [13] Although slavery put sugar in their tea, coffee in their cups, cotton shirts on their backs, and pounds sterling in their bank accounts, the institution made English blood run cold and warmed an Anglo-Saxon passion for appropriating the concept of liberty as its own.

Reginald Horsman in *Race and Manifest Destiny* traces the development of Anglo-Saxon mythic identity and its accompanying mystification of race. The myth glorifies and sentimentalizes the savage, hardy, free Anglo-Saxon whose natural liberty was corrupted by the imposition of an unnat-

---

[12] Seymour Dresher, *Capitalism and Anti-Slavery* (London: Macmillan, 1986), 138; Eltis, 5–6.

[13] In Marxist terms, the slave owner prior to abolition of the slave trade could ignore a fundamental requirement for a steady supply of labor: procreation. Subsistence, in a slave economy, was no longer bound "to the means necessary [to produce and maintain] the labourer's substitutes, i.e. his children." Karl Marx, *Capital*, in *The Marx-Engels Reader*, 2d ed. (New York: Norton, 1978), 340. Once the trade was abolished and effectively suppressed in the British colonies the problem of an inadequate subsistence economy for the planter became evident and produced imaginative though ineffective solutions. Monk Lewis, for example, institutes "The Order of the Girdle" which accords special preferments—dispensations from punishments and privileged hearings for special favors—to slave mothers whose infants survived their fourteenth day, an image of the perversity later found in the Nazi valorization of Teutonic motherhood. Matthew Gregory "Monk" Lewis, *Journal of a Residence Among the Negroes in the West Indies* (London, 1845), 66.

ural autocratic rule.[14] The myth in part underwrote the development of the concept of precedent, inventing a "spirit of English law" and thereby bolstering the position of those who would limit the monarchy and royal prerogative.[15] After Waterloo, the myth shifted from domestic to imperial significance: "Englishmen and Americans increasingly compared the Anglo-Saxon peoples to others and concluded that blood, not environment or accident, had led to their success."[16] The discourses that produced and participated in a theory of racial superiority compiled evidence wherever it could be gleaned: anecdote, found in traveler's journals such as those of Edward Long, Bryan Edwards and "Monk" Lewis; science and pseudoscience, drawn from Linnaeus and Buffon and including a wide variety of historians, philosophers, physicians, phrenologists and philologists willing to engage in the debate between biblical monogenesis and polygenesis. They were literary and popularized: Disraeli, Carlyle, Kingsley, Kipling and Trollope all lent a hand, finding a forum in broadly distributed publications including *Blackwood's*.[17] Who exactly was to be included in this superior pedigree was problematical. Blacks, browns, yellows, reds and non-English speaking Celts were excluded, while Scandinavians, Teutons and Englishmen were included, but the location of classical Greeks and Romans and the Hebrews was less clear cut. While theorists argued about the

---

[14] Reginald Horsman, *Race and Manifest Destiny: The Origins of American Racial Anglo-Saxonism* (Cambridge: Harvard UP, 1981). Imposing Christian consolation and communal camaraderie onto a pre-Christian Anglo-Saxon culture is inherent in the myth. The existential anguish in, for example, "The Wanderer"—the lament of an Anglo-Saxon warrior deprived of his lord and fellows—is silently erased, and the vision is more post-Norman. The myth creates a happy, primitively democratic crew who joyfully embrace Providence rather than the isolated "eardstapa" who must wearily "wyrde [fate] wistondan" without earthly or transcendent direction. Bruce Mitchell and Fred C. Robinson, *A Guide to Old English*, 4th rev. ed. (New York: Basil Blackwell, 1986), I. 15. Thus the Anglo-Saxon became a figure who was at once free, heroic, and brutally civil.

[15] The seventeenth century experiment with republicanism (1649–1660) inspired a flurry of justifications of regicide and social contract theory. Milton's political tracts, Locke's theoretical works, and later Rousseau's indictments of civilized man are perhaps the most obvious contributions.

[16] Horsman (note 14), 62.

[17] According to Elizabeth Gaskell, the Brontë children had ready access to Mr. Brontë's library and his subscriptions to periodicals that published articles engaging in this debate. Although we do not have more than fragmentary pieces of the "Gondal Sagas," Emily's and Anne's juvenile productions, we do have a considerable corpus of Charlotte's and Branwell's juvenilia, some of it in tiny handsewn booklets entitled "The Young Men's Magazine," fashioned after *Blackwood's*. Glass Town, the children's imaginative colony ruled by four Genii, was located in Africa. And we know the children took a lively interest in current events and controversies. Elizabeth Gaskell, *The Life of Charlotte Brontë* (New York: Penguin, 1975), 112–19.

innate character (docile or brutish) and the ultimate fate (extinction or refinement) of the "inferior" races, agents of the second empire made the essence of the matter clear by mid-century.[18] "All is race; there is no other truth," wrote Disraeli; Robert Knox echoes that sentiment, "Race is everything, literature, science, art—in a word, civilization depends on it." The January 1844, *Edinburgh Review* aphorizes: "Of the great influence of Race

---

[18] Some defenders of slavery typically characterized the black slave as docile, dependent and loyal. In an anonymous 1836 review attributed to Edgar Allan Poe, the author writes: "The peculiar character . . . the peculiar nature of the negro" differs in "passions and wants and feelings and tempers in all respects" from the white man. These differences create a relationship "of loyal devotion on the part of the slave to which the white man's heart is a stranger, and of the master's reciprocal feeling of parental attachment to his humble dependent . . . [T]hese sentiments in the breast of the negro and his master, are stronger than they would be under like circumstances between individuals of the white race." Furthermore, "the habitual use of the word 'my' . . . is a term of endearment. That is an easy transition by which he who is taught to call the little negro 'his,' in this sense and *because he loves him,* shall love him *because he is his.*" [Edgar Allan Poe], Review of *Slavery in the United States* by J. K. Paulding, in *The Complete Works of Edgar Allan Poe,* ed. James A. Harrison, 17 vols. (New York: Thomas Y. Crowell, 1902), 8:270–72. For a discussion of the place of the review in the Poe canon, see Joan Dayan, "Romance and Race," in *The Columbia History of the American Novel,* ed. Emory Elliott (New York: Columbia UP, 1991), 89–109 and "Amorous Bondage: Poe, Ladies, and Slaves," *American Literature* 66 (1994): 239–73. George Frederick Holmes echoes Poe's theory of racial difference: "Thus what would be insupportable to one race, or one order of society, constitutes no portion of the wretchedness of another. The joys and the sorrows of the slave are in harmony with his position, and are entirely dissimilar from what would make the happiness, or misery of another class." George Frederick Holmes, review of *Uncle Tom's Cabin,* in *Slavery Defended: The Views of the Old South,* ed. Eric L. McKitrick (Englewood Cliffs, N.J.: Prentice-Hall/Spectrum, 1963), 107. Others characterized blacks as brutes. Edward Long catalogs the characteristics: "A covering of wool, like bestial fleece. . . . Their bestial or fetid smell. . . . In general, they are void of genius, and seem almost incapable of making any progress in civility or science. They have no plan or system of morality among them. Their barbarity to their children debases their nature even below that of brutes. They have no moral sensations; no taste but for women; gormondizing, and drinking to excess; no wish but to be idle. . . . They are represented by all authors as the vilest of the human kind, to which they have little more pretension of resemblance than what arises from their exterior form." Edward Long, *The History of Jamaica, Or, General Survey of the Ancient and Modern State of that Island* (London, 1774), 352–53. Finally, S. T. Coleridge asserts that "the Africans are more versatile, more easily modified than perhaps any other known race." He then draws a distinction between the "savage" and the "barbarian"; "The American Indians are savages: the Africans (to speak classically) barbarians." Both the past and future of the former are uncertain, but the latter are capable of "progress[ing] from barbarism to civilization, through its various stages" because there is evidence that others have done so. Presumably Coleridge refers to Anglo-Saxons. [Samuel Taylor Coleridge], Review of *History of the African Slave Trade* by Thomas Clarkson, *Edinburgh Review* 12 (July, 1808): 378.

in the production of National Character, no reasonable enquirer can now doubt." [19]

Wuthering Heights is the site in which the problematics of an Anglo-Saxon mythology saddled with the fact of slavery and the "fact" of race are revealed, if not resolved. Brontë locates her plantation colony not on the margins of the empire, some exotic island half way around the world, but in the heart of Yorkshire. In the novel the Heights, corrupted by the introduction of the racially other, is the place where the figures of a system of bondage work out their relationships. These relationships are represented according to principles common to abolitionist, anti-abolitionist, and Anglo-Saxon racialist discourses available at the time the novel was composed. Heathcliff, Hindley and the elder Catherine are the agents who act out these relationships and principles. The Grange, like Mother England, is an estate isolated from a planter economy by both breeding and seeming cultural independence. At one point Isabella writes that the distance between the Heights and the Grange is tantamount to "the Atlantic" (128). Despite its insularity, the Grange becomes contaminated. Although the racial other is forced back to its quarters, a second generation, a "new series," of relationships and principles ensues, represented by Heathcliff, Isabella and Linton Heathcliff. Penultimately, that other is eradicated and the impending marriage of the younger Catherine and Hareton is a conventional, approved resolution. However, as in mid-century England where the problems of race and slavery did not vanish with emancipation, the book resists a tidy ending. [20]

---

[19] Quoted in Horsman (note 14), 70, 71, 60.

[20] For a fine analysis of abolitionist expectations of the effects of emancipation and their subsequent disappointments see David Eltis, "Abolitionist Perceptions of Society after Slavery," in *Slavery and British Society: 1776–1846*, ed. James Walvin (London: Macmillan, 1982), 195–213. Coleridge was convinced that the "most intelligent of the African tribes" would adopt Christianity (and presumably the industriousness described in Max Weber's *The Protestant Ethic and the Spirit of Capitalism*) because it was "a religion professed by a race confessedly so superior to them" (Coleridge [note 18], 373). Marx fairly chortles over the discomfit of the Jamaican planters who cannot entice the Quashees (freed slaves) to work for more than subsistence. "Loafing" is the "luxury good" and they "observe the planters' impending bankruptcy with an ironic grin of malicious pleasure, and even exploit their acquired Christianity as an embellishment for this mood of malicious glee and indolence" (Marx [note 13], 250). As Eltis points out: "Other races failing to react in the expected manner . . . did nothing to inhibit the development of a respectable intellectual base to racism" (212). Heathcliff combines self-interest with industriousness, what abolitionists had hoped for; Emily Brontë represents what happens when the racially other does not adopt the religion and civilized values of the system of rules he surreptitiously and violently appropriates.

Prior to Heathcliff's arrival, the inhabitants of the Heights and the Grange are racially pure Anglo-Saxons, representative of the yeoman and gentry classes. Both farm and estate are productive, well-defended and portrayed as feudally self-sustaining; there is nothing extraneous, no younger brother, no surplus of daughters, with little need for more than occasional commerce with a world beyond Gimmerton. Even after Heathcliff's arrival, there are only rare gestures to a late eighteenth-century rather than a fifteenth-century world: glazed windows, Joseph's fierce Protestantism and Lockwood's bourgeois bungling.[21] Precisely because the setting Brontë creates is one where "time stagnates" (44), we are predisposed to minimize Heathcliff's racial otherness, and ignore the possibility that he is a product of a thriving Liverpool slave trade. It is a setting that harkens to a mythical Anglo-Saxon past, both more brutal and more heroic than Victorian England.[22] When Heathcliff is introduced, the social equilibrium is upset and the Heights becomes the inverse of a domestic ideal marked by pious faith, a serene and orderly household, and cultivated womanhood. Victorian readers would find both their romanticized projections of the past and their idealized perceptions of their present threatened by this

---

[21] Lockwood, the quasi-Anglo-Saxon representative of the outside world, contrasts sharply with this insular world. He is probably nouveau riche: well-heeled, but rootless, lacking property, purpose through industry, and an identity of his own. His pretensions to Byronic heroism are clearly the object of ridicule in the opening chapters: "He suffers from the inanity his author attributes to the average London reader." Carl R. Woodring, "The Narrators of *Wuthering Heights,*" in *Wuthering Heights: Authoritative Text with Essays in Criticism,* 2d ed. (New York: Norton, 1972), 355. With a fool's accuracy, Lockwood applies the glibly figurative to the literal circumstance, describing Wuthering Heights as "a perfect misanthrope's Heaven," and Heathcliff "a capital fellow" (27). Furthermore, he is the master narrator who authors the text's "enunciative possibilities and impossibilities." The text of *Wuthering Heights,* with its dual narrators, might exemplify a "contact zone" as Mary Louise Pratt defines it, and Lockwood's "urban discourse about [a] nonurban world" represents the mid-eighteenth-century hypothesis that "those who live a hundred miles from the capital, are a century [or an ocean] away from it in their modes of thinking and acting." Mary Louise Pratt, *Imperial Eyes: Travel Writing and Transculturation* (New York: Routledge, 1992), 67, 34–35. Much more about the relationship between his discourse and those of Long, Edwards and Lewis (other travellers to primitive areas) needs to be considered.

[22] See Terry Eagleton, *Myths of Power: A Marxist Study of the Brontës* (New York: Barnes and Noble, 1975). This reading focuses on class bondage, which effectively erases the issue of race and institutionalized slavery; however, Eagleton identifies elements that seem central to mid-century discourses on race: "[Heathcliff's] undisguised violence, like the absolutism of his love, come to seem features of a past more brutal but also more heroic than the present" and Catherine and Heathcliff's "relationship articulates a depth inexpressible in routine social practice, transcendent [read: transgressive] of available social languages" (114, 108).

novel, and in fact reviewers warned them that the book was "inexpressively painful" and "too odiously and abominably pagan" for even the "most vitiated class of English readers." [23]

Slavery had long been identified as a corrupting institution, and both Aphra Behn (1688) and Thomas Southerne (1695) depicted slavers and one class of planters as villainous and vulgar. [24] Mr. Hargrave argued in the Sommersett case that slavery "corrupts the morals of the master, by freeing him from those restraints . . . so necessary for controul of the human passions, so beneficial in promoting . . . virtue." [25] Nelly tells Lockwood that

---

[23] Acton, Currer and Ellis Bell, the Brontës' pseudonyms, were each reproached for coarseness, vulgarity and lack of taste. Until Matthew Arnold had a go at *Villette*, *Wuthering Heights* bore the brunt of Victorian indignation. Here I cite first the *Atlas* review of January 1848, and then Elizabeth Rigby's indictment of both *Jane Eyre* and *Wuthering Heights* in the *Quarterly Review* of December 1848. See Miriam Allott, *The Brontës: The Critical Heritage* (Boston: Routledge and Kegan Paul, 1974), 231, 111, for a fuller sense of the awe and outrage the book incited.

[24] Behn on the planters: "The Governour had no sooner recover'd and had heard of the Menaces of *Caesar,* but he called his Council, who (not to disgrace them, or burlesque the Government there) consisted of such notorious Villains as *Newgate* never transported; and, possibly originally were such, who understood neither the Laws of God or Man, and had no sort of Principles to make them worthy the Name of Men; but at the very Council-Table wou'd contradict and fight with one another, and swear so bloodily, that 'twas terrible to hear and see 'em." Aphra Behn, *Oroonoko: Or, the Royal Slave* (New York: Norton, 1973), 69–70. Southerne so vilifies Captain Driver, the slaver, that even the gold digging sisters of the comic sub-plot reject him, although the planters "applaud him" for encouraging "industry" (1.2. 161, 156). The governor is a potential ravisher, and the planters are rabble who speak coarse prose, while the hero speaks eloquent blank verse. Blanford, Oroonoko's impotent champion, speaks to the planters:

> Have you no Reverence of future Fame?
> No awe upon your actions, from the Tongues,
> The censuring Tongues of Men, that will be free?
> If you confess Humanity, believe
> There is a God, or Devil, to reward
> Our doings here, do not provoke your Fate.
> The Hand of Heaven is arm'd against these Crimes,
> With hotter Thunder-Bolts, prepar'd to shoot,
> And Nail you to the Earth, a sad Example;
> A Monument of Faithless Infamy. (5.2.1–10)

Southerne (note 7), 2:85–180.

[25] Walvin, *Black Presence* (note 1), 100. See also Long (note 18), 485. The notion that slavery was a corrupting and contaminating influence on the master was a staple of not only the abolitionists' texts, but the institution's defenders as well. Long comments on the Jamaican *Code Noir* of the early seventeenth century: "Men are too often disposed to be cruel, of their own depraved hearts; and it becomes a Christian legislature not to inflame and encourage, but to repress as much as possible, this sanguinary disposition."

Heathcliff "bred bad feeling" (52). Indeed, his presence immediately provokes behavior compatible with a vulgar planter rather than a civilized society: Hindley "blubbers" and Cathy "spits" at him (52), the former an unmanly response and the latter a filthy one. Cathy "earned . . . a sound blow from her father to teach her cleaner manners," but the polluting relationship becomes well established. Cathy and Heathcliff were "very thick" by the time Nelly is reconciled with the Heights after her own act of "cowardice and inhumanity" (52). Unlike the Grange, at the Heights social order and station are hazily defined as we might expect at the outskirts of civilization. Heathcliff, who has no designated place in the family other than "usurper" and "beggarly interloper" (53), is given Earnshaw's first born's name. Joseph, the bizarre churl, is the authorized spiritual leader (38) and unauthorized steward of genealogical lore (172). Nelly, the "human fixture" (48) whose servant's status is well-defined at the Grange, occupies an unclassifiable space in the social dynamics of the Heights. The fluidity of station and identity at the Heights is most obviously manifested in Catherine's carved variations of her surname and compounded by the doubling of Catherines (37). Lockwood's inability to sort out the familial relationships and the impotence of polite discourse at the "mad tea party" (31–33) indicate that social intercourse is effected by a series of dominations defined by a system other than Enlightenment social contract theory or nineteenth-century English class and family relationships.[26]

After Earnshaw's death, Hindley emerges as one figure in a bondage relationship with Heathcliff. Depicted as the "negligent," "tyrannical" (58), non-industrious, and gratuitously cruel "master" (39), Hindley quits his "paradise on the hearth" only to mete out punishment (39); his rule is through flogging (58) and deprivation (74). Morals, manners and industry are destroyed by the unchecked reign of tyranny. As absolute despot without productive labor and the temporizing influence of his wife, Hindley drinks heavily, resulting in "either his wild-beast's fondness or his madman's rage" (78). He brutalizes Nelly and his son, and ultimately loses the Heights to Heathcliff at cards. Heathcliff, too, is degraded by the relationship; he is banished from the Earnshaws' company, deprived of education, and forced to "continual hard work, begun soon and concluded late" (74). From the beginning "a sullen, patient child; hardened, perhaps, to illtreatment" (52), Heathcliff "yielded with poignant though silent regret" to his servile station: "He acquired a slouching gait," an "ignoble look" and "contrived to convey an impression of inward and outward repulsiveness"

---

[26] See Nancy Armstrong, *Desire and Domestic Fiction: A Political History of the Novel* (New York: Oxford UP, 1987).

(74). In drawing and developing Heathcliff's character, Emily Brontë creates a manifestation of one Victorian understanding of black Africans:

> Whatever great personages this country might anciently have produced and concerning whom we have no information, they are now every where degenerated into a brutish, ignorant, idle, crafty, treacherous, bloody, thievish, mistrustful, and superstitious people.[27]

Cathy tells Nelly, "It would degrade me to marry Heathcliff," and she blames Hindley for bringing him "so low" (84). Here Cathy resists the biologism implicit in most mid-nineteenth-century conceptions of race, and instead attributes Heathcliff's degradation to his environment.[28] But to entertain a theory of a primeval golden age *and* to accept nurture rather than nature as the determining factor in degradation questions the very concept of race, and thus racial superiority. For mid-century theorists such speculation places the savage origin of black Africans and the primitive origin of Anglo-Saxons in a very dangerous and threatening proximity. Race itself becomes a superstition, and brutality, ignorance and treachery characteristics of degeneration in the potential of any culture—and Hindley is offered as a case in point.

If the attempt to distinguish the qualities of race from those of culture produced anxiety, it did so primarily because of the material reality of slavery. Anti-abolitionist discourses tended to exploit what were represented as the Africans' sub-human characteristics, but slavery is an economic institution, and its intimate connection to race is accidental, not essential. The

---

[27] Long (note 18), 354.

[28] Race is a vexed term. Historically it was used to designate kinship, of family, extended family or tribe, of gender, of profession or inclination. Its use as a term to identify a classification of humanity is first instanced by the OED in 1776. In the seventeenth and early eighteenth centuries the term was primarily used to distinguish an aristocratic "race" from parvenus and the mob. See Aphra Behn's *Oroonoko* (note 24), 9, 26, and Michael McKeon's "Aristocratic Ideology," in *Origins of the English Novel: 1660–1740* (Baltimore: Johns Hopkins, 1987), 131–133. One of the great bourgeois victories of the eighteenth century, separating status from blood while appropriating the status of blood, rests in part on reconstruing "race." Despite Locke's *tabula rasa* and utilitarian schemes for education, biological essentialism, now theoretically divorced from class, was on the ascendent; witness for example the popularity of phrenology. See also George Stocking, *Victorian Anthropology* (New York: Macmillan/Free, 1987), in which he notes that "there was an emerging racialism of a harsher, hereditarian sort, which rejected Lamarckian biocultural interactionism and subordinated culture to race." He goes on to quote from Darwin's *Beagle* journal where the scientist speculates about the possible savagery of "'our progenitors,'" and then asserts: "In the 1830s such thinking was less intellectually acceptable than it had been a half century earlier or was again to be a half century hence" (105–107).

economic nature of slavery greatly complicates the Marxist concept of commodity fetishism, which posits that interpersonal relationships are material, while social relationships exist between things.[29] The slave is quite literally a commodity with an exchange value, by definition a thing capable of effecting social relations. Thus, as Joan Dayan points out in "Race and Romance," the slave becomes for the owner the "ultimate possession" and the pleasure of such ownership becomes "addictive."[30] Within the context of bondage, rather than race *per se,* we can begin to demystify the nature of Cathy and Heathcliff's relationship and the problems of confused identity the text poses.

Even the most casual reader senses that the Catherine/Heathcliff dyad is peculiar in its passion and commitment. Both compelling and repugnant, the relationship may pass for love, but as Charlotte Brontë comments in the "Editor's Preface of the New Edition," Heathcliff's "love" "is a sentiment fierce and inhuman" (22). Heathcliff's lack of humanity is a continual concern of the text, but other characters, too, are called "things" and "property" (179), so that the rhetoric of slavery contaminates pervasively. Nelly says that Cathy "was much too fond of Heathcliff. . . . In play, she liked, exceedingly, to act the little mistress; using her hands freely, and commanding her companions." This game of bondage, what Nelly calls "her pretended insolence," provides Cathy with "more power over Heathcliff than [Mr. Earnshaw's] kindness: how the boy would do *her* bidding in anything, and *his* only when it suited his own inclination" (55). This mistress-bondsman relationship, which Heathcliff explicitly characterizes as slavery (108), is rooted in his complete submission to her will, rather

---

[29] See Marx, *Capital* (note 13), "The Fetishism of Commodities," esp. 321. Lukács' "reification" extends the concept of commodity fetishism beyond the objectification and alienation of one's labor to include commodification of "nonmaterial" products—ideas, institutions, values—which both serve to totalize capitalist ideology and further individuate and alienate the self from its products. Georg Lukács, *History and Class Consciousness: Studies in Marxist Dialectics,* trans. Rodney Livingston (Cambridge: MIT Press, 1968, 1971), 83–222. Both theorists employ slavery figuratively or as a fact of "antiquity" that ignores the very real exchange value, the price, the owner could demand for human property. See esp. Lukács, 166–69.

[30] Joan Dayan's "Race and Romance" (note 18) has fundamentally informed my argument. Primarily concerned with how slavery and race were figured in American romance, Dayan notes that in a system of bondage "the conversion of person into thing for the ends of capital" generated a "twisted sentimentality" and a "cruel analytic of 'love.'" Furthermore, the addictive pleasure of absolute domination depends on the slave who becomes "a necessary part of the master's or mistress's identity" so that "extremes of differences [are] blurred in an odd promiscuity" (90). James Walvin also uses the trope of addiction: "Dependence of African slaves had taken on addictive proportions" (*Black Presence* [note 1], 9).

than mutual affection or sympathy of feeling. His service is the material and social extension of her identity.

At the moment of Heathcliff's first departure, Cathy admits that her identity is absolutely dependent on his existence; she tells Nelly, "If all else perished, and *he* remained, I should still continue to be; and, if all else remained, and he were annihilated, the Universe would turn a mighty stranger. . . . I *am* Heathcliff . . . [he is] my own being" (85). She explains that she loves him "because he's more myself than I am" (84). Her "love" is not a "delight, but necessary," his existence is not a "pleasure" but her "own being," and separation from him is "impracticable" (85). Devoid of a veneer of tender sentimentality and gracious civility, love assumes the qualities of addiction. Indeed when Heathcliff leaves, Cathy falls ill and is cajoled back to health by being allowed "whatever she pleased to demand" (91). There is, however, a vast difference between being humored and being obeyed. The former is an act of grace on the part of another; the latter is the self's exercise of power. This distinction emerges when Catherine says that her love for Edgar is like "foliage" while her love "for Heathcliff resembles the eternal rocks beneath" (85) and when Heathcliff sneers at Edgar Linton's "*duty* and *humanity . . . pity* and *charity*," those ideals so central to English civilized domesticity: "He might as well plant an oak in a flower-pot, and expect it to thrive, as imagine he can restore her to vigour in the soil of his shallow cares!" (139). The privileges and obligations, "the deep and growing happiness" (93), of a conventional marriage pale when confronted with the addictive pleasure of absolute possession free of restraint and control of "human" passions. Heathcliff is her ultimate possession: "*My* Heathcliff" she proclaims at their last meeting, "I shall love mine yet; and take him with me—he's my soul" (144). In the manner of the Gothic novel, she does maintain her possession beyond the grave. In *Wuthering Heights,* the supernatural is possession and, as a convention of fiction, discloses an appropriation of the system of rules inherent in institutionalized slavery only to impose those rules on the concept of romantic love.[31] But slavery is a corrupting institution, and absolute possession in *Wuthering Heights* results in disease, anorexia, and self-willed annihilation.

---

[31] Foucault posits: "If interpretation is the violent or surreptitious appropriation of a system of rules, which in itself has no essential meaning, in order to impose a direction, to bend it to a new will, to force its participation in a different game, and to subject it to secondary rules, then the development of humanity is a series of interpretations." Michel Foucault, "Nietzsche, Genealogy, History," in *Language, Counter-Memory, Practice: Selected Essays and Interviews,* ed. Donald F. Bouchard, trans. Donald F. Bouchard and Sherry Simon (Ithaca: Cornell Univ. Press, 1977), 151–52.

Finally faced with a "cruelly provoking" choice between Edgar and Heathcliff, Cathy retreats to her room, refuses to eat, and suffers from hallucinations. Significantly, she cannot recognize her image in a mirror, confusing it with some other face reflected in "the black press shin[ing] like jet." "Overwhelmed" by "utter blackness," the error leaves her trembling, bewildered and ashamed, believing she was back at the Heights "enclosed in the oak panelled bed at home" (116–18).[32] In this scene imagery of blackness, confinement, and insanity are tightly bound to the plantation site and to confused and lost identity. Cathy anticipates death and taking Heathcliff with her: "'I won't rest till you are with me. . . . Be content, you always followed me!'" (119). The bond between mistress and bondsman transcends the laws of nature, and transgresses the bonds of matrimony.

During a three-year hiatus of which we have only vague speculation, Heathcliff acquires a rudimentary gentleman's education, speech and manners, and cash enough to "pass"—indeed to irresistibly attract Isabella Linton who mistakes him for "a rough diamond—a pearl-containing oyster of a rustic" (101). She projects the romanticized version of the Anglo-Saxon hero onto him, picturing him as "a hero of romance . . . expecting unlimited indulgences from [his] chivalrous devotion"; she "cherishes" "a fabulous notion of [his] character" (137). Cathy attempts to dissuade her, characterizing him as a brute: "An unreclaimed creature, without refinement—without cultivation; an arid wilderness of furze and whinstone . . . a fierce, pitiless, wolfish man" (101). Racialist discourses were riddled with paradoxical anecdotal commentary on the nature and depth of feeling in blacks.[33] On the one hand, they were understood to be universally deceitful and ruled by transitory appetites and terrors, and on the other their

---

[32] Physical intimacy was an inevitable by-product of slavery. The domestic slave attended to the most personal of needs including wetnursing, caring for the young and infirm, bathing, and removal of bodily wastes. We can deduce that shortly after his arrival, Heathcliff was put to bed with the Earnshaw children by Earnshaw's orders (51), and Hindley was removed at least by the time he goes to school some three years later. We know that Cathy was "laid alone for the first time" (118) at age twelve and that she and Heathcliff shared the "large oak case" (37). Lockwood invites us to speculate about the sexual nature of the relationship when he notes that the bed was designed for conjugal privacy (37), but Cathy's hallucination accompanies her illness and Nelly's negligent nursing. See Poe (note 18).

[33] See Thomas Jefferson, *Notes on the State of Virginia* (Chapel Hill: Univ. of North Carolina Press, 1954). Jefferson in describing the distinguishing features of the black race explains: "They are more ardent after their female: But love seems with them to be more an eager desire, than a tender delicate mixture of sentiment and sensation" (139). Jefferson's manuscript originally read: "But love is with them only an eager desire, not a tender delicate excitement, not a delicious foment of the soul" (288, n. 8). As noted earlier Charlotte Brontë terms Heathcliff's love "fierce and inhuman." We can speculate

fidelity and selflessness were eulogized and legendary.[34] In creating the "fiendish" Heathcliff, Emily Brontë adds to Long's characterization by incorporating the varied and seemingly contradictory mid-century stereotypes of the African. Isabella taunts him: "If I were you, I'd go stretch myself over her grave, and die like a faithful dog" (157). Heathcliff asserts, "I'd not exchange, for a thousand lives, my condition here, for Edgar Linton's at Thrushcross Grange—not if I might have the privilege of flinging Joseph off the highest gable, and painting the house-front with Hindley's blood!" (60). As slave, Heathcliff is both devoted to his "condition" and capable of vicious rebellion. Only Cathy's will, which has been conflated with his own, prevents him from tearing Hindley's "heart out" and drinking "his blood" (136). The spectre of slave rebellion (a frequent reality in the early nineteenth century) and the viciousness with which they were executed demonstrate how tenuous and fearful the planters' position was.

It falls to Edgar Linton to identify explicitly the more insidious danger in the intimacy of the master-bondsman relationship: Catherine has become "habituated to [Heathcliff's] baseness" and his "presence is a moral poison that would contaminate the most virtuous" (110).[35] Of course English fear of the base, foreign and domestic, is at least as old as Pope's *Dunciad;* however, in *Wuthering Heights* baseness does not threaten dullness, but vitiating energy. Decorum and a rein on her desires are never Cathy's strong suit; the novel makes clear that the brutal heroics that underwrite the Anglo-Saxon myth are incompatible with the myth of civilized Victorian condescension and the domestic ideal, but they are quite at home with the uncontrolled passions nurtured by an undisguised power/bondage relationship. She humiliates Edgar and sarcastically snaps when

---

that Isabella is attracted to the "eager desire" as she agrees to elope. Nelly appears to attempt the Jeffersonian distinction in contrasting Cathy and Heathcliff's "love" to Catherine and Hareton's. Lockwood seems more ambivalent.

[34] See Williams (note 5). The author reprints obituaries from a Liverpool newspaper eulogizing the faithfulness of black servants: "On Saturday, February 26th, 1780, died . . . a merchant who acquired a large fortune in Jamaica; and on Tuesday died his faithful black servant" (554n). The implication, of course, is that the slave had no reason to live once his master had passed away. Selfless heroics were also a staple: "Rushton swam towards a small water cask, which point of safety Quamina had previously attained, and when the negro saw that his friend was too much exhausted to reach the cask, he pushed it towards him, bade him good-bye, and sank to rise no more" (571).

[35] Lady Maria Nugent and Edward Long both worried that in Jamaica the close proximity to black servants corrupted the speech and deportment of the young white ladies of the house. See Dayan, "Race and Romance" (note 18): "Nugent and Long speak from the position of a dominant culture: threatened by the fact of *creolization,* a contamination, as they see it, of the pure civilities of Mother England" (89).

he covers his face, "Oh! Heavens! In the old days this would win you a knighthood . . . We are vanquished!" Heathcliff refers to Edgar as "it" and calls him a "slavering, shivering thing" and a "milk-blooded coward" (111). Isabella, however, retains her romantic notions, the inevitable residue of a mystification of the primitive. At the Heights, Heathcliff has usurped the dominant culture, and he has contaminated the Grange.

At this point the novel begins to dismantle the Anglo-Saxon myth of racial superiority. When we map out a racial archive for *Wuthering Heights,* we find that its "enunciative possibilities" are expanded when cloaked in both the language of "love" and "dispassionate" scientific discursivity. Heathcliff becomes the master of both discourses; he contaminates and pollutes each with the other.[36] He "trains" himself to be methodical and industrious, ruthless and treacherous, temperate and patient, "working like Hercules" to regain his "condition," his place beside Cathy, and "to demolish the two houses" (265). He usurps the power of vision and with it the authority to interpret. Discovering Isabella's infatuation with him, Heathcliff stares at her "as one might do at a strange repulsive animal, a centipede from the Indies, for instance, which curiosity leads one to examine in spite of the aversion it raises" (103). The colonizing gaze has been reversed. Where once Heathcliff wished he "had light hair and fair skin" (66), saw Edgar Linton as "handsome" and himself less so, he is now repulsed by, while still curious about, those features.[37] We are reminded of Lockwood's observation that the people of the region are like "a spider in a dungeon"; they "may concentrate [their] entire appetite" and they can watch so intently that a single neglect puts one "seriously out of temper" (70). Heathcliff ap-

---

[36] As orchestrator of the dual nature of racialist discourse, Emily Brontë "causes a multiplicity of statements to emerge as so many regular events." Located "between tradition and oblivion" (Anglo-Saxonism and racial disorder, civility and unrestrained passion), this hybrid discursive practice "enables statements both to survive and to undergo modification" (Foucault, *Archaeology* [note 10], 130). These "regular events" are not the multiple deaths, Heathcliff's aborted revenge, or the "fusion rather than confrontation of interests between gentry and bourgeoisie" (Eagleton [note 22], 117). The events are instead "the reversal of a relationship of forces, the usurpation of power, the appropriation of a vocabulary turned against those who once used it, a feeble domination that poisons itself as it grows lax, the entry of the masked 'other'" (Foucault, "Nietzsche, Genealogy, History" [note 31], 154).

[37] Visitors to the new world typically were fascinated by animal and plant life not native to the old. "Monk" Lewis (note 13) mentions encounters with centipedes a number of times, and one section entitled "Centipedes," describes an experiment in which a centipede is cut in half, put under "a glass cover" and watched for signs of regeneration from Saturday until the following Thursday when both parts vanish. Lewis laments, "Gone they both are, and I am disappointed beyond measure. I have proclaimed a reward for the bringing me of another" (146–47).

propriates Lockwood's watchfulness and Lewis's spirit of experimentation. He adopts the methodology Jefferson advises for discovering the secrets of racial difference, particularly skin color: "To justify a general conclusion, requires many observations, even where the subject may be submitted to the Anatomical knife, to Optical glasses, to analysis by fire, or by solvents." Heathcliff becomes the planter, acquires human property and creates an empire over which he dominates without the "pure civilities of Mother England."[38] Instead, his interests in ownership are self-consciously "ghoulish" (104) and he says he would enjoy "vivisection" (225). He keeps the doors locked, the objects of his gaze trapped, and guards vigilantly against rebellion. Unlike Hindley, he does not degenerate into indolence and intemperance; unlike Cathy, he recognizes the danger in loving what he owns; his domination is laborious and calculated.

Certainly we can attribute Heathcliff's "courting" of Isabella to his desire to obtain her legacy, but first he admits that his interest is "ghoulish" and he would make her "waxen face . . . the colours of the rainbow" (104). Brutality here changes that first distinguishing mark of the Anglo-Saxon, its color. He never acquires the essential mark of civilization as it is defined by Bryan Edwards—"a display of tenderness towards the female sex." He remains "without cultivation."[39] By erasing this feminine privilege from the language of the dominant culture, Emily Brontë signals her split from a previous literary generation; she defoliates the hedges and transgresses the neat boundaries erected by the Darcys and the Knightleys. Heathcliff, for example, consciously parodies the pretensions of those he has come to dominate: hospitality, family, a discourse and behavior designed to veil sovereign power and brutality. When he says, "I want my children about me" (237), he appropriates the language of "love" uncontaminated by sentiment. We are faced not only with hybrid discursivity, but with the problem of miscegenation in its most threatening form—white gentried female and the racially other male.

Isabella Linton, who should manifest the virtues of the cult of true womanhood, deteriorates, living as she does in such close, unremitting and, finally, sexual proximity to the racial other. When Nelly visits the Heights she notes: "He was the only thing there that seemed decent, and I thought he never looked better . . . he would certainly have struck a stranger as a born and bred gentleman, and his wife as a thorough little slattern!" (134). Heathcliff agrees: "She degenerates into a mere slut!. . . . However, she'll suit this house so much the better for not being over nice,

[38] Jefferson (note 33), 143. Dayan, "Romance and Race" (note 18), 89.
[39] Bryan Edwards, *History of the West Indies* (London, 1793), 39.

and I'll take care she does not disgrace me by rambling abroad" (137). Stripped of the prerogatives of her race, class and gender, Isabella is vulnerable, and the racialist and misogynistic commentary about the lasciviousness of black women so rampant in Edward Long's *History of Jamaica* are cathected onto her.[40]

Through Heathcliff's character, Brontë exposes the "twisted sentimentality" of passions passing as love firmly affixed to bondage. Possession allows Heathcliff to experiment with his "centipede," to discover exactly what it takes to destroy a mystification that attempts to conflate brutality and refined sensibility. The experiment was

> a positive labour of Hercules! . . . No brutality disgusted her—I suppose she had an innate admiration of it, if only her precious person were secure from injury! . . . I've sometimes relented, from pure lack of invention, in my experiments on what she could endure, and still creep shamefully cringing back! . . . The nuisance of her presence outweighs the gratification to be derived from tormenting her! (137–38)

The "gratification" Heathcliff derives from tormenting Isabella emerges from his "ruthless curiosity" and the pleasure derived from the power to watch and examine.[41] Isabella resists, cherishing her "fabulous notions" of his character constructed from romances of an Anglo-Saxon golden age, notions that Heathcliff systematically demolishes. He has succeeded in degrading Isabella and demonstrating that a nineteenth-century concept of "race" with its accompanying classifications and hierarchies is socially constructed, a system with no essential meaning. Emily Brontë has conflated the model novel hero with the conventional novel usurper; he scandalizes

---

[40] Long (note 18) informs us that oran-outangs "sometimes endeavour to surprize and carry off Negroe women into their woody retreats, in order to enjoy them" (360). "Ludicrous as the opinion may seem, I do not think that an oran-outang husband would be any dishonour to an Hottentot female" (364). Finally, "The equally hot temperament of their women has given probability to the charge of their admitting these animals [monkies or baboons] frequently to their embrace. An example of this intercourse once happened, I think, in England; and if lust can prompt to such excesses in that Northern region, and in despight of all the checks which national politeness and refined sentiments impose, how freely may it not operate in the more genial soil of Afric, that parent of every thing that is monstrous in nature, where these creatures are frequent and familiar; where the passions rage without any controul; and the retired wilderness presents opportunity to gratify them without fear of detection!" (383).

[41] See Foucault, *Discipline and Punish: The Birth of the Prison*, trans. Alan Sheridan (New York: Random/Vintage, 1979), 227 and the section on the Panopticon as a laboratory, 203–4; and *The History of Sexuality: Volume I, An Introduction,* trans. Robert Hurley (New York: Random/Vintage, 1978): "A pleasure that comes of exercising a power that questions, monitors, watches, spies, searches out, palpates, brings to light" (45).

because he flouts a fundamental social code — civility towards women and children — and he merits his superior position according to a code that valorizes talent combined with industry.

Nelly, early in her narrative, characterizes Heathcliff as "very near — close handed . . . greedy" (49), and Cathy concludes, "Avarice is growing in him a besetting sin" (101). Although the novel critiques unrestrained capitalism, Heathcliff is not corrupted primarily by the spirit of commerce as opposed to the spirit of law or decency, but by the nineteenth-century spirit of experiment, investigation and examination that Foucault identifies and explores throughout his work. Heathcliff's exercise of mastery is neither impatient nor haphazard; it is executed according to critical, evaluative principles. For a character seemingly over-full of passion to the point of obsession, Heathcliff is remarkably methodical, clinical, and dispassionate. After Linton lures Nelly and the younger Catherine inside the Heights, Heathcliff comments: " 'Had I been born where laws are less strict, and tastes less dainty, I should treat myself to a slow vivisection of those two, as an evening's amusement' " (225). Nelly notes that his response to Hindley's death was devoid of triumph: "He maintained a hard, careless deportment, indicative of neither joy nor sorrow; if anything, it expressed a flinty gratification of a piece of difficult work successfully executed" (164). Instead his "fiendish prudence" (153) focuses on the analytic, a cruel sense of the curious: " 'Now my bonny lad,' " he says to the orphaned Hareton, " 'you are *mine*! And we'll see if one tree won't grow as crooked as another, with the same wind to twist it!' " (164). Heathcliff has acquired another piece of human property, and initially we are tempted to identify Heathcliff with the wind that has twisted and corrupted Hindley. However, we are also invited to understand that the wind is the tyranny and oppression that has twisted Heathcliff and now threatens Hareton, with whom he explicitly identifies (188). Nelly tells Lockwood that Hareton has been "reduced to a state of complete dependence . . . and lives in his own house as a servant deprived of . . . wages" (165). Heathcliff does not debauch Hareton as he did Hindley; he enslaves him as he himself was enslaved.

The pleasure Heathcliff enjoys from his property, both real and human, lies not in its acquisition, nor in its belonging to him, but in its degradation, its demolition, its destruction (265). He wishes he "could annihilate it from the face of the earth" (272). As master, he can debauch, but his interest is in investigating, scrutinizing and experimenting with degradation. Bragging to Nelly, he claims, "I've a pleasure in [Hareton]" because "he has satisfied my expectations . . . I've taught him to scorn everything extraanimal as silly and weak." Hareton now takes "pride in his brutishness" (188); an Englishman should pride himself on his Anglo-Saxon heritage. For Heathcliff, Hareton is a "personification of [his] youth, not a human being" (265). Dispassionately, Heathcliff has attempted to form his ward into a bondsman stripped of his humanity, and in his face he sees reflected his own "wild endeavors to hold [his] right," his "degradation," and his "pride" (266). Heathcliff does not oppress to wrest labor (as Hindley did) or love (as Cathy does) from his human property, but to watch oppression itself, to see what can happen when a human is turned into a thing.[42] By oppressing, Heathcliff can appropriate knowledge to ultimately reject it and embrace his own slavery, not magnanimously, but absolutely; this way he can attain his "heaven" (273), regain his "condition," and obtain his happiness by "dissolving with [Cathy]" (239). It is a conversional, even Hegelian, form of surrender of will.[43]

How readers respond to Heathcliff's love for Catherine is complex. In considering his love, Charlotte Brontë wrote: "Whether it is right or advis-

---

[42] He experiments with a knowledge as Foucault describes it: "A knowledge, which is dissociated from pleasure and happiness, is linked to the struggle, the hate, and the spitefulness directed against it until it arrives at it own rejection as an excess created by struggle, hate, and spitefulness." Michel Foucault, "History of Systems of Thought," in *Language, Counter-Memory, Practice* (note 31), 203.

[43] See G. W. F. Hegel, *Phenomenology of Spirit*, trans. A. V. Miller (Oxford: Oxford Univ. Press, 1977). In 1807, the year Britain outlawed the slave trade, Hegel published the *Phenomenology*, which spiritualizes "lordship and bondage." In Hegel's schema both lord and bondsman seek freedom, understood as detachment from "life" (113) or "natural existence" (117). The former achieves freedom through "staking one's life" and thus demonstrating that one is not "submerged in the expanse of life" and instead recognizes that there is "nothing in it [life] which could not be regarded as a vanishing moment" (114). The lord is appetitive and relates immediately to the world of things by negation, by enjoying them. In contrast, the bondsman works on things, and "through his service rids himself of his attachment to natural existence" (117). Significantly, it is the slave's self-consciousness that progresses through the dialectic to achieve an *Aufhebung*, escaping "the nightlike void of the supersensible beyond, and step[ping] out into the spiritual daylight of the present" (111). Heathcliff's demise bears an uncanny resemblance to the progress of the "Unhappy Consciousness." He loses his appetite, both literal and figurative. His labors have effected a change so that all objects, animate and inanimate, resemble his object of desire; Catherine and Hareton "are the only objects which retain a distinct material appearance to [him]"; he has to remind himself "to breathe" and his "heart to beat" (266). His existence is "devoured" and he is "swallowed" by anticipation (266). Like Heathcliff, for the Unhappy Consciousness, "Action and its own actual doing remain pitiable, its enjoyment remains pain, and the overcoming of these in a positive sense remains a *beyond*" (138); Heathcliff looks on a "fancied object" that "communicate[s], apparently, both pleasure and pain, in exquisite extremes" (271). "His soul's bliss kills [his] body, but does not satisfy itself" (273). In Hegel's terms, he "has successfully struggled to divest [himself] of [his] being-for-self and has turned [himself] into [mere] being . . . aware of his *unity* with this universal, a unity which . . . no longer falls outside of [him] since the superseded single individual is the universal" (139). Nelly reminds us he died with a "frightful, life-like gaze of exultation" (274).

able to create beings like Heathcliff, I do not know: I scarcely think it is" (22). Love is not bound to lust, a condition our critical antennae would quickly sense and quickly dismiss or condemn. Instead, the absolutism of Heathcliff's love is defined in terms of bondage, and it is chilling to suspect that at some level we find enslavement spiritual—as Poe and Hegel did— or worse, viscerally appealing. Like Isabella, "no brutality disgust[s]" us; perhaps we have an "innate admiration of it" as long as we ourselves suffer no injury. Slavery is condemned as perpetrated by Hindley and Heathcliff, but at the same time it is quite literally romanticized.

What is not romanticized or made appealing is miscegenation, as manifested by its sole issue: Linton Heathcliff. The corruption attributed to hybridization in mid-century racialist discourses is rendered in Linton Heathcliff. He manifests most of the worst accidents and mistakes mixed blood could represent for mid-century England: disease, viciousness, treason, cowardice, duplicity, unmerited power, shiftlessness. The problem of the mulatto is rampant in the discourses about institutionalized slavery. "Monk" Lewis notes, "They are almost universally weak and effeminate persons . . . one black is considered as more than equal to two mulattoes." They make the lives of their own slaves "wretched," and the misery of Jamaican slaves would be greatly relieved if mulattoes were prohibited from becoming slave owners. Warmed to his subject, Lewis goes so far as to support the prohibition of "domestic slavery," limiting the institution to "plantation labour" which he views as economically essential to both colony and motherland.[44] As a side effect, removing blacks from the household would increase geographic and cultural distance between the races. Thomas Jefferson is even more explicit about his fear of miscegenation and more adamant about securing geographic separation. In comparing classical slavery with its modern version he argues that Greek and Roman slaves were white and once freed indistinguishable from their former masters. They might mix "without staining the blood of [the] master." Black slaves, however, when freed must "be removed beyond the reach of mixture."[45]

---

[44] Lewis (note 13), 55, 180–81.
[45] Jefferson (note 33), 141–42. This policy was enacted. The American effort at "repatriation" of Africans was Liberia, already established as "the independent African state of Maryland" prior to 1834. As with emancipation, the British preceded the Americans in relocating freed blacks. In 1787 the abolitionists were able to secure parliamentary sanction for the Sierra Leone Company:

The persons more generally fixed upon for colonists, were such Negroes, with their wives and families as chose to abandon their habitations in Nova Scotia. These had followed the British arms in America; and had been settled there, as a reward for their services, by the

Emily Brontë creates Linton Heathcliff in the mold of the racialist stereotypes and anxieties of the time. As a mulatto, he exploits his weakness, paleness, the younger Catherine's good heart and better nature, and his position as "little tyrant" (229). From the beginning he is an "ailing, peevish creature" (161). Nelly assesses him on first sight as a "pale, delicate, effeminate boy" with a "sickly peevishness" that Edgar Linton had escaped (174), and calls him "the worst-tempered bit of sickly slip that ever struggled into his teens! Happily . . . he'll not win twenty" (205). Heathcliff is appalled by his "property" — "that's worse than I expected . . . Though it *is* something to see you have not white blood" (180). Linton is variously termed "paltry creature," "the vapid thing" (187), a "distorted nature" (214), "a feeble tool" (216), "confirmed invalid" (219), "abject reptile" (222), and a "cockatrice" (229), venomous and deadly. He is a "little tyrant" who would "undertake to torture any number of cats if their teeth be drawn and their claws pared" (229). Even though Heathcliff is "bitterly disappointed with the whey-faced whining wretch" (181), he orders Hareton to obey him and has "arranged every thing with a view to preserve the superior and gentleman in him" (181). Although Linton may not fully understand the dynamics of power, when he has it he exercises it without restraint. The younger Catherine is condemned to attend to him alone until his death, and of that event she comments, "He's safe, and I'm free" (242).

It is only just that we question the source of Linton's spinelessness, spitefulness, sickliness and moral turpitude. His mother may have been silly, duped by a mystification purveyed by trashy novels and romantic claptrap, but she did not lack backbone. Pregnant and bleeding, she revolted against her master, and refused to seek the nearby protection of her brother, electing instead to strike out on her own. That she died ought not to be held against her in a novel littered with corpses. Much could be said against Linton's father, but effeminacy, cowardice, and weakness of will are not among his flaws. However, for discourses that shroud a fear of racial mixture by positing the inferiority of the mulatto, Linton serves a purpose; he is a wretch who erupts as the locus of corruption and pollution in the novel. When Linton flies into a rage, Joseph cries, "That's the father! We've alla summut uh orther side in us" (212). In Linton, Heathcliff is the "other side," the source of contamination. With Heathcliff, Emily Brontë cri-

---

British government. [Thomas Clarkson, *The History of the Rise, Progress, and Accomplishment of the Abolition of the African Slave Trade by Parliament*, 2 vols. (1808; rpt., London: Frank Cass, 1968), 2:343.]

The British rewarded their Black loyalists with settlements thousands of miles from the shores of Mother England, reducing the threat of intimate proximity, miscegenation, and its offspring.

tiqued racialist presuppositions about Anglo-Saxon superiority; but with Linton she reimposes the taboo against miscegenation. The enduring result of miscegenation is narrowly avoided by Heathcliff's abstinent lifestyle, Cathy's "infernal selfishness" (143) and Linton Heathcliff's poor health. The possibilities innate in hybridization, according to contemporary racialist theory, are de facto exterminated by the author. The mulatto in *Wuthering Heights* is an enunciative impossibility. The stain of Heathcliff's blood will not smudge any little faces in the local region nor spread generation after generation until the entire population is infected. The Heights and its environs will revert to Anglo-Saxon racial purity.

This fatal solution is not quite as final as one might expect; the reconstituted community at the close of the novel is not left culturally unpolluted. First, we are hard pressed to remember that Hareton is Frances and Hindley's son. Both Nelly and Heathcliff mark his physical resemblance to the elder Catherine. His filial loyalty is to Heathcliff, not his father, and the younger Catherine is forced to desist from trying to alienate that affection. Furthermore, the parallels between Hareton and Heathcliff are both implicit and explicit. Heathcliff sees his own youth in Hareton (265). When Heathcliff arrived at the Heights he spoke "some gibberish that nobody could understand" (51); when Isabella speaks to Hareton for the first time after she moved to the Heights, "he replie[s] in a jargon [she] did not comprehend" (127). Heathcliff hangs Isabella's "little dog" when they elope (137); when she makes her escape from the Heights, she sees Hareton "hanging a litter of puppies" (160). Both defile the mother tongue and affront a British sensitivity to cruelty to animals. Although Hareton is Hindley's by blood, we are inclined to think of him as Heathcliff's "immaculate" creation, embodying his masculinity and vigor—traits systematically denied a racial hybrid, but afforded the racial other and the racial ancestor.

The other disquieting element that stubbornly persists at the ending of the novel is imagery of bondage, chillingly domesticated and civilized. Our last extended look at Catherine and Hareton is rendered by Lockwood, to whom Terry Eagleton attributes "aesthetic false moves" and "a coy, beaming sentimental self-indulgence." Eagleton may be correct in asserting that the "language used" unconsciously describes a "cultural transfusion." [46] If so, it is plasma extracted from whole blood, a "masked other." The domestic scene that Lockwood relates is riddled with a "twisted sentimentality" of "playful" bondage [47]: "'Recollect, or I pull your hair!'" Catherine threatens. When Hareton's attention lapses, it is recalled "by a sharp slap on

---

[46] Eagleton (note 22), 118.
[47] For citations of these terms, see Foucault, "Nietzsche, Genealogy, History" (note 31) and Dayan, "Race and Romance" (note 18).

the cheek" (253). The economy of slaps and kisses, so sweetly told and mit-igated by visions of "smiting beauty," is reminiscent of Cathy's "pretended insolence" that enslaved Heathcliff. Nelly assures us that the younger Catherine's "anger was never furious; her love never fierce" (165), but we should remember that she "gave [Hareton] a cut with [her] whip" (212) and "beguiled Hareton" to labor for her (267). Are we to suppose that Catherine and Hareton's relationship is but an impoverished reflection of the "love" Heathcliff and Cathy shared? I think not. We should respect it for the virulent strain of ideology it is, a "surreptitious appropriation" and a malicious parody. Lockwood himself feels "impelled to escape them again" (276). Heathcliff's domination dissolves in the grave, but bloodless, he and his mistress are given wide berth and a space to walk, and we can be seduced into thinking that bondage has been quarantined to the spirit world. However, Heathcliff's "masked 'other,'" Lockwood's sentimental discourse, enters to appropriate a vocabulary of brutal domination.[48] Eco-nomic exploitation is eroticized, and "love" flourishes most hardily at the site of oppression.[49]

By 1846 institutionalized slavery was part of the British Empire's past; the fiendish, monstrous, inhuman practice was abolished and suppressed, and those with sunny dispositions imagined that it was dead and buried. However, as the volume of discourses related to slavery and the Anglo-Saxon myth of racial superiority testify, it lay in "unquiet slumber" (276). *Wuthering Heights* suggests that mastery and bondage are not accidents of race, or history. The plantation site is abandoned "for the use of such ghosts as choose to inhabit it" (276) and to become a crumbling reminder that, given the opportunity, all are capable of infinite brutality and falling victim to the addictive pleasure of possessing another human being.

---

[48] See also Pratt (note 21), where she identifies a similar phenomenon, coining the term "anti-conquest" for "the strategies of representation whereby European bourgeois sub-jects seek to secure their innocence in the same moment as they assert European hege-mony" (7). However, Lockwood's pretensions to imperialism are as ludicrous as those to Byronicism: he is a parody of the "'seeing man'... whose imperial eyes passively look out and possess." Even so, his very ineptitude, his inability to see, is disquieting if we en-tertain the concept that discourse is a machine not only of representation but also of sur-veillance, like the Panopticon. Foucault says of the Panopticon: "There is a machinery [read: discourse] that assures dissymmetry, disequilibrium, difference." In contrast to the classical deference to ethos and testimony, "it does not matter who exercises [its] power. Any individual, taken almost at random, can operate the machine." Motive — "curiosity," "thirst for knowledge" or "perversity" — is irrelevant. This language of love "is a marvelous machine which, whatever use one may wish to put it to, produces ho-mogeneous effect of power" (Foucault, *Discipline and Punish* [note 42], 202).

[49] Dayan (note 18) succinctly expresses this relationship between love and oppression.

Part Four

THE LITERARY
AND CULTURAL CONTEXTS

THE BRIDEGROOM OF BARNA

Bartholomew Simmons

As noted earlier, Emily Brontë was an avid reader, and one of her favorite journals was *Blackwood's Edinburgh Magazine*. In November of 1840 she read "The Bridegroom of Barna," a short story by Bartholomew Simmons (1804–50), a minor Irish poet and fiction writer whose collected poetry was published in 1843. (His most famous poem was "Napoleon's Last Look.") Set in Ireland among feuding families, "The Bridegroom of Barna" bears a number of similarities in characters and plot to *Wuthering Heights*. It is reproduced here for the first time in conjunction with the novel. The Irish dialect is translated from Niall O'Dónaill's *Foclóir Gaeilge-Béarla*. [ED.]

Begone! — outstrip the fleet gazelle —
The wind in speed subdue;
Fear cannot fly so swift, so well,
As vengeance shall pursue!

Mrs. Hemans

I

What traveller that is familiar with Ireland, and has walked or ridden along the roads of that country, has not remarked the unwearying disposition the peasantry who happen to journey in the direction he is proceeding in, evince to enter into conversation with him, or, failing that, to at least shorten and sweeten their way by following close at his heels, whether he be on horseback or a pedestrian? As they are naturally a most inquisitive,

---

Blackwood's Edinburgh Magazine (Nov. 1840): 680–704.

as well as social race, this disposition on their part is peculiarly favourable to the gratification of their propensities. Should you, for instance, be accompanied by a friend, there are nine chances to one that they become familiarly acquainted with your private business or family history; and even if alone, and disposed to repel all attempts to be communicative, they are sure not to quit you, without being enlightened upon some part of your personal affairs. If you ride — they will "take the weight" of your horse, calculating by the state the animal is in the exact distance you have travelled; by its breed and grooming the probable amount of your property; and as they are resolved not to give up the chase until you are run to earth at the next park-gate or market-town to which you are bound, they leave you with a tolerable guess at the cause of your journey. If you walk — the matter is still more easily settled; you have less chance of baffling them: and the style of your dress, the appearance of energy or fatigue, the knapsack of a tourist, or the unencumbered ease and delicate cane of a morning visiter, are all satisfactory manifestations of your intentions or pursuits. How often have I amused myself in crossing the scent, by suddenly stopping short, and affecting to wait for some invisible acquaintance in the rear, and thus letting these persecutors get ahead, where I endeavoured in vain to keep them! They will still linger behind, and if you hasten to outstrip them by superior speed, you but overtake a fresh group of tormentors, nor can you reasonably expect any relief until the close of the day, or the arrival at your destination, effects your deliverance.

I had just pulled up at the summit of a long hill, in one of the wildest districts of the county Tipperary, which I had been ascending for a tedious half-hour, in a chill, though bright March evening — in order to alight and walk my mare down the corresponding declivity, that unveiled its lengthy and precipitate way into a champaign country of extensive and bleak appearance.

Having loosened the saddle-girths a little, to relieve my faithful steed, I turned to pursue my way, when I perceived still lingering near me a stranger who had kept close upon my track with unwearied pertinacity, from the town of Ballymore, a distance of seven or eight Irish miles, and all whose attempts to enter into conversation, however graciously offered, I had most perseveringly resisted, not from a feeling that there was any thing obtrusive in the individual, but simply that I was "not i' the vein." As, however, I perceived that although we were at a crossroad, (a spot where four roads meet,) my fellow-traveller was about to take the one I had selected, I was now induced to bestow a little more attention upon him. He was an undersized, athletic-looking young man, perhaps about twenty years of age; bull-necked, with a powerful chest, his countenance harsh and massive beyond his years, with a mouth which would have indicated undisguised ferocity, were it not that the upper part of his face in some degree relieved this expression, or rather diverted attention from it by a broad forehead, and a quick, bright, but restless eye. Altogether he would have given assurance of a tremendous physical maturity, but either naturally or accidentally the mould had been marred—his right arm was wanting, as the empty sleeve pinned to the breast of his jacket too plainly showed; but as if determined to compensate the loss by all the means in his power, he carried in his left hand a club, or, as it is termed all over Munster, a *wattle,* of such prodigious dimensions, and so loaded at the heavier end with lead, as at once to excite my surprise and—shall I own it?—distrust, in a country where I knew, by a recent police enactment, such murderous weapons were prohibited. And yet there was something fantastic about the fellow's appearance notwithstanding. Instead of the customary frieze dress of the peasantry, he wore an old and much-rubbed shooting-jacket of black plush, in the button-holes of which he had arranged sundry gay feathers, the ultimate use of which might be inferred from a quantity of fishing-tackle twisted round his cap, which was huntsman-shaped, and covered with a bristling fox-skin of a fiery-red hue; his feet were bare, and he had his strong corduroy trousers tucked up very high, probably to afford him the greater facility in travelling.

As the gaze with which I regarded my companion was not to be mistaken, even by stronger assurance than he was able to muster in his face at the moment, he very civilly touched his cap and said, "He'd be bound he knew where I was going, and he'd be proud to show me the way."

"And pray, my fine fellow, where do you suppose I am going?" I had the curiosity to ask; "or how have you been able to learn any thing of my movements?"

"O by gonnies!" he said, "I know well. Didn't I not see your honour in Ballymore this morning talkin' to Father Mick, and laughin' with him; an' by the same token you'd be sure to meet him this evenin', as, of all things, you'd like to see an Irish weddin'; and then I knew at wonst that you'd be at Hugh Lawlor's weddin'. 'Tis there Father Mick an' half the parish 'll be this evenin', an' there I'll be myself, with the help o' God. See," he added, not waiting to learn how this introduction was received—"see, sir, over the hill yonder, about a mile an' a half, you can jest spy the smoke of the doin's at Davy Nugent's. Hugh Lawlor is to have Miss Ellen afther all, an' 'tis the boys of Eliogarty are glad to have him back at last; they thought they'd never see him agin, good, bad, or indifferent."

---

frieze: coarse woolen cloth, often striped.
o by gonnies: oh, you simpleton!
doin's: doings, festivities.

"And do they all carry such slips of palm as that pretty one in your fist," I could not help saying, "when they go to welcome back a friend?"

The fellow grinned. "What business would I have up in this counthry without my wattle, sir, when they're all Cumminses about us here, an' I a Dharrig?[1] Only to be shure, now that Masther Hugh is back, an' to be married to a Cummins, I suppose we'll have some sort of pace an' quietness. Gie me the rein, your honour, an' I'll lead the mare easy, an' you can keep off the stones on this smooth bit o' road."

"No, I thank you; but let me ask what was the interesting business that deprived the barony so long of Mr. Hugh's presence?"

"Yes, sir."

"You don't hear me, I believe. Pray, what kept Master Hugh away so long?"

"Wisha, 'tisn't myself very well knows, sir," was the reply, after a slight pause and an inquisitive glance.

"People said a deal about his bein' away. He was fond of Miss Ellen since they wor childer; but his bein' a Dharrig, an' all belongin' to her Cumminses, in coorse they wor morthal enemies. But Hugh, havin' neither father nor mother, nor one belongin' to him since he was a gorsoon; an' havin' fine farms, and bein' his own masther, nothin' could keep him from goin' about Barna, that's Nugent's—jest yondher—an' bein' a great scholar entirely, fit for Thrinity College, shure—Ellen was breakin' her heart for him, an' used to meet him out late in the evenin' unknowent to her family—an' she caught could, an' was near dyin', (shure she was never well since,) an' thin Hugh came oftener to find out how she was—an' her brother Tom watched him, an' they had the divil's own murdher about it. Lawlor wanted to go away quietly, an' not to mind Tom Nugent's blackguardin' till he drew a caneswoord upon Lawlor, an' tould him he was a Captain Rock, an' was out with the Whiteboys[2] the night—The mare has a stone, by your leave, sir."

Before I had time to see what the matter was, he had disengaged a stone from the off hind hoof of the animal, and resumed.

Dharrig: name of rival family.
Wisha: exclamation indicating dismay, emphasis, or surprise.

[1] "The two principal clans or factions of the county Tipperary were distinguished by the epithets of *Dharrig* and *Cummins,* for which we have never learned a satisfactory reason." [*Blackwood's* note.]
[2] The Whiteboys were a secret association of Irish rural workers organized in 1761 to protest high rent and tithes. The members wore white shirts to better identify themselves at night. In 1842 they murdered Ambrose Power in his own house. [ED.]

"An' so, whatever strugglin they had betuxt them, Tom Nugent was run through with the sword, an' left for dead, an' wasn't expected for a long time. An' Lawlor kep' out o' the way, an' Mrs. Nugent, who was on her deathbed, gave him her curse, an' the same to her daughter if she ever had any thing to do with him ever afther. Still, for all that, when the ould woman was gone, and when Miss Ellen kep' always so bad, dyin' in love for Hugh, the father an' the brother thought it a sin to see her goin' to the grave before their face—the creatur!—an' she the only girl o' the whole family, an' a fine fortun', an' a great education entirely at the nunnery in Thurles— so, at long an' last, they forgiv an' forgot—an' Tom Nugent died ov a decline, an' then the sisther was the only one left to the ould man—an' Lawlor kem back to Barna; an' bee gonnies! you an' I'll see their weddin' this blessed night, ples God."

"But how do the Dharrigs like Master Hugh's match, my friend?" I asked. "He must, I suppose, be a great favourite with them." At once I perceived a strong change to pass over his face. His countenance fell, and a hideous expression of hate fastened on it; but, as if afraid to let the feeling be observed, he quickly resumed his lively tone. "A great favourite is it? Ah, 'twas he that was! There wasn't such a boy in the five counties for runnin'—leapin'— throwin' a stone, or any one thing; but, O Lord! O Lord! th! th! th! see what a sight o' people are crowdin' down yondher, in all directions, to Barna!"

By this time we had descended the declivity, and had gained the level road, which, after straggling for about half a mile over a sullen moor, led into traces of cultivation, and finally opened through broad fields, gay-looking, and green with the early wheat, occasionally absorbing into its line a *boreheen*, (or by-road,) with an additional share of travellers, apparently wending in the direction we were going, until by the time we had passed the gentle ascent, above which the chimneys of Barna had long been peering, the numbers had increased to a goodly crowd of the most diversified appearance; and all, as my companion asserted, evidently bound for festivity. Snug-looking farmers on horseback, with their wives mounted behind them; jaunty young men, of that doubtful rank, known nowhere but in Ireland, designated "half-sirs," conspicuous by the ambitious cut of their bottle-green or stone-blue riding-coats and peppery nags; *jingles,* laden with gentry from the neighbouring towns; quilt-covered carts, filled with colonies of village coquettes, clad in all the awful armour of rural beauty; with a host beside, that may best be enumerated by quoting the satisfactory catalogue compiled upon a more ancient and celebrated occasion.

---

decline: consumption.
th! th! th!: tut! tut! tut!

There were pipers, and fiddlers, and
    tailors,
And cobblers, and weavers, and nailers,
And fifers, and sogers, and sailors,
        Assembled at Ballyporeen.

Amongst the foremost of the scrambling pedestrians, were to be seen two or three couples of *boccoghs*—the sturdy beggars of the country, a hateful, and generally a most profligate set of scoundrels—one acting a stone-blind object, in a long loose coat of grey freeze and a filthy nightcap, led by another with a shrivelled arm, which he thrust, with little ceremony, upon the attention of the passengers; both together shrieking out an abominable supplication in Galt, with all their might and main, letting the harmony pause after the following fashion:

Good Chrest—yans give your charity—
To the poor blind object—
Never see the blessed—
Light o' day—for Jesus—
Sake have pity on the—
Poor blind object—(etc. *da capo.*)

Great was the commiseration bestowed upon those afflicted sufferers by the tender-hearted of the softer sex, as they hurried on. Upon the masculine portion of the crowd, they appeared to produce little effect; and the stroller at my side—who, by the way, seemed to know everyone, and to be universally known—evinced a most unqualified contempt for those mendicants.

"Bad 'cess to yez! Bryny Boccogh, an' your blind eyes, you villyan! 'tis you that'll have another tune in your throat to-night afther you clear your sight with eight or ten dandys of punch"—here a fresh group of characters caught his attention—"Ah! Jacky-the-Dance, no fear you should miss Lawlor's weddin'. What a double-shuffle you'll cut upon the barnfloor by-'n-by! Padeen-na-piperah, how is every bit of you? Oh, murdher! what a call there'll be to-night upon your chanter! Kantheen asthore, take care of your father's pipes, an' keep the childer away from him when he's playin', fear they'd make a hole in his music. Hah, dhar dhieu!" he exclaimed of a sudden—"look at all the Cumminses going yondher the field—'tis a black day for some one the day he tuck up with them!"

Jacky-the-Dance: Jack, the dancing-master. [*Blackwood's* note.]
Padeen-na-piperah: Proper name meaning "Padeen is a piper."
Kantheen asthore: Proper name meaning "Kantheen the treasure."
dhar dhieu: My God!

Thus my itinerant acquaintance rambled on, occasionally receiving the salutations of his neighbours, in the shape of an "Ah, Bush, are you there?" "Yerrah, Bush, what brings you to this quarter?" "Bush, you villyan, you're up to some mischief now, I'll be bail!" and so forth; and it was observable that the heartiness of Mr. Bush produced by no means a corresponding share of jocularity on the part of his acquaintances. On the contrary, I thought they all seemed to regard him with coolness, and some to shrink from his recognition altogether with aversion.

We had now approached the scene of intended festivity. Turning short off the high-road, a narrow lane or avenue, skirted by clamps of elder and black thorn trees, brought us to a rude open gateway, passing through which, the house and messuages of Barna stood before us. The dwelling was a long, irregular building, no doubt formerly of only one story, but which appeared in later years to have been raised another, enlarged and dignified with a slated roof; a neglected flower-bed or two sloped below the windows, and with a screen of climatis and woodbine that clambered over the door, showed some softer spirit had once shed an influence about a spot sufficiently harsh in its general features. A huge range of buildings, as usual in Irish farmhouses, projected at right angles, like wings, from the dwelling, and with the main building formed three sides of a square; the fourth being occupied by an immense stone-paved yard, at the extremity of which were piled a heap of ploughs, carts, and other utensils of husbandry, that had been hastily cleared away to leave the area free upon this festive occasion. The whole was environed by an extensive garden and orchard, and sheltered in the rear by some venerable lime-trees and elms.

All within and around the place was a scene of the highest bustle and animation; the yard was thronged with the country guests getting themselves to rights after the journey, and resounded with laughter, congratulation, and music. The humbler class of visiters were ushered at once to the banquet prepared for their reception, in the long range of lateral buildings already mentioned; while those of a higher rank, or the immediate connexions of the family, were introduced to the dwelling-house, and received by the hosts themselves. On my arrival, I was met by Father O' Hea, the worthy priest, under whose auspices I ventured, prompted by curiosity, to appear at Barna, an uninvited guest. He had already been occupied—for it was Shrovetide—in uniting several other creatures, impatient for happiness, in different parts of the country, and had just arrived in time to be my chaperon to the bridal circle. It requires slight preface to establish your claim at any time to Irish hospitality, above all, upon a wedding occasion;

Shrovetide: the three days preceding Ash Wednesday.

I therefore felt no surprise on receiving at the threshold a cordial welcome and shake of the hands from old Davy Nugent himself, a ruddy, respectable little man, in a cauliflower wig and top-boots. We were ushered, by him, to an interior apartment, which, though of capacious dimensions, was crowded with the elite of Mr. Nugent's fellow parishioners. My attention, however, in the midst of this gay, but incongruous assembly, was at once riveted by the bride and bridegroom; and whether the sequel of their extraordinary story has had any thing to do in heightening the interest they excited, I know not; but it seems to me now, after the lapse of several years, that they appeared from the moment I first beheld them two things totally different from the class to which they belonged—a pair marked out, as it were, by nature to be memorable in their generation.

As young Lawlor, the bridegroom, advanced to assure me, being a stranger, of his satisfaction at meeting any friend of his respected pastor, he necessarily first engaged my attention. There was something indescribable in the man. Scarcely arrived at maturity, his frame had all the fulness and development of one in the prime of life; and, aided by a commanding stature, and an ease of manner and fluency of address which courts will not sometimes bestow, and which yet sometimes may be found in cottages, he was admirably calculated for making an impression upon those he addressed. I was about to say an agreeable one—but it was not so; his dark handsome face and deep flashing eye would have been resistless but for a certain furtive expression that every now and then—at all times—in the repose of thought or excitement of argument, hastily overshadowed them, causing the smile to vanish, and the glance to shrink from yours, and then was gone in a moment; but not until it had jarred the pleasure reflected by his presence, as the dip of a flitting wing breaks up the surface of a summer lake. I saw him but this evening, yet in that brief space I hoarded the vivid recollections of an age of observation. I could not but remark him if it were only for the strong relief in which he stood out from the crowd around, and an air of abstraction, from which he was never entirely divested through all the festivity, save when his eyes rested upon the form, or his voice responded to the accents of Ellen Nugent; "for then ear, eyes, and heart would all awake."

"This," he said, bringing me forward, "is the fair girl who has condescended to take charge of my happiness;" and I bowed low before one of the brightest and most delicate creatures I have ever beheld. Her pale gold hair, deep blue melancholy eyes, and pure colourless check, combined with a form light and faery-like as ever danced in a moonbeam, reminded one less of an earthly being, than of some mournful angel doomed for a while to hover amongst mankind, waiting for the appointed moment to wing home to its native world. As my friend, Mr. Bush, had intimated, I perceived traces of recent ill health in this interesting girl, whose excessive fragility of frame might well awaken apprehension. While her betrothed lingered at her side, she looked one of the happiest of the happy. It was only during his momentary absence that her spirits seemed to waver; she then evinced symptoms of anxiety and dejection, such as persons exhibit who are conscious that a beloved object is exposed to danger that by their presence only can be averted. Knowing the peculiar circumstances of her story, I was not surprised at this; but I could not avoid feeling there was less appearance of heartfelt felicity about this young couple than the agreeable termination of so disastrous a courtship might warrant.

After waiting some time for a Doctor O'Drizzle, a principal accessary, I understood, to all merry-meetings, it was announced that this important personage had arrived, and a summons to dinner was the immediate consequence.

"Mrs. Mackesy, allow me the pleasure, ma'am—to the big parlour, ladies and gentlemen, if *you* please—Tim Carroll, see that the neighbours outside are comfortable—Father Hennessy (to the coadjutor) you're young and hearty, will you help Miss Nelly (a venerable spinster) to do the honours to the boys and girls that haven't room with us?"

Thus gabbled old Davy Nugent, as he marshalled us to the big parlour, which well deserved the appellation: at all times a goodly-sized apartment, even in Eliogarty, where architects are less circumscribed than in Marylebone, the room had been hastily enlarged to three times its dimensions, by the simple and accommodating principle of removing a partition, and letting into it what very much resembled a beautified barn. Here the chief banquet was spread, and graced by the presence of the most important guests, amongst whom, probably as being the greatest stranger, I found I had a distinguished place. After events have so impressed upon my recollection every trifling detail of a scene, which would otherwise have melted into indistinctness among the occurrences of an active life, that I must be pardoned such reminiscences. Yet under the most ordinary circumstances, a genuine Irish wedding is a scene not easily forgotten; and the present one might have served as a specimen *par excellence* of that high festival of good fellowship and fun—"Father O'Hea, grace if you please;" and in a moment the hundred-and-odd eager faces and voluble tongues were seized with a becoming gravity, while the priest uttered a benediction less characterized by its length than fervour; at the same time I observed the greater number of the guests describe some mysterious signs upon their foreheads, and plump we all sat down, and then the long array of turkeys, hams, and sirloins, no longer smoked in vain. Dire was the tumult! The windows of the apartment, though it was chilling spring, were necessarily open to temper the atmosphere within; and the pronouncing of grace was at once the signal to our fellow-travellers in the adjacent buildings to sympathize with us, and to a brigade of pipers to open their harmonious batteries upon every quarter of the establishment. They were ably supported by a reserve of beggars, who, the moment attention was properly diverted from matters of minor importance, beset every window and avenue, and with their squabbling, shouting, and objurgations, literally "filled up each pause *the bagpipers* had made."

"Tim Carroll—a-rue—will *you* go out and see that Bill Fagan keeps away them vagabones from the windows—let him get a flail—do you hear me—*a flail!*" "Father," interjected the gentle voice of Ellen Nugent, "not on this evening—let the poor creatures have it their own way tonight. I see that sad boy Tom Bush is back again in the country; I thought"—she suddenly stopped and looked away. "Ellen—my pet—that fellow was never born to be dhrowned—Mrs. O'Shaughnessy, the pleasure of a glass o' wine, if you please—Doctor O'Drizzle, may I trouble you—Mrs. O's glass—now, good people, take care of yourselves—see if ye can make your dinners!" etc. etc.

As I happened to sit near young Lawlor, I had occasionally some chat with him, as well as his manifold occupations would admit, and found him as superior to his class in intelligence as in appearance. I took an opportunity to ask respecting my pedestrian acquaintance, of whom I had just heard mention, and received by no means a satisfactory character of him.

He was a foundling, and derived his name from the bush or thicket in which he had been discovered—had been brought up, the evil, unaided, wretched childhood and youth of an Irish country pauper—had got into habits of the most inveterate vice—was turbulent and brutal in his conduct; and, in an affray between the faction to which he attached himself and their opponents, received an injury which led to the loss of his arm. He was skilful—Lawlor added—as a *marker* for the country gentlemen, and generally knowing about field sports; but he had lately been imprisoned for some offence, and had, my informant supposed, but just now returned.

These remarks induced allusions to the present state of the country, a subject upon which Lawlor was not communicative. He seemed careless of disclosing his opinions to a stranger, and confined himself to comments on the supineness of the neighbouring magistrates, to which he principally attributed the increase of crime and insubordination; an opinion in which he was supported by no less an authority than the viceroy himself, who, on a late occasion, had expressed his sense of the service of those functionaries, in terms that pretty plainly implied he considered "they loved their own barns better than the public weal."

---

a-rue: I'm sorry.
a flail: a whip.

Though Lawlor was "one of the people," and a Catholic, with, it might be supposed, all the prejudices and sense of wrongs—real or imaginary—of his class and creed, I found him disposed to impress me with an idea of his liberality in politics. He painted Whiteboyism and secret meetings in the most odious colours, until the very force of his language led me to suspect its earnestness. We had not, however, much time for such disquisitions: the mirth, without and around, waxed "fast and furious." We had dined, and were lapped in the joyous indulgence of the hour succeeding dinner; the port and sherry were lubricating the tongues inside, while poteen and porter were lending *tone* to the throats without; the pipers played brisker than ever, while boccoghs and beggars danced in the yard with the wild delight of slaves in a saturnalian emancipation. A ring having been cleared before the windows, in the midst of it was placed a smooth wooden platter or trencher, and Mr. Bush coming forward, made his best bow to the gentry in the parlour, and flourishing his wattle, proceeded to dance a hornpipe upon the dish, carefully confining the sphere of his saltation to its limited circumference. This, in more senses than one, is the *ne plus ultra* of an Irish peasant's accomplishments; and to do Tom Bush justice, he performed his task to perfection, concluding, as they say in the playbills, with a "paralysing" brandish of his weapon, and another obeisance to the company. A fresh tumbler of punch was, by Hugh Lawlor's directions, handed to him—a refreshing compliment it would be degenerate in a host or bridegroom to omit at the close of such a piece of ingenuity. The vagrant, placing his cudgel under his arm and raising aloft the beaker, advanced to the window to return thanks. "Healths apiece to ye, genteels, an' my blessin', Masther Hugh, an' the blessed Virgin's on you an' Miss Ellen every day ye see a pavin' stone, an' may ye be as happy as the day is long!" He had just uttered the benediction, and was about to confirm it by draining the glass, when it was shattered to fragments in his grasp, cutting his solitary hand severely in the crash. A stone flung from the rear of the crowd, either by design or accident, was the cause of this untimely and ominous interruption. Yielding at once to the impulse of his savage nature, the fellow snatched his bludgeon, and turning round, without enquiry or hesitation, felled the person who stood next him to the ground. This happened to be no other than Tim Carroll, an official high, as we have seen, in the household of old Nugent, and still higher in his estimation and that of his followers, who at once burst through the crowd upon the offender, and laid him low by the side of Carroll. A general fray now ensued. Bush, it will be remembered, belonged to the faction of the Dharrigs, to whom he had strongly recommended himself by his reckless and abandoned daring. Several of this clan, as was natural, had attended the wedding of their principal chief, and now instantly rose *en masse,* and rushed from the different tables at which they had been carousing, to avenge their prostrate and insulted favourite. Arming themselves with loosened paving stones, (for they had left offensive weapons at home upon this occasion,) and raising their cry of combat—"Here's Dharrig!" they dashed upon the defenceless Cumminses with resistless effect. The stones flew in every direction, sweeping down all before them with the devastation of grapeshot, dashing through the open doors, and shivering to pieces the windows of the surrounding buildings. So sudden and unexpected was the outbreak—scarcely occupying as many seconds as it has taken words to describe it—that not one of any influence amongst the assembled guests had time to stay the tumult before it had risen to a height that threatened the most disastrous consequences. Before the dismayed host, seconded by his reverend guests, the clergymen, could gain the yard, the Cumminses—in other words—the dwellers about Barna and its vicinity, including all the immediate retainers of the Nugents—had rallied, and were doing deadly battle, hand to hand, with their opponents, while fierce shouts of—"Here's Dharrig!"—"Here's Cummins!" were blent with the shrieks of affrighted women, and the loud battering of the missiles, as they told upon the walls and windows of the edifice. At imminent peril to themselves, Davy Nugent and the priests flung themselves among the combatants, and, with uplifted hands and voices, besought them to have mercy upon each other, and respect for the holy sacrament they had assembled to celebrate. "The ould masther," as I found he was familiarly termed, limited his exertions to indignant expostulation; but it cannot be concealed that his reverend assistants enforced their remonstrances with the more logical application of two stout horsewhips, whose arguments were too convincing to be long resisted, and the rival factions at length retired—

As mountain waves from wasted lands
Sweep back to ocean blue!

I was so amazed at this scene of strife and clamour, that I scarce noticed the effects it had upon my companions. I saw, however, that Hugh Lawlor sprang up at the first cry of his faction, but Ellen Nugent was instantly at his side; she clung to his arm, terrified at the scene without, but doubly anxious, it seemed, to prevent her lover from mingling in it, although he assured her repeatedly it was necessary that he should act as a mediator in the conflict. It was to no purpose; she appeared filled with a dread of his leaving her presence for a moment, and he was at last obliged to yield, and wait the efforts of her father's and the priests' interference.

When peace was established, it was found that the number of wounded happily bore slight proportion to the combatants; and that, with the exception of Tim Carroll, who was severely hurt by the left hander he had received, no serious results were to be apprehended to those engaged in the affray. Hugh Lawlor having now been permitted by his fair fiancée to join her father, took the opportunity of severely reprimanding Bush, who, thanks to the thickness of his pericranium, was fast regaining his faculties, for the wanton enormity of which he had been guilty, in committing the assault that had led to so inauspicious an interruption of their harmony. He ordered him at once to depart, and not make his appearance again at Barna, adding, that a strict watch should be kept upon him in case the life of Carroll should be endangered. Far from exhibiting any symptoms of contrition, the fellow replied in a tone of mingled sullenness and defiance, muttering, it appeared, in an undergrowl, some taunting words, to the effect that it would be well if some people felt the same dislike to bloody hands that they did to broken heads. Whatever might be implied by these words, they seemed to exasperate the bridegroom to frenzy—he wrenched the fatal cudgel from the grasp of its owner, and dragging him to the gateway, beat him from its threshold like a dog. Slowly, and with hell-fire glaring in his eyes, Tom Bush, still facing his ejector, withdrew. When he had got some distance from the gate, he pointed significantly to the branch of a mighty elm that projected over the avenue, shook his hand fiercely at young Lawlor, and plunged into the darkness of the gathering night, with which peals of distant thunder, announcing an approaching storm, now began to mingle.

There were very few spectators of this occurrence. Unluckily, in Ireland scenes of popular violence and strife are too frequent to produce much impression—the moment, therefore, the shortlived battle of the factions had subsided, the revellers returned with a tenfold zest to the conviviality of their respective circles. The tables, which had been so plenteously bestowed, and so rapidly relieved of their goodly viands, were in the meanwhile removed—the apartments were gaily lighted up, and preparations for dancing commenced. Hugh Lawlor had by this time rejoined us, quite unruffled by the incident that had just occurred, save that his face, I thought, looked paler than when he had left us; but he was at the side of Ellen in a moment more, and every other thought was lost in the looks of eagerness and delight with which he drank in her beauty. The cheerful glass, with its accompanying toast and joyous laugh, now circulated merrily—the old related their choicest stories—the young gentlemen who happened to be unpaired, told each other of their hardest rides over the stiffest countries; while those who had a pretty partner at their side, (and they were the majority,) whispered those tales that sound sweetest in the ears of a single auditor. I perceived that Father Mick was absent for the last quarter of an hour, and now a little sleek headed man entered the room, and, looking up towards the head of the table at old Davy Nugent, made a low bow;

whereupon Ellen Nugent turned very pale, and then red, and then still paler; and young Lawlor sprang up, and catching her hand, gently drew it within his arm; and then all the gentlemen rose, and each seized a lady, and Davy Nugent led out, with a jaunty air, Mrs. Mackesy, bobbing like a peony in her scarlet bombazine. And so we went back to the small parlour, or, as they would call it in a fine house, the drawing-room. And there was Father Mick in his alb and surplice, looking quite venerable, and the holy water and his breviary before him on a little table, and near him the sleek-headed herald before mentioned—the clerk of the chapel—a useful attendant upon the occasion. And then there was a crowding and pressing forward; and I being a thin man, and easily slipped over in a throng, found myself very much in the rear. But I could see the top of Hugh Lawlor's stately head, and could imagine him whispering some words of encouragement to Ellen, perhaps bidding her remember his long and arduous, and once hopeless suit, and blessing this hour that so brightly repaid him for all. After some low-voiced conversation for a few minutes, Father Mick opened his breviary, and every one knelt down; a few words were said; a prayer uttered, and an amen pronounced; and Ellen Nugent rose up for life and in death the wife of Hugh Lawlor. Then the rushing was greater than ever; but Lawlor was before them all; he had folded his Ellen to his bosom, and laughing, as he disappointed those who sought to anticipate him, bestowed upon her pure lips a most emphatic kiss; whereupon I could not close my ears to the conviction, that a mighty rustling and smacking resounded through the apartment, even as if every woman in the room was being kissed—not excepting Mrs. Mackesy herself, who, however, gave old Davy Nugent a reproachful punch on the head as she was wiping her mouth, which set his wig marvellously awry.

The sudden burst of bagpipes, reinforced by a strong detachment of fiddlers, that now resounded from every corner of the abode, announced the impatience of the humbler guests for the presence of the fair bride and her party. Leaning on the arm of her husband, Ellen led the way to the apartments assigned for dancing, and taking their place at the head of some forty or fifty couple, the happy pair led off the country dance to the appropriate measure of *Haste to the wedding*. The reign of innocent and frolic mirth was now fully established; and it was early dawn that saw the conclusion of the nuptials of Barna. As I had to travel some miles in an opposite direction to that which I had come, for the purpose of paying a long-

---

bombazine: fine fabric of silk and cotton usually worn to funerals.
alb: long white linen robe worn by priests at mass.

promised visit to a friend, I took my leave early in the night, waiting merely to contribute a trifle to the collection made for the priest—one of the principal sources of his support in a country where no provision is by law established for the Roman Catholic clergy.

II

While all was light and gaiety within the bridal mansion of Barna, one of those tempests which, during the equinox, visit the islands of the Atlantic with such extraordinary violence, was raging far and near without. The wind swept the hills with the roar and fury of a hurricane, and seemed to pause only in its career when outbellowed by the thunder, which burst forth in tremendous and long-continued peals through the advancing night. The rain descended in torrents, drifting in sheets along the country, and swelling the mountain streams until they rose above their channels, and rushed down to aid in the conflict of the devastating elements. Amid the tumultuous din of merriment and music at the abode of Davy Nugent, such a storm, if heard at all, was little heeded; but in the quieter abodes of the surrounding country, its terrors were impressively felt and were long remembered. Amongst those who sat listening to its effects, crowded round a cheerful and happy hearth, that contrasted strongly with the desolation outside, was the family of Major Walker, a gentleman of independent fortune, and a magistrate for the county, who resided about four miles distant from the scene of our narrative, but still higher *up* the country, where, after sinking into moor and morass, and assuming the wild features of mountain districts, the land rises and unites with the principal chain of hills that intersects Tipperary. The house, which was a spacious one, was well adapted for its position—it was strongly as well as handsomely built. The place had been but a few years occupied by Major Walker, who had planted extensively around it; but the plantations were not grown, the shrubberies were stunted, and in the midst stood the house, wrapped in a fearnought of weather-slating, and imparting to the whole, what it only borrowed itself, a look of solitary bleakness. Far different, however, was the aspect of the mansion within. The bright drawing-room fire, around which the family were this night seated, blazed upon a cheerful group, surrounded by all the comforts of social existence, that are met with nowhere in greater profusion than in the abodes of the Irish gentry. Wax lights were glancing upon tables strewed with portfolios and books. One of the latter turned down upon its open pages, an idle work-stand, and a piano with expanded music—appeared to have been just abandoned, as if unable to amuse or interest amid the howling of such a tempest. Upon another table was the tea-equipage, with its still simmering urn; while by the fire, in *fauteuils* and easy chairs, were seated the owner of the mansion, a tall grave gentlemanly man of about fifty—his lady, some few years younger—their daughter, a fine florid bright-cheeked girl of seventeen—and two sons, a couple of years, perhaps, the juniors of their sister. A lady and gentleman, Mr. and Mrs. Craven, visiters from a distant part of Ireland, completed the circle, which had gradually narrowed as the violence of the storm increased.

"William, my boy," asked Major Walker, "have you seen to the fastenings of doors and windows tonight?"

"I have indeed, sir—John Bryan and I went through the house at six, as usual. You are not apprehensive, I hope, that doors and windows, proof against bullets and Captain Rock, can be affected by the storm?"

"I am not—but it is wise to take precautions against both."

"Of the two," observed Mr. Craven, "the tempest would be far the more merciful intruder."

"I fear so," Major Walker replied; "for, though I have no reason to think I am unpopular, the very fact of my being in the commission of the peace marks me out for odium—it is certainly a dreadful state of things!"

"Well," cried Charles Walker, "if Captain Rock should come to pay us a visit he will meet a warm reception—there are eight of us men, including servants, with three blunderbusses, two guns, three cases"—

"How can you go on so, Charley?" said his sister; "good gracious!" she exclaimed, "how it does blow! One is at a loss to say which is safer, the outside or inside of the house. What a bad night for Ellen Nugent's wedding, poor thing! I understand half the country were invited to it."

"I don't think," said her brother William, "we had such a storm as this since the night Garryvoe bridge was carried away, when Fogarty the postboy was drowned at Templebeg ford."

"He couldn't have better luck," said Charles; "he was connected, they say, with all the bad boys about the country; and it was strongly suspected he knew something of poor Milo Byrne's murder."

"That was a frightful affair, if I recollect rightly," observed Mr. Craven, "the newspapers were full of it for days—but I do not exactly remember why it excited so much horror?"

"From its unparalleled atrocity," replied his host. "Poor Byrne was a man of easy fortune, an old neighbour of mine before I left Upper Ormond for this part of the country—he lived about seven miles away, at a fine old place that his family—a Catholic one—had for a number of years. They are

---

fauteuils: armchairs.

not exactly gentry, but gentlemen farmers, and Milo was a worthy representative of a respectable stock. He was a fellow of the most inoffensive disposition, universally beloved for his hospitality and kindness of heart—an excellent landlord, and an indulgent master; and so well known through the greater part of Tipperary for his benevolence and charity, that, as a convincing proof of his popularity, it is believed, (however extraordinary such a thing may appear in Tipperary, where we live with the knife almost at our throats)—that at Curraheen, (the name of his place) they never took the precaution of placing more than an ordinary latch upon the doors at night. He used to say he never injured any one—never drove for rent—never ejected a tenant—never turned a beggar away empty—and that, therefore, there could be no temptation for people to come at night to seek the spoil or redress they were welcome to by day."

"And yet he met with such an untimely end!"

"Untimely indeed! It was a fine moonlight night in October—about eight o'clock, Byrne was seated with his family, I believe, reading the newspaper aloud to them—when"—

"Papa! do you hear nothing?" exclaimed Miss Walker, starting suddenly up, as a fresh burst of the hurricane shook the house to its foundations.

"There is no cause for alarm, my love. As I was saying, poor Byrne, it appears, was reading aloud, when the front door of his dwelling was opened, and a number of men, all armed, their faces covered with crape, walked into the room. In other cases of atrocity, insult is generally added to outrage; but, according to the testimony of the unfortunate man's family, the intruders used no words of menace or reproach. They entered with the usual salutation—which, it was observed, they expressed in Irish, a language little spoken in this county—and, addressing Byrne in a respectful manner, said they wanted to speak with him outside. He rose and followed them, two of the party being left in the room to repress any alarm its inmates might attempt to make. In a few minutes more his wife, with the quick ear of anxiety, caught the voice of her husband in earnest expostulation in front of the house, apparently requesting to be allowed to speak with her. In a short time one shot was fired—a dreadful pause—the sentinels were called off; and, when his terrified family rushed out, Byrne lay stone dead at his own threshold."

"And the cause of all this?" enquired Mr. Craven.

"Was the most revolting and incredible in the annals of crime. The murderers, on leaving the scene, met some of the farm servants; and, with a kind of inconsistent justice, frequent in this passionate and distracted people, desired them to proclaim that the men who killed Milo Byrne were actuated by no ill-will towards him—on the contrary, that they respected and esteemed his character — *but his life was the last surviving one in White Will Redmond's lease;*[3] *a man that ruined, they said, their families and themselves; and, by cutting off Byrne in the prime of life, they deprived their oppressor so many years the earlier of an income of about four hundred a year — a deadly and more lasting revenge, they added, than taking away his life."*

"Horrible! Were the murderers brought to justice?"

"Not one of them," replied Major Walker, "It is now more than two years since the transaction, and nothing has transpired to throw light upon the matter. The interest it excited is gradually dying away amongst more recent occurrences; but its barbarous wantonness will never let it wholly be forgotten."

"Well, I always feel confident," interposed Mrs. Walker, "that the perpetrators of that evil deed will yet be discovered. The murderers of so blameless a man will not die unpunished. Even, if all living agency fails, the very dead will rise" ——

As she spoke, a peal of thunder broke above the storm with a crash, as if the very mountains had rent asunder, and were toppling on the dwelling; and, while the awestruck circle awaited the cessation of its stunning roar, a loud knocking at the hall door reverberated sharply and distinctly through the house, as though the fiend of the tempest was demanding entrance.

The little party instantly sprang up — the already excited females clinging in dismay to their protectors. Major Walker, as calm as usual, rang the bell, while his eldest son advanced to the door of the apartment, and impressed upon the servant the needless caution (in Tipperary) that upon no pretence was the nocturnal visitant to be admitted.

Again the thunder rattled round the hills; and the knocking, which had ceased for a moment, was more violently renewed than before. The voice of the servant was now heard in parley with some person, who, it appeared, eagerly sought admission; and, after the lapse of a few minutes, the domestic ascended to the drawing-room.

"The ould boy himself, I do verily b'lieve, Major, is outside. The cross o' Christ betune us an' all harm! sure such another night no Christhan would ventur out in! I 'ont take it on me to swear whether 'tis man or beast is there; but whichever it is, he keeps cursing and bellowring that he wants to see you, an' that he won't go till he does."

---

[3] "In Ireland, where a number of persons are to be frequently found, in a townland or parish, bearing the same name, the peasantry distinguish them by appellations generally having reference to their personal appearance. Thus there are White — Red — and Black Patrick Sullivan, according to the difference of hair or complexion in those respectable individuals." [*Blackwood's* note.]

"Did you not tell him, Bryan, that no stranger is allowed into my house after nightfall upon any account?"

"Faith an' shure I did, over an' over, Major; an' 'twas little use for me; — 'didn't you tell me your masther is at home,' ses he; 'shure 'twouldn't be out sich a night as this he'd be,' ses I, 'nor any one else that was about any thin' that's good,' ses I; 'well, go up and tell him that I'm come a long journey on weighty business,' ses he, 'an' if I go without seein' him, the sin of it be on his own sowl,' ses he, (them were his very words, savin' your favour, Major;) 'whisper your message through the keyhole, can't you,' ses I, 'an' I'll take it safe an' sound for you,' (by the same token I could hardly hear my own ears with the wind and thundher;) with that, my dear life, he hot the dure such a sthroke, I thought 'twas dhruv in in my face; and then such an oath as he swore. 'I'll have *you* yet,' ses he, 'where there'll be no oak be-tune us;' 'wisha I cross,' ses I, 'an' in the name o' God be off out o' that, whoever you are, an' come again in the mornin.' 'I can't come in the day-light at all,' ses he, soft as if he put his mouth down to the keyhole; 'I can't come in the daylight, Bryan,' (how well he knows my name, God help us!) 'I must gi' my message to the masther afore twelve to-night, or not at all; an' if he does not take it the sin of it be on his own sowl, an' go up an' tell him so,' and so I came up to let you know what he ses."

"Go down, then, again," said Major Walker, without hesitation, "and say, what I suppose this person is well aware of, that no gentleman, in the present state of the country, allows his doors to be opened to let in a stranger at such an hour as this. If his errand is on magisterial business, tell him he can go to the police barrack at Capparue, only two miles off, and they will attend to him instantly."

"Thrue for you, sir; shure 'tisn't out of our senses we'd be to open the dure, when maybe 'tis Captain Rock, or some one far worse, is there," and Bryan descended with the message.

The little party listened in breathless attention to learn the effect of this second denial. While the servant was engaged in the foregoing recital, the knocker continued to be plied violently at intervals, showing that the visi-tant by no means relinquished the expectation of being admitted. They could now hear Bryan's voice again announcing his master's inflexible res-olution: they heard no more; nothing but inarticulate sounds outside, blown away by the tempest, and again John Bryan appeared before them.

"You never heard how he swore, your honour, when I gev him your message; I could hear him muttherin' to himself when I put my ear to the keyhole; at last I thought he was gone away entirely, when by this an' by that up he comes again, an' the dure gets another pelt. 'Are you there?' ses he; 'what do you think o' yourself?' ses I. 'Well, up again wid you,' ses he, 'an' tell your masther I'm come for some money he owes me this long time, an' here's the receipt.' With that I sees this weeny bit o' paper thrust through the keyhole," and raising his hand, Bryan extended a scrap of dirty paper to his master.

Major Walker glanced at it, and started; after a pause of some minutes, he said—"I must see this person."

"Is it now, your honour?"

"Instantly: tell them to place lights below in the study," he said, turning to his daughter; "and do you, Charles and William, get Hartnett to the next room, over the hall-door, and keep a good look-out to see that this is no stratagem of Rockites to get in upon us. If there is but one person outside, make no noise while the door is opened: should any more make their appearance or offer for the house, clear away with the blunderbusses—it will be check enough until the door is fast again."

So saying, Major Walker descended, followed by the trusty Bryan, having first supplied themselves with pistols from the armoury closet on the landing-place.

To those of our readers who are only accustomed to the order and tranquility that prevail in countries where the laws are feared at least, if not respected, and where every man's house is literally his castle, the precautions just mentioned may appear the exaggerations of some imaginative storyteller; but they whose birth or business has bound them to the distracted country in which our narrative is laid, will, very probably, perceive that the sketch is more remarkable for feebleness of outline than for depth of colour. To such the marvel would be, not that a country gentleman should place a little garrison under arms when his house door was to be opened after dark, but that, under any pretence, he should permit it to be opened at all.

On reaching the hall, Bryan was directed to undo the fastenings of the door, while his master stood at the entrance opening to the study, and watched with some anxiety a process which, any where but in Munster, would not be an important one. As the last bar was heaved away, and the bolts undrawn, a terrific gust of wind, mingled with the groan of thunder, fiercely blew the door wide open, and the nocturnal visitant sprang in as if winged with the red lightning that at the moment went hissing through the sky.

John Bryan, who had been flung to some distance by the unexpected blast, instantly closed and fastened the door, and the stranger stood alone before his master.

"Humph!" said Major Walker, after closely eyeing the intruder; "I think I have seen *you* before now?"

"Glory be to God! if it isn't Tom Bush after all, the villyan; but dhar dhieu! more like the ould"—

"Jack Bryan—none o' your jaw—or it'll be worse for you!" interrupted the fellow, pulling from the breast of his coat a large clasp-knife, with the blade unclosed, and looking with his flashing eyes—his savage face ghastly with passion, strongly contrasting with the fiery-red cap by which his wild and haggard looks were surmounted, more like

Angry demon sent,
Red from his penal element,

than an inhabitant of the living world.

"I wish to speak with you, Major, i' you please, about that bit o' paper I sent you just now."

"Come this way," said Major Walker, leading the way into the study; "and do you, Bryan, wait in the hall until I call."

They entered the study, and Bush immediately shut the door, seeking, in vain, to adjust the bolt by which persons inside were saved from intrusion.

"There is no occasion—we shall not be interrupted; come forward, and let me hear what you have to say." And the magistrate seated himself within reach of the bell-pull, placing the reading-lamp, the only light that had been supplied, on the table, so as to diffuse its ray as equally as possible through the room.

But Bush did not choose to advance more than a few paces from the door: he kept aloof from the circle of light emitted by the lamp, and stood within the flickering shade that enveloped the greater part of the apartment; his form half bent, his chin resting on his hand, and his eye glistening like a rattlesnake's about to spring upon its prey.

"I have here," said Major Walker, "the piece of paper you sent in. It is the advertisement proclaiming the reward of four hundred pounds offered by Government two years back for the discovery of the murderers of Mr. Milo Byrne of Curraheen—are you able to give any information on the subject?"

"If I worn't able, 'tisn't here I'd be now," said the fellow, after a pause. "Where's the pen an' ink, Major?"

"I am quite ready to take a memorandum of any thing you wish to say, previous to your deposition being duly made out, which can be done to-morrow," said Major Walker, at the same time drawing to him writing materials, and taking up the pen.

"Tomorrow! thon-na-mon-dhoul! it must be tonight, Major! I'll scald the heart in him, and spile his pleasure—if I swung for it! Promise me, by

---

thon-na-mon-dhoul: damn you!

all the blessed books in the house, that if I put my hand upon the man that killed Milo Byrne, you'll get him taken that minnit? Promise me that, or hell to my sowl!" swore the ruffian, "if I ever open a lip upon the matter if you were to have me torn between wild horses."

"Go on, then," said Walker, anxiously, "I promise you."

"Put down—first an' foremost—last Michaelmas-night two years."

"Very well—what of it?"

"Put down, a dance at John Regan's, at the Rag,[4] Major, an' that the boys an' girls wor comin' laughin' an' roystering away from it, an' when they came as far as Bill Molumpy's borheen—five o' the boys—an' I was one of the five—turned off to go home a short cut through the fields;" again he paused, as if doubtful whether his auditor was sensible of the value of his communication, perceiving that it was not entirely committed to paper.

"Proceed, my good fellow; depend on it I shall omit nothing important in your story."

"Well an' good—while we wor goin' through the fields, it biggun to rain cats an' dogs upon us, an' we got undher a big black thorn hedge for shelther, an' then the boys biggun to chat about the girls, an' to brag about their sweethearts, an' all that—at last we biggun to talk of Hugh Lawlor an' Miss Ellen Nugent, an' the long courtship there was betune them. I suppose you often hear of it yourself, Major?"

"I think I have—well?"

"Well, at this time, Hugh Lawlor was on his keepin', on account of hurtin' Tom Nugent, Ellen's brother, in some dispute there was about Hugh's comin' about Barna to see her—an' we wor sayin' what a sin it was for the poor fellow to be kept out o' the counthry, account of it—an' then Lanty Mara, one o' the boys ses—'well, by Gor!' ses he, 'it 'll be worse for them that has a hand in breedin' disturbance betune 'em—an' Hugh Lawlor isn't the man to let it pass with them, tho' he keeps himself so quiet,' ses he. 'An who's blempt for it?' ses Jack Dogherty, (another o' the boys was with us.) 'Them,' ses Lanty, 'that's the cause of all Hugh's throuble of late— them that tould Harden of Marnane to take the parks o' Marnane from Lawlor, afther his father an' gran'father bein' tenants at will upon 'em for many a long year—shure it took a good hundred a-year from him.' 'But Lanty,' ses Jack, 'if Lawlor wasn't belied, you know people used to say, that he was captain o' the gang the night they broke up the parks; that Harden's father tould him, with his dyin' breath, never to have undher any thing but

<hr />

[4] "Public-houses in the remote parts of Ireland, where they cannot afford painted sign-boards, are sometimes distinguished by a wisp of hay, or a sod of turf, suspended over the door. The hamlet alluded to above, obtained its appellation from a house of this kind, whose decoration was a rag tied on a pole, thrust through the thatch." [*Blackwood's* note.]

pasture.' 'Well, an' what of it?' ses Lanty; 'shure the tenant had a right to make the most o' the land, an' when Lawlor asked leave to till it, he was refused, an' then five hundred o' them kem at night, with ploughs, an' broke it up; an' Harden, of course, blamed Lawlor, an' had him ejected, but sorrow the more notice he'd have taken of it, if it worn't for White Will Redmond, who put him up to gettin' a warrant agin the poor boy, adding to his trouble, an' 'twas long before he could show his face in the counthry, till Harden dropped it.'"

"But what has all this to say to the business in hand, fellow?"

"Plenty, Major, lashins an' lavins! never fear. Well, then, Lanty told us that White Will was doin' all in his power to spile Lawlor's chance with Ellen Nugent, bekase he wanted to get her for his own son, an' Davy Nugent liked the match well, account of the property—over £400 a-year—that White Will had; an' at last Jack Dougherty said, what a good deed 'twould be to give White Will a beatin', and that he supposed it 'twould be somethin' in our way from Hugh Lawlor—'Bee the law!' ses Mara, 'if you knew but all, there's a way to spite him worse than beatin.' 'But when I mean beatin',' ses Dougherty, 'I mean doing the thing well—clean off.' 'There's a better way by far,' ses Mara, 'if people had the coorage to be thrue to one another.' 'Can't you speak out,' ses Jack, 'like a man?' ses he. 'No I wont,' ses Mara, 'there's Darby Kieran there—Lawlor's own man, that never threw in a word since we biggun to speak of the matter, an' he knows more than any one about it.' 'I'll tell ye what, boys,' ses Kieran, startin' up, 'any one that's for the thing, let him meet me to-night week, at six o'clock, at the Cross of Drumm, an' we'll see more about it; an' Bush,' ses he, 'you're a good boy an' a shure one—do you come too—we'll want you.' Have you all that down, Major?"

"All that is necessary," replied the listener; "pray get on, the night is growing late."

"Well, to make a long story short, we met at the Cross o' Drumm—put down first and foremost Darby Kieran, Major—Jack Dougherty—Lanty Mara—a boy of the Clearys, from the parish of Golden—Long Jack Moher, an' myself. Kieran brought whisky, an' we took three glasses a man, an' then he swore us."

"Who?" said the magistrate.

"Darby Kieran swore us on the prayer-book to be thrue to one another on what we wor goin' to do—but hell to the word else he'd tell us—'an' Bush,' ses he, 'you know all the places as we go along, an' you must quiet the dogs,' ses he, 'you know all their names,' an' with that we went to the gripe where the guns war hid—an' we got crapes from Kieran, an' we darkened ourselves, an' off we went—an' shure enough 'twasn't to White Will's we wor goin'"—another pause.

"What else?"

The informer bent forward, but did not advance a step. "Put down in that paper," he said, "that we took the high-road that led to Milo Byrne's gate, an' when we got about a mile up the road, Kieran whistled, an' a man, with his face dark like ourselves, jumped over the hedge—an' Darby went up to him, an' they spoke easy—an' then Kieran came back an' bid us follow the captain—that was the new-comer—an' off we set an' never stopped till we came to Curraheen gate, that was wide open. The strange man turned up, but never spoke a word; so up we went to the house, an' easy enough 'twas to get into it; an' sure you know the rest"—

"But you have told me nothing—positively nothing," said his anxious hearer.

"Do you tell me over again if there's thruth in what that paper I sent you ses? on the virtue of your sowl, is there a free pardon for every one but the man that fired the shot?"

"So the Government promise," said Major Walker, "and I am confident they promise truly."

The fellow proceeded. "They brought out Byrne—an' the moon was shinin' as bright as day—an' he was quite easy an' pleasant like, 'till they bid him kneel down. 'For what?' ses he; 'to say your prayers,' ses one o' them, 'an' prepare for death.' With that he leapt up, you'd think the height of the house, an' axed what had they agin him, but no one answered; an' they put a blunderbuss to his broast, an' axed him had he a mind to say his prayers; so with that they forced him down upon his knees, an' then I suppose he knew he was for death, for he begun an avy-maryah; but he couldn't finish it, he was in such a hurry. 'Boys,' ses he, 'let me only spake to the wife,' ses he; an' still the captain never spoke a word, but made a sign, and one o' them riz the gun, an thrun it away from him agin, sayin' in Irish, that Byrne never hurt him or his, and that he could not pull the thrigger. With that, the tall man kem forward—levelled—an' fired himself, an' Milo Byrne dhropped like a bullock!"

"But who was this man?—this captain?"

"By that blessed timber, Hugh Lawlor himself!" said Bush, his voice dropping to a whisper, and his face becoming still whiter in the shadow of the room. "Hugh Lawlor!" he said, lifting his hand and striking on the table—"he that's marryin' tonight—'twas he that shot Mr. Byrne with his own hand. An' now I give myself up to you, Major, an' remember, you promised to take the murdherer the minnit he was pointed out to you."

The bell was rung violently—

---

avy-maryah: Ave Maria.

"Bryan, tell Hartnett to saddle Spring and the chestnut mare, and go up and bid Mr. Charles get himself ready to be off with me to Capparue barracks in a quarter of an hour."

III

Barna was shining far through the stormy night, with the blaze of a hundred wedding lights. Roof and rafter shook to merry music and uproarious revelry, and the jocund dancers thronged with untiring steps every corner of the edifice. The elder portion of the assembly, ranged along the sides of the apartments, or huddled together in the corners, intent upon the joyous groups that rustled by, discussed the comparative merits of their young acquaintances, some as to their personal graces, others as to their artificial accomplishments; and ever their remarks were qualified with a, "My service to you, Mrs. Ryan!" or, "Mr. Keating, your good health!" followed by a trifling sound resembling the jingle of a spoon in a tumbler, and a bland but scarcely perceptible smacking of the lips, and on they went upon the subject again. Many a rustic beauty obtained her due meed of praise that evening—many a diffident beau was patted on the back with an approving, "That's your sort, Phil!" and long continued and vehement were the differences of opinion upon the comparative deserts of the girls of Borrisoleigh and Nenagh. Upon one topic alone did any unanimity prevail, and on that there was not one dissentient voice—that Hugh Lawlor and his bride were the handsomest couple that had been married in Eliogarty for twenty years.

Fatigued from dancing, and overcome by the heat, that fair and delicate bride now stood, leaning on the arm of her husband, in the recess of a window to which he had led her upon reaching the bottom of the set; and the plain but ample curtain with which the window was furnished, while it afforded them a kind of retirement, was doubly welcome by its screening off, in some degree, the glare and warmth of the room.

"Ellen, darling Ellen!" murmured the low deep voice of Lawlor, "you are weary of this scene—you have over-exerted yourself—you look faint—let me implore you to retire."

"I am not weary *now*, Hugh," and she slightly pressed the arm against which she leaned her forehead; "besides, I have promised to dance the next set with John Butler of Pallace."

"The stupid fool!"

"Come, sir, don't be pettish; I thought you would be tonight the happiest and most grateful swain that ever won a wife after so long and weary a wooing as ours."

"And so I am, my own beloved girl," he said; "how little did I think two years back that I should stand here as blest as I do this hour—holding you close to this heart that you may hear beating loud with its fulness of love and truth to you! Are you indeed at last my own for ever?" and he folded her closer to his side.

"God only knows, dear Hugh—(Gracious powers! how it lightens! did you ever see such flashes?)—often and often I think of that nasty Nanse, the fortune-teller—that woman you are always so kind to—that you gave the cabin to when Cregan ejected her. I never liked that woman, Hugh; do you remember her look, and what she said the day she first examined my hand?—'A bride wedded'"—and the innocent girl paused—

"'And never bedded!' I do well, dearest; 'twould be bad for Nanse that all her predictions had so poor a chance of being realized. What a start!— the thunder is certainly terrific; but you are sadly nervous. John Butler of Pallace! Let me lead you from this place."

"Hugh, will you never check your hasty temper? ah! remember all that it has cost us. I own, whenever I hear you burst out thus, and that your look grows so dark, I always fly back to that hideous time when you used to be obliged to steal over here like a thief at night—when we had no place to meet but by Dempsey's Heap,[5] for we knew no one else dared come near it. How savage you used to be then with everyone in the world!"

"With *everyone?*"

"But me, Hugh; you were never cross to me. Oh, yes! *once,* when I asked you in a joke, after a long absence, what kept you away—was it Milo Byrne's murder? and you grasped my neck so, and held back my head to look at my face, and said—ah, Heavens! I have made you angry again! Come away from this spot—indeed, indeed you hurt me—you grip my arm so"—

"Stay, girl! what did I tell you when I looked in your face?"

"I don't remember—I don't indeed."

"By all your hopes of heaven, you do!"

"Something about your not minding twenty murders sooner than lose this face—or lose myself—or some such foolish saying. Ah! come from this spot—I cannot bear the lightning. Come, I will even retire—I will say I am fatigued"—

"Ellen Nugent—I beg pardon—Mrs. Lawlor, the set is waiting for you to lead off: permit me. Lawlor, there's Harriet Burke dhroopin' alone like the last rose of summer—she says you engaged her three sets ago—there goes the pipes, and *Sir Roger de Coverley* for ever!" and away swept John Butler with the passive bride.

---

[5] "In the southern parts of Ireland, wherever a murder has been committed, the spot is marked by a heap of stones—the accumulated contributions of passers by." [*Blackwood's* note.]

"Right and left—hands across—down the middle;" and in ten minutes twenty merry couple were footing it away to drone and chanter. "Well done, Masther John!" "Luck to your own purty foot, Miss Ellen!" "Now for it, Miss Harriet—set the girls of Borris a pattern!" "Ah, Mr. Lawlor, you take the shine out o' them all!" interjected the servants, as they stood crowded inside and outside the door, waiting until a cessation in the dance afforded them an opening to slip unharmed through the throngs, laden with trays of sparkling glasses filled with positive lemonade, comparative negus, and superlative punch, for the refreshment of the dancers, and the edification of the high contracting parties who looked on, imbibing from the proceedings, as we have said, a large portion of pleasure, with a modicum of potation. "See how them Thurles girls dances"—(the domestics went on)—"well, the dickens wouldn't tire them; I give it up to them." "Oh, Masther Ned, the foot is off me! that I mightn't die in sin, but that boy threads like a coult. Yeh, who's that pushin' there behind?" "Nanse the fortune-teller!" "Wisha 'iss a-graghal, let me jest have one peep at the quality," and the sybil edged into the room.

"Oh, then! blessins down upon you Miss Ellen, this night—it does my heart good to look in your purty face!"

"Thank you, Nanse; do you remember telling me my fortune?" and the bride flew on.

"Yerrah, Master Hugh, I wouldn't doubt your step to be the nimblest in the room!" and still Nanse edged forward, as Lawlor danced to his place at the bottom of the set. "You had always the swiftest foot in the barony."

"Oh, I hear you, Nanse!" said the modest bridegroom.

"If you do,'" she said, stooping forward until, unperceived, her mouth came close to his ear, "*heed me*—see if your foot is able for a jig without pumps now—the red-coats an peelers are crossin' the bawn-field—they'll be on you in five minnits; but try one good run for your life at any rate!" —

IV

If on a bright sunny day, while some gallant vessel, with every sail set, went careering, all life and bravery, before the wind, the ammunition-store exploded, and in place of the stately shadow that a moment before danced upon the waves, left them one wide scene of wreck and devastation, the ruin could not be more sudden and irreparable than that which one hour effected in the happy abode of Barna. The cold peevish morning broke upon a little world of the most abject misery. Here were seen guests

---

Wisha 'iss a-graghal: I'm surprised this sweetheart is here.

hurrying from the spot, as though it had been the centre of pestilence, not of pleasure, their faces sickly from the exhaustion of revelry, and wild with horror. There, groups of the lower classes, the peasantry, the neighbours, the servants of Davy Nugent, standing sullenly with folded arms around the mansion, communicating their surmises in whispers, full of apprehension and dismay. Within the house the derangement consequent upon the termination of unbounded festivity, was heightened by the confusion produced in the search of the military and police through the apartments. The furniture lay in heaps, sideboards and tables shattered or overturned, where they fell with their piles of glass and china, as the terror-stricken revellers rushed away upon the entrance of the authorities. The servants were nowhere to be seen; and in chambers that a few hours back shook with the noise of music and the dance, all was now silent as the grave. A couple of greyhounds and a favourite terrier seemed the only things that remained to tell where so much life had lately been; they strolled lazily and unquietly through the lower part of the house, occasionally going to the foot of the stairs, placing their forepaws upon the lowest step, snuffing anxiously up the ascent, and, after a comfortless wag or two of the tail, turning away to repeat their rounds again. Yet, lonely and abandoned as that house appeared, how much of terrible Affliction — of Hope for ever prostrate — and blasted Youth, and despairing Old Age, did it contain!

In an upper and remote chamber that needed no artificial darkening — for the ancient trees of the orchard grew with their broad branches against the windows — knelt, at the foot of a bed, two female servants, their heads bent down upon the coverlet, and enveloped (as is the custom with the women of their country in affliction) in the folds of their ample aprons. On one side sat their wretched master, his aged head bent down upon his breast in that kind of stupor exhibited by one who has suddenly received a stunning blow, from which he vainly strives to rouse himself to life and recollection; while opposite to him, with looks of anxiety and horror, stood the venerable priest, whose blessing had so lately been pronounced upon the bright frail head of her he now watched, extended before him, in doubt whether the death or life contending in her frame was finally to triumph. There lay Ellen Nugent, crushed as utterly by her sudden disasters as were the delicate blossoms that leant upon the window-stone, all withered by the thunders of the night. From the moment the officers of justice burst into the dancing-room, she never uttered a word. A moment before, she had been turned in the dance by her husband, her fingers still trembled from the light kiss he had secretly dropped upon them as he touched her hands; the next instant there was a cry — the room was full of armed men — she heard one beloved name hissing from every lip. She sprang forward. With that glance of love, almighty in its power to search for The One amid the Ten Thousand, she saw that Lawlor was not there. She felt her eyes broadening; the faces round her spread into monstrous aspects; then all things turned the colour of blood; a noise as of the sea swam in her ears, and the rest was forgetfulness. She was borne insensible to the couch where her distracted friends now watched the first symptoms she had yet exhibited of returning consciousness.

And where was Lawlor? . . . Far away, amid the wildest fastnesses of impracticable mountains, the morning saw him shrink to cover, like the stag from the hunters—a doomed and guilty man: his flight alone sufficient evidence of guilt; his guilt most dire assurance of his doom. That any one, however degraded in soul or lost in principle, could be found, in an age like the present, capable of committing the enormous atrocity with which his flight avowed him stained, may well be matter of horrible surprise; but that it should be perpetrated by one like Lawlor, gifted with intellectual attainments of no common order, and raised by fortune sufficiently above those of his class to free him from contact with all that impedes humanity of heart and refinement of manners, involves a moral anomaly as extraordinary as it is appalling. That such persons, however, are capable, in one frenzied hour, of the commission of deeds the most fiercely at variance with their natures, has ere now been abundantly proved; and it has been attempted to account for such preternatural excesses, by attributing them to monomania or hallucination. In the instance at present under contemplation, the motives bear so remote a relation to the crime as to warrant in a great degree such a conclusion. "It is the only way," to use the words of the most thoughtful of living writers,[6] "that we can account for one deed at war with a whole life, blasting, indeed, for ever the happiness, but making little revolution in the pursuits and dispositions, of the character."

From an early age we have seen that Lawlor was left his own master. Endued with feelings of high susceptibility and strong passions, he unfortunately lacked a guide to restrain them when they could alone be taught control. Then came his inauspicious attachment to Ellen Nugent. The long, and bitter, and hopeless opposition that attachment had to undergo, no doubt gave his spirit an inflexibility and sullenness that gradually hardened a heart not naturally ill-disposed, and imparted to it a selfishness by which it was finally corrupted. To his lonely and affectionate spirit, Ellen was all the world—the only living thing that he felt necessary to his existence; and, as he grew to manhood, the potency of this master-passion

---

[6]"The author of *Eugene Aram,* one of the most magnificent and impassioned productions in our language." [*Blackwood's* note.] Baron Edward Bulwer Lytton (1803–73), English novelist, published *Eugene Aram* in 1832. [ED.]

affected more or less all his social proceedings, until the possession of his mistress became with him almost as much an object by which his skill in baffling his foes (for so he deemed all who did not favour his suit) was to be estimated, as one that was to confirm the happiness of his life. By degrees the impediments to that happiness gave way. The wounded brother of his beloved recovered to fall by the slower but surer hand of disease. The irritated mother, too, resigned her enmity and her breath together. But then came White Will, with his impressive purse and his long train of persecutions; and if ever a crime, by its dreadful originality, indicated the revenge of a master-spirit, it was that by which Lawlor, so fatally for himself, resolved to cross his enemy. The deed was done. By the death of Byrne, Redmond was reduced to comparative poverty, and with his wealth subsided his pretensions to claim Ellen Nugent as the bride of his son; and the desperate but devoted lover at once effected the humiliation of his enemy, and secured the hand of his long-worshipped mistress.

V

Months passed away, and Lawlor still continued to elude the officers of justice — but this was all that could be ascertained of his fate; and Time, that veers alike through the most buoyant hours of bliss and the profoundest nights of affliction, saw his hapless bride revive to a state of languid health and mournful resignation. She again attempted to resume the little daily round of domestic duties, and to whisper peace to her infirm father, when she knew there was no peace in the sinking heart that prompted her. From the fatal evening of her nuptials, she never pronounced the name of her husband, nor was it ever breathed in her hearing. She had loved him with a love surpassing that of women. She had for his sake long encountered the stern anger of her brother — the loss of her father's confidence — the reproachful upbraidings of her mother, whose dying injunction, sealed with a solemn curse, that she should not wed with Lawlor, she had disregarded. The more loud the whispers of calumny spread, that his life was irregular — that his pursuits were unlawful — the more perseveringly she fought in his cause, with all that generous devotion and fidelity that none but her glorious sex can feel or practise. "Were Hugh here," she would scornfully say to his detractors, "you dared not insinuate in his presence the stories with which you are so ready to wound the feelings of his only defender. Pronounce them to his face, and I will judge by your boldness whether they are deserving of belief." And now — that idolized one, no longer her lover, but her husband, was, like the first murderer, a fugitive upon the earth, with a curse as deep as Cain's pursuing his footsteps; and she — but no — she had no more to hear of him in blame or obloquy; for, coarse as the people were by whom she was surrounded, their hearts too deeply sympathized in her early sorrows not to respect the eternal silence that sealed her lips. Of one thing only, connected with Lawlor's fate, it was thought she could not be ignorant—that her abode was watched by the emissaries of justice, from a supposition that she was so passionately beloved by the criminal, that he would at some period attempt to visit her: but on this subject too, it is needless to say, she never ventured a remark; perhaps she felt the current of her existence drying away too surely, to care further about any event by which it might be momentarily ruffled or illumined.

It was far in summer. At the close of a sweet evening in July, Ellen sat alone in the window of her chamber that opened upon the deep soft grass and refreshing umbrage of the orchard by which the greater part of the mansion was overshadowed. The air was sweet with the fragrance of lime-trees, and slumberous with the lulling hum of the bees that clustered in the branches. The melancholy girl had thrown the window entirely open, and sat reclined, with her head thrown back, resting in a reverie against the wainscot, scarce conscious of the departing sunset, whose lingering tints, as they fell upon her wan, fair forehead, and the long locks of pale gold that descended to her shoulders, invested her whole aspect with that mournful and spiritual beauty that subdues us in the immortal pencillings of Guido. To a careless eye she would have seemed intently listening to the mellow song of the blackbird, that gushed at intervals upon her ear; but the sweetest sounds of earth had no longer charms for Ellen. Her spirit was far away, in petitions to Him who had chosen, for His own wise purposes, to break so bruised a reed as her pining and tortured heart. The warm tint of evening faded from her face, and the twilight night of summer came down amid the green recesses of the orchard, and still she sat motionless, drinking the holy peace of the scene. All at once she was roused by a shadow encroaching on the faint light admitted through the window; and, starting up, she saw the tall figure of a woman standing close to it. It was Nanse, the fortune-teller, who curtsied low when she saw that she was perceived, but preserved that respectful silence by which, with inmate good sense or taste, the Irish peasantry evince the sense of the sorrows of their superiors, when they feel that they are beyond human consolation. Associated as this woman was with some of the most painful recollections of her past life, Ellen naturally felt shocked upon recognising her; but she was too sorely inured to little trials of this kind not to overcome them; she therefore, upon recovering herself, enquired of the woman the cause of her being so late about the house.

"Pickin' a few herebs about the orchard I was, Miss Ellen," was the reply, "for a poor girl that's not very well. I was just goin' away when I saw you, an' I made bould to come over an' ax afther your health; an' proud I am to see you sittin' there lookin'"—but she dared not finish the hollow flattery.

"What is the matter with the girl?"

"Wisha, Miss, nothin' but downright frettin'; she was married last Shroff was a twelvemonth; but I'm loth to keep you in the damp, Miss; the dew is very entirely to night, and you're not very sthrong."

"I don't mind it," said Ellen swerving from the blow, and making an effort to be resolute. "Who did she marry?"

"A boy of the Donoghues, Miss; an' the match didn't turn out well at all, at all."

"Why?" persevered Miss Nugent.

"Sorrow-a-one o' me knows," replied Nanse; "but they don't live together—their people came betune 'em, I b'lieve: they used to say he was wild, an' all that; but sure, at any rate, that's no reason for separatin' man an' wife afther being married before the althar."

Ellen's heart died within her; she enquired no further, but bid the woman a scarcely audible good-night.

"The best o' good-nights an' blessin's, Miss," said the herbalist, about to depart; but pausing, she added, "I b'lieve that masther is not at home tonight, Miss; I saw him go yonder the road this mornin', as if for the fair of Nenagh."

"My father is not at home; did you want him?"

"Oh geh! no Miss; good-night, an' luck attend you."

"Mother of Him whom you watched upon the cross through the long and killing night!" murmured the distracted girl, when again alone, "look down upon me with pity; you, whose sinless soul was wrung with more than mortal agony, teach a helpless and erring creature to struggle with the lot that is wearing her to the grave!" and she raised her eyes to the brightening stars. When she dropped them again, Lawlor was standing close to her; his very breath almost mingling with the rich shadows of her hair. One frantic shriek, as she sprang with an electric shiver from the spot, gushed to her lips; but, with an instinctive sense of the result, she stifled it ere it passed them, and with a groan sank upon her knees before the window, her hands in vain motioning the intruder to depart.

"Ellen," he murmured, "Ellen, hear me!"

She made no reply, but remained bent in an attitude of supplication and dismay, until she perceived him attempting to enter the apartment; with a stifled sob she rushed forward and essayed to close the window against him.

Shroff: Shrovetide. (See page 399.)

"Very well," he said, "it is a matter of indifference to me; for you and for your love I have become what I am—I have lost them both, and life is intolerable; here, then, I remain until I am observed and given up to justice."

"No, no!" she almost shrieked, "do not drive me to distraction—wretched, sinful, outcast man, what have I done to deserve this trial?"

"Ellen, my life, my bride, hear me!—the world and all its prizes—pleasure, wealth, fair fame, are to me henceforward what they are to the dead. I had long ceased to value them; one thing alone, your affection, bound me to earth; that, that is gone too, this terrible hour convinces me. What, then, have I to dread? No; here I remain—let me die at least within the air you breathe."

"Madman! will you kill me? Every path about the house is beset by armed men thirsting for your blood."

"I know it Ellen, yet I have ventured, and dared them all. Oh, darling! what have I not dared, in this world and the next, to be for ever within sight of the beauty from which I am debarred for ever? Yet one hour with you, only *one hour,* Ellen, if it were but once in the long dreary year, and I could bear to live."

"May God assist me!" cried the frenzied girl. "Oh, Hugh! live—live to repent what has come between us, and left us blackened and withered wretches upon God's fair world."

"Give me one sign, one proof then, Ellen," said the impassioned criminal, "that you still have not lost all the fond love you so often vowed me; let me clasp you once more to this breaking heart, and, degraded and branded as I am, I will be more boundlessly happy than thrones could make me out of your sight. Say that you disclaim me, that I am not your husband, wedded in the sight of that church you reverence so deeply; shut me out from your presence, all of heaven I have long dared to hope for, and give me up to a shameful death; or afford me one hour's shelter in peace and rapture by your side—May I enter?"

There was no reply—he sprang through the window and extended his arms—shuddering, she recoiled from him, but only for an instant—with one broken gasp she darted forward and fell senseless on his bosom.

VI

The hush of midnight had long been on the earth; the broad round summer moon had risen and filled it with mellow light, and was fast hastening to her setting, when a strong party of police, headed by their officer, and accompanied by the nearest magistrate, Major Walker, turned rapidly from the main road and proceeded up the avenue that led to Barna. They were within a short distance of the mansion, when the foremost man of the party stumbled, and nearly fell over the recumbent figure of some person whom the excessive darkness, occasioned by the thick foliage that overhung the pathway, had until that moment prevented him from perceiving.

"Who is here!" exclaimed the man, as he grasped the figure, which had now assumed an upright posture, presenting the outline of a very tall female enveloped from head to foot in the dark blue cloaks worn by her class in Munster. "Who and what are you?"

"Wisha! only poor Nanse the fortune-teller—a-ragal!" was the reply, and the cloak was thrown open, and an apron exhibited filled with a goodly collection of herbs.

"(Go on, Corporal White, with four men to the house, and keep guard upon the windows until we join you;) and is not this a pretty hour for you to be here?" said the officer, "and about no good either, I warrant."

"Never fear that, sir," rejoined a policeman; "no time will do Nanse but one o'clock o' moonlight nights to pick her herbs for pishoges an' charms, an' all that."

"Wisha, God bless you, Tim Kiely! you were always pleasant—let a poor woman be goin', captain."

"Not till you answer one question—how long have you been here?"

"Faiks, an' a good while, your honour; I was for a bit o' the time in the orchard."

"Did you observe any one come or go this way? or meet a stranger about the house to-night?"

"Haith an' I did so—I won't be telling you a lie at this hour in the mornin'!"

"Who, who? what kind of person?"

"Yeh! who would it be but him ye're lookin' for—don't I know well what ye're about?"

"Where is he then?—Out with it, woman, at once—every minute is worth a guinea."

"If it is then, captain jewel, wouldn't you be afther sharing with a poor creature? Pay me well," she said, lowering her voice, "an' I'll tell ye somethin' worth knowing."

"Speak it out, and I promise you you shall be rewarded," said Major Walker—"Do you know any thing of Lawlor?"

"How much o' the *four hundred* will I get, Major?"

"Never mind the woman!" said the officer; "come on, Walker, we lose time."

---

a-ragal: term of endearment.

"Well," exclaimed Nanse. "I depend upon twenty pound at least—twenty goold sov'rens.—I saw Lawlor this blessed night."

"Where, where?"

"Fastenin' down the window o' Miss Ellen's room yondher in the orchard," said the hag, "jist after the clock struck ten."

"By heaven! then," said the officer, "he's gone long since—he would never be fool enough to pay so long a visit—let us dash on, however, and search the house."

"Old Nugent is not at home," said Major Walker; "that poor girl his daughter is in miserable health; and if I thought, as you say, that this dreadful fellow was away again, I would not for worlds subject her to the scene I witnessed in that house before."

"Promise me the twenty guineas," said Nanse, "an' I'll soon find out for you whether he's in the house or no."

"Twenty devils! You shall have five guineas in the morning if you can learn by any means that Lawlor is now in Barna House."

"Oh, I'm not goin' to sell my soul for five guineas yet," bartered the fortune-teller; "make it ten, an' I'll be thrue to you."

"It *shall* be ten if we make him prisoner—if we seize him dead or alive."

"Well, 'tis a bargain. I'll go up to the house an' knock, and ax for a dhrop o' vinegar for a child in the fever, an' never fear I'll soon get in; the girls in the house know well that they daren't face Miss Ellen in the mornin' if they refused to let a body in for any thing they want for a sick person."

"But still, how will this find out what we want to know? The girls won't tell you."

"The girls don't know themselves. Peg Casey will have to go to her misthus for the key o' the pantry, an' won't I have my ear cocked? If she gets into Miss Ellen's room without any throuble or knockin', you may go look for *him* somewhere else; but if the door is locked, an' she can't get in by the latch, my hand to ye but ye're made men."

"Don't delay an instant in letting us know: if you keep us waiting we will follow you into the house."

"Now mind," said Nanse, "that this is the token: if Lawlor is within, I'll come out and go away up by the right-hand side o' the house into the haggard; don't ye stop one minnit, but make for the door before Peg Casey boults it afther me, an' ye are in without a bit o' noise, an' then ye know what to do yerselves."

---

misthus: mistress.

The party advanced, and in a minute or two joined their companions, who were stationed at each corner of the mansion. After having disposed a strong guard upon the windows that opened to the garden, the officer with the main body withdrew to some distance in front of the house, and the spy was directed to perform her office.

Resolutely Nanse advanced to the door, and commenced a gentle but pertinacious knocking, from which she did not desist until a voice was heard to enquire the cause of the disturbance. The response was given as Nanse had agreed upon; she was admitted, and the door again closed and fastened.

The police party now waited with intense anxiety for the reappearance of their messenger, upon which probably depended the capture of a criminal for whose apprehension so large a sum had been offered (the county volunteering to double the Government reward) and the delay in whose detection was considered through the kingdom an imputation on the vigilance of the local authorities.

Ten minutes had hardly elapsed when the door of Barna House was once more opened, and the fortune-teller appeared. With joy the excited party saw her turn, as she had preconcerted with them, to the right of the house, and enter the haggard. At once they dashed forward, but not in time to anticipate Peg Casey in reshutting the door, which they found effectually secured. They loudly knocked, and demanded entrance in the king's name, but no answer was returned. By the orders of Major Walker the guard on the rear of the house was now reinforced, so as to prevent all possibility of escape in that direction, and the men in front were commanded instantly to force the door.

But the doors and windows of an opulent farmer in a retired part of Ireland, and that part Tipperary, possess a provoking stubbornness and obstinacy, that it would sometimes require the energy of the engineers of the Ghizni gate to subdue. Of this class was the one in question; and the rage of its assailants rose in proportion to the resistance it presented to their efforts to break it open; nor was it until a full half hour had elapsed, and a temporary battering train had been procured from the nearest forge, that the party, amidst the yelling of dogs and the piercing shrieks of women, at last effected an entrance.

"Coward!" said the officer, "he might have struck one fair blow for his life, at all events."

Lights were procured, and every apartment was instantly visited. At one alone they met a fresh delay. It was the chamber, the servants said, of their young mistress. To this the officer himself proceeded: the door was made fast—he imperatively knocked for entrance, but receiving no reply, he directed it to be forced. But even here, when the slight door had given way, the entrance was blocked up; the whole furniture of the apartment, including a heavy old-fashioned bedstead (upon which the lovely inmate of the chamber was wont to repose) being piled across it.

The police, however, soon scrambled through these impediments; the lights were brought forward, and gave to view the fainting form of Ellen Nugent stretched upon the floor, supported by a female servant, who, apparently unconscious of, or unconcerned at the scene before her, was occupied in chafing the burning temples of her mistress. But the room contained no one else; and the disappointed party were about to retire, when one of them perceived, by the chinks in a partition, that a narrow closet was attached to the room: he eagerly rushed to it, opened it, and dragged forward, wrapped in an immense fearnought coat and slouched hat—Nanse the fortune-teller.

It were vain to attempt describing the scene that followed.

"Take this woman," said Major Walker, "and make out her committal, as an accomplice after the deed"—

"With all my heart!" cried Nanse—"there is many a mile between the poor fellow and you now Major; and so you thought I was goin' to sell the blood of him I often an' often nursed upon my knee in his father's kitchen—God rest his sowl! No—if he war twenty times the unfortunat' he is!"

VII

The delicate constitution of Ellen Nugent never recovered the repeated shocks of that trying and terrible night. On awaking from the long swoon into which she had not fallen until the loud knocking of the police for admission assured her of the escape of Lawlor, she was seized with fever and delirium, which threatened for several days a fatal termination. During this time she raved incessantly about her unhappy husband, whom she seemed to see constantly by her side, and to whose imaginary entreaties, that she would fly with him to some foreign land, she answered with expressions of the most impassioned devotion. Sometimes she fancied she beheld him in the hands of justice, and prayed and supplicated to be allowed to watch his fate and share his grave. Her disorder, however, yielded to the skill of the physicians—reason again assumed its control—and she once more became rigidly silent respecting the name and the affection for which her heart was breaking. As the lovely autumnal season of her native island set in with unusual mildness, it was hoped that with care her health would be re-established; but when winter came, symptoms of consumption—a disease that had already been fatal to more than one of her family—appeared, and it was evident that her days were numbered. The sweet patient herself was the first to feel the conviction; and the smile of satisfied resignation and thankfulness with which she received its confirmation from the lips of the physician, showed that Hope—that last seed to wither in the hearts of the young and gentle—had long perished in hers. "What have I to do with earth and earthly things?" she said: "my poor old father will not long stay after me, when he misses his spoiled Ellen from his lonely hearth—and then we will sleep together in the same quiet grave, and I shall know what it is to be at peace at last." Winter passed away—the faint perfumes of the early flowers of spring arose from the neglected garden; and ere they had disappeared, one more frail and fair than they was gathered to the dust. Her grave lies in the old churchyard of Abbeymahon; its soft turf is ever bright and green, though the rude letters on the stone by her gentle head are fast becoming illegible:

PRAY FOR THE SOUL OF
ELLEN ———,
ONLY DAUGHTER OF DAVID NUGENT
OF BARNA,
WHO DEPARTED THIS LIFE THE
2D DAY OF APRIL, 1821,
AGED NINETEEN YEARS.

———

It was the third morning after her interment that Tom Bush entered the guard-room of the police barrack at Capparue, where he had for many months been obliged to reside for that protection which such a place alone could afford in Tipperary to an informer—of all miscreants the most odious in the eyes of its turbulent and fierce-spirited peasantry. He had occasionally, for the purpose upon which his revengeful spirit was bent, been permitted to make excursions through the country in the disguise of a mendicant—that generally assumed by his degraded profession—carefully contriving to conceal the great defect by which he was rendered so notorious, beneath his manifold and ragged habiliments, and which he was enabled to do the more securely as he mostly travelled in the night, skulking along deserted roads and other by-places, in his visits to those remote mountain fastnesses where he thought there was any likelihood of furthering the object he had in view.

"Well, boys!" he exclaimed, in an exulting tone, as he entered the room—around the ample fireplace of which several of the men were crowded—and proceeded to divest himself of his soiled and tattered out-

side garments, exhibiting all the appearance of having that moment returned from a long and weary journey—"Well, boys, I have him at last!"

The men, with a simultaneous impulse, jumped up, eagerly enquiring,
"Where—where?"

"Never mind, I'm jest cum from the chief—he knows all about it, an'
he'll be over here directly—only let ye be ready against nightfall. We'll have
a long journey to go, an' the sooner we get to the end of it afore the moon
rises, the better."

Further than this, Bush would not be communicative.

Early in the evening, the men comprising the little force stationed at
Capparue, headed by their officer, and under the guidance of Bush, set out
upon the excursion. By their starting so early, it was evident their destination was a distant one. They were reinforced, as they proceeded, by the
men at two stations in advance on their route. As night darkened, the party
no longer confined themselves to the main roads of the country, but struck
forward on those which led to the mountains by the least circuitous routes.
This, however, rendered their journey tedious and fatiguing, and would
have made it, without the escort of a guide, an impracticable one, from the
nature of the country to be traversed. The paths, for the most part, lay
through swampy moorland, and not unfrequently across vast tracts of bog,
where all traces of a footway disappeared; and where, without the aid of
one thoroughly acquainted with the way, a single step to the right or left
would have buried the whole party in the deep watery slough that spread
far and wide around. It had rained heavily on the preceding day, which
served still the more to impede their exertions, and a sharp spring frost,
which was setting in, made the slowness of their progress doubly irksome. At length they crossed the chain of wild hills that divides the county
of Tipperary, on the south, from that of Cork; but, despite of all their efforts, the moon had long risen above the stupendous range of the Galty
mountains—through which their road now wound—before they came in
sight of the spot which their officer at length informed them was to be the
termination of their march—the churchyard of Abbeymahon. They could
see it plainly at a considerable distance—the ruined tower of the Abbey,
and the grey walls by which it was surrounded, crowning the summit of a
lonely hill directly before them, and glancing white in the broadening
moon.

On approaching the place they halted; and Bush, motioning them to
preserve unbroken silence, crept stealthily up the ancient road that led, by
a winding and steep ascent, to the burial-ground. After a short absence he

---

chief: the chief constable.

reappeared, and beckoned to the party to follow. Imitating the stealthy pace of their conductor, and pressing silently forward without waking a single echo by their tread, they reached the wall of the grave-yard, outside of which the officer disposed his men so as to form an unbroken line of sentinels around the enclosure.

Advancing to a rude stile that led into the cemetery, the spy directed the officer's attention to a scene within it, which, when fully comprehended by the spectator's astonished gaze, made the blood run tingling and freezing through his veins.

By the side of Ellen Nugent's new-made grave sat the murderer Lawlor, enclosing in his arms the form that had once comprised all earth's love and beauty for him, and which, like a miser, with mild and maniac affection, he had unburied once more to clasp and contemplate. The shroud had fallen from the upper part of the body, upon which decay had as yet made slight impression. The delicate head lay reclined upon that shoulder which had been its home so often, and over which now streamed the long bright hair like a flood of loosened gold, the wan face turned up to his as if it still could thrill to the mad kisses in which he steeped it, while he had twined one of the white arms frantically about his neck.

"Ellen!" he said, "Ellen, speak to your murderer! Speak to him who now for the first time holds you to his heart without one answering throb — without one word from those lips that never allowed me to kiss them, and kept that cheek so white, before. Darling! remember the hour in the happy summer-house when you first pledged your faith to mine, with my lips on those eyelids that all the warmth of my heart will never waken into life again. Remember this, and say upon this grave, that you forgive the wretch who killed you because he could not live without your love!"

"Now's your time, captain," whispered Bush, "this is the second night of his comin' an' takin' her up — give the word an' we're on him."

"Advance, men!" said the chief constable, and sprang into the enclosure.

Lawlor was on his feet in an instant — his frenzied eyes glaring with the fierceness of a roused tiger — grasping a carbine, which until then had lain unperceived with the mattock and other implements he had used in opening the grave. The moment he rose he saw Bush advancing with the officer — he levelled and fired — and fell himself, at the same instant, dead by the side of his unburied bride. One of the men, alarmed at the danger to which his officer was exposed, had discharged his musket at him from behind, but not before Bush, the informer, had fallen beneath the unerring aim of the foe he had betrayed.

The remains of Ellen Nugent were recommitted to the earth. An inquest was held on the spot upon the body of her husband, and a report thereof transmitted to Government. Hugh Lawlor was the last of his family, and his corpse was unclaimed by friend or relative; but the strangers who dug his grave did not venture to separate in death the hapless pair who in life could never be united.

Wuthering Heights and Gothic Feminism

Diane Long Hoeveler

Literary critics approach fictional works like blind people feeling their way around an elephant. A critic who examines a certain area of the text and attempts to draw conclusions from that isolated aspect will gain only a partial understanding. *Wuthering Heights,* like all literary classics, needs to be approached in many different ways in order to see its complexity. We have considered the author's early writings and the little we know of her biography. We have also looked at her genealogy, her travels, and her reading in a variety of sources. The following article considers the novel in relation to one of the dominant literary forms of the period: the female gothic. *Wuthering Heights,* along with Charlotte Brontë's *Jane Eyre* and *Villette,* is in many ways the last expression of the nineteenth-century female gothic tradition in British writing.

If the family, according to late eighteenth- and early nineteenth-century bourgeois novelists, was the only certain reality in a perilously shifting world of values, it is possible to see why the gothic, particularly as it was developed by women novelists like Ann Radcliffe and Mary Shelley, would seek to discredit or at least redefine the family. Established and reinforced to ensure inheritance rights based on legitimacy and male supremacy, the patriarchally marked family functions as a sacred totem in society, an order that is not only above the law but also the basis of the legal system. What gothic fiction by women attempts to do, in a covert manner, is to subvert the privileges and assumed prerogatives of the family as a patriarchal institution. Much is made, therefore, of incest, matricide, patricide, intense sibling rivalry, symbolically cannibalistic tendencies in the parents, and dreams of escape by pursued and persecuted children. The gothic family provides a theater in which members enact both a mythic

From *Gothic Feminism: The Professionalization of Gender from Charlotte Smith to the Brontës.* University Park: Pennsylvania State UP, 1998.

struggle for species survival and a more personal quest for individual validation. The female as author, narrative voice, and protagonist participates in a literary fantasy that totally reshapes or even annihilates human history in tracing the fate of one family. The dream that motivates much of *Wuthering Heights* is that families will ultimately self-destruct, allowing women to live and function as individuals. [ED.]

[. . .] Emily Brontë's portrait in *Wuthering Heights* of the perverse and indestructible nature of family relations functions on several levels as a severe indictment of patriarchy. We can initially begin our analysis by examining the character of Emily Brontë's first version of the gothic feminist heroine, Catherine Earnshaw, as she undergoes an emotional and sexual struggle without ever being aware of any of the forces conditioning her to accept familial and social conformity. Even as a very young child, Catherine does not fit the Victorian standards of the docile, submissive child. She is described at this stage as a "wild, wicked slip" whose "spirits were always at high-water mark," "spirits" that are in evidence in her dealings with all the others at the Heights (55).[1] As Nelly Dean observes, "she never was happier than when she was defying us with her bold, saucy look, and her ready words" (55). These sharp words even strike the hallowed figure of her father, who is continually harassed by what he considers her impudent ways. The night he dies he finds her docile and gentle, which causes him to remark, "'Why canst thou not always be a good lass, Cathy?'" Cathy's reply would have been unheard of from the typical Victorian child-heroine: "'Why cannot you always be a good man, Father?'" (56). This is not the voice of a child who fears being the object of a beating. Remember that her one request from her father's shopping excursion was that he bring her home a whip for playtime activities.

From this brief description of Catherine as a child, the Victorian reader familiar with novels like Dacre's *Zofloya*, not to mention the underground pornographic novels of the day, would have immediately identified and typed Catherine as a future specimen of the "Bad (read *passionate*) Woman."[2] This ideological construction concerned a high-spirited girl who

---

[1] All parenthetical references are to this New Riverside Edition.

[2] Pornography was widely read and easily accessible during the Victorian period. This topic is discussed in numerous sources, most recently in Iain McCalman, *Radical Underworld: Prophets, Revolutionaries, and Pornographers in London, 1795–1840* (Cambridge: Cambridge University Press, 1988).

was led to indulge her passions with a lover who subsequently considered it his duty to betray her and marry a virgin. This fate does not await Catherine because she chooses the other alternative proffered by her society—the idealization of sexual repression and its sublimation in a "safe" marriage. In other words, Catherine chooses the path of the Radcliffe heroine; she marries a safely feminized man but unfortunately she does not live happily ever. Brontë subverts our expectations by demonstrating the inadequacies of the Radcliffean formula; she forces her heroine to actually live with her weak husband and actually become pregnant, and the indignity of childbirth is not suffered lightly by most gothic feminists (Wollstonecraft's *Maria* comes to mind). But by continuing where Radcliffe chose to conclude her narrative, Emily Brontë exposes the falsity and futility of "love and marriage" as the "happy ending" for women. Her heroine dies and the next generation barely survives, having learned very little from the errors of her predecessors.

The representation of Heathcliff, however, is essential at this point to a fuller understanding of the personality and familial dilemma of Catherine. As a child he too is depicted as socially rebellious and unacceptable. Physically, he is a "dark-skinned gipsy," as "rough as saw-edge and hard as whinstone" (27, 50). The implication is clear: Heathcliff is a force of nature, a wild and untamable embodiment of pure, diffuse sexual energy. His influence on Catherine is strong, and Nelly has to admit that "they both promised to grow up as rude as savages. . . . [They] grew more reckless daily . . . [becoming] unfriended creatures" (58). But what was considered by Victorian standards to be the most threatening aspect of both Catherine and Heathcliff is their unchanneled and unleashed energy that appears to take on a vaguely sexual character. That Catherine and Heathcliff should have become initially attracted to each other seems obvious to us, both from a psychological and a literary perspective. Freud notes that "the choice of a [sexual] object . . . has already frequently or habitually been effected during the years of childhood. The simplest course for the child would be to choose as his sexual objects the same persons whom, since his childhood, he has loved with what must be described as damped-down libido." [3] The gothic genre frequently depicts a quasi-incestuous attraction between pseudosiblings, and in several ways that characterize the gothic novel, the early relationship between Catherine and Heathcliff is meant to suggest a primitive pseudomarriage, a union of soul mates who do not

---

[3] Sigmund Freud, *The Standard Edition of the Complete Psychological Works*, trans. James Strachey, 24 vols. (London: Hogarth Press, 1953–74), 7:225.

engage in a sexual relationship but who act and think of themselves as a dyadic, androgynous unit.[4]

Catherine and Heathcliff sleep in the same bed as children and join as allies against Earnshaw and his young wife, as well as that other, equally perverse "couple" in the family, Nelly and Joseph. The novel, in fact, is filled with displaced marital relationships, suggesting that the need to form "families," surrogate or biological, is a distinctly human need, found in all people who can only define themselves if they are in relation to others. The early childhood "marriage" of Catherine and Heathcliff is rudely sundered by two events: the death of Mr. Earnshaw and contact with an alien and oddly civilized world, Thrushcross Grange. During one particularly ominous evening ramble when they stumble on the Linton household, both of the children, now budding adolescents, view this effeminate household as a bizarre aberration of human interaction, with its tea cups and polite conversations. This opinion is confirmed when there is a sudden assault on Catherine—as real as it is symbolic. A guard dog literally drags Catherine, kicking and screaming, into the other, proper world, with its other, proper husband. The dog senses that Catherine is its appropriate prey, not the unregenerate Heathcliff. And it is the animal in Catherine that is seized and wounded by the Linton dog.

When the Linton children welcome Catherine into their household they ritualistically wash her feet, and we can see from this action that Catherine is being constructed as the scapegoat who will be offered up for the continuance of their bourgeois world. Indeed, Catherine is initiated into this new realm through gifts of cakes and a ritualistic combing of her hair (the taming of her free and wild tresses suggests a disciplining of her sexual energy). Catherine becomes for the Lintons a sort of fetish, a feminine icon, a new object that they can shape into social conformity, and they appear to succeed admirably.[5] After several weeks of social recuperation and brain-

---

[4]For varieties of "Freudian" readings of Wuthering Heights, see Wade Thompson, "Infanticide and Sadism in Wuthering Heights," in Wuthering Heights: An Anthology of Criticism, ed. Alastair Everitt (London: Cass, 1967); and Michael D. Reed, "The Power of Wuthering Heights: A Psychoanalytic Examination," in Psychocultural Review 1 (1977), 21–42.

[5]Charlotte Brontë herself began the critical denigration of Heathcliff as something less than human in her comment, "Whether it is right or advisable to create beings like Heathcliff, I do not know: I scarcely think it is." See her "Editor's Preface to the New Edition of Wuthering Heights," reprinted in this volume (19–23). More recent critical essays on Heathcliff's problematic status in the novel include Patricia Parker, "The (Self-)Identity of the Literary Text: Property, Propriety, Proper Place, and Proper Name in Wuthering Heights," in Identity of the Literary Text, ed. Mario J. Valdes and Owen Miller (Toronto: University of Toronto Press, 1985); John Allen Stevenson, "'Heathcliff

washing, Catherine returns to Wuthering Heights a demure, fashionable little lady who has been reformed by "fine clothes and flattery." Nelly observes that Catherine is no longer a "wild, hatless little savage," and although Heathcliff makes one effort to be accepted by this other society ("'make me decent, I'm going to be good. . . . I wish I had light hair and fair skin'"), he is unable to be assimilated because he will not or cannot deny his nature as easily as Catherine has (62, 65–66).

Catherine's "civilizing process," her conversion to bourgeois values, however, is far from complete. Nelly notices that Catherine is now "full of ambition, [which] led her to adopt a double character without exactly intending to deceive anyone." Unable to transform her natural and wild spirit, nor to accept completely the imposed politeness and repression of the Lintons, Catherine is torn between Heathcliff and Linton, passion and its denial. When Nelly tells us that Catherine has been forced to "adopt a double character" (73), we recognize the guise of the gothic feminist all too clearly. The masquerade of passive-aggression, the posing and counter-posing for effect, the appearance of compliance while one actively and covertly subverts, these have always been the characteristics of the professionally feminine woman. The gothic feminist has always been torn between her own nature and her own best social, economic, political interests, her own impulses and her own survival, hence her "double character."

On the one hand, Catherine's pseudomarriage to Heathcliff is a denial of the traditional, patriarchal family, a relationship in which she is not defined by her father or his status. It is a relationship that they have entered freely, as equals, and it is a relationship that she has entered into without the intercession or involvement of her father or brother as broker. As a pseudomarriage, it denies the practice of "traffic in women." In a freely chosen alliance with a nameless and illegitimate young man, Catherine finds a means of repudiating masculine and specifically patriarchal values. With Heathcliff she is beyond social norms and conventions; she is not a daughter, a sister, or a wife; she fancies instead that she is an individual who has found an idyllic escape from the realities of repressive roles. But just as history begins with the establishment of names, defined clans, and powerful totems or claims on turf, so must history begin for Catherine with her realization that human beings, particularly women, do not exist apart from the men who can provide them with names and status. In this new world there can be no room for Heathcliff the nameless, as he continues to represent the freedom and aboriginal rebellion that must be denied as well as destroyed before society can progress.

After his only and feeble attempt to reform and conform, Heathcliff reverts even further into his "heathenism." Lately, Nelly observes, he has seemed "possessed of something diabolical" (72). His disdain for the Lintons as rivals for Catherine has been established, and he pleads with her not to turn him out "for those pitiful, silly friends of yours!" (75). But Catherine cannot fail to notice the social and economic superiority of Linton to Heathcliff, although the contrast—which is actually financially based—is represented as physical or even topographical. Linton, she notes, is similar to "a beautiful, fertile valley," while Heathcliff in contrast reminds her of a "bleak, hilly, coal country" (76). And although Catherine is seduced by Edgar's money, position, and manners, she knows in her heart that such a choice is "wrong," for its price is the fulfillment of her sexual nature. She exchanges the fire of Heathcliff for the frost of Linton, a choice that all Brontë heroines are forced to confront. We can recall here the contrast between the fiery Rochester and the icy duty of St. John Rivers. Catherine, however, denies her sexual nature and marries against herself or at least against her body's best interests. The sorrows and follies that ensue are the result of this unnatural choice, and yet, Brontë suggests, this is the best choice that has been held out to women, not simply by their society but by women authors like Ann Radcliffe and Mary Wollstonecraft. Brontë's indictment of the "reasonable woman" is also an indictment of the entire tradition of splitting head and heart and valorizing the former at the expense of the latter.[6]

After her famous "I am Heathcliff" speech to Nelly, a set piece that effectively sends up the absurdity of the Shelleyan epipsyche and the Byronic sister-muse at the same time it reifies the ideal, Catherine confesses that she loves Heathcliff but would be embarrassed to be his wife. Heathcliff flees, hearing only that Catherine has decided to marry Linton. A violent storm of nature occurs at just this point in the text to emphasize a similar state in the human realm. The lightning that splits the tree and knocks down part

---

[6] I am obviously indebted to Sandra Gilbert and Susan Gubar's influential reading of *Wuthering Heights*, "Looking Oppositely: Emily Brontë's Bible of Hell," in *The Madwoman in the Attic*, (New Haven: Yale UP, 1979) 248–308. I also admire the discussion of the novel to be found in Terence Eagleton's *Myths of Power: A Marxist Study of the Brontës* (London: Macmillan, 1975), 97–121. For discussions of the specifically female configuration of Emily Brontë's creativity, see Margaret Homans, *Bearing the Word: Language and Female Experience in Nineteenth-Century Women's Writing* (Chicago: University of Chicago Press, 1986), 68–83; and Patricia Yaeger, *Honey-Mad Women: Emancipatory Strategies in Women's Writing* (New York: Columbia University Press, 1988), 177–206.

of a chimney clearly foreshadows the fate of the estate and paternal legacy of both the Heights and the Grange; both will be threatened if not destroyed later by Heathcliff's vengeance (87).

But what are we to make of the novel's gothic antiheroine, Isabella? She is clearly meant to be Catherine's double or foil, a class-based critique of Catherine's more natural and wild temperament. But her marriage to Heathcliff, so painfully detailed, is little more than a beating fantasy with the other woman as the victim, Nelly as the voyeur, and Heathcliff as sadistic and paternally displaced aggressor. The episode also seems to suggest that for Brontë marriage is a form of institutionalized torture and sexual depravity for women. Isabella's wallowing in masochistic postures at Heathcliff's feet suggests her need not simply to humiliate her brother's class-based snobbery but to debase herself as well.

All of my remarks thus far have been examples of fairly traditional readings of the book's mechanics and theme. And on a literal level the novel is a fairly straightforward romance, using standard romance devices (betrayal, separated soul mates, thwarted sexual longings) with a few gothic touches for effect (Catherine as the ghost haunting Lockwood, Heathcliff as cannibalistic vampire-usurper of the Earnshaw estate). But the initial and instigating motivation of the novel, the choice of Linton over Heathcliff, forms the first crucial act that inaugurates the establishment of the patriarchy over the anarchy and sexual energy that Heathcliff represents. Seen from another perspective, however, what we are witnessing in *Wuthering Heights* is the return and revenge of the earlier and repressed sentimental tradition and its hero, Edgar Linton, who triumphs over the gothic literary movement and its representative, Heathcliff. The novel pits these two genres against each other in a bifurcated attempt to resolve the popular literary heritages that have shaped women's romantic attitudes for the past century. It is as if the sentimental erupts into this gothic text and will not die. The sentimental hero wages a life or death battle with his nemesis, the gothic antihero, and he wins a partial victory. In other words, the sentimental will not die in *Wuthering Heights,* but then neither will the gothic. The reconciled and chastened couple in the last scene of the book, Catherine II and Hareton, exist as residual vestiges of both traditions. They would appear to embody Brontë's final suggestion: that the sentimental needs passion to be authentic while the gothic needs taming, but both impulses finally bring women only to the pages of a book, which is where, after all, they both began.

Let us return, however, to the beginning of the novel and recall that Mr. Earnshaw originally brings Heathcliff into the family by introducing him as a substitute for an earlier, dead son with the same name. Supposedly Earnshaw found the child an orphan in Liverpool, but there is always about Heathcliff the suggestion that he is actually Earnshaw's illegitimate child, and certainly Catherine's query to her father on the night of his death, "why cannot you always be a good man?" suggests some sense on her part, if only unconscious, that her father has not been the paragon of sexual virtue that he might have been. The entry of Heathcliff into the family results in his intense rivalry with Catherine's "real" brother, Hindley Earnshaw, for the love and attention of the father. The fact that the father is unable to mediate between the factions that form over Heathcliff's new status suggests that the family as a unit is a fragile and shifting entity that requires continual vigilance lest it be destroyed or mutated.

Why does the elder Earnshaw bring an interloper into his home and why does he insist that Heathcliff, with that strange adopted single name, be accepted as his son? These are questions that are obviously meant to be unanswerable, but they suggest depths of paternalistic insecurity and paranoia. Was Earnshaw afraid to die with only one male heir? Was Heathcliff his insurance policy should his "real" son prove either weak or unsuitable? Ironically, the introduction of Heathcliff into the family creates both the problems and the solution to those problems. Heathcliff wreaks havoc on the estate of Wuthering Heights, but he also strengthens the second Catherine and the eventual heir, Hareton, through his sheer negative presence. By being such an effective blocking figure, he tempers and shapes both their characters more than their own parents were capable of doing. As the embodiment of the bête noire, Heathcliff becomes the active evil force that has to be confronted and overcome if the gothic feminist is to shape and redeem the old world into something vibrant and new. Heathcliff reminds us of Montoni or General Tilney or many of those dark brooding slightly Byronic gothic tyrants who do not deserve to hold their estates. His corruption is more sympathetically presented by Brontë, who sees her gothic villain as himself a victim of class prejudice, but finally Heathcliff has to be destroyed if the world is to be safe for the daughters of gothic feminists. Heathcliff, like the rest of those earlier gothic patriarchs, stands as an anachronism.

All of this is not meant to suggest that Heathcliff is not first and foremost a literary character. He is but he is also somewhat of a principle (and surely the fact that he is both is not contradictory, although it has spawned a vast critical debate). As a literary character, Heathcliff is a foundling, exuding the aura of illegitimacy and sexual rebellion, a sort of Byronic gothic antihero intent on destroying others as well as himself. But as a principle, he embodies many other dark and fearful aspects of the human mind. In particular, he represents the family's fear and revulsion toward open or aggressive sexuality. He appears to represent the untamed, uncivilized male principle at war with the increasingly potent forces of feminine domesticity, but he also paradoxically represents the very forces that would destroy patriarchy and the entire system of male privilege.

After Catherine decides to marry Edgar, changes begin to develop in both Heathcliff's and Catherine's personalities. His bitterness and frustration turn him into the "devil" and "ghoul" that he is later seen to be by Nelly and his wife Isabella. The change in his sexual nature is predictable. Consider Freud's observation: "sexuality in most males contains an element of aggressiveness—a desire to subjugate; . . . there is an intimate connection between cruelty and the sexual instinct. . . . this aggressive element of the sexual instinct is in reality a relic of cannibalistic desires" (*Standard Edition* 7:159). To claim that Heathcliff is in some symbolic manner a throwback to our cannibalistic heritage is, perhaps, a bizarre claim. But there is some justification for this interpretation if we consider the dominance of oral imagery throughout the text, the profusion of scenes in which food is literally oppressive and the characters are depicted as either starving (Catherine I and the dying Heathcliff) or gluttonous (Lockwood and Joseph). In several ways the urge to metaphorically consume the beloved lies within the gothic and the romantic traditions. This urge originates from the ethos established by Percy Shelley and Byron—a desire to be one with one's spiritual and physical complement.

Part of the incestuously driven Byronic legacy concerns just this urge on the part of the male to absorb the feminine and thus to be become androgynous—at least that is the dream if not the accomplished reality of Romantic poetry by men. That Brontë has written her novel as an extended gloss on *Manfred,* as well as on *Frankenstein,* has been noted by other critics.[7] But the novel also needs to be situated within the gothic family saga tradition that emphasizes and explores perverse sexual and generational relations. Heathcliff in the latter part of the novel is not much different from Ambrosio, Lewis's obsessed monk, or Walpole's mad Manfred, with his mania to produce yet one more male heir. But whereas these works by men explicitly develop the theme of familial and dynastic ruin, Brontë's approach is distinctively covert. She would like to destroy the foundations as well as the generational power of the family, and her scathing depictions of

---

[7] Gilbert and Gubar in *Madwoman* situate *Wuthering Heights* in a line of descent that originates with *Frankenstein* (249); they also compare the novel to *Manfred* (259). Joseph Wiesenfarth, "*Wuthering Heights:* The Gothic Tradition Domesticated," in his *Gothic Manners and the Classic English Novel* (Madison: University of Wisconsin Press, 1988), sets Heathcliff within the tradition of gothic villains, comparing him to both Zofloya and Mathilda in Lewis's *Monk* (77), while Robert Kiely places the work within the "romantic" tradition in his study *The Romantic Novel* (Cambridge: Harvard University Press, 1972).

all the marriages in the novel stand as her clearest attempt to do so. Emily Brontë dreams of a world in which there is neither marrying nor giving in marriage; she dreams of a world populated by passionate but nonsexual forces of energy. She dreams of a world not dependent on the use and abuse of female bodies. She has her heroine Catherine dream, quite literally, of heaven. But dreams, as we know, are always sites of repeated trauma and reenactments of woundings that live on indefinitely in the psyche. Catherine's repetitious dreams reenact over and over again the sundering of her original union with Heathcliff.

If Heathcliff has been sexually mutated by his rejection by and forced separation from Catherine, so has she. This fact becomes evident in her sudden development of hysteria and her eventual death by anorexia complicated by pregnancy (a death that eerily foreshadows Charlotte Brontë's own demise). Freud sees the development of hysteria in women as caused by repression in adolescence, and it seems that Catherine I might have recently been seen by Freud, for her symptoms sound ominously like his diagnosis. The fever Catherine suffers after Heathcliff runs away leaves her "saucier and more passionate and haughtier than ever" (88), while the doctor's orders are to allow her "whatever she pleased to demand, and generally [to avoid] aggravating her fiery temper" (91). But Catherine's health is finally destroyed by her pregnancy. We learn of her condition almost indirectly, as if the author were as embarrassed about it as Catherine appears to be. And our response to the pregnancy is amazement—somehow we are unable to imagine a sexual relationship between Catherine and the effeminate Linton. So between her bodily distortion and willful starvation, Catherine effectively destroys herself while in the act of creating her biological successor, her mirror-image daughter who will bear the same name and eerily reenact another version of the same feminine destiny.

Heathcliff's return to the Heights after a three years' absence begins the final and inevitable working out of the fates of Catherine and Heathcliff. Catherine's process of repression and forced socialization has proceeded far enough so that she is able to describe Heathcliff as "an unreclaimed creature, without refinement, without cultivation, an arid wilderness of furze and whinstone . . . a fierce, pitiless, wolfish man" (101). This is the supposedly civilized Heathcliff, the Heathcliff who has spent three years amassing money and a veneer of cultivation, the Heathcliff who has returned to compete on an equal footing with Linton for the affections of Catherine. Catherine is not particularly interested in this new, monied Heathcliff. She is more interested in the aboriginal Heathcliff, the man who provided her with the appearance of amorality and antisocial deviance, all safely controlled, of course, by the incest taboo operating on them. Seeing herself as "dirty" and of the lower classes is a sort of game with Catherine, a posing for effect while she retreats safely into the world of privilege whenever she wants. On the night of Heathcliff's return, Catherine coaxes Edgar to receive him by setting up two tables, one for the siblings Edgar and Isabella as the "gentry," and one for the pseudosiblings Catherine and Heathcliff as the "lower orders" (95).

The amusement and happiness of Heathcliff's return, however, do not last long. Heathcliff accuses Catherine of having treated him "infernally" and swears revenge, though not on her directly (108). He calls Linton "this lamb . . . a sucking leveret . . . the milk-blooded coward . . . the slavering, shivering thing" (111). His overt implication to Catherine is that she has replaced Heathcliff's sexual superiority with Linton's impotency. Catherine not only appears to recognize the error of her choice, but she admits to suffering, to being "tormented . . . haunted" (115). Catherine, however, never really had the freedom to choose Heathcliff as a mate, and to cling to that idea is a delusion at best. The social and economic facts are such that an intelligent young woman does not choose to marry a nameless, illegitimate pauper as a husband, no matter what the sexual attraction. In gothic novels written by men, the female character often insists on marrying the man of her choice, no matter what his social or economic status. The intense desire to follow her passion into the abyss of social rejection is a potent male fantasy, one that recurs throughout gothic novels written by men.[8] But female authors do not indulge their female characters in such a manner, for they understand all too well the consequences of familial power. As an adult woman, Catherine is game playing; she wants to be the wife of the propertied and secure Linton, but she wants to play at being a social outcast with Heathcliff. There is never any question about whom or what will be chosen at the conclusion of the game.

Although Catherine's waking life may be under her control, her unconscious life as manifested in her dreams is not. In the first dream she describes to Nelly, she has died, has gone to heaven, and is unhappy there because she is not with Heathcliff. She finds herself thrown out of heaven to wander on the moors around the Heights, unable to accept the world of the body or the world of the spirit (84). The dream fingers the wound of her separation from Heathcliff and her marriage to an alien, nonfamilial man, but it is also prophetic in at least two ways. Catherine's vision of heaven proves to be very much like the condition of her marriage to Linton. Patriarchal codes told her that she would find happiness in such a marriage, yet

---

[8] For instance, Joseph Andriano discusses the female figure as a Jungian-inspired anima who haunts gothic literature written by men in his *Our Ladies of Darkness: Feminine Daemonology in Male Gothic Fiction* (University Park: Penn State Press, 1993).

she finds none because the cost of the marriage is the denial of both her sexual and her second self. When Catherine says, "'Heathcliff is more myself than I am,'" or "'I am Heathcliff,'" she expresses that he is the masculine component of her nature, a component that society has taught her to fear and repress (85). Her unhappiness in a heaven without Heathcliff is as inevitable as her unhappiness in a union with Linton. She wants incompatible social realities; she wants passion and respectability, and it is Brontë's point that such a combination is not possible for repressed and successfully socialized Victorian women.

Catherine relates another dream after her hysteria-produced illness, a dream that focuses on the quasi-incestuous oak-paneled bed at the Heights. She describes herself in this dream as aching with "some great grief" and discovers that she cannot remember the last seven years of her life. This discovery provided by her unconscious reveals that her sexual development as a woman abruptly stopped when she was "converted at a stroke into Mrs. Linton . . . wife of a stranger: an exile, and outcast, thenceforth, from what had been my world" (118). Catherine's unconscious mind will not allow her to dupe herself into believing that she ever successfully converted her fiery nature into the frosty restraint that the Lintons required. Catherine longs to awaken from the nightmare that is her life: "'I wish I were a girl again, half savage and hardy, and free . . . and laughing at injuries, not maddening under them! Why am I so changed?'" (118). The processes of repression and socialization have taken their toll. Her only hope of escape lies in death and a future reunion with Heathcliff in the spiritual realm: "'they may bury me twelve feet deep, and throw the church down over me, but I won't rest till you [Heathcliff] are with me'" (119). It would appear that the memory of symbiotic oneness with Heathcliff in that oak-paneled bed is the most potent of Catherine's life. Heaven for her can only be imaged as a return of the repressed, a resurrection of the childhood bed and a return to a womblike existence with one's split-off and fragmented self.

After Catherine's recovery from her attack of hysteria, Heathcliff arrives for what turns out to be their final meeting. Nelly notes that Catherine has been changed physically by her illness, or more probably, by her attempt to conceal and reject her pregnancy. She is "unearthly," "dreamy and melancholy," while she seems to "gaze beyond, and far beyond . . . out of this world" (141). In their final meeting it is evident that their life-long frustrated love can find release only in causing pain, torture, or destruction to each other. This species of sadomasochistic love glories in knowing that each is the cause of the other's suffering. Catherine says, "'I care nothing for your sufferings. Why shouldn't you suffer? I do,'" while Heathcliff knows that Catherine will not be at peace, and that heaven will "be a land of exile to her," while at her death he will be plunged into the "torments of hell" with his "soul in the grave" (143). Heathcliff's final indictment of Catherine's treachery touches the core of the social dilemma she faced: "'Why did you betray your own heart, Cathy? . . . You have killed yourself. . . . What right had you to leave me? What right—answer me—for the poor fancy you felt for Linton?'" Catherine's answer, unfortunately, does not reveal the extent of the social and familial pressures she faced, nor is she particularly aware of all the facets of her choice. She replies, "'I've done wrong, I'm dying for it'" (145).

Death is the only release for Catherine and she accepts that death with a "calmness" and "peace" that have been unknown in her last seven years of life. It is surely no coincidence that Nelly describes Catherine's death as "like a child reviving" (149). Death is Catherine's only possible return to childhood and the free innocence she had experienced with Heathcliff in a sort of polymorphously perverse realm of infantile sexuality. Her salvation comes in escaping a society that could accept her only if she denied her nature and assumed an alien one. Like Catherine, Heathcliff's only escape is through death. His death is the inevitable working out of the spiritual principle that both he and Catherine embodied, and which worked to unite them in spirit after death. The happiness that was denied Heathcliff in life by a society that was threatened by his anarchical presence is obtained by him in death. Heathcliff knows his fulfillment is in a union with Catherine's spirit, not in any socially acceptable conception of an afterlife. His last words are almost identical to the sentiment expressed by Catherine's dream of heaven without Heathcliff: "'I have attained *my* heaven, and that of others is altogether unvalued and uncoveted by me!'" (273). The Tristan/ Isolde *Liebestod* impetus here—the love/death spiral—suggests the basic pessimism implicit in the "melodramatically tragic" strain in female gothic novels. Sexuality and heterosexual passion lead to death for both Heathcliff and Catherine I, because the genre was in the grip of tragedy's replacement, melodrama, the need alternately to celebrate and punish victims. Both Heathcliff and Catherine certainly had unique psychic configurations that led to a predisposition toward incest and dreams of parricide, but finally both are simply characters in a novel and have no real childhoods because they have no ontological existence. Both are signs—coded manifestations of "masculinity" and "femininity"—and the interaction between the two is what the novel as a text is about.

When Emily Brontë chose to retell the Heathcliff/Catherine I narrative, this time with two slightly different constructions of gender, she presented a "happy ending." But that ending has always puzzled or angered its readers, and most critics agree that the second half of the book is its weak section, a sort of extended afterthought.[9] I think not. The second ending tells us that the bourgeois civilizing process has worked and triumphed. Women may be forced to marry oafish men, but those men will turn out to be, after all, educable. Men will continue to exist in female gothic texts, but these men will not be the dark, brooding, and sexually potent gothic heroes we saw in Heathcliff. They will be a sort of amalgam of sentimental Werthers with just a touch of fire. The final world that Emily Brontë depicts for us at the conclusion of *Wuthering Heights* is a world of readers or would-be readers sitting calmly before the hearth as domestic altar, with the professionally feminine girl-woman as Sophia, goddess of wisdom and savior of the civilizable man.

---

[9] The general critical consensus that the second half of the novel represents an adulteration of the first half, not only in characterizations but in its control of narration and theme, has been most recently discussed by Bette London, "*Wuthering Heights* and the Text between the Lines," *Papers in Language and Literature* 24 (1988), 34–52; and Anita Levy, "The History of Desire in *Wuthering Heights*," *Genre* 19 (1986), 409–30.

CHRONOLOGY

MAJOR EVENTS IN EMILY BRONTË'S LIFE

1818   Emily Jane Brontë born on July 30 in Thornton, near Bradford, Yorkshire. Emily was the fourth daughter and fifth child of the Reverend Patrick Brontë and Maria Branwell Brontë.

1820   Brontë family moves to Haworth in Yorkshire, where Patrick Brontë serves for the rest of his life as perpetual curate of the Anglican Church.

1821   Maria Brontë dies, possibly from uterine cancer or aggravated complications from six pregnancies and deliveries.

1824   Emily Brontë enters Cowan Bridge School, where her three older sisters are students.

1825   Eldest daughter, Maria, dies on May 6; Elizabeth, the second eldest, dies on June 15. On June 1, Emily and Charlotte leave the typhus-infected school.

1826   Patrick Brontë gives his son Branwell twelve wooden soldiers in June. Branwell shares the toys with his three surviving sisters; together the children enact and write an elaborate series of plays and sagas about the soldiers.

1827   The play *The Islanders* is begun by the children, each of whom chooses a male character to enact his or her island adventures. Emily Brontë's hero is named "Gravey" and his island is "Arran."

1829   The islands have transmuted into four African kingdoms, grouped together as the Glasstown Confederacy. Emily Brontë's kingdom is now named "Parrysland."

1831   A new literary work, known as the Gondal saga, is begun by Emily and Anne, now writing in collaboration.

1835   Between July and October, Emily Brontë studies at Miss Wooler's school at Roe Head. When she becomes depressed and physically ill, Charlotte recommends that she be sent home for her own safety.

1836   Emily Brontë's earliest dated poem, July 12.

1837   Emily Brontë leaves home to teach at Law Hill School, Halifax, in September. Exactly how long Emily remained at this school is in dispute, but it may have been less than six months.

1838–1842   Emily Brontë lives at home in Haworth, writing poetry connected with the Gondal saga.

1842   Emily Brontë studies at Constantin Heger's school in Brussels from February through November with her sister Charlotte. Concentrating on French and music, Emily impresses Heger as a highly "masculine" woman. In his French class she writes a series of essays that have survived. In November she returns to Haworth on learning that her Aunt Branwell has died, and she never leaves home again.

1844   Emily Brontë copies her poems into two manuscripts, one called *Gondal Poems* and one marked "EJB."

1845   Emily Brontë's poems are found by Charlotte, who insists that they are publishable and that the three sisters should collaborate on a book of poems. Although the date has been vigorously disputed, some scholars believe that Brontë began *Wuthering Heights* in December of this year. Others place its composition much earlier.

1846   Using pseudonyms, the three sisters publish *Poems by Currer, Ellis, and Acton Bell* at their own expense in May. By July, *Wuthering Heights* is under consideration at publishing houses.

1847   *Wuthering Heights* is accepted for publication by T. C. Newby, who also accepts Anne Brontë's *Agnes Grey* while rejecting Charlotte's *The Professor*. Newby publishes the two novels in December, trying to capitalize on the earlier success of *Jane Eyre* published in September.

1848   Branwell Brontë dies as a result of drug and alcohol poisoning on September 24. On October 1, Emily Brontë attends his funeral and contracts a serious respiratory infection. On December 19, she dies of complications from pulmonary disease (then known as "consumption").

1850   Charlotte Brontë reprints her revised version of *Wuthering Heights* in December, attaching an editor's explanatory preface essentially apologizing for her sisters' literary flaws and brief biographical sketches of her two dead sisters. She also publishes some of Emily Brontë's poems, choosing those works that she thinks may counter criticism of her sister's character.

WORKS CITED

Alexander, Christine, and Jane Sellars. *The Art of the Brontës.* Cambridge: Cambridge UP, 1996.

Allott, Miriam, ed. *The Brontës: The Critical Heritage.* London: Routledge, 1974. [Contains the full early reviews cited in the Introduction, from *Jerrold's Weekly, Atlas,* and the *Examiner.*]

Bradner, Leicester. "The Growth of *Wuthering Heights.*" *PMLA* 48 (1933): 139–41.

Brontë, Emily. *The Complete Poems of Emily Jane Brontë.* Ed. Clement W. Hatfield. New York: Columbia UP, 1941.

———. *The Poems of Emily Brontë.* Ed. Derek Roper and Edward Chitham. Oxford: Clarendon, 1995.

———. *Wuthering Heights.* Ed. Hilda Marsden and Ian Jack. Oxford: Clarendon, 1976.

———. *Wuthering Heights.* Riverside edition. Ed. V. S. Pritchett. Boston: Houghton Mifflin, 1956.

———. *Wuthering Heights.* Ed. William M. Sale, Jr., and Richard J. Dunn. 3rd ed. New York: Norton, 1990.

———. *Wuthering Heights.* Ed. Clement Shorter. *The Works of Emily Brontë.* Vol. 2. London: Hodder, 1911.

———. *Wuthering Heights.* Ed. Thomas J. Wise and John Alexander Symington. *The Brontës: Their Lives, Friendships, and Correspondence.* Vol. 3. The Shakespeare Head Brontë. Oxford: Blackwell, 1931.

Chitham, Edward. *The Birth of* Wuthering Heights. New York: St. Martin's, 1998.

———. *The Brontë's Irish Background.* New York: St. Martin's, 1986.

Eagleton, Terry. *Healthcliff and the Great Hunger*. London: Verso, 1995.

———. *Myths of Power: A Marxist Study of the Brontës*. London: Macmillan, 1975.

Gaskell, Elizabeth. *The Life of Charlotte Brontë*. London: 1855.

Hewish, John. *Emily Brontë: A Critical and Biographical Study*. London: Macmillan, 1969.

Heywood, Christopher. "Yorkshire Landscapes in *Wuthering Heights*." *Essays in Criticism* 48 (1998): 13–34.

Hoeveler, Diane Long. *Gothic Feminism: The Professionalization of Gender from Charlotte Smith to the Brontës*. University Park: Pennsylvania State UP, 1998.

Leavis, F. R. *The Great Tradition*. New York: Doubleday, 1948.

Plath, Sylvia. *The Collected Poems*. Ed. Ted Hughes. London: Faber, 1961.

Ratchford, Fannie E. *The Brontës' Web of Childhood*. New York: Columbia UP, 1941.

———, ed. *Gondal's Queen: A Novel in Verse by Emily Jane Brontë*. Austin: U of Texas P, 1954.

Simmons, Bartholomew. "The Bridegroom of Barna." *Blackwood's Edinburgh Magazine* Nov. 1840: 680–704.

Stoneman, Patsy. *Brontë Transformations: The Cultural Dissemination of Jane Eyre and Wuthering Heights*. London: Prentice-Hall, 1996.

Visick, Mary. *The Genesis of Wuthering Heights*. Hong Kong: Hong Kong UP, 1958.

Von Sneidern, Maja-Lisa. "*Wuthering Heights* and the Liverpool Slave Trade." *ELH* 62 (1995), 171–96.

FOR FURTHER READING

Allott, Miriam, ed. *Emily Brontë:* Wuthering Heights, *A Casebook.* Rev. ed. London: Macmillan, 1992.

Armstrong, Nancy. "Emily Brontë in and out of Her Time." *Genre* 40 (1982): 243–64.

Barker, Juliet. *The Brontës.* London: Weidenfeld, 1994.

Berg, Maggie. Wuthering Heights: *The Writing in the Margin.* New York: Twayne, 1996.

Bersani, Leo. *A Future for Astyanax: Character and Desire in Literature.* London: Boyars, 1978.

Davies, Stevie. *Emily Brontë.* New York: Harvester, 1988.

Dry, Florence. *The Sources of* Wuthering Heights. Cambridge: Heffer, 1937; rpt. 1977.

Frank, Katherine. *Chainless Soul: A Life of Emily Brontë.* Boston: Houghton, 1990.

Gérin, Winifred. *Emily Brontë: A Biography.* Oxford: Clarendon, 1971.

Gilbert, Sandra, and Susan Gubar. *The Madwoman in the Attic: The Woman Writer and the Nineteenth-Century Literary Imagination.* New Haven: Yale UP, 1979.

Haire-Sargent, Lin. "The Problem of Heathcliff in Film Versions of *Wuthering Heights.*" *Nineteenth-Century Women at the Movies: Adapting Classic Women's Fiction to Film.* Ed. Barbara T. Lupack. Bowling Green: Bowling Green State UP, 1999), 167–91.

Holbrook, David. *Wuthering Heights: A Drama of Being.* Sheffield: Academic Press, 1997.

Homans, Margaret. *Bearing the Word: Language and Female Experience in Nineteenth-Century Women's Writing.* Chicago: U of Chicago P, 1986.

453

Kavanaugh, James. *Emily Brontë.* Oxford: Blackwell, 1985.

Mellor, Anne. *Romanticism and Gender.* New York: Routledge, 1993.

Miller, J. Hillis. "*Wuthering Heights:* Repetition and the 'Uncanny.'" *Fiction and Repetition: Seven English Novels.* Cambridge: Harvard UP, 1982.

Newman, Beth. "'The Situation of the Looker-On': Gender, Narration, and Gaze in *Wuthering Heights.*" *PMLA* 105 (1990): 1029–41.

Petit, Jean-Pierre, ed. *Emily Brontë: A Critical Anthology.* Harmondsworth: Penguin, 1973.

Pykett, Lyn. *Emily Brontë.* Savage: Barnes, 1989.

Sanger, Charles Percy. "The Structure of *Wuthering Heights.*" *Wuthering Heights. An Authoritative Text with Essays in Criticism.* Ed. William M. Sale, Jr., and Richard J. Dunn. 3rd ed. New York: Norton, 1990.

Stoneman, Patsy. "Feminist Criticism of *Wuthering Heights.*" *Critical Survey* 4 (1992): 147–53.

Tayler, Irene. *Holy Ghosts: The Male Muses of Emily and Charlotte Brontë.* New York: Columbia UP, 1990.

Van de Laar, Elisabeth. *The Inner Structure of* Wuthering Heights: *A Study in an Imaginative Field.* Hague: Mouton, 1969.

Vogler, Thomas A., ed. *Twentieth-Century Interpretations of* Wuthering Heights. Englewood Cliffs: Prentice-Hall, 1968.

Williams, Meg Harris. *A Strange Way of Killing: The Poetic Structure of* Wuthering Heights. Worcester: Clunie, 1987.

Winnifrith, Thomas J., ed. *Critical Essays on Emily Brontë.* New York: Hall, 1997.

FILMS AND VIDEOTAPES

Abismos de Pasión. Dir. Luis Buñuel. Perf. Jorge Mistral and Iraseme Dilian. Producciones Tepeyac, 1954.

Wuthering Heights. Dir. Robert Fuest. Perf. Timothy Dalton and Anna Calder-Marshall. American International Pictures, 1970.

Wuthering Heights. Dir. Peter Hammond. Perf. Ken Hutchison and Kay Adshead. BBC, 1978.

Emily Brontë's Wuthering Heights. Dir. Peter Kosiminsky. Perf. Ralph Fiennes and Juliette Binoche. Paramount, 1992.

Wuthering Heights. Dir. Paul Nickell. Perf. Charlton Heston and Mary Sinclair. Videocassette. Westinghouse Studio One Television Production.

Wuthering Heights. Dir. William Wyler. Perf. Laurence Olivier and Merle Oberon. MGM, 1939.

Wuthering Heights: *A Critical Guide to the Novel.* Videocassette. Princeton: Films for the Humanities and Sciences, 1997.

CREDITS